To Mom
whom I love
very much,

Tom '92

OUTERCOURSE

MARY DALY

OUTERCOURSE

The Be-Dazzling Voyage

CONTAINING RECOLLECTIONS FROM MY
LOGBOOK OF A RADICAL FEMINIST PHILOSOPHER
(BE-ING AN ACCOUNT OF MY TIME/SPACE TRAVELS AND IDEAS
—THEN, AGAIN, NOW, AND HOW)

HarperSanFrancisco
A Division of HarperCollins*Publishers*

OUTERCOURSE: *The Be-Dazzling Voyage.* Copyright © 1992 by Mary Daly. Illustrations copyright © 1992 by Sudie Rakusin. Photograph copyright © 1992 by Gail Bryan. All rights reserved.

Printed in the United States of America.

FIRST EDITION

Library of Congress Cataloging-in-Publication Data

Daly, Mary.
Outercourse: the be-dazzling voyage / Mary Daly.—1st ed.
p.   cm.
Includes bibliographical references and index.
ISBN 0-06-250194-1 (alk. paper)
1. Daly, Mary.   2. Feminists—United States—Biography.
3. Philosophy—Religious Studies—Social Ethics.
I. Title.
HQ1413.D23D34 1992
305.4′2′092—dc20
[B]   91-58914
                                                                            CIP

92 93 94 95 96 HAD 10 9 8 7 6 5 4 3 2 1

*To my mother, Anna, who launched my Craft
and refuels it constantly in the Expanding Now,
and to Other Foresisters and Cronies across Time
who have stayed on Course
in their own unique ways
and who know who they Are*

CONTENTS

Prefatory Notes   xi

Introduction: The Spiraling Moments of *Outercourse*   1

THE FIRST SPIRAL GALAXY
BE-SPEAKING: MOMENTS OF PROPHECY AND PROMISE
(*OH!*–1970)

Prelude to The First Spiral Galaxy My Original Travels—
   to the Year *Oh!*   19

Chapter One Early Moments: My Taboo-breaking Quest—
   To Be a Philosopher   22

Chapter Two Onward by Degrees   42

Chapter Three Student Days in Europe: Metaphysical
   Adventures and Ecstatic Travels   58

Chapter Four Philosophical Conclusions and Beginning
   Be-Speaking: The Summons to Write *The Church
   and the Second Sex*   71

Chapter Five Spiraling Back to Boston and Beyond   87

Chapter Six Reflections on Philosophical Themes of
   The First Spiral Galaxy   109

THE SECOND SPIRAL GALAXY
BE-FALLING: MOMENTS OF BREAKTHROUGH AND RE-CALLING
(1971–1974)

Prelude to The Second Spiral Galaxy Pirating in the Mist   129

Chapter Seven The Time of the Tigers: The Harvard Memorial
   Church Exodus and Other Adventures   134

Chapter Eight The Writing of *Beyond God the Father*—
   and *Some* Consequences!   146

Chapter Nine My "Feminist Postchristian Introduction"
   to *The Church and the Second Sex*: Approaching
   The Watershed Year   172

Chapter Ten Reflections on Philosophical Themes of
   The Second Spiral Galaxy   185

THE THIRD SPIRAL GALAXY
BE-WITCHING: MOMENTS OF SPINNING
(1975–1987)

Prelude to The Third Spiral Galaxy Spinning and Weaving
Through the Mist   195

Chapter Eleven The Qualitative Leap Beyond Patriarchal
Religion   200

Chapter Twelve The Spinning of *Gyn/Ecology*:
My Thunderbolt of Rage   210

Chapter Thirteen Spinning Big: The Explosion/Expansion
of *Pure Lust*   240

Chapter Fourteen Sinning Big: The Merry Merry *Wickedary*   292

Chapter Fifteen Reflections on Philosophical Themes
of The Third Spiral Galaxy   321

THE FOURTH SPIRAL GALAXY
BE-DAZZLING NOW: MOMENTS OF MOMENTOUS RE-MEMBERING
(OFF THE CALENDAR, OFF THE CLOCK)

Prelude to The Fourth Spiral Galaxy Ahead to the Beginning   335

Chapter Sixteen On How I Jumped over the Moon   337

Chapter Seventeen Green *Logbook* Entries from the Moon   346

Chapter Eighteen Doors to Four: Lucky Dis-coverings
and Happy Homecomings   372

Chapter Nineteen Patriarchy on Trial: Whistle-Blowing
in The Fourth Spiral Galaxy   385

Chapter Twenty Sailing On: Ports of Re-Call on the Subliminal
Sea—Ports of Entry into the Expanding Now   400

CONCLUDING–BEGINNING
THE GREAT SUMMONING AND THE GREAT SUMMATION   407

Notes   417

Publications of Mary Daly   455

Index   459

ILLUSTRATIONS

By SUDIE RAKUSIN

Moments of Prophecy and Promise   17

Moments of Breakthrough and Re-Calling   127

Moments of Spinning   193

Moments of Momentous Re-membering   333

PREFATORY NOTES

L eaping into and across the Moments of living and writing *Outercourse* has been an astonishing adventure. Launching this book on its own Voyage into "the world" is a Taboo-breaking Act. Hence predictably it will inspire further A-mazing Events—especially since it is Surfacing in the early 1990s, a period in which atrocities escalate and Righteous Rage Re-surges. This is a Time of Realizing Elemental Powers, which involves Re-awakening of Memory and of words.

In *Outercourse* I employ numerous New Words which I have Dis-covered over Time and which were compiled in the *Wickedary* in 1987.* While many of these were comprehensible from their Original contexts in my earlier books, others were explained at length without being concisely defined. The *Wickedary* explicitly defined the New Words that had appeared in my previous books and introduced yet Other New Words. In order to con-vey in *Outercourse* the historical Background of these New Words I have used a system of moon symbols in conjunction with *Wickedary* definitions.† The following symbols signify which of my books is the Original source of the word defined:

● *The Church and the Second Sex*. The most recent edition (Boston: Beacon Press, 1985) contains the original text (New York: Harper and Row, 1968) and the "Autobiographical Preface" and "Feminist Postchristian Intro-duction by the Author" from the 1975 Harper Colophon edition, as well as the 1985 "New Archaic Afterwords."

◗ *Beyond God the Father: Toward a Philosophy of Women's Liberation*. The most recent edition (Boston: Beacon Press, 1985) contains the original text (Boston: Beacon Press, 1973) and an "Original Reintroduction by the Author." The British edition, published in London by The Women's Press in 1986 (reprinted in 1991) contains the original text together with my "Original Reintroduction."

---

*See *Websters' First New Intergalactic Wickedary of the English Language*, Conjured by Mary Daly in Cahoots with Jane Caputi (Boston: Beacon Press, 1987; London: The Women's Press Ltd, 1988).

†This is the same system used in the *Wickedary* (see pp. 59–60 of that work).

◑ *Gyn/Ecology: The Metaethics of Radical Feminism*. The most recent edition (Boston: Beacon Press, 1990) contains the original text (Boston: Beacon Press, 1978) and a "New Intergalactic Introduction by the Author." The most recent British edition (London: The Women's Press, 1991) contains the original text (London: The Women's Press, 1979) together with my New Intergalactic Introduction.

○ *Pure Lust: Elemental Feminist Philosophy*. The most recent edition (San Francisco: HarperSanFrancisco, 1992) contains the original text (Boston: Beacon Press, 1984). The British edition is published by The Women's Press in London (1984).

The absence of any symbol accompanying a definition signifies that the word defined first appeared in the *Wickedary*.

My *Logbook of a Radical Feminist Philosopher*, from which I have drawn in writing *Outercourse*, does not have material existence. It lives in my Memory, which is always expanding. Thus *Outercourse* does not contain my *Logbook*, but simply some Recollections drawn from it, to which I sometimes refer as "*Logbook* Entries." These Recollections are interwoven throughout *Outercourse* with philosophical/theoretical reflections. In this way they become incarnate in *Outercourse*.

My *Logbook of a Radical Feminist Philosopher* is a distinct entity. It is an inexhaustible Source from which I may draw further Recollections and philosophical questions, insights, and theories in my work as Metapatriarchal Philosopher/Pirate.

My work as a Pirate, Righteously Plundering and Smuggling back to women gems which have been stolen from us by the patriarchal thieves, requires precision, accuracy, and meticulous scholarship. It also demands that I break rules which restrict creative expression. My capitalization, for example, is capitally irregular. It expresses meanings within ever changing contexts which I have created. Hence seeming inconsistencies are consistent with a more important Rule of Radical Feminist Creativity, which is: "Throw off mindbindings/spiritbindings. Reach for the stars."

ACKNOWLEDGMENTS

Several friends offered encouraging and constructive comments on the manuscript at various stages. In particular I thank Barbara Hope, Geraldine Moane, Suzanne Bellamy, Emily Culpepper, Jane Caputi, Myrna Bouchey, Krystyna Colburn, Mary Ellen McCarthy, Annie Lally Milhaven, and Karen O'Malley. Joyce Contrucci worked untiringly and with expertise on the tasks of "idea-proofreading" and scrutinizing of the manuscript, contributing many shrewd and useful suggestions. Robin Hough performed invaluable services as yeoman working in the galleys.

For their important work I thank my agent Charlotte Cecil Raymond, my editor John Loudon, and Joann Moschella, editorial assistant at HarperSan-Francisco. Barbara Flanagan was my helpful and efficient copy editor and indexer. Nilah MacDonald labored Wickedly on the index. Marge Roberson and Judith Contrucci provided skillful assistance in the final preparation of the manuscript.

I am grateful to Sudie Rakusin, whose Elemental illustrations powerfully enhance the book, and to Gail Bryan, the Crafty photographer who produced the Frontispiece.

I am thankful to my Familiar, Wild Cat, who is an Outercoursing Cat, yowling to go Out, especially at night when the moon is full and I am writing up a Storm. She has encouraged and inspired me by sitting proudly in the box containing the manuscript of The Fourth Spiral Galaxy of this book, thereby signifying her identity as a Fourth Galactic Cat who is eager to continue Voyaging Now.

THE SPIRALING MOMENTS
OF *OUTERCOURSE*

The Voyage of *Outercourse* is Metapatriarchal Time/Space Travel, which takes the shape of quadruple Spiraling. Its parts (Spirals) describe clusters of Moments, each involving/requiring gigantic qualitative leaps into Other dimensions of the Background.

As I Re-member my own intellectual voyage as a Radical Feminist Philosopher, I am intensely aware of the struggle to stay on my True Course, despite undermining by demons of distraction that have seemed always to be attempting to pull me off course. These I eventually Dis-covered and Named as agents and institutions of patriarchy, whose intent was to keep me—and indeed all living be-ing—within the stranglehold of the foreground,* that is, fatherland. My True Course was and is Outercourse—moving beyond the imprisoning mental, physical, emotional, spiritual walls of patriarchy, the State of Possession. Insofar as I am focused on Outercoursing, naturally I am surrounded and aided by the benevolent forces of the Background.†

Since this has been my own experience of Outercourse, I have thought it Crone-logical that the philosophical/theoretical dimensions of this work be woven together with Recollections from an imaginary—though factually accurate—volume, which I have entitled *Logbook of a Radical Feminist Philosopher*. I believe that these Recollections shed much light on the major theoretical subjects under consideration, since they contain Revoltingly Intellectual Bio-graphic information that is deeply intertwined with the philosophical quest/questions of this book.‡

---

*foreground◑ is defined as "male-centered and monodimensional arena where fabrication, objectification, and alienation take place; zone of fixed feelings, perceptions, behaviors; the elementary world: FLATLAND" (*Wickedary*). For an explanation of the meaning of the moon symbols (●, ◕, ◑, ○) used throughout this book, see the Prefatory Notes.

†*Background*◑ as used here means "the Realm of Wild Reality; the Homeland of women's Selves and of all other Others; the Time/Space where auras of plants, planets, stars, animals, and all Other animate beings connect" (*Wickedary*).

‡For a brief history of the genesis of this intertwining, see Chapter Sixteen.

THE TITLE OF THIS BOOK: *OUTERCOURSE*[*][1]

The noun *course* is multileveled in meaning. Among the definitions in *Webster's Third New International Dictionary of the English Language*† is "the act or action of moving in a particular path from point to point (the planets in their courses)." An "obsolete" meaning is "RUN, GALLOP." It has as an "archaic" definition "a charge by opposing knights." It also means "a life regarded as a race: LIFE HISTORY, CAREER." *Course* means "a progressing or proceeding along a straight line without change of direction (the ship made many courses sailing through the islands)." A final relevant definition is "the track or way taken by a ship or the direction of flight of an airplane: the way projected and assigned usu. measured as a clockwise angle from north."

The meaning of *course* in *Outercourse* envelops and transforms all of these dimensions. Thus my Voyage as a Radical Feminist Philosopher has involved multidimensional courses. It moves in particular paths—not "from point to point," but from Moment to Moment, and, beyond that, from Spiral Galaxy to Spiral Galaxy. It often feels like running, galloping (like a Nag or a Night Mare). It involves a warrior aspect—not as "a charge by opposing knights," but as an A-mazing Amazonian battle against the necrophiliac nothing-lovers who manufacture, spread, and control the dead zone—the foreground. It is life regarded as a *Race*, that is, participation in the Wild onward rushing movement of all Lusty Life.

The course of *Outercourse* is far from a "straight line" in the usual sense; it is not "linear," but Spiraling. Its Moments are usually unpredictable. However, there is implied in *Outercourse* a Sense of Direction. Thus, despite seeming deviations and sidetracks and peripheral excursions, seeming inconsistencies and changes of direction, there is a kind of Metastraight Line. That is, in a wide view, there is a Fierce Focus to this Course. Implied in *Outercourse* is a Ferocious Refusal to be sidetracked from the Final Cause of the Voyager, that is, her indwelling, always unfolding goal or purpose, perceived as Good and attracting her to Act, to Realize her own participation in Be-ing.

While *Webster's* describes *course* as the way "usually measured as a clockwise angle from north," the Course of the Voyage of Radical Feminist Philosophy moves Counterclockwise, that is, in a direction contrary to the clocks and watches of father time. It is the Time Travel of those who are learning to become Counterclock-Wise, that is, knowing how to Live, Move, Act in Fairy Time/Tidal Time. It is the Direction of Sibyls and Crones who persist in asking Counterclock Whys, Questions which whirl the Ques-

---

*I am indebted to Nancy Kelly for the word *Outercourse* (Conversation, Fall 1987).

†Hereafter, this dictionary is referred to simply as *Webster's*.

tioners beyond the boundaries of clockocracy and into the flow of Tidal Time.[2] Those moving in this Direction Sense that we are on our True Course.

The path/paths of our True Course, as seen from some perspectives, could be called an *Innercourse*, since it involves delving deeply into the process of communication with the Self and with Others—a process which requires deep E-motion, deep Re-membering, deep Understanding. Since it involves Amazonian Acts of Courageous Battling, it could also be called *Countercourse*. However, its primary/primal configuration is accurately Named *Outercourse,* for this is a Voyage of Spiraling Paths, Moving Out from the State of Bondage. It is a continual expansion of thinking, imagining, acting, be-ing. Outercoursing is Spiraling which has its Source in Background experience—in intuitive knowledge that it is by Moving on that Voyagers Dis-cover the Answers as well as the Questions. As Linda Barufaldi observed, it is not by wallowing in the "issues" and pseudoproblems manufactured by therapy and other re-sources that we progress, but rather we "bump into" solutions by moving on in our own lives, following the Final Cause.[3]

As I explain in this book, the ship/vessel/craft of my own Voyage as a Radical Feminist Philosopher and Theologian has been my Craft—as theoretician, writer, teacher. The practice of this Craft is Voyaging, which is a form of Witchcraft. My Craft is a kind of Mediumship, coursing between/among worlds.

This Voyaging is becoming, and it is the Seeking/Seeing of Seers. *Philosophy*, etymologically speaking, is not wisdom, but love of wisdom. Wisdom itself is not a thing to be possessed, but a process/Voyage. Radical Feminist Philosophy, then, is a Questing/Questioning that never stops and never is satisfied with the attainment of dead "bodies of knowledge." It is participation in ever Unfolding Be-ing.

THE MOMENTS OF OUTERCOURSE

> I was looking at the flower bed by the front door; "That is the whole," I said. I was looking at a plant with a spread of leaves; and it seemed suddenly plain that the flower itself was a part of the earth; that a ring enclosed what was the flower; and that was the real flower; part earth; part flower. It was a thought I put away as being likely to be very useful to me later.
>
> —*Virginia Woolf*[4]

The word *moment* is derived from the Latin *momentum*, meaning "movement, motion, moment, influence." It is believed to be rooted in the verb *movēre*, meaning "to move" (*Webster's*). Virginia Woolf suggests that "moments of being" are experiences of seeing beyond the "cotton wool of

everyday life" and understanding context. As she said of the flower in the
flower bed: "That is the whole."

The Spiraling Voyage of Outercourse is comprised of Metapolitical
Moments, which make up Spiral Galaxies. These are Moments/Movements
of participation in Be-ing which carry Voyagers beyond foreground limitations. They are Acts of Hope, Faith, and Biophilic Bounding. They are Acts
of Qualitative Leaping.

Even our seemingly "little" Moments are like leaps into/in a Great
Moment. Thus they partake in the truly Momentous. When women Realize
the Momentous potential of our "ordinary" Moments we find ourSelves
Spiraling. Such experiences are not "merely momentary." They carry us into
an Other kind of Duration/Time.

The Spiraling Moments of Outercourse, then, are utterly unlike mere
instants. *Instant* means "an infinitesimal space of time . . ." (*Webster's New
Collegiate Dictionary*).* The definitions of *infinitesimal* are enlightening. It
is said to mean "taking on values arbitrarily close to zero . . . immeasurably
or incalculably small." The adjective *instant* gives the show away. Thus we
have "premixed or precooked for easy final preparation (instant mashed
potatoes)" (*Webster's Collegiate*).

Instants, then, are units of foreground time. They are incalculably small.
They are mere points in time. They do not imply Motion, Movement,
Momentousness, Momentum. They are elementary, foreground imitations
of Moments. They do not open into the Background. They do not imply
Qualitative Leaping. They do not participate in Spiraling Movement and
therefore do not imply ever deepening experiences of Future, Past, and Present which overlap and which are in dialogue with each other. Like "instant
coffee" and "instant success," instants resemble the "real thing" only to those
whose senses have been dulled by imprisonment in the dim cells of the foreground.

In contrast to mere instants, Moments are incalculably large. They can
be viewed as windows and doors through which we leap and race into the
Background. They influence us; they are of great consequence, for they
point us in the direction of Elemental Time/Tidal Time. Moving in Spiraling
Paths, they hurl us on an Intergalactic Voyage. This leads us to the subject
of the Intergalactic Movement of the Moments of *Outercourse.*

THE INTERGALACTIC MOVEMENT OF MOMENTS

The Spiral Paths formed by Moments/Movements of participation in Be-ing
constitute the four Spiral Galaxies of *Outercourse*. These Spiral Galaxies

---

*Hereafter, this dictionary is referred to simply as *Webster's Collegiate*.

are, like the galaxies of the universe, in perpetual motion.* Like stars, the Moments of Outercourse are born. They happen in the Twinkle of an Eye/I.[5] They come into be-ing through Gynergetic Acts of women whose Focus and Force have their Source in the Background.

One Moment leads to an Other. This is because it has consequences in the world and thus Moves a woman to take the Leap to the next Moment. A comparison with the relations among stars in a galaxy is thought-provoking. An astronomer writes:

> In a galaxy, the stars are separated by vast distances. But the stars do interact because of gravity. Stars feel each other's gravitational fields. . . . In a galaxy, the force of gravity controls the interactions between stars.[6]

In a Galaxy of Outercourse the Moments are sometimes separated by vast distances. But the Moments do interact because of their subjective reality and connectedness in the consciousness of the Voyager and because of their interconnecting consequences in the world. The Focus of the Voyager directs the interactions among the Moments.

The accumulated Gynergy of Moments extends the curved arms of a Galaxy in Outercourse. At a certain point in this whirling progression, the accumulated Gynergy of Moments enables the Voyager to take a Qualitative Leap and thus begin a New Galaxy. Since the Focus and Momentum are from the same Source/Force, the New Galaxy Moves in harmony with the preceding one.

This book describes the Paths of four such Spiral Galaxies of Moments. Perhaps we should bear in mind that *The American Heritage Dictionary*† describes a *galaxy* as "any of numerous large-scale aggregates of stars, gas, and dust . . ." The Voyager of *Outercourse* has to confront a great deal of "gas and dust," not all of which is beautiful cosmic material. Much of the gas and dust between Moments is thrown in our way by the demons who attempt to block our Voyage. Thus Exorcism remains an essential and demanding task in the Intergalactic Voyage which is Outercourse.

This process of Exorcism, in combination with its inseparable companionate activity/experience, Ecstasy, provides essential Force and Focus for Outercoursing.[7] These combustible components fuel our Crafts. They make the Voyage *Be-Dazzling*, that is

> eclipsing the foreground/elementary world by the brilliance of be-ing (*Wickedary*).

---

*A *spiral galaxy* is defined as "a galaxy exhibiting a central nucleus or barred structure from which extend concentrations of matter forming curved arms giving the overall appearance of a gigantic pinwheel" (*Webster's*).

†Hereafter, this dictionary is referred to simply as *American Heritage*.

As the Voyager Moves farther and farther Out, the Light becomes brighter. The foreground fades and its demon inhabitants/rulers are overcome by the Powers of the Background. They are eclipsed by the brilliance of be-ing—which is participation in Be-ing.

Be-Dazzling is the Outrageous Challenge and Hope that moves the Craft/Crafts of Outercourse. In this Age of Extremity, we can settle for nothing less. The alternative to Be-Dazzling is precisely Nothing.

The following sections briefly summarize The Four Spiral Galaxies of *The Be-Dazzling Voyage* which is *Outercourse*.

THE FIRST SPIRAL GALAXY
BE-SPEAKING: MOMENTS OF PROPHECY AND PROMISE (*OH!*–1970)

In my own history, the early Moments involved Be-Speaking, that is, foretelling, speaking of what will be. Be-Speaking brings about psychic and/or material change by means of words. As I have experienced such Acts of Be-Speaking, they were and are* Moments of Exorcism of patriarchally inflicted *aphasia*, that is, inability to Name Background reality as well as foreground fabrications and the connections among these.† One of my own early Acts of Be-Speaking was a letter published in *Commonweal* in 1964, responding positively to an article in that magazine by Rosemary Lauer entitled "Women and the Church." I announced that I was ashamed that I had not written the article myself and foretold a barrage of such Feminist writings, proclaiming: "This is both a prophecy and a promise—they will come."[8]

So I was Be-Spoken into Be-Speaking by another woman's writing. That letter—published when I was still a student in Fribourg, Switzerland—had a chain of breathtaking consequences. It led to the writing of my first Feminist book, *The Church and the Second Sex*, to my subsequent harassment and firing from Boston College, and to the months of student demonstrations, activism, and publicity resulting in my promotion and tenure. It led also, and most significantly, to my own radicalization. In other words, Moment after Moment of prophetic Be-Speaking caused the world to speak back. As this dialogue gathered Momentum I was hurled beyond man-made, fictitious, foreground illusions about "the future" and came into Touch with

---

*There is a problem of tense here. Since the Spirals are not linear—since I have come to the same yet different place of Spiraling at later periods—the past tense is not adequate. Many of these Moments recur in different ways. Thus they were, but they also are, and will continue to be.

†I am indebted to Louky Bersianik for the idea of a Feminist interpretation of the word *aphasia*, as well as *amnesia* and *apraxia*. Responsibility for further expansion and development of these concepts is my own. See Louky Bersianik, *Les agénésies du vieux monde* (Outremont, Quebec: L'Intégrale, éditrice, 1982), especially pp. 5–9.

the Background Future. When I went back to teaching in the fall of 1969 I had already begun to change drastically. I had begun to see through the particularities of my experience with Boston College to the universal condition of women in all universities and in all institutions of patriarchy. I had experienced my first explicit encounters with the demons of *assimilation*—especially taking the form of tokenism—and won. I made the Leap into The Second Spiral Galaxy of my Outercourse.

THE SECOND SPIRAL GALAXY
BE-FALLING:
MOMENTS OF BREAKTHROUGH AND RE-CALLING
(1971–1974)

By Seeing and Naming the connections that had been largely subliminal in the earlier stage of Voyaging, I Moved into The Second Spiral Galaxy of my Outercourse. This involved Acts of Exorcism of the *amnesia* inflicted by patriarchal institutions, religion in particular, and by the -ologies which they engender and which in turn serve to legitimate them. Exorcism of *amnesia* required Acts of Unforgetting—Seeing through the foreground "past" into the Background Past—beyond the androcratic lies about women's history. I found that Breaking through to knowledge of a Prepatriarchal Pagan Past opened the possibility for Radical Naming. It became clear that Re-Calling was the clue to real Momentum. As Orwell had written in *1984*:

> "Who controls the past," ran the Party slogan, "controls the future: who controls the present controls the past." . . . All that was needed was an unending series of victories over your own memory.[9]

My Unforgetting sometimes took active political form, for example in 1971, when—in cahoots with Cronies—I instigated the Harvard Memorial Church Exodus. I had been invited to be the first woman to preach at a Sunday service at Memorial Church in its three-hundred-and-thirty-six-year history. After plotting with a few friends at Harvard I accepted and turned the occasion into a Call for an historic Exodus from patriarchal religion. The hundreds of us who walked out experienced the action on different levels. For some of us it was an Act of Be-Falling.* It involved Moving into Archaic Memory. It also was itself a Memory of the Future—an action which affects/effects the Future. By participating in this event, some of us experienced an ancient, woman-centered spiritual consciousness.

Beyond God the Father belongs to this Galaxy. The writing of that book, followed by the writing of my "Feminist Postchristian Introduction" to the

---

Be-Falling is "the Original Ontological Sinning of Fallen Women who follow the Call of the Fates" (*Wickedary*).

1975 edition of *The Church and the Second Sex*, moved me into further Acts of Be-Falling. I encountered and repelled demonic forces of *elimination*, who/which erase women's histories and our very lives.* I was hurled, then, in the direction of The Third Spiral Galaxy.

THE THIRD SPIRAL GALAXY
BE-WITCHING: MOMENTS OF SPINNING
(1975–1987)

Moments of Spinning Move us into the Background Present. As I have experienced these, they have been Moments of Exorcism of the *apraxia* (inability to Act) inflicted upon women. I do not mean by this that I became more "activist" in the usual sense of the word (although I have continued to work in that way also) but that I have become more Active in my *creative* intellectual work. This has meant that I have Moved beyond "following" or simply reacting to patriarchally defined methods of thinking, writing, public speaking, and teaching. My activity in this sense has become more approximate to my ideal of Be-Dazzling—eclipsing the foreground world with the brilliance of be-ing.

The year 1975 was a Watershed year. By the time the "Feminist Postchristian Introduction" was actually published in 1975 I had moved on to writing and delivering a paper entitled "Radical Feminism: The Qualitative Leap Beyond Patriarchal Religion." This paper was delivered at a conference of sociologists and theologians held in Vienna, under the auspices of the infamous Cardinal König, archbishop of Vienna.

In rereading that paper I am struck by the fact that such words as *Postchristian* had become unimportant to me. Such a term had focused attention on where I had been and not where I had arrived. To keep stressing it would be comparable to a woman's harping on her divorce and identifying herself as a "divorcée" years after the event had occurred. Qualitative Leaping is not merely beyond christianity but beyond all patriarchal religion and identification. Moreover, it is not merely "beyond," but toward and into something else, which I have Named *Spinning*.

In the Course of this Galaxy I wrote and published *Gyn/Ecology* (1978), *Pure Lust* (1984), and (in Cahoots with Jane Caputi) *Websters' First New Intergalactic Wickedary of the English Language* (1987). The process of writing those books and confronting their consequences involved encounters with the demonic forces of *fragmentation*, which cut women off from our true Present and from our Presence to our Selves and to each Other.

My conflicts with these forces and with other personifications of "the Deadly Sins of the Fathers" occurred throughout the Metapatriarchal Jour-

---

*These would, of course, attempt to re-turn, but this was a significant victory.

ney of Exorcism and Ecstasy, which is a basic experience and theme of this Galaxy, first Named and explained in *Gyn/Ecology*. Uncovering and vanquishing the demons requires a mode of creativity which is Spinning. It involves finding threads of connectedness among seemingly disparate phenomena.

A vast shift in my mode of writing is evident in *Gyn/Ecology*, which is Metapatriarchally Metaphorical. This Shape-shifting continued/continues throughout *Pure Lust*, which is a work of Elemental Feminist Philosophy. Re-Weaving Webs of connectedness between women and the Elements is an essential theme of this book, which Fiercely Focuses upon the demonic destruction of nature as well as women and upon Metamorphic means of Weaving the Way Out.

The *Wickedary* also is a work of overcoming fragmentation, bringing together the insights of this Galaxy through the Weaving of Wild Words. It follows in the Wake of *Gyn/Ecology* and *Pure Lust*, fighting against the ever worsening conditions of the foreground, and Moving toward the expansion of women's Powers of Sensing cosmic connections—Powers which enable us to Presentiate/Realize a True Present.

Thus the works of this Galaxy Move more and more into the Be-Dazzling Light. In this Light, the Voyager readies herSelf for her Leap into The Fourth Spiral Galaxy, which takes her Off the Calendar, Off the Clock, into Moments of Momentous Re-membering.

THE FOURTH SPIRAL GALAXY
BE-DAZZLING NOW:
MOMENTS OF MOMENTOUS RE-MEMBERING
(OFF THE CALENDAR, OFF THE CLOCK)

In order to Name the most advanced stages of the demonic dis-ease of *fragmentation* I employ the word *dis-memberment*. The encroachment of the Age of Dis-memberment—a condition which manifests itself in the multiplication of divisions within and among women—involves also the breakdown of nature by phallotechnocrats and the splitting of women from nature.

In this age, Sisterhood can seem like a lost and impossible dream. The knowledge and memories that were reclaimed in the so-called "Second Wave" of Feminism re-turn to a subliminal level in our consciousness. As I see our situation in the 1990s, women are challenged to Spin and Weave the broken connections in our Knowing, Sensing, and Feeling, becoming Alive again in our relationships to our Selves and to each Other. This will require the practice of psychic politics and it will require Time Travel—Re-membering our Future and our Past. What is needed is a Spiraling series of Victories over the dis-memberers of women's Present and of our Memories, including Memories of the Future.

Such a series of Victories, that is, the Spiraling Moments of Momentous Re-membering, cannot be viewed as a linear progression. When the Voyager comes into The Fourth Spiral Galaxy she experiences an Overlapping of the Moments of her earlier Travels—a conversation Now with those Moments. The repetitious aspect of Spiraling enriches the experience of Movement, especially when The Fourth Spiral Galaxy has been reached. Yet the most crucial Moments are always Now, and that is why Now is always the special target of the dis-memberers of women's lives.

It is essential to know that all of the Spiral Galaxies are interconnected, that all of the Moments *implicate* each other. Herein lies the hope for resolving miscommunication arising from "generation gaps" and time warps experienced by women in the Age of Dis-memberment. *Implicate* has as an archaic definition "to fold or twist together: INTERWEAVE, ENTWINE." It also means "to involve as a consequence, corollary, or natural inference: IMPLY" (*Webster's*).

I am suggesting that there is an organic interdependence/interwovenness among the Spiral Galaxies of *Outercourse*. There is a task before us, then: the task of actively *explicating* the connections. One definition of the verb *explicate* is "to unfold the meaning or sense of: INTERPRET, CLARIFY." It also means "to develop what is involved or implied in" (*Webster's*).

The question is: Who can and will do this? Clearly a woman at her first Moment of Be-Speaking could not be expected to do this. Explication is the task of those who have Moved for some Time on the Be-Dazzling Voyage and who therefore can have an overview of its Spiraling Paths. These women are the Memory-Bearing Group—those who have "been around" and can Re-Call earlier Moments, and who can *bear* the memories and knowledge of destruction.

The Hope that such women can be Heard lies in the fact that participation in the Background Present is the underpinning of *all* of the Moments of Outercourse, even the earliest. Insofar as a woman is Alive and Spiraling at all she must have some glimpse of the Background Present. Therefore any potentially Radical Feminist has the capacity to Hear—if not always to understand all—the messages of the Memory-Bearing Group.

Re-Calling my own Voyage, I know that my ability to begin Be-Speaking was rooted in my capacity for Living in the Present, unmasking the foreground present at least to the extent of experiencing desperation, of Fiercely struggling for Focus, and of daring Outrageous Acts in order to break free and live my own Life. This capacity for be-ing in the Present is the core requirement of Outercourse.

In The Fourth Spiral Galaxy, Voyagers Move into the Age of the Cronehood of Feminism. It is probably the case that the so-called "First Wave" of Feminism, in the nineteenth century, did not enter the Age of Cronehood, even though there lived individual Crones, such as Sojourner Truth and Matilda Joslyn Gage. As a collective Movement, Feminism was derailed and diminished by the forces of patriarchy. The sadosociety had effectively blocked the possibility of fully seeing the multiracial, multiclass, and indeed planetary dimensions of the Feminist movement. Phallocracy had muted the Sense of intensity/urgency/desperation to Move on to Moments of Momentous Re-membering.

In the "Second Wave," although there has been a dreary amount of expenditure of energy in reinventing the wheel and fighting fragmentation, we are faced with the fact that a Qualitative Leap into Cronehood is necessary. This is the age of seemingly irreversible contamination—the time of the (foreground) triumph of phallotechnology. It is a desperate time of biocide, genocide, gynocide. Desperation combined with Furious Focus can hurl a significant New Cognitive Minority of women into The Fourth Spiral Galaxy.

While Feminists within the patriarchal era have always been a cognitive minority, the New Cognitive Minority includes the Memory-Bearing Group of women who have Lived through earlier Moments. It includes our Foresisters/Cronies from the Past who are Presentiating their Selves Now to those whose Sense of Cosmic Connectedness is awakening. The Fourth Spiral Galaxy, then, implies entering Other dimensions of Awareness and Movement, evoking Radical changes at the very core of consciousness.

The Moments of The Fourth Spiral Galaxy began when I began working on *Outercourse*. I have written all of *Outercourse* from the perspective of this Galaxy of Time Traveling. From the vantage point of this Megagalaxy/Metagalaxy I have retraced my earlier Moments, which assume richer meanings as I revisit them. Although the events described Originally happened "back then," in the earlier Galaxies, the Re-Calling of them is occurring Now, and the result is utterly Other than a simple collection of memoirs. It is participating in New Spiraling Movement. This is not quite like any writing that I have done before. It is a series of Acts of Momentous Re-membering of my own Voyage.

THE MEANING AND ROLE OF RECOLLECTIONS FROM MY *LOGBOOK OF A RADICAL FEMINIST PHILOSOPHER*

> *Log* [short for *logbook*]: "a daily record of a ship's speed or progress or the full record of a ship's voyage including notes on the ship's position at various times and including notes on the weather and on important incidents occurring during the voyage."
> —*Webster's Third New International Dictionary of the English Language*

> *Logbook*: "A Daly record . . . et cetera."
> —*Websters' Second New Intergalactic Wickedary of the English Language*

It is clear from the preceding material in this Introduction that this book is both autobiographical and philosophical. The *Logbook* exists largely in my own Memories and in my collection of published and unpublished writings. I do not keep written journals, except those Written in Memory.

Recollections from my *Logbook* do not constitute a clearly distinct entity or separate part within this book. The information from my *Logbook* is interwoven with philosophical analysis in the Course of this Voyage, in which Intellectual/Spiritual/E-motional/Physical/Sensory Travels are inseparable.

The purpose of Recollections from my *Logbook* is to Re-Call the Ideas, Experiences, Passions which constitute the Moments of my Voyage. These can Now be seen and understood from the Be-Dazzling perspective. It is my Hope that these Re-Callings will be helpful to women—mySelf included—in overcoming the time warps that mark the Age of Dis-memberment—the foreground "present" that impedes our Living a true Present/Presence. It is my Hope also that this Re-membering will generate more Gynergy for further Be-Dazzling Voyaging.

SYN-CRONE-ICITIES: HOW THE PHILOSOPHICAL AND BIOGRAPHICAL DIMENSIONS OF THIS BOOK FIT TOGETHER

Syn-Crone-icities○: "coincidences" experienced and recognized by Crones as Strangely significant (*Wickedary*).

The philosophical and biographical dimensions of this book intertwine through multiple "coincidences." That is, they are *coincident*, which according to *Webster's* means "occurring or operating at the same time: CONCOMITANT, ATTENDING." *Coincident* also means "occupying the same space: having the same position, direction, or setting." It means "having accordant characteristics or nature: HARMONIOUS." The philosophical and biographical dimensions or aspects of *Outercourse* participate in the same Time. They share the same position and move in the same direction or setting—the Be-Dazzling Voyage. Thus they have accordant characteristics: they are Harmonious. The philosophical theory and the biographical events recorded here are parts of the same Quest.

Recollections from my *Logbook* are the major source for the philosophical theorizing in this book. One key example is my Realization—through Re-Calling my early experiences—of the enormous and complex role of subliminal knowledge in myself and in other women. Indeed it was my subliminal knowledge of the extent of patriarchal oppression and of the existence or at least the possibility of an Other Reality that guided me and gave me the Courage to keep going through the early stages. When it would have appeared that I was a cognitive minority of one, I was—I Now Realize—strengthened by my subliminal knowledge of similar subliminal knowledge buried in other women.

Looking at the *Logbook* material, I Now understand that all of my Voyaging as a Radical Feminist Philosopher has been over and through a Sea of subliminal knowledge—which I have Named "the Subliminal Sea." As the Voyage has progressed, such knowledge has become more and more overt.

As I Now See it, my Life, my Craft in early stages of consciousness moved on the surface of the Sea of subliminal knowledge that is shared by women under patriarchy. Repeatedly I had experiences of being pushed by a Great Wind, and I could feel the stirrings from the depths of the Subliminal Sea. Eventually there were eruptions from volcanoes in the Sea, in my mind. I came to Name this knowledge "Background" knowledge. I found also that as I Moved more daringly, as I made Qualitative Leaps from Moment to Moment, I was Realizing connections not only within myself and with Other women, but with the Elements of this planet, and with the sun, moon, and stars. I Sensed a cosmic connection.

From my *Logbook* Recollections I have learned that an important part of my task has been and is retrieving the subliminal knowledge of women and Dis-covering ways of communicating this. One reality to be confronted is the fact that the Subliminal Sea—like the oceans of the earth—has been contaminated. It has been polluted by man-made subliminal messages (of the media, of myths, of religion, of all the -ologies, et cetera). Yet, since these messages are reversed derivatives of deep Background knowledge, even these are doorways/viewers into the Background. Part of my task is to devise means of using them in this way.

If women continue to lose our Deep Memories, then the images propagated by the pornographers, the obscene experiments of the reproductive technologists, the mutilation and murder of women's bodies by the sons of Jack the Ripper, and the mutilation and murder of women's minds by omnipresent woman-hating propagandists will go unprotested. Unprotested also will be the rape and murder of the planet.

My *Logbook* material (together with other sources, of course) has supplied me with information about the almost ineffable need for transformation of consciousness, and it has given me clues about ways to go about making such changes.

Outercourse is not sterile cerebration any more than it is a mindless and distracted collection of "interesting experiences." A unifying Focus accounts for the "coincidence" between the philosophical and biographical dimensions of this book. An Outercoursing Voyager experiences participation in a complex Chorus of Be-ing. She is aware of a Background Harmony, of a Telepathic/Telegraphic Connection which is nothing less than an Intergalactic concert of Be-Dazzling Intelligences. This book is an attempt to convey the Sense of this Concert, this behind-the-scenes Eccentric and Outlandish Reality that is Present in everyday occurrences and that can enable us to Re-Weave the Integrity of our Lives.

BE-SPEAKING:
Moments of Prophecy and Promise
(*Oh!*–1970)

Moments of Prophecy and Promise

CHAPTER ONE

EARLY MOMENTS:
MY TABOO-BREAKING QUEST—
TO BE A PHILOSOPHER

As a student in a small, working-class catholic high school in Schenectady, New York, I was a voice crying in the wilderness when I declared that I wanted to study philosophy. Even the sensitive and generous Sister who was always encouraging me to write for publication had no way of empathizing with such an outrageous urge.[1] Moreover, the school library had no books on the subject. Yet this Lust of my adolescent mind was such that I spun my own philosophies at home. I have no idea where I picked up that Strange propensity.

As a result of help from my parents plus winning the Bishop Gibbons scholarship (awarded on the basis of a competitive exam in religion) plus saving money from my supermarket check-out job, I managed to go to a small nearby catholic college for women. Being an inhabitant of the catholic ghetto, I had never even heard of such schools as Vassar, Radcliffe, or Smith. Even if I had heard of them, they would not have been accessible—nor would they have appeared desirable. I wanted to study *"Catholic philosophy,"* and the path of my Questing Journey led logically and realistically to The College of Saint Rose in Albany, New York.

Ironically, the college did not offer a major in philosophy, although a required minor consisting of eighteen credit hours in that subject was imposed upon all students. The difference in my case was that I loved the subject. This love persisted, despite the boringness of priest professors who opined that women could never learn philosophy, and whose lectures consisted of sitting in front of the class and reading aloud from the textbook, thereby demonstrating their ability to read English. They appeared to be thoroughly mystified by my interest, and the mystification was no doubt associated with the fact that they had never experienced enthusiasm for this pursuit in themselves. While they sat and droned, I sat and wondered at the incongruity of the situation. This wondering itself became incorporated into my own philosophical questioning. I did not yet understand that for a woman to strive to become a philosopher was to break a Terrible Taboo.[2]

Although those professors contributed little to the furtherance of my philosophical Quest, my own experiences contributed a great deal. There had been shimmering Moments in early childhood. For example, there was the Time, when I was about five or six, that I discovered the big gleaming block of ice in the snow. There were no words for the experience. The air was crisp and it was late afternoon. There was a certain winter light and a certain winter smell when I came upon the block of ice—probably in our back yard. I was all of a sudden in touch with something awesome—which I would later call Elemental. It was a shock that awakened in me some knowing of an Other dimension and I felt within me one of the first stirrings that I can remember of the Call of the Wild. I know that my capacity for meeting ice in the snow in that way has never totally gone away, because recently, while working on this book, I went for a walk on a winter evening and it happened again. This encounter was Strangely familiar.

The shimmering Moments occurred with great intensity in early adolescence. There was the Moment, for example, when one particular clover blossom Announced its be-ing to me. It Said starkly, clearly, with utmost simplicity: "I am." It gave me an intuition of be-ing. Years later, studying the philosophy of Jacques Maritain, I knew that I was not alone with this intuition.[3]

Yet, of course, I was unspeakably Alone with it. It was always calling me somewhere that no one else could tell me about. It would eventually lead me to cross the Atlantic, basically without any money, to obtain doctorates in theology and philosophy in a strange, medieval university where courses were taught in Latin and where my "fellow students" were catholic priests and seminarians.

The encounter with that clover blossom had a great deal to do with my becoming a Radical Feminist Philosopher. If a clover blossom could say "I am," then why couldn't I?

SPIRALING BACK:
EARLY GRADES AND PRIVATE JUNKETS

It would be difficult to convey the foreground dreariness of the forties and fifties in America, particularly for a potential Radical Feminist Philosopher with a Passion for forbidden theological and philosophical learning—it *would be* difficult if the patriarchal State of Boredom had not managed to repeat itself by belching forth the insufferable eighties and nineties, reproducing a time of dulled-out brains, souls, and passions. So I need not ask the reader to imagine or try to remember such a time; she need only look around.*

---

*There is a difference, however. In the course of the last two decades of this millennium it has been and continues to be possible to Re-member the early Moments of this Wave of the women's movement in the sixties and seventies—either directly or through the writings and stories of Other women who were there. It is also possible to Re-Call Feminists of earlier Times.

In those decades, however, there was no point of comparison, no possibility of nostalgia. There was only the self-legitimating facticity of Boredom, with no apparent way out. For me, however, there was the Call of the Clover Blossom. Propelled by the idea that *I Am*, I made exploratory journeys by way of warming up for my Outercourse, which is, of course, the Direction my life has taken.

But I must Spiral back a bit, because before the Time of that existential encounter, there was "elementary school."

Let me assure the reader that I have always, that is, spasmodically, made abortive efforts to conform. For example, in the first grade at Saint John the Evangelist School in Schenectady, when I perceived that many of my classmates had dirty, secondhand readers, I spat and slobbered over the pages of my own brand-new one to make it appear used. When my teacher, Sister Mary Edmund, asked for an explanation, I was speechless. I have no idea whether she understood my motivation for the slobbering, but I do think that I myself had some idea of attempting to "fit in."

One of my classmates in the first grade, whose name was Rosemary, was hit and killed by a trolley car when she was crossing the street in front of her house. There was some confusing story about her not looking both ways and not hearing the sound of the oncoming trolley because the one she just stepped off had started to move. The whole class had to go with Sister Mary Edmund to see Rosemary "laid out." She was wearing a white dress. I did not like being there. The experience did not fit in with anything. It was like a white blob that hung there. It was impossible to understand and was worse than a nightmare.

My second grade teacher was Sister Mary Clare of the Passion, who droned a lot—too much, I thought—about "God's poor." I did not understand why the poor were God's. I had her again in the fifth grade, and I remember a feeling of deep shock when she made fun of a boy in our class who was really poor and whose name was Abram Spoor. She assaulted him with a jingle which went something like "Abram Spoor . . . and he *is* poor."

Upon reflection, I have come to the conclusion that this shocking behavior was inspired not by malice but by a passion for jingles, puns, and wordplay in general. I remember that it was Sister Mary Clare of the Passion who more than once wrote on the tops of papers I handed in to her the title of the (then) popular hymn "Daily, Daily, Sing to Mary." These words would be crossed off with a very light scribbly line—as if to indicate that she had written them there by mistake. I understood that this was meant as a game or a joke, but I did not see anything very funny about it at the time.[4]

Upon further reflection, I Now realize that this woman had a strong creative streak. One day when I was in the fifth grade she told us all to bring in some toy that we had become sick of. The idea was that we would exchange our old toys and everyone would get something new. I brought in a tin monkey with a drum who obligingly banged this instrument when you turned the key. I was ready to discard this because it seemed much too childish for a person in the fifth grade. I remember that Abram Spoor's face lit up with sheer joy when he saw my mechanical monkey and said, "I'd like *that!*"

No doubt this woman had an interesting time watching all of our transactions and reactions. Personally I was delighted with my own acquisition of two oddly shaped books about "Our Gang." But the truly memorable experience of the day was the look on Abram's face and the sound of his voice when he got my monkey. Obviously he had never owned such a wondrous toy in his whole life. I am struck by the accuracy of Sister's insensitive and unfortunate pun. I Now wonder if her puns popped out uncontrollably without consideration of the consequences. Perhaps her weird and lugubrious name—which in all probability she did not freely choose—inspired her to be rather reckless and satirical with words.[5]

Sister Mary Arthur, who was my teacher in the third and sixth grades, was a handsome young woman with shaggy black eyebrows who stormed up and down the aisles hitting the boys—only the boys—with her ruler. She had my unflagging loyalty and admiration.

These Sisters all belonged to a congregation called "Sisters of the Holy Names." Their coifs had stiff white material extending out along the sides of their faces. This headgear must have seriously affected their peripheral vision. So they had to swivel their heads quite a lot, but I didn't think of this phenomenon as too unusual, since that's how it was at Saint John the Evangelist School and I didn't know any other nuns who could serve as a point of comparison.

I missed quite a few days of school during those first six years of my formal education. Even a slight cold was an excuse for staying home in bed and reading my favorite books, such as *The Call of the Wild*, the "Raggedy Ann" stories, and the "Children of All Lands" stories by Madeline Frank Brandeis. It just seemed right to me that I could break the routine and sail off into my own private world sometimes. The special ambrosia served to me by my mother during these outer space voyages was chilled "Junket," which came in three exquisite flavors: chocolate, vanilla, and strawberry. Maybe it also came in raspberry.

The price extorted by my teachers for these blissful free days was lowering of my grade average, which reduced me to being ranked second highest in the class at the end of some weeks. The way they managed to do this was by averaging in "zeros" for tests missed on my excursion days. I thought that this was very unfair, especially because my rival, Sarah Behan, who never missed a day of school, then got to be first, even though her grades were lower. But those Times of flying free, which gave me an enduring Taste for escaping imposed routines, were worth it. I think that my mother, co-conspirator that she was, knew this.

THE WORLD OF GLOWING BOOKS
AND THE CALL OF THE WILD

Well, the years of elementary school skipped along in this fashion. My passion for the intellectual life burst forth at puberty, in the seventh grade to be precise. Since Saint John the Evangelist School ended with the sixth grade, I had moved on to Saint Joseph's Academy. This catholic school was attached to a working-class German parish and provided education for pupils from the first grade through high school. It was staffed by the Sisters of Saint Joseph of Carondelet. Saint Joseph's Academy no longer even exists. But for me that poor little school was the scene of Metamorphic Moments that can be Re-Called and Re-membered. For many of their hundreds of pupils, some of the Sisters who taught there, who were often unappreciated, created rich Memories of the Future. They formed/transformed our Future, which, of course, is Now.

I was an extremely willing scholar. Few understood my true motivation when I followed the high school students around worshipfully, ogling their armloads of textbooks, especially tomes of chemistry, math, and physics. What was really going on was that I was drooling with admiration and envy because they had access to these learned, fascinating books. It never crossed my mind that their attitudes toward these tomes ranged from indifference to loathing. In my own indomitable innocence I saw these as portals to paradise, as magical and infinitely enticing.

Even though, years later, I found out the less than magical qualities of many of those books, this Dis-covery was not an experience of dis-illusionment. My preoccupation with the high schoolers' tomes of wisdom had been grounded in a Background intuition/Realization of the Radiant Realm of Books, which was not an illusion. Therefore, there was nothing at all to be dis-illusioned about. Later on I did find out about the foreground level of most books, but that took nothing away from my knowledge of the Thisworldly/Otherworldly Reality of Books.[6]

My parents had always given me many beautiful books as presents, especially on holidays. So the World of Glowing Books somehow entered the realm of my imagination very early and became a central focus of the Quest to be a philosopher. More than once in high school I had dreams of wondrous worlds—of being in rooms filled with colorful glowing books. I would wake up in a state of great ecstasy and knowing that this was *my* World, where I belonged.

During that early adolescent time I also Dis-covered the "celestial gleam" of nature. Since my father was a traveling salesman who sold ice cream freezers, I sometimes went with him on drives into the country when he visited his customers' ice cream stands. My awakening to the transcendental glowing light over meadows and trees happened on some of these trips.[7] Other Moments of contact with Nature involved knowing the Call of the Wild from the mountains and purple skies and the sweet fresh smell of snow.

These invitations from Nature to my adolescent spirit were somehow intimately connected with the Call of the World of Glowing Books. My life was suffused with the desire for a kind of Great Adventure that would involve touching and exploring these strange worlds that had allowed me to glimpse their wonders and Lust for more.

TABOO-BREAKING:
"THE CONVENT" AS FLYSWATTER

I was reasonably well equipped to follow this seemingly improbable, not fully articulated, yet crystal clear Call. For one thing I was endowed with insufferable stubbornness—a quality which never failed me. I also had the gift of being at least fifty per cent oblivious of society's expectations of me as a "normal" young woman and one hundred per cent resistant to whatever expectations I did not manage to avoid noticing. For example, I never had the slightest desire to get married and have children. Even in elementary school and in the absence of any Feminist movement I had felt that it would be intolerable to give up my own name and become "Mrs." something or other. It would obviously be a violation of mySelf. Besides, I have always really *liked* my name. I wouldn't sell it for anything. A third asset was a rock bottom self-confidence and Sense of Direction which, even in the bleakest periods, have never entirely deserted me.

Looking back, I recognize that all of these assets were gifts from my extraordinary mother. For one thing, she had always made it clear to me that she had desired only one child, and that one a daughter. I was exactly what she wanted, and all she wanted. How she managed to arrange this I was never told. At any rate my father seemed to have no serious objection. For another thing, I cannot recall that she ever once—even once—tried to promote the idea that I should marry and have a family, although she often said that she was very happily married, and indeed this seemed to be the case. She was hardly one to promote the convent either. I was the one who tossed around that threat, chiefly as a weapon against well-meaning relatives and "friends of the family" who intoned that "some day the right man would come along." I never followed through on my threat of joining the convent, but it worked well enough as a defense against society at large.[8]

This is not to say that I never seriously considered entering the convent. I was not exactly insincere in proclaiming this as a goal. It just seemed indefinitely postponable. Perhaps if the Sisters had had the possibility of becoming great scholars, as I supposed monks did, I would have been more seriously tempted. However, I saw something of the constraints imposed upon their lives. They were deprived of the leisure to study and travel and think creatively to their fullest capacity. Even those who taught in college were confined to somewhat narrow perspectives. The Sisters were in fact assigned to be the drudges of the church.* So I couldn't exactly identify with the convent as a goal and just kept moving on in my own way. Later on I read an article in which someone referred to old maidhood as a sort of "budget religious vocation" which was accorded some modicum of respect in the church, especially during the forties and fifties, and especially if the old maid in question was dedicated to her work. I am sure that message had entered my brain and seemed a pretty good deal to me. I know that some women tried to escape "love and marriage" by joining the convent—a strategy that would have worked better in the Middle Ages when many monasteries were Wild places. But I did not see it as a real Way Out. For me, to be an Old Maid/Spinster was the way to be free. Yet I could not fully articulate that idea, even to myself, because even that idea was Taboo. So I just logically acted on it, while waving the banner of "the convent" like a flyswatter when necessary.

ANNA AND FRANK

One point that was very clear in my mother's approach was that I should have everything she did not have when she was growing up. As a very young child she, Anna, had been taken by her grandmother to be brought up among her numerous aunts and uncles because her mother was too poor to take care of all her children. Although she adored her grandmother, my mother's life as a child was hard. She had a lot of housework to do, including the irksome task of cleaning kerosene lamps. Going to school meant trudging on cold and windy winter days across the bridge connecting South Glens Falls, New York, with the town of Glens Falls. Yet she passionately loved learning, and the tragedy of her life was being "yanked out of school" when still a sopho-more in high school to go to work as a telephone operator in Schenectady, a city about forty miles away.†

Anna worked for the telephone company for sixteen exhausting years. She then met and married my father and they bought a house in Schenectady. After a rather long delay I was born. I arrived just in time for The Great Depression. She often said to me that her home became "like heaven when you came."

My mother was thirty-eight when I arrived on the scene. Since she was brought up by her grandmother, Johanna Falvey, who came over from Ire-

---

*This was perfectly in keeping with the drudge role to which all women were/are assigned by the church and by patriarchal society in general.

†I think it was because of the oppression she endured as a child that my mother repeat-edly warned me not to allow myself to be trapped by "family," that is, relatives who would "try to drag you down."

land because of the potato famine, her memories extended far back over time, and she directly and subliminally transmitted a great deal of the old Irish lore to me. Although my great-grandmother had died before I arrived, she was a towering Presence in my childhood—she who had come over on the boat when she was a fourteen-year-old girl, worked as a maid, married, and had twelve children. She could neither read nor write, and she yet knew much of Dickens and the "Lives of the Saints" by heart because her husband, Dan Buckley, read these books to her over and over. She also knew secrets about nature and the weather, and had a gift of healing, and helped take care of other Irish immigrants and their families in her neighborhood in South Glens Falls when they were sick.

On my father's side, the line to Ireland was just as direct, and the female Presence just as strong. Both of his parents had come over from the Emerald Isle. His father had died shortly after he, Frank, the youngest child, was born. His mother was a strong and shrewd woman who ran a business and supported her five children. It couldn't be helped that my father had to leave school after the eighth grade and go to work. Yet he always had a way with words, and put this to some use, for example, by writing slogans for advertising and sometimes winning prizes for these creative endeavors. I remember that one of these slogans was "Eventually, why not now?"

When I was very small I saw copies of a book my father had written and published. It was about how to sell ice cream equipment and there were photographs in it. Copies of the book (which were stored in a big carton) have long since disappeared.[9] I suppose the sight of those books had something to do with the idea I formed in early childhood that some day *I* would write a book.

From both parents I heard the rhetorical question, "Aren't we Lucky to be Irish?" When I had to fill out forms inquiring about my "nationality," I always wrote "Irish." It did not occur to me that I should write "American." Moreover, since I knew it was Lucky to be Irish I thought I must personally be Lucky. No matter how overwhelming the forces were that tried to disabuse me of this impression, it did, in fact, persist. Moreover, I believe that it worked as a self-fulfilling prophecy.[10]

FRIENDS

Despite this peculiar national pride, I don't think that I was particularly obnoxious. In fact, I was a sort of gang leader and had quite a few friends. For example, when I was six or seven there was Carlie Derwig who lived down the street and whose grandfather "came over on the 'big boat' from Germany." Like some of my other boy friends Carlie liked my girls' toys better than I did. He played for hours with my toy washing machine which made lots of suds. When you turned the handle it went wump, wump, wump. Later he turned his attention to toy cars that went zoom, zoom, zoom and I became very bored with him.

After that there was Eddie Mann who lived next door. One day we had a friendly wrestling match and he broke my elbow, so I had to hang from a bar every day for weeks to straighten it out. I didn't consciously feel mad that he broke my elbow.[11] He was a year older and much bigger and heavier than I was, but I knew that I had freely engaged in the contest. What really puzzled me was the fact that his mother made him come over every day with candy as a sort of apology for beating up a girl. I liked the candy but I felt that something didn't make sense about this. Something was wrong about this whole setup. I don't think we played together much after that.

There was a different and deeper kind of wrong, though, which I had experienced much earlier. It was way before I started school and I have the idea that I was four and a half and that my friend Carol Houghton was five and a half. When she came to my house she jumped all over the furniture and broke things. She broke all my mother's rules for good behavior and I felt boundless admiration for her. I loved Carol. When we went to her house her mother read to us from very advanced books like *The Jungle Book*. Then she and her mother moved away and I didn't know where they went and there was nothing I could do about it. I grieved and grieved.

Some of the children in the neighborhood were not exactly friends, but they were in the picture. Hollace Bascomb, who lived on the same street, was older and he was mentally handicapped. He loved to play with my dolls and doll carriage. I didn't mind this, since they did not interest me. I had formerly had tea with my Patsy Ann doll-friend, but that was when I was only about four. After I started going to school my activity with dolls consisted mainly in lining them up about once every few months and playing orphanage. As the director of the orphanage I removed their fancy clothes and dressed them in rags. Then I put their regular clothes back on them and was through with them until orphanage time came around again.

Some of my friends, of course, lived in books. High in my estimation were Doctor Dolittle and Buck, the boydog hero of *The Call of the Wild*. I identified with both. The girls in the books hardly ever seemed to *do* anything interesting except live in other countries sometimes, so there was nothing to think about them and that was very depressing.

I also had friendly connections with my guardian angels and with a number of animals in the neighborhood, with certain trees (a catalpa tree, especially), and with the rosebush and the lilac bush that grew in our back yard, and the dandelions that came back every year.

INDICATIONS OF "SOMETHING(S) WRONG"

Perhaps it was because of my friendship with trees that the horrible thing happened when I was in the sixth grade. It was mid-December and my father and I had gone out to buy the christmas tree. After we had dragged it into the house we were whittling its stump to fit into its holder. Suddenly a wave of horror came over me, which I could not articulate. The feeling haunted and terrified me and I did not know what it meant. Looking back, I would call it an intuition of nothingness. It was a sense of sheer emptiness.

I had always loved christmas trees—the smell of the pine needles and the magical, colorful lights and the presents strewn underneath. It had not occurred to me that the christmas tree in my house had been killed and dolled up, that it only smelled alive after it was dead. I'm sure that on that particular christmas I did not realize any of this explicitly either. But I *knew* that something was terribly wrong before I knew *what* was wrong. Many years later I uncovered some of the layers implicit in that intuition.[12]

I know that I also had subliminal knowledge about other holidays, even though I had no way to articulate this knowing. I felt that there was something horrible about the thanksgiving holiday. It was as if there were a grey fog over it. It was not just that it was a boring holiday comprised of having relatives over for a big turkey dinner. I liked the food and, at worst, the relatives were merely dull. The point is that I had an inkling of something else behind it all—something wrong. I had read the school textbook versions of the origins of thanksgiving and had seen the usual tedious pictures of the pious pilgrims. These were less than inspiring. There was no way I could have known that what the pilgrims were celebrating and thanking god about was the massacre of Native Americans. When I finally did find out about that, my childhood feelings of malaise made perfect sense.

Halloween was something else. It was supposed to be about bad creatures—witches, hobgoblins, and spooks. But I had none of those creepy feelings about Halloween. It did not send out tentacles trying to suck me into some tame world. It was exciting and inviting, calling me into some wonderful place that was connected with the moon and with the night. Halloween costumes were not at all like easter dresses. One year I was George Washington and another year I was a Witch. That was *really* dressing up. And Jack-O'-Lanterns with candles in them were stuff that dreams are made of. In my mind they were connected with the World of Shining, Glowing Books. I loved Halloween.

Then there was easter. I did like toy rabbits, easter baskets, jelly beans, and coloring and hunting for easter eggs. I hated the stuff about easter bonnets and dressing up and going to church. But my sense about the wrongness of easter pointed beyond all that. Even leaving aside the "Resurrection" business, it was supposed to be about the joy of spring. But there was no Wild joy about easter. It was not really about nature but about tame things that held me back from being in nature, like frilly girls' Sunday clothes. If I had had the word then, I would have said that this holiday was really stuck in the foreground.

My intuitions about the evil of dullness and taming were not confined to holidays. Several blocks away from my house there was an "umbrella tree" on Eastern Avenue. This tree was perpetually trimmed so as to appear like an artifact. It was utterly tidy and formal. I had to walk past it several times each week on the way to Saint John the Evangelist School and to the store. Every time I saw it I felt depressed. I would say Now, that what was going on was an awakening of subliminal awareness of patriarchy's perpetual fore-grounding of the Wild, its killing of free and spontaneous expression of Life. The tree wasn't free to be its Self. But of course I didn't know how to say any of this. I just felt unhappy whenever I saw that tree.[13]

Another indicator that there was something wrong in the world was the fate of my two pet white rabbits, Peter and Jacky. One morning I went out to feed them their carrots and found that their tails had been cut off. There was some talk of "bad boys" in the neighborhood. This was a rotten kind of "bad" that I had not realized existed—the kind that puts a horrid film over everything. Later that day my rabbits disappeared. I think I was told that they had run away. I don't know whether I believed that or figured out that my parents had taken them somewhere, but I never saw them again.

One of the rotten bad kind of boys was the big bully who repeatedly tried to corner me on my way to school and invade with his hands while I yelled and kicked. I also had the usual encounters with dirty old men in parks and movie theaters that plague most active little girls. I did not entirely escape their gross manifestations of an insatiable need to expose their inadequacies and "reach out and touch someone." Yet, as I have said, I have been Lucky. So I always managed to escape serious molestation or violation. I could not at that time understand how this disgusting stuff fit together with what was done to my rabbits or with the horrible intuition about the christmas tree, but I did file away all of this important information, and later on—much later on—I made the connections.

I took chances. I remember casually walking home from school one day through Vale Cemetery on Nott Terrace, which was known to be spooky and dangerous. It had a woodsy part with a pond in it where there were no graves and where several children were said to have drowned. Also tramps hung out in that part. I strolled through there past a group of tramps who were eating lunch and I remember that one of them had a knife. I just kept walking past them. I don't think it was a matter of being especially brave. It was partly that I was oblivious and partly that I had a kind of sixth sense which told me nothing bad was going to happen.

When you walked all the way through Vale Cemetery you came to the part near my house which was sunny and where there were lots of graves. I distinctly remember the sunshine over the grass there and sensing that it would not be a bad thing to go back to the earth. There was something right about it.

What really scared me, though, was the movie *Dracula*, which I saw when I was about nine or ten. I went to see it with some other kids and had terrible nightmares for months. I would scream for my mother at night, and for many years it haunted me. I knew that it was tapping into some horrible truth.*

IN THE WAKE OF THE GREAT DEPRESSION

The house we lived in when I was growing up had originally been owned by my parents but they lost it as a result of The Depression. The bank took it. After hearing my parents talk about this I concluded that you really can't own a house. *They* can always take it away.

Anyway, we continued to live in the yellow two-family house which the bank had taken. We rented the first floor. The top floor was occupied by Mr. and Mrs. MacReady and their son Archie when he was not in jail. Mrs. MacReady was a social climber who tried to live beyond her means. Mr. MacReady was a quiet man, and he was depressed. We would see him carrying meals to Archie when he was in jail, and my mother said that he felt ashamed.

I didn't like Mrs. MacReady very much. She belonged to the episcopalian church where the rich people went. Once she invited me to go with her to a christmas play at her church and I didn't want to go but I went. I was very bored. There was always something fake about how you had to be around her. Instead of serving real butter she mixed some kind of yellow coloring with margarine and it tasted awful. I could not act as if I liked it. My mother said she did that so she could save money to buy expensive clothes and make a good impression. I was not impressed.

One day Hollace Bascomb went up into our attic to look through my old toys. I think he may have been looking for my doll carriage. At any rate he opened the window and a bird got in. My mother told me that there was an Irish belief that if a bird came into the house someone would die.

I believe it was shortly after the bird came in that Mr. MacReady hanged himself in the attic. My mother found him when I was at school. She was very upset. She said that Mr. MacReady had looked sad the last time she had seen him, and it was as if he were saying good-bye. I think I was about ten when this happened.

I felt very sad when I realized that my parents were going to die some day. I suppose that understanding came over me gradually but it became clear and focused one evening when I was sitting alone on our front steps. My parents were out, probably shopping, and it was dark. I saw the headlights of cars as they went by. They came and then they were gone. So that was how it was! I grieved a lot when the realization of future loss came back, especially as I was going to sleep.

---

*In the course of The Third Spiral Galaxy I would write about vampirism as a patriarchal phenomenon. See Daly, *Gyn/Ecology*, pp. 81–83, 375.

After Mr. MacReady's suicide, hanging seemed to become almost a popular habit in our neighborhood. Mrs. Priess, who had come over from Germany, where as she said she had "worked twenty years for a feather bed," hanged herself in her attic next door. Her husband, Mr. Priess, who owned that house and worked on it all the time and believed in saving money, became very lonely and depressed. I saw him sitting with his head on the kitchen table. This reinforced my personal conviction that there wasn't much to be said for owning a house and saving money.

Saving money was not exactly in keeping with my parents' way of life. We always had real butter and good food in general. They bought the highest quality that they could afford of clothes and toys and things like that, mainly for me. In my own mind I formed two categories of people—the savers and the spenders. My parents were spenders. Since my father did not have a regular salary, this style of living was not always easy to pull off. We depended upon his "commissions" on sales of ice cream freezers, and these were very irregular. I remember that one winter, when I was growing very fast, all of my dresses were too short, but my mother couldn't afford to buy me a new one right away. I was so embarrassed that I refused to take off my snow pants indoors in front of my friends. They laughed at me, which made me feel that I was peculiar. Still, on the whole, we were very Lucky.

Ever since I was quite small I had enjoyed the feeling of walking along the street with coins jingling in my pocket. I particularly liked having pennies in the pocket of my shorts. I could go to the neighborhood store and buy a large variety of penny candy for five cents, which made me feel like a big spender. The candy—spearmint leaves, candy cigarettes, root beer barrels, chicken bones, and "false teeth" made of flavorful chewing wax—provided an extraordinary gustatory and aesthetic experience.

Looking back, I think the whole subject of money must have been as puzzling to my parents as it was to me. My mother gave me a shiny toy cash register which was a bank for saving nickels, dimes, and quarters. I saved money from my allowance, with her encouragement, for a bicycle. Somehow, also, I picked up the clear impression that it would be a good idea to get a part-time job later on and save to go to college.[14] But the basic idea I learned was that the important thing was to live for the day, because everything was bound to turn out all right eventually anyway.

JUST DIFFERENCES

Shortly after Mrs. Priess hanged herself, a man who lived around the corner did it too, which made him the third one, but I didn't know him. In any case there was just so much I could take in on the subject of hanging. Besides, there were many other things to think about. There was school, for example, and some events were very trying. There was an irritating blond boy named

Peter who gloated over the fact that girls could not be altar girls. I was struck by the injustice of this and I hated him for gloating and sneering.

I don't remember that I ever made the connection between the way Peter sneered at girls and the way people talked about "niggers." I do know that I fought against the irrationality in both cases. When relatives and friends of the family said that "they" were "just different" I would ask over and over again what difference it made just because someone's skin was a different color. I liked to get a tan. So what? And they would reply that there just was a "difference."

There weren't many African Americans (we said "Negroes" then) in Schenectady. Most lived near Lafayette Street which was at least a mile away from our house. I was told that they lived there because they were "poor," but no one explained why they were poor. One family in our neighborhood was thought to be Mulatto, but no one knew for sure, and they "kept to themselves."[15] There were no Negro kids in my school. Still, the subject occasionally would come up when relatives visited, and when I challenged them they ended the discussion by referring to the (undefined) "difference." It was as hopeless as asking why girls could not be altar girls. It went around and around in circles and didn't make any sense.

One day a woman came to our front door taking orders for books for children. On her list was a book about ships which sounded great to me and to my mother too. She was going to order it, but the woman sort of sneered and said it would be *silly* to order *that* for a little *girl*. My mother was taken aback and didn't order anything and the woman left a pamphlet for me about a book called *The Little Engine That Could*. I thought that her pamphlet on *The Little Engine That Could* was the silliest thing I had ever seen. I wondered what I was missing out on that was in that book about ships.

Perhaps the most remarkable inheritance bestowed upon me by my mother was the flood of encouraging messages about *my work*. She was a meticulous housekeeper, but she thoroughly discouraged me from helping with any of the housework.[16] Whenever I made one of my halfhearted offers to do the dishes she would invariably say: "No, you go and do your own work, dear." What that meant to me when I was eight, nine, and fifteen was, essentially, that I had to find out what my work was, and go do it.[17]

I remember that very early on—when I was about nine or ten—I decided that my work was to be a writer. But that left open the question: "Writer about *what?*" What did I know to write about? At the time I tried my hand on a few poems. One, for example, was on the subject of "My [nonexistent] Dog," and another was an edifying piece on "My [utterly inauthentic] Love" for my classmates Charlie Duffy and Clement Higby (a triangular nonaffair).

I was in the eighth grade at Saint Joseph's Academy when the bombing of Pearl Harbor happened. We were at war. My consciousness was saturated with messages about "the war." My father had to relinquish his freedom and work in a factory (General Electric). My mother, who hadn't been employed for many years, became a switchboard operator at the Van Curler Hotel. We took in as a roomer a woman who also did war work at G.E. There was rationing. There were air raid drills and practice blackouts. We had lived through The Depression and now there was this, and it was very interesting.

No doubt my behavior was sometimes outrageous and took its toll on my parents. When I was in the eighth or ninth grade my father expressed his dissatisfaction with my tomboyish ways. I remember his commenting to my mother: "Mary just doesn't have any personality, does she?" I did not respond positively to this obliteration of my soul. His comment had been occasioned by my appearance one day when I came home attired in blue jeans, a red plaid lumberjack shirt, and a rough cap—an outfit which I had purchased with great satisfaction at Sears Roebuck with my savings. My mother also expressed her displeasure at the fact that I always wanted to wear "boys' things." I did not think of these as "boys' things," but simply as stuff I liked.[18]

Even before that I had begun detecting some elusive difference between myself and my parents. I think I was about eleven when I demanded to see my birth certificate because of my suspicion that I had been adopted. Even that proof, when produced, was not satisfactory. I worried that there could have been a switch of babies in the hospital. There really was no absolute proof of my identity.

ENIGMAS, DISCOVERIES, DISRUPTIONS

I had Strange philosophical worries. I pondered with perplexity the idea that George Washington was the first president of the United States. If he was "first," what could have been before that? What could "first" possibly mean? I saw a great gaping blank that must have been before, if he was the first. I had been afflicted with this particular concern at a very young age—perhaps five or six. If I ever had tried to express it, no one had said anything that resolved the problem. It remained an enigma.

Later on I had other anxieties as well. I worried that I might suddenly and unaccountably become pregnant. I had the impression that some girls were actually afflicted in this way and then became "unwed mothers." The reader will have to understand that sex education was not exactly stressed at that time in Irish catholic culture. To me it sounded something like catching leprosy—a possibility which also worried me since several of my teachers had spoken admiringly of saints who got this disease.[19]

Menstruation was a different story. In the seventh grade the school nurse, who always wore a dark blue dress, informed me of this impending event and told me that when I saw blood in the toilet I would be frightened and scream at first but would get used to it. One day I did see red and was not at all frightened, but I screamed bloody murder because I thought this was what one did. I was trying to conform. When my mother came rushing into the bathroom I did not explain that I was merely fulfilling the expectation of the school nurse. She believed I was frightened and I did not disabuse her of this belief. I suppose that I did not want to spoil the high drama of the occasion.

In high school I loved science and math. I felt that these subjects did something good for my brain, making it feel clean and clear. I disrupted classes frequently by asking questions that teachers had a hard time answering. With one nun in particular, this propensity worked greatly to my disadvantage. She taught a wide variety of subjects—as did all four of the Sisters who constituted the entire high school faculty—and among these was physics. I was the only girl who elected to take that subject and she determined to drive me out of the class filled with boys by humiliating me in front of them. She succeeded. So I took third-year German, which was fun, especially since it was taught by an excellent teacher, Sister Genevieve Greisler, who always had a twinkle in her eye.[20] But I was angry that I was missing out on physics.[21]

I also fooled around somewhat boisterously in class. This was in large measure due to the fact that I had to sit there while the teachers explained things which I had understood immediately, for example, the rules of grammar and math, over and over for the benefit of those who were slower at learning. This group consisted largely of boys. Indeed it mainly consisted of most—though not all—of the boys in our class of twenty-six students. It was not just that they didn't study. The problem was that they just didn't get it. This situation had a couple of advantages. One was that the subject matter, for example, syntax, was indelibly imprinted in my brain from so much needless repetition. Another—and more important—advantage was that I was now basically equipped to see through all the myths of male intellectual superiority—forever. It would not be possible for me to be tricked by patriarchal propaganda on that subject, ever. This was possibly the most important lesson that I learned in high school. What I could not understand was how anyone could possibly believe such outrageous propaganda.

Sometimes I was kicked out of the classroom into the hall for indefinite periods—maybe even for hours—for being disruptive. One of my favorite teachers was my primary kicker-outer. However, there was no malice or injustice in her action. Possibly she decided that it was either her or me and chose her own survival. I rather enjoyed the notoriety and my vacations out in the halls. I remember that one of the nuns called up my mother one day and told her she would like to murder me. I don't think I took this literally. I suspect that my mother was amused.

ADVENTURES, EXPLORATIONS, ALTERNATIVES

My gang leader propensities led to my becoming president of "The Polka Dots," an organization which consisted of the girls in our class (there were about twelve or thirteen of us). We began it in the ninth grade and it continued throughout high school and even for a while afterward. Our homes were dispersed throughout the Schenectady area, and "The Polka Dots" was our answer to the resulting isolation. We met at our respective houses every month and did things like go on very long hikes and explorations together. We really enjoyed each other's company, sharing good food and hilarious conversations, laughing uproariously at our own jokes. We even had a mascot named Polky. This was a nondescript, floppy-eared, polka-dotted, stuffed animal. She/he/it was always present at our meetings, having been passed on at the end of each session to the Polka Dot at whose house the next meeting was scheduled to take place.

I also enjoyed solitary adventures. The love of jingling coins in my pocket had never deserted me. Now, however, my penchant for penny candy was replaced in large measure by a desire for hamburgers. So I would sometimes take off on my own at lunchtime for the "White Tower," a hamburger stand within walking distance of Saint Joseph's Academy. There, for twenty-five cents, I could purchase two "junior" hamburgers, a piece of pie, and a coke. I took great pleasure in the smell of the onions frying while I sat in proud independence in my booth waiting for my order. Invigorated by this exotic repast I would return to confront the ordinary trials of school.

My best friend during the six years at Saint Joseph's was Clare Hall. In the seventh and eighth grades we did things like smoking cigars together and sneaking into protestant churches. Throughout the ensuing years Clare was a loyal and active Polka Dot. One of our problems was finding interesting activities to while away the school lunch hour. Our imaginations were fertile and our spirits restless, so we organized such activities as investigating the local jail on the pretence that this visit was required as a social science project.

In the seventh and eighth grades and in the early years of high school I was popular with some of the boys, who bestowed boxes of Fanny Farmer chocolates and other goodies upon me. I did not really get what the fuss was all about and no doubt failed to respond appropriately. Anyhow, the candy stopped coming. This probably had a lot to do with the fact that I deliberately became a sort of slob as the years of high school went on. I suppose this behavior implied some kind of choice in the direction of marginality, taking the form of "unattractiveness." I became known as "the brain," but I did not dislike this appellation, since I greatly valued this part of my anatomy.

School dances were awful. The girls were supposed to stand around and hope to be picked out by some male to be his "partner." Part of my problem was that I could not (or would not) learn how to "follow" a dance partner and would invariably end up leading, which I couldn't do correctly either.

The junior and senior proms were grim events. Most of the boys in our class would not invite the girls. So many of us had to ask boys to "take" us, or else not go.[22] I felt humiliated about asking a boy, but the "choice" of not going was unthinkable. So I went through with it even though I hated the idea of going at all. The whole prom phenomenon was an inescapable mind-fuck, masked as pure delight.

There were no sports for girls at St. Joseph's Academy. The one sport offered was basketball, and that was reserved for boys. Girls could be cheerleaders. I could not understand this phenomenon of cheering for boys. Still, on practice days, when my friends who were cheerleaders wore identical green sweaters to class, I wore my own green sweater to school, even though it was a different shade of green. I remember doing this, but I am not sure that I understood why I was doing it. I was, of course, trying to bond and identify with my friends.

I made other choices. For example, I chose to go with my classmate Ann Hogan to junior training classes for the Women's Army Corps (W.A.C.). We were supposed to learn to march in step and to shoot rifles in a rifle range at the armory. I was not adept at marching in step and I remember being yelled at—"Hey, you on the end!" So—I was walking in the wrong direction, so what? When I tried shooting a rifle the noise stunned me.

I don't think I returned to W.A.C. training more than two or three times. Clearly, not only cheerleading for the boys but also the military life were crossed off my list of possible avenues of self-expression. I brooded, not for the first time, over the possibility that I was a little odd—perhaps downright peculiar. Maybe I was a misfit?

ODD THINGS

One thing that had always—since I had learned to spell—made me feel peculiar was the address of our house. It was "6 Grosvenor Square." I had to spell it for people who did not live on our street and explain that the "s" in "Grosvenor" was silent. Either they pronounced it "Gross-venor" or else they pronounced it right and spelled it wrong. Combined with "Square" and "Schenectady" this was a funny address, especially to anyone who was not from Schenectady. So I had to recite: "'Grosvenor' is spelled G-r-o-s-v-e-n-o-r. Yes, it is 'Square' and not 'Street.'" If they were not from Schenectady my recital went on: "'Schenectady' is spelled S-c-h-e-n-e-c-t-a-d-y. It is an Indian name."

Our street was only one block long and one day some officials changed the numbers on the houses and ours became something like "1306 Grosvenor Square." This made it even queerer. Even "they" must have come to recognize this because they changed the numbers back again.

This alone may not seem very strange but there were other things. For example, I did not have a real middle name. My mother's explanation for this was that she didn't want to saddle me with too many names. I would choose my confirmation name and that would be enough. Four names would be too many. So when I was confirmed at the age of nine I picked the confirmation name "Frances," after my father. My mother's middle name was "Catherine" and that had been another possible choice. She told me it didn't matter which one I chose but when I decided on "Frances" I could see in her face that she was disappointed. But then she said that was wonderful and I stuck with my decision. That was partly because we reasoned that I was named "Mary" after my mother's sister and so adding "Frances" balanced it out to represent both sides of the family. So it turned out to be "fair."[23]

Anyway, when I wrote "Mary Frances Daly" it seemed phony, because I knew that it was only a confirmation name. Whenever anyone asked my middle name I felt peculiar saying "Frances" because it wasn't real, really. Combined with my funny address, it meant more and more explanations. Much later on, when I signed my name "Mary F. Daly" for banks and social security and junk like that it still felt phony and it seemed that the "F" belonged only to the fake documents of that phony world. No one who *knew* me called me "Mary Frances," except for one teacher who didn't know me at all. Maybe "F" stood for "fake," "false," "funny," or "fraud," or—come to think of it—"foreground."

Another odd thing was my father's name. It was Frank X. Daly. He said he was named after saint Francis Xavier. This in itself was not so unusual. However, he pronounced it "X-avier." It was many years before I learned that most people said "Zavier." There were other funny things about the way my father talked sometimes. For example, he pronounced "film" like "fillum." Moreover, he wore his hat perched in an odd way on his head. Much later on, when traveling in County Clare, Ireland, I realized the reason for some of these peculiarities. Even though my father was born in America his parents were from over there, which would explain a great deal about him. So when I discovered that people in Ireland actually say "fillum" and that the older men in Clare wear their hats perched on their heads it all began to fit together. Also, I noted that the people in that area like music and have a way with words and are very shy. So I came to understand in a different light my father's attachment to his piano, his way with words, and his embarrassed shyness.

Such odd things really are too numerous to mention. But together they signaled my growing Sense of Direction as Subliminal Sea Sailor, Boundary Dweller, and Outlandish Outsider.

SPIRALING ON

At any rate, as I moved on into high school I wrote more and more essays and poetry. I had an irregular column in the Albany diocesan newspaper, and a few of my poems were published in national anthologies of poetry by high school students. Sister Athanasia Gurry, who was my English teacher for four years, was consistently inspiriting in this direction.

The present tense would also be accurate here, because I can still Sense the Presence and influence of this extraordinary woman even as I am writing these lines. Her constant encouragement and love and her own remarkable spirit and creativity transformed that small parish school into a time/space that, for me, often shimmered with intimations of transcendence—which I can Re-member Now.

With the very modest means at her disposal in that school, Sister Athanasia orchestrated extraordinary accomplishments. For example, she organized and managed a delightful library for the high school students. It was there that I first encountered such geniuses as Emily and Charlotte Brontë. Although it is true that I bemoaned the fact that it contained no philosophy books, that complaint was absolutely peculiar to me. It would have been— and was—unreasonable to expect philosophy texts to materialize there in that day and age.

Another Memory of the Future which she created was our graduation. Class Day, which involved weeks (maybe months) of preparation, was a beautiful event. There was a formal dinner at the Van Curler Hotel at which we sang songs we had practiced during the preceding weeks.[24] One particularly moving song was called "Green Cathedral."[25] Its melody and some of its words are permanently embedded in my Memory. Clare was salutatorian and I gave the valedictory address. I remember this as a polysyllabic oration on a subject not of my own choosing—"Pax ex Justitia" ("Peace from Justice")—which was inflicted on me by the principal, Reverend Leo B. Schmidt, who was pastor of Saint Joseph's Church and who was memorable for the fact that he wept a lot, particularly during his own sermons. The subject was no doubt considered appropriate because World War II had ended just the year before.

The actual bestowing of our diplomas took place in the church. I enormously enjoyed marching down the aisle in rhythm with "Pomp and Circumstance," and would gladly have continued marching for hours. Perhaps I am still marching to it. The sense of pride, beauty, and hope that the whole event created has never gone away.

It was Sister Athanasia especially who, together with Sister Genevieve,[26] inspired and fueled my determination to reach for the stars. I remember having a strong sense that my decision—and Lust—to become a writer implied a willingness to forego some other things, but it was a completely unambiguous choice. I felt strongly that I wanted to throw my life as far as it would go.

One summer day, while I was lying on the grass near one of the local swimming holes, I had my encounter with the clover blossom that gave me an intuition of be-ing. Then I really began to know *what* I should write about. So I began my Taboo-breaking Quest—to be a philosopher.

CHAPTER TWO

ONWARD BY DEGREES

For years I had looked forward with longing to attending college, and I had wanted specifically to go to The College of Saint Rose. In some ways Saint Rose did fulfill my dream. I took challenging courses taught by women who were very competent in their fields. They were *demonstrating* that women could be college professors. Moreover, they cared about their students.

These women were all Sisters of Saint Joseph of Carondelet. They belonged to the same Congregation as the Sisters who had taught at Saint Joseph's Academy. Since I was accustomed to having teachers who were intelligent and inspiring, it is possible that I took these qualities for granted. I had no point of comparison.

Well, that is, I had no point of comparison as far as *women* were concerned. However, there were the priests. They taught *all* of the courses in philosophy and religion, which were considered subjects too exalted for the female mind but were required of all students anyway. They taught with abominable incompetence, and they could not have cared less.[1]

It was especially unfortunate that all of the philosophy courses were taught by these fellows, since this was the subject I truly loved. Everything else was of secondary interest to me. Had the college offered a major in philosophy, I would have chosen this, despite the quality of teaching, because at least I could have studied the books.

As I have explained earlier, the college imposed upon all students a required minor in philosophy consisting of eighteen credit hours (in addition to our freely chosen minors).[2] Some of the priests were very vocal in expressing their contempt for women's intellects. Although the Sisters did not express their opinions about the ability of women to learn philosophy, I doubt that they agreed with the priests, but the whole matter was fraught with ambivalence. On the one hand, a "Catholic higher education" was considered incomplete without the study of "Catholic philosophy." On the other hand, since many of the Sisters had themselves studied at Saint Rose, they certainly knew about the calibre of the priests' teaching. Undoubtedly many of them had acquired an unacknowledged distaste for that subject as well as for the study of "religion."[3]

For me, this ambivalence was excruciating. Even though philosophy was wretchedly taught, it was *there*, and I devoured the textbooks. But I profoundly wanted more—much more.

THE HIDDEN BROKEN PROMISE

Throughout my twelve years of school I had been in coeducational environments. Now, in this college for women, I felt an aura of dullness. It seemed that something was missing. I thought, then, that the missing factor must have been the presence of boys. But this was too simple an explanation. I would say Now that my early experience of coeducation had masked the condition of women in the real world. This was especially the case since all of the real authority figures—over both girls and boys—were women. (The pastor and the priests who dropped in occasionally to "take over" religion classes were obviously figureheads.)

At Saint Rose—virtually a world of women—I was directly confronted with evidence of the stunting and taming of women conditioned in a society which I later learned to call "patriarchy." Not until many years had passed—in 1968, during the cresting of the women's movement—would I first experience the Real Power of Presence of women to each other in Women's Space, as we took over classrooms and buildings, coming together for our *own* purposes.[4]

There was no Feminist context and no vocabulary to enable me to Name what it was that was missing in that college for women. What I unconsciously longed for was what Emily Culpepper in the 1970s Named *Gynergy*—"the female energy which both comprehends and creates who we are; that impulse in ourselves that has never been possessed by the patriarchy nor by any male; woman-identified be-ing."[5]

This was not a space that could Spark Gynergy. That is, it was not Women's Space, any more than convents, ladies' auxiliaries, women's prisons, women's clubs, or other women's colleges were then or are today—even though there are oases on the Boundaries of some colleges now, taking the form of Women's Centers, Women's Studies classes, and Feminist activist groups.

What I Sensed was the repression and oppression of all these women together but not together—an enforced narrowness of horizons. This was not a finishing school. The teachers were well-prepared and enthusiastic. Many of the students were very bright. Nevertheless, an all-pervasive subliminal message was that we were indeed finished, by definition. We were not destined for greatness. That message hung like a miasma over everything. If being there was not quite like living mentally in a straightjacket, I did sometimes feel as if my spirit was stuffed into a Victorian corset. I longed to be free.

But of course there were no words available to communicate these feelings, this lack. There should have been explosions of Background Feminist consciousness. After all, Sappho, Matilda Joslyn Gage, and Virginia Woolf had gone before. But these and almost all Foresisters had been completely erased.

Still, I was as emotionally attached to my "Alma Mater" as anyone. My college did offer good things, after all. I had camaraderie with other young women who were "getting an education" and having good times together. But the whole setup was also an illusion. It was a broken Promise, but nobody admitted that, and nobody could say what was the Promise that was broken.

Looking at the situation from my Present perspective, I see that these four years in an all-female educational environment were so heartbreaking precisely because of this hidden broken Promise. Buried among the wreckage of women's dreams under the oppression of patriarchy has been the dream of a Feminist University—a School in which women could unravel the lies of phalloscholarship and Dis-cover our own history, literature, science, philosophy.[6] Women's colleges have been—and still are—dim foreground simulations of such Places of Study. They have been like disneyland, mimicking the Wild Realms of Nature. They have aroused expectations of something wonderful—something which they cannot offer and cannot even speak about, except in broken words and sentences, occasionally Disclosing glimmers of what might have been and could still be, if only a few women could allow themselves to See.

The fact is, however, that the women in my college at that time could *not* do this. The patriarchally imposed blinders and mindbindings were thick and tight. The tragedy was that everyone was crippled by the invisible broken Promise—struggling to survive. I would like to believe that some were also struggling, in their own ways, to break free.

I had good and loyal friends in college, especially my roommates Kay Fitzpatrick and Mary Jane Fina. We all visited each other at our parents' homes and had genuine conversations. I don't really know whether they or any of my other friends shared my grief over the broken Promise. This did not appear to be the case. Looking back, I am certain that I was not able to articulate my grief at that time, when such words as *Feminism* and *Lesbianism* were never spoken. This was the late forties, the time/space of dulldom, when/where we were not even supposed to know that dullness existed.

Of course I did not *appear* to be grieving over such an elusive Promise. If my yearbook is a reliable indicator, I was considered witty, as well as scholarly and extremely active—hardly a "sad sack." If my memory is a reliable source, I was always ready for a mischievous adventure. What was going on here was a subliminal grieving which could be recognized as such only many years later. Insofar as there was overt, identifiable grieving, this was over my father's illness and his death in June of 1949, at the end of my junior year.

My father had suffered a heart attack when I was in high school and he was sick and later slowly dying during my college years. My mother, who was fully aware of his approaching death, did her best to conceal her sadness, but there were times when her tears welled over. So I did indeed grieve over his illness and death and over her situation. But I know that this was distinct from my sorrow over the broken Promise of that college for women, although it may have masked this Nameless experience.

After graduation, Mary Jane went to medical school and Kay, who had majored in English, entered the convent. We went our separate ways and lost contact after a short time. Within a few years, most of my classmates were married. The common joke that the only desired degree was the "Mrs." had functioned as a self-fulfilling prophecy.

Part of the broken Promise syndrome had been the blunting of female friendship. There was a Terrible Taboo against deep psychic connections among women as well as the emotional and physical expression of such connections.* This Total Taboo blocked energy, friendship, and creativity on all levels.†

I think it is significant that my experiences of female friendship in college were somehow less robust, healthy, and spontaneous than my childhood and high school experiences. The latter blossomed in environments that were less weighed down by the Terrible Taboo. Perhaps this is because these coeducational environments were less loaded with the *potential* for female bonding and therefore less repressive.

It is also possible that the subtle and unacknowledged effects of class differences had something to do with the less spontaneous and less Sparky character of most of my relationships with my classmates in college. For although this institution was referred to by the nuns as a college for girls of the working class, this was not entirely true. There was a range of economic backgrounds. I am Now able to see that I received countless subliminal messages concerning my "inappropriate" behavior and style from classmates who came from upwardly mobile middle-class backgrounds. The fact was that I never did "fit in," and that my (mutually) chosen friends were mostly from economic backgrounds that somewhat resembled my own.

What made all of this so difficult was the fact that I did not consciously understand the unacknowledged class snobbery and therefore could not confront it directly. This befuddlement, combined with the fact that all, or nearly all, of the students seemed to be planning on marriage, threw me into a kind of mystified marginal situation.

Since I was cast into this situation I was quite acutely aware of what I Now call "the dull tone." This was not an experience that I enjoy remembering, and I have had to overcome some resistance to recalling that time, which

---

*Terrible Taboo○ is defined as "the universal, unnatural patriarchal taboo against women Intimately/Ultimately Touching each Other; prohibition stemming from male terror of women who exercise Elemental Touching Powers" (*Wickedary*).

†Total Taboo○ means "prohibition against the Terrible Totality of female bonding—against direct physical and emotional contact and especially against the exercise of the Spiritual Touching Powers of women" (*Wickedary*).

was marked by the drone of that tone. Now, in Naming the dull tone, I am aware of its oppressive/repressive implications that I was not then able to Dis-cover or decode.

I don't know if my roommates or other friends ever would have become Radical Feminists, but I do know that a certain quality of energy was stopped dead in many by the universal patriarchal Taboo and that an enormous Female Potential was affectively/effectively blocked—a Potential that, if unleashed, could change the course of the world. The Potential that I am identifying here is Elemental/Spiritual Power.

So part of the broken Promise was the stunting of spiritual/psychic knowledge. On an academic level, college religion courses were unchallenging and uninspiring, functioning to reinforce traditional beliefs about women's role. These did not arouse my interest but they did stir my anger, which was a major contribution after all. That smoldering Rage stayed with me over the years, as I accumulated countless other pieces of evidence of phallocratic erasure and enslavement of women and Dis-covered the connections among these. Years later my Rage finally burst into the flames of Pyrogenetic Passion, providing fuel for my Be-Dazzling Voyage.

Reflecting upon those years, I recognize that the great advantage bestowed upon me by my marginal situation was that it was also an opportunity. It had the potential to become liminal—that is, to be a threshold to Other and New perceptions. For while I may have appeared reasonably comfortable to my teachers and classmates, I was not. I was Nagged by my smoldering subliminal knowledge that something was wrong and that Something Else *could be.*

This was then an inchoate knowledge, but it relentlessly drove me on to become able to Name what it was that was Nagging me. It drove me to successive Acts of Be-Speaking, which themselves were for years inchoate, because the context could not permit anything more. But over the years I gained Momentum, and so when the Time/Space was right—beginning in the early sixties—my Be-Speaking could become explicit and the Call of the Wild could ring Loud and Clear. In that future Time, my marginality would be transformed into Active Boundary Living.*

In the meantime, at The College of Saint Rose I majored in English because there was no major in philosophy and because I knew I wanted to be a writer. I did in fact write throughout college—essays, poetry, and short stories. I was editor of the college literary magazine in my junior year and year book editor in my senior year. I wrote incessantly, often getting up in the middle of the night to write a couple of poems.[7]

---

*Boundary Living⊕: "Realizing Power of Presence on the Boundaries of patriarchal institutions; Presentiating the Background in the midst of foreground conditions by communicating contagious Courage, Pride, and Other Volcanic Virtues" (*Wickedary*).

Although I took an exorbitant number of courses in many fields, I did want to maintain my high average and at the same time engage in a variety of "extracurricular" activities. This required that I acquire an acute Sense of Timing, especially when it came to studying for exams. It was necessary to know exactly when was the last split second before I had to stop "fooling around" and start cramming.

The one who came to my aid in this matter was known to me as "the little Green Man in my head." This personage was—and still is—The Timer. Although my first clear memories of the manifestations of this entity are associated with taking exams in college—probably because I was then often in tight situations—it is possible that I had already encountered "him" in high school.[8]

At any rate, the unusual excrescence of "credits" on my transcript was embarrassing to the Registrar—or so she told me. One reason for this phenomenon was that I was looking for something that was not in the courses. Many of these were, by the "normal" standards of patriarchal education, very good. But I was Searching for Something Else. I suppose I kept hoping that in one of them I would hit the jackpot.

I acquired much knowledge that would be useful—even essential—later on. The College of Saint Rose was a substantial springboard for many Qualitative Leaps that I would have to take in the Future. Without realizing what I was doing, I was preparing for those Leaps.[9]

RUNNING FOR MY LIFE: THE CALL OF THE DREAM . . . THE DREAM OF GREEN

After I graduated from college this "accumulation syndrome" repeated itself in a magnified manner. Instead of simply amassing courses and credits I accumulated degrees. This was difficult to do in view of the fact that I had absolutely no money and no connections. It was also the case that I knew I had absolutely no choice. It was evident to me that my survival—my very life—depended upon climbing my way "up" the academic ladder by the exercise of my brain. As a secretary or high school teacher in Schenectady I would have perished of alienation and despair.

I knew that it was imperative that I go away to graduate school, but this decision was not easy. Since my father had died, my mother had only me, and there was very little money. The parish priest told me that I should stay at home with my mother and work in Schenectady. I knew in my core that he was wrong. Although he made me feel confused and guilty by giving bad advice—*bad* in every sense of the word—I had no choice but to go. My mother's understanding and generous spirit were, as always, extraordinary.

My survival instinct was clear and certain. I had had some experience with jobs when still in high school, so I knew what the odds would be against someone Odd like me if I stayed in Schenectady. I had worked in a hamburger stand for a short period, but I was fired for eating the hamburgers and drinking the milkshakes instead of serving them to the customers, and especially for arguing about ideas with the boss. I had also worked in the Schenectady Public Library, but was fired for reading the books instead of serving the clients, and most certainly for being insubordinate to the librarians. I was not fired from my job as packer in the supermarket, but my obliviousness was perceived as stupidity. This was understandable, because I had a habit of putting bread and eggs in the bottom of the bags and piling heavy items on top. Once I overheard a middle-aged customer who had been eyeing me with distaste remark to her companion: "What dumb girls they have working here!" I found this remark thought-provoking.

So, after obtaining the B.A. I determined to get a master's degree in philosophy. However, there were serious obstacles thrown in my way by the system, which I still did not understand as *patriarchy*. (How could I? The word was never used by anyone in 1950—nor was the word *sexism*.) The only respectable university available to me as an inhabitant of the spiritual, intellectual, and economic catholic ghetto was The Catholic University of America in Washington D.C., which offered me a full-tuition scholarship. The hitch was that one could have a scholarship for the M.A. only in the field in which she/he had majored as an undergraduate. I mention this tedious detail because it was one more thwarting of my Quest to study philosophy. Rather than not go to graduate school at all I took the scholarship and got my M.A. in English, taking philosophy courses on the side.

Here I was once again in a coeducational environment. I experienced a lifting of the weight that I had felt at Saint Rose, which I Now understand as the heaviness of the subliminal broken Promise, the shattered dream. I didn't have to notice that feeling of inexplicable nostalgia. Catholic University was exhilarating in its own way. I was beginning to get a real taste of the intellectual life.

The other students in the graduate program in English were good companions. There was a complex wittiness about them that I liked. Of course, "the boys" became aware of my Feminist views (which couldn't be identified precisely as "Feminist" in that era) and hated these ideas. When my closest friend there, Ann Walsh, announced that she was getting married I agreed to be her "maid of honor" but was secretly appalled.

During that first year at Catholic University I had an extraordinary dream one night. I had spent tedious hours that afternoon and evening engaged in the arduous task of translating passages from Middle English into modern English. When I finally went to bed that night my brains were fried. It had definitely not been an invigorating experience. However, I fell into a deep sleep and I dreamt of something that was of absolute importance to me. There are no words that can convey the content exactly. I have always remembered it as "The Dream of Green." I dreamt of Green—Elemental

Green. When I woke up, the message was clear—clear as Be-Dazzling Green. It was: "Study philosophy!" It was saying: "This tedious stuff is not what you should be doing with your life. Do what you were born to do. Focus on philosophy!"

It is possible that The Dream of Green was triggered by something in the Middle English texts I was reading, some of which were mystical and Elemental. It could have been connected with the fourteenth-century poems *Gawain and the Green Knight* and *Pearl*. But what mattered was its absolutely thunderous message. Of course, the problem remained: How *could* I, with no money?

During my second year in that program I wrote my master's dissertation in the field of literary theory.[10] It was an analysis of the theory of John Crowe Ransom. I chose that area despite unwritten rules that no master's dissertation should be done in it. It was generally reserved for doctoral work. I argued and fought to do this, because it was as close to working in philosophy as I could get. Moreover, the professor who taught literary theory was James Craig La Drière. We didn't communicate well personally, but he was a great teacher. From him I began really to learn to think. I could not then realize that his excellence was in large measure contingent upon male privilege.* The fact was that in comparison to him the Sisters who had taught me in college were limited and limiting—competent and committed though they were. I could not yet understand that this was one more manifestation of the tragedy of the broken Promise. The comparison was unfair, but the fact was that this privileged male professor who was at best indifferent to me was my first outstanding exemplar of a teacher who was a sophisticated scholar and systematic thinker.

Professor La Drière was my M.A. dissertation director. One priest professor, a W. J. Rooney, who was a reader, was especially discouraging. He complained that my dissertation showed a lack of a "philosophical *habitus*." I wasn't quite sure what such a *habitus* was, but I was determined to find out. The priest's criticism was cruel, since what I really wanted to study was philosophy anyway, and his institution was preventing me from doing so. However, it stung me into an even fiercer determination to obtain a doctorate in philosophy and *to be* a philosopher.

I think it was at about this time that I decided to destroy all of my poetry. I judged it to be "flabby" and lacking the rigor of a "philosophical *habitus*." This was a somewhat dramatic act, but I really decided that if I were ever to write lyrically/poetically again, my work would be strong and absolutely precise. It would be philosophically poetic.

---

*Despite the reality of male privilege, the fact is that La Drière was the first gifted male teacher whom I had ever encountered. Moreover, he was an exception among his colleagues at Catholic University.

It is only Now, in Re-Calling the experience, that I Realize more of the content of the message of the hedge. It Said: "*Continued* existence." At that time, and for many years afterward, I could only understand this as referring to a future continuing existence. As a member of the catholic church I was forbidden to believe in reincarnation, that is, in "past lives," or in simultaneous multiple lives or forms of existence. Such a thought would be unthinkable. I remember thinking that "continued existence" did seem an odd expression. Why the implied past tense? Why not "continuing"? However, I Heard what I Heard and then interpreted it within my limited context of christian belief.

Now, as I Re-Call the Be-Speaking of the hedge, I Realize that there are possible Other Temporal dimensions in the message.[13] The words imply something like "I was, and am, and will be." So that unique Moment has Spiraled back again and the Be-Speaking is richer in its possibilities. It Discloses more about the Unfolding of Be-ing. The meaning of the Original message Unfolds even as I am writing this, and my Memory of my Moment of Hearing the hedge Dis-closes itself as *Metamemory*○. That is, it is

> Deep, Ecstatic Memory of participation in Be-ing that eludes the categories and grids of patriarchal consciousness, Spiraling into the Past, carrying Vision forward; Memory that recalls Archaic Time, Re-Calling it into our be-ing; Memory beyond civilization (*Wickedary*).

One day I found the passage in Aquinas about women being "defective and misbegotten" as a result of "defect in the active force [the male seed] or from some material indisposition, or even from some external influence such as that of a south wind, which is moist."* I rushed over to one of the other eleven women in the program, who was considerably older than I was and somewhat intimidating, and yelled "Look at this!" To which she responded, "That's no offense to *your* dignity."† I was stunned and attempted to make her see but only managed to sound like a raving maniac. So I filed away in my mind the whole experience. Years later the opportunity would

---

Summa theologiae I, q. 92, a. 1 ad 1. In a telephone conversation in July 1988, when I told the story of the Great Wind that blew me to Saint Mary's—and elsewhere—Jane Caputi noted the interesting contrast with the "south wind" which Aristotle and Aquinas credit for the existence of women. Indeed, this is thought-provoking. I have experienced many Leaps and synchronicities as be-ing carried by a Great Wind. These have been Leaps into greater Self-Realization as a deviant/defiant—and, by patriarchal norms, defective—woman. Indeed, I am Now inclined to think that the "south wind" of Aristotle and Aquinas is a patriarchal reversal of the Great Wind which Calls and Carries Wild, Deviant Women on our True Course.

†This kind of Self-censorship, Self-delusion, and Self-denial was and still is commonly used by Catholic women in order to silence the "immature," i.e., troublesome, questioners among them. It is transmitted into the minds of the masses by such clichés as "equal in dignity," "equal in the eyes of God," and so on, and on.

come to expose this passage within the context of my own analysis. At that Moment I understood, not for the first or the last time, what it means to be a cognitive minority of one. It was an opportunity for developing the spiritual muscles to be able to stand alone, keeping my own consciousness intact. This was a skill that I would badly need in the Future.

One of my friends at Saint Mary's was Betty Farians. Betty was also potentially a Radical Feminist Philosopher. Although neither of us had the vocabulary to Name our identity in this way at that time, the driving Force was there in both of us, the longing and the Sense of Outrage. Years later our paths would cross again and again. In the sixties we would both join Saint Joan's International Alliance, an organization of catholic Feminists who fought for equality of women in the church and all over the world.[14] In the seventies we worked together to organize women in the Boston Theological Institute—the consortium of theological schools in the Boston area. But even then, back in the early fifties, Betty was a rebel who Lusted for justice and fought for it, a rugged individualist and true lover of nature.

I got my Ph.D. in religion at the ripe old age of twenty-five. One of the great side benefits of this was that I would no longer have to be called "Miss Daly." Although "Miss" was less horrifying to me than "Mrs.," it irked me deeply. So I was not shy from then on in insisting that I be addressed as "Doctor" rather than "Miss." I had not yet read Virginia Woolf's *Three Guineas*, with its elaborate description of the "odor" attached to the term "Miss," but even then I *knew*.

I felt unsatisfied with this degree and still wanted a doctorate in philosophy *per se*, so I applied for admission to The University of Notre Dame, which was across the road, and which proved to be obstinately bigoted and oppressive in its policies toward women. I was refused admission to the doctoral program in philosophy there solely on the basis that I was a woman.

In addition to this rejection, I was suffering fall-out from my falling out with Sister Madeleva, who had been turned off by my uppityness as a poor graduate student who wanted to reform her pet project, the doctoral program in theology. I had been one of the leaders of a revolt demanding the removal of a professor from whose dryasdust teaching we learned nothing. So the poet/prophet whom I had admired so deeply withdrew her offer of a teaching job at Saint Mary's, which would have supported my study at Notre Dame, *if* they had admitted me.

Faced with this double catastrophe I got the message that my Time there was over. I felt an excruciating Sense of desolation. It was like being kicked out of a dimension of existence which had been Paradise, and where I had tasted of the Tree of Knowledge and found its fruit delicious. I remember going to an Alec Guinness movie (*Kind Hearts and Coronets*) with my friends in South Bend after receiving the bad news, and watching it in misery, laughing at the funny scenes and at the same time feeling utterly abandoned.[15]

SURVIVING THE GRIND OF THE GRIM FIFTIES (1954–1959)

So I proceeded to look elsewhere for a teaching job in theology, naively thinking that this would present no problem and that I could somehow pursue my dream of a doctorate in philosophy while teaching for a living. After receiving rejections from at least two dozen colleges, I accepted a teaching job for the fall of 1954 at the now defunct Cardinal Cushing College in Brookline, Massachusetts, which was just opening as a two-year college. Since there were very few students there the first year, I was saddled with teaching also in the high school attached to it—a position which I resented and hated. After the first year I did teach full time at the college. After a short period I *was* the entire theology and philosophy faculty there.

In the mid-fifties my mother moved from Schenectady to Brighton, Massachusetts, where we shared an apartment. I could not at that time realize what the loss of her home meant to her, although, of course, I knew it was very hard. It is Now, however, in the writing of *Outercourse* that I have Remembered parts of her story that place that event in context. As I explained in Chapter One, she was brought up by her grandmother. Her own mother died a few years after her grandmother took her, and she was to some extent the servant of her adult aunts and uncles. Their house was not really her home. Then, when she married my father, she had her own home for the first time. So, the act of selling most of her furniture and moving from Schenectady was excruciating for her. Yet we knew of no other solution, and it was good to be together.

It was a bleak period. Although I learned quite a lot by preparing my wide variety of classes at Cardinal Cushing College, something was terribly missing. This was not an actualization of my dream of being a philosopher, of Living the life of the mind. I could not even find words for my unbearable sense of loss and the dreary greyness that hung over the 1950s. I struggled to climb out of the mire by taking graduate courses in philosophy late afternoons at Boston College and in the summers at various universities, including Notre Dame (which allowed females in during the summer session), Laval University in Quebec, and Saint Louis University.

In addition to that I audited some of Paul Tillich's lectures at Harvard Divinity School. There were virtually no other catholics around the Divinity School in that pre-ecumenical period, but I was warily welcomed into the "flock" by the registrar.

I sat in the back of the Sperry Room while Tillich lectured. He had a powerful charisma but there was something about it that I did not like. I attended only sporadically—torn between attraction to Tillich's intellect and repulsion for his miasmic charisma. I am not sure whether, when sitting in the back of that lecture hall, I had any premonition of my battle with that corrosive force that would take place many years later. Probably I did not have any foreknowledge of that. But it was important that I saw and heard Tillich in person—that my knowledge was not confined to his books.

It was during that grim time of the mid to late fifties that I heard myself say to a friend: "I want to write a book." I remember that I did not say it with great confidence. My voice felt weak and uncertain and I barely believed my words. The mind-poisons that permeated the atmosphere in America during that period had been eating away at my sense of purpose and undermining my Self-esteem, and there was no Feminist movement to help me make sense of what was happening all around me, i.e., brain death, soul death. The word *Feminist* still was not used—unless perhaps to refer to some weird old ladies who had lived in the last century and had been derisively called "suffragettes." As for the word *Lesbian*—that was unspeakable, unthinkable. It suggested hideous perversion, something to be hidden in the filthiest basements of conscious awareness.

At some point I found Simone de Beauvoir's *The Second Sex* in a bookstore—probably in Cambridge. I remember standing there reading it—drinking in great gulps like a woman who had been deprived of water almost to a point beyond endurance.[16] My gratitude to her was enormous. Still, there was no context, no movement, in which to Realize her message.

THE GREAT WINDFALL: MY DIS-COVERING OF FRIBOURG

So I had to Move on in my own Quest. Since I had not been able to get a job teaching theology in a college which might be said to have an intellectually challenging atmosphere, I believed that what I needed was a "better" doctorate as a ticket of access to an environment in which I could breathe and expand.

At the core of my be-ing I still wanted to be a philosopher, but my experience when accumulating forty-two graduate credits in philosophy had not been entirely gratifying. A smog of deception as well as dullness had hung over many of those courses. Besides, the Great Wind that had carried me to Saint Mary's in Indiana to study theology was still blowing mightily.

I thought that if I got the highest of higher degrees in theology—which for a catholic then meant the doctorate from a Pontifical Faculty of Sacred Theology—I would have a chance of getting a job teaching challenging courses to very bright students and have time for my own work. Since The Catholic University of America was the only university in the United States which conferred that ultimate degree, I wrote to the Dean of the School of Theology, repeatedly, and received no reply for a long time.[17] I had studied Latin, Greek, Hebrew, as well as German and French. I had more than the equivalent of an M.A. in philosophy, and a Ph.D. in religion, but they could not bring themselves to reply. The crude bigotry of that wretched institution was blatant in this case. The only "problem" was that I was a woman, and they didn't even have the courage to say that with minimal courtesy.

I was very Lucky that they rejected my application, because I had to turn my attention to bigger and better things. There was no other university in the United States that could offer such a degree, so I began to think of Europe. After considerable effort I found out that the French and Belgian universities would not admit a woman for this degree. The only possibilities would be in Germany or in Switzerland, because in those countries the Faculties of Catholic Theology and of Protestant Theology were incorporated into the State universities, and the German and Swiss governments did not permit exclusion of women on the basis of sex.

There was one slight problem. I literally had no money. My salary at Cardinal Cushing College hardly permitted saving money, even if I had been so inclined. My mother was living with me and needed my assistance. However, I felt sure that somehow I could resolve all this.

I made a list of catholic bishops in order to inquire about loans for the continuance of my theological education. First I wrote to Cardinal Cushing of Boston, who replied by sending me a "holy card" containing a prayer for a "religious vocation." After tearing this up in a rage I wrote to John Wright, then Bishop of Pittsburgh, who was known as a liberal who encouraged (male) lay theologians.* He responded almost immediately with a small gift of money (five hundred dollars) and a loan of twelve hundred dollars from the Medora A. Feehan Fund. It was and is gratifying to know that the money came from the estate of a woman.

Meanwhile I had applied both for a Fulbright scholarship for study in Germany and a Swiss student exchange scholarship. The Swiss came through. Moreover, I found out that I could teach at Rosary College's junior year abroad program in Fribourg, Switzerland, to support myself, as well as live in one of their apartments as "chaperon" for the students there. I also learned that I was definitely admitted for the fall of 1959 to the Faculty of Theology at the University of Fribourg.

I stared at a map of the world in absolute star-struck wonder. Seeing the map of Europe was like already being there. Finding Fribourg there on the map was the beginning of my Great Dis-covering. It would later inspire the ideas of Wanderlust/Wonderlust which I developed in *Pure Lust*. Just Now, while writing this paragraph, I have opened the World Atlas and am Living the experience in a different way. I Re-member Fribourg in clear detail and I Re-Call with a vividness that is Stunning countless other places that I visited in Europe and the Middle East during the long vacations. Looking at the atlas right Now, I seem to *be* in all of those places—that is, to be here and there at the same Time.

I went through some anguish over leaving my mother. She decided that she would stay with her sister in California, but I had misgivings about that.

---

*Because of his decency, sensitivity, perceptiveness, and even magnanimity, which transcended the constrictions of the conventional prelate's role, I refer to this individual here and hereafter in this work simply by his own proper name.

I was still haunted also by the guilt instilled by the parish priest in Schenectady years before, when I had left for Washington to save/find my Life. That guilt had followed me also when I had left for Saint Mary's. Now I was leaving again—crossing the ocean to a foreign country—and my mother was sixty-nine years old.

Yet my sheer desperation to find what I had to find and the Great Windfall of happy circumstances that were coming together to make this event happen triumphed over everything. The summer before I left she and I spent a few weeks in Ottawa, Canada, where I was teaching summer school at the University of Ottawa. I remember that we frequently took evening strolls and looked at the stars. I think we both Sensed that our separate yet intertwined Voyages would require heroic feats, astronomical changes, and astral communication.

CHAPTER THREE

STUDENT DAYS IN EUROPE:
METAPHYSICAL ADVENTURES
AND ECSTATIC TRAVELS

In September 1959 I flew to Europe for the first time. I landed in Paris and was filled with wonder and ecstasy at every sight and sound. This was all like a fairy tale, and it was happening to me. After the deadly alienation of America, arriving in Europe was like finally coming home. I visited a friend in Paris and then boarded a train for Fribourg. I stared with something like disbelief at the beauty of the country as the train rushed through the lush green world of Switzerland. I was carried by the same Wind that had brought me to South Bend seven years before.

Fribourg was something that I never could have imagined existed—except in story books. The magical, otherworldly sight of the *basse ville*—the medieval part of the town—had my eyes popping. The sound of Swiss cow bells was celestial. The whole *aura* of the place was enchanted. The air *smelled* different. The smog of dullness that hung over life in America was missing! I almost couldn't stand the relief. Although I didn't know it yet, Fribourg would be my home for the next seven years.

METAPHYSICAL ADVENTURES

Even before the semester began I saw the white-robed Dominican priest professors walking on the streets of Fribourg. What made them especially funny looking was the fact that most of them wore their robes quite short—perhaps seven or eight inches from the ground—but did not wear trousers underneath. This was "the European look." The American priests and seminarians would not be found dead without trousers.* I wondered what classes would be like at the university, which was wryly "christened" by some of my American classmates as "dear old F. U."

At the Villa des Fougères, where Rosary College's junior year abroad program was housed, I taught theology and philosophy courses to young

---

*I was informed by American seminarians that the European Dominican priests were forbidden to wear trousers underneath their robes in order to make it more difficult for them to sneak off or run away. I am not sure whether this explanation is apocryphal or accurate, but at least it is entertaining.

American women. There I met Sister Kaye Ashe, who later was appointed director of the program. We soon became Be-Laughing friends, and this friendship was a bright light throughout the ensuing years in Fribourg. Cackling with Kaye over the incongruities of life in Fribourg became one of my favorite part-time occupations.

At the university I took about eighteen hours a week of classes each semester, which were taught in Latin by Dominican priests who came from several different countries and consequently had different accents speaking Latin. For the first couple of months I sat there and understood almost nothing. Then the fog lifted. It was an extraordinary intellectual experience to hear lectures on the mathematics of "the Trinity" in Latin. "Why are there three Persons instead of four?"[1] The refined commentaries delivered by the professors on the *Summa theologiae* of Thomas Aquinas were expert masterpieces of precise and elegant logic—which would appear convoluted only to one who did not accept their bizarre premises. I thrived on this metaphysical logic. I soared with it. It belonged exactly to the time/space of medieval Fribourg and I was enjoying the exhilarating ride.

I detested courses in "Sacred Scripture" and church history. I found them unchallenging. The lack of inherent logic in the bible depressed me. But the courses in theology itself were exquisitely complex. Essentially they were Greek metaphysical treatises carried into the realm of mysticism, but constrained by the limitations of christian myth. I took what was helpful from them. It was not that I had consciously sorted it all out. Rather, I think that there was/is an innate natural wisdom in my psyche that knew this was the route for me to take into the Background in the early sixties. It was not simply a gathering of information but a training of the mind. It exercised that part of my brain that had loved math in high school. It was also a metaphysical adventure. Without this training/experience, I could not have written *Beyond God the Father*, *Gyn/Ecology*, *Pure Lust*, the *Wickedary*, or *Outercourse*. All of these books have drawn upon the athleticism of the mind that I learned then—a kind of intellectual Karate. They also have involved a decoding of the symbols and myths and ethics of the Western patriarchal theological tradition, which I am able to do because I have learned it so well.

This metaphysical adventure could only have happened for me in Fribourg, that time/space of the Middle Ages which was also filled with young American students on their junior year abroad, from whom I learned a great deal.* In Fribourg I was far away from the mental/emotional/physical/imaginative confines of America, and close to many other countries, other cultures, which were accessible during the long spring and summer vacations.

---

*It was clear to me, as it had been even in adolescence, that my style was teaching in order to learn—not learning in order to teach. (Later I would add: teaching in order to write—not writing in order to teach.)

I especially loved the arduousness of the intellectual life of a Thomist scholar.* I loved and still love abstract thought and I deeply distrusted symbols because of what I then perceived as their fuzziness, their sloppiness.† It was fortunate that my pursuit of this quintessentially abstract theological study was combined with living in a Strange country and with many opportunities for adventurous travel. My travel experiences were very vivid, specific, and concrete. These adventures in New and Archaic worlds formed a kind of counterpoint to the work of abstract study, so that there was something like a unified and moving harmonic texture in the experience as a whole. It was a way of be-ing that anticipated what I would later call "Spinning."

The more I studied and the more I traveled, ripping away cultural limitations and mindbindings, the less frequently I went to church. I was not afflicted with piety or missionary zeal. I had no desire to be a priest or to minister to anyone. My Lust was for the Life of the Mind. The simple fact is that the more I studied and explored, the more I was in touch with mySelf, and going to church became odious.

If there was an exception to this, it had to do with cathedrals consecrated to Mary that I visited when traveling around Europe on vacations, and with one shrine in particular that is near Fribourg.‡ The latter is a shrine to Our Lady of Bourguillon, where innumerable cures have taken place. Although the shrine itself was hideous, I sensed a strong Presence there, and it was a place where, without knowing what I was doing, I invoked the Goddess. The Presence there is Prechristian/Metachristian. It is ultimately Pagan, Potent, and Natural. It was and is a wellspring of my life.

---

*I capitalize the words Thomist and Thomistic whenever they occur in this book because of my regard for the intellectual training and treasures which I acquired in my study of that tradition. This study strengthened and sharpened my intellectual powers—both rational and intuitive—preparing the way for the creative work that was to come. See Chapter Four.

†When I refer to "abstract thought" in this positive sense I am referring to philosophical concepts which have a solid basis in reality and which enable one to perceive similarities and to make distinctions. I am very much aware that there is also a kind of empty abstraction which permits verbal maneuvers that are not grounded in experience. These are pseudo-abstractions. They are, in fact, distractions. As for my former contempt for symbols: I think that this was a result of the fact that the symbols of patriarchal society are all patriarchal and therefore fuzzy. They have to be, because they are vehicles of deception. Inevitably they serve as uppers for males and as downers for women. Later, when I began to See through the veils of male symbol systems, reversing their reversals and arriving at more Archaic and Original mythic thought, I came to be at home wielding the creative power of Metapatriarchal Metaphor. See especially Chapters Twelve and Thirteen.

‡I had no interest in the masses and ceremonies held there, but I Sensed the Power of these Spaces.

It had always been a fact that the ecstasy I experienced from Nature and from the Realm of Books was quite distinct from piety. The joy and exhilaration that I Realized studying in Fribourg had nothing whatever to do with religiosity. It was the exuberance of Intellectual/E-motional/Spiritual/Elemental Life.

At the end of the first academic year I passed final exams for the Baccalaureate in Sacred Theology, *summa cum laude*. Given the fact that I already had a Ph.D. in Religion from St. Mary's College, in a program staffed by Dominican theologians, it would seem bizarre that I had to take these exams. The fact was that the esteemed faculty held that program in contempt and therefore required that I jump through all the European hoops—preliminary to their super doctorate—to prove myself. Indeed, when I showed the American diploma to one of the professors he laughed. The unspoken message was that this had been a program of study for women and therefore laughable.[2]

The baccalaureate exams were oral, and I chose to take them in Latin rather than in French—calculating that the examiner, a French Dominican priest, would not have quite such an unfair advantage if we both had to speak Latin than if he could use his native tongue. So I spoke in crude Latin, which felt to me like pig Latin, supplemented with sign language and vivid facial expressions when I couldn't think of the exact word.

During the second year in Fribourg I rented a room in the home of a Swiss family. Madame charged me a tip for serving me dinner and provided neatly cut squares of newspaper as toilet tissue. My room was unheated during the day (Madame stayed in her heated kitchen), so I went to the university and studied in empty classrooms. In the middle of that year I acquired a second job, teaching philosophy to young men in the junior year abroad program of Georgetown University. I had been refused that job when I applied because the jesuits did not want to hire a woman. However, since their male philosophy teacher suddenly disappeared in the middle of the year, they were willing to try me out. I kept that job for the remaining five and a half years I was in Fribourg. At the end of that year, which, like the first, had involved taking seventeen or eighteen hours of classes a week, I passed the final oral exams for the Licentiate in Sacred Theology, *magna cum laude.**

Theological scholarship by women was considered a joke in Fribourg. Whenever a professor would mention in his lecture a book or an article by a female scholar (and such occasions were extremely rare), a good number of my two hundred or so classmates—priests and seminarians from all over

---

*There is nothing quite equivalent to the licentiate in the American educational system. The licentiate is higher than a master's degree and less than the doctorate. It is the final great hurdle before the student is entitled to begin writing her/his doctoral dissertation.

the world—would loudly indicate their amusement. Their way of laughing at this or any other statement that seemed funny to them was to stomp on the floor under their desks. That way the professor could not detect the "guilty" party.

Yet their attitude toward me was not one of contempt. It seemed to be a combination of fear, astonishment, and admiration. As I wrote in the "Autobiographical Preface to the 1975 Edition" of *The Church and the Second Sex:*

> The oddness of this situation was compounded by the fact that my classmates were nearly all priests and male seminarians, many of whom were from Latin countries. It was further compounded by the fact that in the crowded classrooms there frequently were empty places on each side of me, because my "fellow" students feared the temptations that might arise from sitting next to a female.[3]

When I would meet the hordes of black-robed Spanish seminarians on the streets of Fribourg, their eyes were modestly cast down, while I stared. The terror of a woman in their midst was clear. Yet there was no general sense of hostility from these students. The nature of their admiration was revealed after I passed the formidable examinations for the Licentiate in Sacred Theology. They publicly applauded and compared me to John Glenn, who had just orbited the earth. The comparison struck me as astronomically thought-provoking. But, after all, it is true that we were both "firsts."

Despite the fact that I had two teaching jobs and that I had managed to get my Swiss exchange student scholarship renewed for yet a third year, money was still a problem. The loan from the Medora A. Feehan Fund had been intended only to cover expenses for the licentiate, and I was determined to stay on and get the doctorate in theology. So I wrote again to John Wright explaining this intention. He increased the loan by three thousand dollars, which arrived in three installments.

By now I had acquired a third job, teaching in yet another junior year abroad program. This was the program of La Salle College of Philadelphia and there were at least twenty male students enrolled in it.

So when I began my third year in Fribourg I was teaching a total of about thirty young women and thirty young men, plus taking advanced seminars for the doctorate in theology and several courses in philosophy as well.[4] All of this activity required quite a lot of dashing around, since the programs were held in three different buildings scattered around Fribourg and the university was yet a fourth location. So I bought a Velosolex motor bicycle and zoomed all over town on it. I loved that motor bike and took frequent trips out into the Swiss countryside. Riding it felt like flying. I was assured by "fellow Americans" that I presented an astonishing sight dashing around on that vehicle.

During that third year I was renting a room with another Swiss family in Fribourg. Here, at least, there was heat in the winter months. I began work on my doctoral dissertation in theology, which was on "The Problem of Speculative Theology." The texts I had to work on were in Latin and French, and I spent many hours in the university library.

In case the reader gets the impression that all of this sounds like work, work, work, rest assured, it was. The point is that I *loved* what I was doing. Also, there was a lot of play, play, play and ecstatic travel. I don't know how that was possible, but it was. At some points I taught as many as twelve or thirteen credit hours a semester and worked hard preparing this variety of courses in philosophy and theology. But there was also the fact that my students and I had good times together, frequently hanging out in Fribourg's tea rooms and beer halls, rejoicing in the fact that we were there and not "back home." We also went skiing and on picnics and trips together. I gave oral exams in philosophy on the roof of the Villa des Fougères, while sipping wine with my victims in this exotic inquisitorial atmosphere. In some ways, the living was easy.

ECSTATIC TRAVELS

I traveled a lot by myself, spending summers in Paris and Madrid and taking off for places like London, Dublin, and Rome. I traveled by train, second class, and stayed often in third or fourth class *pensioni* (in Italy), cheap hotels, and convents that took in female travelers. I once picked up a flea that stayed with me for weeks. I roamed the streets of all these places, often at night, and felt virtually no fear. I always met interesting sister wanderers from other countries and we would investigate castles and museums together. I recall one thought that recurred over and over as I sped or hiked through beautiful countryside. It was, simply: "I am the Luckiest woman in the world." I think I even said it out loud.

These adventures in Europe were Moments that expanded my world. A few years before, a friend from Yugoslavia, whom I met in Canada, had told me that if I went to Europe my mind would "blow up like a balloon." She did not mean that I would become an "air head," but that my consciousness would become enormously larger. Her description proved to be prophetic. Having been sprung free from America, I experienced my aura expand. From the Moment of that first landing in Paris I felt that I had come Home. Sitting at sidewalk cafés on the Boulevard Saint-Michel, staring at the gargoyles on Notre Dame, wandering the streets of Montmartre—I entered an Other Time/Space. I know that I often smiled to myself as I stared at wonder after wonder, and this expression of my state of bliss was mistaken as an invitation by some of the creepy-crawly men who approached apparently available females from all sides. "Mademoiselle?" The whispers invaded my Space. They thought I was smiling at them?! I was not accustomed to latin male behavior, but I learned to cope. On return trips I brought along a learned tome, which provided something to be seriously engrossed in when necessary, as well as serving as a potential weapon.*

On Italian trains the reaching-out hands were sometimes unendurable. I found that an umbrella could serve as a useful jabbing instrument, but I didn't usually carry an umbrella. So I discovered ways of stalking and glaring. I had neither the skill nor the inclination to adopt the studied blank look that was considered effective by Latin women. Perhaps mine was not the most successful method in a no-win situation, but *I* felt better.

Still, all of this was a minor annoyance. Italy was sheer beauty. Sometimes I stayed at Italian convents which offered cheap accommodations for women, with quite good conditions. The convent I occupied in Venice was literally a palace. In such places I often met European travelers who were as poor as I was, and as eager to explore new terrain.

The Stunning thing about my early travels in Europe was the utterly surprising phenomenon of having all the magical images that had populated my imagination since childhood actually materialize and come alive. In Rome, for example, when I first saw the Forum and the Colosseum at night I was transported. I had seen pictures in my Latin textbooks in high school. Now they really existed! So I was Space/Time traveling, participating in the Fourth Dimension.[5]

Sometimes nursery rhymes would come alive. When I first saw London Bridge I expected it to be "falling down." At other times, I would come upon the Originals, the Sources of American imitations. I had always loved Gothic architecture. Gazing at Notre Dame or at Chartres, I was Seeing— and experiencing with all of my Senses—the real thing. Sometimes the experience was of Seeing/Sensing the Origin of some work of art. I had always felt some affinity for El Greco. Traveling in Spain, I Saw what it was that had inspired him.

In short, I had come from a place of derivatives, fakes, and phony everythings to the Sources. It was as if I had lived imprisoned in a sort of disneyland and was suddenly released into the real world. I was like someone who had known only plastic trees and flowers and who now was let loose in a verdant place—a forest or a jungle. Countless doors and windows in my brain were thrown open and I gulped the fresh exhilarating air. I had been suffocating in a state of sensory deprivation, and that state was behind me.

None of this really says it all. The fact is that the aura/auras of Europe were/are different; they were/are Archaic. They matched my soul. This was

---

*The one I frequently used was the French edition of Aquinas's *Summa theologiae*. This came in a set of several small paperbacks and thus was convenient to carry. It had several other advantages. I could get some of my studying done while traveling. Also, anyone who saw what I was actually carrying and reading—I sometimes read it while waiting for the *Métro* or on the street—was likely to be horrified, intimidated, or simply turned off.

a world of radiance and splendor. It was Be-Dazzling. My traveling to and through Europe was an inherent part of my Voyage into the Background.*

Sometimes I would see groups of American tourists being herded off their tour buses and ordered around. I thought it would be virtually impossible for them to have an Original adventure. I felt sorry for them that they had waited all their lives for their tour of Europe which wasn't real at all. Re-Calling this, I am reminded once again that I am Lucky to have had parents who believed in living one day at a time instead of saving for a foreground future. I also see that their nonquenching of my adventuresome spirit made this sort of Metatraveling possible for me, and that these adventures were essential for my future work as a philosopher/writer.

My first trip to England and Ireland (in 1961) involved a bout of seasickness crossing the English Channel. I had taken the train up through France to Calais and had to cross over to Dover on a rough sea. The area around Canterbury seemed mystical/magical. I felt in touch with the time and tales of Beowulf and Grendel. I saw a place where weavers had lived and worked. Although I knew nothing about weavers at that time, I had a strong intuition that there was something special about them.

I took the train and night boat over to Ireland and made the mistake of renting a cot and blanket, consequently becoming a walking flea-bag. In this condition I arrived in the land of my ancestors. It was raining, of course. I wandered the streets in amazement. I stopped before an apparently empty anglican church and was surrounded by red-headed children begging for pennies. "Why are you goin' in *there*, Miss?" they asked. Good question. I went in anyway and found that a late afternoon service was about to begin. There was a procession of males—one or two in robes and others in surplices. Somewhere in a corner I saw one doddering around in quaint black breeches. It was a scene out of an old Alec Guinness movie that had never been made. The congregation consisted of one properly dressed lady, and the males sang Vespers to themselves. I was mesmerized for a few minutes and then left to give the children their pennies. I think I agreed with them that it was a bad, haunted place.

---

*Of course, this does not mean that Europe *is* the Background. I am only too well aware of the oppression of women, as well as racial and class exploitation and the destruction of the Wild there and all over the world. But in Europe, there were and still are Memories embedded in the land and in the culture/cultures that render the Background more accessible to me. These Deep Memories of Archaic Reality are not as faded and decayed as they are in America. It is important to understand also that this is a description of what Europe meant and still means to *me* on my own personal Voyage. Since my roots are not Native American, I cannot feel rooted in the North American continent. It is possible that someone else would find that her Background experiences are triggered especially by traveling to America or Asia or Africa. The important thing is that such experiences/ Memories can be triggered.

Next I visited Trinity College to see the open pages of the Book of Kells. In the evening I went to Jury's Hotel to enjoy its famous song and dance show and became suitably sentimental over my Irish coffee. I stayed in a convent that had newspapers for toilet paper and chatted with the good-natured nuns. After a trip to Glendalaugh I boarded a train for the West. The Ring of Kerry was misty and spooky. Convinced that I had encountered a family banshee at Ross Castle, I curled up in a fit of terror in my bed at the B and B where I was spending the night. This, however, was not my deepest Encounter with Ireland. That Moment would occur many years later.* The Deep Background of Ireland was still hiding its face from me.

My living in Switzerland—my home base—was in itself an Ecstatic trip. The streets of the *basse ville*—the old town—of Fribourg transported me into the Middle Ages. The sound of the musical cow bells literally carried me into Fairy Time. The big town clock in Bern, with its multitude of moving little people and animals, was a childhood dream come true. The Alps, especially in the Jungfrau region, were—to me—*real* mountains, majestic beyond belief. They were no more like the Catskills and the Adirondacks of my native New York State than Chartres was like—or reducible to—Saint John's Church in Schenectady.

One of my sister travelers was Dorothée Gysi, whom I met in Paris, and who happened to be from Bern, which was not far from Fribourg. With Dorothée I went on adventures in Switzerland. One of the most memorable of these was a winter study-vacation in a chalet high in the Alps that was owned by her family. In order to get there we took the train to Brig and then a terrifying cable car—up beyond anything accessible by train. (It was a cable car often used for transporting lumber as well as people. A few years later I heard that several people were killed when it finally crashed.) The trip on this vehicle went so far up that in order to reach the chalet one then had to go back down a short way. The only way of accomplishing this last lap of the trip in the winter or early spring was on skis. Expert skier that I was not, I managed to get down there, mainly on the seat of my ski pants.

In this inspiring haven I worked on my dissertation while Dorothée did her own studying. From this perspective it was impossible to think of Switzerland as a tiny toy country that specialized in cuckoo clocks. Here it was a realm of majestic power and peace. Working on "The Problem of Speculative Theology" did not feel at all out of place in this rarified but absolutely Elemental atmosphere.

---

*In 1984 I spoke in Liberty Hall in Dublin, after *Pure Lust* had come out and after *Gyn/Ecology* had become quite well known in Ireland. That time I traveled to Belfast and Cork and met good friends. But the Great Adventure started to Unfold when I returned in 1987 and *really* began to encounter Ireland. See Chapters Thirteen, Seventeen, Eighteen, and Twenty.

THE GREAT REUNION

During all this time in Europe I was a free Alien, not caged in by the alienation of "belonging." I dreaded one thing—returning to my "native land," with its smog of unreality and mind-numbing sameness, and not being able to escape again. I had nightmares of going back for a visit and breaking a leg or having some other accident that would prevent me from returning to Europe and my free life there as a scholar visiting Strange lands.

Going back for a visit had been out of the question financially, anyway. There was no way that I could pay for a plane ticket to any part of the States, and certainly not to California, where my mother was living. What I really hoped was that I would find a way to make it possible for her to come and stay in Fribourg. I continually tried to find a way.

By the end of my third year in Fribourg (summer 1962) I was earning enough from teaching in the junior year abroad programs, so that—combining this with my student exchange scholarship and the loan from John Wright—I could afford to rent an apartment and send my mother an airline ticket to come over.

Since the only affordable ticket was with Icelandic Airlines, which did not fly into Switzerland but only to Luxembourg, my mother bravely flew from California to that tiny country. So I went by train to meet her at the airport. On my way from the train station to the Luxembourg airport a Strange thing occurred. I saw a maroon Pontiac parked on the side of the street. It was of an old (mid-1940s) vintage with the standard silver Indian on its hood. The car was exactly like the Pontiac my father had owned during the last few years before he died in 1949. This "coincidence" was startling. I had never seen a maroon 1940s Pontiac during all my travels in Europe. (Nor have I noticed one since.) It felt like a clear message that my father was around and that he had had something to do with making this reunion possible.

It was moving to see my mother coming off the plane. We had not seen each other for three years, even though we had written to each other several times a week. I saw that she looked a lot older. We stayed in a hotel in Luxembourg for a day or two and then took the train to Fribourg to settle into the first of the three apartments that we were to occupy there. ·

During the fourth year in Fribourg (1962–1963) I taught in the junior year abroad programs and took an enormous number of courses and seminars in the Faculty of Philosophy, while continuing to write my theological dissertation. The long vacations made it possible to do quite a bit of traveling.

Although my mother's health was failing, we traveled together adventurously, at first around Switzerland and later to other countries. We often went to Bern on Sundays for dinner and an American movie. Bern, with its enticing arcades, was in another canton and seemed like an other world from Fribourg, even though it was (then) a mere twenty-seven minutes from

Fribourg on the *Schnellzug* (fast train). One of our favorite trips was to Interlaken, which was the starting point for a round trip up the Alps in the Jungfrau region, to Wengen and Kleine Scheidegg and back down by way of Gründelwald.

We often marveled at our living and traveling together in Europe. She would say: "They [the folks back home] will wonder where all the money is coming from, when the postcards arrive. They'll think we must secretly be rich!" The fact is that we were living on my very modest income from teaching, my mother's social security pittance (thirty-eight dollars a month), and—during those first years of her visit—my small additional income from the Swiss exchange student scholarship and the renewed loan. Once we were both over there and comfortably established in an apartment, expenses were minimal. Still, it seemed like a miracle.

There was a New level of communication between us. This had not been possible during my long and turbulent adolescence and young adulthood. Now, at the age of thirty-four, I was able to Re-Call our earlier connection, the happiness of my childhood, and my inestimable gratitude to her and admiration for many qualities, especially her sensitivity and unique, profoundly touching sense of humor. All of this was still in evidence in full force. One day, when she was returning home from the hair dresser's in Fribourg, she commented upon her own diminished ability to walk, simply by reciting from a nursery rhyme: "Hippity hop to the barber shop, to buy a stick of candy." This was pure vintage Anna, who was not one given to moaning and groaning.

She forgave everything. Even though I was peculiar enough to get degree after degree, she saw that I was recognized as a popular teacher and that I was happy, and so she was relieved. There was a harmony of understanding that brought back shining memories. All of this was intensified by the beauty of our surroundings and sense of reunion and adventure together. It was intensified also by our indirectly acknowledged knowledge that life is short, and that this Time was a special gift. My mother was my Boon Companion.* Her Presence in Fribourg was a companionate blessing.

MY DOCTORATE IN SACRED THEOLOGY:
AN ASTONISHING PHENOMENON

By the end of my fourth year in Fribourg (summer 1963) I had completed my dissertation for the Doctorate in Sacred Theology and had passed my final examinations for that degree, *summa cum laude*. The whole phenomenon of my attainment of that degree is, from my Present perspective,

---

Boon Companion is defined in the *Wickedary* as "an intimate friend; one who arrives in Tidal Time; a companionate blessing."

astonishing but comprehensible. As I have already said, it can be understood only within the context of my Quest during that time, which was still before the "Second Wave" of Feminism came crashing through.

One of the astonishing aspects of that achievement was my doctoral dissertation itself, on "The Problem of Speculative Theology." Looking at that document in the Present Time—having carefully hidden it from myself for years—I Now am amazed to See what was really going on.

It was with some trepidation that I took it off the shelf in the spring of 1988, blew off the dust, and began to analyze its contents as possibly representing some preliminary Moments of the Be-Dazzling Voyage. I noted with some slight chagrin that its author was "Mary F. Daly." Oh, well. I then began to read. What I found in this work was a Passionate defense of the life of the mind, and especially of knowledge for its own sake, carried to the ultimate degree.

My dissertation was a fierce and intricate argument against certain Augustinians who held that theology was primarily practical, and in support of the Thomistic position that it is primarily speculative wisdom—that is, knowledge for its own sake. This is one way of describing it on a foreground level. However, reading it Now, I can clearly see what I was trying to get at. In my analysis of Thomistic texts, I had found passages suggesting that theological knowledge has a "dynamism to go beyond itself," a "tendency to overreach itself," that is, to attain understanding that is beyond reason, but in an inherently rational way. I was arguing that theology overreaches blind faith in its seeking for understanding, that it "tends to a certain participation in the vision of God." To put it simply, I was fighting for intellectual autonomy.

Of course this was written in terms that I would not use Now, but the dissertation was an elegant argument for the possibility of rational knowledge that goes beyond appearances to the very core of reality. If I were to try to explain the intellectual process that I see going on in this dissertation, I would say that I was writing and thinking in a language that could not say what I was trying to say. I detect a kind of Metaknowledge running through my arguments. I think I was functioning in what might be called "a subliminal mode." That is, I was writing in code without realizing this. Much later on, when I was writing *Beyond God the Father, Gyn/Ecology, Pure Lust,* and the *Wickedary,* this experience of having been obliged to think subliminally was very useful. Having been sensitized to this multileveled nature of discourse, I was enabled to reverse the process and decode patriarchal theological and philosophical texts, thus exposing their hidden messages.

The obtaining of my Doctorate in Sacred Theology involved many amazing events. One of the most Stunning of these had to do with the university's requirement that all doctoral candidates in theology take the "Anti-Modernist Oath" after final examinations. This involved kneeling in front of the white-robed Dominican Dean of the Faculty of Theology and putting one's hands on the bible which he held in his lap.

Since Modernism involved many ideas with which I was fully in agreement, e.g., trusting one's individual inspiration without reliance on "authority," there was no way that I could perjure myself in this fashion.[6] However, if the candidate did not take this oath, the doctoral degree would not be conferred.

The reason that I hadn't foreseen this crisis was that for the earlier degrees (the baccalaureate and licentiate) the "Anti-Modernist Oath" was taken in a group. We all stood there while one student rattled off the thing in Latin. The student chosen for this role was invariably a Spanish seminarian, because the Spaniards could rattle off Latin faster than anyone. Since I hadn't been obliged to *say* anything, I hadn't felt that I was perjuring myself on these earlier occasions.

The doctoral situation was different. I would have to say the abominable thing alone, and I could not in conscience do that. I began to wonder if, after all these years of struggle, I would not get the doctorate after all. Then at the last minute, without having any idea of what they were doing, the esteemed members of the Faculty of Theology saved me. Since I was the first woman ever to earn this degree, they were faced with a unique situation. They decided that, although they could not bar me from the degree, they did not want a woman to be allowed to take the "Anti-Modernist Oath," because the implication of taking that oath was that she would be legitimated to teach in a Pontifical Faculty of Theology (for example, at The Catholic University of America). So they forbade me to take it. I almost exploded with relief and laughter in the face of the professor who pompously announced this solemn decision. As usual, I was very Lucky.

CHAPTER FOUR

PHILOSOPHICAL CONCLUSIONS
AND BEGINNING BE-SPEAKING:
THE SUMMONS TO WRITE
THE CHURCH AND THE SECOND SEX

The summer of 1963 was a decisive time. Having obtained my doctorate in theology, which was my sixth degree, in June, I was in no mood to stop my career of accumulating degrees. I loved Fribourg and still had my three teaching jobs there. I was addicted to zooming around on my Velosolex and to spending vacation time in other countries. Moreover, the University of Fribourg had an excellent Faculty of Philosophy. So I decided that the stage was set to act directly toward achieving the purpose that had been with me since high school. Now I was free to enroll formally in the Faculty of Philosophy and write my doctoral dissertation in that field.

I had, in fact, been taking philosophy courses throughout the academic years 1961–62 and 1962–63, while writing the theological dissertation.* All that remained to be done was to take a few more seminars and write the dissertation in philosophy. With my record in Fribourg I had no trouble sailing on into full-fledged status as a doctoral candidate in philosophy.

When my friends stared and intoned, "Mary, *not* a *third* doctorate!" I became more stubbornly confirmed than ever in my purpose. So I was launched on what might have seemed to be my career as the world's oldest child prodigy. "Will she ever stop?" they groaned. "Not as long as I can get away with it," I thought. "It gets easier by degrees," I said.

During the academic years 1963–64 and 1964–65 I happily continued living with my mother, teaching and taking philosophy courses and seminars. I worked hard on my doctoral dissertation in philosophy. I also traveled.

ASTONISHING ADVENTURES

The most spectacular and adventurous traveling with my mother occurred on our trip to Greece. This was in the spring, probably of 1964. We took the train, second class, all the way. This meant going across Switzerland and

---

*See Chapter Three.

northern Italy, then through Yugoslavia and continuing down through Greece to Athens. The train was packed, and the stamina required for this long trip was no small matter. I remember being relieved at the appearance of young boys selling shishkebab through the train windows when we got to Greece.

In Athens we somehow Lucked into a simple but clean and beautiful hotel room with a wonderful view of the Acropolis. My mother loved this bright room. We visited Piraeus, the port of Athens. I recall eating what I thought to be a delicious fish dish and then being told that it was baby squid and that it had been smashed with rocks. I washed down the rest of my dinner with ouzo and tried to forget about it.

We took several tours, and I remember going to Corinth and to Delphi and seeing the Temple of Poseidon on the coast at sunset. The colors of the ocean and sky were so vivid that—to those from a less colorful locale—these appeared almost "artificial." We took a boat ride also to a beautiful small island (Delos) which was covered with bright flowers.

The most astonishing event was our visit to Crete. We crossed over by boat, and it was a rough crossing. Everyone was sick. Crete itself was unlike anything I had seen. We traveled by ordinary buses into the countryside. I was amazed to see that all of the other passengers were perpetually crossing themselves (backwards, from my roman catholic perspective). I didn't see that we were passing many churches or shrines and could not determine what occasioned all of this crossing. I finally thought perhaps it was the bumps in the road that inspired such apparently desperate expressions of piety. I noted that the women crossed themselves about twice as frequently as the men. The driver, however, crossed himself very, very frequently.*

There were inexplicable small events on this bus trip. For example, in the middle of absolutely nowhere, with no village or house in sight for miles around, the bus stopped and let off a passenger as if this were an ordinary stop. I stared out the window to see if he would disappear into a cave or a hole in the ground, but the bus kept bumping on. At another stop a woman got on carrying a basket with a cloth covering its contents and a hen sitting on top of the cloth. I don't know why this seemed so peculiar—not annoying—just interesting and peculiar. At least the hen did not cross herself.

We went to the Palace of Knossos, of course. I did not consciously understand its prepatriarchal significance. Such insights would not become accessible to me until years later.† Yet there must have been something

---

*There was a shrine on the dashboard with several burning votive candles placed before a statue of some unrecognizable (to me) saint. This in itself was enough, I thought, to make everyone in the bus quite nervous.

†On a return visit in 1976 I really understood the Archaic significance of Crete, and that trip greatly influenced the writing of *Gyn/Ecology*. See Chapter Twelve.

powerful that pulled me to visit Crete. Like my first visit to Ireland, this trip, in retrospect, seems like a first preparatory "touching base" with something too powerful to be Dis-covered all at once. And, of course, this travel was taking place in the early sixties, before I knew what to look for.

Our return trip on the train from Greece to Switzerland was full of unexpected surprises. When we had made it through Yugoslavia the train suddenly stopped at a town just before the Italian border. Everyone was ordered to get off the train. My mother was dozing when this happened and I had just fought my way through the crowd to and from the W.C. In any case, neither of us was able to pick up any explanation for this rough expulsion. I tried to get one in English, German, and French.

Finally we found out that there was a train strike in Italy and so the train could go no further. We were on our own to find a place to stay for the night—or, indefinitely. I looked into my wallet to see how much money was left and discovered to my horror that all of my money had been stolen. I recalled that a particularly suspicious looking character with an ingratiating smile who had been sitting directly across from me had watched all of my movements. He was now nowhere in sight. I concluded that he must have taken the money while I was away from my seat and my mother was sleeping.

It didn't matter who had taken the money at that point. The fact was that it was gone and we had to do something. It was late afternoon and we walked to the local travel agency. I explained our plight to the young woman who worked there and asked when we might catch a train to get home to Fribourg. All of this communication had to take place in inadequate German, since this was the only language we had in common.

The young woman invited my mother and me to stay at her home, so we did. We were invited to dinner and the encounter there was very moving. The woman's grandmother and my mother communicated nonverbally and liked each other immediately. My mother told me that the old Yugoslavian woman reminded her of her own grandmother. When I asked what she meant, my mother said: "It's the way she does things. For example, look at the way she washes the dishes." I saw that she used no soap but thoroughly rinsed the dishes, just using her hands in the hot water. Apparently that was how my great-grandmother had done it. Also there was a cat who reminded my mother of her grandmother's cat. The kindness of those women was very touching.

I could not possibly ask these people to loan me money, and we would need some for meals and for the Swiss train after arriving in Zurich, in order to get home to Fribourg. So I decided to go to the parish priest, and asked for a loan for the equivalent of forty dollars—or Swiss francs—I can't remember which. The man looked terrified and probably was sure that he would never see his money again, but he did loan it to me. I realized that he must have lived in a state of perpetual fear, because I saw people stealthily making visits to the church, then crossing themselves, looking around, and hurrying away. Clearly they were devout people who were afraid to be seen going near the church in that communist country.

The next day the train did move on and we got back to Fribourg safely. I sent the priest an international money order, but I could never know for sure whether he actually received the money. My mother and I often talked about that eventful trip.

MY DOCTORAL DISSERTATION IN PHILOSOPHY: PARADOXES

I went back to work on my doctoral dissertation in philosophy, which was entitled *Natural Knowledge of God in the Philosophy of Jacques Maritain.* This would actually be completed in the spring of 1965, in time for me to take final examinations for the doctorate in July of that year.

The experience of taking this volume off the shelf during the process of writing *Outercourse* and encountering it for the first time in many years was comparable to my recent renewal of acquaintance with my theological dissertation. The philosophical work was also written by one "Mary F. Daly," an ardent Thomist scholar, who referred to herself, in the academic convention of the time, as "we." Having already familiarized mySelf with her style in my study of her earlier dissertation, I was ready to plunge into the subject matter.

It was not surprising to see that this work too is a passionate treatise on the intellectual life. Like the theological dissertation, it is extremely technical. Of course it deals with different subject matter, and writing it involved close reading of Maritain's copious works in French. Yet the theme of knowledge that has a dynamism to go beyond itself continues like a haunting refrain. The primary concern here is the "intuition of being," which to me was a subject of intense interest. I wrestled with Maritain wherever I thought he was in danger of slipping into a kind of "soft" intuitionism. Although I agreed with him that "it is this intuition that effects, causes the metaphysical habitus," I worried that his line of thinking could fall into an easy assumption that "this quasi-mystical intuition could play the role of substitute for the *work* of philosophy."

The point is that although I cherished this intuition, and could see no use in philosophizing without it, perhaps even in living without it, I wanted a clear defense of intellectual rigor/vigor. This insistence on having it *all*—intuition *and* arduous reasoning that is rooted in intuition—was of deep importance to me. I loved both modes of knowing, which I recognized as essential to each other. Sickened by the downgrading and caricaturing of intuition and the relegation of this pathetically reduced "talent" to women—which of course also implied the safeguarding of "reason" as the prerogative of males—I was struggling to Name this game which had been played by academics for centuries. It was indeed one of the masters' major mind-fucks of the millennia.

I Now realize that my work on this dissertation, as well as my theological work, had an extremely important role in preparing me to write all of my books, although, of course, I had no idea at the time that these would come into be-ing. Through my work on this dissertation I strengthened my ability to go to the heart of a problem, to make connections logically, to trust my own intuitions while demonstrating their implications rigorously, and to articulate my arguments in a way that is inherently clear in itself—which is quite a different matter from being a good "debater" who argues only to score points but does not seek the truth. Later on, as a Radical Feminist Philosopher, I would draw upon these skills and the confidence that came with them. I would need them, especially because my own free creativity, knowledge that overreaches itself, needs to be Fiercely Focused.* To put all of this in a somewhat oversimplified way: I had to learn the rules extremely well in order to break them with precision.

So my training as a Thomist theologian and philosopher became my Labrys, enabling me to cut through man-made delusions to the core of problems and to Dis-close the deceptive deadly devices that are used by the academics, media men, and culture controllers of patriarchy—devices such as erasure and reversal. As the challenges have become greater, my work has become Wilder and I have continued to draw upon that training in precision. An essential aim of my task has been the development of a philosophy that sustains both the daring free play of intuition and the rigor of rational analysis.

It may seem paradoxical that I went to learn from the medieval masters and their disciples and later came to the point of Realizing the necessity for overthrowing the patriarchal masters of all kinds. However, I do not experience this as inconsistent with the direction of my own Be-Dazzling Journey. There has been an inherent consistency in this Quest, which has required continual breaking through blockages, tearing off mindbindings, reversing of reversals, Dis-covering what has been defaced and erased and buried—in other words, working as a Crafty Pirate.† And since I am a woman-identified philosopher in a patriarchal world it makes sense that it is turning out this way, which is the way of Outercourse.

Another paradox is the fact that those years of study, culminating in my writing of the philosophical dissertation, increased my understanding of and respect for intuitive powers, including those of so-called "simple" or

---

*As the disabling devices of phallic fragmentation and dis-memberment have worked to undermine the insights of Feminism—especially since the mid-1980s—the importance of Furious Focus becomes evident. For example, we can see the necessity for avoiding disintegration into anti-intellectuality and, at the seemingly opposite end, dryasdust elite/effete academic studies and discussions (sometimes under the aegis of "Women's Studies" or "Gender Studies") that turn back the clock and endlessly reiterate tired old "problems" that were intelligently discussed and moved beyond two decades before.

†See "Prelude to The Second Spiral Galaxy" for further discussion of Piracy.

"uneducated" women. I became better equipped to analyze how patriarchal "education" can blunt and stunt such powers. The direction in which my study was pointing me was away from academic elitism and toward Realizing our common knowledge.

This paradoxical understanding was reinforced by my gradual realization that some of my professors were less admirable than the doctrines they taught. One example stands out. An esteemed professor of new testament, who specialized in the idea of "charity" (*agapē*) in the epistles of saint Paul, took it upon himself to try to destroy the possibility of my teaching in the junior year abroad programs, which would have meant economic disaster for me, as well as the end of hope that I would be able to continue my study, and ultimately the destruction of my reputation. This much admired priest went to the director of one of the junior year abroad programs and announced to her that I was an immoral person and should not be allowed to teach. Since I was not engaged in "immoral" behavior even by his standards, the incident was bizarre.

Luckily the director politely laughed the saintly scholar out of her office. When she told me about it later, I felt a peculiar horror at the lowdown nastiness of this priest. The experience helped to prepare me for variations of the same theme of priestly christian charity that would occur later. At that time, I saw this as the grotesque behavior of one individual, and even experienced some "guilt," wondering what I had done that was bad enough to elicit this underhanded punitive behavior. Later I would come to recognize it as one manifestation of ordinary, banal, institutionalized evil, specifically, misogynism. I would also question more closely the lofty ideology of christian virtue that could legitimate such woman-hating.

Yet the attitude of the Dominican professors was not unequivocally or universally one of misogynism. Some members of both the Faculty of Theology and the Faculty of Philosophy genuinely tried to be helpful. The director of my doctoral dissertation in philosophy—M.-D. Philippe, O.P.—was a genuine scholar and a person of integrity who respected my work. I have no reason to think that he would be pleased with my Feminist books, but I would expect a more complex reaction than the predictable arrogant hostility of many others. In any case, at that time, he was a good dissertation director and a brilliant teacher.

THE SUMMONS TO WRITE A BOOK

It was during that period of working on my dissertation in philosophy that The Momentous Thing began to happen. In December of 1963, *Commonweal* magazine published an article by Rosemary Lauer, a professor of philosophy at St. John's University in New York, entitled "Women and the Church," in which she argued for the equality of women in the catholic church. That article was magical in its effect. It awakened in me the power to speak out and to Name women's oppression. That is, it awakened my sleeping Powers of Be-Speaking.

In response to that article I wrote a letter to *Commonweal* announcing that I was ashamed of my own silence—ashamed that I had not published such an article myself. After proclaiming that there should be a deluge of such essays and of scholarly books which study the history of the problem of women and the church, I wrote:

> This much I know: the beginnings of these articles and these books (how badly we need these books especially!) are already in the minds and on the lips of many of us. And—this is both a prophecy and a promise—they will come.[1]

This was before the cresting of the "Second Wave" of Feminism, and I was referring to future books by myself and other women. These words came out of my typewriter before I was even confident that I could write such a book. I did not even know that I knew such a thing until the words were right there before me.

Without realizing consciously what was happening I had leaped into the whirling movement of Moments of *Be-Speaking,* that is

1 : Auguring, foretelling, Speaking of what will be **2 :** bringing about a psychic and/or material change by means of words (*Wickedary*).

The Momentum of that Original Moment of Be-Speaking propelled me into the writing of my first Feminist articles. One of these was published by the Swiss Feminist Gertrud Heinzelmann in her anthology, *Wir schweigen nicht länger!—We Won't Keep Silence Any Longer!*, a collection of statements by women to the "Fathers" of the Second Vatican Council.[2] Another was "A Built-in Bias," published in *Commonweal*, in January 1965.[3] The publication of this article had Momentous consequences.

In the spring of 1965, while I was hard at work on my dissertation and teaching yet another batch of American junior year abroad students, my *Commonweal* article was having its effects—all unknown to me. A publishing consultant who worked for a London publisher (Geoffrey Chapman, Ltd.) had read the article and was trying to find me. As I wrote in the "Autobiographical Preface to the 1975 Edition" of *The Church and the Second Sex*:

> Some weeks later a letter from a British publisher in London found its way to me in Fribourg, after visiting several wrong addresses. It contained an invitation to write a book on women and the church, developing the ideas in the *Commonweal* article. . . . The letter was like a summons, and I knew clearly that the time was right for the First Coming of *The Church and the Second Sex*.[4]

Looking back at this Moment, I am struck once again by the fact that it was an Act of Be-Speaking by another woman that had triggered the chain of events that made it possible for me to actualize my own Be-Speaking Powers. The Gynergy that was released by her Courageous Act opened my

(Third) Eye/I. It ripped off the blindfold that had covered my eyes and the gag that had kept my mouth shut, enabling me to See and to Name "the mystery of man."

It is in the nature of Moments that one Moment leads to another. This is because it has consequences in the world and thus Moves a woman to take further Leaps. My Act of "writing out loud" my own thoughts had real consequences. Thus the "summons" to write a book that came from the British publisher was like a Call from the cosmos itself—an unrelenting Call. The letter finally found me, after being blown through all those wrong addresses by the Great Wild Wind that had carried me this far. The phenomenon was both very Strange and very familiar. So when the letter did reach me, I understood what I had to do. Of course the Calling had been reciprocal. By writing "A Built-in Bias" I had summoned this summons. On a deeper level still, the Call of the Clover Blossom that had lured me to Fribourg was behind it all, beckoning me on to further Be-Speaking.

There followed an accelerated Spiral of Moments. In May 1965 the contract for *The Church and the Second Sex* was signed (with Geoffrey Chapman of London). I was slightly distracted from this project by the fact that I had to complete and defend my doctoral dissertation in philosophy—a task which I did accomplish in July of that year, while wrapping up yet another semester of teaching. There remained only the problem of publication of the dissertation, which was required by the university.*[5]

The completion and defense of my doctoral dissertation was the grand culmination of my Quest through the mazes of academia. I don't mean that by my acquiring of that degree I magically became a philosopher, as if that could be accomplished by conferral of a degree. Rather, it was a kind of rite of passage. Moreover, for me—although I could not yet articulate this—it established a Right of Passage on my Piratic enterprise of Plundering treasures stolen by phallocratic thieves and Smuggling them back to women within academia itself. That is, it was a patriarchal professional legitimation for my Absolutely Anti-patriarchal, Unprofessional career of seeking and Dis-covering lost/stolen knowledge and of Re-membering my own Lost Senses and Lost Senses of words. In Other words, it was a Momentous Moment on my Voyage of becoming a Radical Feminist Philosopher.

ROME 1965: INVESTIGATING
THE SECOND VATICAN COUNCIL

In the fall of 1965 I took a train to Rome in order to conduct my own personal investigation of The Second Vatican Council. I checked into a relatively bug-free *pensione* and began my wanderings of the streets of Vatican City.

---

*I requested and received a further increase of my loan from the Medora A. Feehan Fund to cover the expense of publication. This brought my accumulated debt to $5,200, which was a lot then, but I knew that I could and would pay it all back.

No one had invited me, of course. I had no official role. However, I felt quite at home among hundreds of other deviants who were there to lobby for their various causes. I bonded with other catholic Feminists and hob-nobbed with theologians and students as well as journalists. A couple of the latter were willing to loan me their identification cards so that I could sneak into saint Peter's when the council was in session and view the fantastic scene.

My visit to Rome was packed with intense, multicolored, multileveled experiences. I saw and heard the pompous cardinals, who seemed like silly old men in red dresses, droning their eternal platitudes. I engaged in intense conversations with catholic thinkers and advocates of social change. We shared an exhilarating sense of hope, an impassioned belief in the possibility of change.

Among my serendipitous encounters was one special meeting with the gentle Irish journalist, Gary MacEoin. Sitting in one of Rome's friendly restaurants, Gary very simply described to me the secret art of how to write a book. It was true that I had written doctoral dissertations, but I was mystified by the problem of how to go about beginning to write a *Book*. The project seemed massive and unmanageable. When this friendly journalist showed me how he set up the structures of his books, the mystery was cracked in one easy lesson.* I was ready to begin writing *The Church and the Second Sex.*

I was somewhat impoverished by the expenses of a month's living in Rome (even in my budget *pensione*) but vastly enriched in every other way. I now had countless memories of exciting encounters and conversations—of exchanges of energies that had electrified every day. My imagination also had been Sparked by a Stunning array of visual experiences. There had been the Moment, for example, when just outside saint Peter's I suddenly found myself within a few feet of a pathologically weighty cardinal in his flaming red attire literally being lifted out of his limousine by two sturdy members of the Swiss Guard who apparently had been assigned to get him to the council on time. His eminence saw me gaping and gave me a look of pure hate. I would never forget those dark beady eyes and that look of utter misogyny. Indeed, one could say that this was, in a certain way, a Moment of Inspiration.[6]

---

*Gary dashed off a quick outline of his process. Although I cannot Now remember all of the details, I recall the basic structural elements. He suggested that I write a letter to a friend describing what I wanted to do. He said that he generally began with a chapter whose function was "setting the scene." This presented the contemporary context. Then there would be a chapter analyzing the problems inherent in "the scene." This was followed by historical chapters presenting the background of these current problems. His final chapters offered new approaches to solving these problems. Although all of this may seem very general, it was just what I needed to Spin off from. My block about structuring a book was gone forever. This memory of the procedure was reconfirmed in a discussion with Gary while in the process of writing *Outercourse* (Conversation, Boston, June 1990).

So I returned to Fribourg with clear, sure determination that I would and could and had to write this book. It was already in process, since my unconscious Self had been working away on it, Spinning and Weaving connections at every Moment.

A YEAR OF GRACE

That seventh and last academic year in Fribourg was a year of grace. In "theory" I should have returned to the States and imprisonment in some full-time teaching job by September of 1965, since I had finished my degrees. However, I didn't want to go back yet or, in fact, ever. My resistance to returning at that time was Right on Course. Had I returned, I would have missed that Stunning Time in Rome as well as other exploratory adventures, such as my trip to the Middle East. Most important, I would have missed that year of freedom to live and write in Fribourg, following the Call of the Wild, supported, of course, by my triad of junior year abroad teaching jobs.

I would have been tempted to stay on in this State of Bliss for an indefinite period. However, I naively made a tactical error by registering in the fall of 1965 with the Swiss foreign police under the category of "worker" rather than "student," which had been my previous status. Since I had decided not to go for a fourth doctorate and was no longer registered at the university, this seemed to be a logical move. However, a particularly rigid employee in the office of the *police des étrangers*—a pious catholic who had previously been employed by the university—decided that I should be subjected to the letter of the law. This meant that since I was no longer officially a student I would have to get out of Switzerland by the end of the summer of 1966. Moreover, when the police called my apartment and discovered that my mother was living there, they ordered her to leave also.

Kicked out of Fribourg! The thought and anticipation of leaving was very painful. I spent the academic year 1965–66 intensely engaged in the writing of *The Church and the Second Sex*, hoping to get it finished before I was doomed to leave this magical place that I loved and return to the country that had never really felt like my "native land." I also kept in contact with a few women who were working for the cause of Feminism (then perceived as "equal rights"). Among these was the indomitable Gertrud Heinzelmann who for years had been fighting for women's suffrage in conservative Switzerland[7] and who turned her attention to the catholic church at the time of The Second Vatican Council. There were also the courageous elderly English women who had founded and sustained "Saint Joan's International Alliance"—an organization of catholic women who for decades had fought patriarchal injustice. One American member of that organization whom I met and came to know in Rome, an ardent and constant fighter for equality of women in the church, was Frances McGillicuddy. Another was Betty

Farians, whom I have mentioned earlier.* These friends would continue to be important to me after my return to the United States.

DIS-COVERING THE MIDDLE EAST: OTHERWORLDLY DIMENSIONS

In the spring of 1966 I decided to travel to the Middle East. I determined to seize the opportunity, since I was fated to return to the United States and since, relatively speaking, it was not so far from Fribourg. The trip was out of the question for my mother, but she had no objection to my going. There were some who thought that such a journey, undertaken alone, was perilous. A hair dresser in Fribourg, when I told her of my travel plans, gasped as she cut my hair. *"Vous allez toute seule? Quelle horreur!"* ("You're going all alone? How horrible!") To me, however, the prospect was hardly one of horror but of high adventure. And indeed, as it turned out, it was exactly that. My wanderings around Europe had indeed been eye-openers/Eye-openers. My trip to Jordan, Lebanon, Syria, and Egypt added utterly Other dimensions.

In Jordan I was in a Super Natural stoned state, without the aid of pot, hashish, or any drug.† The place itself did it. My most vivid experience was a trip across the desert from Jerusalem‡ to the ancient city of Petra. I was picked up at four a.m. at my hotel by an Arab wearing the traditional white robe and headdress, who announced that he would be my tour guide and taxi driver for the long trip. During the ensuing hour he collected several other tourist-passengers. It was important to get an early start, so that we could return that night. Also, it was essential that we reach our destination before the mid-day heat. During that dash through the desert I saw herds of running camels and a group of wandering Bedouin.

When, after several hours of this bizarre travel, we neared our destination, we approached an extraordinary gorge. Here the car could go no further, so we traveled through the gorge on donkeys, led by small boys. The sound of my donkey's feet clip-clopping on the stones in the gorge echoed in that Strange place, and it echoes Now in my mind. This astonishing procession brought us to a rose-red temple with graceful columns and sculptures of winged war-maidens and Arab war-horses. Beyond this was a mountain-ringed oval space. This is where the vanished city of Petra had

---

*Further information on Betty's work can be found in Chapters Two, Seven, and Eight.

†Neither pot nor hashish ever noticeably (to me) affected me. I've never tried anything else. Juno knows I tried with hash. I bought a large slab of it from one of my American male students who had smuggled it from Istanbul. Since I found it difficult to inhale, I swallowed large quantities of it in tea—all to no avail. Those around me who had taken the same stuff were profoundly stoned.

‡At the time, part of Jerusalem was still in Jordan.

My Middle Eastern trip had taken only about two weeks, reckoned in foreground time/tidy time, but in the dimensions of Elemental/Tidal Time it was like an experience of countless years. I returned to Fribourg deeply refreshed and eager to continue work on *The Church and the Second Sex.*

EXPULSION FROM PARADISE: SENT BACK "HOME"

During that last year in Fribourg I had written letters of application for teaching jobs in the States. I had a number of offers—each of which sounded more gruesome than the next. Doors to teaching positions both in philosophy and in theology were open to me at reputable colleges from East coast to West coast. I did not at the time understand that this was in part because the Age of Tokenism had begun. My truly troublesome nature was not yet understood in the U.S., and my record looked very good to departments seeking token women. What I did understand was that this meant closure on the ecstatic and free existence I had known in Fribourg, and imprisonment in academic banality. My sense of impending loss was profound.

Indeed, impending loss in the deepest sense hung over me that year. My mother's health was visibly failing, and I knew that she did not want to end her days in a foreign country. She wanted to go home. On some level I recognized that going "home" would also mean the loss of my dearest friend and companion within a fairly short period of time. This knowledge intensified my sense of the preciousness of every Moment in Fribourg—that Fairyland that had become the incarnation of my World of Glowing Books, the Time/Space of my dreams.

I completed the first five chapters of *The Church and the Second Sex* in Fribourg. Although I finally had my doctorate in philosophy, the Great Wind that had taken me first to Saint Mary's and later to Fribourg was still blowing. It was the Wind that had carried the invitation to write a book on women and the church and that had reached me, despite the many improbable addresses it first visited, and it was the Wind that had carried me to Rome. Translated into practical/political terms, what the Wind now was howling was that theology departments were where the hope of action was, since after The Second Vatican Council some theologians were at least open to ideas of social change and were beginning to seek out colleagues who would challenge the status quo.

It was imperative also that I teach in a coeducational university. A good number of the males in my classes had shown enthusiasm for discussion and exploration of ideas, and that was the bottom line, or so I thought then. I had vivid nightmares of being marooned in a dulled/dulling catholic women's college—a fate which I envisioned as unbearable. My experience of teaching the young women in the junior year abroad program of Rosary College had been largely positive. Still, combined with memories of my life as a student and later as a teacher in catholic women's colleges, it had convinced me that I would not be happy continuing at such institutions, where most of the students and faculty seemed to be immersed in the feminine mystique.

I was plagued by a Nagging Sense of Something missing at those places. That Something was a Lust for learning and for bonding with women. This lack was a continuation of the broken Promise syndrome, and my horror of it was profound. Even though I liked the students and had good times with them, the thought of returning "home" to face hordes of young women fixated upon the goal of becoming the Wives and Mothers of America was unbearable. It seemed that this would be like becoming trapped/zapped in a zone of the living dead.

After considering offers for positions at several universities and colleges, I signed a two-year contract as assistant professor in the theology department at jesuit-run Boston College.* I was so naive that I didn't even know enough to bargain for an associate professorship or for tenure right at the outset. Given my years of teaching experience and degrees that would have been a reasonable request. I wasn't even aware of the distinction between assistant and associate professor. Such academic details had not been a part of my world.

My signing of the contract had been preceded by some correspondence with the chair of the department, who wanted me to teach courses in "Christology." The fact was that for years I had found the christian fixation on the "divinity of Christ" and on the figure of Jesus disturbing and profoundly repulsive. I think that I knew on some level that this divinization of maleness served to legitimate patriarchy. Of course, I did not explain the problem in these terms, but expressed my strong preference for more philosophically oriented courses centering on "the problem of God." I had no ethical dilemmas about teaching this kind of course, since I still saw "God" as a genderless word, not necessarily implying images of maleness. So I was lighthearted when the chairman agreed to my choice of subject matter. I was slated to teach in the "Honors Program," and wide-ranging exploration of philosophical ideas that would challenge very bright students was what was wanted. It seemed that once again my Luck was with me. I could expect to teach freely in a stimulating environment.

All the same, I felt that I was being corralled back into prison. Leaving Fribourg was an experience of being expelled from Paradise, comparable to my departure from Saint Mary's. I wept on the train leaving Fribourg for the last time, and my mother felt sadness and distress also. Together we sat there and cried shamelessly, as over a vast and senseless loss.

---

*A major factor influencing my decision to accept Boston College's offer was my desire to be on the East coast. Although I had received job offers on the West coast, that felt too far from Europe. I wanted to be geographically "near" to Fribourg. Moreover, the Boston area was, at least, familiar.

We did not return to Boston immediately or directly. I had shipped several large footlockers of books and clothing to Boston and in August we traveled by train with two or three suitcases for a final vacation in Europe. We headed for the Adriatic coast of Italy, which I had discovered a few years earlier, thanks to Gertrud Heinzelmann, who had invited me to spend a few days with her in Pesaro. I remembered that the beaches there were wonderful and that good, clean hotels right on the beach were accessible for very low prices. We needed a place to rest and recuperate after the physically and emotionally exhausting weeks of packing, selling furniture, and ultimately moving out of Fribourg. Pesaro was the perfect answer.

Italian women were impressed with my mother's beauty. At the age of seventy-six her hair, even though it was mostly grey, had obviously been black. Her eyes were blue, but her skin had an olive tinge. This feature had been considered a blemish by her Irish grandmother and aunts but to the Italians she seemed somewhat Italian. I remember one chambermaid exclaiming: *"La Mama è bella!"* Indeed, she was.

My mother enjoyed the rest and the beauty of the sea coast but she felt something fearful when she heard the sound of the sea at night. I was saddened by the fact that she experienced it this way. To me, that sound was an ecstasy-evoking sensory experience and it had been one of my greatest memories of my first time in Pesaro. I had not taken into account the fact that the pounding of the sea carries many kinds of messages.

Our plan was to return to Boston by way of Dublin. When we talked about it in Pesaro, my mother said: "Maybe I'll meet my grandmother in Ireland." I knew that she was referring to that ultimate reunion, and that her speaking of it in this way was elicited by the relentless and awesome sound of the sea.

The process of returning to America was poignant. We did stop briefly in Ireland. My mother did not meet her grandmother then, but there was an unacknowledged understanding between us that that Event was impending. When our plane for Boston reached the North American continent I stared down with distaste and dismay, and with the doomed feeling of having come full circle. I could not yet realize that this "return" was *not* a dead circle, but rather an essential part of the Spiraling Voyage.

CHAPTER FIVE

SPIRALING BACK TO BOSTON AND BEYOND

It was mid-September of 1966 when my mother and I checked into a hotel in downtown Boston. Ahead of me was the task of hunting for an apartment. Having put off my return until the last possible instant, I was faced with the reality of having to begin teaching classes in two days' time. I recall sitting in that dreary hotel room and turning on the television set. American TV! Something I hadn't seen for seven years. A *Tarzan* film was on. A familiar old depression crawled over me and haunted the room.

For a while it seemed—not that my Luck had really failed me—but that Fate was pushing me harshly in a direction that I resisted. But there was no time for resistance. The relentless struggle for survival had me running breathlessly. I had to become reacquainted with American money, American supermarkets, American public transportation. Strangely enough, I found all of this much harder to comprehend than the currency, shops, and transportation systems of Switzerland or of any European country I had visited. I was a homesick alien, experiencing the alienation that I had known here before, but this time *consciously*: Now I knew *what* it was that was missing—the exhilarating intellectual life, adventurous travel, cultural Diversity, reconnection with my roots, and joyous psychic freedom that I had experienced in Europe.

CIRCLES, CONTRADICTIONS, ERASURES, REVERSALS

It was with a heavy heart that I boarded a trolley (now known as "the T") for my first encounter with Boston College as a new faculty member. As the trolley approached the neighborhood of BC, I passed "Cleveland Circle," which was close to the area where I had lived before leaving for Fribourg. It reminded me of my fear that I had come "full circle"—that I was stuck back in a rut that I had believed had been left behind forever. This perception was "enhanced" when I walked around that neighborhood, desperately hunting for an apartment that my mother and I could move into. As I approached Cleveland Circle I glimpsed an enormous red neon sign that said "CIRCLE." It was, in fact, a sign for "Circle Cleaners," but its message to me was "back again."

Looking back, I see the CIRCLE sign as a warning against the traps of Stag-nation. Although I didn't yet understand this, my return to Boston would make possible the continuation of the Spiraling Journey beyond stagnant circling. It would involve Moments of moving further and further on the Be-Dazzling Voyage. But in order for those Moments to occur I would have to take chances, jump off a few cliffs, and fly with the Fates. All of this would be made much easier by the fact that the Great Wind that I had ridden to Saint Mary's at Notre Dame and later to Fribourg was still blowing and that there would be many opportunities to hop on for a ride.

Meanwhile, I began my teaching career at Boston College. It turned out that virtually all of my students were males, since women were not yet admitted to the College of Arts and Sciences, but were relegated to the School of Education and the School of Nursing. At any rate, I liked my students and immediately assigned them difficult but interesting reading lists of books that ranged from Nietzsche to Martin Buber to Arnold Toynbee to Paul Tillich to Jean-Paul Sartre.

It struck me as strange that whereas women were not deemed fit to be admitted as students in Arts and Sciences at BC, I was welcomed as a teacher not only of ordinary male students but especially of "honors students." This was one of many spooking experiences with which I was bombarded every day on campus.

My situation was actually one of living a contradiction. Without understanding the setup, I had accepted a job as token woman in an all-male theology department in a jesuit university. Naively, I had believed that I had been hired because of my extraordinary qualifications for the job. On a certain level, of course, this was true, but it was not true in the straightforward way that I had understood the case. A major clue emerged when I realized that a rabbi and a protestant theologian (both males) had also just been hired. In fact, our photographs appeared together in *The Boston Globe*. My colleagues even joked about the fact that if a Black protestant female theologian had been hired they could have had three for the price of one, and I laughed along with them. However, I still didn't understand the full implications of this. I didn't yet have an analysis of the meaning of tokenism.* How could I? This was 1966—the period immediately preceding the blossoming of the "Second Wave" of Feminism—and I was just back from Fribourg. So within this context I could hear the joke and get the point, but I could not *really* grasp the depths of the problem. Re-Calling this fact reveals the horror of the imposed doublethink of patriarchal institutions.

The double-edged character of my situation, which involved my perpetual and unchanged lower caste status as a female under patriarchy combined with my status of earned privilege as faculty member—and as a

---

*Years later I did develop increasingly complex analyses of tokenism. See *Beyond God the Father, Gyn/Ecology, Pure Lust,* and the *Wickedary.*

unique faculty member—gradually revealed itself. The clues emerged haphazardly. Their degrees of explicitness varied from grossly overt to subtle to spookily subliminal. My recognition of these clues was intense and visceral. It involved a kind of E-motional knowledge which was absolutely certain yet unverifiable by ordinary standards for "rational" cognition.

The reader must understand that there was no accessible body of Feminist analysis of academia in 1966.[1] Nor was there any available cognitive minority of Feminists with whom one could discuss events and decipher their meaning. All the same, one of my strongest assets was my capacity to feel keenly the importance of occurrences that signified my sexual caste status and to detect a pattern in these occurrences.

At the beginning of my first semester, for example, a male (good old boy) member of the philosophy department ostentatiously introduced several new faculty members, i.e., several men and myself, to a group sitting at a table. Whereas all of my colleagues were introduced as "Doctor" so-and-so, I was presented last, and as "Miss Daly." It felt like a cosmic joke. I had returned to this country with three doctorates and this was how they would handle the situation. I hadn't yet learned any strategies for confronting this kind of undermining tactic guised as "respect." It was a setup designed to make me feel outraged and impotent, and of course like an imposter, old maid, and creep. Since no one else seemed to notice anything strange about it, I had to file away my perception—i.e., clear knowledge—of what had happened.

More subliminal messages came from slips of the tongue, or rather, slips of the ear, and from grotesque silences. For example, when meeting with my chairman about courses I would like to teach I mentioned literature and mythology and alluded to the fact that I had earned an M.A. in English. He looked confused and said, "You got an 'A' in English?" He actually had not heard, but when I repeated the statement his eyes glazed. I felt as if I had belched. On another occasion, when I was requesting an opportunity to teach some courses in philosophy, I mentioned that I had a Ph.D. in philosophy as well as a doctorate in theology from Fribourg. I felt that I had to allude to this obvious fact since it was being consistently erased. When I did mention it, the esteemed chairman stared at his desk and then proceeded to fill and light his pipe very slowly, with ostentatious attention to detail. I felt like a mental patient who had just let out a string of obscenities in the presence of a fatherly psychiatrist.

Worst of all, since I was not given to bragging about my degrees, but even felt a little embarrassed by them, I was made to feel like a reversal and caricature of myself—a loud-mouthed braggart and pedant who just couldn't stop talking about my own qualifications. Certainly, I was set up to appear to myself as a "sick" spinster who was fixated on her academic achievements and given to inappropriate pronouncements—a most unattractive and unfeminine creature, a hopeless misfit.

The comedy of the situation was obvious, but since this was happening *before* I had had a chance to encounter the women's movement in this country, I was bereft of Be-Laughing companions—Crones and Cronies—to take away the crazy-making feelings and Howl away the pain. The few friends who were able to get the joke were, of course, males. One of these suggested that I bring a lipstick to the chairman's office and slowly and ostentatiously begin putting it on whenever he started the pipe performance. Not a bad suggestion for 1966!

All of these experiences, neatly or chaotically filed in my Memory, pushed me toward further Moments of Prophecy and Promise and laid the groundwork for later theorizing about such patriarchal strategies as erasure and reversal.

At the same time that I was encountering the spookiness and precariousness of my life as a successful woman in an environment charged with disguised hostility I heard and saw and felt that America had changed. The stultifying society which I had fled in 1959 was rapidly transforming into a country of Hope. The Civil Rights movement had been in full swing for some time, and there was something in the atmosphere that felt *right*. This was strongly conveyed to me by the rhythm and words of popular music, which was utterly unlike the dreary, depressing blare of the music of the forties and fifties. Psychics would say that the vibrations were different, and that is what I Sensed. These were similar to the vibrations that I had felt in Rome the year before. Something *good* was happening.

This does not mean that I didn't miss Fribourg. My connection with that time/space was so deep that just the thought of Fribourg made me happy. It was an Ecstatic Memory. One of my continuing bonds with this Reality was my work on *The Church and the Second Sex,* which had been interrupted but never abandoned.

Among the interruptions were my first public lectures on women and the church. Of particular significance was the lecture I gave at the College of the Holy Names in Oakland, California, in April 1967. Many nuns attended. I noticed in the course of my speech, as I exposed the misogynism of the fathers of the church and of medieval theologians such as Thomas Aquinas, that many in the audience—especially the nuns—were glaring at me in anger. I gradually realized, to my astonishment, that their anger was directed not at the misogynism I exposed but at me for exposing it. I somehow knew at the time that the discovery of this mechanism of transferral of anger was Momentous, and I automatically filed the experience in my psyche for future reference.*

---

*This mechanism continues to be operative. In the conservative eighties, especially, it functioned to hold back women from Radical Feminism and woman-identification. Women who had taken very strong pro-woman positions—who had fought for women *as women*—were targeted as "man-hating," "racist," "classist," et cetera, and were conned into paralyzing false guilt. See especially The Third Spiral Galaxy of this book for further analysis.

I finished the book in the summer of 1967 and waited. I did not fully realize at that time that the writing of this, my first Feminist book, would profoundly affect/effect the Outercourse of my life. It was an Act of Be-Speaking that would hurl me into conflicts that I had never anticipated. The book itself had seemed to me to be eminently sane and reasonable—and indeed it was. Yet it was very radical in its impulse and in its Time.* I was, after all, "merely" trying to reform the catholic church, and that act was too threatening to be gracefully accepted by my employers and the powers they represented.

MY MOTHER'S DEATH

During the fall and winter of 1967 I still did not foresee consciously the tumult that would be caused by my book, which was due to appear in the spring. This was not only because I was extremely busy teaching, but because something infinitely Momentous and painful was happening. My mother was dying. I was about to lose my dearest friend.

During that period, long-time friends stepped in and eased the conditions of our lives. Particularly memorable was the Presence of Bill Wilson, who had been my student in Fribourg and who was then doing graduate study in theology at Princeton. His sensitivity and helpfulness were remarkable. Also outstanding in kindness were Pat and Joe Green, whom I had first met while in graduate school at Catholic University, and with whom I had reconnected at a party in Boston in 1967. They were *there* at crucial times, and that helped me to carry on.

My mother and I had been very close during my childhood, but adolescence and early adulthood had brought years of grief and struggle between us. Our time of living together in Brighton before I went to Europe and then especially our great period of reunion in Fribourg had involved a transcendence of that conflict. This reunion recaptured the early ecstatic dimensions of our communication and recapitulated the glowing Moments of my childhood, while moving on to deeper understanding between us. We had not merely come "full circle." Rather, our progress was spiral-shaped. My mother was not simply my mother, but also my sister and friend.

---

*At the time of writing this chapter I was interviewed by a journalist who—after I described the contents of *The Church and the Second Sex*—exclaimed: "So you were a liberal feminist before you became a radical feminist!" This comment illustrates the many problems of communication that are posed by time warps. My Be-Speaking was Originally Radical in its impulse, and insofar as I have been true to that impulse I have moved in Be-Dazzling directions. Had I published that book, or one making the same arguments, in 1985 or even in 1975, the interviewer's remark would make sense. Given the fact that I wrote it between 1965 and 1967, her comment was chronologically out of place, that is, anachronistic. As I see it, the adjective *Radical* describes the Original impulse and not merely the material content of an act, and the act should be viewed in its historical context.

During our travels together we had shared in a deep way our love of natural beauty. We had gazed in awe at the mountains of Switzerland, delighted in the sunny meadows of Italy, avidly absorbed the vivid colors of the skies and coastal waters of Greece. My mother's remarkable sensitivity to beauty was manifest even to the last moments of her life.

A few weeks before her death we still went for drives to see the magnificent New England autumn foliage. We were able to go on these drives because after a year of teaching I could finally afford to buy a car, so I had acquired a shiny new gold Plymouth Barracuda (which I was destined to keep for twelve years). She was very happy about this car because it symbolized something. I think that what it meant to her was that I had "arrived"—that after all the years of studying and of teaching for low wages and no "benefits" I had achieved a kind of economic recognition and security. I think also that my car may have carried messages of some kind of connection with my father, whose car had been his most significant possession—the vehicle that was necessary for his work as a traveling salesman, and that made possible scenic trips into the country with my mother and me.

So somehow many things were coming together in these Moments of our lives together. Although my mother did not live to see *The Church and the Second Sex* in its final book form, she did see the final page proofs from the publisher with the dedication to her. She was not well enough to read much of it, but she had the pleasure of holding it in her hands. She had been an inspiring and consoling Presence during the entire writing process, at first in Fribourg and then in Boston. So we shared a Sense of satisfaction when finally that dream/project was Realized. Neither she nor I could have guessed the extent of the price I would have to pay for this achievement.

Meanwhile, every Moment was precious. I Re-member vividly a particular event on one of our very last autumn trips. We were driving home after sunset and caught sight of an incredibly colorful maple tree glowing in the dusk. My mother gasped: "Oh, you beauty!" And indeed she was speaking *to* the tree. I was able to glimpse then something about the capacity for ecstasy that was characteristic of her and that she had transmitted to me. That capacity was at the core of the profound bond between us. We shared an intuitive knowledge that we participated in something glorious, something wonderful, something sometimes very funny.

Reflecting upon my mother's conversation with the tree, I understand better Now the source of the glow that touched so many things in my childhood, such as shiny lollipops, friendly neighborhood dogs, the stores we visited on shopping trips downtown, the dandelions and buttercups that I offered her in childish bouquets. There was a quality in her aura that was in harmony with the life around us.

On the last night of my mother's life we talked almost until daybreak, recalling our good times together. We talked about how Lucky we had been to have shared that time in Europe and to have visited such fantastic places.

She told me that I was everything she had always hoped I would be. A few hours after this final extraordinary gift of total acceptance and approval she died at home. It was a sunny morning—December 15, 1967. I had tried to call an ambulance but—Luckily—it arrived too late. She was spared the horror of returning to the hospital and suffering prolonged "treatment."

I remember the way I said the word "No" when I saw that my mother had died. It was No to the unspeakable loss that I had dreaded since childhood. It was the ancient awful No that countless other daughters had gasped at such a Moment throughout thousands of years. Now it was my turn to say it.

During the next few months I went through the motions of my life—teaching, going out with friends—but the gaping wound of loss was always there. During that time I was forced to search for further dimensions of meaning, to move psychically beyond where I had been. I felt then, and have felt ever since, that my mother was beckoning me across barriers of time and space that had appeared insurmountable before.

THE PUBLICATION OF
THE CHURCH AND THE SECOND SEX: BIZARRE PR

During the winter of 1968 *The Church and the Second Sex* came out in England. It was published in the United States in the spring. Once again, in yet another way, my world split open. My American publisher, Harper & Row, sent me on publicity tours involving live appearances on television. I was literally hurled before the TV camera with golden opportunities either to perform brilliantly or fall on my face in front of millions of viewers. My first performance was on the "Alan Burke Show" in New York City, from which I emerged triumphant. Shortly after that I debated with William F. Buckley, Jr., on his videotaped show, "Firing Line." Buckley attempted to discuss my book without having familiarized himself with its contents. Although he lacked the wit to cover his ignorance, he did display considerable skill in getting the last word just before each commercial break. However, after each "pause" I managed to come back with a refutation of his ill-logic. After the show, friends seated in the studio audience told me that they saw him pushing a button under his seat whenever he decided it was the opportune time for a "break." Although I could not see this, it did not seem improbable, since the commercial seemed invariably to immediately follow his punch lines.

One of the most incongruous of these media-mediated experiences was my appearance on the "Our Man Mark Show" in Cleveland, a daytime show whose target audience was housewives and small children. I was featured together with Blinko the Clown, who told the "boys and girls" how they should drink their milk. Following this act, without missing a beat, the host introduced me in solemn, sonorous tones as "the Boston College theologian, author of *The Church and the Second Sex*." Although my outfit was no match for Blinko's, I felt a similarity in our roles, and I accepted the challenge.

There were many other bizarre performances, but the most Stunning was my appearance—live—on the "Frank Ford Show" in Philadelphia in May 1968. I was informed at the last minute by my publisher that I would be on a program with members of the Cryonics Society, comprised of persons who planned to have their bodies frozen at death, against the day when future science would be able to thaw and reanimate them. Their motto was: "Freeze —wait—reanimate." My sole source of information on cryonics at the time was one article, which I read on the plane to Philadelphia. Arriving at the television studio just before the show was about to go on, I found that I was to appear alone with this group. I felt as if I were surrounded by aliens. Before I knew what was happening, I heard myself being introduced as "*the theological expert on cryonics from Boston University.*" The subject of women and the church was not discussed on the show, but I did give as my official opinion the pronouncement that there was no contradiction between cryonics and christian doctrine on immortality. My comment was warmly received by the cryonics people. Moreover, incongruously, a copy of *The Church and the Second Sex* was flashed on the screen for thirty seconds or so. I rushed to the airport in the wild hope of escaping Philadelphia with a few remnants of my sanity intact. Later I heard from a friend of mine who was then living in that city—Jane Furlong Cahill, who had studied theology with me at St. Mary's in the fifties. Jane had watched the show in astonishment and commented that I hadn't seemed "quite your usual self." Indeed!

OTHER MOMENTOUS EVENTS

On a seemingly completely different level, another Momentous event occurred that spring of 1968. I was vacationing for a few days with friends in Florida—Pat and Joe Green—and we went to a catholic church in Fort Myers on easter Sunday. I had stopped going to church gradually before that, but the fact that my friends had their small children along must have influenced the decision to attend. At any rate, the sermon was dedicated to the subject of Bingo, and as I gazed around at the blank-faced, lily-white congregation in easter attire I experienced an overwhelming desire/need/ decision to leave.

We were sitting near the front. Just as I stood up and strode alone down the long aisle to the exit, the organ began to play. Unbelievably, the hymn that resounded through the church as I departed was "Daily, Daily, Sing to Mary"—that paean which my teacher had found it amusing to tease me with in my childhood. I had considered the joke unfunny and boring. At this Moment of Be/Leaving, however, I Heard the hymn take on dimensions of cosmic hilarity. For years I had been struggling to avoid church. This, however, was a Great Departure and Debut. I was Moving Out—Leaving/Leaping further in this First Spiral Galaxy of Outercourse.

The spring of 1968 was also the Time of my first Momentous experience of Women's Space.* A Tae Kwon Do demonstration was given by three women who were Black Belts to an all-women audience in a classroom at a large university in Boston. I recall vividly the rush of energy/Gynergy that I felt as I stepped into that room. Shortly after I arrived and sat down somewhere near the back of the room, an outraged male who had been denied entrance to this women-only event stalked into the room and was asked to leave. He yelled that he had a right to be there, since it was *his* room in *his* building in *his* school. When he refused to leave, two women in their white Karate uniforms simply picked him up and carried him out. When this happened the waves of Gynergy intensified to an astonishing degree. I knew that I was experiencing something New. Women were claiming our own Space. As I Now reflect upon that event, I would say that we were Realizing *Nemesis*.† I did not experience the tragedy of the broken Promise in this Space. This was a Moment of Promise in which the brokenness was transcended, and I glimpsed the potential of woman-identification/integrity.

THE WAR OVER *THE CHURCH AND THE SECOND SEX*

The academic year 1968–69 was filled with the activities associated with teaching and public lecturing. *The Church and the Second Sex* brought unwanted fame to Boston College. That winter I was given a one-year terminal contract; that is, I was fired.

I did not employ an attorney, nor did I compromise in any way.‡ Although I did not yet have a vocabulary to describe the demonic phenomenon of *assimilation*, I knew the danger and somehow side-stepped it.§ There was nothing "normal" in this Spiral of events, and I think this is precisely because their Origin, their Fire, their Focus, and, consequently, their Outcome came from the Background.

---

*Women's Space⚲, as defined in the *Wickedary*, is "Space created by women who choose to separate our Selves from the State of Servitude: FREE SPACE; Space in which women actualize Archimagical Powers, releasing the flow of Gynergy; Space in which women Spin and Weave, creating cosmic tapestries; Space in which women find Rooms, Looms, Brooms of our Own."

†*Nemesis○*, according to the *Wickedary*, means " **1** : Virtue beyond justice, acquired by Inspired Acts of Righteous Fury; Virtue enabling Seers to unblindfold captive Justice **2** : participation in the powers of the Goddess Nemesis; Elemental disruption of the patriarchal balance of terror; Passionate Spinning/Spiraling of Archaic threads of Gynergy."

‡I did actually consult with an attorney for an hour or two. This attorney—Irvin Cobb, in Boston—and I came to the conclusion that since I was not willing to compromise, I had absolutely no use for an attorney. This insight proved to be absolutely correct. A few years later I did employ attorneys who specialized in "academic freedom" and "women's rights," and these experiences confirmed the original insight. I realize that some women in academia (and, of course, elsewhere) say they have been aided by attorneys. I do not doubt their word. But the price, not only in money, is exorbitant. Working against one

In 1975 I published the following account of this "Spiral of events":

Although the administrators never bothered to give any reason for the termination of our happy relationship, the press and just about everyone else put two and two together. An uppity Second Sex was just too much for the church. And for Boston College students that was precisely the issue: Was their university a place where ideas could be expressed freely, or was it "the church"?

My "case" became a *cause célèbre*. It was 1969, a year of demonstrations, and the students wanted a symbol in their crusade for "academic freedom." I was it. There were several months of struggle. An estimated fifteen hundred students demonstrated. Twenty-five hundred signed a petition. All of this was ignored by the administration, whose nonresponse brought forth a seven hour teach-in. Several professors fired from other universities spoke, students spoke, I spoke. Some local self-declared witches came and hexed Boston College, reminding us of the churchly habit of witch-burning. The next day the students began picketing the president's house, and the administration building was decorated at night with brilliant red graffiti (faint traces of which remain to this day, despite the costly use of modern technology to blast them away). The campus became a circus grounds, and television cameras were quick to arrive on the scene. The story was front page news in the Boston papers, duly reported in the *New York Times*, and recounted in a syndicated column which was published in major newspapers across the country. My case was receiving national, international, supernatural publicity, and the Jesuits could no longer hide behind their rosary beads.

The bureaucratic machinery began to grind. A special meeting of the university academic senate was held and a "faculty review committee" was elected to investigate the case. Since the committee was merely advisory to the president and since it was bound to "confidentiality," even a unanimous decision in my favor would not guarantee victory. When the academic year ended with no decision announced, it seemed that my fate was sealed.

The spring of 1969 had been an incredible time. From the roof of my apartment building, I could see the tower of Boston College's administration building, Gasson Hall. I recall having a strong intuition that there was some primary warfare going on, whose dimensions could not be reduced to the "issue" of academic freedom. It was an archetypal battle between principalities and powers, of which this "case" was a blatantly noticeable instance. In cruder and more immediate terms, I recognized that it was—and was more than—a war between

---

patriarchal institution with the "help" of another inevitably involves situations that are humiliating, draining, and profoundly destructive. It requires muting one's own instincts, denying ninety per cent of what one knows from her own experience. The fact that such recourse is sometimes necessary for survival is a depression-provoking illustration of life under the reign of the fathers, sons, and holy ghosts.

§ The deadly sin of *assimilation* is discussed in *Gyn/Ecology*, in the *Wickedary*, and in Chapter Six of this book.

"it" and me, and I willed to go all the way in this death battle. Perhaps the survival of "it" did not depend upon the outcome, but mine did. The practical/personal/political issue was simple. Under the insidious guise of "confidentiality" my teaching career was being destroyed. The university officials had refused to give any reasons publicly or to me privately for my firing, but the well-known phenomenon of grapevine innuendo would destroy my college teaching career.

Summer came, and since summer was the season when troublesome students were out of the way, the administration could be expected to behave in the way characteristic of university administrations. I would be quietly executed in my own absence. Such were my expectations when I arrived in June at a small college in Oregon to teach a summer course. Then the absurdly improbable happened. On the day of my arrival a telegram appeared in Oregon from the president of Boston College, informing me, without congratulations, that I had been granted promotion and tenure.

It was a strange victory. Apparently the book which had generated the hostility which led to my firing had generated the support which forced my rehiring. I now had the relative safety of a tenured university professor, subject of course to the possibility of harassment at any time in the future. But something had happened to the meaning of "professor," to the meaning of "university," to the meaning of "teaching." The "professors" from the various "fields" who had been my judges, the judges of my book, had themselves never written books, nor had they read or understood mine. Standing in negative judgment of my teaching, they were in fear of the students who had no use for their "teaching." I began to understand more about the prevailing "Beta consciousness" of academics, dwarfed by a system of "education" which made them unfree, uncourageous, and radically uneducated. Nor could I live under the delusion that this phenomenon of soul-shrinkage was peculiar to this one university or to church-related universities or to those engaged in this particular field. Letters and conversations, especially with women, during and following the event, made it clear that this was a universal disease of "universities," which were microcosms reflecting the patriarchal world. I recognized that Boston College was not unusual. Perhaps, indeed, it lacked the more sophisticated means of oppression employed in the "great" universities, and there was even something like idealism that wove its way through the destruction and helped to make possible this absurd triumph.

It was the universalist quality of this personal "revelation" that was important. I began to understand more of the implications of the feminist insight that "the personal is political." The interconnections among the structures of oppression in a patriarchal society and the destructive dynamics which these structures generate in their victims became more and more visible. In other words, I understood more clearly the nature of the beast and the name of the demon: patriarchy.

The procession of consequences of *The Church and the Second Sex*, then, was a transforming process. So I moved into a more advanced class in a newly founded invisible counter-university, the Feminist Universe, whose students from all over the planet were beginning to discover each other.[2]

PATRIARCHAL WAR TACTICS:
SUBLIMINAL UNDERMINING

When I returned to BC a new set of experiences nudged me along in my process of understanding patriarchal tactics. I had been a popular teacher and had no reason whatsoever to expect this to have changed. However, when I entered my classroom in September of 1969 I was faced with very small classes. I felt confused by this and was too naive and nonparanoid to look for murky explanations. I still did not understand the complexity of the machinations that are associated with academic harassment.

One particularly unnerving experience involved going to teach one of my courses in the assigned classroom for the first scheduled class and finding that the room was literally devoid of students. I was facing an empty classroom. My feeling of shock in the face of this crazy-making situation was intense. I felt utterly spooked.[3] I waited a few minutes and two or three students came into the room, announcing that their chess club was scheduled to meet there. I was not able to get an explanation for this phenomenon when I mentioned it to my colleagues. I believed that I had gone to the right room at the right time. Was I insane? The situation became "straightened out" in a spooky way. At the next scheduled class time for the course there was a handful of students. I felt very strange indeed, but could not get to the bottom of it all. There seemed to be no explanation. I remember developing at that time a peculiar feeling of horror in the corridors of Carney Hall, where I had my office, and where the theology department was located. Something was happening that was not visible to me.

Strangely concomitant with all of this was my continuing and increasing popularity as a public speaker.[4] Some of the sense of unreality that had arisen from this bizarre situation was relieved a few months later when a group of my (male) students came to me and expressed their ideas about "what was going on" to keep students away from my classes. Putting their information together, they came to the conclusion that many were being systematically discouraged by some of my "colleagues" from taking my classes. So these young men took it upon themselves to spread the word about the quality of my classes, and the problem was partially resolved. The "colleagues" continued with their efforts to discredit me and to use subtle and not so subtle methods of mystification. For example, some proclaimed to easily intimidated students at registration time that my courses were "extremely difficult" and to others that my courses were already filled.

Young women who were enrolled in the School of Education and in the School of Nursing were beginning to attempt to register in my classes, and the "extremely difficult" line was particularly effective in driving them away. Because of their conditioning and their condition as women, they tended to have less self-confidence than male students. When they heard from the faculty who were "manning" the pre-registration desks that I assigned long and hard reading lists, many were discouraged. A few brave souls made it through this obstacle course—which, of course, I didn't yet know about.

I think that it was at about this time (the fall of 1969) that The Recurrent Nightmare arrived. It returned over and over again for years, taking different forms. The classic form of The Nightmare has been as follows:

> I never did finish those doctorates. So I go back to Fribourg and try to find my old professors. When I arrive I find that the streets have changed. When I do find one of the professors he tells me that a chapter or some footnotes are missing from my dissertation (or dissertations). I get lost trying to find the missing parts. I wake up with a sense of horror.

As the years went on The Nightmare took variant forms. In its most drastic form the plot was something like this:

> I do not yet have my B.A. I am quite elderly—almost doddering—and I am attending night school attempting to obtain this degree. I am in a large auditorium-like classroom, seated near the back, taking notes in order to pass the course. I am wearing a dowdy kind of dress and am feeling quite confused and addle-brained.

The message is clear. I never really did get any of those degrees.* A woman could not get them. A woman could not be legitimated by patriarchy's institutions of higher education. Doctor Mary Daly does not exist. I am an Imposter.

The image of myself as The Imposter and the repeated experience of The Nightmare would intensify in the seventies, partly as a consequence of subliminal undermining by some so-called colleagues. Meanwhile, laughing

---

*A specious sort of probability adheres to these absurd dreams as a consequence of the fact that at the University of Fribourg in the sixties the system of grading and of recording degrees was literally medieval. As students we had small *tabellas* or notebooks in which the professors recorded the grades for courses with their signatures at the end of each semester. (Grades were *optime, valde bene, bene, sufficienter, or insufficienter.*) I don't know what would happen if one lost one's *tabella*. When I defended my doctoral dissertations in theology and in philosophy, the fact that I had obtained the doctorates with honors was recorded in each case by hand by the appropriate Dean. Thus the fact that I had obtained the Doctorate in Sacred Theology *summa cum laude* was written by hand in a big book by the Dean of the Faculty of Theology. He attempted to add: "She did not take the Anti-Modernist Oath" but I stood there looking over his shoulder and protested loudly to this, fearing that the information would be used to invalidate my degree later on. So he crossed those words out. Later the diplomas were mailed to me, but I feared that if I lost these I could never prove that I had those degrees at all. Indeed, in my travels and many house moves I have temporarily lost the cylinder of diplomas several times. Something about all of this contributes to the fragility of my sense of Reality about those degrees. I should add that the University of Fribourg did not have graduation ceremonies. It is conceivable that the fact of being handed diplomas publicly would have helped to confer/confirm the degree.

about all this with friends helped to exorcise its subtle spooking effects, but a massive task of creative exorcism awaited me.

CREATIVE EXORCISM AND EYE-OPENING EXPERIENCES

At any rate, when my naiveté and idealism about academia were confronted by patriarchal foreground fraudulence I did not become "crazy" and "bitter"—the outcome desired by the twisted tricksters—but I did become Wilder, more Raging, Daring, and sure of my own insights and intuitions. I also further developed my Be-Laughing skills.

In 1969 I met the African American Feminist poet and civil rights activist Pauli Murray, who at the time taught at Brandeis University. We became good friends, sharing academic and other horror stories and developing a Be-Laughing camaraderie. I learned a great deal about how racism as well as sexism corrodes the lives of those living under patriarchal power. Our friendship generated many important Moments.

Among these Moments was a trip with Pauli to Bethesda, Maryland, where we attended a seminar organized by a group of church women and comprised of Feminists from a variety of professions. A "futurist" who presented himself as an affiliate of a "think tank" authorized by President Nixon (and whose name I cannot remember) addressed the group. He told us that by the most "optimistic" standards, the "X-factor" might survive in human society for another twenty years. By "X-factor," he said, he meant something like what is commonly called "free will," and/or "spirit." The reason he gave was the growing need for governmental control of "crazies" who might harm millions of people, for example, by poisoning the drinking water.

Reflecting upon this from a Fourth Galactic perspective, in which it is more obvious than ever that the government is comprised of and supportive of crazies, this idea of deviants as the dangerous ones is hilarious. However, the "futurist" prophecy of doom had a ring of truth and impressed me so deeply that I told the story to all of my classes and have continued to tell it each year. The exact number of years was not the essential point, but what mattered was the declaration of negative prophecy and promise, the statement of necrophilic purpose, which I would Now also call a description of the ultimate foreground future, as foretold by a foreground futurist.[5]

Another set of Eye-opening experiences that occurred during this time was engendered by the flood of mail following the publication of *The Church and the Second Sex* and the publicity that attended my "case"/cause at Boston College. Some of the letters concerning the book were based upon newspaper articles rather than on reading the book itself. These, especially, tended to be rather bizarre. One letter in particular that stands out in my memory was from a priest who argued that women could not be priests because God did not come to earth as a woman. Furthermore, this correspondent argued,

"He" could not have come as a woman because "He" was destined to die on the cross. If "He" had come as a she this would mean that a female would have been hanging half naked on the cross and would have been an occasion for impure thoughts in the minds of people (who, presumably, would own or see crucifixes with half-naked female jesuses hanging on them). Therefore, this correspondent concluded, it is obvious that women can never be priests, because God could never do such a thing, that is, become an occasion of sin.

I have merely summarized this letter here. The priest's descriptions of the women jesuses, et cetera, were somewhat graphic. Naturally I was astonished by this communication. I am sure that I laughed almost to the point of tears. But the most important effect was that it clued me in to the nature of male fantasies about the crucifixion. Probably I did not consciously understand the wider implications and thought of this fellow—or tried to think of him—as a rare kooky individual. But I think that on a subliminal level I got the message concerning foreground fantasies. So, a few years later, when I read Hannah Tillich's exposé of her husband Paul Tillich, the famous theologian, who was obsessed with watching pornographic films of crucified women, I was not totally unprepared for her startling revelations.[6]

There were many positive and intelligent letters, of course. However, given the chaotic nature of my life at the time, I could not answer all of them. Recently, in the process of writing this chapter, I resurrected the two huge stuffed manila envelopes containing correspondence concerning *The Church and the Second Sex* and found that one envelope was labeled "Nut Mail" and the other, "Non-Nut Mail." It was startling to find that the envelopes were about equal in weight. Equally thought-provoking was the fact that when, in my rush to get at the letters, they spilled out on the floor and became mixed together, I found it virtually impossible to sort out some of the "Non-Nut Mail" from the "Nut Mail." So I stuffed them back as best I could and went on with my writing.

A TRYING TIME OF TRANSITION

The fall of 1969 marked the beginning of drastic changes. I began to see through the particularities of my experience with Boston College to the universal condition of women and all those oppressed under the institutions of patriarchy. This seeing through did not happen all at once, however. Even as my Spirit was rushing ahead, something in me dragged its/my heels a little. That November, for example, I published an article in *Commonweal* dissociating my position from that of the priest-theologian Charles Davis, who had left the church. I wrote:

> It may happen, of course, that one may come to decide that the existing structures of Catholicism are so alienating and dysfunctional that the social reality

called "the Catholic church" must be rejected. This appears to be the case with someone like Charles Davis. Although I respect this position and am more in sympathy with this honest criticism than with official Catholicism, I am not sure that it is radical enough. The basic problem with this stance is the isolation and ineffectiveness to which those who adopt it seem to be doomed. For my part I am still willing to work in my own way (lazily) at a mutually transforming confrontation with my own heritage, still being naive enough to think that in some sense I can win.[7]

This article was a classic specimen of cautious liberalism. It lacked conviction and the fighting spirit of *The Church and the Second Sex* and of my later writings. It was hardly an example of Be-Speaking. Nor was my 1970 article, "The Problem of Hope," even though this did manage to deflate the then-popular "theology of hope." I suggested that "perhaps we are being dazzled by a future-talk which may be combined with a sort of 'bibliolatry.'"[8] Here the dead give-away (give-away of deadness) was the use of qualifying terms and phrases, such as "perhaps," "may be," and "sort of"—quite a few precautionary measures for one little sentence. The article was also full of the pseudogeneric "man," "he," et cetera, ad nauseam.

During 1969–70 I also worked hard on the manuscript of a book which had several tentative titles. Among these was *Catholicism: Death or Rebirth?* Another was *Catholicism: End or Beginning?* One might say that this was the beginning of the end of my concern over the fate of catholicism. Probably the question mark at the end of each title was the most significant part. At any rate, this project failed to sustain my interest. It fell apart in the middle. Or, one could say that it was an abortive effort. The publisher with whom I had signed a contract for this book (Lippincott) agreed with my sentiments.

Even though I couldn't go on with it, I suffered from this rejection of my work. Later, however, I realized that this termination was a case of the proverbial "blessing in disguise." It would have been embarrassing if the thing had been printed, especially since within a year or two of its demise I was thoroughly in disagreement with its frame of reference. I think I simply saw that I had been framed by that frame and wanted to break out of it.

Another related painful event was the fact that my publisher was allowing *The Church and the Second Sex* to go out of print. Already in 1970 I was informed that it probably would not go into a third printing. This information was heartbreaking and I thought that the situation was deeply wrong. There were countless women who needed the information in that book.* I felt blocked and erased, but there was no way I was going to give up.

It was partially because of my activism that I was able to move on. During that transitional period of 1969–70, as I was getting ready to move out

---

*It did in fact go out of print in 1971 but appeared in a New incarnation in 1975 with the "Autobiographical Preface" and "Feminist Postchristian Introduction." For the story of that rebirth see Chapter Nine.

from The First Spiral Galaxy, I was engaged in exploring avenues of political action. During my first years back in the States I had attended some of the "peace movement" gatherings that were part of the scene in America in the sixties, and had found them ineffably draining. My sense had always been that as a woman I really could have no say in what was going on. I had felt alienated, disemboweled, castrated with every attempt to participate in these groups. If this was "revolution," I concluded, it had little to do with me.

I next moved on to meetings of the National Organization for Women, both in Boston and in Worcester, Massachusetts. These NOW meetings were more positive than my other experiences with political groups. It was at a Boston meeting of this organization in 1969 that I first met Andrée Collard, whose friendship and ideas became more and more important to me over the years. Despite such personal benefits, however, something was missing in NOW. It failed to spark my imagination.

In the spring of 1970 (May 15–17), a "National Conference on the Role of Women in Theological Education" was held at a retreat center in Groton, Massachusetts.[9] I organized this event together with Jan Raymond, who was then studying for her M.A. in theology at Andover Newton Theological School and taking my courses at Boston College. Consultants who partici-pated in the program included women who were on faculties of various insti-tutions: Peggy Way (University of Chicago Divinity School), Nelle Morton (Drew Seminary), Elizabeth Farians (Loyola University, Chicago), Pauli Murray (Brandeis), Marlene Dixon (McGill), Sister Marie Augusta Neal (Emmanuel College), and Arlene Swidler (editor of the *Journal of Ecumeni-cal Studies*). A number of women students attending theological schools in the Boston area also participated.

We were not exactly a dull crowd. On the first evening of our conference, as we were seated in the dining hall, members of another group were also taking their places in another part of the hall. Suddenly a male voice blared over a loudspeaker, thanking "our heavenly father" for the food. The sono-rous, droning voice was unbearable to all of us. Characteristically, it was Betty Farians who let this be known by shouting ("inappropriately"), "God is *not* our father!" The ensuing silence was Stunning.

In the course of that conference we drew up proposals regarding Women's Studies within the Boston Theological Institute, a consortium of theological schools in the Boston area. We outlined a rationale for a research center and Institute on Women to be initiated within the BTI.[10] Our ambi-tions were sky high. I personally imagined Women's Studies as taking over theological education in particular and universities in general. My optimism was unbounded and, from a Fourth Galactic perspective, not entirely un-founded. Despite all the setbacks, it is only fair to say that a great deal has changed since 1970.

Although I really could not fit into the mode/mood of NOW, I saw it as having an important role in the complex mosaic of the women's move-ment. For a short period of time in 1969–70 a group of my friends and acquaintances even held "NOW Religion Task Force" meetings in my apartment on Commonwealth Avenue. Despite the seriousness of the title, these meetings were often rather raucous events attended by a variety of characters who had as our common purpose the unmasking and undoing of patriarchal religion. We were virtually rolling on the floor with laughter a good deal of the time. Among our members was a young protestant minister (whom I remember as "Caroline") whose usual/unusual outfit consisted of a black miniskirt and shirt topped with a roman collar and motorcycle helmet. The roaring of her noisy vehicle announced her arrival each time. All in all she could be said to have incarnated the spirit of our group.

So by 1970 my apartment had become a center of Radical Feminist activism and intellectual life. That was where my mother and I had lived together during our first year back in the States after returning from Switzerland, and it was there that she had died in December of 1967. I Sensed that the space was suffused with her Aura and Presence. She was an abiding Presence during countless meetings, sessions of Spinning ideas, and Sparking conversations. She had been especially Present during my writing of *The Church and the Second Sex* before her death, and she continued to be There while I went on writing.*

MOMENTOUS PRESENCE:
THE PRESENCE OF MOMENTOUS TIME

An enduring reminder of my mother's Presence was and still is a phenomenon that began happening shortly after her death. She had a small traveling clock near her bed, which I had given her several years before. The clock stopped when she died, at about twelve past eleven in the morning. A week or so later my watch stopped while I was sleeping, at 11:12 p.m. I was staying overnight at the home of Pat and Joe Green in Natick, Massachusetts, after returning from my mother's funeral in Glens Falls, New York, the hometown of her childhood. That was the beginning. Since then, through all the years since December 1967, the 11:12 phenomenon has repeated itself in various ways.

I cannot begin to recall the many times that I have walked into a room or down a street where/when a clock announced that it was exactly 11:12. This has happened in various cities and countries. Sometimes I have been with others and sometimes alone when it has occurred. A typical example involved stepping off a train during a return visit to Fribourg in 1968 and being immediately face to face with the large station clock, whose hands

---

*Many articles were written in that apartment, as well as *Beyond God the Father*, the 1975 "Autobiographical Preface" and "Feminist Postchristian Introduction" to *The Church and the Second Sex*, and *Gyn/Ecology*. When I moved from there in the summer of 1979 I was leaving a space of intense life and Radical Feminist creativity.

were precisely at 11:12.* Significant though less spectacular have been the countless times that I have glanced at my watch or clock or telephoned for "the time" at precisely this time. Indeed, throughout the writing of this book I have experienced this phenomenon. Sometimes after working long into the night I have awakened in the late morning and found the hands of the clock to be exactly at 11:12.

Particularly interesting was my realization that the 11:12 phenomenon was/is contagious. Throughout the late sixties and continually into the Present time of writing, my closest friends and collaborators began and continued to have this experience. It meant/means something important, but what? For years—decades—I have wondered about this and mused over various possible explanations. I have thought about the obvious psychobabble explanations such as "autosuggestion," but that in no way touches the astonishing complexity of the event. Clearly one could say that those experiencing 11:12 are self-programmed to be on the lookout for 11:12 and have a heightened awareness of clocks at such times.

To which I would reply: Even if all of this were true, so what? None of this speaks to the depth of the event. Moreover, none of this answers the question: Why? What does it mean? I have run through a number of "explanations" of the recurrent experience over the years. It remains partially opaque and infinitely rich. It is multilayered. Comparable to a koan, it is a constant reminder of the limitations of mere linear reason and a catalyst for Leaps of Re-membering and awakening of Lost Senses.

Clearly it is about Time.† Certainly the synchronicities/Syn-Croneicities involved in the experience of 11:12 cannot be "explained" in reductionist categories. And most certainly all of this is quite outside the scope of the alienating, simplistic, mind-muddying "mystical" categories of new age "spirituality." From my Present perspective, I can See and Name the 11:12 experience as a way of marking Moments in the Intergalactic Movement which is the Be-Dazzling Voyage. It is not exactly that each 11:12 has been a distinct Moment, but clusters of these signal the Presence of a Momentous Time.‡

---

*A special example in the 1980s occurred when I was living in Leverett, Massachusetts. See Chapter Thirteen.

†One outgrowth of reflections upon this "koan" is *Appendicular Web Four* of the *Wickedary*: "Jumping Off the doomsday clock: Eleven, Twelve . . . Thirteen."

‡The 11:12 phenomenon seems to be connected with the Timing entity known to me since college days as "the little Green Man/Woman." This, in turn, is related to "The Dream of Green," which occurred when I was working for my M.A. in English at Catholic University, and which reminded me that it was Time to move on in my Quest to be a philosopher. In the process of writing this book I have Re-Called the fact that my "Dream of Green" happened after studying the fourteenth-century poems *Gawain and the Green Knight* and *Pearl*. It is interesting that *Pearl* consists of 101 stanzas of 12 lines each. See Chapter Two.

There have been and are dimensions in which I have experienced participation in Be-ing ever since early childhood. But after the shock of my mother's death I gradually became aware of Elemental Reality in yet Other ways. In large measure such awarenesses were and are really Dis-coverings of forgotten dimensions that had been covered over by thick layers of mind-bindings manufactured in the factories of patriarchal conditioning. These awakenings have come in Moments of overcoming patriarchally inflicted *amnesia*—Moments of Anamnesia/Unforgetting.

THE SEARCH FOR THE LOST SENSES

My grief over my mother's death and the deep questioning which this evoked propelled me on a Search for what I would Now call the Lost Senses. In January of 1968 I went with Pat and Joe Green to a meeting of the Spiritual Frontiers Society in Natick, Massachusetts, which led to my attending meetings at the houses of various members of that society. This was a new kind of experience for me. I had never before sat in a circle in the dark with a group whose members all saw things that were invisible to me. One, for example, would see a leopard lying on the floor, and someone else would comment on the beauty of its eyes. Someone else would "send" a gorgeous Chinese teapot to another member, who—gasping with admiration—thanked her (or him). Meanwhile, I stared into the darkness, seeing nothing, torn between an urge to giggle and a feeling of indescribable deficiency. After several of these fruitless sessions, I stopped attending.

Although these experiences seemed then and still seem comical to me, I don't believe that these people were "crazy" or that they were hallucinating. They simply were "tuned in" to different aspects of reality than I had experienced. They were rational, serious, intelligent, and kind, and I had no reason not to respect them. One important result of my adventures with "Spiritual Frontiers" was that it was through this group that I heard of Gladys Custance, a Spiritualist medium gifted with exceptional powers.

Before my Momentous encounter with that woman actually occurred, however, I did meet a number of others who were reputed to have psychic powers, but who somehow failed to communicate what I felt I needed to know. One particularly astonishing experience occurred when I accepted an invitation to give a five-day series of lectures at the Chautauqua Institution in Chautauqua, New York, during the summer of 1970. Entering this place was like stepping into a total time warp. Situated on a beautiful lake, the "Institution" was founded in 1874, and going there was, indeed, a trip into the nineteenth century. It prided itself upon its summer programs, which combined lectures, symphony concerts, operas, plays, summer schools, religious activities, and summer sports. My lectures—on the general theme of "Christians in Crisis"—were scheduled from Monday through Friday at 4:30 (on such subjects as "Faith and Doubt," "The Death of God and the

Problem of Myth," and "Alienation and Existential Courage"). These talks, which drew increasingly larger crowds every day, were held in an improbable place—a large fake ruin of a Greek (or Roman) temple.

Since I had plenty of free time I went on short trips. Somehow at Chautauqua I heard about the town of Lily Dale, which was filled with Spiritualist mediums. Perhaps Chautauqua put me in the mood to go to such a place. At any rate, the idea of visiting there was irresistible, so I went. The streets of Lily Dale were lined with houses that had signs on their lawns announcing that they were the residences of mediums, astrologers, et cetera. I chose one medium—a woman of about seventy, who told me she was a speech teacher and came to Lily Dale in the summers. I was shaken when she warned me that some of the objects in the room had been "apported," and could disappear at any time. There were dozens of small statues around, and I stared at them suspiciously. Meanwhile, the medium's dog lay down under a chair (either hers or mine) and went into a deep sleep. That woman gave me my first "reading," the content of which I can barely recall. It did not strike me as impressively accurate. The scene, however, was unforgettable.

This experience in itself could have seemed to be a dead end, but it probably had the effect of whetting my appetite for a more satisfactory reading. I think it was no coincidence that in August of that summer I followed through on the idea of going to Cape Cod in order to have a reading with Gladys Custance. That Moment revealed the extraordinary quality of Gladys's gift. It was the first of many such encounters with and through this remarkable woman—encounters with dimensions and worlds that I came to recognize as Natural and Real—beyond "belief."

I maintained contact with Gladys Custance, "checking in" with her every year, and we became good friends in the years preceding her death on March 27, 1988. Now, in The Fourth Spiral Galaxy, as I am writing this book, I am Realizing the Momentous extent of her influence on my life and writing ever since our first meeting, and I look forward to ever greater Spiraling adventures.

LEAPING INTO THE VORTEX
OF THE SECOND SPIRAL GALAXY

The quality of my writing changed after that summer of 1970. It Leaped. By the end of that year, as I Moved within the interwoven contexts of the rising women's movement, of friendships charged with intellectual E-motional energy, and of the spiritual realms of awareness that were becoming more accessible, my writing, teaching, and public speaking began to thrive in New ways.

Having hurled my caution to the winds, I mySelf was hurled into cracking the code of the patriarchal system and Naming connections among manifestations of patriarchal oppression. I was active on many fronts.[11]

Despite the fact that my pro-choice position on abortion brought down the wrath of "colleagues," I spoke at rallies, for example, at the rally organized by the Massachusetts Organization for the Repeal of Abortion Laws in October 1970. A special Moment of Prophecy and Promise occurred in November, when I attended an ecology seminar at the Northeastern University Warren Center in Ashland, Massachusetts. I dropped a bombshell simply by remarking that the cause of ecological problems was patriarchy and that the destruction of the environment and the oppression of women were linked. This Act of Be-Speaking created such a controversy that finally someone shouted that the group (consisting entirely of males and myself) be divided into two groups—"those who wanted to talk about ecology and those who wanted to talk about 'women's lib!'" But the group could not be divided, and the discussion was an Eye-opener.

Since the radical impulse of my travels in The First Spiral Galaxy was relentlessly moving me outside christian frameworks, the focus of my interest and energy was shifting profoundly. For example, the article which I had sent to Robin Morgan in 1969 at her request for her anthology *Sisterhood Is Powerful* was already beginning to be a minor cause of embarrassment to me shortly after that book was published in 1970.*

The cumulative intensity of New Moments enabled me to Move into the vortex of The Second Spiral Galaxy. Before moving into the story of that Galaxy, however, I will turn to the task of philosophical reflection—from my Present vantage point—upon the Elemental Events as well as the foreground conditions of The First Spiral Galaxy. It is my hope that this process of Discovering more about the meaning of those early Moments will encourage Other Voyagers to regain Gynergy for continuing their own Be-Dazzling Voyages.

---

*It was an increasing source of embarrassment as the anthology became a feminist "bestseller," and as I rapidly became more radical. In a conversation about the manuscript of *Outercourse* Emily Culpepper recalled that she considered not cross-registering into my Women's Studies courses at Boston College in 1971 because that article was so conservative. She did take the courses anyway and was pleasantly surprised (Transcontinental telephone conversation, October 1990).

CHAPTER SIX

REFLECTIONS ON PHILOSOPHICAL THEMES OF THE FIRST SPIRAL GALAXY

The reflections in this chapter on early Moments of my Voyage have been recorded—speaking in foreground terms—in the early 1990s. In Other (Background) Words, they have been written from the vantage point of The Fourth Spiral Galaxy, the Galaxy of Time Traveling—a Megagalaxy/Metagalaxy made up of Moments of Momentous Re-membering. Moreover, the preceding—and the following—chapters of *Outercourse* have also been written from a Fourth Galactic perspective. That is, the Recollections from my *Logbook* also are Fourth Galactic phenomena. By Time Traveling I can retrace earlier Moments, as with a Pen of Light. These take on New significance and assume more levels of meanings as I revisit them in the Fourth Dimension.

THE CRAFT OF THE FOURTH DIMENSION

These Time Traveling adventures have been possible because of my Craft. The word *craft* means, among other things, skill and cunning. Wild women sometimes refer to our strength, force, skills, and occupations as Witchcraft. My own particular Craft involves writing and the forging of philosophical theories.

Craft is etymologically related to the verb *crave*. As Voyager I have Spiraled and continue to Spiral with my Craft because I crave something, because I have a strong longing for something. That "something" is the free Unfolding and expansion of my be-ing. Propelled by Wonderlust, by Wanderlust, my Quest *is* the expansion and communication of my be-ing.

I have come to see that taking charge of my Craft has been one of my primary/primal tasks, for this is overcoming the "woman as vessel" motif that prevails in Stag-nation. Women under phallocratic rule are confined to the role of vessels/carriers, directed and controlled by men.[1] Since that role is the basic/base reversal of the very be-ing of Voyaging/Spiraling women, when we direct our own Crafts/Vessels we become reversers of that deadly reversal. In this process we become Crafty.

From my Present perspective I See that it is in The Fourth Spiral Galaxy that the Craft of the Crafty Voyager can truly begin to Move as the Craft of the Fourth Dimension. For there is available a personal/political/historical/Elemental context in which the earlier Moments can be Seen. This context contains previously subliminal Background knowledge which has to some extent become overt, that is, explicitly Realized, over Time. Such knowledge throws Light on my Sense of Direction and Sense of Intention across Time.

So I can Now steer my Vessel back to revisit and Re-member the Moments of The First Spiral Galaxy (and The Second and The Third). Since I have Spiraled this far, I can be Present to the earlier Moments in ways that I was not Present "then." I can know these Moments in far wider and deeper Ways than were then accessible. This New knowledge and subsequent New Naming of them increases their Momentousness and their Momentum. Thus the perspective of The Fourth Spiral Galaxy speeds up the Swirling Movement of the Other Galaxies. The accelerated Momentum is cumulative. The logical/Crone-logical result is a kind of Intergalactic Whirlwind.

The experience of looking back/re-experiencing the early Moments from the perspective of this stage of my Craft's Movement Dis-closes the previously hidden Fourth Spiral Galaxy, which is not merely "the next one," as in the series: "1, 2, 3, 4." Rather, The Fourth Spiral Galaxy is a Metagalaxy that is in a Sense comprised of, but also more than, the Others. It has special dimensions of Self-consciousness and Sea-conciousness because my Course is retraced Here/Now in Deep Memory. When as Webster I draw out Webs of connections with my Pen of Light, this Moves my vision around and forward. Thus these Shimmering, Be-Dazzling Moments of Re-membering eclipse with the Brilliance of Background Be-ing much of the foreground smog that had hung over earlier Moments.

The Craft of the Fourth Dimension, then, does not merely "fulfill" my Moments of Prophecy and Promise, but rather it reawakens Powers of Prophecy and expands my Promise, for my horizons as Voyager expand. To put it an Other way: In contrast to backward-looking "memoirs," my Memories are like Galvanizing Intergalactic Gallops that recharge my Craft, which at Times feels like a racing Steed or Nag and at Other Times seems to be a Broom. For this is a kind of Time/Space travel that defies simple labels and descriptions.

MY PIRATE'S CRAFT

From the perspective of Momentous Re-membering I realize that my Craft of the Fourth Dimension is also my Pirate's Craft. I am and have been a Pirate across Time. In fact, I Now see my whole life as an increasingly daring Piratic enterprise, which has involved Righteously Plundering treasures of knowledge that have been stolen and hidden from women and Smuggling these back in such a way that they can be seen as distinct from the mind-binding trappings in which they have been hidden and distorted by the patriarchal thieves.

During most of The First Spiral Galaxy I was Plundering treasures and storing these up for Future use. Although I did teach for a living, mostly to support myself through graduate school(s), this early teaching was not consciously subversive, and so it could not be called Smuggling in the sense of Re-claiming treasures by Naming them in New Ways or rendering their hidden liberating potential accessible to women. I did, however, prepare myself for this Crafty occupation by years of studying. Of course, I did some preliminary Smuggling in my publications of the 1960s, in the early Feminist articles and in *The Church and the Second Sex*.* All the same, my primary Piratic occupation in The First Spiral Galaxy was Plundering.

Since I did not consciously understand the meaning and purpose of my Plundering then, I would Now say that my methods and intent, as well as much of the content of my Piratic Plundering, especially prior to the mid-sixties, were known to me only subliminally. Yet this subliminal motivation and knowing was strong enough to carry me ahead in my Pirate's Craft, which speedily Soared into Other Galaxies.

SUBLIMINAL KNOWLEDGE:
THE LIFE-SAVING SOURCE

Looking Now at my early Moments, I see these as involving a Rising of Background knowledge into consciousness. Such Surgings often but not always occurred in times of intense activity and in the process of speaking or writing. For example, I have described my E-motional glimpses in childhood beyond the foreground façades of Halloween and other holidays. Throughout my studies of medieval theology and philosophy I had, I think, some potentially explosive Sense of an Other reality behind christian myths and symbols, which Sparked and sustained my interest, for example, in such seemingly dull affairs as "the Divine Trinity." Certainly, my letter on "prophecy and promise," published in *Commonweal* in 1964, was an explosion of subliminal knowledge.

Often these Realizations of Background knowledge were—and still are—like eruptions of a volcano. This is because the knowledge exploding into consciousness is Terribly Taboo. Sometimes they were more gradual and subtle, like awakening from sleep. The point is that the knowledge was there, waiting for a chance to erupt.

This had everything to do with my situation as participating in a cognitive minority whose Other participants were unknown to me. Indeed, I was, in my immediate environment, a cognitive minority of one. There were, of course, Other women with comparable cognition, each of whom

---

*Geraldine Moane emphasized the reality of Smuggling by Radical Feminists in the course of conversations about Piracy (Conversations, Newton Centre, Massachusetts, August 1988).

experienced her life as that of a cognitive minority of one. Virtually none of us had any Name for our identity, however, and virtually none of us knew each other.

In recent years I have frequently heard myself saying to audiences that a cognitive minority of one cannot survive, referring to sociologist Peter Berger's dictum that "the subjective reality of the world hangs on the thin thread of conversation."[2] Often at some point in the same lectures I have also heard myself saying: "Even if I were the only one, I would still be a Radical Feminist." This may seem a little Strange, even self-contradictory. Reflecting Now upon the *Logbook* material of The First Spiral Galaxy, however, I Re-member that I was then in the situation of "being the only one"—the only one known to myself, at any rate—and that I have Survived.

I think that my Surviving through The First Spiral Galaxy had to do with the fact that there has always been a Sea of subliminal Background knowledge shared by women under patriarchy. So I have never been completely alone in my knowledge. My Sense of Aloneness was, I think, due to the fact that such knowledge was more conscious/explicit in my case. I would hazard a guess that my Survival was possible because I was also in possession of subliminal knowledge of the subliminal knowledge in Other women. This would surface in some individuals in expressions of insight, fragments of understanding that would burst out—only to be contradicted by the same women in a babble of patriarchal clichés. But they had clues, and so did I. The existence of this Sea of shared subliminal knowledge accounts for the fact that when I have managed to Be-Speak, some have understood right away. It also accounts for the fact that in the bleak fifties I understood Simone de Beauvoir's *The Second Sex* immediately and welcomed it with unspeakable gratitude. Such understanding is, as a number of women have described it, like an "awakening" to something familiar, or like "coming home." For under patriarchy, the subliminal realm is where women's Reality Lives.

SAILING THE SUBLIMINAL SEA

As a Crafty Pirate I have dared to sail this vast Realm of mindspace/minedspace which I Now Name "the Subliminal Sea."* This contains deep Background knowledge, together with countless contaminants—the man-

---

*I hope that it is clear that my theory of a Sea of subliminal knowledge in women under patriarchy is not to be confused with Jung's "collective unconscious." My analysis is from my own experience and is in no way Jungian nor is it derived from Jung. The fact that Jung did hit upon some interesting knowledge that is ultimately from Archaic sources does not make him an originator of these ideas, nor has it prevented him from polluting such ancient knowledge with oppressive permutations. A similar process of pollution is

made subliminal and overt messages disseminated through the media and other channels for the purpose of mind manipulation.

Reflecting upon my travels in The First Spiral Galaxy I Re-Call the experience of being pushed/directed by a Great Wind. Traveling in that early Time involved sailing the surface of the Subliminal Sea, Sensing its depths, while not being overtly conscious of the contents of those depths, at least not to a sustained degree. Occasionally I had conscious glimpses, and these were enough to keep me on Course. I could feel through my Craft the swishings and swirlings that rocked the boat, so to speak. Some of these, I think, were the result of E-motions and psychic sensations that smoulder in Undersea Volcanoes, just under the threshold of conscious awareness, whose eruptions inspired/fired my Moments of Prophecy and Promise.

DRAWING OUT CONNECTIONS
IN THE FIRST SPIRAL GALAXY

I Now approach the awesome task of drawing out connections within and among Moments of The First Spiral Galaxy in the Light Now accessible to me. In the process of Searching through the first five chapters of *Outercourse* I have seen that certain threads of connectedness are Present. I did not intentionally put them there when I was writing Recollections from my *Logbook*. Yet there they are, plainly visible to me from the Craft of the Fourth Dimension. Sometimes they form fantastically coherent Webs. I shall Now trace an extremely important Web, which will serve to illustrate this phenomenon.

A Sense of Direction

The Web which I shall Name "A Sense of Direction" would appear to be easy enough to trace. My account of my Original decision to become a Radical Feminist Philosopher is recorded in the "Prelude to The First Spiral Galaxy." It is clear from the description of early Moments that already in adolescence I Dis-covered that my Quest was to become a philosopher. I was launched on this Quest by the Be-Speaking of a clover blossom which Announced its be-ing to me, thereby bestowing upon me an ineffable gift—an intuition of be-ing. This Be-Speaking also gave me a kind of "Interior Compass."* It

---

observable in some "New Age" babble. Both Jungianism and "New Age" seduce women into the pit/pitfall of the stereotypic eternal feminine. An important clue that this is mushthinking is the obvious lack of Passion, especially of Rage on behalf of women and nature—the primary targets of patriarchal necrophilia.

*Transcontinental transtemporal telephone conversation with Emily Culpepper, June 24, 1989.

In the process of Naming these seemingly contradictory directions of my Craft's Movement, I shall attempt to show how these four counterpoints were related in The First Spiral Galaxy to the problem of overcoming obstacles that were intended to divert me from my True Course. As I have explained in the *Introduction,* these obstacles included *aphasia*—the patriarchally inflicted inability to Name Background Reality as well as foreground phenomena and to Re-Call differences and connections among these. *Aphasia* is a basic block to Acts of Be-Speaking. Another omnipresent obstruction was the perpetual patriarchal projection/injection of man-made, fictitious, foreground illusions and fears about "the future," which were/are designed to block vision and Movement into the Background Future.

Despite these hindrances I did Be-Speak and I did Move on Course, experiencing Moments of Prophecy and Promise. This was of necessity a tumultuous and complex adventure. My Craft was buffeted in many directions by the Great Wind, which kept me alive, agile, and alert to my Final Cause/Sense of Direction.

Throughout all of this early Voyaging I was engaged in primal warfare, struggling to overcome the demonic assaults of the as yet unNamed Deadly Assimilators. As I later came to understand, *assimilation*◑ is

> gynocidal/biocidal *gluttony* which expresses itself in vampirism/cannibalism, feeding upon the *living* flesh, blood, spirit of women and Others while tokenism disguises the devastation of the victims (*Wickedary*).*

Although it involved warfare, the prevailing experience of Spiraling toward the Threshold was not grim. It was Outrageous, Perilous, Ludicrous, Ecstatic, Elemental. It involved matching, complementing, antithetic combinations of Moments/Movements stirred up by the Wild Wind that was pushing and Calling me beyond the limits of the foreground. I shall turn Now to the task of describing these antithetic Movements of my Craft in The First Spiral Galaxy, as I understand them at this Time.

The First Counterpoint

Right from the beginning I was drawn to the splendour of the Elemental individual realities in the world, as known through many Senses. The catalpa tree, the lilac bush, and the rosebush in our back yard, and the dandelions and buttercups that glowed with glorious yellow made me ecstatic. The warm shining sand in my sandbox Touched my soul. The smell of burning leaves and of fresh snow brought intoxicating messages. The trees swishing

---

Assimilation is one of the *Deadly Sins of the Fathers*◑, which are "the primary manifestations of patriarchal evil, incarnated in phallo-institutions and in those who invent, control, and legitimate these institutions; biocidal blockages/obstructions to Wild Women's Otherworld Journeying" (*Wickedary*).

Wildly before a storm gave me brainstorms/heartstorms. The moon told me things specific and precise in a language that was both private and universal. The purple sky carried me to places beyond the realm of thought and imagination. The beauty of my mother's eyes and hair and especially of her hands Be-Dazzled me. Her voice sings in my ears Now, a quarter of a century after her death. And I Re-member how we sat in the grass when I was very small and ate chocolate ice cream with wooden spoons, and that we were happy together, simply happy.

So I should have loved myths and symbols, right? And poetic and mystical thinking would have seemed vastly preferable to math and logic, yes? But no, it was not so simple. First of all, I loved math and logic, which always felt like invigorating exercise for my brain. Second, the myths and symbols available to me, for example, in nursery rhymes, fairy tales, literature, and religion, were quintessentially patriarchal, and thus despite pseudoglorification of "Woman" and nature, they were woman-hating and often nature-hating to the core. Of course, because of the *aphasia* inflicted upon me, I did not know how to Name this situation as "patriarchal" and "misogynist." (And if I had known, who would have listened to me?) Yet I Sensed subliminally that there was a plot afoot—that this was a Dirty Trick. Symbolic/poetic works were always putting women down, while at the same time women were relegated to this type of thinking, which was often associated with something disparagingly called "women's intuition." The whole setup was fraught with what I later would call "reversals." It was (and is) fundamentally a veiled phallocratic mind-fuck.

In contrast to this, abstract thought—from math to logic to Aristotelian metaphysics—seemed relatively uncontaminated. But abstract reason was not enough. I wanted it all—the rich imagery and the rigorous reason that should accompany each other in the fullness of Intellectual Life.

This Lust for Intellectual/E-motional/Spiritual Integrity is reflected in my doctoral dissertations written in Fribourg, both of which championed abstract, metaphysical reasoning that is rooted in deep intuition. In very different ways, both exemplify reasoning that is grounded in the intuition of be-ing, which arises from encounters with concrete Elemental Realities. Those dissertations represent years of studious struggle to achieve harmonic reconciliation of different modes of knowing/thinking. That struggle strengthened my Craft, preparing the way for the more daring, imaginative, and creative works that I would Weave in the Future.

The Second Counterpoint

Crone-logically speaking, the second contrapuntal whirling dance involved the tension between my Lust to become a philosopher and the Call to become a theologian. The clover blossom that had graced me with its Be-Speaking during my adolescence was never really silenced. It howled and whispered into my Inner Ear, echoing through the Labyrinthine years in Passages of Time: "I am."

In foreground terms, my Quest to become a philosopher was thwarted at every turn. The College of Saint Rose, the only college accessible to me, did not offer a major in philosophy. The Catholic University of America, the only university accessible to me for graduate study, would not give a scholarship in philosophy to one who had not majored in philosophy. The University of Notre Dame would not admit women into its doctoral program in philosophy. Although I struggled against these conditions, taking copious graduate courses in philosophy and teaching it to college students, it did appear that demons were blocking gateway after gateway of my philosophical voyage.

In contrast to that struggle, the Course in the direction of theological study was Strangely smooth. The Great Wind got me to Saint Mary's and to Fribourg, blowing obstacles out of the way. As a result of going to the extent of obtaining the "highest of higher degrees" in theology at the University of Fribourg, I managed to keep riding that Wind and acquire my doctorate in philosophy, finally.

Even this was only the beginning of this intricate second counterpoint. While I was writing the philosophical dissertation the summons came from the London publisher to write a book on women and the church. So my Craft darted around on both sides of the boundary between these two "fields." When I was obliged to return to the States, I grudgingly sent out letters of inquiry both to philosophy and to theology departments.

In the process of corresponding with "chairs" about these depressing options—depressing because they meant re-turning "home"—it became obvious that in the mid-sixties theology was a much Windier Course. While the philosophers navel-gazed, muttering irrelevancies among themselves, the theologians were beginning to be concerned with social movements. So, although I had offers from departments in both areas, it became clear that I would have more flexibility wearing my theologian's hat. Attired in that style of millinery I went to Boston College, which I chose mostly because I preferred to be in Boston, on the edge of the Atlantic, as close as possible to Europe.

When *The Church and the Second Sex* was published, the Weather became Windier. My Craft was in the Eye of a Cyclone. After that storm abated (only briefly, of course) I found it possible to reflect upon the twistings and turnings of my Craft in relation to philosophy and theology. I recognized that I was able to teach philosophy—the kind of philosophy that I loved—under the aegis of theology. I saw clearly that philosophy as it was currently taught tended to be "abstract" in the negative sense, that is, abstracted/distracted not only from social and political concerns, but also from deep E-motional and Psychic Reality—in a word, from the Lust for Wisdom. Theology also fell short. Its symbols were, to say the least, limited and limiting. It retained its thinly veiled eternal tendency to be dogmatic, narrow, and woman-hating. Yet, there was room for Dancing around its boundaries—for intellectual creativity.

Luckily, I was becoming more and more Dis-illusioned. The experience of having been buffeted around quite a bit was knocking me into my Senses. I Sensed that for me to follow my Original Quest and *be* a philosopher would mean Sailing Way Out. I was on my way to understanding, more deeply than before, that a Radical Feminist Philosopher cannot be contained in any "field." She must break the brokenness of women's Original Promise and thereby become Prophetic. This Prophetic dimension, which is Be-Speaking, opened the way for Stormy reconciliation in later Galaxies between my Lust for philosophy and the Re-Sounding Re-Calling of theological questions and Quests.

The Third Counterpoint

Concomitant with the first and second counterpoints was a third. As a student and later as a teacher in colleges and in a junior year abroad program for women I had experienced the phenomenon of women who were "together" but not really *together*, either within themselves or with each other. They were divided from their Selves and from other women. These institutions functioned as foreground simulations of a Reality later Realized as *Women's Space*. I could not have Named *Women's Space* at that time (that is, before 1968), since I had not yet experienced that Stunning phenomenon. I did experience the lack of a certain shared vitality. Yet my knowledge of what it was that was lacking was still mostly subliminal. What I Sensed was the tragic phenomenon which I Now call "the broken Promise" of colleges for women. My breaking away from incarceration in such pseudo-Women's Space involved joining the faculty of a coeducational university. Paradoxically, this was, for me, a movement toward unbreaking the broken Promise.

I was at that time in agreement with Simone de Beauvoir's theory that coeducation is more liberating than single-sex institutions. In *The Church and the Second Sex* I wrote:

> Isolation in one-sex institutions promotes unrealistic notions about the other sex, as well as about one's own. In the vacuum of the imagination which is not supplied with general experience of personal encounter and dialogue, the sexual stereotypes thrive. Obsession with sex then plays a compensatory role.[3]

There was an element of truth in that passage, but my naiveté about coeducation is Now astonishing to me. Having taught for years in a coeducational university and having visited and spoken at hundreds of these, I am only too well aware of the overwhelming "obsession with sex" that prevails in such places. But then, in the sixties, I wrote:

The advantages of coeducation are evident. It provides opportunities for normal day to day encounters, on a level other than that of dating. The two sexes learn to work together.[4]

Sure they do!*

I Dis-covered more and more about the wonders of coeducational colleges and universities in the late sixties (and of course throughout the seventies and eighties and into the nineties). But these horrifying revelations did not erase my Original (though subliminal) insight concerning the broken Promise of women's colleges. They did make me aware that in all institutions of patriarchy women are marginal beings, and that there is more than one form of patriarchal deadly/deadening education, whose tentacles are multitudinous/multifarious. To paraphrase Gertrude Stein:

> Their origin and their history patriarchal education their origin and their history patriarchal education their origin and their history. . . .
>   Patriarchal education makes no mistake. . . .
>   Patriarchal education is the same.[5]

In the late sixties, after the Original publication of *The Church and the Second Sex,* I did Dis-cover the ecstatic energy of Women's Space. I was approaching the point of understanding how this Reality would have to be created "on the Boundary" of patriarchal universities and colleges, but it could not happen just yet. Together with Other women, however, I was rapidly Sailing on our communal Quest toward formulating the still subliminal/sleeping Crafty Question: How to Move in the Direction of breaking the brokenness of women's bodies, spirits, memories, minds by patriarchal institutions of education, most specifically, of "higher" education, while at the same time Righteously using these institutions?

---

*In the 1975 "Feminist Postchristian Introduction" I wrote: "Subsequent experience demonstrated that 'equality' in fact did not happen in the so-called coeducational institutions, which feminists now generally perceive as subeducational. The 'normal day to day encounters' were not infrequently rape in one form or another (physical or mental), especially following the 'sexual revolution.' The instances when male members of the university 'community' did work together with female members nonexploitatively were not frequent enough to affect the general atmosphere or to alter the normal functioning of sexual politics. Not only were administrators and professors by and large sexist (even if not 'intentionally' so), but the curriculum content was also hopelessly androcentric. Today, we are experimenting with new forms of woman-centered, woman-controlled studies which make it possible to learn our own history and think our own thoughts. Of course, since 1975 A.F. is still a transitional time, our methods of surviving subeducation are shifting and diverse. Our programs, courses, and centers are separate spaces created on the boundary of these 'educational' institutions. It is through living 'on the boundary' that women gather energy to use the resources worth using at these institutions and to create our own resources" (Daly, "Feminist Postchristian Introduction to the 1975 Edition," *The Church and the Second Sex,* p. 45).

The swirling contrapuntal movement that carried me into conscious awareness of this Question and into Realizing the beginnings of concrete political solutions hurled my Pirate's Craft—as well as the Crafts of many Cronies—toward The Second Spiral Galaxy. It also hurled me in the Direction of Realizing the Righteousness of Piratic Illegitimate Acts.

The Fourth Counterpoint

My contrapuntal movement of seeking legitimations (degrees) and then refusing academic legitimacy on foreground terms is inextricably connected with Sensing the hidden broken Promise, rejecting its brokenness, and Be-Speaking and Realizing deep Promise. The Unfolding of the Promise required both my seeking of legitimations and my refusal of their foreground consequences, in particular, the "invitation" to sell my soul and become assimilated into a career of professional tokenism. This refusal was necessary for Moments of Prophecy and Promise to continue to happen, that is, for my Be-Speaking and Dis-covering of a Background Future.

For years I had been driven by the fact that none of my degrees, that is, academic legitimations, seemed to be "enough" to bring me freedom. As I then understood "freedom," it meant liberty to live the life of a writer/philosopher/teacher who is not tied down and drained by constraints imposed by mediocre institutions. I believed that by acquiring the "highest of higher degrees" I would earn this privilege. I Now think that on a subliminal level I was seeking something more than I could articulate at that Time. I think that what I really sought was not freedom within academia, but freedom from it. But I did not want simply to leave. I wanted to Be/Leave.

As I came to understand more about academia, I still wanted to be in that world, as it were, but not of it—to be there still, but unconstrained. I wanted academia to support my real work in the world. I would later come to Name this style of be-ing as "living on the Boundary." In this Sense I wanted to Leave, in order to Be, in Other words, to Be/Leave. Although eventually I could no longer believe in academia/academentia, I could Be/Leave *in* it. In Other words, I could be a highly qualified Pirate.

To put it another way, I wanted to Realize my true potential, and academia appeared to be the means for achieving this. Since I did not come from a wealthy or upper-middle-class family, I would have to earn my living. Universities could offer me a meal ticket, or rather meal tickets, as well as congenial environments in which I could do my *own* work, or so I then believed. And, by way of preparation, I could study and accumulate degrees, all of which was gratifying.

My accumulation of legitimations/degrees and my struggle to become tenured/legitimate helped to bring home to me the Realization—by degrees —that I never would or could be "legitimate." My Recurrent Nightmare of losing all evidence of having acquired my Fribourg doctorates brought me closer to this Realization.

My complex contrapuntal movement of struggling for tenure in androcratic academia, specifically at Boston College, while at the same time refusing to conform to cockocratic thought and speech control was a complex maneuver. I kept on writing bold criticisms of the church and its doctrines while continuing to fight to retain my job.

Although *The Church and the Second Sex* was controversial, it was within the range of respectability in the minds of catholics who valued rationality and academic freedom. The antediluvian response of Boston College to that book could be seen as helping me to Move on, but it would be a mistake to give credit where credit is not really due. To be sure, that institution exposed itself, so to speak—allowing me to see through the male veils and glimpse more of the Mystery of Man. However, the fact is that all of the contrapuntal movements of The First Spiral Galaxy were inherently headed in the Direction of ever more Illegitimate Acts.

My transgressing of the boundaries between intuitive and rational modes of knowing and writing and my crossing of lines between carefully delineated "fields," especially between philosophy and theology, were counterpoints/clashes that would inevitably evoke/demand further leaps of daring and creativity. My Dis-covering of the breaking of women's Promise by all patriarchal education heightened my Rage and hence hurled my Craft further. The skills/crafts acquired in my struggle for legitimations had increased and refined my capacity for Unlimited, Illimitable Illegitimacy. So it was that my Contrapuntal Outercourse became more and more Outrageous and Outlandish, and I became Confirmed/Illegitimated in my career as an Outlaw, in my Craft as a Pirate.*

As I approached the point of Breakthrough, my *aphasia* faded fast. My Acts of Be-Speaking speeded up my Craft. As my Moments of Prophecy and Promise became more prolific, generating more Moments, I Saw the temptations of tokenism as totally tawdry tricks—Truly Untempting. My Craft

---

*I have considered the possibility that there were still other contrapuntal movements in the Course of The First Spiral Galaxy. A fifth counterpoint, for example, would be between the life of a scholar/writer/teacher/lecturer and that of an activist. Indeed there were strong tides pulling me into the world of political activism, particularly as the women's movement surged in the mid-sixties. However, rather than seeing this tension as a distinct counterpoint, I Now recognize it as a theme running through the major contrapuntal movements. Already in The First Spiral Galaxy my direction was clearly Metapolitical rather than merely political. That is, I was not struggling for power simply in an institutional sense, but rather in an ontological/metaphysical Sense. At its core, my activism had its roots in my Sense of Background reality. So my work as scholar/ writer/teacher/lecturer became more and more Active, challenging old patriarchal assumptions, opening New doors.

crashed through the blocks and illusions of the foreground "future," fairly flying toward the Background. The attempts of the (as yet unNamed) Assimilators/demons to devour my Craft were foiled by this flying. Looking back, I still see them, their monstrous mouths gaping open, while the Wild Wind tossed me free and away to New Whirling Worlds and Words, that is, to The Second Spiral Galaxy.

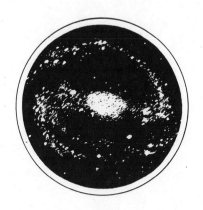

BE-FALLING:
Moments of Breakthrough and Re-Calling
(1971–1974)

Moments of Breakthrough and Re-Calling

PIRATING IN THE MIST

A s I have explained in "Reflections on Philosophical Themes of The First Spiral Galaxy," that early part of my Voyage involved sailing the surface of the Subliminal Sea, Sensing its depths, while not being overtly conscious of the contents of these depths. I did have occasional conscious Sensations, however, and these kept me on Course.

The intensified Momentum of my Craft as I Moved through those early Moments warmed the surrounding waters. Droplets of those Sea waters rose into the air, forming a Mist containing vital subliminal information. When my Craft sailed into this Mist I was bombarded with Messages that had risen from the Subliminal Depths—Messages which I could See/Feel/Hear, and Name consciously. I had crossed the Limen into The Second Spiral Galaxy —the Time of Moments of Breakthrough and Re-Calling.

I Now See that as I sailed into The Second Spiral Galaxy I was commencing my New work as Pirate of the Mist. I did not Name my identity in this way then, although I often spoke of "Righteously ripping off what Rightfully belongs to women." But this is how I Now Re-member and Name that identity.

Of course I had already been a Pirate all my life, accumulating treasures of knowledge that had been hidden from my Tribe. It was this Call to Piracy that had lured me to obtain degree after degree, ultimately crossing the Atlantic and Righteously Plundering another space/time, that is, Europe/the Middle Ages. It had Summoned me to carry this loot back across the ocean seven years later, in preparation for my still unforeseen sophisticated Smuggling operations.

In the Course of The Second Spiral Galaxy my Piratic career Leaped/ Spiraled around and ahead into New and Daring dimensions. As before, I rarely missed an opportunity to attack and board the vessels of the phallocratic erasers of women,* seizing what I recognized, on one level or another,

---

*The names of some of these fellows can be found in footnotes in all of my books, which have been scrupulously researched according to the highest standards of scholarship. Their vessels include their books, which carry their seminal ideas, and the universities, libraries, and professional societies and journals controlled by deadly deadfellows who belong to the same fraternity. True Piracy (Righteously Ripping off these vessels), as I understand and practice this, requires rigorous and meticulous scholarship. Thus my own Pirate's Craft must be and is a Superb, Subliminal Seaworthy Scholar Ship.

as Rightfully belonging to my Tribe. Now, however, my work as Plunderer and Smuggler (two essential aspects of my Piracy) reached Other levels of significance.

My Plundering in The Second Spiral Galaxy involved Seizing and Sailing off with the subliminal meanings which I Dis-covered in patriarchal texts—reversed and buried meanings which are visible only in the Mist. Armed with the Courage to Sail into the Mist I was able to detect and grasp these meanings. This work of Getting the Messages involved adventurous Moments of Breakthrough.

Then, of course, I had to Smuggle this heretofore hidden material back to women in such a way that it could be seen as distinct from its patriarchal trappings. So I began Naming/Defining old material (old stuff) in New Ways, thereby rendering its liberating messages accessible. For example, I redefined "original sin" as women's internalization of blame and guilt, the result of enforced complicity in our own oppression. So also I Plundered the christian doctrine of "the Second Coming," transforming it to mean "the Second Coming of women," thereby Smuggling New and Archaic insights by way of this symbol. Thus old words became New Words, Re-Calling our erased possibilities.

So it happened that my Be-Speaking (overcoming of *aphasia*) led to the overcoming of *amnesia*, another pathological condition inflicted upon women under patriarchy, the State of Erasure. My Piratic enterprise in The Second Spiral Galaxy thus centered on breaking through the foreground "past," the "past" of patriarchally falsified history, and Dis-closing the Background Past.*

This Re-Calling† of Prepatriarchal/Metapatriarchal Reality was a tremendous Piratic adventure. It involved breaking taboos, daring to question "time-honored" beliefs. I had to summon the *Courage to Sin*○, that is

> the Courage to be intellectual in the most direct and daring way, claiming and trusting the deep correspondence between the structures/processes of one's own mind and the structures/processes of reality; the Courage to trust and Act on one's own deepest intuitions (*Wickedary*).

As my Be-Speaking became more Originally Sinful/Illegitimate, it often took the form of Be-Falling.‡

---

*Of course, I could not have used this language to Name the process during the Time of The Second Spiral Galaxy. This description contains words Dis-covered in The Third and Fourth Spiral Galaxies. It is Now that this language is available to me to describe as accurately as possible how I understand what was going on then.

†By *Re-Calling* ○ I mean "1 : persistent/insistent Calling of the Wild; recurring invitation to Realms of Deep Memory 2 : Active Unforgetting of participation in Be-ing; Remembering and giving voice to Original powers, intuitions, memories" (*Wickedary*).

‡For the definition of *Be-Falling*, see the Introduction.

The Unfolding of my career as a Pirate in The Second Spiral Galaxy was a complex process. But my Daring reconnaissance expeditions into the Mist gave me the insights and clues needed for my New work. In the Course of these expeditions, however, I had to ward off the demonic assaults of the as yet unNamed Eliminators. *Elimination*◗, as I later understood and defined it, is

> necrophilic *envy* of Biophilic powers, which demands the eradication of ensouled matter and the fabrication of replacements, imitations, simulations of Life (*Wickedary*).*

It is perfectly logical that I should have been forced to confront the evil Eliminators in the Course of The Second Spiral Galaxy. Having already in The First Spiral Galaxy beaten back the demonic Assimilators, who had tried to swallow me, to fence me into their "future" by embedding fearful illusions and by tempting me into a living death of timid tokenism, I was now free to Re-Call the Elemental Memory of women—to uncover our Past. And so the Eliminators of women's history, the erasers of Deep Memory/Metamemory of Biophilic women, the effacers who perpetually replace the story of our Foresisters' Lives and our Lives with Lies, would naturally/unnaturally try to eradicate me, together with Sister Pirates. That is, they would attempt to negate our be-ing and our work because it rendered/renders their deceptions transparent.

The Eliminators would inevitably display their *envy* of natural Biophilic powers, especially creativity and what they fearfully recognized/unrecognized as success. And so they would resort to their timeworn strategies of erasure and reversal. Since these tricksters' tricks work only in the framework of their own foreground, however, they were doomed from the start. Indeed, they functioned mainly to provide more material for Piratic study and analysis, by exposing not only their own methods and inadequacies but also those of their predecessors (which were, of course, the same).

So I kept on Pirating in the Mist.

Much of my actual Plundering and Smuggling occurred in the process of writing articles and books. I transmitted my treasures of heretofore subliminal knowledge to women chiefly through these writings, but also by means of my Feminist philosophy classes at Boston College, as well as through seminars, academic lectures, public speeches, and workshops across the country and abroad.

It was not that I hid or cloaked anything I had to say. Quite the contrary: I was/am extremely forthright. The real nature of Smuggling has to do with the multidimensional Meanings/Senses of the material I had now begun to transmit. This was/is Explosive Stuff. The articles of the early seventies, as

---

Elimination, like *assimilation*, is one of the Deadly Sins of the Fathers. See Chapter Six. See *Wickedary*.

well as *Beyond God the Father* and the "Feminist Postchristian Introduction" to *The Church and the Second Sex,* are charged with Time Bombs. Or, to Name the situation in another and perhaps more accurate way, they are loaded with materials that can stir up the Volcanoes smouldering within women—those Natural Time Bombs that are so cravenly feared by the phallocrats.

I think it is very important for Other Voyagers to understand the nature of this Smuggling. Clearly, it was not and is not a matter of simply transmitting male-authored ideas to women, to be applied to "women's issues." Nor is it an attempt to absorb "feminist theory" into some prefabricated patriarchal system, as has been the case with much run of the mill "socialist feminist theory," for example.[1] Thus I am not an Aristotelian, Heideggerian, or Whiteheadian "feminist philosopher," trying to gain acceptance as a philosopher in/on male terms. In my view, this would be quite the opposite of Piratic Smuggling. It would be active complicity in the patriarchal system of Assimilation. Ultimately, it would mean Self-elimination. While I have used some male thinkers' works as springboards for my own thought, my work is not sired (or husbanded) by any of them.

My Piratic Plundering and Smuggling had/has its Source in Woman-identification/Self-identification. My task was/is to seize and transmit women's buried tradition/treasure, so that the Quest for the Wisdom masked by the distorted "wisdom" of the fathers can be carried on. So in The Second Spiral Galaxy I began Smuggling Background information gathered in the Course of my E-motional/intellectual/psychic/geographic travels, transmitting material that I was in the process of decoding, working to make this accessible to mySelf and to Other women.

Such Smuggling is Consciousness-Raising. By setting off Time Bombs in women it can release us into our own Momentous Time. By causing Undersea Volcanoes to erupt, it unleashes the explosive force of Memory and the Fire of smouldering passion. Thus dangerous knowledge was launched between the covers of an innocent-looking book—*Beyond God the Father.* On second thought, perhaps it was not so innocent-looking, since the very title is loaded, and since the subtitle, *Toward a Philosophy of Women's Liberation,* breaks the Taboo against women becoming Woman-identified/Self-identified philosophers.

At any rate, that book passed. It passed into bookstores and libraries and into required reading lists, not only for Women's Studies classes, but also for courses in religion, philosophy, psychology, American Studies, sociology, and so on, and on. It was/is, after all, meticulously scholarly and Timely. It uses vocabulary which, in some parts of the book, may appear conventional, if understood only in a foreground sense. Moreover, its author had/has a respectable teaching job and was highly degreed—overdegreed. Who could doubt her legitimacy?

The book passed from woman to woman. Women began to discuss it, to act on it, to spring off from it. Women carried on/carry on. And I carried on/carry on. It is of the nature of Pirates to carry on, because Pirates are far out. We are Outlaws,[2] and our Sense of Direction leads logically to Outercourse.

Specifically, *Beyond God the Father* led logically to the writing of the "Feminist Postchristian Introduction" to *The Church and the Second Sex*. As an Honest Pirate I felt that it was important to Announce forthrightly my New location on my Voyage and to explain the how and why of my apparent shift in Direction. I say "apparent," because my seemingly different Direction was quite consistent with that of my earlier Moments. Indeed, those Moments had led me logically to my Postchristian position. That is the Way of Spiraling, as opposed to mere linear motion. Insofar as there was a Shift, it was consonant with the Spiraling Shape-shifting of the earlier paths of my Outercourse.

As the following chapters reveal, in The Second Spiral Galaxy I was energized by my increasingly conscious understanding that I was not Voyaging in isolation. Having Realized my participation in a Cosmic Covenant of Cronies, I rejoiced in my knowledge that the Verb/Be-ing was Unfolding in an extraordinary way for Wayward Women. Buoyed up by my Newfound Sense of our boundless possibilities I sailed onward through the Mist, following the Call of the Wild, Re-Calling Realms of Deep Memory. I was Unforgetting our common participation in Be-ing, Be-Falling farther and farther, as I broke through to New Words for Absolutely Female feelings and intuitions—for that certain knowledge shared by women Be-Friending and Bonding in Sisterhood.

CHAPTER SEVEN

THE TIME OF THE TIGERS:
THE HARVARD MEMORIAL CHURCH
EXODUS AND OTHER ADVENTURES

The year 1971 was packed with excitement. It was a Sparkling year, a Stunning year. It was a Time of intense Re-Calling.

BREAKTHROUGH: "AFTER THE DEATH
OF GOD THE FATHER"

Early in the spring of that year I published an article which marked my Breakthrough to a New way of thinking. It was entitled "After the Death of God the Father."[1] That article began—Strangely enough—with the following sentence:

> The women's liberation movement has produced a deluge of books and articles.

So I was—perhaps unconsciously—Re-Calling the Self-fulfilling Prophecy and Promise of my letter published in 1964, which had foretold that "a barrage" of articles and books studying the history of the problem of women and the church "will come."[2]

"After the Death of God the Father" went far beyond merely delineating the history of the problem of women and the church. After describing the "deluge" of books and articles thus far produced by the women's movement as focusing on the task of "exposition and criticism of our male-centered heritage," I went on to proclaim:

> As far as the level of creative research is concerned, that phase of the work is finished. The skeletons in our cultural closet have been hauled out for inspection. I do not mean to imply that there are not countless more of the same to be uncovered. . . . What I am saying is that Phase One of critical research and writing in the movement has opened the way for the logical next step in creative thinking. We now have to ask how the women's revolution can and should change our whole vision of reality.[3]

I then proceeded to challenge the symbol system of patriarchal religion and society, declaring that women, as "extra-environmentals" who have not been part of the authority structures, can effect social change. One of my essential points was that by challenging the patriarchal infrastructures women can undermine and withdraw the props that have sustained and given plausibility to the symbol system which, in turn, legitimates these social structures.

Viewed from the Present, this article is mild. It calls for "a diarchal situation that is radically new" and looks somewhat favorably upon Mary Baker Eddy's "Father-Mother God." (I disposed of this about a year later in the process of writing *Beyond God the Father*.) Despite its "diarchal" universalism it is substantially tough—asserting that the women's revolution will become "the greatest single potential challenge to Christianity to rid itself of its oppressive tendencies or go out of business." It did not take me long after that to Realize that oppressive tendencies are not aberrations but the very stuff of christianity, since its symbols are inherently oppressive.

One remarkable detail about the history of this article is the fact that it was in part inspired by *The Sacred Canopy*, a work by sociologist Peter Berger. Ingenuously, I wrote to that esteemed academic, conveying how impressed I had been by his book and how it had influenced my own thought. I explained enthusiastically that I had applied some of the ideas in his book and carried them to their logical conclusions—and enclosed a copy of "After the Death of God the Father."

Professor Berger responded to my letter. He was most displeased that I had sprung off from his analysis in such a manner. Indeed, he had little use for women's liberation, which he seemed to perceive as primarily about orgasms of middle-class women in the suburbs of America. The renowned professor himself had recently returned from Africa and had found *real* oppression there. Of course, he did not mention the specific real conditions of the lives of *women* in Africa. He suggested that I come to New York to speak with him, presumably so he could straighten me out. I responded in disgust, inviting him to visit me in my office in Boston. That was the end of our brief correspondence.

Berger's reaction to my work was an important experience of Dis-illusionment. It evoked Moments of Breakthrough. I gained the insight, never to be forgotten, that one could write a lucid book such as *The Sacred Canopy* (which I still consider an important work, that is, useful to spring off from), while refusing to acknowledge its logical implications. Berger's abstract theory was split off from insight into the realities that I experienced every day of my life.

This incident was a source of inspiration. One message that I received was that patriarchal theorists could know exactly what their society was doing to women while at the same time refusing to know this. To me, this implied an aggressive will *not* to know.[4] The clarity of Berger's theory was so stunning that it seemed to me impossible that he could not see what I was getting at. So any remnants of my naive belief that "the problem" in patriarchy was lack of information and that rational explanation/education was an adequate solution were blown away. This experience helped to hurl me beyond "After the Death of God the Father." I wanted to understand more about the refusal to see and the reality of the Courage to See.

BEYOND DETACHMENT: "THE COURAGE TO SEE"

A few months later I published my article "The Courage to See."[5] Already in "After the Death of God the Father" I had written that "the driving revelatory force which will make possible an authenticity of religious consciousness is courage in the face of anxiety."[6] The idea of existential courage was initially inspired by Paul Tillich's book, *The Courage to Be.*[7] However, in "The Courage to See" I took it into another context, that is, the context of the omnipresent sexual caste system of patriarchy, and applied it to the struggle to see through basic/base assumptions of sexual hierarchy in theology and in popular culture. So the concept of existential courage was radically transformed. Tillich became the target of my criticism for encouraging detachment from the reality of the struggle against oppression in its concrete manifestations:

> . . . just as Tillich's discussion of God is "detached," so is the rest of his systematic theology. His discussion of estrangement, for example, when he "breaks" the myth of the Fall, fails to take specifically into account the malignant view of the man-woman relationship which the androcentric myth itself inadvertently "reveals" and perpetuates.[8]

This article calls for insight regarding such "oversight" in religious thought and in all thought and behavior. It acknowledges that such seeing is difficult:

> It is understandable that most men would prefer not to see. It is also understandable that many women would prefer not to see. Seeing means everything changes: you can't go home again. It is not "prudent" to see too well. Therefore the ethic emerging in the struggle for women's liberation has as its main theme not prudence but existential courage.[9]

WHIRLWINDS: SPEAKING, TEACHING, GROWLING

The entire spring and fall of 1971 were filled with intense and extensive political activism. For example, I spoke at a number of rallies and conferences on abortion, especially in Boston and New York, during that time of struggle against oppressive, woman-killing laws. On March 23 I testified before the Social Welfare Committee of the Massachusetts legislature as the lone catholic who would speak up in favor of the repeal of anti-abortion laws. When I walked up and began my testimony, most of the congressmen rose and walked out. So that's how it was with politicians in catholic Boston!

At any rate, I delivered my testimony for the women who had come, and they applauded enthusiastically.

I was also caught up in a whirlwind of travels and adventures that were hardly restricted to the abortion issue. I gave a number of sermons and talks to church groups, as well as to university audiences.[10] All of these lectures and talks were—in varying degrees of explicitness—"good-bye to the church and all that" messages.

The academic year 1971–72 was the beginning of the Time of the Tigers. I taught my first Feminist classes that year. During the first semester I taught "The Women's Revolution and Theological Development" (as well as other courses, of course). This was followed in the second semester by "Women's Liberation and the Church." These were the first Women's Studies courses offered within the consortium of theological schools known as the Boston Theological Institute (BTI). My students included Jan Raymond, who was then beginning her doctoral studies in the joint doctoral program of Boston College and Andover Newton Theological School. Also Present were three Wild women from Harvard Divinity School—Linda Barufaldi, Emily Culpepper, and Jean MacRae. These four women, together with myself, constituted a very loosely organized but closely bonded group known among ourselves as "the Tigers."

The chief activities of the Tigers among ourselves were Spinning ideas, organizing subversive events, and, in general, having a good time. Several of us also growled frequently, particularly as a form of salutation and greeting, in person and on the telephone.

THE HARVARD MEMORIAL EXODUS:
A METAMORPHIC MOMENT

The fall of 1971 provided opportunities for Fiercely Focused action. One such action stands out especially as an historic Moment. It became known as the Harvard Memorial Church Exodus. This event began to brew sometime in October, when I was invited to be the first woman to preach at a Sunday service in Memorial Church's three-hundred-and-thirty-six-year history. The invitation posed a dilemma. To simply accept would be to agree to being used as a token. To refuse would seem like forfeiting an opportunity. I tried to think of a creative solution.

The solution came when a group of women met at Harvard Divinity School (in Linda Barufaldi's room, to be precise) to discuss the problem. With the encouragement of these Cohorts, I decided that I would accept the invitation and turn the sermon into an action. Together we planned the event, which was to be a call for a walk-out from patriarchal religion.[11] The resulting "Exodus" (on November 14) turned out to be an historic Moment of Breakthrough and Re-Calling.

In order to give the sermon I was obliged to sit up in the sanctuary during the first part of the service. It was evident that the ministers and choir had got wind of the fact that "something" was going to happen. The pastor had delegated his assistant to conduct the service, seating himself discreetly among the congregation, and thus sparing himself some embarrassment. Some of the members of the choir were suppressing giggles of nervous excitement. Obviously "nonsexist" hymns had been judiciously selected for the occasion.

Scriptural passages were read by two women (Cohorts). Liz Rice read from the old testament (1 samuel 15:23): "For rebellion is as the sin of witchcraft." Emily Culpepper, wearing her bright red "Witch Shoes," read from the "new" testament, specifically from pauline epistles. I Re-Call the look of absolute satisfaction and glee on Emily's face as she intoned from 1 timothy 2:11: "Let the woman learn in silence with all subjection," and so on, and on.

The way was thus prepared for the sermon. When the Moment came I solemnly mounted the steps up into the gigantic, phallus-like pulpit. My address began: "Sisters and other esteemed members of the congregation: There are many ways of refusing to see a problem." I discussed the need for the Courage to See and to Act, affirming that "externalized action, or *praxis,* authenticates insight and creates situations out of which new knowledge can grow."

As the sermon moved toward its dramatic ending I fervently hoped that I would not have to go through the humiliation of being almost alone, accompanied by six or seven staunch comrades, stalking out of the church. But whatever the consequences, I would have to go through with it. So I went on:

> We cannot really belong to institutional religion as it exists. . . .
>
> The women's movement is an exodus community. Its basis is not merely in the promise given to our fathers thousands of years ago. Rather its source is in the unfulfilled promise of our mothers' lives, whose history was never recorded. Its source is in the promise of our sisters whose voices have been robbed from them, and in our own promise, our latent creativity. We can affirm *now* our promise and our exodus as we walk into a future that will be our *own* future.
>
> Sisters—and brothers if there are any here:
>
> Our time has come. We will take our own place in the sun. We will leave behind the centuries of silence and darkness. Let us affirm our faith in ourselves and our will to transcendence by rising and walking out together.[12]

I need not have feared the embarrassment of walking out almost alone. Hundreds of women and some men began stampeding out of the church the Moment I finished. Far from being "the leader" of a "flock," as some journalists chose to perceive it, I was caught in the middle of the stampede. By the time I managed to run down out of the enormous pulpit half of "the flock" were rushing ahead of me. So I just joined the crowd.

Some of the brightest and funniest Moments happened afterward on the steps outside the church. We roared as we heard the concluding hymn being sung by those who had chosen to remain inside for the rest of the service. It was a hymn to "the Holy Spirit"—chosen for the occasion, no doubt, because of its "inclusive" language—and it was being sung entirely, or almost entirely, by male voices. The deep voices dutifully droning the hymn on the inside contrasted sharply with the cackling and cheering of the predominantly female crowd outside. In the midst of this joyous chaos, members of the press pressed us with questions. They had been notified of the event by Feminist activist and publicist Mary Lou Shields, who also fielded their questions. Soon after that we rushed off for a self-congratulatory brunch.

The Exodus sermon was a qualitatively different Act of Be-Speaking from those of The First Spiral Galaxy. It was not Be-Speaking from within a patriarchal institution, nor was it an attempt to reform/change such an institution. It involved a Seeing of connections and a Radical Departure. Thus it was also a summons to Acts of Be-Falling.

As an event, the Exodus was a manifestation of the *Courage to Leave●*, which is:

> Virtue enabling women to depart from all patriarchal religions and other hopeless institutions; resolution springing from deep knowledge of the nucleus of nothingness which is at the core of these institutions (*Wickedary*).

For some of us who walked out that day, our Act was indeed a departure from all patriarchal religions. As Linda Barufaldi wrote:

> It [the Exodus] involved admitting into my consciousness the painful fact that the Judeo-Christian tradition . . . its culture, its doctrine, and its community, is male-oriented and male-dominated. It is not mine.[13]

Not everyone who walked out experienced the Exodus in this depth or made the same commitment. Some returned to Harvard Memorial Church or to some other church on following Sundays, presumably in the hope of changing the institution "from the inside." Certainly not everyone who heard or read about the walk-out understood it in such depth. Many perceived it as simply a "symbolic" act. Among those who reduced it in this way were some who wanted to tokenize and co-opt it. At least one minister wrote to me and asked if I would come and preach in his church and "do the same thing." Obviously he saw it as a mere repeatable performance. I responded with outrage: "No, of course not; I really *meant* it when I said I was walking out." This was incomprehensible to him.

Employing the language later developed in *Pure Lust,* I would Now describe the Exodus as a Metaphoric event. The word *metaphor* is derived from the Greek *meta* plus *pherein,* meaning "to bear, carry." As a Meta-phoric event, the Exodus *carried* those who participated with deep convic-tion into Metamorphic Moments/Movements, changing our lives, hurling us beyond the imprisoning cells of patriarchal religion. I am not saying that this happened all at once, but that we were on our way, since one Moment leads to another.

While the patriarchs did not succeed in co-opting the Exodus, they have in large measure managed to erase it from history—though not from the Memories of the participants. By writing this I am Re-membering it. I am publicly—and for the record—Unforgetting a Deep Moment of Break-through and Re-Calling. By Re-Calling that Re-Calling I participate in the process of overcoming the dis-memberment of women's history and break-ing through to our Background Past.

WILD HOPES, FIERY FRIENDS, DARING DEEDS, WICKED WORDS

1971 was exactly the kind of year in which an event such as the Exodus could happen. There was widespread faith within the Feminist movement in the possibility of a complete change in women. Radical Feminists *looked* differ-ent because we *were* different. We looked Wild, Angry, and Absolutely Nat-ural. I was then (and am Now) deeply Moved by the illustration on the cover of *Notes from the Third Year: Women's Liberation*—a collection of articles by Radical Feminists published in 1971. That illustration is a collage of two women's faces. On the right is a photograph of the head of a pre-Feminist woman. Her hair is carefully curled. Her face, caked with makeup, is expressionless, dead. On the left is a photo of a woman whose consciousness has been liberated. Her hair is casual and free-style. Her face is free of makeup. She is bursting with energy, and she is laughing.

The Moment that I saw the cover of this issue I felt an enormous surge of hope. It seemed to me that The Change had happened once and for all. Plastic women, I thought, were a thing of the past. Soon I would never have to see dead, robot-like female faces anymore.

On an obvious level that hope was unrealistic. Within a few years fem-botism, or fembotitude,[14] would be back in full force. Deadened/"fixed-up" faces and bodies, fashioned by fashionable makeup and clothing, would return. But I knew then and know Now that my hope was not unfounded. Despite all the work of fashion designers and media-men of all kinds, the imaginations of millions of women were stirred. Even if the Memory has dropped to a subliminal level, it is not gone.

In 1971 I published an article in *Notes from the Third Year* entitled "The Spiritual Dimension of Women's Liberation."[15] The appearance of that arti-cle functioned as a proclamation to mySelf and to the women's movement at large that I had moved beyond the political position of *The Church and the Second Sex*. It also demonstrated movement into dimensions beyond those of the article, "Women and the Catholic Church," which had been published in 1970 in Robin Morgan's widely distributed anthology, *Sisterhood Is Powerful*.

Although the world of christian theology and of things even remotely churchy was fast receding from the center of my scope of interest, I continued to be active on the Boundary of that milieu. For example, in the fall of 1971, at the national meeting of the American Academy of Religion held in Atlanta, a women's caucus was formed. I proposed that we should also establish a section (called a "working group") on Women and Religion. What this meant was that this large professional organization of theologians and scripture scholars would have to allot "official" time and space every year for women to present papers in Women's Studies. It was decided that I would be program "chairperson" of the section for the following year. Thus began a forum for women, a place of our own to create and Spin on the Boundary of a huge male-run congress. The stage was also set for some fascinating activities the following year on the part of the Tigers.[16]

Of special significance also was the fact that Betty Farians came to Boston to be the Executive Director of the Women's Institute of the Boston Theological Institute for that entire academic year.* Betty instigated a flurry of activities in her efforts to organize women in the various theological schools of the Boston area and to encourage women faculty to offer courses in Women's Studies. She struggled valiantly to move obtuse and misogynist deans and other bore-ocrats to assist women and to hire faculty with Feminist consciousness. It was a frustrating and often infuriating job. Yet Betty's Presence and commitment helped to create an atmosphere of camaraderie and comedy that helped to keep our revolution rolling.

It was during that Time that Nelle Morton, the widely known and respected Feminist theologian from Drew University, visited my class. We sat in a circle and discussed the situation of women with Nelle, who announced that she was fed up with trying to work with men. Clearly the Time for the creation of Women's Space was more than overdue. Nelle, then about sixty-seven, with her grey hair in an attractive sort of pony tail, was speaking with us in her Tennessee drawl, and the scene was unforgettable.

An important "good-bye to the church and all that" talk, delivered to an audience that had already left or had never been "there," was my speech at the historic Radical Feminist Conference on Prostitution held in New York in December 1971. I explained that saint Augustine and Thomas Aquinas after him had reluctantly affirmed the expediency of prostitution, justifying this by comparing prostitutes to the sewers of a city. According to this traditional

---

*During the spring of 1971 Jan Raymond had served as Interim Coordinator while studying full time to finish her master's degree at Andover Newton Theological School.

doctrine, prostitutes help to preserve the institution of marriage and to keep wives "pure." As a consequence of this public Be-Speaking, I broke through to deeper recognition of the fact that all women are sewers in the eyes of the fathers and theologians of the church.

The buildup of such actions and insights, combined with Sparking conversations with other Feminists, especially the Tigers, carried me into 1972 in a surge of energy. Some of this creative energy was expended in organizing. That winter and spring, for example, I worked together with Jan Raymond on the project of soliciting and choosing the papers that would be presented in the "Women and Religion" section of the National Meeting of the American Academy of Religion, which was scheduled to take place in Los Angeles in the fall of 1972. We had the sense that there was something Momentous about this task. It was an experience of creating Women's Space in—and on the edge of—a conservative and improbable environment.

The most powerful manifestations of this tidal wave of energy were in my writing. In February 1972 I published my controversial article, "Abortion and Sexual Caste."[17] It was not because of a personal/private agenda that I took on this issue. I have never needed an abortion. But my commitment was and is to the cause of women as women.

In the article I cited my favorite and irrefutable set of statistics, which I had frequently used on panels and discussions of religion and abortion: "One hundred per cent of the bishops who oppose the repeal of anti-abortion laws are men and one hundred per cent of the people who have abortions are women."[18] I thought it clear and obvious—and outrageous—that men had appropriated the right to dictate to women in this matter. I saw that the main issue was really power over women.

"Abortion and Sexual Caste" had as its purpose the placing of the abortion issue in the context of the sexual caste system:

> Since the condition of sexual caste has been camouflaged so successfully by sex role segregation, it has been difficult to perceive anti-abortion laws and anti-abortion ethical arguments within this context. Yet it is only by perceiving them within this total environment of patriarchal bias that it is possible to assess realistically how they function in society.[19]

In discussing the problem of camouflage I showed that the anti-abortionists (especially the catholic church) hide the fact that opposition to the repeal of anti-abortion laws is interconnected with misogynistic practices such as the exclusion of women from the ranks of the clergy. Although a contemporary Feminist might be inclined to say that this interconnection is obvious, the fact is that it was not obvious in 1972 and still isn't evident to many women, because abortion was and is singled out as unique:

> If . . . one-sided arguments using such loaded terminology as "the *murder* of the unborn *child*" are viewed as independent units of thought unrelated to the

kind of society in which they were formulated, then they may well appear plausible and cogent.[20]

I think that the editors of *Commonweal* had a difficult time dealing with the vitriolic response of many of its readers to my article.[21] I had gone too far, and I was never again invited to publish an article in *Commonweal,* the leading liberal catholic magazine. This was one more indication to me that it was time for me to move on—and Out.

Yet it was ironic that my good-bye article in *Commonweal* was on abortion. This issue was not at the center of my own interests. I hardly saw the right to an abortion as the ultimate goal of the Feminist movement, or as an expression of the epitome of Feminist consciousness. But I refused to see it as disconnected from other issues and I Named the connections.

Ostensibly my crime was taking a pro-choice stand on abortion. In reality my crime was my Choice to See through and Name the workings of the sexual caste system. The events culminating in my departure from the ranks of *Commonweal* writers constituted important Moments of Breakthrough and Re-Calling.

The following month (March 1972) *Andover Newton Quarterly* published an important issue devoted to the subject of women's liberation. This contained articles by Nelle Morton, Elizabeth Farians, and Jan Raymond as well as myself. There was also an essay by a male professor on "Jeremiah and Women's Liberation"—not exactly a topic of burning interest to any woman I knew. My article, "The Spiritual Revolution: Women's Liberation as Theological Re-education," contained concepts that were later developed in *Beyond God the Father.*[22] It also presented ideas and expressions that I discarded a few months later in writing that book. For example, in the article I wrote of "sisterhood as church,"[23] but I soon realized that I did not want the women's movement to be called a "church."* I came to see this as inherently contradictory. Another expression used in this article which I later came to find problematic was "sisterhood of man."[24] In *Beyond God the Father* this is described as a "deliberately transitional" expression.

VOLCANIC TABOO-BREAKING: RE-CALLING MY LESBIAN IDENTITY

If 1971 was a Sparking year, 1972 was Volcanic. *Notes from the Third Year* contained an interview by Anne Koedt, entitled "Loving Another Woman."[25]

---

*In *Beyond God the Father* I created the expression "Sisterhood as Cosmic Covenant." After that Breakthrough and Re-Calling I could never identify with the expression "Womanchurch," which became popular in the 1980s, and which seemed to me to be a regression.

It was a transcription of a taped interview with a woman who talked about her love relationship with another woman. Just as Rosemary Lauer's article of 1963 had Be-Spoken me into Naming and Realizing my Prophecy and Promise as a Feminist writer, awakening my Powers of Be-Speaking, this interview Be-Spoke me into Moments of Breakthrough and Re-Calling my Lesbian identity. Reading it in 1972 Be-Spoke me into Be-Falling.

In this interview the (anonymous) speaker said:

> I guess it was also a surprise to find that you weren't struck down by God in a final shaft of lightning. That once you fight through that initial wall of undefined fears built to protect those taboos, they wither rapidly, and leave you to operate freely in a new self-defined circle of what's natural. You have a new sense of boldness, of daring, about yourself.[26]

And, as the same woman emphasized:

> . . . it very quickly became natural—natural is really the word I'd use for it. It was like adding another dimension to what we'd already been feeling for each other. It is quite a combination to fall in love with your friend.[27]

My friend and I read this piece together and soon sprang into action. From that Moment nothing was ever the same again. That relation ended after a few years but the transformation was permanent. I Re-Call looking out my office window at trees whose branches met and having an overwhelmingly powerful intuition that expressed itself in the words "The trees came together." I would Now call that experience "an intuition of Elemental integrity."

Enormous forces were unleashed by this Dis-covering of an Other dimension of my identity. I had already glimpsed the Promise of women together and I had written and acted boldly. Now I could live and create more boldly—even while Moving through various kinds and degrees of turmoil.

Why hadn't this possibility been obvious before? Clearly there had been a Taboo against it. When I had broken the Taboo sexually and Realized how very Natural/Elemental this was, I began to understand more and more explicitly the vast dimensions of what I would later Name the *Terrible Taboo,* which is also a *Total Taboo* against exercising Touching Powers.*

---

*These expressions are defined in Chapter Two. *Touching Powers*○ are "Pyrogenetic Powers of Communication, actualized by women who break the Terrible Taboo and thus break out of the touchable caste" (*Wickedary*). The expression *touchable caste*○ Names the "fixed status imposed upon women and all of nature; condition of those condemned by phallocrats to be touched—physically, emotionally, intellectually, spiritually—by those in possession of a penis; condition of those systematically subjected to phallic violation, e.g., by rape, battering, medical experimentation, and butchery" (*Wickedary*). See Daly, *Pure Lust*, Chapter Six.

These words were Dis-covered much later, of course. But in the early seventies I knew clearly that the physical and spiritual dimensions of the Taboo were closely intertwined. The Totality of my Breaking the Taboo opened the way for Re-Calling Original Integrity—and for Spelling Out this knowledge in words and actions that would reach other women. This process would be Realized much more fully in The Third Spiral Galaxy.

Breaking the *Terrible Taboo/Total Taboo* is not a simple affair, so to speak. I did not think then, nor do I believe Now, that the fact that a woman relates sexually with another woman necessarily means that she has broken the Taboo in the most profound way. In my view, then and Now, there are many dimensions of woman-identification. I will have more to say about this in the Course of The Third Spiral Galaxy. The task at hand, however, is Remembering the Moments just before, during, and after the writing of *Beyond God the Father*. I will leap into that Whirlwind in the following chapter.

I remember thinking how bizarre the word "cute" had sounded. The Moment ended quickly, and the reading and discussion continued without any further incidents. Judging from the apparent normality of everything that followed, I think that it is not unfair to believe that for most of the women there "the incident" simply slipped back into the Subliminal Sea. After all, there were no words for it and there was no context in which to place it.

At such Moments the Voyager is aware of the Heat/Energy that fuels her Craft and that causes the contaminant-filled Mist to rise up from the Sea. She must Sail through the Mist, which contains Background Knowledge as well as man-made mind-pollutants. Each Moment pushes her further in her own Direction. She learns to Move in and through the Mist. As she gains enough confidence to See through the Mist she is actually nourished and energized by her own effort. She is undoublethinking her way out of fatherland, Breaking through to and Re-Calling her Original knowledge. She can do this when she recognizes that the illusions that are contaminating her mind and the minds of those around her are reversals of deep Background Reality, reversals which feed off and falsely imitate Elemental Images and Ideas.

I think it is because the all-male christian trinity is such a reversal that the lecture at Harvard and the talk in Madison were such powerful experiences. They were Pyrogenetic Paradigms of my later experiences of reversing this reversal.[5] I know that even Now the significance of these events may not be totally explicit to me, for such Misty Moments have a way of Unfolding their meanings more and more in the Spiraling that continues.*

Moreover, from a Fourth Galactic viewpoint I see something particularly ominous about the christian trinitarian reversal, namely its blocking of Realization of the Fourth Dimension. The christian trinitarian god is by dogmatic definition immutable/changeless. He is perfectly dead; his processions go nowhere. In contrast to this, Goddess symbolism has been moving and complex, often emphasizing swirling, Spinning quaternity as well as dynamic threefoldness.[6]

The Biophilic Fourth Dimension is about Movement and Depth. It signifies that which is hidden as well as that which is manifest. It is about the Be-Dazzling rootedness/context that makes a Sense of Direction and Unfolding possible. As Virginia Woolf wrote: "That was the real flower: part earth, part flower."[7] And, of course, the View from The Fourth Spiral Galaxy enables me to See that the "fearful symmetry" of the "Tyger burning bright in the forests of the night" and getting ready to spring was the perfect

---

*Thus in The Third Spiral Galaxy I would come to understand the christian trinity as a take-over and symbolic sex change of the Triple Goddess, and to see the mind-boggling implications of this reversal. The father, son, and holy ghost have been used to legitimate such atrocities as the witchcraze in Western Europe and the use of nuclear weapons. Godfather, Son, and Company continue to justify rape, genocide, and war with their trinity.

metaphor for the configuration of energies that characterized the Time of *Beyond God the Father.* It was during that Time and in that book that I identified the Moving power of the Final Cause, which I Now associate with the Fourth Dimension. The "Tyger" Forecasts/Foresymbols the Fearsome Pyrogenetic Focus and Power of Movement which is Realized by means of the Craft of the Fourth Dimension.

MY WORK AS A PIRATE

In the Course of The Second Spiral Galaxy I had just begun confronting the double crosses of male mysteries. It was a fast-moving time of beginning Breakthroughs. I had not yet had a chance to see all—or most—of the implications of my New Dis-coverings. For example, I did not yet explicitly see mySelf as a Pirate, even though I was actively engaged in that profession.

As I sailed further into the Mist I fought off the thought police who were patrolling the Subliminal Sea, such as university bore-ocrats and other aca-demented busybodies. I attacked "legitimate" vessels, for example, "scholarly" volumes used to transport materials that functioned to destroy my Tribe. Breaking into these vessels/containers, I wielded my Labrys to hack away the trappings used to conceal important meanings and messages from women. For example, in writing *Beyond God the Father* I hacked away false meanings of *transcendence, courage, revelation, revolution, sisterhood.*

I carried away armloads of the stuff the patriarchs had stolen from my Tribe and which they had converted/reversed to serve their own purposes.* Sometimes my Righteous Plundering involved reversing their reversals, such as the myth of the Fall—the myth of feminine evil, conceptualized as the doctrine of "original sin"—showing that the myth itself is evil, providing the setting for women's victimization by perpetuating hatred of women by both men and women. Sometimes it involved reclaiming ideas in order to place them in a clarifying context so they could be liberating for women— ideas such as "final cause" and "covenant." Darting through the Mist by means of my Craft I salvaged much material.

I set up shop, so to speak, in a comfortable cove, from which I had an excellent view of the Subliminal Sea. I felt at home there in the Elements, sorting out my material and shaping it into a work of my own creation. From Time to Time I sailed off on brief excursions, always returning with more ideas for my Work, which grew and took on clearer form with each new day. I found mySelf Re-Calling more and more—understanding ever more

---

*Later in my travels I would come upon a few Treasure Islands, such as Crete and Ireland, where some of women's Wonders had mistakenly been left intact by the robbers. I would be able to experience these firsthand. At this earlier Time, however, even though I had actually visited the aforementioned islands already in the Course of The First Spiral Galaxy, I was not yet prepared to discern the Presence of such Treasures.

deeply that women have had the power of Naming stolen from us. I gradually came to understand the enormity of the patriarchs' pillage of women's energy. This pillaging of energy was a necessary condition of their production of monstrous distortions, and the distortions themselves were designed to sap women's energy—by depleting our Self-esteem, by killing our memories, our hopes, our confidence, our courage. I realized that by distorting and erasing women's Past they had ravaged and purloined our Present and Future. I worked to reclaim our Reality.

Actually, in foreground terms, my Cove at the Time was my apartment on Commonwealth Avenue in Brighton (which I inhabited for thirteen years, beginning in 1966). This had been and continued to be the vortex of ever more intense intellectual and political activity. Here I was joined frequently by Cronies, and central among these in 1972 were, of course, the Tigers.

SOME BE-MUSING MOMENTS

There were many Be-Musing Moments when the Tigers were together in my Cove.* One beautiful evening in late summer or early fall of 1972 was especially Momentous. We were all sitting in my living room (which really was a Living Room—the Workshop where I was writing *Beyond God the Father*), and we were engaged in an intense discussion. It is possible that we were discussing the point which I Originally and frequently summarized in the one-liner: "If God is male, the male is God."

At any rate, Linda has reminded me that for her that evening was a Moment of Realizing that she couldn't be a christian any longer. It is possible that no one made that statement out loud, but it was absolutely clear to all of us. This does not mean that this was the first Time that it had been clear. But our various Moments of Realizing now came together with explosive force. All of our eyes/Eyes met—ten Eyes. We sat in complete silence for some Time as the sun set and the room grew dark. It was a Moment of "Interface of all the Realms."[8]

With my Fourth Galactic telescope I see such Moments as immeasurable communal Movements of breaking through the Mists of the Subliminal Sea. This does not mean that all the individuals there were Moving with the same speed or with equal force, but we were synchronously crossing Limen after Limen in our individual ways. We all were responding to the Call of the Wild, actively Unforgetting our participation in Be-ing. Separately and together we were on the Boundaries of many worlds.

Be-Musing means "be-ing a Muse for oneSelf and for Other Muses; refusing Musing to a-Musing scribblers; Spinning great dreams and reveries of Female creations, of Lesbian nations" (*Wickedary*).

It is true that the Harvard Memorial Church Exodus had occurred almost a year before this Time. The primary signification of that event had been Departure from the *institutions* of patriarchal religion. This Moment in 1972 was a distinct though related experience. We now Realized in our separate ways the depth of our transformation. We were not christians in any sense—not even "noninstitutional" christians. No way!

In the future some christians would try to claim me as perhaps a post-modern, secularized, gnostic, new age/old age catholic or christian—or whatever disguised variety of "beyond christian" christian happened to be in vogue. But—how can I say it clearly enough?—I was becoming *Other* than christian. I had not considered all of the implications yet, but I would continue in that direction, as subsequent chapters, and my subsequent books, demonstrate.

Of course the Tigers played a lot, in our own ineffable fashion. Sometimes we went out for dinner after class and before meetings. One favorite haunt was "Beacon Restaurant," now extinct. On some occasions we brought along our, uh, mascot. This was a green beanbag frog named François, an inhabitant of my apartment on Commonwealth Avenue. At such places as "the Beacon" we sometimes gave François his own place at the table, with a small plate. If anyone thought we were crazy, we could say: "Right!" After all, we constituted a cognitive minority of five—no, six.

At meetings of the "Women's Institute" of the BTI, sessions were sometimes tiresome, especially because a few new members were into Robert's Rules and the letter of the law. Linda, in particular, was inclined to develop headaches during these trying times. I recall vividly how she wore dark glasses under the fluorescent lights and leaned back with François on her forehead, functioning as a pseudo-ice pack.[9]

Indeed, an entire mythology developed around François. Emily tuned in to his "feelings" of solitude and found him a mate—a "female" green beanbag frog named Joan, who was on sale among the dented cans in a Cambridge supermarket. It went on like this for years, until François literally lost his beans and faded into oblivion.

My excursions from my Pirate's Cove in 1972 to the public realm were fairly wide-ranging.[10] I carefully attended to the reactions of these diverse audiences and carried this feedback home to the Cove.

One particular excursion was outstanding mainly for its bizarreness. I was asked to give a talk at the Eighth Annual Law Enforcement Seminar at the Statler Hilton in Boston. I am not sure why they invited me or why I accepted, but I do know that the event transpired on May 5, 1972, and that I spoke to a crowd of policemen. Probably having a "lay woman theologian" was thought to be "hip," or at least a demonstration of absence of sexism within their ranks. According to my recollection I was also asked to give the "invocation" but refused. Emily and Linda came along as my psychic Amazon bodyguards in that police-infested place. They accompanied me on stage and sat on each side of me. As Linda Re-Calls this phenomenon, their intent was "to Cast a Spell and expand the aura of Womanpower, demonstrating Presence that is beyond tokenism."[11] Of course, I would have gone on with it anyway, but my "bodyguards" added another dimension to the experience. I have almost complete amnesia about the content of my speech to the police[12] and have trouble believing that this actually happened, but it did. It was the sort of improbable thing that did occur in 1972.

TURNING MY SOUL AROUND

Most of the time I was back home in the Cove sorting out my loot, studying it, putting the pieces together. The Subliminal Sea continually offered me helpful bits of information. Sometimes ideas were inspired by conversations with friends. At Other times they were sparked by the Strange and synchronous/"coincidental" appearance of books and articles. It is clear that conversations with each and all of the Tigers wove a context of Hearing and Speaking in which a book such as *Beyond God the Father* could be created and flourish. Nelle Morton's Presence and influence also were immeasurable.

Often, when sitting down to write *Beyond God the Father,* I Heard/Be-Spoke to mySelf certain words, which constituted a powerful mantra/Spell. These words were: "I have to turn my soul around." I would Hear/Say these words in my mind often in the Course of writing. I know that on one level—the clearest and most explicit—this meant that I had to turn vigorously and decisively away from preoccupation with busyness. I had to turn my back on a distracting and draining range of vibrations—meaning preoccupation with the kind of interchange involved in a whole gamut of activities, including shopping, going to the dentist, arranging travel schedules, answering correspondence, examining bank statements, getting the car fixed, paying bills, et cetera.

Of course, I did manage to pay my bills (that was the bottom line), and I did the other necessary chores, but I did not let them take over. I had to wrench my soul free from the endless "roof brain" chatter associated with "lists of things to do." The way I experienced this psychically was expressed in the words: "I have to keep beta outside the door." "Beta" meant all that stuff pertaining to the world of busyness. I could literally see beta trying to push through my apartment door, which seemed to bend inward from its aggressive force.

The earlier part of the day belonged to beta, but as the afternoon wore on, my brain waves changed. The door was sealed shut. Once my soul was turned around I had entered another realm. As I sat at my typewriter, the inspiration came. What was happening, in fact, was that my Craft was departing from the linear world. It was Spiraling. So of course my soul was turning around . . . and around.

Sometimes the phone would ring, bringing messages from my friends. Frequently it would be Emily or Linda, each of whom introduced herSelf with her own distinctive version of a Tiger's growl. They, especially, were into the cosmic dimensions of this Metaphor, and we growled to each other in proud salutation, on the phone, on paper, and in person. Often the calls were from Jan, who brought important suggestions of books and articles to read, and of special passages relevant to what I was writing at the Moment. Just as my Craft seemed to be slowing down she would bring a load of fuel and I was off and away again.

Jan's comments on the work were not only scholarly but deeply thoughtful and discerning, characteristically laced with wry wit. Emily, the visionary, shared her dream world with me. We crossed the Boundaries between dreams and "reality" in unconventional conversations. Jean was more reserved, but her comments sparkled with gems of insight. It was she, for example, who stressed that women, having been denied equal access to the printed word, still have primarily an oral tradition. This became the first footnoted comment in the Preface to *Beyond God the Father,* where I explained that my references to conversations are meant to be a reminder of that tradition, as well as an effort to set precedent for giving women some of the credit due to them, finally. Barufaldi (Linda, that is) bounded into ideas with boundless enthusiasm and flashes of Witchy intuition.

Those conversations were Positively Weird. They were often introduced with a specific scholastic axiom, namely: "The final cause is the cause of causes, because it is the cause of the causality of all the other causes." These words would be said "out of the blue," so to speak. They were a mantra of the Tigers. No need for an explanation. The mantra/Spell was a philosophical axiom which I frequently tossed out in class, partly for fun. And now it had a New Meaning. Linda had said it: "*We* are the final cause."[13]

Together we formed a spunky, funky group and sort of had the world by its tail. We were a phenomenon of the early seventies and of a Moment whose Momentousness would be forever. We had found and were founders of Radical Feminism. We were our own Foresisters—although there had been thousands of others, of course. We knew that for us, at least, nothing would ever be the same again. We also believed that the world would never be the same. From a surface/foreground point of view we were dead wrong. But from a Fourth Galactic Perspective the Chance/Wager/Hope is that we were and are right. Because if the Vision is true, then the Hope is real. Because if the Moment was Momentous, its Momentum also *is* Momentous. In The Fourth Spiral Galaxy the Hope continues to Spiral, Here and Now, through the Mist, in the Direction of Be-Dazzling.

So I wrote and wrote my heart out. I wrote like a house afire. I knew that I was on the right Spiral. So it makes Sense, from a Fourth Galactic Point of Hearing, that even as I write this chapter I am still profoundly in accord with *Beyond God the Father.* Even though—and especially because—it belongs to an Other Galaxy, I understand it deeply.

Significantly, I went on many trips to Onset, Massachusetts, during the Time of writing the Breakthrough articles of 1972 (just as I had in 1971), and while Crafting *Beyond God the Father*. Onset, which is at the beginning/onset of Cape Cod, was the home of Gladys Custance, the Spiritualist medium who was co-pastor (together with her husband, Kenneth Custance) of the Spiritualist church in that town. As the reader will recall, I had first encountered Gladys Custance in 1970,* and her subsequent influence upon my life and work has been tremendous. I did not fully realize the extent of that impact in those early years.

Onset had/has attractive features, including an extraordinarily beautiful beach. I was irresistibly pulled by this place, drawn by its mellow, sweet vibes and haunting light, which were relaxing especially on sunny summer afternoons at the beach. Unlike most other resort towns at the Cape, it seemed to have died at about the turn of the century. It could be described as quaint and old-fashioned. It was and is, in fact, a center of tremendous Spiritual Power.

Frequently I went there alone for a swim and a couple of hours on the beach. Occasionally I went with all of the Tigers. Sometimes I went with Emily and Linda and sometimes with Jan. I also visited there with a number of other good friends. In fact, I seemed to be continually introducing my friends to the wonders of Onset.

In the early 1970s the water was sufficiently unpolluted, so that swimming was generally in the picture, together with picnics on the sand. Once when all of the Tigers were there we trooped into the "Ladies Room" of the Onset Hotel (now defunct and converted into condos) in order to change into our bathing suits. As we marched out, wearing our clothes over our suits, we were forced to go past a group of drinking bums at the bar. (These were of the variety that I would later call "snools.") One of these deadfellows slurred something like: "Have a good time in the bathroom, girls?" There was a long second of dead silence. Then Emily drawled (her Southern accent was still very pronounced, so to speak, in those days): "Why don't *you* go to the bathroom and get ahold of yourself?" There was another second of shocked silence. Then, in spite of themselves, the snool's buddies exploded in raucous laughter *at him*, and implicitly at themselves. We kept right on stalking haughtily past them and out the door.

This kind of gleeful triumph was typical of the Time. We were in the process of learning tactics for dealing with such assaults. It is significant that the Timing was perfect and our Victory complete. This became a Memorable Moment of Tiger lore—not at all incompatible with the mystical Background Moments associated with Onset and elsewhere. One Moment flowed into the Other. The Labrys-like combination of Exorcism and Ecstasy, a major theme of The Third Spiral Galaxy, was already coming into be-ing.

---

*See Chapter Five.

The matter of Timing had always been important to me. As I explained in The First Spiral Galaxy, ever since college days I have had a Sense of Timing which is related to unconscious/subliminal knowledge. I often referred to this Sense as "the little green man in my head." Later, on more sophisticated and complex levels, this Time-keeper became helpful in the complex work of writing and living Radical Feminist Philosophy. (Of course, I Now think of this creature as a little green woman—especially since she must accomplish more complicated and subtle Woman-identified tasks.) What she appears to do is arrange things so that my writing is in harmony with a wide context of interrelated happenings.* When the Time is right, the book can be written. *The Church and the Second Sex,* for example, appeared at the precise Moment when many women were eager for its Incendiary Message. So also, *Beyond God the Father* was written when its Time had arrived. And, of course, this was the Time of turning my soul around.

PIRACY, ALCHEMY, ATHLETICISM . . . BE-ING

As I have said, my work as a Positively Piratic Plunderer and Smuggler was essential for the creation of *Beyond God the Father*. I Righteously exhumed ideas from a wide variety of sources, giving all due credits, as a meticulous scholar should. I examined gems of partial insight (partial because confined within patriarchal trappings) in the writings of philosophers—among them Aristotle, Nietzsche, Whitehead—and in the works of theologians—especially Aquinas and Tillich. I took off with and from the findings of anthropologists such as Bachofen and Briffault—again with scrupulous scholarly integrity. I examined the theories of modern thinkers as diverse as Herbert Marcuse, Peter Berger, Paulo Freire, Thomas Szasz, and Jürgen Moltmann. I sorted out nuggets of partial, i.e., patriarchally distorted, knowledge and placed these in a Metapatriarchal context,† so that they could radiate richer meanings. This changing of context transformed the old limited and limiting meanings, so that New Meanings could be Dis-covered.

Thus my work as author of *Beyond God the Father* was not only that of a Pirate but also that of an Alchemist. Each time I returned from my adventures in the Mists of the Subliminal Sea I quickly settled down to work in my Cove and Conjured my Alchemical Craft. With this Craft I transformed the damaged but partially genuine gems of insight that I had acquired in my High Sea adventures. The secret of my Alchemical powers lay in my ability to Dis-cover and create an entirely Other setting for these treasures, that is, Radical Feminist Philosophy.

---

*Hence her work is profoundly connected with what I have come to call "the 11:12 phenomenon." See Chapter Five.

†The word *Metapatriarchal*◑ was not Dis-covered until later, but it describes the context of the writing of *Beyond God the Father*. It means "situated behind and beyond patriarchy; transformative of and transcending the Static State" (*Wickedary*).

My work in the Cove also involved—and of course still involves—Spiritual/Intellectual Athleticism. Naturally I used some of the bits and pieces of booty that Rightfully belongs to women in order to construct a kind of springboard, from which I dove into the depths of the Subliminal Sea. I then returned to the surface carrying clusters of deeply buried jewels of information that made it possible for me to see the Background of partial and foregrounded insights.

However, none of these aspects of the work, i.e., Piracy, Alchemy, Athleticism, fully explains the magical way that *Beyond God the Father* came into be-ing. Indeed, this very word, *be-ing,* is an example of the complex convergence that went into the making of that book. Since the Moment of my intuition of be-ing in adolescence (which I then, of course, would have spelled *being*) I had been on my round-about, that is, Spiraling, philosophical Quest. This had led me not only to pursue graduate study culminating in the doctorate in philosophy but to something beyond that. I was Moving in the direction of creating and participating in my own philosophy. Rather than being a follower or promoter of the philosophical system of any man, I wanted to break the Taboo and *be* a philosopher, mySelf. *Beyond God the Father* was a first incarnation of my *own* philosophy of be-ing, which was—and continues to Unfold as—an Elemental Radical Feminist Philosophy. My whole life had been leading to this.

It is obvious that this philosophy of be-ing has not been created in isolation, but rather in a context of participation. My Quest has converged with the Quests of myriads of Sister scholars across Time. My colleagues/collaborators included/include Matilda Joslyn Gage, Jane Ellen Harrison, Mary Wollstonecraft, Simone de Beauvoir, Pauli Murray, Elizabeth Gould Davis. My Cronies while I was creating *Beyond God the Father* included not only these and countless Other Foresister Pirates of the Past, but also contemporary Cohorts such as Nelle Morton, Betty Farians, Robin Morgan, and the Tigers. These Companions all cooperated in our mutual task of Discovering the Context.

The bonding in Sisterhood in the early seventies and conversations that ensued led to a consensus, with Nelle Morton especially, that Be-ing is a Verb.* To stress that Ultimate Reality is a Verb, and an intransitive Verb, I began to hyphenate it: *Be-ing.*†

---

*This insight occurred in a conversation with Nelle, probably in 1972, in her home in Madison, New Jersey.

†The word *Be-ing*◉ refers to "the constantly Unfolding Verb of Verbs which is intransitive, having no object that limits its dynamism." It is "the Final Cause◉, the Good who is Self-communicating, who is the Verb from whom, in whom, and with whom all true movements move" (*Wickedary*). When *be-ing*◉ is not capitalized, it refers to "actual participation in the Ultimate/Intimate Reality—Be-ing, the Verb" (*Wickedary*). In *Beyond God the Father* I did not yet consistently hyphenate *Be-ing* or *be-ing* in order to spell out, so to speak, my intention of Naming the Verb and participation in the Verb.

THE UNIFYING THEME
OF *BEYOND GOD THE FATHER:*
THE WOMEN'S REVOLUTION
AS AN ONTOLOGICAL MOVEMENT

At the very core of the philosophy of *Beyond God the Father* is the Realization that the women's revolution is about participation in Be-ing. That is, it is an ontological movement. As outsiders, or extra-environmentals, women are especially equipped to confront the structured evil of patriarchy. So, as I wrote, women are in a unique sense called to be the bearers of existential courage in society. In its deepest sense, this implies Breakthrough to Realization of the existential conflict between the female Self and patriarchal structures that have given crippling "security." Women acting upon this knowledge confront the "anxiety of nonbeing,"* and this confrontation is revelatory, driving consciousness beyond the fixation upon "things as they are." "Courage to be is the key to the revelatory power of the feminist revolution."[14]

Clearly, I was using Paul Tillich's *The Courage to Be* as a springboard. But whereas his analysis was restricted to universalist, humanist categories, *Beyond God the Father* released the ideas into the context of the social, political, ontological realities of women's lives under patriarchy.

The basic thesis of *Beyond God the Father,* that the movement for women's liberation is an ontological movement, is the consistent, organic, unifying theme from the beginning to the final page, where I advocate "forging the great chain of be-ing in sisterhood that can surround nonbeing, forcing it to shrink back into itself." Moreover:

> The power of sisterhood is not war-power. There have been and will be conflicts, but the Final Cause causes not by conflict but by attraction. Not by the attraction of a Magnet that is All There, but by the creative drawing power of the Good Who is self-communicating Be-ing, Who is the Verb from whom, in whom, and with whom all true movements move.[15]

It is important to keep in mind this unifying theme when studying the many and diverse Breakthrough concepts in *Beyond God the Father*. Among these interrelated ideas are: revelatory courage; the unfolding of God; living "on the boundary"; new space; new time; power of presence and power of absence; methodolatry and methodicide; the "original sin" of women; sisterhood as revolution; the scapegoat syndrome; the Great Silence (about a woman-centered society before patriarchy); patriarchal strategies for stopping women's movement, such as reversal, particularization, universalization, trivialization, spiritualization; the Second Coming of women; the Second Coming of women as the Antichrist; Christolatry; The Most Unholy

---

*I would Now write "anxiety of nonbe-ing."

Moment? Does the Wind have a Sense of humor? The answer, clearly, is yes. I am reminded also of my role as Pirate on the High Sea of subliminal knowledge. All right, so this was merely a paved highway, and I was sailing with Cronies in my beautiful gold 1967 Plymouth Barracuda. So what? High Sea or High Way, the fact is that I was on my True Course as Pirate and here—in the form of unexpected treasures on the Way—was more confirming evidence of that fact. Moreover, my beloved Great Barracuda (for which I was rather notorious) was—despite her fishy name—quite at home on the highway.

I returned to my regular teaching at Boston College in September 1973, knowing that *Beyond God the Father* would be out in November. There was excitement in the Atmosphere.

That academic year I taught courses with titles such as "Religion and the Oppression of Women," "God-language in Modern Philosophy," and "Women's Liberation and Ethics." These were packed, and nearly all the students who signed up for them were women. I did also teach other courses, including "Revolution and the Struggle to Be Human." Nearly all the students in this course were male. It seemed that not too many women were interested in struggling to be human.

Jan Raymond, who was writing her Ph.D. dissertation under my direction, was assigned to be my teaching assistant, which relieved some of the pressure on me, especially of reading papers and grading. During the second semester of that year Jan also taught courses in Medical Ethics at BC on a part-time basis, as a teaching fellow. But Jan was no fellow. She was a Sister Radical Feminist teaching courses in the same department and her Presence as a colleague was encouraging. Too encouraging. I had great hopes that the bonding of women teaching Feminist Studies could happen even in that institution. I did not yet fully realize how threatening to the priestly and academic patriarchs were the combined Presences of two women who refused to sell out and become tokens, choosing instead to follow the paths of Feminism and Woman-identified bonding. But the story of the events leading to that Realization belongs to a later chapter.*

Meanwhile, my dashing around the country on the lecture circuit continued. The range and variety of institutions visited was expanding in new directions and the pace was intensifying. One astonishing tour that took place in October 1973 involved speaking as a "Visiting Scholar" at six colleges in the vicinity of Richmond, Virginia, in three days. I gave one lecture each afternoon and evening. The colleges were Randolph-Macon College for Women, Sweet Briar College, Mary Baldwin College, Longwood College, Bridgewater College, and Madison College. I was rapidly chauffered around to and from these places by a dashing driver. When, upon return-

---

*See Chapter Eleven.

ing to Boston, I recounted the story of this experience to my friends, one of these—Robin Hough—elaborately portrayed his impression of my chauffeur in Virginia as a sort of celestial motorman who helped me to deliver my cosmic messages. According to this graphic depiction, I dropped in at each of these strange places from Outer Space, as it were, set off my explosives (which I would Now call Time Bombs), and soared off with alarming alacrity.

AFTER PUBLICATION I:
REVIEWS AND RESPONSES FROM WOMEN

Beyond God the Father appeared in November 1973. It was very favorably reviewed in a large number of newspapers and journals. Widely read publications that gave it positive reviews included *The New York Times Book Review, The New York Review of Books, The Washington Post Book World.* On the local scene, there was the unforgettable review entitled "A Woman's Prophetic 'No'" in the *Boston Sunday Globe* (1/13/74). This was co-authored by Brita Stendahl, then lecturing at the Radcliffe Institute, and her husband Krister Stendahl, long-time Dean of Harvard Divinity School. And there were many more.[26] Yet, for almost a year after the book's publication, acquaintances in New York City said the only way they could obtain a copy was by writing to the publisher and asking to review it. In other words, there were distribution problems.

The book, however, could not be stopped. It was quickly getting around the United States . . . and beyond. Evidence of this sort of quiet Wildfire (which has never been put out) came largely in the form of extremely moving letters, mostly from women.

My Amazon Assistant who helped in answering these early letters was Linda, who officially was my "research assistant" during the academic year 1973–74. This "research" helped Linda to pay the rent during her one year in the "joint doctoral program" of Boston College and Andover Newton Theological School. (She subsequently fled the program in order to avoid a situation which to her felt like brain death.) At any rate, we often read the letters together in Wonder.

Having searched for and found my files of *Beyond God the Father* letters, I am again—Now—Be-Dazzled by the words of these women. These letters are entirely different from those responding to *The Church and the Second Sex,* published five years earlier. These are written in an entirely Other dimension. Although a few focus on agreeing with or disputing "points," this is not the general tenor.

There are certain recurrent ideas in these letters, themes which have repeated themselves hauntingly in my Memory. I have not needed an excellent power of recall to Re-Call them, since many of these themes have been repeated over the years in remarks by women, especially after public lectures. I call these recurring ideas/feelings that were conveyed by women in response to *Beyond God the Father* "themes" because they cannot be pinned down—or up—to abstractions or to emotional reactions. They could be called "melodies." They are not identical with each other, but they are profoundly interrelated. They reinforce and complement one another. In a Sense, or in many Senses, they can be said to harmonize, like Re-Callings of the Wild.

These letters were—and continue to be—ineffably encouraging, beckoning me to Move onward, reinforcing my Courage to Write. They told me beautifully, intricately, that there are many of us. They said: Write on!

I answered some but not all of these. I tried. But I was in a perpetual energy crisis—a condition that has impeded my answering correspondence concerning every one of my books. My life as a professor in the oppressively mad world of academentia and as a public lecturer, activist, and Wild woman demands energy. And, in a special way, my life as a philosopher/writer demands energy.

So I have made choices—then and Now. I have chosen to put my Gynergy into my books, which are, in a Sense, letters posted from my Craft to the women of my Tribe. In these missives from the High Sea I have tried to answer their/our/my questions and raise more—ever more—hair-raising ones, while sailing on the Quest beyond *Beyond God the Father*.

Re-turning Now to these letters, I note some of their themes from a Fourth Galactic viewpoint. For one thing, the correspondents explain in a variety of thoughtful and eloquent ways that on some level they were Discovering what they already knew. Clearly, the repeated affirmations of this Re-cognition came out of the Subliminal Sea. A woman from Nebraska wrote:

> You took the top off my head. You electrified me. I felt as if—this may sound contradictory—I were *discovering* things for the first time and *recognizing* them as authentic, recognizing them as things I had so long felt myself. What a reinforcing experience! Basically, I guess, I felt that I myself developed greater confidence in my own perceptions because they were yours too.

That woman, clearly, had experienced herSelf as a cognitive minority of one. But now her Time had come: she could join forces. This theme of women recognizing their *own* hidden thoughts and feelings was expressed over and over again. One woman wrote that the experience of reading *Beyond God the Father* had been like walking through the garden of her own mind. A woman who was—and presumably still is—a potter wrote:

> Every few sentences I am underlining and saying: "Yes. Yes, this makes sense out of my own experience."

A woman from Colorado had this to say:

I remember that I felt almost incandescent after reading it for the first time. It was everything that I knew and felt in my heart but could never put into words.

A second recurrent theme was the insistence of women writing these letters that they had never written such letters before. I believed them and I understand why they felt impelled to write. This motivation was rooted in what I would Now call an E-motional Explosion of their own subliminal knowledge. They were impelled to express this, to Be-Speak.

A third theme was exuberant, volcanic Hope. As one correspondent from a town in Massachusetts wrote:

I feel like we might really make it. I feel like we might really have a *right* to exist.

Combined with expressions of Hope a fourth theme was often in evidence. There were clear descriptions of the sanctions for acting on that Hope. A reader from Vermont expressed all this:

Reading your book, *Beyond God the Father*, made me feel once again that maybe there is hope for those of us who can no longer function in this society authentically, especially when you speak with such authority about the Cosmic Covenant we could create in the nothingness that lies beyond patriarchal space. But how to do it? I've tried so many times all without success. And I'm growing tired for trying. The traps are so subtle, the punishments for daring to speak so cruel. Yet I know, you see, exactly what you are saying. And I know that those of us who have "seen" and felt the urgency of this responsibility must DO something. . . .

At this point I am feeling so isolated and well understand the dangers of this to my psychic, emotional and intellectual health, and of course feel a great urgency to protect myself from . . . creeping despair disorders.

I have cited this letter at length because it could have been written in 1984 or in 1992. It was written in the spring of 1974.

Yet the sense of exhaustion and isolation was not overwhelming in these letters. A fifth theme was the experience of energy surges:

I've just finished Chapter Two, and I am bursting with energy. . . . As we DREAM, so shall we BE.

The themes of excitement, exhilaration, vitality run throughout this correspondence. One woman wrote: "Energy flows wider and fuller." It was and is clear to me that the flow of energy was experienced because women were confronting their own subliminal E-motional knowledge.

Such experience of energy/Gynergy implies a sixth theme, which was very explicitly expressed in several letters—that is, coming into contact with one's own psychic powers. Some women wrote of their Sense of expansion of spiritual powers and described experiences of clairvoyance and synchronicities. These women were Living the Ecstatic process of reclaiming our own powers. As a college teacher in New Jersey put it:

I am moved to write you that I didn't read your books (*The Church and the Second Sex* and *Beyond God the Father*). I danced them, lived them, and celebrated them. . . . You have taught me that the church doesn't own transcendence nor the questions that surround the transcendent.

I think that the author of those words already *knew* this. It was simply that reading these books Be-Spoke her into saying/writing "out loud" what she subliminally knew. She felt legitimated in her own understanding.

A final—and hardly the least—theme is Lesbianism. Lesbian Feminists recognized its author as one of their own. Yet very few chided me for not Coming Out yet. Their criticism of my section on "Heterosexuality-Homosexuality: The Destructive Dichotomy" in Chapter Four was good natured—and it was right.[27] Anyhow, as one Lesbian wrote:

We promote you as our articulation.

Right. Right on. And I did really Be-Speak about that later.

AFTER PUBLICATION II:
BACKSIDES, BACKLASH, AND BEYOND

Shortly after the appearance of *Beyond God the Father* peculiar events happened around Boston College. One of these "happenings" was a publication party held at Andover Newton Theological School, attended by the faculty and administration of the Joint Doctoral Program of ANTS and BC.[28] The authors supposedly being honored were Professor Roger Hazelton of Andover Newton, who had recently published a new book, and myself.

I recall vividly that although the Andover Newton faculty were courteous and gracious to me, my male "colleagues" from BC, on the whole, were not. A few stood with their backs to me throughout. Reflecting upon this phenomenon, I think it must have been somewhat difficult for these fellows to "circulate" while displaying only their derrieres in my direction. I remember in particular the large behind of one fellow, notorious for his wangling ways, who managed to help himself repeatedly to refreshments, which required passing me with his fundament pointed precisely and prettily toward me. I wondered what sort of social coercion (ecumenism, perhaps?) brought these lads to such a party held in my honor, and motivated such bizarre behavior. Were they mortally offended that I had written another book, and—worst of all—that it was already a success?[29]

Of course this display of tail feathers could be interpreted merely as a befuddled and disoriented mating ritual of peacock-identified professors. But there is a far more straightforward explanation that occurs to me Now. The exposition of backsides was, I think, an announcement of intention, a prefiguring, so to speak, of the backlash to come.

Backlash did rear its ugly behind at a meeting of the senior faculty of the theology department, comprised of about twelve apostolic men and myself.

This group of men and I sat around a sort of seminar table. One of them started it. Gazing around knowingly he said: "Let's see. We don't have any-one in our department who is doing anything in philosophy, do we?" Since I was the only one among them who had a doctorate in philosophy* and who had taught the subject for years and who had just published a work of philos-ophy that had been widely acclaimed, I was shocked. I also realized that I was in a classic no-win situation. Had I protested: "Wait a minute! I've just published . . ." they would have stared vacantly and/or sneered. (I knew this tactic from other experiences.)† Had I walked out in a huff at that point, I would have felt defeated. I knew and they knew that I had no ally in that room. There was no one with whom I could even make eye contact and laugh. They were bonded solidly/stolidly in this ritual of erasure. So I toughed it out and stared straight ahead in silence, mentally already out of that room, waiting for the Moment when I could Leave physically and Rave with my friends.

These men could not understand that they were giving me rich material for analysis. What I was living through was not dissimilar to the experiences of many Other women who have displayed strength and belief in their Selves—not only in academia/academentia, but also at board meetings/ bored meetings of all kinds. What I was living through was linked to the experiences of women who have struggled to save their Selves when patron-ized, battered, and/or raped by predatory pops, pimps, or husbands, or when undermined by sickening physicians, pompous priests, jockocratic judges, or bullying bosses, or when simply drained by droning clones or sapped by sneering snools in the street.

I may not consciously have realized this then, but I do Now: *All* of those women were in that room with me then, and they are still with me Now.

They were saying . . . They are saying: "Pay attention to this. This is very important for you to understand. Help us to understand. Analyze this. Spit it out. Rage. Weep. Laugh. Create a language to express what this means. Show the connections. Make us see the connections. We have all been here. At the conference table. At the dinner table. We who are so able—called 'unable.' Put your own cards on the table. You are not alone. You will never be alone. We are with you. We *are* you. We will always be with you. Even when we don't understand—or when you don't understand —we are with you. Write on. Please keep writing on."

And so, of course, I did. Of course I did.

---

*My doctoral dissertation in philosophy had, of course, been published and had been acquired by university and seminary libraries in the U.S. as well as in Europe. See Chap-ter Five.

†See for example Chapter Five.

MY "FEMINIST POSTCHRISTIAN INTRODUCTION" TO *THE CHURCH AND THE SECOND SEX:* APPROACHING THE WATERSHED YEAR

During the summer of 1974 I wrote my "Autobiographical Preface to the 1975 Edition" and my "Feminist Postchristian Introduction" to *The Church and the Second Sex,* which was scheduled to appear in paperback in the winter of 1975. This itself was a Strange experience of Time Travel, anticipating to some degree my Present Intergalactic Tour.

Back in 1970 my publisher (Harper & Row) had informed me that *The Church and the Second Sex* probably would not go into a third printing. It did go out of print, and in 1971 the rights for the book had reverted to me. The trauma and anguish caused by this obliteration of my work were enormous.* Then, in January 1974 Leslie Moore, an editor at Harper Colophon Books (an imprint of Harper & Row), wrote to me, expressing great interest in bringing this book out in paperback.[1]

PLUNDERING THE EARLY DALY:
A BE-LAUGHING LARK

So the decision was in my hands, and the situation posed an interesting dilemma. Since I had moved far beyond the stage of Feminist analysis represented by that 1968 book, I didn't want to perpetuate ideas with which I now disagreed. On the other hand, my first Feminist book contained valuable information, which would be difficult for most women to find elsewhere, and at the same time it had itself become an important historical document, representing a significant stage of thinking and analysis.

So I decided to bring it out again. As I wrote in the new "Autobiographical Preface":

> Since I was, in an earlier incarnation, the author of that book, I am in a unique position to bring it forth again in a new light, to tell its story and then, in the new introduction, to become its critic and reviewer. And so it was the Morning of the Second Daly. I saw that it was a good idea.[2]

---

*I have described that experience in The First Spiral Galaxy (Chapter Five).

And Now, more than ever, I See that it was a good idea. Once again, the theme that seems to recur so often in my life was manifesting itself with Be-Dazzling clarity: I was Lucky that it had all turned out this way, very Lucky.

Writing the "Autobiographical Preface" and the "Feminist Postchristian Introduction" that summer was a tremendous High. I cackled with glee as I pounded the typewriter. Even typos were inspired. In the passage cited above, for example, I had intended to write "Morning of the Second Day." But unconsciously I typed the right word. It was a message, one might say, from the Subliminal Sea.* This was indeed a Second Daly who was now writing about *The Church and the Second Sex* as comparable to "the journal of a half-forgotten foremother, whose quaintness should be understood in context and treated with appropriate respect."[3] I actually did refer to the early Daly as "she" and "her," wondering "out loud," so to speak, why any woman would want equality in the church. *I* had known for three or four Woman-Light years that a woman struggling for equality in the catholic church, or in any christian church, is involved in an inherently contradictory situation. As I now had come to see it, the entire system of myths, symbols, creeds, dogmas of christianity contradicts the idea and the possibility of equality.

Despite my efforts to remain respectful and tolerant, I was truly befuddled by the early Daly's apparent obtuseness:

> Flipping through a few pages, I noted that the author had used the rather pompous editorial "we" instead of "I" and had written "they" to refer to women, instead of "we." Why did she say "we" when she meant "I" and "they" when she meant "we"? I noted with a sense of embarrassment for her that she used the term "man" as if it were a generic term. I perceived that she had hoped to reform christianity.[4]

I still quite agree with my wry and extensive critique of the early Daly in the "Feminist Postchristian Introduction." I also agree with my whimsical caveats as the 1975 Daly concerning my own criticisms of that quaint, half-forgotten foremother. I was right to temper these criticisms, as when, for example, I wrote: "I think that in fairness I should admit that in her circumstances I would have done no better."[5] However, my perspective Now is not totally identical with that of the author of the "Feminist Postchristian Introduction," who was writing in the Course of The Second Spiral Galaxy. At that Time, my sense of separation from The First Galactic Daly, that is, "her," was acute. I think that Now I understand "her" even better than did her Second Galactic critic.

My point in going into this is to introduce a reminder of the way I Presently Re-member the adventures of all the Galaxies recorded in this

---

*The copy editor at Harper, unfortunately, failed to grasp the message and changed my "typo," i.e., *Daly*, back to the biblical *Day*. Luckily I caught his or her error when proofreading the galley, and changed it back to *Daly*.

book. This Re-membering Dis-closes a Sense of Direction that has always been there, becoming ever more explicit as it has Unfolded. In the Light/Sound/Scent of this Sense I can recognize my identity with the Voyager of both The First and The Second Spiral Galaxies in the Powerfully Present Now. In Other words: I am she.

By the Power of Re-membering I Realize that the writing of my "Feminist Postchristian Introduction" was in fact a way of introducing mySelf to the problems, perils, and challenges of thinking, writing, feeling, be-ing Postchristian. This exercise was indeed my own individual Introduction to Postchristian Explorations. It was, after all, written just shortly before my Leap into The Third Spiral Galaxy. I was then almost at the beginning of the next Galaxy.

I had, of course, introduced the "Postchristian" concept before, in my paper on "Post-Christian [*sic*] Theology," delivered at the Annual Meeting of the American Academy of Religion in November 1973. In that paper, which had been offered as a "footnote" to *Beyond God the Father,* I had been very direct:

> I propose that we face the possibility of a contradiction inherent in the idea "feminist Christian theologian." I suggest that the idea "feminist theologian" implies an evolutionary leap in consciousness beyond "Christian" and that the word "feminist" does something to the meaning content of the word "theologian." . . .
>
> After stepping outside the circle of Christian theology we find ourselves in unexplored territory.[6]

Now, in 1974, I had to introduce mySelf by means of *praxis* to this way of be-ing and writing in unexplored territory because, as usual, I had no role models readily available. I had to become Self-taught through this and Other Acts of Be-Speaking. Certainly, there had been other women who had "left the church." Simone de Beauvoir had become an atheist and saw little or no value in religion. But "Postchristian," to me, did not mean merely "atheist." I longed passionately for the transcendence that was held prisoner and choked by religion and theology and for the emergence of *Feminist* philosophy/theology. As I had written in the 1973 AAR paper:

> Tillich described himself as working "on the boundary" between philosophy and theology. It appears that a feminist's work should be not merely on the boundary *between* these (male-created) disciplines, but on the boundaries *of* both, because it speaks out of the experience of that half of the human species that has been represented in neither.[7]

What this work involves is risking raising the questions that arise from women's process of becoming, which to the male-controlled theological and philosophical establishment are nonquestions. So I had also written:

> For some of us the transcendence question mattered, matters, will matter so much that "changing the subject" means risking the nonquestions that theolo-

gians cannot stand to hear. I do mean *risking*. Not only because this is dangerous for one's personal survival (job, health, bread). I mean especially *risking failure* to follow through on our own deepest, most authentic insights; risking failure in the most important undertaking of our lives, which is to ask the best nonquestions possible.[8]

These passages from the earlier paper are helpful, I think, in offering a glimpse of the intellectual/spiritual/E-motional Source/Background of my "Feminist Postchristian Introduction," which was an example of such working on the Boundary and of such risking.

As I have said, that Act of Writing was an extraordinary High. Every Moment of every day was precious and I jealously guarded my Time. Each day I happily hurried to my typewriter, knowing that my Muse was right there, waiting and raring to go. I was not willing to be distracted, to lose track of my Muse, to become a-Mused. It was an experience of Time that I would later Name "Tidal Time."[9]

Of course, I took "time off." But that was so I could run home to Real Time. If I dashed to the beach, basked in the sun, swam in the salt water, that was well and good: the Voice of the Tide sent me back to my typewriter, back to my task, which was not really distinguishable from play. It was a Be-Laughing Lark.

I giggled unashamedly at the early Daly while doing an extremely serious analysis of her work. I experienced no contradiction in this. Perhaps the experience was comparable to how a snake feels when she sheds her skin. Perhaps it was not comparable to anything. But I was indeed shedding a lot of foreground fears and fixations that had afflicted the early Daly. In other words, I was shedding layers of nothingness, and therefore experiencing a Lightness of be-ing. I was enjoying a great Breakthrough into the shimmering light of Be-Dazzling. By this writing I was eclipsing my former foreground phobias with the brilliance of Background be-ing. So *of course* it was fun.

Was my writing of the "Feminist Postchristian Introduction" an Act of Piracy? Yes, Positively. Having shamelessly assumed my rightful place as the world's leading Dalyan scholar and disciple I righteously Plundered her work. I salvaged and praised the things I could agree with.

In addition, I used her book as an opportunity to criticize ideas that I could by then see were holding women back. I did this benevolently:

> It is my opinion that Daly would have listened to these views and considered them, were I able to make such a time trip into the past and make myself visible and audible. But unfortunately, voices from the future are harder to hear than those of the past. Here is her book, solid and visible before me. I have the distinct advantage of understanding her better than she could comprehend me.[10]

Thus I made clear my vantage point and my position of authority in this matter. I used the device of the "Feminist Postchristian Introduction" to Smuggle to women important New knowledge. By explaining, point by point, my differences with the early Daly I blazed a trail across the seven Woman-Light years that separated me from the time of that "reformist" writing of the past. By doing this sympathetically, I tried to convey my own intimate understanding of the "Christian Feminist" position as well as the reasons for my conclusion that both rigorous logic and experience, if honestly and courageously attended to, inexorably lead to the dismissal of this position as inherently self-contradictory. As Pirate, I Smuggled to women my map of the Way Out of the impossible doublebinds of doublethink that I myself had experienced.

It was important for the success of this Smuggling operation that the appearance of the New edition of *The Church and the Second Sex,* specifically its frontispiece and cover, convey the accurate, powerful clues that would attract readers who were ready to receive its messages. The frontispiece of the 1975 edition, designed by Emily, had several important elements. There was the head of a woman, with her hair streaking behind her, flying above and away from the church, represented by a church building with a steeple. Superimposed on the woman's head was the women's symbol, with a clenched fist extending into its circle. The church was circumscribed by the masculine symbol, with its arrow pointing upward, and the church steeple was erect within the arrow. The drawing was/is very powerful visually. As I examine it Now I admire its clarity and absolute absence of ambivalence. It says directly that the Spirit/Spirits of women are departing from the church. In fact it says that we are already Out and soaring away with awesome power and speed.

The cover, ultimately, was remarkably good. At first, the publisher was going to bestow upon my book a cover which sported a woman's head with bizarre wrappings around it. The background appeared to be a pale blue sky with clouds which showed through spaces in the woman's head, which made her look something like a lobotomized "air head."* When I saw this I stared in horror, and then called an emergency meeting of the Tigers. My Cohorts and I agreed that the cover illustration and print should be red and black against a white background. Mary Lowry and I examined typefaces at a local shop, settling on "Hobo" as the most imaginative. This typeface suggested originality and a kind of spookiness, and there was something comic about it. It was perfect. So we pasted up a dummy cover.[11]

I flew down to New York at my own expense to deliver the product and argue strongly for its acceptance. This was on August 19, 1974. The women I had to deal with at Harper's were very agreeable and cooperative. So through our combined efforts and ingenuity that aspect of the book's coming into be-ing was, so to speak, covered.

---

*Significantly, the artist had forgotten to add under the title: "With a New Feminist Postchristian Introduction by the Author."

SOME POSTCHRISTIAN TRAVELS AND ADVENTURES

Having written that Time-traveling Time Bomb I was ready for some more earthly travel and adventure. My lecture travels were enlightening, especially in the realm of understanding environmental destruction.

In *Beyond God the Father* I had written a passage entitled "Earth, Air, Fire, Water: Ecology and the Cosmic Covenant," calling for a Great Refusal of rapism, which involves "refusal to rape earth, air, fire, water, that is, refusal to objectify and abuse their power."[12] I had warned that nuclear reaction threatens our lives and the life of the planet and had cautioned that if we remained locked in the "Looking Glass Society" (patriarchal mirror world of deadly reversals and projections) "life *will* depart from this planet."[13] These insights had come from reading, discussions, and personal reflection. In late 1974, however, I was introduced more directly to the reality I had glimpsed and foreglimpsed.

In August I gave an address at a symposium on "Women and the Environment" held at Gonzaga University in Spokane, Washington, in connection with Expo '74, which was billed as a major series of International Symposia on environmental issues. This informative context provided a general and gentle introduction to my next visit to the state of Washington, which was in early October.

On October 3 I went to speak at Richland, Washington. I knew nothing about Richland and was completely ignorant of what I was flying into. The program ("Community Seminar") in which I had been invited to participate was called "1974–1984, Decade of Choice." There was a clue in this, but I couldn't possibly have understood the context until I arrived and had spent some hours in Richland. I flew into Seattle and then took a small commuter plane (Execuair) into Richland. Stepping out of the plane I found myself in the dazzling early afternoon sunshine gazing off into fields of grasses waving in the wind. But then I noticed that the beautiful fields were fenced off—by barbed wire as I recall—and that there were uniformed fellows and warning signs near the fences. I did not understand why I couldn't stroll into that invitingly beautiful golden land. I did not yet know that millions of gallons of radioactive waste were stored there.

Gradually strange bits of information were given to me as I was driven to my motel and during the ensuing hours. For example, I was told that the people of Richland were proud of the enormous fruits and vegetables that were raised in the area, and whose growth was facilitated by the wonderful warm water coming from the nearby nuclear reactor. It also appeared that nearly everyone in Richland was opposed to the Nuclear Regulatory Commission.

I recall sitting in an auditorium waiting to give my speech. I was preceded by a buddhist monk who spoke—endlessly it seemed to me—on flower arrangement. I remember staring in shock, wondering what I was doing there and how I would get out of this one. I did go through with it, of course, speaking from *Beyond God the Father.*

Later that evening the two women who had organized the event took me out for an unforgettable evening at a local bar. A middle-aged woman wearing a wig played music from the 1940s on an organ (or piano—I'm not sure which), and couples danced as if they were in a stupor. The stiff movements and blank faces of the couples made me think of dancing corpses.

While I stared in horror, my companions described the lives and mentality of the inhabitants of this town, which is the location of Hanford Reservation, "home" of nuclear generating plants and of the infamous huge high-level radioactive waste storage facility, of which the residents of Richland were very proud. These people lived very much in a dead-time zone, glorying in their role in atomic energy research that had led to the manufacture of atomic bombs in the forties. The high school football team called themselves "the Atomic Bombers" and wore sweat shirts bearing the mushroom cloud as an emblem.

My companions also explained that men and women were almost segregated in that place. The husbands, they said, went off to do their top secret nuclear research every day and had to hide all information from their wives, all or most of whom were seeing psychiatrists. (I was sure that some women must have been doing such research also, but I don't remember that topic being discussed.)

The town was pathologically pro-nuclear beyond belief, and the women who invited me were trying to find a way to get out of there with their children. Their purpose in inviting me was, of course, to raise consciousness. Having had my own consciousness considerably raised/razed by that unusual day and evening, I gave my second talk on the following morning on "The Women's Revolution and the Future." Then I flew off, carrying with me a permanently altered state of awareness.

I Now recognize the women who organized this "Community Seminar" as Pirates who Plundered its funding in order to Smuggle me in. In return, I Smuggled as much information to Richland as I could, and I Plundered that place for the real top secret information—the still largely disguised fact of the creeping madness of nuclearism, and I Smuggled it to women.*

---

*Many years later—on May 23, 1988, to be more precise—when I was in Portland, Oregon, for the purpose of speaking at Portland State University I met a woman at a potluck supper who had grown up in Richland and had attended high school there. I was excited to meet her, especially when she confirmed everything that I had learned in 1974, and more. She confirmed that women as well as men did research at Hanford, and told me about people there who had cancer but denied vehemently that it had anything to do with their work and/or location. She described her high school class ring, which sported as its insignia a mushroom cloud. This woman, who was about thirty, had fled Richland as soon as possible after finishing high school. Our meeting was, for me, a Strange encounter, which helped me to Re-member my impressions of that scene of horror.

For years my students have heard the story of Richland and its corpse people. We have discussed its significance as a symbol of something larger and more hidden than Richland itself. This account became part of my treasure trove of true adventure stories, which includes the story of my 1969 encounter in Washington, D.C., with the "Futurist" who "optimistically" predicted the end of the "X-factor" (free will) within twenty years from that time.

There were other interesting lecture trips that fall, which I viewed as Amazonian escapades.[14] Moreover, *Beyond God the Father* was issued in paperback, which made it accessible to more women, and more likely to be assigned in classes. Despite these distracting attractions, there was a heaviness in the air.

MEANWHILE ON THE "HOME" FRONT

In September 1974, having sent my "Autobiographical Preface" and "Feminist Postchristian Introduction" off to the publisher, I had returned to teach my classes at Boston College. My classes in Feminist Ethics were packed with excited and exciting students. My course in "Philosophical Foundations for Revolutionary Ethics" involved strenuous study and analysis of philosophical texts.

Since I was aware that promotion to the rank of full professor—with its attendant salary raise—was, to say the least, overdue in my case, I made inquiries with the department chair, Robert Daly, s.j. (no relation) and discovered that the full professors had already chosen their own candidates. I was told, however, that since I was an associate professor with tenure I could apply on my own initiative. The full professors in the department would of course judge my application "objectively." Their objective decision would then be passed on to the equally objective promotions committee of the College of Arts and Sciences. Non-full professors in the department would be consulted but could not vote.

The whole atmosphere surrounding my application for promotion was murky. The fact that I had to put myself up rather than being "invited" or "presented" (the obfuscating jargon which the "full" professors chose to describe their "objective" mode of selection) was not a good sign. Still, I knew that it was Time to take a stand. I had published two major books and many articles, had devoted more than my share of time and energy to committees, and had taught with great success. So that October I did apply.

Among the documents that I had to "submit" were, of course, my curriculum vitae, copies of publications, and copies of student evaluations. I had accumulated hundreds of evaluations over the years, and the majority of these, from both female and male students, were extremely positive. Since I had begun teaching Radical Feminist courses in 1971, more and more of my students had been women. After I returned from my sabbatical and from teaching at Union, that is, beginning in the fall of 1973, the majority were women and by the spring of 1974 my "student population" was overwhelmingly female. This was naturally the case, given the focus of my interest and the general vitality of the women's movement.

It was the responsibility of the theology department chair to assist candidates for promotion in preparing their dossiers. My chair indicated to me that courses in Feminist Studies were looked upon as insignificant by the theology department. He asked me to submit course critiques from 1970 because this was the last year in which men students predominated in my classes. He let me know that evaluations from women students would have less credibility with the department in showing my qualifications as a teacher.[15]

So I did submit published critiques from male students from 1969 as well as from 1970, which clearly placed me in the category of first-rate professors, university-wide. I also submitted the critiques from women and men up to and including 1974.[16] Although no one among my friends and friendly colleagues could believe that I would be refused full professorship, I Sensed that the atmosphere was ominous. I focused on things that mattered. I wrote and taught and traveled and lived very intensely while I waited for the patriarchs to hand down their decision, which was to be announced in January 1975.

That fall semester was also one of suspense for Jan. She was continuing her very successful teaching of Medical Ethics at BC on a part-time basis. Meanwhile the department announced a full-time job opening for the following academic year (1975–76) in the very area in which she was teaching. She applied, and was advised by the department chair that it would be good for her candidacy if she submitted a "statement of faith," since members of the faculty supposedly had been asking what her faith position was. She was assured that this was only for purposes of answering the questions of anyone who might ask. So Jan wrote an eloquent and honest statement, not knowing that this would be circulated as part of her dossier and presented to the full committee considering her candidacy.[17] She continued to work hard and waited for the department's decision on her job application, which would be made known in January.

THE TICKING OF THE TIME BOMB

Meanwhile, my Time Bomb, the 1975 edition of *The Church and the Second Sex,* was ticking away at the publisher's on its way to publication in January 1975. The "Autobiographical Preface" contained the story of my being fired and re-hired at Boston College, as well as other adventures, and the straight-shooting "Feminist Postchristian Introduction" was explosive material.

I had not given a thought to timing things in such a way that the promotion decision at Boston College would precede the appearance of the new edition. My focus was on getting the book out as soon as possible, because

I was eager to see it in print. My correspondence with my editor at Harper Colophon indicates that I was trying to speed up production, so that the book would be out by November or early December. I had consistently been very forthright publicly about my views on any topic that I considered Timely and important, including my own history at Boston College—on television and radio and in newspaper interviews. I was perfectly aware that withholding my views would never save me—and I had no desire to be "saved" anyway.

I had also worked hard proofreading to meet the deadline of *Ms.* magazine for its December 1974 issue, which contained excerpts from *Beyond God the Father* and the new "Autobiographical Preface." By November, *Ms.* was on the stands and thousands of readers could know, by opening it to the first page of the excerpts, that *The Church and the Second Sex* contained a "Feminist Postchristian Introduction." I was hiding nothing.

That issue of *Ms.* was important historically. I don't know how fully aware the editors were of what they were doing, but they were in fact making very explicit the distinction between "Christian Feminism" and Postchristian Feminism by having as their cover story of that issue an article by Malcolm Boyd entitled "Who's Afraid of Women Priests?" Boyd's article was occasioned by the ordination of eleven women to the episcopal priesthood.[18]

Postchristian Feminists most certainly were not and are not interested in being "ordained priests." Most of us were not and are not interested in becoming priestesses either, although I doubt that any of us object to being called "pagan."*

The early Daly had fought for the ordination of women to the catholic priesthood, because she saw the denial of this possibility as deeply connected with all the other injustices perpetrated by the church. This perception of connection was, of course, accurate. However, since the early seventies I had seen the idea of women's ordination in the catholic church as an absurd contradiction and had often publicly compared it to the idea of a Black person seeking office in the Ku Klux Klan.† The resurrection of this idea and the fact of its being highlighted by *Ms.* in December 1974 gave me a shocking experience of time warp. I saw this as a quaint repetition of an

---

*According to *American Heritage*, *pagan* is derived from Late Latin *paganus*, meaning "civilian (i.e., not a 'soldier of Christ')," and from the Latin *paganus*, meaning "country-dweller." According to the *Wickedary*, *Pagan* means "a Background dweller: Heathen, Wholly Her-etical Hag." N.B.: *Skeat's Concise Etymological Dictionary of the English Language* explains that *paganus* means (1) a villager, (2) a pagan, because the rustic people remained the longest unconverted.

†Since the episcopal/anglican church claims to be part of the catholic church and since it uses the same woman-obliterating symbol system, I saw its ordination of women as mired in the same set of contradictions. For example, a woman giving a blessing "in the Name of the Father, Son, and Holy Ghost" is in effect proclaiming that "God" is male, and thereby legitimating the patriarchal social system in which the male is "God."

idea whose time had come and gone, an idea marked/marred by built-in obsolescence.

What I was Sensing was, I believe, one of many signals of the beginning of the time of time warp. The foreground fathers were trying to draw women in, to seduce us into spinning our wheels just when we were raring to go and ready to Spin on our heels, away from the death march of patriarchal institutions. We were approaching The Watershed Year.

APPROACHING THE WATERSHED YEAR

Throughout the summer and fall of 1974 there were signs that 1975 would be a Watershed Year. Not only were there ominous signals from the foreground but also exciting beckonings from the Wild Realm that I would later call the Background. I know Now that there was a surging of Creative Sources as well as opposing forces that were just about ready to burst forth. I also felt it then, but probably much of my Sensing of imminent changes was Subliminal Sensing.

Right in my immediate environment there was emerging a New cluster of Cronies. I did not yet fully understand the significance of these women's Presence/Presences. What was coming into be-ing was definitely a Background phenomenon—a convergence of New energies. The Tigers were still there and going strong. It was not the case that they were displaced/replaced, but simply that yet an Other convergence was occurring. To put it another way, a different but complementary convoy of Cronies was arriving.

Most of these women had been and/or were at that time in my classes, which included "Philosophical Foundations for Revolutionary Ethics" as well as "Feminist Ethics." I did not yet know them well, but their intelligence, creativity, and woman-identification were evident. Despite differences, all shared a Common Sense of excitement—an exhilaration and hope that characterized the women's movement at that Time. Like the Tigers, these women knew that they were embarking upon a creative adventure, that they were participating in a special Moment in history. We shared this vision and this passion in the unlikely context of Boston College. Among these women were Fran Chelland, Eileen Barrett, Denise Connors, Pat McMahon, Jane Caputi, Linda Franklin, and Peggy Holland. The surging of Gynergy among these Cohorts was still in its incipient stages, but our Moments of Breakthrough were hurling us Hagward/Nagward with Breakneck Speed.

Just as this A-mazing Movement was gaining Momentum in my proximate environment, the whirling dance of woman-identified knowing/be-ing was transpiring/trans-spiraling synchronously in distant parts of the world. In December 1974, for example, Anne Dellenbaugh, a young American woman studying in Japan, went to the American Center in Kyoto and found the issue of *Ms.* that contained an excerpt from *Beyond God the Father.* The Center subsequently acquired the book. Anne, who was then contemplating studying to become a buddhist monk, read the book as soon as it arrived and almost left Japan immediately to come and study with me at Boston College. As she told me several years later, when she was actually in my class, she "got it" immediately on the deepest gut level.[19] Although I cannot claim that I "knew" that a woman named Anne Dellenbaugh was inhaling *Beyond God the Father* in Japan, I did know that Big things were happening in a New Time/Space.

Indeed, everything around me was happening so fast that there was very little time for reflection. The dreary grinding of the wheels of oppressive academic bore-ocratic procedures was draining. The writing and production of my Postchristian work required active expenditure of energy, as I have described. The highs of friendships, teaching, and traveling also demanded, and gave back in return, tremendous quantities of energy.

One Promising event on the horizon was the Second International Symposium on Belief sponsored by the Giovanni Agnelli Foundation and his eminence Cardinal König, Archbishop of Vienna. The Symposium was scheduled to be held in Vienna, January 8–11, 1975. I had been invited to deliver a paper and gleefully accepted the invitation. It would mean an exciting intellectual adventure and a free trip to my beloved continent of Europe. The "line-up" of participants revealed that all were theologians or sociologists and that the vast majority were, of course, males.

Luckily, I would not have to feel isolated, surrounded by stuffy academics. My friends Robin and Emily, who represented the epitome of Unstuffiness, just happened to be planning a trip to Europe during that winter vacation. This was a wonderful "coincidence"/convergence. It was obvious to the three of us that they should attend the Symposium. To facilitate this, I arranged that my paper be scheduled for the day after their arrival and requested a double room. Since the Symposium was paying for the rooms of participants and their spouses, I wrote to the organizers: "Since I obviously do not have a wife, I would expect that you were planning to reserve a single room for me. However, since my two friends are not rich, it would be helpful if they could share my room." My request was granted.

So Robin and Emily would be there to hear my paper in that alien environment, and we would have a Roaring Time in Vienna and then move on to other places of interest. It was clear that the trip to Vienna would be an *Event*—Something to look forward to and, later on, Re-member.

In November I wrote to the organizer of the Symposium, Professor Rocco Caporale, making very explicit the fact that "my frame of reference is Radically Feminist and Postchristian, no longer catholic," so that I would not be invited under any "false assumptions." I sent the paper later that month, with the title "Radical Feminism: The Qualitative Leap Beyond Patriarchal Religion." Professor Caporale wrote back in December that he had received it and liked my thinking, warning me that I could "expect a good dose of controversy, all for the better."

The preparation of that paper during the fall of 1974 had indeed involved a "Qualitative Leap" moving me far beyond my "Feminist Postchristian Introduction," which would be in the bookstores in January.* During the process of writing, my "Qualitative Leap" paper even Leaped beyond itself. I had at first given it the mild title "The Sins of the Fathers," but then moved on to Naming what it really was about.

So there was a Tidal Wave of creation involved in the writing of that paper, hurling me toward the truly New year of 1975. The foreground conflicts of that time were, I think, in some way connected with this Positively Creative Wave, and they provided fuel for my Leaping in the direction of The Third Spiral Galaxy. The Fierce Focus of my heightening understanding of patriarchal evil, combined with the mounting Fires of my Rage, Naturally inspired more Moments of Breakthrough. But they also whirled my Craft into the vortex of an Other Galaxy, comprised of Qualitatively Different Moments—Moments of Spinning. In that Third Galaxy I would learn powerful ways of exorcising *apraxia*—the patriarchally embedded inability to Act,† and I would Spin beyond the foreground "present" into the Background Present.

But the story of The Third Spiral Galaxy belongs to later chapters. At this point it is important to reflect upon philosophical themes of The Second Spiral Galaxy. These reflections, which constitute the subject matter of Chapter Ten, are important preparations for Re-membering the Great Leap that was yet to come.

---

*The word *beyond* in this context does not signify any disagreement with the "Feminist Postchristian Introduction." It simply means that my ideas had continued to develop in New ways. Thus the word here has an entirely different meaning from *beyond* in *Beyond God the Father.*

†See *Introduction.*

CHAPTER TEN

REFLECTIONS ON
PHILOSOPHICAL THEMES
OF THE SECOND SPIRAL GALAXY

Reflecting upon my Moments of Breakthrough and Re-Calling, I am astonished at the intensity of that Time. By foreground reckoning, The Second Spiral Galaxy spanned a mere four years. But during that short span of Pirating through the Mist I made Momentous discoveries. I saw ever more clearly how patriarchal theory is split off from the social reality that it attempts to describe. I saw the reason for such splitting of theory from reality, namely, bad faith. The theoreticians simply did not want to know the realities of oppression, most specifically the oppression of women. By pointing out the discrepancies and filling in the blanks, so to speak, I broke an important academic taboo and implicitly announced my identity as an Outlaw, as a Pirate.[1]

Characteristic of this Galaxy was the bonding of women in Sisterhood, which I experienced ontologically as the "Cosmic Covenant."[2] A worldwide network was developing, and this provided a context of cognition and love that emboldened me to steer my Craft into the Mist and keep Naming/Re-Calling the Realities that rose up in my path.

DILEMMAS AND BREAKTHROUGHS

Often the important Acts of Breakthrough were occasioned by the emergence of dilemmas. As I sailed the High Seas I experienced these dilemmas as situations that "came up," apparently forcing me to choose between two odious alternatives, which were like treacherous male-made maelstroms designed to drag down and suck away my Craft from my True Course. The challenge was to somehow Sail between, around, below, or above these maelstroms and, beyond that, to convert the dilemmas into occasions for Spiraling creation.

I Now see two examples of such dilemmas in the Course of The Second Spiral Galaxy as especially paradigmatic. One of these examples was the invitation to preach at Harvard Memorial Church in the fall of 1971. The second was Harper & Row's design in 1974 to bring out a paperback edition of *The Church and the Second Sex*.

In both of these instances I was faced with two unacceptable options. In each case the first option—mere acceptance of the invitation—would involve assuming the role of token and functioning to legitimate an institution which I had come to recognize and Name as inimical to women, that is, christianity. Thus, allowing the re-emergence of my early catholic book would be comparable to accepting the "honor" of being the first woman to preach at a Sunday service at Harvard Memorial Church. Clearly, a decision in favor of "acceptance" in both cases would mean being party to a gross deception: I would be allowing my Radical Self to be assimilated.

The second obvious option in both dilemmas was outright refusal of these "opportunities." However, such refusal would mean paying the price of erasure/elimination/silencing of mySelf.

It might appear that I could have accepted both offers in good conscience, and without compromise, by introducing some criticism. It might seem that I could have preached a sermon that was moderately or even stridently critical of christianity, and that I could have produced a "revised" edition of *The Church and the Second Sex*. I did give these possibilities some thought. However, it rapidly became clear to me that a merely "critical" sermon would still be within the category of "sermon," and that a merely "revised edition" of *The Church and the Second Sex* would still be "more of the same," involving an infinitely tedious task of revision and refinement.

In each case I was challenged to find a creative solution. So at Harvard I gave an "Exodus" sermon which was in reality an anti-sermon, a clarion call to *leave* that whole scene—the church with its sermons and token women preachers. The point was to turn this "honor" on its head. "Good-bye to tokenism!" is what I essentially said. So hundreds of women and some men said No both to assimilation and to erasure of Feminism by stampeding out—smiling and proud of ourSelves. This was my invention of a Transcendent Third Option—the option to overcome the dilemma by facing it head on, smashing through the veils of mystification, Naming the game.

My decision to write the "Autobiographical Preface to the 1975 Edition" and the "Feminist Postchristian Introduction," and to add these at the beginning of the untouched original edition of *The Church and the Second Sex* was also—and in a more sophisticated form—the creation of a Transcendent Third Option. It was an Act of Sailing past the twin perils of tokenism/ assimilation and Self-erasure/elimination into something entirely New. For Now the reader could (and still can) have before her in one compact volume the early Daly's book and the radical critique—a tangible record of Intergalactic Travel.

So it happened that these paradigmatic solutions to patriarchally produced dilemmas became Metamorphic events. They mended and healed some of the fragmentation caused by such dilemmas, and they anticipated and prepared the Way for my Qualitative Leap into The Third Spiral Galaxy, the Galaxy of Spinning.

This "anticipation" is perhaps not too surprising, since certain Moments of The First Spiral Galaxy had also been Foreglimpses into The Second. My early intuition of be-ing and my Fribourg dissertations, for example, contained Promise of the ontological unfolding of the philosophy of women's liberation in *Beyond God the Father*. And the "prophecy and promise" that "these books will come" expressed in my *Commonweal* letter of 1963 anticipated later productivity. Moreover, my Lucky Leaps of that earlier Time, such as the Leap across the Atlantic to Fribourg, prefigured a continuing theme.

From my Fourth Galactic Perspective, I See that there was an Unfolding Sense of Direction in all this Leaping. I also See that this mode of Movement continued to be inspired by desperation as well as ingenuity, although in the Time of The Second Spiral Galaxy my Sense of Desperation was somewhat lessened and my Ingenuity was intensified. This, of course, had something to do with the fact that my daring endeavors were successful. It had everything to do with the Presence of Sisterhood, since the women's movement was then in full swing.

THE COURAGE TO SAIL ON,
OR CONTRAPUNTAL MOVEMENTS, CONTINUED

The aforementioned dilemmas were political and ethical/metaethical as well as intellectual. I had to learn to steer my Craft Craftily in order to resolve and transcend them, and this meant actively participating in the Unfolding of New Be-ing.

I Now See these specific Moments of facing and transcending dilemmas as manifestations of the contrapuntal movement that has characterized most of my Voyaging. The reader will recall that in my "Reflections on Philosophical Themes of The First Spiral Galaxy" I Dis-covered four counterpoints. This quadruple counterpoint continued into The Second Spiral Galaxy, where/when my Craft persisted in seeking Transcendent Options.

The first counterpoint centered around the tension and struggle for harmony between my love of abstract thought and my love-hate for symbolic modes of expression. In the early years I had struggled in my dissertations to resolve the apparent conflict between these modes of knowing/thinking/speaking by defending rationality that is deeply rooted in intuition. In *The Church and the Second Sex* I had challenged the silly symbolism of "the eternal feminine." But in the Course of The First Spiral Galaxy I had not yet taken on the vast corrosive symbol system of christianity.

I did take on this system in The Second Spiral Galaxy, in my 1971 and 1972 articles and especially in *Beyond God the Father*. My tackling of these symbols involved abstract analysis. I used my Craft of philosophical and theological reasoning, arguing on the enemy's own turf, which I knew only too well. I also used theoretical analysis to confront patriarchal strategies, such as reversal, erasure, trivialization, spiritualization, universalization, and particularization.

One of the most important achievements of that book and other works of The Second Spiral Galaxy, was, I think, my early synthesis of abstract reasoning and Metaphoric expression.[3] This synthesis is evident in a profusion of ideas, such as New Time—New Space, the "original sin" of women, prophetic dimensions in the image of Mary, existential courage and transvaluation, Sisterhood as Cosmic Covenant, the Final Cause as Cause of Causes.

This New Naming/Re-Calling was possible because I had decided to overcome male methodolatry and reclaim the right to Name. Since I had decided to "go the whole way" with Radical Feminism, the Way was wide open for Tremendous Contrapuntal Creativity. As Pirate I had broken the chains of dogmatic mindbindings and was ready to Sail through the subliminal-laden Mist, smashing the masters' myths. My Craft danced through the Mist in an exuberant exercise of polymorphic, polyphonic, polymetric, polyrhythmic Piracy. I Plundered and Smuggled like an Outrageous Outlaw Dis-covering Other Laws, the Laws of my own Muse. I was becoming free for the work of Metapatriarchal creation.

The second contrapuntal movement—between philosophy and theology —was a continuing theme. It had been puzzling to me for many years that my desire to study philosophy seemed to be thwarted at every turn. Moreover, the Great Wind had persisted in blowing my Craft in the theological direction. I had attempted to resolve the dilemma by obtaining doctorates in both "fields," each of which seemed partial and ungratifying without the other. And in fact I came to understand through experience that each was/is incomplete without the other because intuitive/rational Wisdom is absolutely Natural and at the same time translucently Transcendent.

So it was consonant with this insight that *Beyond God the Father* had as its subtitle "Toward a *Philosophy* of Women's Liberation." Indeed, smashing the symbol of the Godfather and his associates is precisely what makes possible the Outercoursing Voyage toward a *philosophy* of women's liberation. This is the case because such theological symbol-smashing breaks down barriers to genuine and free philosophical thought. Moreover, it opens the way for Dis-covering the Treasure Trove of symbols and myths that have been stolen and reversed by the theological thieves.

When I began to break through to these Treasures I was enabled to examine them, play with them. When I tore them free from their dead casings of patriarchal theological systems they sparkled and sparked me to make up my own Metatheological Metaphors. These Metaphors carried my Craft, so that I felt like a gull sailing with the Great Wind, which kept calling and moving me over the shining Subliminal Sea.

As I moved to New Boundaries of both theology and philosophy the Light of understanding began to break through the Mist, making it possible to See and Name complex connections, that is, to Leap in the Direction of The Third Spiral Galaxy.

The third contrapuntal movement, since my college days, had centered around the problem of "women together but not really together." It had focused on the struggle to break the brokenness of the hidden "broken Promise" of foreground simulations of Women's Space—Space claimed by women for our own purposes, such as thinking our own ideas together, strategizing, planning, creating.* In the mid-sixties, this problem had led to my choice to teach in a coeducational university rather than in a college for women. The latter would, I thought, inevitably be ghettoized. Hence I had innocently seized an opportunity to experience firsthand the horrors of "coeducation." The counterpoint to my opting for coeducation was my increasingly extensive and intensive involvement in the Feminist movement.

As I moved further into The Second Spiral Galaxy I found myself working toward a dynamic and risky resolution of this problematic situation. I achieved such a resolution by the creation of Women's Studies "on the Boundary" of patriarchal coeducational institutions. Thus "the Tigers" emerged from my graduate classes at Boston College, which included women studying at other coeducational schools, such as Boston University, Brandeis, Harvard Divinity School, and Andover Newton Theological School. In addition, many other women from the Boston area began to benefit from my creation of Feminist philosophy and ethics classes, which were pivotal for intellectual and political activities that affected the wider environment.

The fourth contrapuntal movement involved an increasing tension between seeking academic legitimations—from degrees to tenure and promotions—and, on the other hand, refusing to censor my own speech and writing for the sake of such "rewards." Whereas in The First Spiral Galaxy, my academic pursuits were still within the bounds of "loyal dissent," by the Time of The Second Spiral Galaxy I could no longer stay within these bounds. To be more precise, I had to throw off the mindbindings/spiritbindings of catholic/christian myths, symbols, and dogmas.

This did not imply a choice to leave (in the usual sense) academia or the specific institution at which I was a tenured faculty member. The two odious alternatives—assimilation into tokenism on the one hand and Self-elimination on the other—were designed to divert my Craft from its Course. My only Hope lay in Dis-covering a Transcendent Third Option that would carry me past this dilemma. What I Dis-covered was the possibility of Boundary Living. This involved creating a Space in which women could find rooms, brooms, and looms of our own, Spinning and Weaving tapestries of our own creation. My concept of Women's Studies required nothing less than this.

---

*For a complete definition of *Women's Space* see Chapter Five. See *Wickedary*.

Moments of Spinning

SPINNING AND WEAVING THROUGH THE MIST

In The Third Spiral Galaxy I continued my work as a Pirate sailing through the Mist of the Subliminal Sea, taking on the massive symbol system of patriarchal religion. In the works of this Galaxy, however, I went far beyond the scope of *Beyond God the Father* and my "Feminist Postchristian Introduction." My analysis was no longer restricted to christianity or to the "judeo-christian" tradition, but extended to the omnipresence of patriarchal myths and symbols on this planet and to the atrocities legitimated by them. Moreover, my synthesis of abstract reasoning and Metaphoric expression evolved explosively in these works, as New Words proliferated. In addition, since I had decided to "go the whole way" with Radical Feminism, the Way was wide open for A-mazing and Spinning, in Other words, for Exorcism and Ecstasy. So by symbol-smashing I broke down barriers to creative thinking, and my focus became Fiercer.

SPINNING CONNECTIONS, LEAPING, BE-WITCHING

Already in 1975 the demonic agents of fragmentation* were seriously threatening the Newly Re-Called Integrity of Feminists and our expanding Network. By means of the thought-stopping/action-stopping machinations of their media, their educational institutions, their religions, their politics, they were inducing *apraxia* in many women, that is, inability to Act as Radical Feminists.

The Imperative to overcome the man-made illusions of the foreground present and to Realize our Active Presence that is rooted in the Background became clear to me. It was Time for *Spinning* ◑, which is

> **1 :** Gyn/Ecological creation; Dis-covering the lost thread of connectedness within the cosmos and repairing this thread in the process; whirling and twirling the threads of Life on the axis of Spinsters' own be-ing **2 :** turning quickly on one's heel; moving Counterclockwise; whirling away in all directions from the death march of patriarchy (*Wickedary*).

---

*fragmentation ◑, one of the primary manifestations of phallocratic evil (Deadly Sins of the Fathers), is "patriarchally enforced *sloth* which enslaves women and other living creatures, severing them from their Original Capacities to Act, to Realize their potential to glimpse their Final Cause; the stunting and confining of Elemental growth, movement, and creativity by mandatory subservience assuming the forms of enforced passivity and/or ceaseless busyness" (*Wickedary*).

Together with other Spinning Voyagers I Dis-covered more about our connectedness with each Other and with the cosmos. This enabled us to be increasingly Present to ourSelves and to each Other. Our Presence together in the Present kindled Female Fire/Gynergy.

The Fire's Heat caused more droplets of Mist to rise over the Subliminal Sea, and the Fire's Be-Dazzling Light shined through the Mist. This became brighter as I became more Active in my Craft, Craftily Spinning as well as Knotting and Unknotting, Realizing the Vertigo of creation.

In this Searing/Seering Light I recognized and Named hidden patterns. The process itself of Seeing and Naming connections among apparently disparate phenomena generated more Heat and Light, making possible the increasing Momentum and complexity of my Moments of Spinning.

It was not the case that such Be-Dazzling Light had ever been entirely absent. It had been there incipiently, even brilliantly, in earlier Moments. In The Third Spiral Galaxy, however, it acquired intensified Power and Focus. It was not yet "all there," of course, nor is it fully Realized Now, as I write this Fourth Galactic account. However, the Fiery Heat and Light of that Time made possible New Qualitative Leaps which eventually would bring me into the vortex of The Fourth Spiral Galaxy.

These Leaps were transformative/transmutational. My entire be-ing, including my writing process in The Third Spiral Galaxy, became a surprising adventure/experience of *Be-Witching* ○, that is

leaping/hopping/flying inspired by Lust for Metamorphosis; Macromutational moments/movements of be-ing (*Wickedary*).

My Be-Witching Powers were Charged/Inspired by the fact that Radical Feminists had embarked on the A-mazing enterprise of changing our Lives. There was a New and Determined Daring in the air in the mid-seventies. I would Now say that many were beginning to acquire Pyrogenetic Virtues— Virtues which fueled the Fires of Gynergetic Action.

PYROGENETIC VIRTUES*

The Virtue of Rage

As a Third Galactic Pirate I was Fired by Righteous Rage. It became clear to me that Woman-identified Rage is not simply a feeling, and that it is not negative. This Rage on behalf of women is not mere anger.[1] It is a Passion

---

*In writing of *Pyrogenetic Virtues*, I use as a springboard the classical philosophical concept of a virtue as a good, operative habit which is acquired by repeated acts. Radical Feminist Piratic Pyrogenetic Virtues, transcending patriarchal "good" and "evil," reverse the inherent reversals of phallic morality. Hence they are *Wicked* revelatory operative habits which we acquire by repeatedly performing A-mazing Amazonian Acts.

and a Wicked Virtue which, when unleashed, enables Furies to sever our Selves from the State of Severance, breathe Fire, and fly into freedom. As I wrote in *Pure Lust*:

> As she is drawn into the Spiraling movement of Be-Friending, a woman becomes a friend to the be-ing in her Self, which is to say, her centering Self. The intensity of her desire focuses her energy, which becomes unsplintered, unblocked. This focusing, gathering of her dissociated energy, makes possible the release of Rage. The Metamorphosing Sage rides her Rage. It is her broom, her Fire-breathing, winged mare. It is her spiraling staircase, leading her where she can find her own Kind, unbind her mind.
>
> Rage is not "a stage." It is not something to be gotten over. It is transformative, focusing Force. Like a horse who streaks across fields on a moonlit night, her mane flying, Rage gallops on pounding hooves of unleashed Passion. The sounds of its pounding awaken transcendent E-motion. As the ocean roars its rhythms into every creature, giving birth to sensations of our common Sources/ Courses, Rage, too, makes senses come alive again, thrive again.[2]

This quickening and sharpening of Senses is an essential prerequisite for Seeing hidden connections and Naming them. When I sailed into The Third Spiral Galaxy I was propelled/impelled by Illuminating Rage, which awakened my capacity for detecting subliminal patterns of patriarchal atrocities. As I Named these patterns my understanding of them became more and more overt and the evidence was absolutely compelling.[3]

Awakened by the Eye-Opening force of Pyrogenetic Rage, I Plundered and Smuggled back to women information about worldwide phallocratic gynocide. This was an agonizing process of Exorcism, but it also hurled my Craft around and ahead in the direction of Ecstasy. As Virginia Woolf explained this phenomenon:

> It gives me, perhaps because by doing so I take away the pain, a great delight to put the severed parts together. Perhaps this is the strongest pleasure known to me.[4]

Ecstasy, however, was/is not derived from putting "the severed parts" of patriarchal atrocities—of the State of Atrocity—together and then merely gasping at the unspeakable horror. Rather, such knowledge was/is compelling and expelling. When a woman really faces the horror she is morally compelled to Act (overcome *apraxia*) and to begin changing/Be-Witching. She becomes empowered to expel the demonic embedded Self-censor within, who has blocked her from Spinning. She dares to begin Be-Witching.

The Virtue of Courage

My mounting Rage encouraged me to greater Acts of Courage. I came to understand that each Act of Pyrogenetic Courage leads to further Daring Deeds. I Dis-covered the fact that Spiraling Courage takes many New and Wicked forms.

Before Pirating into this Galaxy I had known that at its core, Courage is ontological, that it is the Courage to Be through and beyond the patriarchal State of Negation, participating in the Unfolding of Be-ing, continuing on the Journey always. I knew that Ontological Courage is revelatory, that it implies the Courage to See.

In The Third Spiral Galaxy my Plundering and Smuggling operations were indeed revelatory, leading me to learn through personal experience that such Courage is truly Outrageous, transforming a woman into a Positively Revolting Hag who goes on reversing the reigning reversals, becoming ever more Offensive, more Tasteless.

As an Offensive, Tasteless, Haggard Pirate I was inspired to acquire the Courage to Leave the doldrums of Stag-nation, Sailing off with as much loot as my Craft could carry. I tried to foster in mySelf and in Others the Courage to Live Wildly, that is, to refuse inclusion in the State of the Living Dead, to break out from the molds of *archetypal deadtime (a.d.)* ●,* to take leap after leap of Living Faith, becoming Fiercely Biophilic.

The Courage to Sin/Spin

Spinning on, I came to See more of the previously hidden connections among Courageous Acts themselves. I saw that the deepest thread of connectedness among them was/is the Courage to Sin.

I am not alluding here to the petty sort of sinning which is forbidden and therefore deceptively incited by the "major religions" of phallocracy. I am talking about Sinning Big. For a woman on this patriarchally controlled planet, to be is to Sin, and to Sin is to be. To Sin Big is to be the verb which is her Self-centering Self.

In The Third Spiral Galaxy I was Sinspired to Sail farther and farther Out on my Quest as an Outlaw, as a Terrible Taboo-breaking Radical Feminist Philosopher/Pirate. I found out that the Courage to Sin is also the Courage to Spin. My Sinspiration was Spinspiration, so I Spun three Wicked books in that Time—*Gyn/Ecology, Pure Lust*, and the *Wickedary*. I became more and more Metapatriarchally Metaphorical.

My Focus was on overcoming fragmentation in all of its forms. Having mended and Spun threads of connectedness in *Gyn/Ecology*, I Moved on to the Crafting of Elemental Feminist Philosophy, which is the work of *Pure Lust*. My Craft then turned to the task of fighting fragmentation through the Weaving of Wild Words. Thus the *Wickedary* is both a summation and a continuation of the Movement of this Galaxy. It became increasingly evident that my Craft as a Radical Feminist Philosopher is also Witchcraft.

---

*See *Wickedary*.

Other Piratic Virtues

In the Light of this Be-Witching Sinning/Spinning, I could hardly help see-ing the need for acquiring Other Virtues.[5] I have singled out three for spe-cial attention here.

First, I came to Realize the importance of the Virtue of Nemesis. My Piratic explorations in this Galaxy made it clear to me that "justice" is not possible under patriarchy. What is called for is Nemesis, which is a Virtue beyond "justice," acquired by Inspired Acts of Righteous Fury. It is participa-tion in the powers of the Goddess Nemesis, and it foments Elemental disrup-tion of the patriarchal balance of terror.

Having seen through the façades of "justice" I became free to cultivate the Virtue of Disgust, the habit of feeling and expressing profound revulsion at the conglomerates of toms, dicks, and harrys—and their henchwomen—who are hell-bent on destroying all Life.

Hand in hand with Disgust came the Virtue of Laughing Out Loud. This Lusty habit of boisterous Be-Laughing women bursts the hypocritical hier-archs' houses of mirrors, defusing their power of deluding Others. Indeed, the cackling of Crones together cracks open the man-made universe, creat-ing a crack through which cacklers can slip into Realms of the Wild.

As my Craft swirled and twirled through this crack I proclaimed that Laughing Out Loud is the Virtue of Crackpot Crones who know we have Nothing to lose. "We are the Nothing-losers," I cried. Hearing each Other's cackling, crowds of Cronies appeared, and together our Crafts Spun around as we danced on the wide open Sea. In such Moments of Spinning we saw that the "Lunatic Fringe" is the truly moving center of the women's move-ment, comprising those who choose always to Survive/Thrive on the Bound-aries, refusing compromise.

Charged up by such Spinning I often had Moments of Glimpsing that something even more Momentous might—perhaps—occur. These were, of course, Foreglimpses of The Fourth Spiral Galaxy, but I could not Realize this yet. I was, after all, caught up in the swirling Movement of the Third Galactic Present.

The story of that Time must Now be told.

CHAPTER ELEVEN

THE QUALITATIVE LEAP BEYOND PATRIARCHAL RELIGION

January 1975 marked the arrival of The Watershed Year, the year my world split open, in the most Positively Revolting ways imaginable. That year heralded my entry into The Third Spiral Galaxy. It was a startling Time, characterized by a convergence of many events which Moved me into utterly New dimensions of thinking, living, loving, writing, be-ing.

That Time was truly Volcanic. The turmoil of Background beckonings and New creativity erupting from the Subliminal Sea, and—on a very different level—the grindings of academic bore-ocracy, tossed my Craft on into Moments of Spinning.

THE SYNCHRONISTIC SYMPOSIUM IN VIENNA

During the second week of that January I embarked on a bizarre adventure which turned out to be a fitting initiation into The Third Spiral Galaxy. As I have already explained, I had been invited to deliver a paper at the "Second International Symposium on Belief," scheduled to be held in Vienna and sponsored by Cardinal König of Vienna and the Agnelli Foundation.[1] The majority of the participants in the symposium were world-renowned male theologians and sociologists of religion, who were interested in "objectively looking at" contemporary religious movements in which they did not participate. From my perspective their papers were for the most part pedestrian, pedantic, and—in a word—dryasdust.

Since the situation could not have been more incongruous, I decided to be congruous with its incongruity by wearing my usual cords and boots. I sported a terrifying Tiger T-shirt, which I thought was appropriate for the delivery of my paper, entitled "Radical Feminism: The Qualitative Leap Beyond Patriarchal Religion."*

Among those in attendance was Cardinal König himself. The appearance of his eminence inspired me, in a perverse sort of way, to be as ferocious as

---

*The original version of this paper was published in Italian as "Femminismo radicale: al di là della religione patriarcale," in *Vecchi E Nuovi Dei*, a cara di Rocco Caporale (Torino: Editoriale Valentino, 1976), pp. 357–87. A shortened version, simply entitled

possible. With unmitigated gall—or maybe simple forthrightness—I launched forth on my rapid-fire presentation of Radical Feminist ideas.

I enjoyed subsequent memorable exchanges with his eminence at his luxurious palace, where a reception was held for Symposium participants. Not willing to miss out on the full experience, I joined the receiving line. In the course of our handshaking and smiling for the benefit of photographers, König exclaimed: "So, you teach at Jesuit-run Boston College!" Flashing a gleeful smile I responded: "Yes, and they would like to get rid of me but they cannot." Beaming at the cameras, his eminence snapped back: "I am not so sure about that!"

The setting and circumstances of the reception were astonishing. Prominent among the works of art was a huge painting of the crucifixion, which had been slashed by the nazis. Scurrying female servants in black uniforms carried trays of refreshments for the guests.

Fortunately, my friends Emily Culpepper and Robin Hough had managed—in the course of their winter vacation in Europe—not only to attend the Symposium as my guests, but also to accompany me to the Cardinal's reception. Robin acted as my unofficial photographer at the palace—since the Cardinal had an official one there—so that I would have my own pictorial record of the event. In fact, I even went through the receiving line and the official handshaking and smiling twice, so that these striking photos could be obtained. In addition, Robin outdid himself in his photographic documentation of Emily and me smoking cigars in various impressive poses. These items had been passed out on silver trays, together with champagne, by the harried female servants to the men present. We simply could not pass up this opportunity to help ourselves.[2]

AN ANALYSIS OF MY VIENNA PAPER/ *QUEST* ARTICLE

Although "Radical Feminism: The Qualitative Leap Beyond Patriarchal Religion" was actually written in the fall of 1974, its élan, its content, and its purpose (presentation at the 1975 Symposium) converged to carry it into this Galaxy. It was indeed an initial Third Galactic Phenomenon.

It is significant that the original paper, published in its entirety only in Italian, began by posing "two strange dilemmas" and moved on by explaining my solution to both. The dilemmas arose from my expectation, which proved to be more gruesomely accurate than I could have anticipated, that most of

---

"The Qualitative Leap Beyond Patriarchal Religion," was published in *Quest: A Feminist Quarterly*, vol. 1, no. 4 (Spring 1975), pp. 20–40. The *Quest* version has subsequently been reprinted in a number of anthologies.

the Symposium participants would be pompously patriarchal and abysmally, willfully ignorant of the basic meaning of the women's movement.*

I explained the first dilemma as follows:

> First, I do not wish simply to rewrite ideas which I have written elsewhere. Yet there is a background, or frame of reference, or context, in which this paper is written . . . a context discussed at length in a number of articles and in two books.[3]

In other words, I did not wish to bore myself by beginning at "square one" for the benefit of this prestigious group of men.

The second dilemma was explained in my paper as follows:

> Feminist theory is brought forth within a certain environment, the supportive *hearing* of a cognitive minority of women who recognize our situation as extra-environmentals in a male-ruled system, and *whose sense of reality is different from the prevailing sense of reality.* We are primarily interested in speaking to each other, because this is where we find authentic communication. Others may read and comment upon our work, but genuine *hearing* is something else. My presence here is an experiment, questionable and problematic to myself. In a very real sense it is a contradiction. But then, as Whitehead recognized, a contradiction can be a challenge. Whether the challenge is worth the effort remains to be seen.[4]

Having thus unflatteringly but truthfully addressed these colleagues at the Symposium, putting them in their rightful place, as I saw it, I proceeded to resolve the dilemmas just described by presenting a Prolegomenon consisting of twenty-three theses. These theses, or premises, summarized the development of my theory to date, providing an abbreviated context in which the New ideas being presented could be understood.†

It is interesting Now to recognize that my resolution of the dilemmas posed by presenting this paper to such a group followed a paradigm already established in The Second Spiral Galaxy. That is, I again Dis-covered a

---

*The Anglo-Saxon participants, especially, appeared to experience no emotion. Their blank stares gave me the impression that I was simply an unoccupied chair. However, several Italian participants were very much excited by my ideas. Their reactions were extremely positive. If my memory is correct, it was they who arranged a television interview with me. As I recall the situation, the questions were asked in Italian, which I did not understand, but I gave some sort of answers anyway, before escaping as quickly as possible.

†It is of historic interest, I think, that an editor who included "The Qualitative Leap" article in his 1990 anthology, believing that this had been written originally for *Quest: A Feminist Quarterly*, wrote the following statement: "Because Daly did not anticipate an argument from her audience (preaching, as she was, to the converted), she does not employ a rhetorical strategy explicitly designed to change people's minds." See *A World of Ideas: Essential Readings for College Writers*, ed. by Lee A. Jacobus, Third Edition

Transcendent Third Option, Spiraling past the twin perils of tokenism/assimilation and Self-erasure/elimination.[5] I could not settle for going to Vienna only to drone "acceptable" academented abstractions. Nor could I stand to refuse this opportunity. So I accepted it as a Call to perform an Act of Defiance. I went as an Offensive, Tasteless Tiger, Fiercely growling and roaring Radical Feminist ideas. Thus it was fantastically fitting, I think, that this transitional paper/article itself served as my initial Qualitative Leap into The Third Spiral Galaxy.

In fact, my Lust for Transcendent Third Options characterized the whole paper, which was like a series of acrobatic Acts of Leaping for such Options. I say "Leaping *for*" because I couldn't yet quite make the Daring and Wicked Verbal Leaps that would be possible later. However, I was Hopping high, and in the right direction. This paper was an invigorating exercise. It was a kind of initial tryout for the Third Galactic works to come.

My critique in my Vienna paper/*Quest* article of the word *androgyny,* which I had frequently employed in *Beyond God the Father,* exemplifies this phenomenon of High Hopping.[6] Recognizing that my use of *androgyny* had been a failed attempt to express an intuition and incipient experience in women of wholeness which transcends sex-role stereotyping—the societally imposed "eternal feminine" and "eternal masculine"—I sought to undo the damage.*

I pointed out that in speaking to audiences across the United States I had sometimes had the impression that people hearing this term vaguely envisaged "two distorted halves of a human being stuck together."[7] I saw this image reflected also in the activities of a woman who is successful in a career on male terms (for example, a high-ranking business executive) and at the same time a model housewife. As I wrote then:

> In fact, this career housewife as described fails to criticize radically either the "masculine" or the "feminine" roles/worlds. She simply compartmentalizes her

---

(Boston: Bedford Books of St. Martin's Press, 1990), p. 608. Since that article was originally written to be presented almost exclusively to the *unconverted*, this misunderstanding is ironic. Moreover, certainly I was not "preaching." But the perception that my strategy was "not explicitly designed to change people's minds" is accurate. Rather, as Pirate, I was Plundering my rightful heritage, preparing the way for Smuggling it back to women. The fact that my first audience for this material was patriarchal is irrelevant, because I was not trying to convince them. Of course, I was speaking to my two friends and to mySelf, and perhaps to whatever capacity for Hearing was there in anyone else present. Mainly, however, I was Be-Speaking into the ether, that is, Auguring, foretelling, speaking into be-ing.

*In Chapter Eight of this work I have presented a Fourth Galactic critique of my usage in *Beyond God the Father* of such words as *androgyny, God, homosexuality,* and *human.* Here, however, I am giving an account of my thought process as reflected in the critique of these terms in the 1975 article.

personality in order to function within both, instead of recognizing/rejecting/transcending the inherent oppressiveness of such institutions as big business and the nuclear family.[8]

I continued:

When one becomes conscious of the political usages of language, she recognizes also that the term *androgyny* is adaptable to such mystifying usage as the expression *human liberation* has been subjected to. That is, it can easily be used to deflect attention from the fact that women and men at this point in history cannot simply "get together and work it out," ignoring the profound differences in socialization and situation within the sexual caste system. Both *androgyny* and *human liberation* function frequently to encourage false transcendence, masking—even though unintentionally—the specific content of the oppression of women.[9]

After showing that the image conveyed by the word is that of a "feminized" male—a fact demonstrated by the frequent and earnest insistence of male christian theologians that there is no problem because "Jesus is androgynous"—I pointed out that dressing up old symbols doesn't help. Radical Feminism is not about "liberating the woman within the man."[10] It is about the liberation of women, all of whom live under an oppressive patriarchal system.

Nor is Radical Feminism about "liberating the man within the woman." I had discussed the use of *androgyny* as an unsuccessful attempt at finding a Transcendent Third Option to the twin perils of "masculine" and "feminine" sex roles—unsuccessful because it combined them both, leaving us with the worst of both worlds, or rather, the worst of one world, namely patriarchy. So I experimented briefly with *gynandry* as a replacement, since it at least puts the female "half" first. However, I immediately noticed that this failed to "dissolve the inherent dependency of the word itself upon stereotypes" and "encourages on some level a perpetuation of stereotypes." Hence I decided that both terms are in fact transitional words, or more precisely "self-liquidating" words, which should be understood as having "a built-in, planned obsolescence."[11]

It is significant that I did not Move on in this paper/article to the invention of words which are beyond the scope of "merely transitional" or "Self-liquidating"—at least, not for the concept of woman-identified wholeness. Reading this text Now, I see that this is because the entire article is itself transitional, leading into the Metapatriarchal World/Whirl/Words of *Gyn/Ecology, Pure Lust,* and the *Wickedary.*

In a section entitled "Wanted: 'God' or 'The Goddess'?" I argued cogently enough for dismissal of the former in favor of the latter. However, I did not Spiral ahead to the rich creation of Other words to Name the Reality of self-transcending immanence. Moreover, while I dismissed the idea of female christian priests in favor of pagan priestesses, I did not then Move on to the Weaving of Wicked Words Naming Realities connected with the idea of "priestesses." In these sections I was taking care of unfinished business from The Second Spiral Galaxy and setting the stage for the Otherworld Journey, which had been Named at the outset of the article.

The Great Explosion of Third Galactic New Words would begin with the Spinning of *Gyn/Ecology.* Already, however, in this early 1975 paper, I was advocating "the qualitative leap toward self-acceptable deviance as ludic cerebrator, questioner of everything, madwoman, and witch."[12] I wrote:

> I do mean witch. The heretic who rejects the idols of patriarchy is the blasphe-
> mous creatrix of her own thoughts. She is finding her life and intends not to lose
> it. The witch that smolders within every woman who cared and dared enough
> to become a philosophically/spiritually questing feminist in the first place seems
> to be crying out these days: "Light my fire!" The qualitative leap, the light of
> those flames of spiritual imagination and cerebral fantasy can be a new dawn.[13]

Reading through "The Qualitative Leap Beyond Patriarchal Religion" Now, I am surprised to see how many of the basic themes of *Gyn/Ecology* are already there. The following partial list will serve to indicate the extent to which "The Qualitative Leap" article actually was itself a Leap toward the Otherworld of *Gyn/Ecology.*

First, I described Radical Feminism as the becoming of women and as "very much an Otherworld Journey." Second, I introduced the theme of the Deadly Sins of the Fathers as demonic manifestations of the internalized godfather, asserting that the Otherworld Journey involves encounters with these demons and exorcism of them. Third, I Named Exorcism and Ecstasy as two aspects of the same Journey. Fourth, I introduced the idea of Amazon expeditions into male-controlled fields in order to righteously plunder them, while avoiding being shrunken into the mold of the twice-born Athena, Daddy's Girl—the mutant who serves the masters' purposes.[14] Fifth, I described patriarchal processions in the tradition of Virginia Woolf's *Three Guineas*[15] and located their paradigm in the processions of the all-male trinity of christianity.

"The Qualitative Leap" article was, then, not only in the circumstances of its original presentation at the Symposium in Vienna, but also in its contents, a complex Moment of Spinning. It was an initial Third Galactic phenomenon involving many Acts of Be-Witching. It generated much Be-Dazzling Light, enabling my Craft to Spin and Spiral further into the Present, through the Newly illuminated Mists of the Subliminal Sea.

THE FATHERS' FOLLIES:
DENIAL OF FULL PROFESSORSHIP

In the winter and spring of 1975 I continued to be buffeted by swirling energies.[16] It would be an extraordinary understatement to say that there was much excitement in the air. On the exhilarating side, there was my expectation that my Time Bomb, the New edition of *The Church and the Second*

Sex, was about to be released into the atmosphere. On the draining side, there was my anticipation of Boston College's decision regarding my application for promotion to the rank of full professor.[17]

By any and all standards of academia/academementia this was a highly appropriate time to have applied for the full professorship. My qualifications were impeccable.* The university's decision, unbelievably, was negative. My students and many other supporters demanded an explanation, so the department chair "explained" to interviewers from *The Heights,* the Boston College student newspaper: "She has made no significant contribution to the field. In terms of achievement, Mary's case seemed to rest on *that book [Beyond God the Father]* and it is not a distinguished academic achievement."[18]

Significantly, Jan Raymond was denied even an interview for a faculty position in ethics at BC. Questioned by interviewers from *The Heights* as to whether Raymond's association with Daly was the actual reason for the denial of an interview, the department chair is reported to have said: "Yes, in the sense that she approaches most subjects from a basically feminist perspective." According to the same *Heights* article, "Fr. [Robert] Daly went on to say that the department would be out of balance if two people were approaching things from a feminist anti-Christian perspective."[19] (The theology faculty consisted of more than thirty members at that point.)

On February 14, 1975, a meeting was held between fr. Thomas O'Malley, then Dean of the College of Arts and Sciences, the university attorney, my attorney, and myself. The university attorney, Philip Burling, admitted that the student reports were "favorable," that the outside experts' reports were "favorable," and that the only negative report came from within the theology department.[20] I was told to go to the department to hear their reasons.

Hence there was a subsequent meeting (February 24, 1975) between a senior theology professor (fr. Richard McBrien), Burling, my attorney, and myself. Fr. McBrien stated that the department found my publications, particularly *Beyond God the Father,* to be deficient in scholarship. Also they considered them "popular theology, unworthy of consideration for promotion." My publications were compared by fr. McBrien to those of fr. Andrew Greeley, who was denied promotion at the University of Chicago because

---

*I had published (in addition to dissertations) two major books—*The Church and the Second Sex* and *Beyond God the Father: Toward a Philosophy of Women's Liberation.* By the fall of 1974 the latter was used as a required text in universities and seminaries across the country and was excerpted in several publications. In addition I had made contributions to more than ten books and had published more than twenty articles in professional journals as well as in Feminist periodicals. I had done substantial committee work in a variety of areas, had given more than seventy public lectures, and had presented papers at learned [*sic*] societies. I was listed in a dozen or so *Who's Who* dictionaries and encyclopedias. I also had seven degrees, three of them doctorates.

of his popularizing works. Burling then compared my case to that of Erich Segal, whose novel *Love Story* was not considered a scholarly writing entitling him to promotion in the classics department at Yale. I terminated the meeting in disgust at this point.[21]

"SISTERS, WE MEET ON BLOODY JESUIT GROUND"

A group of women students from Boston College and Feminists from various other universities organized to protest the absurd denial of my promotion. We created a Sparkling event which was a kind of Metaresponse, not only to my situation, but to the conditions of oppression of all Feminists in "higher education." This event was a "Forum on Women in Higher Education," held in Roberts Center, a gymnasium at Boston College, on February 27, 1975. Approximately eight hundred women packed the gym.

The program began with a self-defense demonstration, which was followed by a dramatic presentation in which "Quotes from the Foremothers"[22] were read Fiercely by a number of students. Dressed as Foremothers, Linda Barufaldi (Gertrude Stein), Emily Culpepper (Elizabeth Oakes Smith), and Carol Adams (Susan B. Anthony) sat and Gossiped together on stage while the audience eavesdropped.

Robin Morgan, moderator of the Forum, greeted the audience with the battle cry: "Sisters, we meet on bloody jesuit ground!" After reading a poem she had written for the occasion, which was dedicated to women fighting for freedom in academe, she introduced Linda Franklin, a Boston College student, who read an article from *The Heights* outlining the history of my case.[23] Besides myself, speakers included Christiane Joust (Tufts University), Lila Karp (SUNY at New Paltz), Marcia Lieberman (University of Connecticut), Nelle Morton (Drew University), Denise Connors (Boston College), Jan Raymond (Boston College), and Adrienne Rich.

The speeches constituted massive, impressive testimony to the fact that Feminists were being purged from academia.[24] Yet the atmosphere was not grim. The otherwise boring milieu of the gym was transformed by forty or so huge portraits of Foremothers. These were the creations of Boston College student Pat McMahon, who painted these splendid representations on bedsheets. It was also transformed by the event that was transpiring, so that it became a Time/Space of whirling, zinging Gynergy.[25]

The revelations of this Forum, combined with Boston College's disparagement and attempted erasure of *Beyond God the Father* as well as *all* of my work—and indeed of my very be-ing—fomented enormous explosions in my psyche. They unleashed my powers and hurled me further on my Intergalactic Voyage.

I was thrown into greater and greater freedom. Since *Beyond God the Father* had been super-scholarly and yet had been called "unscholarly" by the cynical and deceptive fathers of reversal, I was now liberated into the possibility of qualitatively Other Daring Deeds. It was not the case that I would become *less* scholarly. Indeed, I was now free to become even more so—and to leap creatively further into the Background.

Moreover, the True Horror Stories of Radical Feminists driven out of academia that year kindled my Righteous Rage, which was/is Creative Rage. I knew then, fully, that my scholarship and originality would never be adequately rewarded within the "system," and that my Rewards would be utterly Other, chiefly in the work itself and in what this communicated to other women.

THE FOREGROUND AND BACKGROUND CONTEXTS OF THE WATERSHED YEAR

The wide foreground context of The Watershed Year included the media's foreclosure on the women's movement. This was typified in a cover story in *Harper's* magazine entitled "Requiem for the Women's Movement." The picture on the cover was of a woman in mourning, wearing "widow's weeds." The intended message was obvious.*

There was, however, a Deep Background context: Despite signs of regression, the Movement was Moving, Spiraling farther and farther. More and more women were "coming to consciousness," that is, waking up and awakening each other from the patriarchal State of Sleeping Death. Moreover, there was a widespread eagerness—a profound Lust—for Leaping beyond the patriarchal constrictions of Mind/Spirit/E-motion that were still holding us back. Indeed, the women's movement was not dead. It had, to some extent, gone underground/undersea, but/and it was Alive with expectation and hope.

Despite erasure by the media and other patriarchal institutions, there was by 1975 a substantial body of Feminist writings, as well as art work, music, films, and organizations of all kinds. And despite the widespread purging of Radical Feminists from academia, Women's Studies existed and was expanding—and some few Radical Feminists did manage to survive on the Boundary of academia and of Women's Studies itself. In addition there was a large women's Network, which was rapidly becoming international/global. This had not yet settled down too comfortably into "women's communities," nor had the massively passivizing effects of the therapeutic establishment or of "New Age" style "Goddess spirituality" dampened the Radical Impulse.†

---

*Periodically throughout the 1980s and into the 1990s, the media masters have continued to hum the same boring refrain—frequently using the voice of a "nonextremist, well-balanced" woman—for example in *Time*.

†Nor is that Impulse defeated Now. Many Furies and Harpies are committed to the task of fanning its flames so that ever greater combustions/conflagrations will continue to Self-ignite. Indeed, the Spiraling of this book is evidence that the Voyage continues.

The dream of a "Feminist University," too, was alive and well among women in 1975. A manifestation of this was "Sagaris," a Feminist summer school held in Lyndonville, Vermont (at which I taught courses during the first session). In many ways, no doubt, this experiment "failed," but even as a flawed incarnation of the dream, it created a Memory of the Future—a hope that Something Else could be.

Given this history and this context, my way was prepared for the expansive expeditions and exploits of Exorcism and Ecstasy that were forthcoming. Although I could not know explicitly that *Gyn/Ecology, Pure Lust,* and the *Wickedary* would Unfold, I did Sense that something enormously exciting was about to occur.

Doorway after doorway of my imagination was flung open as I raced through the Labyrinthine passages of my own mind, Facing and Naming the myths and actual atrocities of Goddess-murder all over this planet and their interconnectedness—and A-mazing the masters' mazes in order to Dis-cover and celebrate Gynocentric Ecstasy.

Gyn/Ecology Unfolded and Unfolded. I began to contemplate the possibility that it might become a work of nine volumes. I do not say this as a joke or by way of exaggeration; it is indeed what I believed. Then I thought that there would be three volumes, of which *Gyn/Ecology* would be the first. I had a general idea that this book would deal chiefly with the first three sins on my list of Deadly Sins of the Fathers, which are Processions, Professions, Possession (deception, pride, and avarice). I thought the second volume would be about the next two sins, namely, Aggression and Obsession (anger and lust).[3] The third volume, I then believed, would be about encounters with Assimilation, Elimination, and Fragmentation (patriarchal gluttony, envy, and sloth).[4] I did not yet realize that the writing of *Gyn/Ecology* itself would take three years.

In May 1975 I had applied for a Rockefeller Foundation Humanities Grant, and in March 1976 I was awarded a very substantial grant from that foundation. Since I was on unpaid leave of absence from my teaching job at Boston College, this grant was literally a life-saver. It allowed me the time to write this lengthy work and to pay much-needed research assistants.

As I began the rewriting of *Gyn/Ecology,* that is, the second draft, something, or rather, somethings, Strange started to happen. For one thing, the whole shape of the book shifted radically. Indeed, the entire writing process became a Stunning experience of *Shape-shifting*○. This word is, I think, accurately defined as

> transcendent transformation of symbol-shapes, idea-shapes, relation-shapes, emotion-shapes, word-shapes, action-shapes; Moon-Wise Metamorphosis (*Wickedary*).

Moreover, in the Shape-shifting process the writing became more and more condensed. Whole pages sometimes became one paragraph or perhaps one sentence. The Fire and Focus were intense, burning away what seemed to be unnecessary words, forcing me to create New Words.

Often the New Words arose as a result of Searches through the dictionary, which involved the uncovering of etymologies, definitions, and synonyms, which in turn led to further word-hunts and Dis-coverings.[5]

Clearly, then, the chapters changed; the outline changed; I changed. I sometimes broke into incantations, chants, alliterative lyrics. As I wrote in the original Introduction to *Gyn/Ecology*:

> At such moments the words themselves seem to have a life of their own. They seem to want to break the bonds of conventional usage, to break the silence

imposed upon their own Backgrounds. They become palpable, powerful, and it seems that they are tired of allowing me to "*use*" *them* and cry out for a role reversal.[6]

There was nothing contrived about this process. I did not sit down and think that this work required a "different style" and then attempt to create it. I simply risked Leaping into the process of Gynocentric writing, which meant that the work, in a real sense, created itself.

Part of the Peculiar phenomenon of the writing of this book was its Timing. My Muse or Muses invariably waited until evening to arrive and stayed around until I was more than ready to collapse with fatigue. Since the inspiration tended to become stronger during the wee hours of night, I struggled and fought against the temptation to stop just when the Spinning was at its Beginning.

Although I was not in a "trance" when writing *Gyn/Ecology,* I was in a special mode of creative consciousness. This gathered Momentum throughout the writing of the book, crescendoing at the end of Chapter Ten, in the sections entitled "The Dissembly of Exorcism" and "The Celebration of Ecstasy." The inspiration for these last pages literally poured over me when I was taking a shower, after which I immediately rushed to my typewriter and got the words down with alarming alacrity.

This "special mode of creative consciousness" arose in part from a will to overcome all phallocratically imposed fears and *Move* on the Journey of Gynocentric Creation. The fears that haunted me were legion. I was worried, at first, that no one would publish such an Outlandish book, and then that even if it did find a publisher, it would receive only horrendous reviews or dead silence from the critics. I was haunted by the spectre of being considered "off the wall" because of its Outrageous style and ruthless unveiling of patriarchal myths and atrocities. I was afraid that noncomprehending editors would say the style was "gimmicky."[7] Of course, I was expecting the worst.[8]

However, since I had a Network of Radical Feminist friends, it was not possible to imagine—for too long a period of time—that I was a cognitive minority of one. Moreover, after I had written some of the New material I experimented with presenting it in my public lectures at colleges around the country. The audiences were warmly enthusiastic and en-Couraging, so I was spurred on to become an ever more Positively Revolting Hag.[9] Indeed, the emergence of *Hag*-related words, as well as such Names as *Crone, Spinster, Harpy, Fury,* and Other New Words, was an integral part of the writing process, and when I spoke these aloud to women I was committing Acts of Be-Speaking. I was speaking the words into be-ing. Nor was I alone in this process. Wild women Heard me into Be-Speaking, and together we were forging a Metalanguage that could break through the silence and sounds of phallocratic babble.

Among my political/personal Acts of Be-Speaking, beginning in 1977, was my habitual announcement on stage, in the course of public lectures, of my Lesbian identity. Although this had been known for years by my friends and was obvious to Others from my writings, as well as my style of acting and be-ing, there were still many others who, for their own reasons, preferred not to know. So I made it a point, on certain occasions, to be very explicit, for example, by spelling the word out loud on stage: L-e-s-b-i-a-n.

I cannot say that for me, personally, coming out publicly as a Lesbian felt like my most radical and dangerous Act of Be-Speaking. Even then, in the seventies, I knew that the word *lesbian* by itself, if used to describe only "sexual preference" or a personal life-style, lacked the deepest, most radical spiritual power. So I surrounded it with New Words to fill out and expand the Reality of Lesbians/Feminists who Live in Tidal Time—who Act Metapatriarchally/Metapolitically.[10] This Call from the cosmos to Name and Name again the Elemental/Spiritual Touching Powers of women summoned me on to ever bolder Acts of Be-Speaking.[11]

Somewhere on the Journey of writing *Gyn/Ecology,* especially when I was working far into the night, a sort of formula came to me, which could be called a *mantra,* or perhaps more accurately a Witch's Self-determining Spell. The words, as I Re-Call them, were: "No matter what happens to me afterward (or, as a consequence) I WILL write this book." The Spell carried me through the dark nights of my soul's Journey and onward into more Be-Dazzling adventures.

A comparable phenomenon had happened a few years before in the process of writing *Beyond God the Father.* At that Time, the mantra/Spell had been simply: "I have to turn my soul around."[12] When I came to the writing of *Gyn/Ecology* I still had to keep the everlasting attacks of "beta" (or busyness) at bay, of course. But I had by then already turned my soul around. That is, I was *continuing* the Metapatriarchal Voyage begun during the Time of *Beyond God the Father.* Now the task was a more intensified turning. It was the task of Weaving connections in such ways that I was in fact Spinning the integrity of my own be-ing and knowing, experiencing Vertigo, and Moving into uncharted Realms.

SOME BE-LAUGHING AND BE-MUSING MOMENTS

Experiencing Vertigo and Moving into uncharted Realms involved not only cosmic adventures but also comic episodes, shared Be-Laughingly with my Traveling Companions/Cronies. I Re-member these in a seemingly haphazard way, that is, not chronologically, but Crone-logically.

Peggy Holland, who was one of my inspired Search assistants, has Re-Called a typical incident during the Time of the writing of *Gyn/Ecology.*[13] We were returning from one of our frequent trips to Cambridge for a quick supper at "The Turtle Café," and some frantic xeroxing of manuscript pages at "Gnomon Copy," in Harvard Square. When we jumped into the car, anxious to get back to my apartment on Commonwealth Avenue and continue working, I was in the perplexed state of an Intergalactic space cadet struggling to cope with mundane foreground realities. I started the car, zoomed as far as the first stop sign, and abruptly stopped. Peggy sat in the passenger seat, expecting me to get moving again, since no cars were in sight. Finally, when she asked what was going on, I explained patiently that I was waiting for the sign to say "Go." Peggy burst into gales of uncontrollable laughter. Stunned, I moved my foot from the brake to the gas pedal and we were off, laughing ourselves half the way home.[14]

In case this strikes the reader as just "silly," let me assure her/him that it was/is. By the adjective *Silly* (derived from the Middle English *sely, silly,* meaning "happy, blessed"), I mean:

> Happy, Blessed, Graceful—applied esp. to giggling Gaggles of Geese and Gossips (*Wickedary*).

This State of Silliness was understood and shared by Charlotte Cecil Raymond, my editor for *Gyn/Ecology,* who has referred—with a touch of nostalgia—to "the heightened state" of that Time.[15] Charlotte's office, which was on the third floor at Beacon Press, was the scene of hard labor together, particularly as the book entered the galley and page proof stages. I would come armed with a bag of "Trail Mix" and we would drink quantities of Beacon's undelicious coffee.

One memorable day Charlotte stayed long after normal working hours, accompanied by her two-year-old daughter, Alyssa, who squealed and toddled around the office while we struggled with the proofs. At irregular intervals I would leave the office in order to get more coffee from the first floor coffee machine. At some point Charlotte noticed a trail of nuts and dried fruit on the floor. Curiously she began following the trail, which led out the office door, along the length of the hall, around the bannister, and down the steps to the first floor coffee machine. I met her on my return trip upstairs. Explosive giggling fits ensued. Despite, or perhaps because of, such incidents we managed to accomplish good work and to Brew Brainstorms in that office. It was Charlotte's idea to add the "Index of New Words"—a sort of embryonic *Wickedary*—to *Gyn/Ecology.* It was also she who suggested that I should be identified on the jacket of that book as a "Revolting Hag." Since this was an expression that I had proudly claimed and explained in the book, I Revoltingly agreed that it would be an appropriate appellation for mySelf.[16]

Gleeful experiences were abundant during the Moments I worked on *Gyn/Ecology* with Emily. At times we would be literally rolling on the floor, doubled over with mirth. Upon reflection, we have agreed that the key ingredient of this blissful, creative merrymaking was a Sense of Freedom.[17] We were breaking the Taboo against seeing through the pious pomposity that masks androcratic absurdity. For example, when we were discussing a passing reference in the manuscript to "pope paul the sixth," we concluded that

The hermit crab's life-style was, as I divined it, "amphibious, multibious be-ing." Applied to Voyagers, this suggested that we have "the agility that comes from integrity of Self, which makes it possible to move on the dangerous boundary-zones of patriarchal institutions."[23]

An entertaining and memorable instance of interspecies communication occurred when Denise and I were traveling in Switzerland during the summer of 1976. We took a mountain train up into the Jungfrau region of the Alps and got off at the station called "Wengen" and then proceeded up the alp to a place called "Kleine Scheidegg." Climbing up further we found ourselves surrounded by cows, whose musical bells carried us into a kind of fairyland.

Gradually one cow, who separated herself from the others, commanded our attention by her striking behavior. She seemed to be a loner among her own kind, but was very much attracted to us. Since her nose was dripping voluminously, we loaned her the beach towel we had brought along to sit on, which could serve as a sort of Kleenex to alleviate her problem. The towel became no longer usable by us, but we kept it as a souvenir, referring to it simply as "the cow towel."

When the unusual cow tired of our companionship she wandered further up the alp and sought out the company of a solitary artist—a painter who was poised and ostentatiously posed on the very edge of a high mountain ridge with his easel and canvas. This fellow was flamboyantly flourishing his brush and, to top it all off, so to speak, he was wearing an artist's beret. The bovine intruder walked up behind him and comically stood looking over his shoulder. She appeared to be gazing at his artistic endeavor.

Knowing something of the cow's nasal condition, we were not surprised to see the pretentious painter swing his arm around and try to wave her away. The stalwart animal was not discouraged by the insulting gesture, but merely stepped back and then moved forward again and again in her determination to look over his shoulder. The painter appeared to become almost hysterical in his efforts at swatting her away. No doubt he felt that his image was being damaged by the intrusion of the persistent creature. We watched all this, sitting on the mountain grass, convulsed with laughter at the scene.

Naturally, I Now recognize the comical cow of Kleine Scheidegg as a great Divining Familiar, whose mission was to exhibit and communicate the Virtue of Laughing Out Loud. Even as I am writing these lines I can imagine her looking over my shoulder at the page, and I want to wave a towel and Laugh Out Loud—with her—especially at the absurd idea that animals have no Sense of Humor.

On that same trip to Europe Denise and I went to Crete and visited—among other places—the Palace of Knossos and the Herakleion Museum. The famous restored paintings of the blue dolphins on the walls of Knossos are powerful aids for Spinning in many Senses: They offer clues for Dis-covering the lost thread of connectedness within the cosmos, specifically between women, animals, and the Elements. They also provide inspiration for Spinning away from the patriarchal necrophilic system that negates such connections, destroying women and nature. Moreover, the dolphins inspire Courage to Spin in the Sense of "to last out, extend." For these are ancient paintings. They are messages of hope, swimming to us from the Past. The dolphins are Subliminal Sea dwellers, bearing Good Tidings into the Future and into the Present, Be-Speaking Tidal Time. They elicit Memories of the Future.

The place of animals in a woman-centered society, such as Crete had been, was also suggested by the Minoan Snake-Goddesses in the museum in Herakleion, particularly the smaller statuette whose hands grip/span writhing snakes. Indelibly impressive also was/is the fresco of bull-jumping, which has been transferred from the east wing of the Palace of Knossos to the Herakleion Museum. The bull is charging violently, while the three acrobats, two of whom are women, are leaping with amazing suppleness over his horns to his back and to the ground. The exceptional acrobatic skill of the bull-jumpers is inspiring for Ludic Leapers who are acquiring New Athleticism, whirling and twirling in Gyn/Ecological communication with each Other, so that we can outlast/outlive the State of Stag-Nation.

The Minoan animals and women of the Background Past became Present in these representations. Indeed, they are Present to me Now as I write this. Their messages/meanings worked their way into the content/style of *Gyn/Ecology.* They are joined with Other Divining Familiars whom I have met on my travels and who have guided me into my Future.

Throughout my travels I was, of course, as always, doing my work as Pirate. When I was Plundering the Treasure Island of Crete I was preparing to Smuggle back to women some of its wonders in *Gyn/Ecology.* Of special significance for this Smuggling operation was/is the symbol of the Labrys, the ancient sacred double-ax, which came alive in my imagination as a consequence of seeing the numerous huge Labryses in the museum in Herakleion.[24] The Labrys, which is a basic Metaphor not only in *Gyn/Ecology* but throughout the works of The Third Spiral Galaxy, has inspired many New Words.[25]

The jacket of the original cloth edition of *Gyn/Ecology* Announced the Cretan influence. The Labrys which is the slash in the title was copied from a small souvenir Labrys which I acquired in Crete and which I carry with me always on my key chain. The dolphins on the back of that jacket are copied from a post card replica of the fresco at Knossos. The Labrys has always remained on the American edition, and the dolphins, which had temporarily disappeared from the paperback edition, happily returned on the 1990 edition, which contains my "New Intergalactic Introduction." I take this to be a promising omen for the 1990s.

Not only Divining Familiars but also Domestic Familiars played an important part in the Unfolding Life of *Gyn/Ecology*. I refer here to two Stunning Felines, whose Cat/atonic influence and Cat/egorical Imperative inspired this work.* Their story is as follows:

On Labor Day, 1975 a cat in Quincy, Massachusetts, gave birth to a large litter of kittens. The "owners" of this cat family sought good homes for the promising and beautiful offspring. Among their acquaintances was Denise, who had been inspired to seek out two tiny kittens who would be "little spirit sisters." The two chosen ones were a beautiful calico and a striking tabby. The latter was introduced as "the runt of the litter" and was described by her "owners" as "just like a girl," because she cried a lot. The Wondrous qualities of the calico were immediately clear. She became the Familiar of Denise, who also Dis-covered the less obvious genius of the tabby. The tabby's promise of a brilliant future was indicated by her remarkable grey toes. She became my personal Familiar.

For many months it was impossible to find suitable names for these young felines, since their respective characters had not yet manifested themselves. So they were simply called "Calico" and "Tiger." As time passed, however, it became clear that "Tiger" was a natural athlete and a retriever. She had a fondness for green beans and would do a sort of complex triple pirouette as she leaped to catch and retrieve any green bean tossed in her direction. "Calico," on the other hand, was a keen observer, especially of her sister. Her beautiful, piercing, Eyebiting eyes followed every detail of her sister's sport from a regal distance. So it subsequently became clear that the real name of "Tiger," the activist, was Wild Cat, and that the true name of "Calico," the Seer, was Wild Eyes.

The fact of their fundamental but complementary temperamental differences did not mean that these sisters had nothing in common, however. The commonality was evidenced in many ways even in kittenhood. For example, both had the same favorite television program—"Wild Kingdom." Their way of "watching" this show was to crouch together on top of the television set, feeling the vibrations and listening to the roars, squeals, howls, chirps, et cetera, of the principal characters on the show.

The companionship of these gifted and loving Sisters contributed great inspiration to the writing of *Gyn/Ecology*. They were/are constant reminders of the Wonder of cats and of all the Other animals who share this planet with Wild women. They Re-Called/Re-Call the Presence of the Background, which is where all animals Live. Wild Cat and Wild Eyes helped to make *Gyn/Ecology* Wild.[26]

---

*Cat/atonic○ means "healing exhilaration achieved through the companionship of Felicitous Felines" (*Wickedary*). *Cat/egorical Imperative*○ means "the Call of the Wild, the Summons of the Weird, conveyed through the Mediumship of a Feline Familiar" (*Wickedary*).

GYN/ECOLOGY AND THE CALL OF THE WILD

In *Gyn/Ecology* my Spinning became Wilder and Wilder. I Spun more and more New Words, New Metaphors. Dis-covering my true identity as a Hag, I was swept away, farther and farther into the Background, by the Wild Wind, which had become my Broom, my Night Mare. I unraveled reversals, finding the Archaic Origins of myths and symbols that had been stolen and twisted to serve the masters' purposes. I Re-Considered everything, Re-Weaving threads of connectedness.

Throughout this process I was Fiercely following the *Call of the Wild*❶, that is

1 : the recurring invitation to bound out of the State of Bondage 2 : the Elemental Sounds of Otherness which awaken Be-Longing, summoning women to embark upon Journeys of Exorcism and Ecstasy (*Wickedary*).

On this Swirling Journey I strove to Re-Weave and mend Background Tapestries of Archaic meanings. I also Named connections among foreground phenomena—connections that were masked by the demonic deceptions of the State of Separation/Severance/Fragmentation.

I wrote to expose the atrocities perpetrated against women under patriarchy on a planetary scale and to show the profound connections among these Goddess-murdering atrocities. To this purpose I Dis-covered the Sado-Ritual Syndrome.*

My Plundering and Smuggling back information about worldwide atrocities required investigation of patriarchal re-sources. It was an agonizing process. I had to look at the horrible material—which often included photographs of the maimed women, especially in the cases of footbinding and genital mutilation—read it over and over again, write about it, rewrite early drafts about it, proofread it over and over. The horrors burned themselves into my brain; yet this knowing had to happen and be communicated.

As I uncovered the connections I began to Spin ever more Wildly, and my Voyage became more Vertiginous. I was Fired by the white heat of accumulating Rage, which hurled my Pirate's Craft around and ahead to the Ecstatic be-ing of The Third Passage of *Gyn/Ecology,* that is, to Spooking, Sparking, and Spinning.

---

*Since *Gyn/Ecology* was published, the agents of patriarchal evil have invaded women and nature with more and more virulent attacks. Their tentacles have grown and multiplied. I have found that the seven-point Sado-Ritual Syndrome (explained on pages 130–33 of *Gyn/Ecology* and applied throughout The Second Passage) continues to work very well as an analytic tool for unmasking the escalating horrors of the sadosociety and for showing the connections among these.

The essential components of the Sado-Ritual Syndrome are: (1) obsession with purity; (2) total erasure of responsibility; (3) inherent tendency to "catch on" and spread; (4) use

My Moments/Movements of Spinning became more and more Be-Dazzling as I sailed further through the Mists of the Subliminal Sea. In the Be-Dazzling Light I saw astonishing and complex connections, and as a result of the Acts of Seeing, the Light became stronger. In other words, there was a Spiraling progression/intensification of Luminosity. Such complex progression was a form of verbing/be-ing that was characteristic of *Gyn/Ecology.* This brings me to the subject of the Metapatterning Movement of that book.

THE UNIFYING THEME OF *GYN/ECOLOGY:* THE METAPATRIARCHAL JOURNEY OF EXORCISM AND ECSTASY— METAPATTERNING

Just as the basic thesis of *Beyond God the Father*—that the movement for women's liberation is an ontological movement—is the organic, unifying theme of the diverse concepts in that book,[27] so the central motif of *Gyn/Ecology*—that the women's movement is a Metapatriarchal Journey of Exorcism and Ecstasy—is the organic, unifying Source of the pattern-detecting which characterizes this work. The pattern-detecting of *Gyn/Ecology* is, in fact, *Metapatterning* ○, that is

> process of breaking through paternal patterns of thinking, speaking, acting; Weaving the way through and out of male-ordered mazes; Metapatriarchal Erratic Movement (*Wickedary*).

---

of women as scapegoats and token torturers; (5) compulsive orderliness, obsessive repetitiveness, and fixation upon minute details, which divert attention from the horror; (6) readjustment of consciousness, so that previously unacceptable behavior becomes accepted, acceptable, and even normative; (7) legitimation of the ritual by the rituals of patriarchal scholarship.

To list a few current "developments": A ten-billion-dollar pornography industry has developed and continues to escalate; its images of the torture, murder, and dismemberment of women and girls are everywhere, "inspiring" more and more rapists and sex murderers to copy these images. Woman battering and incest are alarmingly widespread. The reality of these horrors has always been there, but in recent years there has been an increase not only of information about them, but also of the "practices" themselves. There has been an upsurge of international trafficking in women. Women of color are the primary victims of this atrocity as well as all other crimes. The demand for child prostitutes is enormous, especially around military bases and as "tourist attractions." The new reproductive technologies have developed at an alarming rate, taking on forms that reduce women to subhuman "subjects" of experimentation. The torture of animals in laboratories and in agribusiness beggars description. And the Life-killers continue to kill the earth and its inhabitants. In 1991 the atrocity of "the Gulf War" manifested the escalation of patriarchal necrophilia.

Among the connecting and connected analytic themes through which the Metapatterning Movement of *Gyn/Ecology* is Realized are: the eight Deadly Sins of the Fathers; deadly deception through myth and language; necrophilia as patriarchy's essential message and modus operandi; the Sado-Ritual Syndrome: the re-enactment of Goddess-murder and dis-memberment; Spooking; Sparking: the Fire of Female Friendship; Spinning.

The connecting threads in *Gyn/Ecology* also include Labrys-like, double-edged pairs of words which carry the Journeyers of this book into Other dimensions. These Act as *Metapatriarchal Metaphors*○, that is

> words that function to Name Metapatriarchal transformation and therefore to elicit such change; the language/vehicles of transcendent Spiraling; words that carry Journeyers into the Wild dimensions of Other-centered consciousness by jarring images, stirring memories, accentuating contradictions, upsetting unconscious traditional assumptions, eliciting Gynaesthetic sensing of connections, brewing Strange ideas (*Wickedary*).

The following pairs of words illustrate the Labrys-like dimensions of Metapatriarchal Metaphors:*

foreground—Background

Exorcism—Ecstasy

necrophilia—Biophilia

tame—Wild

man-made maze—Labyrinthine Passage

gynocide—Gynocentric be-ing

chronology—Crone-ology

all-male trinity—Triple Goddess

torture cross—Tree of Life

flying fetuses—Spiraling Spinsters

supernatural—Super Natural

self-centered—Self-centering

re-search—Search

patriarchy—Otherworld

possession—Dis-possession

spooking (patriarchal)—*Spooking Back/Enspiriting*

total tokenism—Amazonian Female Bonding

---

*In those cases where both "sides" of the Metaphor are capitalized, both have Background meanings; for example, both *Exorcism* (of patriarchal demons) and *Ecstasy* are implied in Journeying beyond the foreground. My capitalization of Metaphors sometimes corresponds to the style of *Gyn/Ecology*, sometimes not.

newspeak (Orwellian)—*New Words*

fembot—the Enspiriting Self: Hag, Spinster, Crone, etc.

Uncreation—Creation

Sometimes connecting threads are manifested through whole "Tribes" of New Words. There are, for example, the Words of the *Hag*-Tribe, such as *Haggard, Hag-ocracy, Hag-ographer, Hag-ography, Hag-ology.* Again, there are Words of the *Crone*-Tribe, including *Crone-logical, Crone-ography, Crone-ology, Crone-Power, Crone-Time, Chaircrone, Fore-Crone. Gyn*-Words include not only *Gyn/Ecology* and *gynocide,* but also *Gynaesthesia, Gynergy, Gynocentric, Gynography,* and *Gynomorphic.*

In *Gyn/Ecology* my Craft Leaped/Spiraled still farther than my earlier works toward reconciliation of different modes of Knowing/Naming. This work is truly an Offspring of *Beyond God the Father.* Hence it Springs Off into The Third Spiral Galaxy. Its range is wider/Wilder. Its Focus is Fiercer. It is a Deed of Dreadful/Dreadless Daring. Its Reasoning is Raging, and its Metaphors are Macromutational. Its form/movement is Shape-shifting. *Gyn/Ecology* throws caution to the Winds.

Gyn/Ecology's Metapatterning is massive and Metamorphic—attempting nothing less than transformation of tamed women into Wild Witches. This requires that its Raging Reasoning be rigorous/vigorous. The scope of its task does not permit indulgence in irrationality. Rather, it demands Super Rationality. Bursting the bounds of previous discourse, *Gyn/Ecology* reaches for the stars.

Since *Gyn/Ecology* was/is a Journey of Exorcism and Ecstasy, its effects continue to be unpredictable. I will discuss some of the consequences of this Act of Be-Witching in the following sections.

THE PUBLICATION OF *GYN/ECOLOGY*: ACQUIRING THE ART OF A-MAZING

Whereas *Beyond God the Father* had tiptoed into the world, gradually attracting readers and steadily, quietly gaining momentum, *Gyn/Ecology* came crashing in like a long-awaited, longed-for Thunderbolt. It was a discharge of lightning, that is, atmospheric electricity, accompanied by rumbling thunder.

This book had been long awaited and longed for because there were electrifying powers in the Atmosphere. When it began to appear in bookstores —in December 1978—there was a widespread Knowing among women that it was Time to Spin connections that were becoming visible in multitudinous lightning flashes of Terrible insight. Many were ready to Hear the explosive sounds that Naturally follow such flashes in the path of an electrical discharge. Indeed, many had been looking and listening intently, hoping the storm would come soon. Electrified Searchers were aided in finding *Gyn/Ecology* by the multitude of reviews that appeared.[28]

The Background climate, then, was Electric. There was a heightening capacity for Be-Dazzling among such women, who felt ready for almost anything. We were ready for the Brewing of Elemental Brainstorms, for meteoric manifestations of Gyn/Ecological Knowledge, Passion, and Female Bonding.[29]

Meanwhile, there was not "smooth sailing" for my Craft on the foreground front. Attendant/dependent upon the manifestations of Background light and fire came foolish phallocratic displays of pseudolight and pseudoheat. Although such puerile "fireworks" are undeserving of the attention of Voyagers as anything more than foreground phenomena, they do require examination and analysis in order to acquire the Art of *A-mazing* ➋, which is

> essential process in the Journey of women becoming: breaking through the male-ordered mazes of the State of Reversal, springing into free space (*Wickedary*).

By *maze* ➋ I mean

> man-made set of tracks/traps leading nowhere which masks/hides the true Labyrinthine path leading into Wild Reality, the Background (*Wickedary*).

It is important at this point, then, to practice this Amazonian Art and examine the foreground tracks/traps intended to block *Gyn/Ecology* and the continuation of Gyn/Ecological Voyaging.

INVASION: THE STRUGGLE FOR A CLASSROOM OF MY OWN

Even before *Gyn/Ecology* was published, foreground fix-masters had busied themselves with their attempts to stop the process. Since I was on unpaid leave of absence for the purpose of writing this book, I was in need of income. My Rockefeller Foundation Humanities Grant, awarded for the academic year 1976–77, was extraordinarily helpful. Unfortunately, however, it could not help me during the first year of my leave (1975–76) when I was almost totally dependent upon lecture invitations in order to survive. And that avenue of support was being deliberately blocked.

One member of the theology department, who had been assigned to my former office, habitually blocked phone calls to me that came through my old extension. Many of these calls were invitations for speaking engagements at colleges across the country. He variously told callers that my home phone had been disconnected, that I had moved, and he even hinted that my extended leave from Boston College was for therapeutic reasons. Moreover, he attempted to discourage callers from contacting me by mail, intimating that I rarely came by to collect my mail. All of this, of course, was a lie, yet representative of the devious tactics which the theology department had used for years in trying to discourage students from taking my courses.[30]

I first realized that these interventions were happening when a professor at Dartmouth College called me at home and described her experience of trying to reach me at Boston College to invite me to speak at Dartmouth. She warned me that someone was not so subtly intimating that I was having a breakdown. So I asked a friend to call my former office extension from my apartment, pretending to be inviting me to speak at a nearby university, while I listened on an extension phone in an adjoining room. The experience of hearing my own reality grotesquely distorted/reversed was shocking. So also was the response of my "colleague" when I interrupted the conversation, addressing him by name, and asking him what he thought he was doing. Without missing a beat, this righteous professor of catholic theology responded casually: "Gee, Mare, I was only trying to help ya." I put a stop to this "help," and the lecture invitations came flooding in again. So I survived, and I did write *Gyn/Ecology*.

When I returned to teaching in September 1978, the book was at the publisher's, almost ready to be unleashed/released into the world. I could almost hear it snapping its teeth in gleeful anticipation. To the naive or insensitive observer, things appeared to be relatively peaceful at Boston College. I Sensed that this was a deceptive "peace." It was significant that each previous attack had followed the publication of a major new book, although typically these works were never cited by the administration as reasons for their assaults. So clearly it would be no coincidence if a third wave of hostility and persecution were to follow the publication of *Gyn/Ecology*. Meanwhile, I was kept busy with teaching, traveling, speaking, and, of course, Living. In late November early reviews began to appear, and by December the book was "out." It was beautiful.

On January 23, 1979 the ugly attack began. Three "visitors"—fr. Frank Paris, a maryknoll missionary priest, Marsha Fowler, and Sharon Webb—arrived to attend my Feminist Ethics class. This was not the first week of the class, and the visitors were not officially enrolled. The students were disturbed by the sneering demeanor of the visitors. They understood that their intent was to disrupt and requested that they leave. I asked fr. Paris and his female companions to respect the wishes of the class. They gave the impression that they had decided not to take the course and walked away. In fact, I later learned that they had walked directly to the office of the theology department chair (rev. Robert Daly, s.j., who just happened to be in his office at 5:30 p.m.) and that the latter, without investigating the situation or conferring with me, immediately invited the visitors to register formal complaints and offered them his typewriter. He also suggested that they might wish to press legal charges.[31]

The following morning I received a special-delivery home-addressed letter from Chairman Daly, plus the three visitors' letters of complaint. These astonishing letters, among other things, accused both me and the students of verbal assault and of threatening physical assault.[32]

On January 29 the Dean of the graduate school (Donald White) ordered me to send, within twenty-four hours, letters of apology to fr. Paris and Marsha Fowler[33] and also to write a statement saying that I supported the University's "policy of no discrimination on the basis of sex or ideology."* I was told that I was receiving a reprimand, to be placed in my file, and that if I failed to comply with the Dean's orders I would be suspended without pay.[34]

On January 30 my Feminist Ethics class was again visited by fr. Paris, who, still unregistered, was accompanied by his remaining female accomplice and fr. Robert Daly. As I commented in a statement to *The Heights*:

> This was a serious encroachment of my rights as a faculty person. A chairperson does not do visitations. . . . It was an intimidating and degrading thing for him to come supposedly supporting these visitors who were never registered.[35]

Paris and his remaining supporter, still unregistered, attended yet a third class (on February 6), and subsequently alleged "verbal assault and harassment" by me and the class members.[36] The university administration used these allegations as an excuse to send monitors into all of my classes. This began on February 12.[37] I canceled the first monitored class shortly after it began, since I needed time to work out a strategy.

When it was time for the second class that day—which happened to be "Mythic Patterns of Patriarchy"—I was ready. The monitor this time was fr. Daly himself. I had instructed the students to sit in a circle. Hence the chairman was obliged to sit in this circle, with large, strong women at each of his elbows, while I lectured on the witchcraze in Western Europe during the so-called "Renaissance," alluding to the role of the jesuits in such atrocities against women, and reading from the letters of fr. Daly and his fellow bureaucrats at Boston College as examples of the continuing witchcraze. I also read from the visitors' letters and from my own letters to the university. Students in the class then asked fr. Daly to respond to these statements and confronted him about his purpose in the class. He responded that he could not discuss any "substantive matters" and was only able to say that he was doing his duty, since he had been sent by the university administration. I had informed *The Heights* about this impending event, so student reporters were present for this scene. Two wide-eyed young men avidly and enthusiastically took notes on this unusual class.

My next step was to call in journalists and photographers from local newspapers. My "colleagues" who had been willing to serve the university as monitors were in a tight spot. It seemed that none of them really wanted their pictures in the newspapers. Apparently even they recognized that such

---

*I have never refused to teach *bona fide*, registered, qualified male students nor have I refused admission to any student on the basis of ideology.

blatant invasion would not be interpreted in a favorable light. So after two or three more monitored classes they disappeared. Their departure was no doubt hastened by the fact that I addressed them in front of the class, describing their participation as "extreme harassment," after which students also confronted them in the presence of the press.

On February 23 a letter from President Monan of Boston College informed me that monitoring of my classes would be discontinued.* The letter rumbled on about the "complaints" lodged against me, which were "serious enough to violate fulfillment of contractual obligations." In a subsequent interview with *The Heights* I indicated that the recent publication of *Gyn/Ecology* was probably what triggered the university action against me. My summation of the situation at that time was:

> The administrators at Boston College have neither the courage, nor the wit, nor the scholarship to refute my ideas. Therefore they must resort to lies and petty harassment.[38]

On March 12 a letter signed by all the registered members of my Feminist Ethics class was published in *The Heights* under the headline "Daly's Class Speaks Out Against University." The following citation is extracted from that document:

> Throughout their investigation of Professor Mary Daly's classes, Boston College has NEVER SOUGHT the observations of the students in Feminist Ethics II. Instead they have listened solely and entirely to the accusations of three visitors to that class. . . . Monitoring a tenured faculty member was unheard of until the university began monitoring all classes taught by Professor Mary Daly. . . .[39]

The letter ends with laudatory comments about the class and my internationally known work.

The saga, however, had not yet ended. On March 14, there was another meeting between myself and university officials at which a demeaning and absurd document was presented for my signature. Of course, I did not sign this statement, according to which I would "agree" to a number of disgusting conditions, including the stipulation that "during registration periods, University personnel will attend her courses as observers."[40]

Instead of signing the document I fired back a letter indicating the following: that as a matter of conscience I could not sign something which in my judgment does not conform to the facts; that I would continue to admit

---

*By this time Frank Paris, who definitely was not even registered at Harvard Divinity School, as he had claimed, and therefore had not a shadow of a right to be in my class, had terminated his missionary work as a plant in my class and had returned to his teaching job in the Philippines. I was told that he was saying masses for me. His female supporter also vanished from the scene.

qualified students into my classes; that I expected the Boston College administration to honor my status and credibility as a tenured faculty member and my rights to academic freedom attendant to that status, and to see to it that correct information concerning my classes be duly distributed to students.[41]

So that was the end of that round.*

PYROGENETIC CONCLUSIONS AND BEGINNINGS

Did such puerile persecution spell defeat? Speaking for mySelf, the answer is No. Once again Boston College had functioned as a laboratory and microcosm, enabling me to understand even more deeply not only the banal mechanisms of phallocratic evil but also possibilities of transcendence.

Such machinations are doubtless intended to intimidate, drain, defeat, and sicken their victims—the "uppity" ones, specifically Feminists. There is no question that the events just described were exhausting for me and all of the women involved. The triumph consisted in transforming this exhaustion into woman-identified energy—reclaiming our Fire from the ashes of androcratic asininity.

My own primary/primal mode of reclaiming Fire—of perpetuating Pyrogenesis—has been Be-Speaking by means of writing, lecturing, teaching —through and beyond the atrocities and the State of Atrocity. My major Act of Be-Speaking in direct response to the 1979 Sado-Ritual took place in the context of a Sparkling Event organized by a group of Feminists known as "*Ad Hoc* Hagographers." This Event/Rally, which was called "We Have Done with Your Education,"[42] was held at Morse Auditorium at Boston University on April 8, 1979.

---

*Well, not exactly. The final tactic that Boston College used before the end of the spring semester 1979 was to withhold the annual amendment to my faculty contract which would have stated my salary increment for the academic year 1979–80. (The university sends increment notices to all returning faculty on February 28 of each year. The notices, which are required by the provisions of the university statutes, must be signed and returned by March 15.) I placed a series of phone calls to university administrators and received nonanswers to my questions concerning the whereabouts of my salary increment notice. When I finally managed to contact Chairman Daly (April 5, 1979) I told him that I considered the university's actions to be "serious violations of legal rights and faculty rights" (*The Heights*, April 9, 1979, p. 17). Although I did eventually receive my notice weeks after it was due, it was self-evident that the withholding was a punitive measure. No doubt the delay until semester's end was also designed to protect Boston College from public embarrassment over the minimal increment allotted to me after the publication of yet another major work. This anxiety-producing delay was an omen of the financial harassment/hardship that would prove to be the basic/base strategy of the 1980s. See especially Chapters Thirteen, Fourteen, and Nineteen for further details.

According to a major Feminist newspaper of the time, close to one thousand women attended this support Rally, which drew a standing room only crowd from as far afield as Nebraska.[43] Besides myself, speakers included Jan Raymond, Adrienne Rich, and Andrée Collard. The Moderator was Emily Culpepper. There was a Stunning musical performance by Willie Tyson and Susan Abod.

The printed program made the intention of the Rally clear:

> The fathers of Boston College are seeking to silence the voice of Radical Feminism. They would bind women's minds with the lies of patriarchal education. Mary Daly insists on Naming these lies and exhorts women to do battle against the mindbinders.

Appropriately, the event began with a choral reading by nine women (students), entitled "A Call to Hags, Harpies, Crones, and Furies." The members of the chorus recited brief historical accounts of atrocities committed against women throughout the ages of patriarchy, including witchburnings of the so-called "Renaissance" and recent rapes and murders in the Boston area. They announced: "We have come to make the connections."

Jan Raymond, then on the faculty of Hampshire College in Amherst, Massachusetts, acted as the evening's Crone-ologer. She reviewed my "decade of harassment" at Boston College as "the amazing record of a survivor." Dividing the ten-year period into "three waves of harassment," Jan delivered her lengthy speech, "Mary Daly: Complete Crone-ology," with a flair and, at points, with costume. She donned a clerical collar when citing from jesuits and other priests at Boston College, and produced an "impressive" pipe which she puffed professionally when citing nonclerical BC deans and attorneys.[44]

Adrienne Rich spoke of the bland rationalization of woman-hatred and woman-torture by scholars. Identifying as a freedom-loving woman, she named the fact that "our struggle, radically understood and radically pursued, is the struggle against planetary extinction."

Before introducing the next speaker, Emily Culpepper made note of the breadth of the Feminist network, pointing out the banner which hung behind the podium proclaiming:

> Dispossess BC! Dismember Academe! Nebraska Spinsters support Mary Daly!

The crowd roared approval when she added:

> May Boston College tremble!

Andrée Collard, who was teaching at Brandeis University, discussed the profound connections of women to nature and animals. She showed the strong links between the patriarchs' need to control and dominate nature and their treatment of women. She warned that once a woman declares the immorality of patriarchal values she becomes dangerous. She is no longer one of their intellectual clones.

When it was my turn the evening had already been long, but our energies were still rising. I spoke of the Fire of woman-identified energy. Citing Virginia Woolf's *Three Guineas,* I proposed that we "set fire to the old hypocrisies."[45] I spoke of the harassment of Hags in academia and elsewhere, and proclaimed that it is necessary to reclaim our own treasures while avoiding the traps of tokenism. I advocated fueling the Fires of our Rage and ended with reading "The Dissembly of Exorcism" from *Gyn/Ecology.* This reading was accompanied by Super Natural sound effects from the chorus.

The 1979 Rally—to which many of us referred simply as "The Event"— sparkled with women's brilliance and collective Hope. By the time that Willie Tyson and Susan Abod played and sang "The Witching Hour"—with the women in the audience singing along—the auditorium was no ordinary place.[46] It had become Women's Space and Time. The vibrations in the room shimmered with the Be-Dazzling Light of Female Fire—the Fire of women's auras/O-Zones Sparked by each Other's Gynergy. That Space/Time was Radiant, streaming with sounds and colors of every tone and hue. That Room of Our Own was blazing and shaking with our cosmic concordance.

So that Convergence was the Background Conclusion to the foreground fathers' persecution. More importantly, it was a Background Beginning of New bursts of Gynergetic Spinning. I am sure that no woman who was Present at The Event has forgotten it. Although some may have dozed off into temporary *amnesia,* we had concreated a Memory that would continue to Vibrate in Tidal Time, carrying the good tidings that Other Events could continue to happen. Something Else could continue to be.[47] And the knowledge of transformation carried by each of the women Present there that evening would subtly affect those around her. The ripple effect would work its way into the lives of many, and the current would be carried deep and far in the Subliminal Sea.

CONTINUING RADICAL FEMINIST PROCESS: *GYN/ECOLOGY* AS A VERB

In the original introduction to *Gyn/Ecology* I wrote:

> Writing this book is participating in feminist process. This is problematic. For isn't a book by its definition a "thing," an objectification of thinking/imagining/speaking? Here is a book in my hands: fixed, solid. . . . It is, at least partially, her [the author's] past. The dilemma of the living/verbing writer is real, but much of the problem resides in the way books are perceived. If they are perceived/used/idolized as Sacred Texts (like the bible or the writings of chairman Mao), then of course the idolators are caught on a wheel that turns but does not move.[48]

To put it another way, I have always seen *Gyn/Ecology* as part of a Movement, including my own Voyage, which has continued since that writing and continues, because I am not a noun, but a verb. When I set it free so it could *be* in the world, I did not see it as a work of perfection. For some women it could be an Awakening shock, for others a Source of information, or a springboard from which they might Leap into their own A-mazing Searches, Words, Metaphors.

Above all, I was acutely aware that I had not done or written everything. I had not written the Last Word. (Otherwise, how could I ever write again?) Rather, I had set free this book, this Thunderbird, in the hope that its Call would be Heard. I hoped that it would soar together with the works of Other women, which were coming and would come from different Realms of the Background. I looked forward to the profusion of New Creation, which I believed could emerge from women of all races, cultures, classes—from all over this planet—speaking/Be-Speaking out of our various and vital heritages.

From my Fourth Galactic perspective I see that this has happened and is happening, because our Time has come. Particularly Moving to me, personally, is the work of women of Ireland, that Treasure Island which I recognize deeply as the wellspring of my Background, my ancestral home. Especially Gynergizing on a global scale is the New abundance of creation from women of color.

Explosions of Diversity do not happen without conflict, however. One of the responses to *Gyn/Ecology* was a personal letter from Audre Lorde, which was sent to me in May 1979. For deep and complex personal reasons I was unable to respond to this lengthy letter immediately. However, when Lorde came to Boston to give a poetry reading that summer, I made a special effort to attend it, and spoke with her briefly. I told her that I would like to discuss her letter in person so that we would have an adequate opportunity to understand each other in dialogue, and I suggested places where we might meet for such a discussion. Our meeting did in fact take place at the Simone de Beauvoir Conference in New York on September 29, 1979. In the course of that hour-or-so-long meeting we discussed my book and her response. I explained my positions clearly, or so I thought. I pointed out, for example, in answer to Audre Lorde's objection that I failed to name Black goddesses, that *Gyn/Ecology* is not a compendium of goddesses. Rather, it focuses primarily on those goddess myths and symbols which were direct sources of christian myth. Apparently Lorde was not satisfied, although she did not indicate this at the time. She later published and republished slightly altered versions of her originally personal letter to me in anthologies as an "Open Letter."

It continues to be my judgment that public response in kind would not be a fruitful direction. In my view, *Gyn/Ecology* is itself an "Open Book." I regret any pain that unintended omissions may have caused others, particularly women of color, as well as myself. The writing of *Gyn/Ecology* was for me an act of Biophilic Bonding with women of all races and classes, under all the varying oppressions of patriarchy. Clearly, women who have a sincere interest in understanding and discussing this book have an obligation to read not only the statements of critics but also the book itself, and to *think* about it.*

GYN/ECOLOGY AND RAGE

Gyn/Ecology can be Seen/Heard as a Thunderbolt of Rage that I hurled into the world against the patriarchs who have never ceased to massacre women and our Sister the Earth. I wrote it in a Time of Great Rage, when women were Wildly Moving, Sinspired by Creative Fury.

Rage, however, can be displaced. In reaction to the Absolutely Righteous Rage of women of color against racism, some women retreat into passivity, hostility, and guilt, often displacing energy into targeting scapegoats.[49] The targeted scapegoats can become de-energized, losing the ability to focus Rage. The winners in this game, of course, are the patriarchs themselves, who, by the way, invented it. Having embedded Self-hatred and horizontal violence into women they leave us to our own devices for becoming distracted into destroying ourSelves, rather than engaging in an honest and thoughtful battle against racism and woman-hating.

Gyn/Ecology is a Thunderous Call to refuse to be distracted from the Gynergizing Focus of Rage. It is High Time that Gyn/Ecological Rage be Dis-covered again and again, for this Rage can inspire the Courage to Spiral on, continuing the process of Radical Feminism.

LETTERS: THE SURGE OF BIOPHILIC BONDING

Throughout the horrors of the academented witchcraze the letters responding to *Gyn/Ecology* came to me. They came to me like healing balm. Reading many of them was and continues to be like sampling an almost infinite variety of exquisite wines. They renewed/Re-New my Spirit.

The letters conveyed many complex things. Simply stated, they poured out love and gratitude and they told me that the long struggle had not been in vain. They gave me something back—renewed Hope, Courage, and Strength. They surged up from the Subliminal Sea, with messages of Biophilic Bonding.

---

*This piece ("Open Letter") has been assigned as required reading by not a few professors in academentia to students in classes where *Gyn/Ecology* itself has not been assigned, or a mere handful of pages of this book have been required reading. This kind of selectivity is irresponsible. It imposes a condition of self-righteous ignorance upon students, often within the setting of "Women's Studies." This is, in my view, a worst case scenario of pseudoscholarship. It is, even if "well-intentioned," divisive, destructive. It functions, at least subliminally, as a self-protective statement about the purity and political correctness of the professor. It can be analyzed in further detail as a manifestation of the seven-point Sado-Ritual Syndrome, as described in *Gyn/Ecology* (pp. 130–33).

The sampling of letters concerning *Gyn/Ecology* that I have reread ranges from December 1978 to August 1991, for, of course, women have Dis-covered the book (as well as my other books) over Time. Since my filing "system" has been less than adequate, this sampling is haphazard. (I reached into the folders and simply took handfuls and read them over again.) Yet my Sense is that these represent something of the range of feeling and thought that characterize the letters as a whole. Almost all are intimate as well as analytic. They are intimately analytic. They are written by women who have been shocked into contact with their own Depths.

I have Dis-covered in these letters a hard-to-Name combination of E-motions, of rhythms and tones, of lights and colors which suggest that the Be-Dazzling Light of the Background is shimmering through the Mist for these women. Because of this subtle complexity, I will not attempt to arrange these letters according to themes—although themes are there.* Rather, I will examine a few of these missives as I would gaze at gems that I have found in the Subliminal Sea. Then, perhaps, I can Spin a few connections.

I will begin with a letter dated December 29, 1978. This correspondent wrote:

> It is a relief to see things in print that I have only thought of in my head. I also feel compelled rather than depressed—a state I'm sure I share with many of my sisters.

Here recognition of previous knowledge is combined with a will to overcome *apraxia*. And this woman had important insight about *how* to move. As she wrote: "I am trying hard to place my anger in the right place." Moreover, her words are Be-Dazzling:

> I wish you all the hope I can give and the happiness which will carry you to yet another horizon.

As I have indicated, the responses of women to *Gyn/Ecology* are marked by a wide range of very intense E-motion. A woman writing from Washington, D.C. in 1979 described the "whole experience" of reading the book as "profoundly disturbing." She meant this in a positive sense, and within a few lines was writing: "Its recovery of language thrills me." And then: "I had to grin and slap the table in just glee."

---

*Some of the themes in a significant number of these letters are similar to the main themes of the *Beyond God the Father* letters. These are: (1) insistence by the writers that they were finding out what they had already (subliminally) known; (2) statements to the effect that the correspondents had never written such letters to authors before; (3) exuberant, volcanic Hope; (4) acknowledgment of the sanctions for acting on that Hope; (5) experiences of energy surges; (6) experiences of coming into contact with one's own psychic powers; (7) affirmations of Lesbian identity. See Chapter Eight.

Many focus almost entirely upon positive E-motion, Spiraling, and energy surges. In an undated letter from Burlington, Vermont, the writer stated that reading *Gyn/Ecology* felt like a four-hundred-page love affair, which made her "feel high." A correspondent from San Francisco wrote in 1979:

> Reading it helped me survive a near fatal earthquake.* . . . My favorite passage is "The Dissembly of Exorcism." It is now my bedtime story/prayer/incantation/dream inducer.

Expressions of horror are recurrent. Writing from Colorado Springs in 1979, a woman described her response to the "gory details" of The Second Passage:

> The effect of your detail on me was to erode my denial and racism. Like so many of the "experts" I also thought Africans and Chinese to be "exotic" (or some such thing), which made me blind. Your treatment—step by step—left me no place to hide and I thank you for the detail (although I was sick, I cried, and finally had to put it aside for a day or two to survive the African genital mutilation passage). I shall never look at the world as I did before. I have moved light years in my view of sisterhood.

The same correspondent expressed her experience of logical progression from knowledge to action (overcoming *apraxia*) when she described, at the end of her letter, her act of communicating to a group of church women her understanding of a sexist sermon they had all just endured, but which most could not criticize articulately.† She wrote:

> I could not listen to his sermon. . . . Afterwards a few women came up to me with a wildness in their eyes—couldn't put their fingers on what was wrong but were furious—not knowing why. I told them what I thought had happened (using what was learned from *Gyn/Ecology*) and eyes and spirits clicked and clacked so much that the room was like . . . filled with electricity.

A woman psychiatrist from Oregon (letter undated) wrote to me of her "state of shock" from the revelations of The Second Passage, and of "hanging half way between vomiting and tearing the enemy to shreds." She added: "It's easy to stumble around in there, instead of spinning away."

Many letters indicate that a major obstacle to "Spinning away" is fear. Writing in July 1980, a woman from Rochester, New York, expressed the problem as she saw it:

---

*The word *earthquake* is used here as a Metaphor, in the sense described in *Gyn/Ecology* (pp. 409–13).

†The sermon had been introduced with a "cartoon" in which Priscilla Pig goes to a Lama to learn the truth of her reality. The Lama is to reveal to her the truth of her being. According to my correspondent: "The last picture shows Priscilla with rapt gaze (down before him) and she says—'Tell me, Great One, what is my truth?' He replies: 'Think pork chops.'"

For me, *Gyn/Ecology* is a powerful and dangerous book. I am compelled to study it, but I am afraid of it. Afraid because I live very close to the boundary, the boundary of marriage, children (ages 2 and 6), job (adjunct English teacher at a community college), friends (who are functioning Catholics and male-centered). I have a responsibility to the people who love me. I am afraid if I enter into the joy of spinning, everyone and everything around me will break from what they will see as destructive feminist energy. . . . Please, if you know a way to Be without being alone, without giving up home, family, friends, job, etc., please tell me.

There are clues to the answer in other correspondence. For example, I am perusing a letter from a woman who wrote from Amherst, Massachusetts, in 1979. She stated:

The layout of the book allowed me to journey/voyage as I read, and now that I have finished I am able to continue on backwards. I have read too much to go where I was before; I have begun to spiral to my center to include the space all around me. . . . The [woman-identified] feelings have made themselves a home in me. Each day as I reject more and more of my socialization, I grow more at peace inside and outside. It is a difficult journey, especially to be alone without much emotional support, but . . . I am slowly assembling my loom on which I will weave my tapestry.

My excitement in reading such letters stems in part from the astonishing fact that the correspondents have seemed to be responding to each other, backwards and forwards across Time. This phenomenon is possible because all participate in the same Background. All sail the Subliminal Sea.

The Sense of psychic connectedness is evident in many letters. For example, a woman writing from British Columbia in 1986 expressed her awareness of Other dimensions:

Gyn/Ecology was the first book [of yours] I read and it was quite accidental how I came across it, almost like a planned accident, if you can call it that. Many things you wrote about I had felt inside of me but was unable to connect it together.*

Clearly there is a connection between awakening to previously known/felt experience and an awareness of "planned accident," i.e., synchronicity —or Syn-Crone-icities. When a woman's Background awareness explodes, she realizes that she does not live in a world of mere "accidents." She begins to break out of the State of Fragmentation; she begins to See and Name connections. That is, she begins to Spin.

More certain than ever of the Background knowledge of women and of our participation across Time in the ebb and flow of the Subliminal Sea,

---

*These words Re-Call another letter from the mid-eighties, whose author wrote: "It [reading *Gyn/Ecology*] is like seeing my mind/journey laid out in black and white."

I will Now Spiral ahead to a recently received gem of a letter from a woman who first read *Gyn/Ecology* in 1990, and who wrote from Milwaukee:

> When I started reading *Gyn/Ecology,* it was like a crack in the horizon. Certain vague, nebulous emotions (whose origins I knew not) that had heretofore haunted me in varying degrees since I was a kid I now saw in a new light. . . . Perhaps you could say I was a female person who wasn't quite totally brainwashed.

It is especially interesting to note combinations of images and realizations in this woman's letter. The "nebulous" emotions of her childhood do indeed appear to me like the Mist of the Subliminal Sea. The fact that she now sees them in a "new light" is characteristic of the experience of The Third Spiral Galaxy, to which *Gyn/Ecology* belongs.

Discussing her dislike of the male voice-over that accompanies the images on "Nature" shows on public television, the same correspondent wrote:

> Even as a young person I knew on some level (that I would only be able to articulate as an adult) that men couldn't see nature as a separate reality from their masculinist mindset, that everywhere they looked, they saw themselves.

I recognized immediately the drone/dull tone she was describing, and her early subliminal understanding.

It was encouraging to see these sentences in combination with the following statement in the same letter:

> *Gyn/Ecology* has greatly moved me. When I stop to consider the phrase "moved me," I realize it would be helpful to elaborate *from* where and *to* what new position!

Apparently even in the process of writing the letter, the writer realized that she was not talking about mere "feeling," but about traveling/Voyaging. She was overcoming *apraxia* and moving toward a "crack in the horizon." The fact that these words were written by a woman Dis-covering *Gyn/Ecology* in early 1990 struck me as a Be-Dazzling omen.

Another letter written close to the same time (November 1989) came from a twenty-three-year-old woman who described herself as very poor. The opening sentence of her letter is:

> Eleven months ago I read *Gyn/Ecology* and for the first time since childhood I was excited by life and wanted to live.

This takes on particular significance when it is Heard in the connection with another statement in this letter:

> Your words flowed into my heart and they were nothing new—I'd always known them deeply.

What this young woman was telling me was that *Gyn/Ecology* triggered her ability to Re-member her own deep Biophilic knowledge which, I would say, had sunk beneath the surface of the Subliminal Sea. She described "the enormity of the change" in her as "astounding." She continued:

> I'd always been too self-hating to speak up, to write my opinions for others to see, but suddenly it wasn't difficult at all. You exist, you see exactly what I see!

Although the writer did not use the word *light,* the experience she has related is what I would call Be-Dazzling. She was enabled to See and Name her connection with Reality because someone else Sees and Names it too. She was Be-Spoken into Be-Speaking. She is not a cognitive minority of one any more, or rather, she knows that she is not alone in her knowledge.

When I was writing this section—in August 1991—a remarkable letter concerning *Gyn/Ecology* and *Pure Lust* arrived from London. Its author, who said she had read *Gyn/Ecology* in about 1982, wrote that shortly after reading it she "threw everything to the four winds and started to travel extensively." She stated: "It's nearly ten years later and I've been mostly living in a tent by the side of a river called the Rio Colorado in Central America."*

When discussing her stark Aloneness she wrote:

> Sometimes I'm afraid, but it doesn't compare to the bubbling inside and the feeling "I am home."

After describing some of her A-mazing physical and psychic travels and adventures this woman wrote:

> I was spinning around for years after reading it [*Gyn/Ecology*]—the Rage was something Volcanic—a lot of volcanoes and angels and mermaids were in my subsequent "paintings."

She put quotation marks around the word *paintings* because she thinks of these as "only messages, so I call them 'Butterfly Wings.'" She began creating these "about two years ago. . . . They've all been given away. They probably number over 200 paintings."

The Butterfly Wing which accompanied this woman's letter, a beautiful watercolor Message, arrived at an important Moment in the writing of this chapter, and it is Now on the wall above my bookshelves. It signals the Surge of creativity that comes when a woman is brave and free. It is called "The Water of Life."

Clearly, there are connecting threads among these letters. These include: Realization of formerly subliminal knowledge; Active overcoming of *apraxia*; a Sense of Change/Metamorphosis; Biophilia; a Lust for Biophilic Bonding; Realization of not being alone; psychic Sense of Serendipity/Syn-Crone-icity;

---

*She plans to get a new tent and go back: "So I'm going 'Home' to stay this time."

Spinning connections; overcoming of fear; Realization of be-ing Alone/ Home; Volcanic Rage; Surges of creativity; Be-Dazzling Voyaging.

So, the letters are there, Be-Speaking me into Moving on/Sailing on, Inspiring the Courage to Write. They were, and continue to be, overwhelmingly Positive, reaffirming my Reality as a Positively Revolting Hag. Surging from the Subliminal Sea, they Re-Call the Powers of Biophilic Bonding. Together they reflect the Crone-logical context,* the Gynergetic Reality which sustains the Spell/Mantra that carried me through my Spinning of *Gyn/Ecology* and my Surviving of the consequences: "No matter what happens [and happened] to me afterward . . . I WILL [and DID] write this book!"

I hope that in its richness, as well as in its incompleteness, *Gyn/Ecology* will continue to be a Labrys enabling women to learn from our mistakes and our successes, and cast our Lives—Now—as far as we can go.

---

*This Crone-logical, Life-sustaining context has been manifested also—and especially —in countless conversations with women all over the United States and in many other countries. Some of these women are personal friends. Others I have encountered in connection with my work as a teacher and public lecturer. The continuing Presence of this Nixing Network of Nags perpetually encourages me to keep on Spinning.

CHAPTER THIRTEEN

SPINNING BIG: THE EXPLOSION/EXPANSION OF *PURE LUST*

*P*ure Lust* sprang out of the rich Volcanic soil of Elemental Passion for Life. It was Fired by the auras of many women and Other Wild creatures. It was Charged with determination to overcome the bores, botchers, butchers, jocks, plug-uglies, rippers, and other snools[1] who control and perpetuate the wasteland which I have Named the *sadosociety.*[2]

Intergalactically speaking, *Pure Lust* Spiraled out of the Momentum of the Moments of *Gyn/Ecology,* continuing the Path of The Third Spiral Galaxy. I was learning to Live "on the Boundary" in an Extreme Sense, Seeing more clearly than ever that I had only Nothing to lose. I had further cultivated the Virtue of Disgust with phallocracy and its rules and rulers. I had developed confidence in my Positively Peculiar Perspective, vowing that I would dare to Spin Wildly, always.

When Spinning *Pure Lust* I continued Exorcising the demons first introduced in *Gyn/Ecology,* who/which are personifications of the Deadly Sins of the Fathers. Whereas the primary Deadly Sins confronted in *Gyn/ Ecology* were *Processions, Professions,* and *Possession* (androcratic deception, pride, and avarice), in *Pure Lust* the main demonic attacks that must be exposed and thwarted come from *Aggression* and *Obsession* (malevolent male violence and phallic lust). These demons parade in line (out of line) after the deadfellows who were fought and conquered in the earlier book, and who must be reconquered again and again, of course, with Re-Newed Force. As I wrote in the Preface to *Pure Lust*:

> As the Voyage continues, the Furious Fighters of these infernal molesters increase in numbers and in spirit-force. Moving onward, upward, downward, we enter now, New Realms of Spheres.[3]

The explosive becoming of *Pure Lust* was, on one level, a battle against the Aggressors/Obsessors driven by phallic lust, which is violent and self-indulgent, leveling all life, dis-membering spirit/matter, attempting annihilation. Early in this process I realized that the word *anger* (which appears in the traditional lists of deadly sins) does not accurately Name a Deadly Sin of the Fathers, whom I came to see as incapable of Deep Volcanic Rage. In contrast to this, phallic Aggression is a manifestation of the deadly dispassion that prevails in patriarchy. Together with its twin sin, Obsession, it comprises the life-hating lechery/lust that rapes and kills. This lust is *pure* in the sense that it is characterized by unmitigated malevolence. It is *pure* in the sense that it is ontologically evil, having as its end the braking/breaking of female be-ing.[4]

At the same Time that I came to understand *pure lust* as ultimately evil, I recognized that this expression can be a Labrys, for the Background meaning of *Pure Lust* is utterly Other than its foreground sense:

> Primarily . . . *Pure Lust* Names the high humor, hope, and cosmic accord/ harmony of those women who choose to escape, to follow our hearts' deepest desire and bound out of the State of Bondage, Wanderlusting and Wonderlusting with the elements, connecting with the auras of animals and plants, moving in planetary communion with the farthest stars.[5]

Thus the struggle Named by the Labrys of this title is between Reality and unreality, between the Natural Wild, which is be-ing, and man-made fabrications that fracture her substance, simulate her soul.

My engaging in this battle was not and is not a matter of simply sitting down and placidly typing out pages. My participation in this warfare has been physical/intellectual/E-motional/spiritual. It has been on a cellular level. It has been an outpouring of Life's blood. It has been Risky, Ecstatic, Lusty. It has required Acts of Pure Lust. My long-range preparation for participation in this Battle of Principalities and Powers has been described in the preceding pages of *Outercourse.* Further matters of Timing and context will be recounted in the following section.

GYN/ECOLOGICAL SPIRALING ON
INTO THE MOMENTS OF *PURE LUST*

My whirlwind Gyn/Ecological lecture tour around the United States swirled on through the academic year 1979–80. I drove and flew north, east, south, west, descending upon colleges and universities, women's bookstores, restaurants, and coffee houses. I was beyond jet lag. I was flying in Spirals.[6]

Meanwhile, back at the "home" front, there was business as usual. As always, I had very bright, stimulating students, many of whom were cross-registered in my courses from other universities in the Boston area. I often felt that I was flying in my classes, where my flight companions were my students. Together with Other books I used *Beyond God the Father* and *Gyn/Ecology* as texts. We explored New dimensions of Feminist Ethics, Discovered mythic patterns of patriarchy, and engaged in Feminist analysis of philosophical and theological texts. The discussions were Spinning and often continued long after regular class hours in nearby restaurants. The year whizzed along without any extraordinary interference from the Boston College administration, although I had a continuing awareness of the possibility of ugly "incidents."

There also were countless Sparking conversations in the house which I had rented that year with Denise in Newtonville, Massachusetts—a place conveniently located between Boston College and Brandeis University, where she had begun studying for her doctorate in sociology. That house was a center of much buzzing social and intellectual activity. Something was brewing deep in my psyche, and that something was *Pure Lust*. This book Naturally had to explode out of the aura of *Gyn/Ecology*.

When I flew to Seattle to speak at the University of Washington on May 12, 1980, the plane obligingly soared right past the volcano Mount Saint Helens, as she belched large puffs of white smoke, warning of her ensuing eruption.* I felt a deep kinship between her need to explode and my own. One could say that my meeting with that volcano was like an encounter with a Divining Familiar.[7] And indeed, why shouldn't a mountain—especially an about-to-erupt volcano—be a Familiar? Our meeting may have appeared to be "accidental." However, I think it not accidentally followed the performance of certain magical ceremonies, such as Spinning conversations with friends and wondrous classes and discussions with students, and meetings with women all over the country, who filled lecture halls, reception rooms, dining rooms, and bars with Sparking communication of auras.

Mount Saint Helens spoke to me of the Elemental Biophilic Powers of the Earth and of women, as distinguished from destructive man-made necrophilic nuclear, chemical, and political pseudopowers. That volcano said to me: "Come on! Explode with me! Our Time is coming."

A few days later, after giving several West Coast speeches—at Seattle, Sacramento, Stanford, Oakland, and San Francisco—I found myself giving my last lecture of that trip, at the University of California at Berkeley, on May 15. I think I had the Sense that it was my last *Gyn/Ecology* lecture in this country, period.[8] It was the end of the academic year, and I was moving on to Something Else, to a New book, to a continuation of The Third Spiral Galaxy.

This was different from my 1970 experience of speaking from *The Church and the Second Sex* and realizing that

> the "I" who was standing before the friendly audiences and tossing out the familiar phrases was already disconnected from the words, already moving through a new time/space. I often heard the old words as though a stranger were speaking them—some personage visiting from the past.[9]

My 1980 experience was not similar to this because I was *not* disconnected from the words of *Gyn/Ecology*, but rather connected with them more than ever—so deeply connected that I was being driven/propelled to draw out their implications further—to Spin forth the successor volume whose

---

*There was a huge eruption of this volcano on May 18.

roots were already there in *Gyn/Ecology.* I was not being hurled into an Other Galaxy, as had been the case in 1970, after publication of the original edition of *The Church and the Second Sex.* Rather, I was Moving on to further Moments within The Third Spiral Galaxy—further Moments of Spinning.

So I Sensed that the Berkeley lecture was not only a culmination but also a beginning. Significantly, the auditorium in which I spoke was in a science building. Knowing that animal experimentation, that is, torture of animals, was practiced there, as in other "educational" institutions, I was inspired to dedicate that lecture to my friend Andrée Collard, who was then doing research for her book *Rape of the Wild,*[10] and who was passionately de-voted to exposing patriarchal destruction of nature, and particularly of an-imals. I also made a number of comments on what was being done in the name of "science" in that place and elsewhere.

Thus the Gyn/Ecological connection, the Elemental connection between Radical Feminism and Ecology was explosively made there. Obviously it was not the first time, but it was a special Time/Moment, that was conjoined in my psyche with my encounter with Mount Saint Helens.* The audience was Wild and enthusiastic, but since the building was being closed and there was no reception scheduled afterward, the women dispersed themselves quite rapidly. I remember the Strange sensation of standing alone on stage, thinking/feeling: "So this is the end of that!"

That particular lecture was taped by the listener-supported radio station KPFA in San Francisco, and it was played and replayed frequently over the years by popular demand. At some time in the mid-eighties this tape was offered as a premium to persons who donated money to that station. The fact that this speech was recorded and made so widely available for so long seems to me about as "accidental" as my encounter with the about-to-erupt volcano.

As the world moved on into 1980, the beginning of the Reagan years and of a decade of increasing conservatism and decadence, we—the women, the cats, the Other Elemental creatures—struggled to stand our ground against the bad vibrations of the political and social environment, against the gathering storms of insidious backlash, and against the confusion and dis-placed anger that were being embedded into our own psyches by a sado-societal system. We Sensed that the world was growing colder, more hostile, more Life-hating and woman-hating.

In the midst of this pervasive malevolence my creativity did not cease, but rather it was intensified. I Sensed the impending attacks against Radical Feminists from a society that was rotting in its core. The challenge was to

---

*I had been making the connection since the early seventies, and it is Present in *Beyond God the Father,* but the vastness of its implications were becoming clearer.

become ever more Fiercely Focused, more Wild and Daring. Our Sister the Earth was in mortal danger. It was Time to muster Elemental Forces within mySelf.

So *Pure Lust* began to take shape in my mind, and its Fires were fanned by the swirling auras of conversations with traveling companions/friends.* In Deep Background dimensions there were Elemental Volcanic explosions of creation as the early ideas of that book Unfolded. On foreground levels I had to face the horror of patriarchally designed implosions—the shattering of many women's confidence/courage to carry on in an environment that was more and more antipathetic not only to Feminism, but to all Natural Life.

The glorious Time of the sixties and seventies was over. That meant that more Courage would have to be Conjured, that the pain of abandonments, betrayals, and acts of horizontal violence would have to be overcome, that Moments of Spinning would have to be cherished and nurtured. The challenge was—and still is—to Re-member "the vigor, eagerness, and intense longing that launches Wild women on Journeys beyond the State of Lechery."[11] The challenge for me, as I see it Now, was and is to continue Spiraling on the Be-Dazzling Voyage which is Outercourse.

Specifically, at that Time, the task at hand was the creation of *Pure Lust: Elemental Feminist Philosophy*. The story of that book must Now be told.

THE BEGINNINGS OF *PURE LUST*

Throughout the summer of 1980 I worked at collecting information and commencing the philosophical analysis that constituted the raw beginnings of *Pure Lust*. Barbara Hope and Anne Dellenbaugh, both of whom were doing graduate study at Harvard Divinity School, were working with me as research, that is, Search assistants. Their help was invaluable as we amassed mountains of material in two unforgettable milk crates (which are Now serving the cause of *Outercourse*). One of these—the green one, I believe— contained files of newspaper clippings. The other—the cream-colored one —held files of notes corresponding to these clippings. There was an enormous amount of information on volcanoes and a specific file on Mount Saint Helens alone. There were "foreground files" on nuclearism and nuclear

---

*An outstanding example of such conversations with traveling companions was a week-long conference sponsored by the Canadian Council of the Arts at Stanley House in New Richmond, New Brunswick, on "Memory and Writing." The conference took place August 17–24, 1980. The women writers Present included Gail Scott, Yolande Villemaire, France Theoret, Louky Bersianik, Nicole Brossard, and Marisa Zavalloni. All gave extremely stimulating talks and the atmosphere was one of Radical Feminist intellectuality at its best. I had already met Marisa and Nicole in March 1979 in Montreal, shortly after *Gyn/Ecology* had been published, and we have subsequently met and conversed in various places, including New York, London, Oslo, Dublin, Boston, and Montreal. They are highly valued friends and Cronies.

explosions—the epitome of contrast to volcanic eruptions. There was a good deal of preliminary work on the obscenely proliferating lethal megamachine that I had begun to call "the sadosociety."

This early work was done in the Newtonville house, where the Furry Familiars Wild Cat and Wild Eyes ruled happily, taking over the house and yard, making it their own universe. Books were strewn all over the living room floor and the screened-in porch. Particularly impressive was the collection of library books on volcanoes. The energy swirling around there was *more* than impressive.

A startling manifestation of swirling Familiar energy occurred one evening when Anne Dellenbaugh and I were seated in the living room reading aloud passages concerning the doctrines about Angels in the writings of Johannes Scotus Erigena and Thomas Aquinas, as well as the doctrines of certain Arab philosophers, such as Averroes and Avicenna.* As we spoke of Angels, those majestic and powerful enlightened and enlightening pure spirits, traditionally considered as intermediate between "man" and "God," the room was Charged with Presence/Presences. Suddenly the two Furry Familiars dashed into the living room and onto the top of the piano, which was directly in front of us. They instantly assumed counterposing queenly positions—sitting tall—at the extreme left and the extreme right of the piano top.

I had never seen anything like this before. The cats had never assumed such positions. They appeared like a pair of Sphinxes who had flown in from a completely Other dimension—who had been Conjured by our reading of the words about Angels.

It would be impossible to see these Sister Felines in a merely ordinary way ever again. They had allowed me to Glimpse the Background, Shimmering in and through their Majestic Presences. It was a Moment of Seeing Elemental Spirits/Animals/Angelic beings—all at once.

I cannot Re-member what Anne and I did or said right after that brief Encounter, but I do know that subsequently Wild Cat and Wild Eyes returned to their familiar Familiar antics. Both enjoyed sleeping on their backs in the summer heat, with their front paws dangling in the air, apparently in a state of deep relaxation and with a Sense of complete safety. Wild Cat retrieved green beans and Wild Eyes watched, as usual. They were delightful "little angels," crouching here and there, playing hard and eating voraciously. They could afford to relax, having made their point that Angels and Animals are in communication with each Other. That was an Unforgettable Message that would work its way into *Pure Lust.*

---

*The idea of Angels here has nothing whatsoever in common with the insipid cherubic images commonly residing/presiding in the popular imagination. Nor does this have much in common with the biblical depictions of "angels." The Angels as understood by Aquinas are beings of great power and superior intelligence. The popular images are completely foregrounded reversals of the Reality of these Background beings.

In order to work intensively on *Pure Lust* I went on leave of absence from teaching for the academic year 1980–81. That fall I moved to a cottage—commonly known as "the cabin"—on a small piece of property on North Leverett Road in Leverett, Massachusetts, about eighty miles west of Boston. This absolutely Charged place had been jointly purchased by Denise and me as a "getaway place" in early September 1979.[12] It consisted of a funky, peach-colored, somewhat ramshackle colonial house which had been built in the nineteenth century and two free-standing buildings—"the cabin" and "the loft"—as well as a barn and a rather large garden in the back. The surrounding lands were extraordinarily beautiful . . . and Wild.

Frequently I would climb up one of the neighboring hills in order to chat with a friend of mine. This was a striking young cow whose demeanor and behavior were Free and Wild. I Sensed that her name was Catherine. Among Catherine's most remarkable qualities were the intelligence and communicativeness of her eyes. Clearly she was not by nature a domesticated animal. I often urged her to follow the Call of the Wild. "Be Free, Catherine!" I would say, and she would nuzzle my hands and skip around in her pasture.

Among the Elementally inspiring features of this setting were a horse pasture across the road and another just a few hundred yards away. The horses sometimes broke loose at night and went thundering down the road. One white mare, in particular, had a propensity for doing this, and a few times I saw her rear up on her hind legs in the moonlight, neighing in the Ecstasy of her Freedom and Wildness. Behind the horse pasture that was across the road was/is a very large hill ("Jackson Hill")—which was almost a small mountain—of incredible beauty, especially in the autumn.

Also breathtaking were the marshlands along the side of this property, which were of exquisitely variegated colors and which housed many inhabitants, including birds, peepers, and rabbits who "came out" frequently at sunset.

The land of this "property" was itself astonishing.* It was on a small hill. Between the house, with its attached "loft," and the cabin further back there was a lovely young fruit tree. Way back behind the cabin and garden there was a large maple tree which really was two trees that had grown up together, like siamese twins, forming one whole. The whole place, particularly at the top of the hill around the large maple tree/s was very windy. When I stood under that tree I could often see its leaves swirling/spiraling Wildly.

There was also the awesome sky. Views of the sunset were beyond breathtaking. But most remarkable was the night sky. On a clear night the

---

*As I repeatedly write the word *property* to describe this place I feel more and more absurd. According to *Webster's*, property is "something that is or may be owned or possessed." It became increasingly clear that neither I nor anyone else could "own" this place. It was not ownable.

moon and myriads of stars were more than visible. I say "more than visible" because the moon and the stars were also tangible. It was impossible not to feel a connection with them—not to be Touched/Influenced by them. They shifted vibrations. They Inspired/Fired feelings, images, words. Often "shooting stars" shot by, and these too carried messages.

The music of the stars and the music of the multitudes of birds and peepers were connected. This was a place of connections. Although I could not have known this at the time of the purchase in 1979, this would be the place of the Spinning of *Pure Lust*.

THE TORNADO

The Wildness of this setting can be Sensed more fully if one knows the story of The Tornado. I am referring to that Whirling Wind which caused tremendous damage there on October 3, 1979, not quite one month after the deed to the "property" had been signed, and almost a year before I moved into the cabin to work on *Pure Lust*.*

The Tornado struck the barn belonging to the farmer who lived next door and hurled huge slats of wood from that structure directly at the old peach-colored house, smashing the windows, damaging the roof, and knocking

---

*On October 16, 1991, I spoke on the phone with three residents of the Leverett area. I was confirming the exact date of The Tornado and asking about their experiences of that Wind. I first called the Leverett Town Hall and serendipitously reached Jane Davis, who remembered the event vividly. She had been teaching botany at the University of Massachusetts in Amherst in the fall of 1979 and had actually taken her class on a "field trip" the day after The Tornado to see its effects. She had brought them to my land, among other places. Together we managed to narrow the date to sometime in late September or early October of that year. When I asked her for her impression of that Tornado, she said: "It was *Strange!*" She was referring, in part, to the way it "hopped around," striking randomly here and there. Jane Davis suggested that I contact Annette Gibavic, who was doing historical research, and had just been at the Town Hall a few minutes before. I called Annette Gibavic and heard that she had found an article the evening before, describing The Tornado at length. The article, written by Georgene Bramlage, headlined "The Black Tornado Surged Through Leverett," had appeared in the *Amherst Morning Record*, October 16, 1979, p. 5. Annette Gibavic read some of this lengthy article to me. This not only established the date—October 3—but also gave graphic details of The Tornado's behavior. Her own word for this was "erratic." This was very interesting to me, since I had written in the Preface to *Pure Lust*: "Chiefly, it is a Work of Feminist Erraticism" (p. x). This causes me to Wonder Now if indeed The Tornado blew those words into my aura. At any rate, I next called Georgene Bramlage, around whose house on Cave Hill Road The Tornado had circled, felling hundreds of pine trees and causing "green air" (flying pine needles). Luckily, I found her at home. When I asked her to describe that Wind she paused and then answered: "Unreal! A Wizard of Oz experience!" From her tone, as well as the tones of the other women, I Sensed that for them it was, in fact, Super Real.

down wires.[13] In addition, that Whirling Wonder knocked the cabin off its foundation of rocks, so that it stood at a dangerous tilt. The large maple tree at the top of the hill, which had been two trees fused together, was split in half. One half, or one twin, remained standing, while the other half/twin crashed to the ground. As for the young fruit tree, the top part (almost half) of its trunk was cut off, while the bottom remained standing.

Within a couple of months the cabin had been moved back onto its foundation and damages to the main house had been repaired. It was sad to see the felled half of the maple tree/s lying on the ground, waiting for the farmer next door to get to the task of chopping it up and carrying it away.

When I moved into the cabin in September 1980 the surviving half of the maple tree/s was well along in the process of healing itself, as vines grew on its shattered side. It was by then a crooked tree, of course, like an illustration for a fairy tale or a gothic novel. The young fruit tree was growing one strong branch straight up alongside where the top of the trunk had been, so that this was beginning to look like a replacement for the top of the trunk.* In this Elemental setting I continued the Searching and began the Spinning of my Elemental Feminist Philosophy.

DIS-COVERING ELEMENTAL FEMINIST PHILOSOPHY

The subtitle of *Pure Lust—Elemental Feminist Philosophy—*says exactly what I meant it to say. Many meanings of the word *Elemental* converge to convey "a form of philosophical be-ing/thinking that emerges together with metapatriarchal consciousness—consciousness that is in harmony with the Wild in nature and in the Self."[14]

> The force of this philosophy has its source in women breaking out of the tamed/tracked modes of thinking/feeling of phallocracy. It is the force of reason rooted in instinct, intuition, passion.[15]

The meanings of *Elemental* that converge to convey this force include its "obsolete" definition, "material, physical." Other definitions include "fundamental, basic, earthy" (*Webster's*). Moreover, the noun *Elemental* was used by the philosopher and alchemist Paracelsus (and others) to name the earth spirits (gnomes), water spirits (undines or nymphs), fire spirits (salamanders), and air spirits (sylphs).

---

*When I revisited that place in 1990, in preparation for writing this chapter, I was excited to see that the maple tree no longer looked so much like a mythic crooked tree, but rather was standing quite straight, full, and strong. As for the fruit tree—its strong straight branch had grown so tall that a casual glance would not reveal that the trunk ended abruptly about halfway between the earth and the top.

The expression *the Elements*○ (the English translation of the Greek word *stoicheia*) means:

> **1 :** the spoken letters of the alphabet; the primal Race of words—their cosmic sounds, meanings, rhythms, and connections **2 :** fire, air, earth, water, constituting the deep Realms of Reality with which all sentient beings are Naturally and Wildly connected **3 :** the larger cosmos including the sun, moon, planets, and stars; the vast context within which the Primal Powers of Witches and all Wild beings must be understood **4 :** Elemental Spirits/Angels/Demons (*Wickedary*).[16]

The interflow of all of these meanings suggests the essential unity and intelligence of spirit/matter. It suggests the vastness of the Background in which we participate, and the need for Stamina on the part of Wild Women reclaiming our integrity by Spinning and Weaving broken connections.

Clearly my Piratic Dis-covering of Elemental Feminist Philosophy required more than study and discussion in the usual sense. It demanded that I risk living through Wilder Moments of Outercourse. The Tornado of 1979 had been telling me this. My "accidental" meeting with Mount Saint Helens just before her eruption had been another clear message. Moreover, it "just so happened" that I was driven by circumstances of my life in the fall of 1980 to actually move out to the place on North Leverett Road. So I was hurled into a Wild environment where I would be able to Live in deeper and richer connectedness than before with the Elements.

I Now See that my move to Leverett was not inconsistent with earlier Spiraling Leaps of my Outercourse. In some ways it is comparable to my move to St. Mary's College at Notre Dame to study theology in the early fifties when I had a powerful Sensation of a Great Wind carrying me.[17] It is also comparable to my crossing the Atlantic in 1959 in order to study at the University of Fribourg, in Switzerland.[18] At that Time also the Great Wind was my true vehicle. The same Wind blew the invitation from a British publisher in the sixties to write a book on women and the church, which reached me in Fribourg after "blowing around" that city to about eleven wrong addresses.[19] It brought me back to Boston in 1966 when I was forced by circumstances to leave Fribourg and return to the United States.[20] It continued Swirling throughout the late sixties and the seventies, as I wrote, taught, fought, laughed, Lived the life of a Radical Feminist.

There are threads of connectedness among all of these Swirling, Windy, Metapatterning Movements. There have always been a Search and an element of desperation. I was driven to/by each of these Wind-riding movements, and at the same Time I was eagerly following the Call of the Wild, which was an overwhelming, pleading Call, and an imperious one.

Strangely enough, in 1979 and 1980 I did not think of The Tornado as connected with the Great Wind. Perhaps this was because its behavior—at least as seen on the surface—was apparently unlike that of the Great Wind, which sometimes carried me like a gull and which also empowered my Craft to sail the Subliminal Sea. In contrast to this benign, empowering Wind, The Tornado came as a violent, destructive force.

Re-membering The Tornado Now, in Fourth Galactic Time, I Realize its *constructive* aspect. It *was* carrying something(s), like the Wind that carried the publisher's letter to me in Fribourg in the sixties. It was bearing Elemental messages and warnings. Insofar as I was able to Realize these, The Tornado empowered my Craft for the Swirling Moments of Dis-covering Elemental Feminist Philosophy.

These messages were Metaphoric, carrying me beyond the pseudoworld of the foreground. They came from the deeps of the Subliminal Sea, which had been stirred up by this Wild Wind, and they went deep into my soul. They rose with the Mist when I was writing *Pure Lust,* and as I decoded them the Be-Dazzling Light of The Third Spiral Galaxy was intensified.

Many of these decoded messages are recorded in *Pure Lust.* The essential thread that runs through them is the importance of Dis-covering and communicating Elemental Reality, and of illuminating the vast difference between this Reality and elementary pseudoreality, which is characterized by artificiality, and lack of depth, aura, and interconnectedness with living be-ing, and which is marked by a derivative and parasitic relation to Elemental Reality.[21]

It is not always a simple matter to recognize and communicate the differences between Elemental Reality and the elementary world—in other words, between the Background and the foreground. This is in part because of the increasing pervasiveness of the elementary world and because the latter is comprised of derivative imitations of the Elemental world, which are mere *elementaries.**

While it may be easy to distinguish plastic flowers from real ones or even a satellite in the sky from a real star, there are more insidious cases. For example, one may have some difficulty recognizing genuine Passion/E-motion, as distinct from plastic passions. A woman may also have trouble, at first, distinguishing genuine Spinning conversation, which resonates with cosmic sounds, meanings, rhythms, and connections, from academented babble. At times the differences are unmistakable; at other times they are blurred.

---

*elementaries○ are "simulations of and planned replacements for the Elemental, the Wild; fabrications which distort experience of the Elements and which are largely invisible by reason of being all-pervasive; incarnations of phallic myth that constitute the foreground; man-made phenomena lacking depth, radiance, resonance, harmonious interconnectedness with living be-ing. *Examples* **a** : the poisonous fumes and radioactive emissions of phallotechnology **b** : the transmissions of popular media and the erudition of specialized fields **c** : traditional assumptions, spoken and unspoken **d** : shopping malls **e** : plastics" (*Wickedary*).

Learning to trust one's own judgment, one's deep powers of discernment, and to communicate such knowledge and Act on it is an essential task of the Elemental Feminist Philosopher. The process of writing *Pure Lust* was engaging in this task. It consisted of Moments of encountering and Naming Elemental Reality and of peeling away and expelling elementaries. These were Be-Dazzling Moments of eclipsing the foreground with the brilliance of Background be-ing. This brings me around again to the subject of the setting in which these Moments occurred.

LEVERETT IN THE FALL OF 1980
I: SWIRLING CONTINUITY

North Leverett Road offered the kind of throbbing Elemental environment in which my early intuitions of be-ing could be Wildly Realized. In the beginning of *Outercourse* I described the Moment in my adolescence when one particular clover blossom gave me an intuition of be-ing, beckoning me on my Quest to become a philosopher. I have also described the companion Moment/experience which occurred a few years later at Saint Mary's, Notre Dame. This Time the Speaker was a hedge on the campus, who/which Said "Continued Existence." The hedge was simply Unfolding, or making more explicit, knowledge that was implicit in the Be-Speaking of the clover blossom. Insofar as the two experiences were distinct and separate, I might venture to say that whereas the earlier Encounter had summoned me to become a philosopher, the Be-Speaking of the hedge Nudged/Called me further on my theological Course. As Fourth Galactic Time-Traveler, however, I Know that they were ultimately the same Call. I had responded in a variety of ways in many Moments and in each of my earlier books. But in my Weaving of my *Elemental Feminist Philosophy* I was challenged further to create a tapestry of intertwining threads, manifesting the New/Archaic integrity that was intimated in those intuitions/beckonings.

These early Encounters had in common a shocking abruptness but also a gentleness.[22] Both were absolutely Elemental, but their settings—Schenectady, New York, and Saint Mary's, Notre Dame—were not Wild. This is not to say that Wildness was not there. There was incredible Elemental Green in grassy places, but it was rather hidden and therefore startling in its manifestations.

Compared to these, the Elemental Encounters of Leverett were less gentle, and the setting was indeed Wild. As I reflect upon the other than gentle quality of the Leverett experiences, I am again reminded that the scene was set by The Tornado. For me, The Tornado functioned in the deepest Sense like all Metapatriarchal Metaphors. That is, by Naming/Signaling Metamorphosis, it elicited Metapatriarchal transformation.

nudged to Dis-cover the relation of divination to the Elemental world, as I pounced upon words such as *Geomancy, Aeromancy, Hydromancy,* and *Pyromancy*—words meaning, respectively, Divination by means of signs derived from earth, air, water, and fire.

Thus these Words themselves put me in Touch with Other dimensions of the Elements—just as the Elements connected me with the Words. This was not the first Time that I had experienced Other Dimensions. I had known them in early childhood and more strongly in adolescence, when they had shown themselves with abruptness, gentleness, and pure poignancy. I had had, for example, a Sense of direct contact with the moon. There also had been Moments of Seeing the "celestial gleam" over hills and meadows. Especially transporting had been the Dimension of the Purple night sky that was Other than ordinary purple, which I once had glimpsed in adolescence and had vowed never to forget.[26] Of course I did forget for long periods of time, when I was submerged in "the cotton wool of daily life."[27] I also forgot—and would later Re-member—fields that elicited experiences of *déjà vu* as well as Foreglimpses of Ecstatic running through tall grasses and around tufts on winding pathways, on some undefined but joyous Search.[28]

So my Dis-covering of Lost Senses, including the Sense of Deep Memory, involved Diving and Soaring into Elemental Reality in ways that were not entirely unfamiliar, but Strange nevertheless, because they cut through the "cotton wool." I am quite sure that in 1980 I did not Re-member consciously all of the comparable yet different Elemental experiences of my childhood and adolescence. But I do Know Now that those Moments of Spinning in Leverett were also Moments of reconnecting with the early experiences. These were like "parallel" Moments in the Spiraling Paths of Outercourse. Thus my Touching the moon and stars of the night sky in Leverett was enhanced by the Moment of transcendent vision of the Purple sky over Schenectady. The fields of Leverett and my hikes through them corresponded somewhat with experiencing the mystical fields of my childish explorations. I was Re-Calling the Elements and Weaving/Re-Weaving connections with them. I was Re-Claiming Elemental be-ing.

LEVERETT IN THE FALL OF 1980
III: THE BEEHIVE STRUCTURES AND "BA"

Some of the events that happened in that Time/Space were more complex than others. One rather complex concordance concerns "beehive" structures.

That autumn a neighbor sent me a local newspaper clipping about "beehive" structures (referred to as "tombs") that had been found in Leverett. Someone had presented a paper on these at the Deerfield Historical Society. By means of some detective work I tracked down this man and arranged to meet him at a certain crossroads (at the intersection of North Leverett Road and Route 63). My guide took me to the three beehive structures in the area, which were/are quite close to each other.

These structures were all built underground. Each had a large slab of rock covering and hiding its entrance. The walls of the interiors were comprised of rocks intricately and precisely put together. After climbing inside each one I had the sense of sitting in a beehive, looking out at the sky. These did not seem to me to be tomb-like, but rather resembled hideouts or small dwellings.[29]

The three structures were different in size and my experience of each was distinct. The largest was spacious enough to hold five women. The middle-sized one was capable of "accommodating" three. The smallest would contain only one. It was my impression then that the smallest was a rather powerful energy source, whereas the largest structure was the weakest. This may have had something to do with the fact that many people had already "discovered" the large cave, or dwelling, and had used it for a variety of purposes.

I visited the three "beehives" with women who belonged to a study group that had originated in my classes in the spring of 1980 and continued for many months afterward.* We were incessantly involved in intense Spinning conversations, many of which centered around the Weaving of *Pure Lust*. On one of our first visits to these Strange places, a few of us were inspired to chant "Om" while sitting inside.

The night after the first "Om" chanting I was sleeping alone in the cabin and was awakened by a peculiar sound outside my window. What it "said" was "Ba." The letter "a" sounded like the "a" in the word "apple." It did not sound quite human—nor did it sound exactly like a sheep. It was a sheeplike sound but different—more startling and aggressive. Moreover, there were no sheep in that area. Although I was "freaked out," I went back to sleep.

The following day, having half-forgotten the incident, I was looking up "Beehive" in J. C. Cooper's *An Illustrated Encyclopedia of Traditional Symbols*. Suddenly my eye caught an illustration on the opposite page of a bird hovering over an Egyptian mummy. The caption under the illustration read:

On a 13th-century BC Egyptian papyrus, the Ba, the bird of the soul, hovers over a mummy before beginning its flight to the afterlife.[30]

Stunned by this "coincidence" (the illustration was not meant to have anything to do with "Beehive," but rather accompanied the entry on "Birds"), I contacted the women with whom I had chanted "Om" the day before. We went back to the beehive structure and chanted "Om" again. Then I

---

*These women were Anne Dellenbaugh, Barbara Hope, Eleanor Mullaley, Kathy Miriam, and Mary Schultz.

suggested that we chant "Ba." We did, and were astonished afterward to hear the sound of bees buzzing, although no bees were in sight. This experience was repeated throughout the fall, with variations, in the middle-sized structure especially. However, the meaning of all of this was partially obscure.

It was not until years later (in 1987) that I read in *American Heritage* (Appendix on Indo-European Roots), that the root *bhā²* means "to speak." *Bhā²* is the root of the Latin *fārī* "to speak." The past participle of this word is the root of the English word *fate*.[31] So it was before I knew that *bhā* (Ba) means "to speak" that I had the intuition to go and chant this sound with my friends in the beehive structure in Leverett. However, I had read in Cooper's *Illustrated Encyclopedia,* in the entry on "Beehive":

> Eloquence, "honeyed words," an ordered community. . . . In Greece the beehive was often used as the shape of a tomb, suggesting immortality.[32]

I don't think that I was consciously applying this information when I followed my instinct to go and chant "Ba" in the "beehive." Clearly, however, this series of incidents was interconnected with the process of writing an Elemental Feminist Philosophy. These incidents, as I understood them, were "saying" that *Pure Lust* was participation in the work of the Fates, who spin *Stamina,* the thread of life.[33] The Fates are associated with Elemental sounds.[34] They inspire Be-Speaking. They inspired *Pure Lust.*

LEVERETT IN THE FALL OF 1980
IV: MORE MAGIC

A favorite Elemental place was Rattlesnake Gutter Road, which runs off North Leverett Road and winds high up, so that eventually there is a deep ravine on the right, which is full of trees, rocks, and large natural caves. On the left-hand side of the road the ground rises up, and giant trees have wrapped their roots around moss-covered rocks for such a long time that the reality is part roots, part rocks—all covered with the glistening, soft, rich green moss that Gnomes love to use as cushions and pillows.

This Haunt was a haven at all times, but especially on rainy and misty days it revealed itself as an Other world, awakening *Elemental Memory*○, which is the

> faculty that Re-members knowledge, emotions, and experiences beyond the fabricated elementary "recollections" of the foreground; Deep Memory, grounded in primal experience of the Elements; Memory of Archaic Time, where/when the commonplace brims with meaning, the trees and animals speak, and Crones *know* our connections with the moon and stars (*Wickedary*).

Moreover, Rattlesnake Gutter Road was (and is) a Haunt of *Elemental Spirits*○, that is to say,

Spirits/Angels/Demons manifesting the essential intelligence of spirit/matter; Intelligences ensouling the stars, animating the processes of earth, air, fire, water, enspiriting the sounds that are the Elements of words, connecting words with the earth, air, fire, water, and with the sun, moon, planets, stars (*Wickedary*).

Given the fact that it awakened such Memory and was Haunted by such Spirits, that place lured me on in my efforts to participate in the cosmic concordance of *Elemental Sounding*○, that is, "the Speaking of all Elemental creatures in the chorus of be-ing" (*Wickedary*). So I Be-Spoke many Words of *Pure Lust* in this throbbing, vibrating atmosphere of connectedness.

Several times when I was hiking on Rattlesnake Gutter Road climbing into the caves and up among the trees, New Words began their Soundings in my consciousness. When I was exploring there with Barbara, *Gnome*-words naturally popped into our conversations. Indeed, our study group soon became known among us as the "Gnome Group," and our conversations became more Gnomic, that is, Earthy.

At the same Time the stars gave awesome messages of Be-Dazzling connections. The Milky Way was on display and "shooting stars" hurled themselves through the heavens in full view of the cabin. In this atmosphere, words such as *Starchase* and *Star-Lust* were born.

There were also Magical encounters with books. On my frequent trips with Barbara to rather esoteric bookstores near Leverett, especially "Sophia" in Amherst and "Beyond Words Bookstore" in Northampton, I Dis-covered and purchased spiritual and mystical books that were extremely helpful for the expansion and articulation of my Elemental consciousness. Among these were works by the alchemist/philosopher Paracelsus, Madame Blavatsky, and Jane Roberts. I also acquired and devoured several books on auras. I pounced upon works on gnosticism. At other stores I darted for books on stars, nebulas, quasars. I snatched up works by novelists such as Alice Walker and ecologists such as Rachel Carson. I flew with this loot— properly purchased, not "ripped off," of course—back to my cabin/cove. These served as navigational aids for my Craft, as I sailed with the stars, the birds, the women and learned to Hear and Speak Elemental Sounds.

After a short time my Furry Familiar, Wild Cat, joined me in Leverett. She was Ecstatic in the country and especially in the cabin, that archetypically Witchy crooked cottage near the crooked tree. There, in *her* house, she loved to climb the rafters, behaving like a true jungle animal. Whenever she disappeared, the first direction in which I Searched for her was Up. She tried to earn her own living by catching mice, but her generous spirit led her to the practice of bringing me their "remains" as gifts. I tried to refuse these presents graciously, but we had a "communication problem." Since neither Wild Cat nor I cared or care to resolve "issues" by going to a therapist, we agreed to bracket the whole affair. She never told me that she felt "invalidated" by my cold refusal and I never asked her to sit around and "deal" with her "perception." We did not "share" our "problem" with anyone, and we continued—and still continue—to enjoy each other's company and affection, remaining blissfully ignorant of our "interpersonal dynamics." Wild Cat never joined a "twelve-step program" to help her with her mouse addiction. Moreover, neither she nor I are of the opinion that our mothers are to blame for this "block" in our "relationship." Indeed, we have no opinions at all about "our stuff."

TRYING TRANSITIONS:
WINTER, SPRING, AND SUMMER 1981

During the winter of 1981 it was very cold in the cabin, even though it had some (defective) electrical heating system. I am no Eskimo, so I moved back to Newtonville. The Gnome Group managed to meet there a few times. I longed for the Elemental connection, however, so I returned to the cabin for awhile that winter and spring.

On one of my winter trips out to North Leverett Road with Wild Cat as my passenger, my Pinto skidded wildly on the ice in a deserted area on Route 2, somewhere near the exit for Lunenburg. There were cement walls serving as partitions on the road in that area, but at the spot where we skidded it "just so happened" that there were no deadly dividers, but rather there was a wide snow-covered grassy area separating the two sides of the highway. So the car careened off and just skidded for some distance in the snow. Once again in my Life, I was very Lucky.

Leaving Wild Cat in the car I walked over to the road and flagged down a car, asking the driver to notify the State Police. After awhile a police officer arrived and I had to go with him to State Police Headquarters to track down a tow truck. When I returned in that vehicle I found Wild Cat safe but cold, of course. When we got back on the road it was snowing rather heavily, and it was dark. The trip seemed endless.

Somewhere in the mountainous, spooky area near the town of Athol, Wild Cat spoke. It was the first Time that I Realized she could talk. Of course she had "talked"/communicated with me in many ways since kittenhood. This, however, was a human word. What she said was simply one word, with a questioning and infinitely pleading intonation. That word, very comprehensibly uttered, with a slight feline accent, was "Where?" Of course, I tried to console her with scratches, strokes, and spoken reassurances all the scary way home.

That spring and summer of 1981 I was based in Newtonville. Although I had good friends, it was a dry period. My soul was in Wasteland. There were bright spots, however. One of these was the ten-day visit of Erika Wisselinck, who was translating *Gyn/Ecology* into German. This was our first meeting. She came in late June and left in early July. Her trip from her home in Strasslach, Germany, to Boston had been by way of California, where she had visited Nelle Morton.

Erika had nearly completed her translation. It was a monumental task, not only because of the length and intense compactness of the book, but also because the wordplays in English have no strict counterpart in German (or in any other language). Erika's creative genius allowed her to Dis-cover comparable but not always identical wordplays in German. So *Gyn/Ecology* (*Gyn/Ökologie*) Sparked her own Original work.

Erika finished her translation of the last chapter of *Gyn/Ecology* in the Newtonville house. She also began writing her own extraordinary book, then entitled *Anna: Several Days in the Life of an Old Woman.* This is her Original version of the legend of the mother of Mary and of her relation with her daughter and (less significantly) with her peculiar grandson.[35] During that visit we began what has proven to be a lasting friendship. We discussed the twelfth-century Genius, Hildegard of Bingen. Erika's remarks Sparked my interest to the extent that I went down into the cellar and dragged out a dusty volume of the *Catholic Encyclopedia,* which, Strangely enough, did contain very useful information and Background clues about the life and work of this gifted woman, with whom I have Sensed an Electrical connection.

Erika and I traveled to Onset, noting on the way the escalation of de-struction of the environment. We also made an important "business trip" to Amherst, where we consulted with Beate Riesterer, a German scholar and college professor who had been reading over and commenting upon a sec-tion of Erika's translation of *Gyn/Ecology* since April. The scene in Beate's apartment was, from my point of view, very comical. I enjoyed watching and hearing two German Hags arguing and cackling over particular points of translation in German. I felt that we were a conspiracy of Witches brewing and stirring a Gyn/Ecological pot of Wicked Soup, so that women in Ger-many could gobble it up and form more Covens of Revolting Hags.

There were other bright spots that summer. Among these were the steady and enduring friendships of several women, very different from each other, but very Real in their Presence. Among these were Pat Green, Fran Chel-land, Clare Hall, Ann Cobb. Very bright was the return of Emily to Cam-bridge, after being away for two years in California. But my soul was still parched, enduring a seemingly endless Passage through Wasteland.

THE JOURNEY TO AUSTRALIA:
A TIMELY ESCAPE AND MASSIVE EXORCISM

On July 28, 1981, I started on a journey to Australia. I flew to California, stopping to visit my good friend Nelle Morton in Claremont. On the follow-ing day I was driven to the airport by a woman who had been a graduate stu-dent at Claremont and who had visited my classes in Boston. I had noticed that she seemed "off" and strangely detached. On the way to the airport she narrated in detail a very hostile dream she had had about me. She told me that in her dream she and I were married. She wanted (and got) a divorce, because I had no passion, no fire, and not much intellectuality either. At the conclusion of this unpleasant narrative she told me that women are threatened by my brain, by my intellectuality, by the fact that I am a philosopher, whereas they are not threatened by novelists or by poets, like Adrienne (Rich). She announced that the dream (in which I was essentially reduced to mush) had freed her of her fear of me.

That conversation helped make me more conscious than before of the Total Taboo against women becoming Woman-identified/Self-identified philosophers—a Taboo implying terrible sanctions, which are imposed not only by men in power but also by their (largely unconscious) henchwomen, who function as Token Torturers. I began to see that this Taboo is far deeper than the Taboo against women becoming theologians. This is in part because theology, traditionally understood, implies submission to authority—of the bible and/or a religious institution. A philosopher, on the Other hand, is an autonomous seeker of wisdom who freely explores and Names Reality. Under patriarchy *this*—more than anything else—is forbidden to women. This Taboo is embedded in women's psyches, so that they become Self-censors and censors of each other. The Nag-Gnostic philosopher who breaks this Taboo will inevitably become the target of "sisters"/censors who fear and envy her Ecstasy, her Freedom, and her Fiercely Focused Sense of Purpose.

Armed with that load of thought-provoking and horrifying ideas and images I boarded the plane for Sydney. The day before leaving Boston I had had the feeling that I was escaping "here" just in time. The bad times of the early eighties were taking their toll among Radical Feminists. I recall conversations with Robin Morgan in the course of which we spoke, almost in whispers, of *how* bad it was—physically and psychically—among women. No explanation was needed. It was simply an all-pervasive condition. It was "in the air." So also was the fear of nuclear holocaust, which was very much on our minds at that time.

In Sydney I stayed at the adjoining homes of Suzanne Bellamy and Janet Ramsay. These women were not strangers to me. Suzanne had begun corresponding with me in 1975, after she had read *Beyond God the Father* and lectured on it to six hundred students in a course at the university where she was teaching. Both women had stayed at the Newtonville house during their visit to the U.S. in January 1980 and had visited my Feminist Ethics class, partly to serve as psychic bodyguards against the possibility of an invasion by other "visitors"—the monitors that the administration had implicitly threatened to send again.[36]

It would be difficult to find suitable adjectives to describe my experience of Australia. Suzanne and Janet and their three cats—Cinnamon, Bianca, and Sylvia—were very generous and kind, providing an atmosphere where I could recuperate from my multileveled jet lag. I Re-Call day trips, especially into the Blue Mountains. At a wildlife park I met koalas dining on eucalyptus leaves and had a surprising encounter with an emu. The latter, who was extremely tall, was out for an evening walk on a path which I had egotistically assumed was reserved for humans. I did not see this personage approaching, and nearly collided with it. Its remark was a loud inimitable sort of gronking sound, and it almost knocked me down as it continued on the path. It reminded me of a European professor haughtily pacing and cogitating after an evening meal. We also went into "the bush" for a hike. For the first time I heard the loud laughter of kookaburras. The Be-Laughing of these Strange Australian birds was startling and contagious.

Next I went to central Australia with Suzanne and Janet. We flew to Alice Springs on Sunday, August 9, and on Monday we drove three hundred and fifty kilometers on a red sand road to Ayers Rock. After walking around part of it we drove to our main destination, the Olgas, which are a collection of twenty-eight domes of conglomerate rock, separated by deep valleys. As I climbed up and around the Olgas, walking through the Valley of the Winds, I was more and more confirmed in my impression that I was not just on a different continent on the other side of the globe, but on another planet. The landscape/rockscape was not like anything I had ever seen. There were multitudes of fantastically colored Wild parrots, and here and there I met a kangaroo. We returned to Alice Springs, staying at a ranch on the way. On Friday we went to King's Canyon and took a side trip on our way back to Alice, going past two-million-year-old meteorite craters. The drive to the craters in the sunset was ineffable—a world of red, orange, and violet. We saw the craters in the light of the full moon. It was August 14—the eve of Lammas—one of the four great feasts of Witches. The place was eerie beyond belief. It was an unearthly, Martian-like scene.

On Saturday we went to Simpson's Gap and Standley Chasm. The aridness of the canyons, gaps, and gorges exacerbated my thirst, literally, on many levels. I looked eagerly for water, everywhere. Once, when I found some in a dried-up river bed, I was overcome with a sense of relief, for I had felt as if my soul was dying.

The animals never failed to give signals of Biophilic encouragement. In addition to the winsome large kangaroos, the astonishing variety of strange lizards and breathtaking parrots, there were dingoes (wild dogs), wallabies hiding (but visible) in the rocks, soaring kites who caught bread that was thrown into the air at a campsite, camels (not indigenous to Australia but *there* all the same). These animal friends inspired me.

On Sunday I decided to blow my savings and took a flight from Alice to Cairns, in northeastern Australia, in order to explore the Great Barrier Reef. I found myself in tropical Australia. Although it was August and therefore winter, the place was extremely hot. I saw the astonishing coral, and I swam in the ocean. I took an overnight bus trip into the mountains, and it was there, after the long arid Passage of my soul's Journey, that I experienced the miracle of beginning to feel in Touch once again with the Powers of the Elements. Having dozed off on the bus at night during the return trip, I was awakened by the Touch of Something. That Something was the Moon shining through the window. It seemed to be tapping me on the shoulder. Startled, I looked out and saw in the distance a fire on the side of a mountain. So I was experiencing the beginnings of a New Realization of Elemental connectedness. I was preparing, deep in my soul, for continuing the creation of *Pure Lust*.

Before I could return to that, however, I had to speak at a Meeting (Conference) in Sydney during the last week of August. This was held in the auditorium of the Teachers' Federation Building. Hundreds of women came —many from far away. Most came with good intentions. However, the few women who came with the intention of disruption and destruction wrought havoc. They wanted a "show," and I was fair game. Several of these individuals stood up and interrupted me loudly. One shouted: "Yankee go home!" Since I am not exactly a flag-waving patriot, I was astonished. Another stood and sobbed with phony hysteria. She whined: "You're not speaking to *me*, Mary." In the course of her ensuing tirade she proclaimed that "housewives" could not understand me.

After each interruption I answered, and I stood my ground. I explained, for example, that the remark about "housewives" was insulting to women who might be "classified" in that category and that many "housewives" had attended my classes and public lectures and had read my books. Moreover, I described the very positive and intelligent response of these women to my work. It was clear that the band of noisy disrupters had not won. It seemed strange to me, however, that most of the other women there did not intervene. I finished my speech and left the auditorium. It was obvious to me that no further discourse could happen in that atmosphere.

A large number of women regrouped later that evening at Suzanne's house, where we held the *real* "meeting." These women were intelligent, sensitive Feminists.* We discussed many subjects, including the backlash against Radical Feminism, as displayed in the auditorium that evening. Several bouquets of flowers and cards of sympathy and apology arrived for me during the next few days. These were kind gestures, but I felt that there was something comic, as well as eerie about this "funereal" scene.

At any rate, I was far from dead. I was beginning to comprehend that my voyage to Australia had functioned not only as a Timely escape and Passage through psychic Wasteland, but also as a massive Exorcism of the demonic forces that assault Radical Feminists. Moreover, I knew that I was ready to Spiral on with *Pure Lust*. I returned to the U.S. by way of New Zealand,

---

*I met many stimulating Hags/Nags in Australia—on hikes in the bush, at picnics and parties, and in the course of doing radio and newspaper interviews. The odd twist of the Meeting in Sydney could be seen as a fluke, or as representative of a negative undercurrent in Australia at that time. At any rate, Radical Feminism in Australia was then and is Now a Living Reality.

stopping over for a few days to visit that beautiful country. I could not stay long, however, because it was Time to Move. Charged/Re-Charged with the will to get back to Spinning, I returned to Newtonville and began preparing for my final move back to North Leverett Road and its Elemental setting.

LEVERETT IN THE FALL OF 1981

In September 1981 I started packing and making arrangements, and in October I moved into the structure known as "the loft." Unlike the cabin—that compact little Witch's house—the loft was one large room. Its various windows looked out on the rabbit-inhabited, multicolored marshland on one side and on the hill out back on another. The window directly opposite the one with the view of the marshland faced a large, extraordinarily communicative tree, whose splendors would be revealed to me in all seasons. The loft had a very efficient gas heater, and the sense of spaciousness allowed my aura to expand.

I also used the small apartment in the main house. This was necessary to house my furniture as well as overnight and weekend guests. Not less important was the fact that it had a bathroom, which the loft lacked. The loft did have a stove and sink with running water but, unlike the cabin, it lacked a shower and—uh—commode. Otherwise it was extremely comfortable. It was *the* place for my writing at that time. The vibes felt exactly right for Spinning Big.

Fran Chelland moved to the cabin shortly after that. She helped me with correspondence and did other work, including composing her own music and writing for the *Greenfield Recorder.* Her Presence was a Be-Witching gift.

The Wildness of the place was surging through my soul. By early November I was making big breakthroughs in writing. Joann Aalfs, who Searched for me at local libraries, did invaluable work, finding important Sources on Gnosticism. Extremely significant were works that she herself owned and loaned to me, especially *The Interpreter's Bible,* a twelve-volume set with Strangely useful exegeses,[37] and *The Interpreter's Dictionary of the Bible,*[38] a four-volume set containing crucial material for my purposes. These works served as springboards for my work on Elements, Elemental Spirits, Principalities and Powers, Angels of the Elements.[39]

An important "interruption" was a trip to California for the purpose of giving a lecture at The School of Theology at Claremont on November 6. According to my notes, I spoke about a number of ideas from the First Realm of *Pure Lust,* such as the sadosociety, the Sadospiritual Syndrome, the meaning of *Pure Lust,* the Race of Women, the Archimage, Elemental Spirits, Traveling Companions. The women at Claremont loved my material. Happily Nelle Morton was there. I had a wonderful visit with her at her home where she read my "New Stuff" with great appreciation. So that whole experience at Claremont encouraged me to Leap and Bound around and ahead with that book. I returned to Leverett in high spirits.

A Strange event occurred soon after my return. It happened on Friday, November 13, in Steiger's—a department store in Hanover Shopping Mall on Route 9, outside Amherst. That evening I went into the store to buy something and happened to wander through the clock department. To my utter astonishment, *nine* clocks were stopped at exactly 11:12—my Be-Witching Hour.[40] When I mentioned this mind-boggling Event to Emily she of course understood my astonishment, since we had had long conversations about "the 11:12 phenomenon"—an experience in which she and Other friends have participated. We conjectured that this exaggerated version of the experience—*nine* clocks—could be seen as a comic/cosmic emphasis of "the message." To me it was as if the clocks were screaming in chorus: "Don't you get it yet?! Hurry up. It's Time! Do your Work!"*

So I did. I Sprang ahead with my writing and lecturing.

WINTER, SPRING, SUMMER 1982

La Crosse, Wisconsin, and The Inquisition

On February 25, 1982, I spoke at the University of Wisconsin in La Crosse. Judging from the response of the audience at the lecture and during the reception that followed, as well as from the letters I received afterward, the event was a great success. I did notice a few people in the audience who seemed a bit creepy but I didn't think much about it at the time. There was a particularly pompous-looking priest lurking in the back of the hall and a group of grim-looking women sitting together. As I was walking down the aisle of the auditorium on my way to the reception, one of these, in a loud voice, offered me the distressing "information" that I would experience a "deathbed conversion" back to catholicism. The others nodded knowingly in agreement, with looks of pure hate.

During the reception a woman reporter from the *La Crosse Tribune* came over to "interview" me. She had only one question: "Are you a lesbian?" I answered "Yes, and what does that have to do with my lecture?" She walked away. Apparently this was a hot subject in La Crosse.

Upon returning to Leverett I went back to my Spinning in the loft. Early in April I received a strange letter, dated March 29, 1982, from J. Donald Monan, s.j., President of Boston College, informing me that "many people"

---

*Now, in The Fourth Spiral Galaxy, I Realize that this Message was echoing the Words of my mother, repeated frequently in my childhood and adolescence: "You go and do your own work, dear." See Chapter One.

had contacted BC about my lecture at La Crosse. Since I was on unpaid leave of absence that academic year for the purpose of writing, I was surprised to hear from those quarters, and especially astonished to find that this missive concerned my speech at La Crosse. Was Torquemada following me around the country?*

President Monan had enclosed a copy of an article from the *La Crosse Tribune* as well as a copy of his reply to a letter sent to him by a rev. Bernard McGarty, who was "Director of Communications" for the Diocese of La Crosse. President Monan wrote to fr. McGarty that "some of the quotations attributed to Dr. Daly amply fulfill the definition of 'blasphemy.'" He informed this individual that "I am currently seeking counsel as to whether those statements, made on a public university campus, constitute a violation of contractual obligations she still retains towards this University."

Within a couple of days I received a "follow-up" letter, this time from William B. Neenan, s.j., then Dean of the College of Arts and Sciences, who "requested" a statement in writing "either affirming or denying the accuracy of the remarks attributed to you as quotations." I was told to send the statement to him by April 23.

So this was the Inquisition—just what I needed to provide peace of mind while writing *Pure Lust!* I wondered: How could one respond? Of course, I sprang into action, first calling the Symposium Chairperson at La Crosse, who informed me that any "negative response" to my lecture was almost entirely a reaction to the irresponsible and distorted journalism of the *La Crosse Tribune*. She had received a number of letters congratulating the Symposium Committee for bringing me to La Crosse and offered to forward these to me. She also agreed to inform persons who were at my lecture of this "situation" and to request that they send letters to President Monan and Dean Neenan describing their response to my lecture, with copies of these letters to me.

On April 21 I wrote to Dean Neenan, explaining that the article in the *La Crosse Tribune* was a complete distortion of my speech. I enclosed copies of letters from women and men that had been forwarded to me from La Crosse, as well as letters from faculty at other colleges and universities where I had recently lectured and had presented substantially the same material as that delivered at La Crosse.[41]

The letters sent to President Monan and Dean Neenan were enlightened and enlightening. Many attempted to explain my stature in the world as a philosopher, theologian, and lecturer. Many also explained that the tempest in the La Crosse teapot stemmed almost entirely from persons who had *not* attended the speech and who had been urged "from the pulpits" to write their (uninformed) opinions (based on the absurd article) to the *La Crosse*

---

*Torquemada, of course, was the fifteenth century Spanish Grand Inquisitor.

Tribune for publication. One professor of history who had been present wrote: "It was the best intellectual jolt this University has had in my fifteen years here." Many reassured the BC administration that the *La Crosse Tribune* article was a gross distortion. Some tried to appeal to the jesuits' reputation for "fairness" and "openness to ideas"(!). Others attempted patiently to explain to President Monan the antediluvian, parochial attitudes that prevail in the La Crosse, Wisconsin area.*

Subsequent letters to me from Dean Neenan as well as punitive action from the university demonstrated that antediluvian attitudes were not confined to La Crosse. I received a second letter from Neenan, dated May 14, 1982, which he sent after receiving my reply of April 21 and the many letters of support. He offered no acknowledgment of all of this testimony. He reiterated the inquisitorial demand: "I repeat my request to receive in writing a statement either confirming or denying the accuracy of the quotations attributed to you."

Since I could not spend time on the worthless and demeaning task of responding point by point to statements attributed to me out of context in a malignant piece of yellow journalism, I did not bother to reply. I had important work to do, especially my writing and public speaking.[42]

Of course, the BC administration was showing no respect for me or for the many highly qualified people who had written to them on my behalf. Moreover, they were using the common oppressive strategy of embedding anxiety. This, as is well known, can block creativity. By not succumbing, and by continuing to write and sustain my public Presence, I was learning more and more about the Battle of Principalities and Powers, which was a pivotal subject of analysis in *Pure Lust*.

On September 16, 1982 Dean Neenan sent yet another letter to me in Leverett, where I was spending my third year of that unpaid leave Spinning *Pure Lust*. He intoned: "I can only assume from the fact that you have not responded directly to this request that you do not take exception to the quotations attributed to you in that issue of the *La Crosse Tribune*." The letter rumbled/rambled on about my "contractual obligations," which somehow

---

*Stark evidence of the reality of these "attitudes" in that area came three years later. On February 7, 1985, a very "parochial" catholic from La Crosse committed a triple murder. His victims were: Rev. John Rossiter, pastor of St. Patrick's church in Onalaska (ten miles from La Crosse), Ferdinand Roth, Sr., a lay minister at the church, and William Hammes, custodian. The killer, Brian Stanley, shot the priest in the back of the head with a 12-gauge shotgun right after Mass and shot the others shortly afterward. The reason for the killings was that Stanley was "upset" that Rossiter had allowed two girls to read aloud from scripture during the Mass. (See *La Crosse Tribune*, February 8, 1985, p. 1.) In a conversation with a woman who belonged to that parish in Onalaska and knew the slain priest, I learned some of the details including the fact that she had seen his blood splattered on the ceiling of the church (Telephone conversation with Mary Brieske, September 21, 1991).

were construed to include the obligation to censor mySelf, or rather, to refrain from "the derisive and deliberately provocative tone of those remarks" attributed to me. So once again I pondered dimensions of patriarchal deception and the Battle of Principalities and Powers.

I did not respond. Most importantly, I kept Spinning, Spiraling on.*

Living in the Loft: Spiraling into Pyrospheres

Although it was draining, The Inquisition contributed to my development of many of the ideas in *Pure Lust*. These concepts include the Sadospiritual Syndrome, women as touchable caste, academentia, bore-ocracy, absence of Presence, elementaries. When I say that this draining intervention "contributed" to the development of ideas, what I mean is that *I* as agent Actively wrenched from the experience *more* knowledge about the fathers' foreground and the elementary world. I did not merely passively *re*-act. Rather, I fought to overcome the *apraxia* which such foregrounding, elementary machinations are designed to reinforce. Hence I became more *Active* than before, using my awakened Senses to understand and Name the deadly phallocratic games, Plundering and Smuggling information gleaned from the experience, Shaping a Sharper analysis of androcracy.

The "contribution" of the patriarchs to my work is not at all comparable to the Gifts of the Elemental world and its Inhabitants. In the case of the former I was/am the true Agent molding the material presented according to the Direction of my Craft. The elementary inquisitors have only Nothing to offer. They merely presented yet another occasion for my Craft to increase in Speed and Spirit-force, in the process of cutting through and exposing their nothingness.

In contrast to the intervenors, the Inhabitants of the Elemental world Actively participated with me in the creation of *Pure Lust*. They did this not in the sense that they were directed by me, but simply by reason of the fact that they were/are their Selves, Actively creating/be-ing. By be-ing, they Gave; they Enspirited me.

The winter snow on North Leverett Road, for example, reawakened my childhood memories of Elemental Snow. At Times it made rather forceful

---

*The final letter from Dean Neenan was dated August 5, 1983. In this missive he reviewed "our" correspondence over the past sixteen months and climaxed his review of his own letters with the following statement: "An indication of the serious intent of the University in this regard is shown by the zero salary increment awarded you for the academic year 1983–84." I had been too deeply involved in my work on *Pure Lust* and Other matters to have given much notice to the zero faculty "increment" that had been "awarded" to me for the following year—the year I would be returning to teaching. Boston College repeated its cross-country tracking of me in yet another context in 1985. For details on this later sadosocietal witch hunt see Chapter Fourteen.

FLYING TRANSITIONS:
FALL 1982, WINTER, SPRING, SUMMER 1983

Throughout the fall of 1982 and the first three seasons of 1983 I Lived and Spun in my Wild domain. The primary/primal work of my Life then was the completion of *Pure Lust*. I was flying rapidly through *Pyrospheres* and into The Third Realm, which is *Metamorphospheres*○, meaning

> Realm of macromutational transformations, where Prudes explore the States of Grace (Be-Longing, Be-Friending, Be-Witching), where Websters see Stamina as its own reward, where Dragons are in our Elements, and where Muses Muse, Compose, Create (*Wickedary*).

The cabin continued to be a place of changes. In September Fran—despite her love of that Witchy place and Life in the country—decided that it was Time for her to relocate in the Boston area. The cabin was empty for some time after that. It seemed to be waiting for the right occupant. This New cabin-dweller was Nancy Kelly, who came accompanied by her Saint Bernard, Zelda, and her Siamese cat, who sometimes bothered to answer to the name Stella. Nancy was at that time beginning her doctoral work in English at the University of Massachusetts in Amherst.

In early September 1982 Denise had moved into the big house, where she had a beautiful study. She was then teaching at Fitchburg State College and starting work on her doctoral dissertation in sociology at Brandeis University. Wild Eyes, her Familiar, enjoyed country living as well as occasional spats with her sister, Wild Cat. During our frequent evening walks on North Leverett Road, Denise and I communed with the stars and communicated Spinning ideas. Often when she came home from teaching we would dash off in the car to supper at various inexpensive restaurants in towns nearby. This was preferable to a continual diet of our own "home cooking."

In October 1982 I left this home base for a brief time to give lectures outside the U.S. First, I spoke at the University of Toronto on October 2. Shortly after that I took off on a Stunning trip to Europe. The German edition of *Gyn/Ecology* had come out in 1981, and this had caused a steady buildup of interest in my work. The beginning of the "European connection" had been Woven, and that tapestry of connectedness with women in Europe was continuing to grow in size and intricacy.

Spiraling into the New European Connection

Although I did not have an invitation to speak in Switzerland, I flew directly from Boston to Zurich in mid-October, and then hopped on a train destined for my beloved Fribourg. After an overnight of Ecstatic Re-membering of my Life there in the Middle Ages I flew on to Graz, Austria, where I met my friend Erika Wisselinck and two other German women—Susanne Kahn-

Ackermann, then Director of *Frauenoffensive* (my German publishing house) and Feminist theorist Heidi Göttner-Abendroth.

This whole congruence was a Witches' plot. I had been invited to be a speaker at an event exotically entitled "Styrian Academy, 1982," sponsored by the Department of Cultural Affairs of the Government of Styria, Austria, which would be held at the University of Graz. I had immediately written to Erika, suggesting that we seize this opportunity for a visit, since the "Styrian Academy" would pay for my ticket. Erika rightly suggested herself to be my translator at Graz. She and Susanne Conjured a cluster of invitations for me to speak on *Gyn/Ecology* in Munich and Cologne and to give a public lecture at the University of Nijmegen in the Netherlands.

Two memories of that Time in Austria are especially vivid. One is of standing before a rather large audience, attempting to speak from notes filled with my own New Words, occasionally glancing over at Erika who was perspiring in her "simultaneous translation booth." I could see the audience, some equipped with headphones, others "toughing it out" in English, looking grimmer than grim. Despite what I thought was a rather witty presentation and despite Erika's excellent translation, some of those academics did not quite get the drift.

The other vivid memory is of walking in the shopping district of Graz with my friends, who were aware of my approaching birthday. As we stood in front of an antique shop I saw an incredible antique bronze snake in the window. Out of the corner of my eye I noticed that Susanne had her eye on it too. I pretended not to notice when they conspired and went into the store to buy the snake. Later, when it was given to me, I made a great show of surprise—or so I thought. At any rate, the "surprise" snake is coiled before me Now, as I Spin this chapter.

I took the train back to Munich with Erika, Susanne, and Heidi. They all had a loud laugh at my expense because I was wearing sturdy hiking boots. But, after all, Susanne had written to me that we would be visiting "the surrounding hills and wine caves" (near Graz). I just thought I would come prepared. As it turned out, we saw the surrounding hills from the train window, but that was beautiful anyway and our conversation together was invigorating and, one could also say, full of intoxicating ideas, even if we were only drinking coffee.

Upon the return to Munich I stayed at Erika's house and talked with many women, including interviewers from the Feminist magazine *Courage,* which was published in Berlin. After my lecture Erika and I went on to Cologne, where we stayed at the home of Ginster Votteler, who organized everything for us in that city, including my talk. Ginster ran a wonderful Feminist bookstore, which we visited. Our breakfast on the roof of her apartment building with a group of women was an awesome experience. Also poignantly memorable was our drive with Ginster to Holland, where we explored the mystical countryside. At the University of Nijmegen I was pleased to meet

Professor Tina Halkes and to experience the enthusiasm of the audience. This was particularly important to me, since much of the material I presented was from my work-in-process on *Pure Lust*. So the visit to Nijmegen was a fitting culmination of the whole trip, which had been an inspiring reintroduction to Europe and a Source of high Hopes and rich Memories, which I carried back in my Craft for the completion of *Pure Lust*.

The Spinning of Metamorphospheres

I spoke at a few universities in the U.S. and Canada that winter and spring of 1982–83,[44] but I was Fiercely Focused on the Spinning of *Metamorphospheres*. Speaking in terms of tidy time, I was scheduled to return to teaching in September 1983, so it was imperative that the manuscript be completed and sent to the publisher that month. Be-Speaking in words of Tidal Time, I was Weaving this work very rapidly, in harmony with *Elemental Rhythms*○, which are

> **1 :** rhythms displaying the infinite interplay of unity and diversity characteristic of Elemental phenomena such as tides, seasons, phases of the moon: TIDAL RHYTHMS **2 :** cadences and vibrations of the wordings of Websters, which are Be-Spoken in cosmic concordance (*Wickedary*).

Emily's more frequent visits to Leverett in these Tidal Times corresponded to the increasingly rapid rhythm of these wordings. We drudged untiringly and Be-Laughingly as always, and her comments were, as usual, very Shrewd.

Denise's wit and canniness helped to make my Realizing of *Metamorphospheres* possible. It was she who Dis-covered Ernest G. Schachtel's book, *Metamorphosis,* which is filled with crucial ideas, especially on memory and on allocentric perception, that served as springboards for my analysis in The Third Realm.[45] Moreover, it was she who suggested the word *Metamorphospheres*.[46]

Poison in the House:
Surviving an Elementary Atrocity

By spring 1983 I was truly soaring with *Pure Lust*. Then, sickeningly, there came a tidy wave of man-made destruction/disruption. This took shape hideously. We had a growing and undeniable realization that there was poison hidden in the walls of the beloved old house on North Leverett Road. The previous owner had filled these walls with urea-formaldehyde foam insulation (UFFI). The implications of this fact became more and more horrifyingly obvious as testimony of homeowners concerning the adverse effects of UFFI on their health received media attention. Formaldehyde gas emitted by the insulation was known to cause respiratory and skin ailments (such as rashes), nosebleeds, stomach problems, fatigue, memory loss. Persons reported that the gas made their families, guests, and pets ill, and that a number of pets died.

It was not necessary to *read* about the symptoms, however. Eventually, Denise's eyes itched badly whenever she spent a long time (several hours) in the house. On one occasion her face became horribly bloated. The previous owner had conveniently disappeared, leaving no phone number or address. I did discover, however, in a file of documents about fixtures and products in the house and the other structures, that the main house had been insulated with "Insulspray," manufactured by Borden Chemical, Division of Borden, Inc.

The house was tested, room by room, by local "environmental specialists." The degree of exposure to the poisonous gas was bad, but not quite bad enough to merit consideration for financial help from the State of Massachusetts to have the stuff removed. The cost of having it taken out, as estimated by "specialists," would be astronomical. Hence that "option" would be out of the question.

Gradually, as the summer wore on, it became absolutely clear that there was no hope for the house, and that it would be very hard to sell, even at a great loss. One aspect of the horror was the realization that the longer anyone stayed there, the more hypersensitive she would become to small amounts of formaldehyde anywhere/everywhere . . . And it was/is just about everywhere—in fabrics, dyes, tobacco, plywood, baby shampoo, *et cetera, ad nauseam.* Confined by these hideous circumstances, Denise used the cabin as her study and I used the loft, spending minimal time in the house.

Despite this elementary disruption, I kept on writing through the summer and into September, when I would be forced to move back to Boston, at least for several days a week, to resume teaching at Boston College. Although I would never willingly have chosen such a "learning experience," this necessity of Living through/against this poisonous penetration reinforced my understanding of elementaries as largely invisible by reason of being all-pervasive. This encounter furthered my analysis of elementaries as products of the negative opposite of *Pure Lust,* which is *pure lust○,* that is

> the deadly dis-passion that prevails in patriarchy; the life-hating lechery that rapes and kills the objects of its obsession/aggression; violent, self-indulgent desire to level all life, dismember spirit/matter, attempt annihilation; ontologically evil vice, having as its end the breaking/braking of female be-ing, the obliteration of natural knowing and willing and of the deep purposefulness which philosophers have called *final causality* (*Wickedary*).

We—the women, the cats—Survived that elementary atrocity in the Elemental environment of North Leverett Road. My own Surviving deepened my experiential understanding of the Sado-Ritual Syndrome, which serves in *Gyn/Ecology* as the structural basis of The Second Passage, and

The connection/fusion of the formerly abstract and elitist vocabulary of ontology with the concrete and often Wild Words that surge to express the variations of Elemental Life breaks ancient Taboos and causes friction. Often it arouses women into Be-Laughing and Be-Falling. This is Pyro-ontology, Pyrosophy. Its purpose is *Pyrogenesis*○, that is

the birthing/flaming of Female Fire; the Sparking of Radical Feminist consciousness (*Wickedary*).

Hence participation in Be-ing comes Alive in *Pure Lust*. Its Elemental Potential is Realized. The *Be*-Words illustrate this Aliveness, for they are manifestations of thinking which is *both* abstract and concrete, Intellectual and E-motional.

In a Fourth Galactic conversation, Jane Caputi told me that when she first read my expression "Elemental Philosophy" she thought this would seem oxymoronic to the morons who preach patriarchal philosophy. The beauty of this expression is that in just two words it dissolves the dualism between "matter" and philosophy.[49] Of course, the full subtitle of *Pure Lust* —*Elemental Feminist Philosophy*—breaks down yet other dualisms.* These include the split between "feminism"—as this is commonly (mis)understood —and philosophy, and the imposed division between women and philosophy. As the full meaning and implications of *Elemental Feminist Philosophy* became incarnated in *Pure Lust,* other dualisms crumbled, such as those between theology and philosophy, between poetry and philosophy, and between mysticism and ontology.

It is in *Pure Lust,* especially, that I have Realized that Moment of Prophecy and Promise that occurred several decades before, when I was studying at Catholic University and experienced the Dream of Green. I had understood the message of that Dream to be: "Do what you were born to do. Focus on philosophy!"[50]

I did not then try to analyze why a Dream which consisted entirely of a Vision of Green should of necessity mean: "Focus on philosophy." But this is what I understood it to mean when I woke up, and that meaning seemed absolutely clear . . . and Natural. I did not then explicitly understand the connection between Green and philosophy, nor would anyone have been able to explain this, if I had spoken about it. But I knew then implicitly that *my* philosophy would be Green.

In my Fourth Galactic Vision and Memory, I See that my Moment of Prophecy and Promise which occurred even earlier—my Encounter in adolescence with the clover blossom which/who Said: "I am"—was also

---

*In the early stages of the Unfolding of *Pure Lust* I had agonized over its subtitle. I debated with mySelf whether it should be *Ontological Feminist Philosophy* or *Elemental Feminist Philosophy*. The reasons supporting the first option are obvious. As I Re-Call conversations with my Cohorts at that Time, it was Anne Dellenbaugh who most strongly argued for the Word *Elemental*. This, of course, is the Elementally accurate Word.

pointing me toward my Future Realizing of my own Green Philosophy.[51] My existential meeting in my early twenties with the hedge which/who Said: "Continued existence" was also a summons into the Green.[52] These *Elemental* Realities had conveyed *ontological* messages. They had Be-Spoken the breakdown of foolish/snoolish dichotomies, such as the unnatural splitting of ontology from the Elemental world. They had Re-Called the Integrity of the Background.

Daring Ecstasy

In order to Spiral on into the process of Elemental Feminist Philosophy I would have to Move more Deeply into the Background. I would have to Realize more of the Background. This is what happened in the Moments of Spinning *Pure Lust.*[53] This meant that the Battle of Principalities and Powers would become more intense, and that the differences between the foreground/elementary world and the Background/Elemental Realms would become clearer. My Labrys would—and did—become much sharper.

A New and Qualitatively Different kind of Daring was needed for my Dis-covering of Elemental Feminist Philosophy. I was forced to Face more fully not only the patriarchal evil of the patriarchs but also the patriarchal corrosion of women's bodies, minds, souls. I had, of course, written explicitly of female Self-hatred and horizontal violence and of tokenism and the scapegoat syndrome in *Beyond God the Father.* I had elaborated further on these themes in *Gyn/Ecology,* developing in that work my analysis of women as token torturers and as "Painted Birds." But I was forced to experience and to Name even more of this evil in the Time of *Pure Lust.*

The Other side of this intensified Courage to express/enact the necessary Exorcism was heightened Daring to express Ecstasy. This above all was the challenge of *Pure Lust*: to Spin and Live Moments of Ecstasy. For Ecstasy is Taboo in phallocracy, the sadosociety. In Daring to Break this Taboo I became open to Other vibrations, which are incorporated into the very texture of *Pure Lust.*

Daring Ecstasy had its consequences. In Weaving this work I encountered Other Traveling Companions, including Elemental Spirits, and I Dared to introduce these to readers who were entering the Race of Wild Women. I Dis-covered Ways of Living in the Background and attempted to Spell these out. I collected and Presentiated equipment—images, ideas, New Words—that might serve to strengthen the Crafts of Other Voyagers.

BACK AND FORTH TO BOSTON

In September 1983, having delivered the manuscript of *Pure Lust* to the publisher, I returned to Boston College to teach, after my long leave of absence. Since my plan was to spend a few days each week in the Boston area, returning to Leverett for the weekends, I decided to rent a room. I found one in a house on Crystal Lake, in Newton Centre. The setting was beautiful and the location convenient, but the room was over a garage and turned out to be quite cold as the fall progressed. The price was right, however. As I cooked my meals on a hot plate I was reminded of student days in Fribourg.

There was no time to contemplate the irony of my situation, however, because there was so much to do. The copyedited version of the manuscript arrived for my inspection, and not too long after that the galleys arrived to be proofread. Emily continued to be a valiant helper with this work. Sometimes we went out to the loft in Leverett, and sometimes we worked in that cold room. My memories of Emily sitting in my rocking chair, wrapped up in a blanket, as we engaged in the hunt for typos are indelible.

Then there was teaching. I reveled in lecturing from *Pure Lust,* which of course was not yet out. There was a sense of great excitement in these classes, where the students were getting "the Words" before they appeared in print.*

There were Syn-Crone-icities in the histories of some of these women. One extraordinary example of this was the story of how Suzanne Melendy, from Eureka, California, "happened" to be in my classes. Back in 1981 Suzanne had Dis-covered *Gyn/Ecology* in a Strange way. She had been Searching for a book on Feminist theory in her local library in Eureka. As she recounted her story to me, she was reaching high on the shelves for some other book when—Shockingly—a heavy tome entitled *Gyn/Ecology* fell on her head. Since she was too short to put it back up, she included it in her pile of books to be checked out and carried it home.

In a Fourth Galactic account of this experience,[54] Suzanne informed me that she had waited awhile before reading *Gyn/Ecology.* When she did finally read it, she understood it to be an "open invitation" to come across the country and study with me at Boston College. She described her subsequent acceptance of this "invitation" as "the obvious and natural thing to do."

So it came about that this young woman, who had virtually no money to spare, traveled three thousand miles across the United States to Boston, only to find out that I was not teaching that year but was off in Western Massachusetts writing another book (*Pure Lust,* of course). She enrolled at BC anyway, with the help of student loans and scholarship money for tuition, and survived by working hard at low-paying jobs. When I did return she was there and in my classes, and subsequent events demonstrated the rightness of her serendipitous experience and acceptance of *Gyn/Ecology's* "invitation."

---

*My classes were not invaded during this time by unwanted "visitors" sent by the administration, but the salient reality of the "zero salary increment" that had been "awarded" to me by Boston College in retaliation for my lecture at the University of Wisconsin in La Crosse was in evidence on every monthly paycheck.

Since my work in the Boston area, combined with lecture trips, was more time-consuming than I had anticipated, the problem of taking care of the Leverett "property" was becoming serious, especially as cold weather was approaching. I discussed this with Nancy Kelly, who had moved out of the cabin in May 1983, and she agreed to move back in October, together, of course, with her dog, Zelda, and her cat, Stella. Nancy then became a sort of overseer of the place during that transitional time.

Meanwhile, my work of proofreading with Emily went on in my spare time. In December 1983 Emily was summoned home to Macon, Georgia, to be Present at a tragic event. Her mother, Helen, to whom Emily had always been extremely close, was dying. The work had to be finished on the book, however. So my friend Sandra Stanley agreed to come from Minnesota for two weeks and help me complete this chore.

There remained the nearly insuperable task of compiling the Index. This was accomplished between January and March 1984 by the serendipitous Suzanne and Ann Marie Palmisciano, a poetically gifted young woman who was also in my classes.[55] They worked in my office, often basically camping out there, and I brought them supplies of food from a nearby gourmet take-out shop. One night, when both were asleep on my futon on the floor, a campus policeman, having seen a light, used the "master key" and entered the office. Ann Marie, startled out of a sound sleep, grabbed the manuscript and slammed it down menacingly in front of the surprised cop, shouting: "Can't you see we're working on a manuscript!?" He left quickly.

In the meantime there were classes, classes, classes,* and my usual round of public lecturing.[56] *Pure Lust* was not published until June 1984 —not exactly an optimum month for books to appear. But there was no time to worry about that, because I had to fly off to England and Ireland.

WEAVING CONNECTIONS IN ENGLAND AND IRELAND

Early in June 1984 I flew to London to participate in the First International Feminist Bookfair. The atmosphere was charged with the interaction of

---

*That semester, Professor Sharon Welch, who was then teaching Theology and Women's Studies at Harvard Divinity School, sat in on my Feminist Ethics class, in which I lectured on *Pure Lust*. It was exciting to have her Presence there, and her comments were helpful to the students. Among the Other outstanding women who sat in on that class at that Time were Krystyna Colburn and Mary Ellen McCarthy, both of whom drove up from Bridgeport, Connecticut, for this purpose, together with women from Bloodroot Restaurant and Bookstore in Bridgeport—Betsey Beaven, Noel Furie, Selma Miriam, and Meg Profetto. It was inspiring to have these women in the class and enjoyable to go for dinner with them occasionally after class. Professor Lorine Getz, then Director of the Boston Theological Institute, sat in on "Feminist Critique of Theological and Philosophical Texts," another advanced course. It was extremely encouraging to have colleagues of such stature in my classes—a reminder that "Sisterhood" was still alive and well.

energies/auras of Feminists from all over the world. I was especially happy to meet my friends Marisa Zavalloni and Nicole Brossard from Montreal, Erika Wisselinck from Germany, and the brilliant French author Michelle Causse. That particular group of Cronies stayed up through the wee hours in my room at Hotel President, attempting to solve and re-solve all the problems of women on a patriarchal planet.

Soon after my arrival I found that I had been scheduled for a public "conversation" at the Institute of Contemporary Arts Theatre in London with the author of a short book purporting to "analyze" Radical Feminism, but in fact attacking it, focusing much of its attack on *Gyn/Ecology*.[57] The "conversation" had been arranged by that author's publisher in order to sell her new publication, which was in bookstore windows around London. Since *Gyn/Ecology* had been published in 1978 (1979 in Britain) and since *Pure Lust* had just appeared in the United States, I was prepared to Present New material from my more recent book. Certainly I had no interest in conversing/debating about the earlier work in order to promote the sales of a hostile book by someone of whom I had never heard.

The struggle for a "lecture room of my own" lasted for two days, and it involved semi-sleepless nights. Promoters of the anti-Radical Feminist tract and would-be imposers of the tedious "conversation" (boring bickering) banged on my hotel room door to attempt to force the issue. I refused and the upshot was that I did give a talk based on *Pure Lust* at the ICA Theatre, while the other author also conducted her own session in another room.

The experience of speaking there on my newest material in the Presence of women from many countries was exhilarating and moving, but the process of having to struggle for that space had been extremely draining. The significance of this struggle was that it displayed the growing hostility and resistance to Radical Feminism that was happening on the level of foreground time/tidy time "simultaneously" with the Re-Surging from the Background of Be-Longing, Be-Friending, and Be-Witching—in Other Words—of Pure Lust. This Groundswell occurred—and continues to occur—in the Realm of Tidal Time. The Ecstatic encounter with the women who chose to come to my talk at the ICA Theatre was made possible by Exorcism of the demonic "divide and conquer" setup—the block that I had been forced to overcome. The experience was a manifestation of the Battle of Principalities and Powers described in *Pure Lust*—a Battle that has continued to Rage through the eighties and on into the nineties. What I learned from the London event—and have had to re-learn repeatedly—is the Absolute importance of continuing to Exorcise the foreground demons and to Re-Call Background consciousness, memories, images, which in these decades of decadence have been pushed back under the surface of the Subliminal Sea. The challenge is to continue *Realizing* the Elemental Powers of women.

That night I flew to Dublin, where I was met by women who were Radical Feminists/Cronies. Even though we had never met before, I felt a close kinship—ties that were Archaic and lasting. I Sensed this especially with Joni Crone and Aileen Ryan, whom I was destined to meet again . . . and again, in the context of Radical Feminism in Ireland. This was the real beginning of my New Irish Connection.

The next evening I spoke in Liberty Hall, which I experienced as a great honor. The Meeting was co-chaired by Joni Crone and Ailbhe Smyth. Nell McCafferty, famed journalist and Wicked wit, introduced me. The crowd was Wild and turbulent and certainly challenging. It seemed to me, from that Time on, that Ireland was seething with Radical Feminists and Lesbians. That impression was not entirely false.

I had already fallen in love with Ireland on earlier visits, but this was Something Else. That first lecture in Dublin was a good introduction, even though I was restrained by the extreme exhaustion that I still felt from the struggle to gain my own space in London. So I was less capable of quickly connecting directly with the immediate concerns of the audience, that is, of Sensing and adapting to this new situation, than I would normally have been. After a couple of days of being with the Irish women, however, I felt more and more At Home.

I was staying at Buswell's Hotel, where—for some reason—I felt just right. Indeed, when writing this Now, the thought of Buswell's makes me smile. Having tea and sandwiches there with my Irish friends was a blissful experience.

My next talk was in Belfast. I was driven there by Mary O'Callahan, who was familiar with the process of crossing the border into Northern Ireland. I was "handed over" to Siobhan Molloy, one of the main organizers of the Feminist Book Week in Belfast. Conversations with these women and others who were introduced to me about the actual conditions of women's lives in that war-torn area were Eye-opening, Heart-opening. The women, ranging widely in age, class, life-style, and views on Feminism, seemed to me to have at least one very strong characteristic in common, for which I felt immense gratitude: They were Absolutely genuine. That is, they were their Selves—All There. They were Real. There could never be any distracting, academented, jargon-infested babble with them. Their Lives were/are too Real to leave room for that kind of decadent indulgence. When I finished my talk, one woman, in typical Irish fashion, stood up and sang a song for me. It was a ballad she had written about her love who had been killed in the war.

I returned to Dublin by train on Friday, June 15. On that train a curious sort of game seemed to be going on. I was fascinated by the Irish people and so, although I tried not to stare, I did keep glancing at individuals. Each of them reminded me of some one of my own relatives in Glens Falls, New York, or some friend of Irish descent, and so I could not stop looking. They, on the other hand, never let me see them staring or glancing at me. All seemed to have their eyes modestly cast down. I felt that they were aware of my existence and compulsion to gawk, yet none of them allowed me to catch them catching me, so to speak. This was exactly the opposite of my experience throughout years of riding on Swiss trains and being stared at rudely and steadily until I began to wonder if my shirt was unbuttoned or my horns were showing. At any rate, before I managed to solve the eye-contact mystery the train was pulling into Dublin.

I was happy to see Joni at the station and to return to my old stomping ground—Buswell's Hotel. That evening a group Named "The Spinsters"—a rather Wild crowd of women who regularly held discussion sessions and celebrations and who had been Loudly supportive during the Meeting at Liberty Hall—were having a party for me. This was supposed to be a small event, but a multitude of "gate crashers" came, and so it was wall to wall women. Wine and other beverages flowed freely. I recall a number of fiddlers playing and singing, much animated conversation, and a few women demonstrating the Irish jig, in an effort to get me to try. It was a not un-pleasantly chaotic evening.

The next day Joni and I took the train to Cork, where I was scheduled to speak. We were preoccupied the whole time with very intense conversation. At one point someone threw a rock at the train window right in front of us. The glass was cracked but did not come crashing in. This was the sort of thing I had half-expected to happen on the way back from Belfast, but I was genuinely surprised that it was happening in the Irish Republic.

In Cork we stayed at the homes of young Lesbian Feminists who had decided to make that city the base for their work as teachers and as activists. Like all the Irish women I met, they were extremely hospitable.

I had dinner with a group of women in a restaurant upstairs from the Cork Quay Coop, an alternative store. We then went to the Ivernia Theatre, where I was scheduled to speak. I remember that the wooden steps there appeared to be hundreds of years old and to have been worn down by thousands of footsteps. I seemed to be walking in those footsteps. The woman who introduced me took that opportunity to describe to me publicly the real conditions of women's lives in Cork, under the heinous oppression of the catholic church. I could see that she was nervous, and that her uttering of that eloquent testimony required enormous Courage.

I began by commenting that I knew they were sick of so-called "Irish Americans"—such as ridiculous Ronald Reagan—"claiming their roots." (Ronald's recent pretentious and politically opportunist visit to Ireland and his assertion of "roots" there had been protested and scoffed at all over that country.) I then went on to Name my own Irish American identity (on both sides of my family), remarking that "in my case, it happens to be true." That drew a laugh, and I felt a rapport that was from the Background.

As in Belfast I was struck by the vast range in age, life-style, and perspective of these women, and I was grateful for their blessed gift of Genuineness/Reality. I remember that I told them the story of my struggle to Survive in the face of harassment by the jesuits of Boston College. These women of Cork did not need an explanation. They understood perfectly, from their own experience of Surviving under the rule of the woman-hating catholic hierarchy in Ireland. One woman did ask why I stayed at Boston College. I did not reply with details about the buddy system of the academic men's club or the workings of grapevine blacklisting or of the purging of Radical Feminists from academia. Rather, the answer that I gave came from someplace very deep and ancient inside me—from the Depths in me that had been elicited by the Depths in them. I gave the truest answer that I knew. This was, simply: "I choose to Stand my Ground."

As I said these words I was a little surprised and startled. I did not re-call having said them before. As I Re-Call them Now, in Fourth Galactic Time, I Hear their mythic, Original truth. The women of Cork Heard me into this Be-Speaking, and they applauded loudly when I spoke the Words. The applause was not, I think, simply for me, but for and from a Deep Background understanding and approval of something we had/have in common.

That something is our Primal, Pre-Celtic, Prepatriarchal Heritage that is not lost but that is hidden in the Subliminal Sea. On some level all of us in that room were aware of that Hidden Reality. We were also aware of the fathers' foreground facsimile of that Reality. Whether the "fathers" specifically in question were the catholic hierarchy in Ireland or Irish American jesuits, they were/are recognizable as what I would call "foreground Irish." They have demonstrated by their behavior that they belong to the male-centered and monodimensional arena where fabrication, objectification, and alienation take place. This is characterized by a derivative and parasitic relation to Elemental Reality.*

In my Fourth Galactic Re-membering of that crucial Moment, I know that my answer/statement—"I choose to Stand my Ground"—struck a deep Chord in the Other women as well as in mySelf. As I Re-member that event Now, I Hear/See that I was Realizing "out loud" my Answer to a very deep question. That question has to do with the significance of living "on the Boundary." Over a decade before my 1984 visit to Cork I had written of Boundary Living.[58]

Since the Background is vast and since the foreground is by its "nature" —or rather, pseudonature—widespread, there has to be some specificity about Boundary Living, that is, about *where* one chooses to Stand her Ground. This choice, if it is Prudishly Prudent, will take into consideration such questions as: Where can I Act most effectively? Where do I have a greater possibility of Presentiating the Background?

---

*It does not matter whether any of the Other women Present at that Meeting in Cork would have chosen to use my words, such as *Background, foreground,* or *elementary.* I am speaking here of a Deep Knowing/Realizing that could be expressed by different women in many different words. I am expressing here, in words of my own Crafting, an awareness that cannot be confined by specific words, although words can help the Hearer to recognize that awareness.

In Cork, in that E-motional Aura of Deep Connectedness with the women Present, I was enabled to connect very accurately with the Sense of the question: "Why do you stay at Boston College?" I was able to respond to it out of the context of my own Radical Feminist Philosophy. I was saying, in a simple and condensed way, that I was choosing to Fight/Act (Stand my Ground) at that precise location on the Boundary between Background and foreground where the demonic patriarchal distortions of women's Archaic heritage are most visible and accessible to me, where my Craft can be most effective in the work of Exorcism—reversing the reversals that blunt the potential for Realizing Ecstasy.*

While staying in Cork I went with Joni Crone and several women from that city to the Old Head of Kinsale. The women from Cork showed me a wall that had been built during the Great Famine by Irish people who were virtually forced by the British to do meaningless slave labor for a few pennies a day in order to ward off starvation.[59] The British were concerned, it seems, that the starving people might become lazy. The wall was extremely well made . . . and it led nowhere, because it had no purpose. I remember that one of the women Touched the wall, commenting upon the craftsmanship. I also Touched the wall.

Foolishly fearing to appear like a sentimental Irish American, I strode off into the fields to hide the tears that were streaming down my face. I wanted to lie down and hug the earth, but instead I looked off toward the sea. Later that day Joni and I looked down at the water together, watching the Spirals in the sea.

After I boarded the plane from Cork back to London, where I was scheduled to give a final speech before returning "home" to America, the tears let loose. I wept for a long time on that plane, overwhelmed with grief for my people, and dismayed that I was leaving Ireland, longing to turn the plane around.

When I arrived in London I tried to use an Irish pound note to buy my supper. Since the Irish accepted British currency, it had not occurred to me that this would not be reciprocal. The person to whom I handed the note rejected it contemptuously, snarling: "We don't accept that stuff." I expressed my Rage and Disgust at this ignorant and arrogant attitude. I think I said something like: "Who do you think you are? You don't have your rotten

---

*In a Fourth Galactic phone conversation with Joni about the trip to Cork, I discussed with her the response of the women there to my answer: "I choose to Stand my Ground." She replied immediately that my statement resonates with a theme in many ancient Irish myths. When I asked her how she understood this, she answered: "If you've tilled the soil, you've put your essence and spirit into it. It [the statement] has to do with integrity. There is something in you that belongs there, that you can't give up." She referred to the Irish film *The Field*, which, despite its flaws, makes this point (Transatlantic telephone conversation, October 15, 1991).

British Empire any longer!" Whatever words I used, they could not have been strong enough to express what I felt.

When I reached my hotel room I threw myself on the bed and turned off the light. Strangely, beautiful fields filled with Wild Flowers came vividly before my closed eyes. There were continually shifting, almost Tangible scenes, each more Be-Dazzling than the next. This Ecstatic "field trip" lasted quite awhile. Then there was the pain. It was an Unnameable grief for my own people—not, at that Moment, for the people of women generally, but specifically for the women of Ireland, for my Foresisters there, and my own Self. I thought of what the british and the christian hierarchs had done to them/us. Then, from deep inside, I Wailed Loudly. I did not care who heard me. I Wailed as long as I had to, wanted to.

The next evening I spoke at Conway Hall in London. It was Sunday, June 17, 1984. Ros de Lanerolle, then Director of The Women's Press in London, introduced me. Ros was gracious and wore a kelly green scarf in my honor. Since the International Feminist Book Fair was over, this was an audience of British Feminists. They were warm and welcoming and, on the whole, it was a happy ending to a trip which I Now know to have been an Ecstatic Beginning, particularly of my Irish adventures and explorations.

LETTERS:
RE-SURGINGS FROM THE SUBLIMINAL SEA

Shortly after I returned to the Boston area in June 1984 the letters responding to the recently published *Pure Lust* began to arrive. Having reread a large number of these letters, ranging from 1984 through 1988, I find Cronelogically connecting themes and threads. Most or all of the themes of the *Beyond God the Father* and *Gyn/Ecology* letters can be traced here. However, there are differences in tone. There are definite signals in the *Pure Lust* letters that the women were writing in the terrible mid-eighties and that they were/are Survivors of these times.

A common theme in these letters is a sense of terrible isolation, combined with a longing for connectedness. The "flavor" of this experience was conveyed by an adventurous woman traveler who wrote:

> Thank you for being out there, for having produced physical evidence that we exist. Even in the States, and I now live in San Francisco, when I am outside my circle of friends I am struck by how absolutely isolated I am.

When this correspondent wrote to me she had been traveling for four months in Nepal and India. She wrote that when she saw the deplorable oppression of women there she wondered what I would say about it. She wrote:

> That way I remind myself that I'm not alone.

She continued:

> A few months back I swapped my copy of *Gyn/Ecology* for a friend's copy of *Pure Lust*—we met in Kathmandu. It has been a pleasure to have to read and reread while making my way through the crowds of men here. The women are mostly silent and kept faceless by their husbands and veils. Up in the hills of India . . . I met an Australian woman with a copy of *Pure Lust*. We are everywhere! But often with too much space in between. . . . Having *Pure Lust* is like traveling with a friend.

In these few sentences this woman conveys several of the themes characteristic of the letters sent in response to *Pure Lust*. There is the Courage of the Survivor/Traveler who keeps going when Alone. There is the Wonder of serendipitous Syn-Crone-icities. There is the mind-boggling knowledge and reassurance that "We are everywhere!" This is Background understanding that coexists with the knowledge of foreground isolation. Moreover, an essential theme is the importance of Radical Feminist books as traveling companions/friends. This, of course, combines with their function as "physical evidence that we exist."

These themes Weave their ways through other letters. A woman from Sydney, Australia, described her experience of serendipity/Syn-Crone-icity in relation to *Pure Lust*:

> It literally fell into my hands in a bookshop just as I had despaired of ever finding originality in writing again. You have made me proud to be a weird, elemental woman. . . . Your book was a homecoming.

A woman from Charlesbourg, Quebec, described the experience of Syn-Crone-icity in a different way:

> It was elemental knowing or my "guides" (as I name them) who led me to read the book just at this time in my life.

This woman also expressed an Elemental connection when she wrote:

> You have connected with me through your book and needing to respond was like a volcano inside me.

The theme of *Pure Lust* as traveling companion was expressed in a variety of ways. A woman from Seeley's Bay, Ontario, Canada, wrote:

> Thanks for sparking me with *Pure Lust*. I keep reading parts again and again and keep it handy.

Writing from Brisbane, Australia, in 1988 a woman who had first read *Pure Lust* three years earlier said:

> I am struck and restruck by its truth and powerful insight, and it remains for me a companion and a confirmation of the journey.

Often the letters are tapestries of conflicting emotions. A correspondent from Islesboro, Maine, wrote:

> I am furious to be so awakened and want to get back to sleep but I am addicted intellectually by what you have said and by what it means to me to see in black and white impeccable scholarship the proof of my own thirty odd year old knowledge/intuition/reality right there in book form.

Clearly, the recognition of her own experience is more powerful than the urge "to get back to sleep."

A similar struggle is described in a letter from Bridgeport, Connecticut:

> All my life I struggled to stay tame. I used all my energy to keep my life within "the boundaries." . . . The first time I read *Pure Lust* I don't think I got a tenth of it, but I could not stop to reread. It was the music I wanted to hear. I could almost dance to it if I read it aloud. And then I began to read. Everything I could get my hands on and to think. . . . You helped me to find my own mind and my own voice.

In some of the letters the primary response expressed is joy. A botanist from Athens, Ohio, wrote:

> I cried through *Gyn/Ecology* but laughed in sheer delight through most of *Pure Lust.* . . . But living joyously, acting in a manner based on ideas that come from trusting one's own mind and senses is indeed a very radical concept. Most of the people I come into daily contact with seem to prefer me depressed. I'm a greater misfit now than I ever was.

From Oneonta, New York, a reader pronounced:

> It is recognizing joy that registers your work—Real weight.

A well-known seventy-year-old Lesbian Feminist writer living in Montreal commented:

> As I read *Pure Lust* I feel vital energy and pure joy filling every one of my aging cells. . . . I really exploded with laughter as I read.

A woman whose address I cannot find wrote:

> Your language opens up new visions and often makes me cackle aloud because it makes so much so clear.

A Light-making Lesbian comedian cackled:

> I think *Pure Lust* is one of the funniest books I've ever read and I thank you for all the new material.

Experiences of metamorphosis were recorded in some of the letters. A correspondent in Los Gatos, California, wrote simply:

I've been greatly changed and strengthened by *Pure Lust*. Knowing you're out there has funded me again and again in my life situation.

Another woman, from Belleair, Florida, stated:

Mary, my world has been turned upside down/right. . . . I shall never be the same person as before I read *Pure Lust*.

The horror of women's experiences in these times is a haunting refrain. Sometimes it is expressed in a general way, as in a letter from San Francisco, whose author comments:

The very fact that your words buoy me up means that I constantly need buoying up in these unbelievably hideous times, so I plan to use *Pure Lust* as an antidote to malaise, rereading several pages each day as a kind of "fix" for my flagging spirits.

In other letters the horror is described in very specific and personal terms, as in a letter from a small island off the coast of Scotland, whose writer explained:

It [*Pure Lust*] fitted in with my experience exactly. Your book has freed me from a feeling of guilt and fear from which I have suffered for ten years. I was sexually attacked by a man and was treated by all, including a psychologist, as though it was all my fault. . . . Now I have read your book, I realize it is all part of the patriarchal plan, and my former self-esteem has returned. I am almost happy again and hope eventually to return to my own lusty, canny old self.

Another very specific Naming of atrocity came from a veterinarian in the Southwest:

I read myself to sleep with *Pure Lust*. At three A.M. I woke suddenly and almost violently. . . . After three long years of suicidal longings I finally *knew* the origin of my shame and self-loathing and why it took so long to share the knowledge of that shame. I have been so conditioned by my parents and the damned church and society to look upon men as gods and me as slime that my suicidal shame had its genesis in the fact that I was ultimately *strong* enough to thwart those four goons and was never physically raped or physically harmed in any way. Indeed I had sent them all to cover in one way or another. How *dare* I thwart those poor darlings! How *dare* I not let them have their way with me! Who in God's Hell do I think I am? I have actually hated myself for being strong—it is incredible! To imagine that depth of submissive conditioning. And after all— "nothing" happened.

A counselor told this woman that she should feel sorry for the men and her holistic friends told her it was just her Karma and that there was some "lesson" for her to learn from the experience. Another counselor told her that there was something about her persona that "invites" such incidences.

But now I have *Pure Lust* and now I know of the Maenads that refused to stand by while I would have made the old conditioned noble sacrifice expected of me.

Not every reader was able to emerge triumphant from her situation in these times. A correspondent from Montreal wrote:

Pure Lust provoked me, stimulated me when I began to read it last June. It pleased me. It confirmed my experiences. But I had nobody to share it with. I didn't finish it. I got hospitalized in psychiatry for a few weeks. I didn't feel like reading anything after that.

I have read such letters with great sadness. I've compared the letter just cited with another, from Clarksville, Georgia. This woman brought *Pure Lust* home to her roommate (love) of sixteen years and they read it together. She declared that this "saved my life—present, past, and future." Clearly, the difference—between despair and exuberance—is not attributable only to the fact that one woman was isolated and the other had an understanding companion. Yet the fact remains that the problem of isolation is a major source of debilitation.

The letters of some women revealed that their authors are gifted with a special spark. An English professor from New York wrote:

I am of the type capable of being intellectually excited and your writing struck me dead center in the brain and gave me one of the highest intellectual highs I have had since I read Nietzsche at 18 in college.

A young woman from Seattle, Washington, wrote:

Each page has sent so many electric charges through me that I need to write this letter to you. . . . Last night I was reading your emphasis on "what is said" about brain differences between women and men. This is something I'd heard before, and I always became FURIOUS and PROUD. This combination would usually shock and dismay the people who were around to hear me.

This young woman went on to explain something about herself:

I taste and feel in colors. I see and feel music. I hear textures. I sense 3-dimensionally things that are "really" 2-D. I didn't think about it until at age 14 I read that it's considered a MEDICAL DISORDER to "mix" the senses. . . . I thought, Well, maybe I'm a born artist; but I also felt ALONE.

A woman from California described her Electrical Connection with *Pure Lust*:

I had an extraordinary experience last year, when I was going through the long and painful process of bringing a sexual harassment charge against a Very Famous visiting professor. . . . I had just bought *Pure Lust* and had been browsing through it. One night as I slept a deep and powerful female voice said to

lake, taking notes, and trying to Sense the order in which this Metadiction-ary should emerge. Frequent swimming breaks helped us break away from the foreground world. No doubt Nixes, Mermaids, Sirens, and Undines were sending essential messages and these were received, subliminally at least.

More than once when we were sitting on the Green grass I discussed with Jane "the 11:12 phenomenon."[2] One Time I said that it had something to do with the *Wickedary,* and Jane responded by counting "Eleven, Twelve . . . Thirteen." We observed that whereas twelve is representative of patriar-chal time, *Thirteen* clearly signifies an Other Time, which is "off the clock."[3]

Jane had in her files issues of the *Bulletin of Atomic Scientists,* which since 1947 has displayed a picture of a "doomsday clock." This represents the degree of nuclear peril as perceived by the editors. In this symbol, "mid-night" signifies the hour of nuclear holocaust.[4] We discussed the "dooms-day clock" as representing the necrophilic means and end of phallocracy.

One evening in July 1984 we were walking around Crystal Lake and dis-cussing *Thirteen* and related subjects, such as the question of how to stop the doomsday clock. A Be-Dazzling full moon was shining on the water, and I had a sudden flash of insight. The expression "face that would stop a clock" floated across my consciousness. I turned to Jane and said: "Maybe the moon's face is the face that could stop the (doomsday) clock!" It was an expression of my strong intuitive knowledge that only Elemental forces can save this planet from destruction by the foreground fix-masters.

Right from the beginning, then, it was clear that the inspiration of the *Wickedary* was Elemental. It was/is a manifestation of *Biophilia* ◑, that is

the Original Lust for Life that is at the core of all Elemental E-motion; Pure Lust, which is the Nemesis of patriarchy, the Necrophilic State (*Wickedary*).

The purpose of the *Wickedary* was the freeing of words from the cages and prisons of patriarchal patterns. Words and women had served the fathers' sentences long enough. The Time for a Witches' dictionary/Meta-dictionary was long overdue.

THE SCHEME OF THE *WICKEDARY*

The goal for the summer was to get the proposal Spelled out. *American Her-itage* was most helpful in providing clues for articles that would constitute the front matter. The first of the preliminary articles in that dictionary—"A Brief History of the English Language"—served as a catalyst simply by sug-gesting the importance of an essay concerning the *Wickedary*'s history.

It was immediately obvious, of course, that the Unfolding History of *this* work, which would Dis-cover hidden Webs of words in ordinary diction-aries, moving into the Archaic Background of these words, would not be "history" in a foreground sense. The word *mystery* emerged as a replacement

for *history. Mystery,* however, is also a problematic foregrounded word.*
This was not clear at first, so the original title of the first preliminary essay
was "The Wickedary: Its History/Mystery."†

Other titles of articles in *American Heritage* set off vibrations in sharply
attuned Inner Ears. These included "Grammar and Meaning," "The Spelling
and Pronunciation of English," and "Guide to the Dictionary." As we brain-
stormed, New ideas for preliminary essays of the *Wickedary* "took off" from
these overtly boring but subliminally suggestive headings.‡

One of the preliminary articles in *American Heritage* was/is, in fact,
very Sinspiring. This is "Good Usage, Bad Usage, and Usage" by Morris
Bishop, who wrote:

> The words of a living language are like creatures: they are alive. Each word has
> a physical character, a look and a personality, an ancestry, and expectation of life
> and death, a hope of posterity. . . . There are magic words, spells to open gates
> and safes, summon spirits, put an end to the world. What are magic spells but
> magic spellings?[5]

Exactly! And the nature of the *Wickedary* was/is to be absolutely
ALIVE. Hence its form had/has to be living. It could not have a mere static
structure.

---

*As I wrote in *Preliminary Web One*: "According to *Webster's* the word *mystery* is derived
from the Greek *myein*, meaning 'to initiate into religious rites,' and also meaning 'to close
(used of the eyes and lips).' It is said to be possibly akin to the Latin *mutus*, meaning
'mute.' These etymological clues can lead Websters a long way in the complex process
of unraveling the mystery of the word *mystery.* . . . Why, we might ask, should initiation
involve an injunction to close the eyes and lips? A miasma of mystification and murkiness
is attached to the very word *mystery.* If we look steadily at this word, Seeing it with Real
Eyes, we understand that it functions within a patriarchal context . . . to block Elemental
Journeyers.

"*Webster's* serves up several definitions of *mystery*, each more unappetizing than the
next. Thus, for example, we read that it means 'a religious truth revealed by God that man
cannot know by reason alone and that once it has been revealed cannot be completely
understood.' . . . It is Crone-logical to point out that one possible reason that a 'religious
truth' said to be revealed by god continues to be unintelligible is simply that it makes no
sense" (*Wickedary*, pp. 5–6).

†It would later become *Preliminary Web One*: The Wickedary: Its History/Metamystery.
Metamystery came to be defined as "depths/surfaces that are hidden by man's myster-
ies/misteries; Wonders of Wild Reality that are behind/beyond the fathers' façades; ever
Unfolding reality glimpsed by Seers and announced by Be-Speakers: the Radiant Integrity of Be-ing" (*Wickedary*).

‡When I later came to the final writing of these succeeding articles, they were called
Preliminary Webs. They are entitled "Spelling: The Casting of Spells"; "Grammar: Our
Wicked Witches' Hammer"; "Pronunciation: Denouncing, Pronouncing, Announcing";
"Guides to the *Wickedary.*" The *Wickedary* Guides included all of the Elements and
specifically many animals. These appeared and Be-Spoke throughout the Weaving of
the work.

After presenting some idea of the introductory essays, the proposal briefly described the Core of the work, which would consist of the words themselves, their definitions and etymologies. It concluded with short summaries of the four appendices.*

So the groundwork was laid for my Weaving of the Preliminary Webs and Appendicular Webs, and the massive chore of assembling the Core lay before us. With gleeful satisfaction we delivered this proposal to the typist.† The summer's work was done, and Jane returned to Albuquerque to resume teaching. The next session was scheduled to take place during the winter break. Meanwhile, I returned to teaching and to my public lecturing.[6] My students were "high" on the process of Spinning ideas from *Gyn/Ecology, Pure Lust,* and Other books. So was I, although my Nag-Self was chomping at the bit, eager to get on with the *Wickedary.*

THE X-MAS BREAKTHROUGH

Jane arrived in mid-December and stayed for three weeks. The task at hand was to begin collecting and arranging New Words which were to be defined in the Core of the *Wickedary.* We began by making lists derived from the "Index of New Words" in *Gyn/Ecology* and its much richer successor, the "Index of New Words" in *Pure Lust.* The lists also included words from *Beyond God the Father* and *The Church and the Second Sex.* In the course of this process we began thinking of a few New New Words, and these were added to the lists.

We worked enormously hard and laughed equally hard. Soon the lists were so unmanageable that we switched to three-by-five-inch index cards, in order to insert Other New Words. At first the cards simply contained only the words and their definitions. Defining the words was no small matter. Even though the majority of these had first appeared in my four previously published Radical Feminist books, many had not been strictly defined. In many cases their meanings had been evident from the context in which they arose. In other instances their meanings had been developed at length and in a somewhat descriptive manner.

As we moved along it became evident that Outrageous examples would enrich the definitions. This could involve a fair amount of added Searching.

---

*These eventually turned out to be Appendicular Webs. As I later wrote of them in the Preface: "Here I have woven four Deliberately Delirious essays. . . . These Delirious essays, or Wanton Webs, are essential to the Tapestry of the *Wickedary.* Unlike the Preliminary Webs . . . these Weavings do not resemble/dissemble the format of normal patriarchal dictionaries in any respect. They simply Spin Off from the Core, in a Biological manner" (*Wickedary,* p. xix).

†When the typist of the proposal, Mary Lawrence, finished her task, the document came to a total of thirteen and one-half pages. Appropriately, she numbered the last page 13½. Clearly this woman was into the Spirit of the enterprise.

At this point the Fates provided a solution. "Coincidentally," Diana Beguine, a remarkably gifted Searcher, came for a visit on New Year's Eve. When she departed she was armed with lists of Wicked Words and Charged with her task of finding Weirdly suitable examples.*

During that X-mas "vacation," therefore, an enormous Breakthrough was made. The Core of the *Wickedary* had been cracked, Dis-closing the general Idea of its form. On the horizon was the adventure of Dis-covering the three major tribes of Wicked Words which would eventually be Woven into three large interconnecting Word-Webs within the Core. Also lying in wait were other difficult chores—as yet not fully foreseen—such as finding the Meta-etymologies of some Words, developing a system of cross-referencing, and creating a set of symbols to signify the works by me in which *Wickedary* words first appeared. All of this was too formidable to be known at once, even by the most Dauntless Wickedarians.

Dauntless though we were, our work was doomed to be interrupted, since both Jane and I had to return to teaching at our respective institutions during the spring semester of 1985. As it turned out that semester was both eventful and revelatory.

SURVIVING SNOOLDOM, SPRING SEMESTER, 1985

It did not escape the notice of Radical Feminists that by the winter and spring of 1985 we were exactly in the middle of that decade of horror. Perhaps sometimes we tried to console ourselves with numbers/dates. After all, we had Survived 1984, the dreaded symbolic year of George Orwell's dystopian novel. Maybe things would get better . . . Or would they? Was the *real* 1984 still on its way? The paralyzing knowledge that "the people" had elected Ronald Reagan for a second term was difficult to deny, but there was, at least, something funny about it. Could things get worse? Looking at the tele-vised face of George Bush, I thought, Yes. But neither my friends nor I could guess what the foreground world of the 1990s would bring. We were spared that gruesome foreknowledge.

The immediate foreground context was a microcosm of the prevailing horror show of the mid-eighties. In the spring semester of 1985 the in-quisitorial cross-country tracking of me by the Boston College administra-tion was resumed. After I spoke at the December 1984 Annual Meeting of the American Academy of Religion in Chicago, an article purporting to report on my lecture appeared in the *St. Louis Post Dispatch* (December 28, 1984). In late February 1985 I received a letter from Dean Neenan who was once again nipping at my heels. Enclosed with his letter was a copy of the

---

*Diana eventually came up with many examples which Jane and I added to our own lists. We later categorized some of these as "Canny Comments" by Hags and Nags and others as "Cockaludicrous Comments" by prominent snools. The remaining ones continued to be called "Examples."

article. In this letter Dean Neenan "requested" from me "in writing a statement either confirming or denying the accuracy of the remarks attributed in that article to you as quotations." Dean Neenan demanded a response by March 18.

I responded on March 17 that the article was "substantially inaccurate, taking phrases out of context and failing to grasp the content and spirit of my lecture." For seven weeks I was left in peace but that was not the end of this witch hunt.

Dean Neenan fired off another missive in my direction on April 12, reiterating his "request," and demanding a response from me by May 1. On May 1, I responded:

> My lecture at the December 1984 Annual Meeting of the American Academy of Religion came directly from my book, *Pure Lust: Elemental Feminist Philosophy.* The article in the *St. Louis Post Dispatch* is a barely recognizable paraphrase of my lecture. If you are concerned about an accurate version of what I said, I can only refer you to my book as a complete source of the text.

Appearing to have lost the scent, Dean Neenan did not reply.

My students were extraordinary. They demonstrated the Survivor qualities necessary for Radical Feminists in such times. They were tough, inventive, brave, humorous, and definitely fed up. They were willing to take risks and did so. They knew the preciousness of the Space provided by my classes and were willing to struggle for it. I recently asked one of these, Lizzie Gelles, who was a first-year student when she was in my courses: "What was important to you about being in those classes?" Her response was immediate: "I knew that I was not alone."*

I was planning to go on leave of absence the following academic year (1985–1986) in order to work full time on the *Wickedary.* I Sensed profoundly that it would be crucial that advanced Radical Feminist Women's Studies continue to be available in my absence, not only for the women at Boston College but also for students at local colleges and at other member schools of the Boston Theological Institute. My students Sensed this also and decided to compose and distribute a petition which would be presented to the Executive Committee of the theology department at Boston College, requesting that Dr. Emily Culpepper be hired part-time to teach in my absence.†

---

*As I listened to Lizzie's reply to this question in 1991, the words of the women who had written to me about *Pure Lust* echoed in my mind. I understand Now, more deeply than ever, the depths from which such responses have come.

†The petition said, in part:

> We, the undersigned, are hereby requesting that the Theology Department of Boston College take into serious consideration the hiring of Dr. Emily Culpepper during the

All of the students distributing the petition gathered signatures, beginning in early March and continuing until late April. Lizzie, in particular, worked at this strenuously day and night for two months, and kept a journal of the experience. The petition finally had approximately one thousand signatures, of which over seven hundred were from Boston College. The rest were from students at other colleges and universities in the area, including member institutions of the Boston Theological Institute, who were interested in the possibility of cross-registering.

In response to this enormous demand, the Curriculum Committee of the Theology Department recommended to the Executive Committee that Dr. Culpepper be hired to teach one (1) course in the spring term of the following academic year. The students replied by sending a memo to the Executive Committee.*

After seemingly endless waiting, evasion, and hassle, the students received a bland refusal to hire Emily at all, essentially giving no reasons why their modest and polite request would not be granted. Once again the boreocrats demonstrated their fear and hatred of Radical Feminists and of "Feminist Theory beyond the introductory level."

While all of this was going on I kept on teaching as Spinningly and Furiously as possible. I spoke at many colleges and Women's Spaces around the United States and Canada.[7] I was Soaring High with the expectation of Spiraling back, around, and ahead with the *Wickedary.*

At the end of the semester a party was held for the graduate and undergraduate students who had attended my upper-division classes. This event was held in the faculty lounge of ANTS (Andover Newton Theological

---

absence of Professor Mary Daly. . . .

In our opinion, Dr. Emily Culpepper has superb qualifications to teach at Boston College. She has written many articles in her area of expertise. Dr. Culpepper received her Th.D. from Harvard Divinity School. She has teaching experience in the field of Feminist Theology and is currently Visiting Lecturer and Research Associate in Women's Studies and Religion at Harvard Divinity School.

In an institution of higher education such as Boston College, we think it is important that the level of academic excellence in Feminist Theology and Philosophy be upheld. If this learning and growing process is to be successful, it is imperative that as students we have the best and most capable professors to continue studying Feminist Theory beyond the introductory level. . . .

We request that Boston College make this opportunity available.

*The memo stated in part: "We welcome the support which the Curriculum Committee has shown. However, this is not sufficient for our academic needs. In our opinion, it would not be unreasonable for Dr. Culpepper to teach two (2) courses, one in the fall and one in the spring. We know of several institutions which would be willing to help with the cost of a part-time Professor. That way Boston College can afford to have Dr. Culpepper teach a class both semesters. We urge you to take this matter under consideration as soon as possible."

School). As has been the case with all of my "class parties," the purpose was not only recreational—although a rollicking time was had by all—but also Metapolitical. It was about Spinning and about *Surviving* ⊙, that is

> the process of Spinsters living beyond, above, through, around the perpetual witchcraze of patriarchy; Metaliving, be-ing (*Wickedary*).

While all of these parties had been crucial for Radical Feminist Surviving, this one was especially so. For then, in May 1985, women were acutely aware of the need to Spin the threads of connectedness which the fathers perpetually tried to break. The students had just been through the experience of having their modest petition for the hiring of Emily as part-time teacher in my absence ruthlessly refused. They *needed* the lucid analysis and strong personal Presence which she could bring in a place and time so devoid of Feminist consciousness. They reflected cynically upon the true value of their expensive education.

The point, then, was how *not* to be defeated. We—the students, Emily, and I—thought about this problem together. I proposed that we begin a Feminist lecture series—not necessarily on the campus of Boston College, but in the Boston area—which would bring in Radical Feminist scholars and activists who would Spark continuing discussions and help carry on the teaching/learning process, despite the growing lacunae in universities.

Both Emily and I argued for Naming the sponsoring group and the series with the acronym WITCH. We didn't really need to "argue," however, since everyone Wildly agreed. There was some discussion of the specific Spelling out of the acronym in this case.* We all decided, finally, among gleeful shouts and suggestions, that it should be "Wild Independent Thinking Crones and Hags." When that Wording finally came out right, an audible "Ahhh" of satisfaction floated through the room. As I am writing this Now, I note with some satisfaction that this manifestation of WITCH continues in Boston.[8]

SPINNING THE WORD-WEBS OF THE CORE

In June 1985 Jane arrived from Albuquerque in her slightly wrecked car, which was loaded with her possessions. This vehicle, which appeared to

---

*WITCH has been an acronym for numerous Radical Feminist groups. For example, in 1969 the New York Covens used WITCH to stand for "Women's International Terrorist Conspiracy from Hell." This activist group made the famous statement: "You are a Witch by saying aloud, 'I am a Witch' three times, and *thinking about that.* You are a Witch by being female, untamed, angry, joyous, and immortal." See "WITCH," in *Sisterhood Is Powerful: An Anthology of Writings from the Women's Movement,* ed. by Robin Morgan (New York: Random House, 1970), pp. 538–53.

have barely made it to a parking spot in front of my apartment, sported a colorful array of bumper stickers. The latter were of interest not only to me, but also, I am sure, to my conservative and inquisitive neighbors.

Jane had been granted a leave from teaching for the fall semester, and the plan was to work steadily through the summer, fall, and winter until her departure in January. As it turned out, the stack of complicated index cards grew and grew. They filled boxes and boxes. By August 1985 it was clear that Jane should try to stay for the full academic year. She obtained an extension of her leave, and the stage was set for a year of uninterrupted work on the Core of the *Wickedary*.

The summer of 1985 was particularly intense. Even the week's "vacation" that Jane, Nancy Kelly, and I spent at Onset on Cape Cod involved preoccupation with dictionaries and the ever present three-by-five-inch cards on which the words of the Core were being "Spelled out" and defined. Everything was *Wickedary*-related. Everything brought Messages that were essential to the Weaving.

It was especially back at Crystal Lake and its environs, however, that Syn-Crone-istic Elemental connections were made. It was here that the importance of animals as Guides to/through the *Wickedary* became evident. A few Strange examples will illustrate this fact.

ANIMAL GUIDES I: WILD CAT

First and foremost among the Animal Guides of the *Wickedary* is my Domestic Familiar, Ms. Wild Cat—informally known simply as Wild Cat. Wild Cat is a *Furry*, that is "Feline friend and companion of a Fury: Purry" (*Wickedary*). She is also a *Glamour Puss* and a *Magnifi-cat*. In the most Serious Sense she is a *Grimalkin*, that is, a Wise Old She-Cat.

During the *Wickedary*-Weaving days, months, years Wild Cat was my constant companion, as she had been throughout the Spinning of *Gyn/Ecology* and especially of *Pure Lust*. She was attentive to her task of sitting on dictionaries, sending Cat/alytic inspiration. She communicated her Cat/egorical Imperative.

One particularly Peculiar happening illustrates Wild Cat's role in Summoning the Weird. On Friday, September 13, 1985, at approximately 12:15 a.m. I noticed that Wild Cat was not inside the apartment. She had disappeared! Since I knew all of her hiding places I looked in them, to no avail. Knowing that she had not gone outside I turned the place inside out, searching for her. I actually searched until about 3:00 a.m., at which hour I fell into a fitful sleep. At about 5:30 I woke up and heard her voice very faintly. It was a muffled meowing that seemed to come from within the walls. I followed the pitiful sound, and finally I was led to the large desk in the guest room, next to the *Wickedary* room. I opened the deep, tightly closed left-hand desk drawer and found Wild Cat scrunched in the back, behind many files. As I helped her out—meowing and scolding me—I felt great relief, of course. However, I was shocked. How did she get in there? I did not recall opening or closing that drawer the night before, and no one else was in that room. The question has remained unanswered.

I felt impelled, of course, to ponder the meaning of Friday the 13th. Barbara Walker, in her entry on "Friday" in *The Woman's Encyclopedia of Myths and Secrets,* wrote:

> Day of the Goddess Freya, called unlucky by Christian monks, because everything associated with female divinity was so called. Friday the 13th was said to be especially unlucky because it combined the Goddess's sacred day with her sacred number, drawn from the 13 months of the pagan lunar year.[9]

Freya, Great Goddess of northern Europe, is the Mistress of Cats. Moreover, she was/is believed to ride through the heavens in a chariot drawn by cats.[10] Although Wild Cat's "message" on that particular Friday the Thirteenth cannot be simply decoded, it is clear to me that she was, at the very least, calling attention to the importance of the number Thirteen and to Female and Feline participation in Other Dimensions.

I suspect that she was also Announcing the significance of her own name, *Wild Cat*○, which means

> **1 :** a Savage, Tempered, or Spriteful Cat, esp. one who engages in a risky or unsafe enterprise; a Radical Cat **2 :** a woman who participates in the qualities of a Radical Cat **3 :** member of a worldwide Wild tribe composed of Witches and their Familiars (*Wickedary*).

By means of such Weird and Canny/Uncanny behavior, Wild Cat made it known that she was/is superbly qualified to Act as Guide for Websters learning to become *Pixilated*○, that is

> **1:** highly creative; Wandering far afield from the disciplines of pedants and schoolmen. . . . **2:** Touched by the Fairies: Pixy-led (*Wickedary*).

Wild Cat has helped me to Re-member the importance of Wandering far afield from the foreground, breaking the spells of twelves, Spelling Thirteen. She has focused my attention on the *Thirteenth Hour,* which is

> the Other hour, beyond the direction of disaster; Time of jumping off the doomsday clocks of doomdom; Hour of Hope: Time beyond the parameters of patriarchal predictability; the Be-Witching Hour (*Wickedary*).

Since Wild Cat has also been my Cat/atonic companion during the Voyage through the writing of *Outercourse,* I have shared the chapters of this book with her. Naturally she has displayed varying degrees of interest.

During my crafting of the preceding chapter she occasionally sat on a copy of *Pure Lust,* looking at me with ineffable intensity. *Pure Lust* is, after all, *her* book. And Now, as I am writing the chapter on the *Wickedary,* she sometimes sits on the most recently typed pages. This is her Intergalactic Seat of Approval, perhaps.*

ANIMAL GUIDES II: DIVINING FAMILIARS

A few incidents will serve to illustrate the ways in which Wild animal guides "accidentally" came upon the scene before, after, and during *Wickedary* working sessions. The Wicked work itself was a kind of series of "magical ceremonies"—magical enough to Conjure "coincidental" meetings with Elemental creatures who were Divining Familiars.[11]

In late July 1985 a cluster of "coincidences" occurred after I Realized that the *Wickedary* should be a complex composition of Webs. Recognizing that it was essential to understand more about spiders and how they make their webs, I called Andrée Collard, who I knew would be a helpful Source of information. Andrée discussed at some length her observations of orb weaving spiders, which are orange-yellow in color. Immediately after that conversation Jane and I walked out to my car and noticed an orange-yellow spider weaving a web between my car and the tree next to my parking spot. In her appearance and activity she matched Andrée's description. For some reason I was inspired to call her "Sara."

Because of Sara's magical appearance I could not bring myself to disturb her and therefore avoided using my car. The following day her web was even more elaborate, and my dilemma remained unresolved. Finally Emily saved the situation by delicately moving Sara and her complex creation from the car to the tree, thereby freeing me to drive.

This was not the end of the story, however. A few days later a couple of other "Saras" were at work inside my car, constructing webs across the back seat. I don't recall how long they stayed. It was in late August, however, that the clincher of the Sara saga occurred. When I got into my car I was startled

---

*Yet there has been a change in the focus of her interest. Wild Cat has frequently (perversely it has sometimes seemed to me) left me alone in the *Outercourse* room. Sitting at the door with her back to me, she has definitively indicated that she wants to go *Out.* For some time I have struggled not to take this personally. And Now, finally, I get the message. I am embarrassed to admit to my slowness in acknowledging that Wild Cat has become an *Outercourse* cat. The many hours of solitude which she enjoys out in the hall, on the other side of the door, testify to the fact that she is developing something like a Feline Fourth Galactic perspective. She is a far-out Familiar, offering me a Course in being *Catty,* that is, "Self-reliant, independent, resilient; having the Wild, Witchy, and Wicked characteristics of a cat" (*Wickedary*). The Virtue of Cattiness is very important for Intergalactic Voyagers to learn, of course.

to find a member of the Sara tribe swinging from my rearview mirror, exactly in the position of a good luck charm.

An Other Momentous "accidental" encounter occurred in early August 1985. Jane and I had gone to the Post Office. She expressed a desire to see some big birds. When we arrived back at Crystal Lake the day had turned misty and the grass appeared *very* Green. And there, beside the water, was an astonishing gaggle of Wild geese who had just dropped by and were having an afternoon snack. Most impressive were their long, sinewy necks, which seemed to coil in all directions. When we approached them they hurried into the water. They swam a short distance. Then they signaled each other with their wings and took off, creating an extraordinary display of Bird-Power. This inspired some ideas about Word-Power as it should be displayed in the *Wickedary*.

First of all, the *Wickedary* words should fly together in a skein. One definition of *skein,* according to *Webster's,* is "a flock of wild fowl (as geese or ducks) in flight."* As I wrote in the *Preface*:

> The Labyrinthine design of the *Wickedary* is organic and purposeful, and it can be compared to a flock of Wild fowl in flight.[12]

Moreover,

> Websters Hear/Know words as birds—often in flight, sometimes at rest on the earth, in trees, or in the water (as geese in gaggles). Consequently, this is a Book of Augury. An Augur is a Soothsayer, "said to mean a diviner by the flight and cries of birds" (Walter W. Skeat, *A Concise Etymological Dictionary of the English Language*). The flight and cries of words/birds help us to Divine the way through the Labyrinthine passages which are the true pathways of the Metapatriarchal Journey of Exorcism and Ecstasy.[13]

Also:

> In our weavings we follow the flights of words, which carry messages, hop, fly, soar, and sing. Like birds, words are winged. . . . The *Wickedary* is a Source Book of such messages.[14]

Another significant encounter with Divining Familiars was Jane's "bee experience" in the fall of 1985. Bees kept flying into the apartment where she was staying. She couldn't seem to stop this invasion, so the idea occurred that these were messengers of some kind. She came to the conclusion that they were Spelling Bees, and these joined the ranks of Guides to the *Wickedary*. Naturally, when I was Weaving *Preliminary Web Two,* which is "Spelling: The Casting of Spells," they buzzed their way into the text. It became literally impossible to write *Be-Spelling* without Hearing also *Bee-Spelling*.

---

*Appropriately, *skein* also means "a loosely coiled length of yarn or thread" (*Webster's*).

Some encounters were less evident in their signification, but they were memorable. In July 1985, for example, a hoptoad hopped up onto the stone step at the front entrance of my building, next to the lake. When approached, it played dead for awhile. Having read that Witches in Europe in the Middle Ages gave milk to their Toad Familiars, I offered this visitor a saucer of milk, but it showed no interest. All the same, the visitor herself was interesting and inspired the expression *Toadal Time,* which is

> the Time of the Toad; Toadally experienced Time; Time of Toadal encounters: eventide; Hopping Time, outside the totaled time of clockocracy (*Wickedary*).

SPINNING/SPEEDING THROUGH THE CORE:
A BE-WITCHING OMEN

Throughout the fall of 1985 and the winter, spring, and summer of 1986 Jane and I were occupied/preoccupied with Spinning the Word-Webs of the *Wickedary*'s Core. Jane would have to leave for Albuquerque in July or August, and it was essential that the basic work on this part of the book be finished by then.* So I kept my number of "gigs" to a minimum.[15]

Marge Roberson, the *Wickedary* typist, worked heroically at the seemingly insuperable task of transferring onto correctly typed pages the complex content of the index cards, which contained the words of the Core, their definitions, etymologies, and Other Weird information, much of which had been Searched out by the Wild Hag Diana Beguine. On June 16, 1986 Jane and I brought these pages, together with my first draft of most of the essays/Webs, to a copy shop in Brookline.

Then a typically Weird, Witchy, Wicked event occurred. When the xeroxing was finished we walked up the street to a restaurant ("Veronique") in order to celebrate with drinks and dessert. When the waitress brought the bill and MasterCard receipt to be signed, the amount came to $13.13. Moreover, she had written on these impressive documents "#13," indicating the number of our table. With Loud Hoots and Cackles we pranced out of the sedate restaurant. This was indeed a Be-Witching Omen, Foretokening a Fascinating Future for the *Wickedary.*

---

*When the *Wickedary* assumed its final form, it consisted of *The First Phase*: Preliminary Webs; *The Second Phase*: The Core of the *Wickedary; The Third Phase*: Appendicular Webs. *The Second Phase* is comprised of three Word-Webs. *Word-Web One* of the Core consists of Elemental philosophical words and phrases and Other key words. *Word-Web Two* is made up of words describing the Inhabitants of the Background, their activities and characteristics. In *Word-Web Three*, travelers view the inhabitants of the foreground from the perspective of the Background. These words describe the characteristics, behaviors, and products of the foreground fellows and their henchwomen.

It was also a culmination. Shortly thereafter Jane would be leaving and I would be taking off for a speaking tour in Norway and Germany. Upon my return I would resume my work on the *Wickedary*.

NORWAY AND GERMANY—AFTER CHERNOBYL

On June 22, 1986 I took off for Europe. My lecture tour, which was to include Oslo, Norway, and several important centers in West Germany, had been in the planning stages for several months, and I had looked forward to it with enthusiasm. Then in late April a hideous "accident" occurred—the meltdown at Chernobyl.

Of course the media in America were less than straightforward in reporting the implications of that disaster. In Germany, however, the "news" was more reliable—far more so than in many other European countries. Gradually, throughout May and early June I heard from my German friends of the radioactive fallout in that country. There were reports that Munich was as contaminated as Kiev. Many women were basically fasting, or trying to live on imported foods and/or foods that had been processed and in storage since before the meltdown.

I briefly considered the option of canceling. When I mentioned this thought to Erika she said simply: "It will be very discouraging for the women if you don't come. They'll think that if Mary Daly won't come here it must be really terrible." I gave the matter some thought and decided to go. "Do it, Daly" was my firm advice to myself from mySelf. I went armed with a huge box of dark green, foul-tasting powder which was supposed to ward off the effects of radiation. I met Erika in Frankfurt on June 23 and we flew together to Oslo, where I was scheduled to speak the next day at the Second International Feminist Bookfair. Since there was a mix-up about lecture halls, a group of us took over a large classroom so that I could speak. The talk was a kind of double feature, combining *Pure Lust* and *Wickedary* material.

I dined alone in the cafeteria of the student hotel where we were staying. Having been told to avoid fresh vegetables, milk, eggs, cheese, butter, meat, fresh fruit, I was bewildered. I chose pasta and then sat staring at my plate in horror. After eating some of this I went for a walk. It was a poignantly beautiful midsummer evening, so I walked to a nearby lake. At ten in the evening it was still quite sunny and a number of people were swimming and lying on the grass. I imagined at the time that they were thinking thoughts of doom in the midst of that beauty. Later, however, I realized that the news about the effects of Chernobyl was more suppressed in Norway than in Germany, so it is possible that the people at the lake were not preoccupied with that atrocity.

Many of the Scandinavian women at the Bookfair were overwhelmed, however. One woman gave me a beautifully crafted Norwegian salad fork and spoon, with a comment to the effect that she would no longer be using them, since the vegetables would be contaminated. Some calculated how many years they might have left and discussed what they hoped to accomplish. All of this was strangely mixed with Spinning discussions and optimistic plans for the future.

At the conclusion of the Bookfair Erika and I flew to Hanover, Germany. We were met by Helga Edelmann-Klittich, who drove us to Bielefeld. A conference, organized by women teaching interdisciplinary Women's Studies at the University of Bielefeld, was scheduled for the 27th and 28th of June in a comfortable new conference center. Women from many other universities in Germany also attended the conference. I spoke on several themes from *Pure Lust*.[16] A great deal of interest was focused that weekend on the problem of tokenism, with many references to *Bemalte Vögel*, that is, Painted Birds. The concept of "The State of Total Tokenism: Painted Birds" is, of course, from the chapter on Spooking in *Gyn/Ecology*, which by 1986 had caught on and spread like Wildfire across Germany.

Although I said some things in German as well as in English, Erika was a much needed translator for the difficult text. Our method of speaking together was that I would say a few sentences and Erika would then translate. We alternated—sometimes in large bites and sometimes in smaller ones. It was partly a matter of playing by ear.

In Bielefeld I heard more and more about nuclear contamination in Germany. Erika and I had dinner at the home of Helga and her husband. They served us an excellent meal, consisting of delicacies that had been frozen or canned and held in storage since before Chernobyl. Inevitably our conversation turned to the recent—and current—disaster. Although the German authorities required testing of vegetables, fruits, milk, et cetera, it was just about impossible to decipher the results. A vocabulary of radiation measurement had evolved which was virtually meaningless to most people. For example, it would be reported on the radio that the broccoli on sale at the market place in Munich contained so many *Becquerel* on a certain day. No one knew exactly what that meant, but it sounded bad, and that was warning enough.

Helga told us that the contamination in the area around Bielefeld (and elsewhere) was so sporadic that, for example, the strawberries on one side of the road would be "clean," whereas right on the other side they were heavily contaminated. The land in many areas was so contaminated that it was life-threatening to sit on it or walk on it. Cow pastures were radioactive. Mothers, especially, were in a state of panic about how to protect their children.

The time in Bielefeld was not all gloom and doom, however. It was there that I met Lilly Friedberg, a truly Sparking and Spinning American woman who had moved to Germany to live, study, and work, and who apparently had no intention of leaving soon, if ever. We were destined to meet again and again, in Germany, Ireland, Switzerland, and Italy. Lilly clearly had joined the Race of Wild Women/Witches.

Weighed down by the knowledge of Chernobyl and at the same time eager to continue on the tour, Erika and I went next to Hamburg, where I spoke in a huge old factory (*Kampnagelfabrik*). This women-only event had been arranged by the Feminist bookshop in Hamburg, and women had come from a number of cities in busloads. Clearly the women's movement was really cooking in Germany. In that speech I began to use the seven-point Sado-Ritual Syndrome from *Gyn/Ecology* to analyze the Chernobyl atrocity. It applied with extraordinary accuracy. The women did not fail to see the connections between the environmental atrocities and the mutilation and massacre of women. The audience was loud and Wild, and the encounters there were extremely powerful.

In Hamburg Erika and I stayed at the home of two strapping young women—Feminists who were organizers of the event—who loaded the table with a variety of cheeses. I did not understand this phenomenon until Erika explained later that these women had been basically starving themselves for six weeks and had come to a decision to "live now," and take their chances. It was horrifying to think that it had come to this. Despite the horror we discussed many things. It was evident that there was great vitality in the German Feminist movement.

On July 2 we moved on to Frankfurt, where I was scheduled to speak at the university. This was arranged by women there in cooperation with the Universities of Marburg, Giessen, and Mainz. Again, the crowd was huge. It was a mixed audience—mostly women and some men. By this time—although Erika and I had perfected our style of alternating English and her German translation—I was eager to say more things in German. So in fact I did toss in quite a few words, phrases, and sentences in German. Sometimes my sentences began in English and ended in German. Some women told me later that it was a strange experience of hearing a speech half in English and half in German, and that it even sounded quite natural.

Following the precedent of Hamburg, I applied the Sado-Ritual Syndrome to the atrocity of Chernobyl. I ended the lecture with a rousing/arousing selection from a draft of the Final Appendicular Web of the *Wickedary,* which was "Jumping Off the doomsday clock: Eleven, Twelve . . . Thirteen." Then, in my usual way, I called upon the Great Original Witch in every woman, who Howls:

Flieg mit meinen Winden—Fly with my Winds

Ströme mit meinen Wassern—Rush with my Waters

Umarme meine Erde—Hug my Earth

Entzünde mein Feuer—Light my Fire!

Since Germany was the country in which the witchcraze in Western Europe had been most cruel and most violent, I felt a special Be-Witching power in the uttering/Howling of those words there, on that ground. The women also Heard that power.*

Our final stop was Stuttgart. We went by train. By then Erika and I felt more and more like a traveling circus. Why not go on . . . and on? At any rate, the speech in Stuttgart was arranged by the Women's Center, called SARAH. Women came on buses from the surrounding areas of Germany and quite a few came from Switzerland. My speech went over well. Particularly poignant for me, however, was the time some of us spent together after the talk. We walked the streets looking for a not too noisy restaurant and finally had to settle for a noisy place anyway. All the same, our group— including Erika, Gerda Gallup, who is a powerful sculptor, and Doris Gunn, a Feminist activist who had come from Switzerland—had Spinning conversations and seemed to share an abiding Presence.

BACK TO BIG TRANSITIONS

On the plane returning to the U.S. the next day (July 5) I had a chance to compare a German newspaper (*Frankfurter Allgemeine Zeitung*) and an American paper (*The International Herald Tribune*). While the German paper had articles about the effects of Chernobyl, I found nothing of the sort in the American paper, which was filled with fluff about the Statue of Liberty and the Fourth of July. I pondered with disgust the systematic moronization of Americans by the media.

Paradoxically, that European excursion had been exhilarating. The International Bookfair in Oslo had been stimulating, but the German women especially gave a boost to my Hope. Their vigor, creativity, intellectuality, courage, and determination were inspiring. Whereas Radical Feminism seemed at that time to be somewhat in the doldrums in the United States, in Germany many women were on the Move.

When I arrived "home" I could not stop myself from speaking glowingly about the women in Germany, because just as disillusionment and *apraxia* were settling in here, they were *there*, alive, active, and strong. I had gained the Hope-full insight that when Radical Feminism seems to be "down" in one area, it may be Rising Furiously somewhere else. As Voyager/Pirate I well knew how to use my Craft to carry Tidings/Messages of such varying conditions to Cronies, reporting my observations of shiftings of the Tides in the Subliminal Sea. So I brought my A-mazing accounts of experiences in Germany to dis-Couraged companions in America.

---

*Following this lecture, a group of Feminist theologians asked me to speak to a small seminar at the university. This also was a positive experience. I was asked if I would consider coming to teach for a semester at Frankfurt, so I suggested that they go ahead and check it out—knowing, of course, that what women want and need is not usually what they will get at patriarchial universities.

I returned to the engaging task of writing the final drafts of the Preliminary Webs and Appendicular Webs of the *Wickedary*. This was a Be-Musing experience of high hilarity and Hopping Hope.

At the same Time, something deeply tragic was happening. Andrée, my good friend of many years, was very sick. Frequently I drove down to Norwell, Massachusetts, where she lived with Joyce Contrucci. Sometimes I went there with Nancy Kelly or with other friends, and often I went alone. The feeling of helplessness was overwhelming. Andrée died on the Equinox, September 23, 1986.

Grief was not so overwhelming that I was stopped for very long from the work of writing. Andrée, great lover of Life and creativity, would have hated that, and so would I. So I kept on writing up a storm. The *Wickedary* is a Biophilic work. It is an affirmation of ongoing Elemental Life.*

Also in the fall 1986 I learned that my good friend Bill Wilson, who had been my student in the La Salle College junior year abroad program in Fribourg in the mid-sixties and with whom I had kept in touch after we both returned to the United States, had died of AIDS in New York. An extraordinarily sensitive and Life-loving person, he was cut down prematurely, wrongly.

During that fall and through the winter and spring of 1987 Emily worked with me, offering Shrewd comments and criticisms. We carefully went over the entire manuscript, polishing and rearranging some definitions and scrutinizing essays, prior to my handing it to the publisher. She also assisted me in the arduous work of galley proofreading.

This was a hard time in her life, as she searched for a teaching job in a world that was increasingly hostile to Radical Feminists. Superb qualifications, including a doctorate from Harvard, excellent publications, and more than successful teaching experience were not enough.[17] We both realized with sadness that she would have to leave the Boston area, and probably the East Coast, in order to obtain a decent job. This was a significant manifestation of the diaspora that was being imposed upon Radical Feminist friends. We had to go—or stay—where we could survive. This added to our increasing sense of isolation.

In March 1987 my friend Josephine Yancey, whom I had met in the late sixties through our mutual friend Pauli Murray, died of what could be called

---

*Hence the dedication is:

In Metamemory of
Andrée Collard
True lover of the Wild
and
to the myriads
of Hopping Hoping women
and Other creatures
who continue to carry on

"environmental racism." At about that time I heard more bad news. Word arrived that Nelle Morton did not have much longer to live. Since I had agreed to speak in Ireland in July, I felt that it would be important to see Nelle before that trip. So I accepted an invitation to speak at California State University at Fresno on May 11, in order to pay travel expenses for a visit with her at her home in Claremont.[18] I did manage to have a couple of days with Nelle. As usual, she was sparkling with intelligence and wit, and we enjoyed Canny conversations that ranged over many topics. The fact that this could be our last visit was not explicitly acknowledged, but the understanding was there. I returned home with a deep sense of sorrow.*

Thus the fall of 1986 and the spring and summer of 1987 brought much sadness. Nonetheless the *Wickedary* swooped and soared as a Winged Work of Word-Magic. It is Now Time to examine the Workings of that Word-Magic.

THE UNIFYING THEME OF THE *WICKEDARY*: SPINNING THREADS, WEAVING WEBS— PRESENTIATING THE BACKGROUND

Searching Now, from a Fourth Galactic viewpoint, for the "unifying theme" of the *Wickedary*—I see that I have not far to look. The *Wickedary* is a Web-Work, consisting of Webs, and Webs of Webs. Each thread of each Web is a *Pixy-path*, that is

> **1 :** trail into the Background where Journeyers are Be-Wildered and forever lost to patriarchy **2 :** pathway that leads between the left and right hemispheres of the brain; path that leads off the map and into the Third Hemisphere (*Wickedary*).

By *Third Hemisphere* I mean

> zone Dis-covered and explored by Contrary-Wise Crones who Spin beyond the compass and off the map; uncharted Zone: Fairy Space (*Wickedary*).[19]

Recently when I asked Geraldine Moane how she experiences the *Wickedary* as distinct from my Other Third Galactic books, she replied:

---

*Nelle died on July 14, 1987. I was extremely glad that I had managed to arrange the trip to see her in California in May. On September 12 a memorial gathering was held at Scripps College in Claremont to celebrate her life. Everyone attending was invited to share a memory of Nelle. I was not able to be there, since I had agreed to address the Illinois NOW Congress (Joint State Conference of Iowa and Illinois) on that date. However, I communicated my "Memory" by phone to Emily, who read it to the group. My Memory was of Nelle "speaking out" at the "Forum on Women in Higher Education" held at Boston College in 1975 (see Chapter Eleven). Nelle had described some of the economic hardships she had endured as a result of not speaking up for herSelf over the years as clearly as she had for others. She proclaimed: "I have not come to speak out for Mary Daly, but to speak out, finally, for mySelf." She then urged all of the women there to speak out for themselves. Her Rage and her message had been very powerful.

It puts you [the reader/Hearer] immediately in Touch with the Background. If you are stuck in linear thinking you can just open it at any point, and a cognitive shift takes place, a Shape-shifting. The structure is such that you can catch any thread and just Hop. This is because the Power is dispersed throughout the book.[20]

Ger also remarked that the *Wickedary* is very much a book that women can *use*. It *propels* us into the Background very easily. It cuts through the foreground context faster than its predecessors. Comparing it to the preceding books, she said:

With the other books there is a sense of going through the foreground into the Background, but in the *Wickedary* you are already there.[21]

As a consequence of be-ing "already there"*—

No matter where you are [in the book] you have a sense of the whole. . . . So you can make more connections.[22]

Crone-logically, the *Wickedary* was Spun after *Gyn/Ecology* and *Pure Lust*. It can Presentiate the Background with special immediacy because my Craft had broken through obstacles and gained Momentum and Power as it Moved through book after book. The *Wickedary* is Original in a unique way because in large measure its Source is my own preceding work. Hence it is an appropriate culmination of The Third Spiral Galaxy.

When the *Wickedary* exposes the foreground, this is from a Be-Dazzling Background perspective. Of course, it is also the case with my Other books that they analyze (and therefore expose) the foreground from a Background perspective. It is not possible to expose the foreground from a foreground perspective! But by the Time of the Spinning of this third Third Galactic work, the "groundwork," so to speak, had already been done. Hence there is a Lightning-like quality to the *Wickedary*. It flashes around, illuminating the scene Erratically.

Word-Web Three of the Core, which defines the inhabitants of the foreground, their activities, characteristics, and products, exemplifies this lightning-like propensity. Upon numerous occasions I have Hopped through the *Wickedary* before audiences of hundreds of women, flipping through the pages and reading passages and definitions at random. The passages from the Preliminary and Appendicular Webs have been Heard with appreciation. So also have the Elemental philosophical words from *Word-Web One,* and words describing the Inhabitants of the Background in *Word-Web Two.*

---

*This does not mean that Wickedarians or readers are permanently and "all the way" in the Background all the time. It means that there is an accessibility to Other awareness that is the result of previous work(s). The Be-Dazzling Light has intensified; Pixy-paths are more visible.

Indeed, these passages and words always have elicited much Be-Laughing. But the words and definitions from *Word-Web Three*, read rapidly, always have crackled and snapped with alarming alacrity the man-made *mindbindings* ➊, which are

> layers of crippling patriarchal thought patterns comparable to the footbindings which mutilated millions of Chinese women for over one thousand years; master-minded myths and ideologies meant to mummify the spirit and maim the brain (*Wickedary*).

In Other words, these Words break the Terrible Taboo. They Touch women, Touching off flashes of insight, releasing powers of Laughing Out Loud. The inhabitants of the foreground—among them the *bores, blobbers, botchers, butchers, cockalorums, dicks, flappers, fundamentalists, plug-uglies, snools*—and their products, such as *academentia, flopocracy, psycho-ology,* and *re-search,* parade before the Hearers' eyes, and Eye-biting powers are awakened. Since to See is to Laugh, thunderous cackling commonly ensues.

Be-Speaking from the *Wickedary* summons cosmic thunder and lightning, as cackling women crack the male-ordered universe, slipping off into the Wild. At such Moments women Move far out on the Subliminal Sea. Some, overcome with fear of foreground fixers, may eventually retreat, but a Memory has been created, and this cannot be totally erased. It can sink into the depths of the Sea, but there is also the possibility that it will be Re-Called and Re-membered.

For the reader of the *Wickedary,* the physical/visual layout of the book conveys a wholeness of vision. The Webs, with their intertwining Pixy-paths—for example, trails created by the cross-referencing of words—suggest *Fairy Space*○,* that is

> Space Dis-covered by Fey Women who Spiral beyond Stag-nation; Space where Weird Women gather and Gossip with Fairies (*Wickedary*).

To understand this definition, it is helpful to Re-Call that the verb *Gossip* means

> to exercise the Elemental Female Power of Naming, especially in the Presence of other Gossips. . . . to divine and communicate the secrets of the Elements, the wisdom of the stars (*Wickedary*).

There is a connection, then, between Qualitatively Other Space and the enhancement of reciprocal powers of Naming and Hearing.

---

*This impression is greatly enhanced by the thirty Stunning illustrations created by Sudie Rakusin, whose Background characters Leap off the pages, awakening the reader's Wicked imaginative powers.

Entering Fairy Space awakens our *Labyrinthine Sense*◑, meaning "the faculty of Hearing the difference between Real, Elemental Words and mere elementary terms" (*Wickedary*). Hence, readers who truly enter the world of the *Wickedary* are Hearers and Speakers. Words, after all, are sounds—not mere scratches on paper.

The Spelling/Spilling of Elemental Sounds into the Ether transforms vibrations. This change of vibrations sharpens the Sense of Direction of Voyagers as we Move farther out of the foreground, beyond the compass and off the map. It also strengthens our Sense of Tidal Time, sending us off the calendars and clocks of the tidily man-dated world.

The *Wickedary,* then, invites Hopping from Web to Web and from uncharted zones to further uncharted zones. The Sense of Spatial Wholeness conveyed by the Webs of this work engenders the longing for Temporal Wholeness. As Nancy Kelly proclaimed, "The 'Beyond' which is the Third Hemisphere sends one 'Beyond the Beyond.'"[23] To put it another way, it propels the Voyager into what might be called the Fourth Hemisphere, which is *Fairy Time*○:

> Time that is off the clocks of father time; Time that measures intensity of experience and therefore can be stretched or condensed; Time that moves Counterclockwise and is accessible to those who ask Counterclock Whys; Time symbolized by the number Thirteen (*Wickedary*).

Appropriately, *Appendicular Web Four,* which concludes the *Wickedary,* brought me to this zone of Time Travel. Crone-logically, my Craft was prepared to Move into The Fourth Spiral Galaxy.

Moreover, since in the *Wickedary* I Conjured Elemental Sounds, that work Naturally opened the way to further communion with Elements in the sense of the larger cosmos, including the sun, moon, planets, and stars. It brought me further into Touch with the vast context within which the Primal Powers of Witches and all Wild beings must be understood. Having suggested a connection between Spinning Webs of words and Intergalactically Voyaging through Time, I Conjured by means of the *Wickedary* a Hopping-off point for the Spiraling Moments of *Outercourse.*

RESPONSES TO THE *WICKEDARY*: LETTERS

Laughing women posted letters to my Craft, confirming my faith in the Lunatic Fringe. One of the first to arrive, coming from a woman in Boston, cackled:

> I bought the *Wickedary* the other day, started reading, and went back the next day and bought four more copies for presents, and I haven't stopped laughing yet. As one of the Cracked Crones behind the fatuous foreground, I am especially appreciative. . . . It is a great relief to realize there's a sizable group out there who are also laughing. I thought I was the only one.

Others wrote in a more serious vein. A woman who described herSelf as "a 60-year-old survivor of the stupid stagnation state" wrote from Berkeley, California:

> I loved every word of it. Thanks to you, Jane Caputi et al., the Background has come to the fore ever more clearly and confirms what I know instinctively. . . . Although I have been able to distance myself mentally from their mad world, I'm still trying to distance myself physically short of death. So far, to no avail. But I keep trying.

Sometimes the response was to a specific word or words. A reader who signed "In Spinsterhood," wrote concerning "enlightening words and thoughts relating to Spinsters":

> I was startled and thrilled to find words for my feelings. I've stumbled and fumbled for years trying to briefly express my way of life and you have done it . . .

The focus was more general in the letter of a folklorist from Berkeley, California, who informed me:

> I have been carrying [the *Wickedary*] with me and dipping into it to remind myself that yes, this is who I am and this is the world view which is mine, even when surrounded by people who have bought into all the lies.

Once again, there is the theme of confirmation coming from one who Senses herSelf to be a member of a cognitive minority. Such acknowledgment of the experience of being confirmed in and reminded of one's Sense of Reality when overwhelmed by the State of Deception occurs repeatedly. One woman from Los Angeles stated simply:

> Thanks again for your wonderful irreverence. It's the only thing that can keep us (reasonably) sane.

This woman enclosed a fairy tale—a "good witch/bad witch saga" that she had written.*

A correspondent from Cambridge, Massachusetts, addressing her letter to "Mary, Jane, and Sudie," wrote:

> Thank you for the joy I felt in reading pure words, root words, branch and stem words, not yet misused into meaninglessness in this year [1988] of presidential candidates.

In contrast to this expression of joy, there was a note of sadness in some letters. A combination of joy and sorrow is expressed in a letter from Columbus, Ohio:

---

*Many women responding to the *Wickedary* and to my Other books have enclosed copies of their own creative work, including poems, stories, drawings, tapes, and accounts of political actions.

Your Crone-logical hits dis-spell the Bull in which we are all swimming/drowning. Dispersing it, however, will require a group effort. . . . Your Words bring tears of joy and sorrow, focusing my rememberings on the agonies and the ecstasies of my own journey, and wondering how in this fabricated hell I can survive another day. . . . Your book took me places I was not thinking about going for a while yet, so I wasn't—nor could I have been—prepared for its power combining with mine in my present mode of "just take it easy, just go to your job. . . ." To see things this clearly saddened me almost beyond endurance and at times I felt as though I could (and would) weep forever.

Women wrote of psychic events. A reader from Mashpee, Massachusetts, described her experience:

I spent two solid days with the book, writing all over it and having a great time. Last night I was picked up by this huge burst of energy and suddenly I was inside this Great Big Witch, but also Seeing her, riding a huge wave, legs tucked in the meditating position, black robe and hat streaming out behind her, across the sky. . . . Now that I've read the *Wickedary* I realize that what has really been plaguing me with pain all these years is Herself/MySelf, buried in tons of snoolshit, Nagging me with vicious vibes every time I tried to be a good little woman in their terms.

The *Wickedary* was characterized by a woman from Fredericton, New Brunswick, as dream-inducing:

I read it before I go to bed at night and have the most powerful dreams!

Laughter combines with Syn-Crone-icity in some letters. A reader from London reported:

Today I was sitting in the garden flitting through the *Wickedary*. I laughed, I felt smug knots of recognition, I was happy that accident brought me to this book. Lots of things meant many things and my mind ranged freely.

A Radical Feminist living in New South Wales, Australia, delightfully related her encounter with the *Wickedary*:

The humor and irreverence are explosive. I can't help leaping about in it. In fact the day the parcel came . . . the first word I "accidentally" turned to was *blob*. Somehow forever after I am doomed in the middle of really serious situations to suddenly think about Blob Hope [an example under the word *blobular*], and I crack up. It's so splendidly silly . . . and so has equal power with the "serious" words.

Reading these letters Now, as the foreground world of the 1990s becomes ever more obscene, I am encouraged to have in my hands evidence that around this planet there are Webs of Wicked women, Be-Laughing, Surviving, Spinning, Be-ing Alone, rejoicing, weeping, Be-Witching, Living into The Fourth Spiral Galaxy.

RESPONSES TO THE *WICKEDARY*: REVIEWS

Many of the reviews of the *Wickedary* were gleeful, witty, and Wicked. Julia Penelope's scintillating piece in *The Women's Review of Books* (December 1987), published under the heading "Erratic, Ecstatic, Eccentric," was itself an Eccentric analysis.

In fact, a number of the reviews' headings revealed delight in Wickedness. Debra Schultz's review in *Belles Lettres* (March/April 1988) is entitled "An Antidote for Academentia." Ann Marie Palmisciano's Be-Musing review in *Sojourner* (April 1988) is headed "The Wickedary: A Be-Witching Book." Carol Lansbury published a rollicking review in *The New York Times Book Review* (January 17, 1988), under the Weird heading "What Snools These Mortals Be." This piece, accompanied by "A *Wickedary* Sampler" and illustrated with cartoons that had me cackling for hours, days, weeks, began with the following forthright remarks:

> Roistering, rambunctious, tickling and tumbling, Mary Daly's *Wickedary* makes a good antidote to last month's celebration of the birth of a male Saviour, sent by a masculine God to deliver the world from sin and death. Blasphemous in her intent, Daly—in cahoots with Jane Caputi—has composed a dictionary, a female counterpart of the 15th-century handbook for witch-hunters, the "Malleus Maleficarum." The *Wickedary* would undoubtedly have sent this merry martyr to the stake had she lived in Salem or in Calvin's Geneva. That's if she hadn't already been burnt for previously published books . . .

Reading these words Now, I am a bit more sober. In the foreground of the early nineties this is Bush's and David Duke's America. The technology and techniques of the prevailing witchcraze are more sophisticated than those available to Calvin and the authors of the *Malleus Maleficarum*. And—in case the reader is wondering—No, I will not stop Now.

There were many other reviews, mainly very positive, for example, in *On the Issues, The Book Reader, The Bloomsbury Review, Plexus, NWSA Journal, Durrant's* (London), *Booklist, Chicago Outlines, Minnesota Women's Press, Iris: A Journal About Women, Golden Threads, Common Lives/Lesbian Lives, Religious Studies Review, Times Literary Supplement* (London). In 1988 *The New York Times Book Review* listed it among "Notable Books of the Year."

I unabashedly find such response Sylph-satisfying.

RESPONSES TO THE *WICKEDARY*: SPOOKS' SPOOFS

I was pleased to learn that the *Wickedary* was/is "notable." Moreover, I would like to believe that Noah Webster shares in this delight, and a couple of "accidents" have encouraged this belief. First, one day—probably in 1986 or 1987—I flipped open the huge *Webster's Third New International Dictionary of the English Language* and read, on the page opposite Noah's picture, that he was born on October 16, 1758. Since October 16 is also my birthday, I thought, Hmmm?!

That fact alone, of course, does not necessarily go beyond the realm of mere coincidence—or does it? At any rate, it just so happened that early in 1987, a few months before the *Wickedary*'s appearance, I went to visit an acquaintance in West Hartford, Connecticut, a place with which I was totally unfamiliar. I became hopelessly lost when trying to find her house, and found myself driving on a street which had a sign indicating that I was approaching Noah Webster's birthplace. This was a bit startling, since I had not known that Noah was born in West Hartford. However, I kept driving around, feeling as if I were in a maze. Again I found myself approaching a sign indicating that I was on the way to Noah Webster's birthplace. I decided to go there and I did see the old house, but it appeared to be closed to visitors. So I just let it go and pursued my original purpose in visiting West Hartford.

On the way home I pondered over the possible meaning of my finding Noah's birthplace. I felt a bit Spooked, because my publisher had recently asked me (as publishers commonly do) for suggestions of well-known persons who might write effective statements (blurbs) for the jacket of the book. I came to the conclusion that neither dead men nor fictional characters should be excluded from this list. I saw no reason to discriminate against such personages. This was, after all, the *Wickedary*! Among those on my list, to whom I planned to attribute appropriate statements, were Mr. Webster, John Bartlett, pope Innocent VIII, Professor Yessir, tom, dick, and harry, Mrs. Malaprop, and Eve.

As I thought about all this in the car, I admitted to mySelf that the blurb I intended to attribute to Webster could be perceived as insulting by that sensitive individual. So I censored my original wording, of which I have, unfortunately, no written record and no clear memory.*

After some careful thought I came up with the appropriate and correct blurb, which was:

> This dictionary is beyond me! Never in my wildest dreams could I have foreseen this book.
>
> —*Mr. Webster*

When I arrived home I wrote this down and read it to mySelf with a Sense of great relief.† I reflected upon the possibility (fact?) that Noah had taken great pains to make his point. Just Now, when writing these reflections, I have turned to the page opposite the title page of *Webster's* and have

---

*If I did have such a record I would not publish it anyway.

†None of my other deceased or made-up blurbers have caused me such anxiety. I might have expected some resistance from John Bartlett, author of *Familiar Quotations*, to whom I attributed the following comment: "Astonishing . . . educational . . . a revela-

carefully read the citations from that learned gentleman which are printed there. The first is:

> a living language must keep pace with improvements in knowledge and with the multiplication of ideas
>
> —*Noah Webster,* A Letter to John Pickering, 1817

Yes, indeed.

There were Other Spooking/Spoofing incidents during the period preceding and following the appearance of the *Wickedary*. These occurred during my adventurous travels Be-Speaking/Be-Spelling Wicked words hither and yon during the summer and fall of 1987. Traveling to and through Ireland in July 1987 was especially eventful.*[24] So also were many trips around the United States in the fall.[25]

One event which involved Spoofing by a Spook merits special attention here. It occurred under improbable conditions in an unlikely place and at a Strangely significant Time. It happened at a session of the Annual Meeting of the American Academy of Religion in a downtown Boston hotel on Sunday, December 6, 1987, between 11:00 a.m. and 12:00 noon.[26] The "session," which was part of the "Women and Religion Section,"[27] had as its theme "Feminist Language." Emily Culpepper presided, and I Be-Spelled from the *Wickedary*.

There was no hint of daylight or of fresh air. The packed large room was windowless, and it abounded with glaring lights.† I could feel a clash

---

tion! I am not familiar with most of the quotations in this work." However, that compiler did nothing (that I know of) to cause me to have second thoughts. Also, I heard not a peep from pope Innocent VIII, who commented: "Blasphemous . . . Dangerous . . . A work of Witchcraft! This book threatens our male members everywhere." It is possible that he agrees with his comment. Moreover, tom, dick, and harry (attorneys for Godfather, Son & Company), who described the book as "An outrageous assault on the interests of our clients," did not threaten litigation. Possibly this is because they too agree with their comment. Most likely it is because of their shaky status as mere figments of my imagination.

*Although I continued to experience the Moments from July through December 1987 as Third Galactic Time, centering around the "coming out" of the *Wickedary*, that Irish adventure was a pivotal Moment of transition into The Fourth Spiral Galaxy. This should not be too surprising, since Spirals, unlike straight lines, have a tendency to overlap. The Time of entry was really a cluster of Moments. Well before that trip I had started writing *Outercourse*. I had begun to Dis-cover its form and to write the first chapter in the spring of that year. So when I spoke in Dublin in July I Wove some initial *Outercourse* material into that Be-Speaking. Because of my Be-Dazzling experiences in that Green place, I have concluded that it is fitting to write about that journey to Ireland in The Fourth Spiral Galaxy rather than in this chapter.

†The room (and indeed the hotel itself) was, in *Wickedary* terminology, a blob, i.e., "common, hideous product of modern architecture—windowless, airless, lifeless structure which reflects the intellectual and moral gravity/depravity of its designers and owners."

between the unnatural electric lights and the Electrical Powers of the Be-Witching Wicked Words. I Sensed the contrast between the stale air and the Wild Wind that blew through the Words themselves. The atmosphere in the room was Charged with conflict. The Be-Dazzling Light was trying to break through.

After I was a few minutes into my talk, as I spoke of the necessity of releasing the Elemental Powers of women and of words, I decided to quote from a BBC tape of Virginia Woolf from the mid-thirties, on the subject of "Words." I had the intention of attempting to imitate her upper-class British accent as I had heard it on the tape, so I said something like: "I'll now quote Forecrone Woolf with her British accent." Then came my rendition of her words, in what I perceived to be a heavy British accent: "Words do not live in dictionaries. They live in the mind."

I stopped abruptly because at that very split second all the lights over the listeners went out. Everyone gasped in astonishment. The light over the speaker's podium stayed on. The audience was in darkness, while I stood there spotlighted, so to speak. It was as if someone (Forecrone Woolf?) had given me the stage lights, which were appropriate to my role as impersonator and clown. So I acknowledged her Presence and her joke by saying very loudly: "Thank you, Virginia." After a brief pause, the lights went back on.

At the end of my talk there was some speculation about how "it" had happened. A few asked me if I had planned it. I had not. I did not even know the location of the light switch or switches. Others thought that perhaps someone had accidentally bumped against the switch at precisely the crucial Moment. I doubted and continue to doubt that. In any case, what if they had? How could one explain the split-second Timing? What accounts for the "accident"? Moreover, there was no way that anyone else could have planned it, since no one could have anticipated what I was going to say and it all happened very quickly.

From a Dalyan viewpoint—and, I *dare* say, from a Woolfian perspective also—such speculations are beside the point. The Spoofing of Spook Woolf either did not happen or else it did. Any way you look at it you choose. For some who were there the incident no doubt slipped into the nether regions of the Subliminal Sea. For Others it was a flash of lightning, a crash of thunder, and a blast of fresh air, encouraging us onward. To me it was a Wicked affirmation of the Electrical Connections made by the *Wickedary*. It was a Sinspiring Shock, a Joking Jolt/Bolt. It was one of the Happenings that hurled my Craft ahead. It was just in tune with the Time of The Fourth Spiral Galaxy.

CHAPTER FIFTEEN

REFLECTIONS ON PHILOSOPHICAL THEMES OF THE THIRD SPIRAL GALAXY

A s I reflect Now upon the Moments of Spinning which characterized/ constituted my Journey through The Third Spiral Galaxy I see that they hurled me deeper and deeper into the Background Present. Each Moment involved Acts of Exorcism of *apraxia*. As I became more active, especially in the realm of intellectual creativity, my Third Galactic Moments become more Be-Witching.

My Craft leaped, hopped, and flew through the three Metamorphic books of this Galaxy, gaining Momentum and complexity as it Moved further and further into the Be-Dazzling Light that shimmers in, upon, and over the Subliminal Sea. Re-viewing the works of that Time, I see their interconnectedness with each Other and their rootedness in Moments and works of the earlier Galaxies. I shall Now Re-Call them in relation to the four contrapuntal movements which have been characteristic of the capering and cavorting of my Craft, as these counterpoints re-emerge in the process of New Creative Resolution which is intensified in The Third Spiral Galaxy.

I See Now that the movement of my Craft in this Galaxy involved fantastic feats of Spinning and Weaving, as I fought with Fury against the encroachment of the demonic forces of fragmentation.

I swirled around and past deadly dilemmas posed by doomdom, Leaping toward finding/creating in each case a Transcendent Third Option. This process involved Moment after Moment of Terrible Taboo-breaking, as I ceaselessly Spun and Re-Spun threads of connectedness, reclaiming and Re-Naming Female Elemental Integrity.

THE FIRST COUNTERPOINT

As the reader recalls, in each of the preceding Galaxies the first contrapuntal movement of my Craft centered around my love for abstract thought and my love-hate for symbolic/poetic/mystical modes of knowing and naming. In The First Spiral Galaxy I had struggled in my theological and philosophical dissertations to resolve this conflict by elaborately defending reasoning that is rooted in deep intuition. In The Second Spiral Galaxy, in *Beyond God the*

Father, I achieved an early synthesis of abstract reasoning and symbolic thinking and expression.[1] In The Third Spiral Galaxy my Craft leaped Light Years beyond my previous synthesis. The old mindbinding, tongue-tying dichotomy really lost its hold over me when my Craft sailed on, by means of the process of Metapatterning[2] to Dis-covering the Transcendent Third Option which is Metapatriarchal Metaphor.

My Journey through The First Passage of *Gyn/Ecology* required that I exorcise patriarchal myth and language, for these function as mindbindings keeping women in the State of Possession. I accomplished this primarily through pattern-detecting, which became a process of Metapatterning. That is, I broke through the paternal patterns of thinking, speaking, acting, and I found mySelf Spinning.

In my Spinning of The First Passage I found that the very process of detecting the patterns of the woman-hating language and myths of patriarchy implied breaking through the mazes of such patterns, Weaving the way into the Background, Dis-covering its riches. This released great quantities of energy, which exploded in the form of New/Archaic Words.[3] These Words functioned as Metapatriarchal Metaphors. By Naming Metapatriarchal transformation they elicited such change. They carried me into Wild dimensions by jarring images, stirring memories, accentuating contradictions, upsetting unconscious traditional assumptions.

Examining the New/Archaic Metaphors Now, it is clear that a large number of these "appeared" in Labrys-like, double-edged pairs. Some pivotal examples are: *foreground—Background; necrophilia—Biophilia; supernatural—Super Natural; re-search—Search.* My seeing through the foreground words elicited the Background Words.[4]

Similarly, my seeing through the myths of patriarchal religion Re-Called Archaic woman-centered myths and symbols. For example, I was able to unmask the all-male trinity as a deadly reversal of the Triple Goddess. This is, of course, a symbolic sex change which has served to legitimate the necrophilic patriarchal possession of spiritual awareness. Again, I was empowered to See and Name the torture cross of christianity as reversal of the Tree of Life, which legitimates and perpetuates pointless man-made suffering and the destruction of life on this planet.

By Spinning/Weaving the way into the Background, then, I created in The First Passage of *Gyn/Ecology* a New Context in which Super Active Knowing, Naming, and Acting could take place. The Act of Metapatterning itself worked to overcome *apraxia.* Accompanying the explosion of Metapatriarchal Metaphors—such as Spinster, Hag, Harpy, Fury—there came an immediate message/challenge to Act differently in the world. For example, I could not say "I am a Positively Revolting Hag" without trying to live up to this challenging eruption of words. Of course, the fact that I could say this at all was an indicator that I had begun to Act *Otherwise,* that is "in a Weird way, in a Deviant direction" (*Wickedary*).

The heightened energy which was generated in this New Context empowered me to Spin on, Naming connections among apparently disparate phenomena. I was enabled to break the old patriarchal taboo against making connections. This opened the way for further pattern-detecting.

So in The Second Passage of *Gyn/Ecology* my Craft darted ahead to a further manifestation of Metapatterning Movement, again demonstrating the connectedness between abstract analysis and mythic modes of thought. I overcame the academented dichotomy between "irrelevant" patriarchal myth on the one hand and analysis of the actual rape, mutilation, and massacre of women on the other. The many atrocities perpetrated against women on this planet are interconnected with each other—as I demonstrated by Discovering and applying the seven-point Sado-Ritual Syndrome—and they are legitimated by patriarchal Goddess-murdering myths all over this planet. As I wrote in the Prelude to that Passage:

> In the following pages I will analyze a number of barbarous rituals, ancient and modern, in order to unmask the very real, existential meaning of Goddess murder in the concrete lives of women. I will focus upon five specific righteous rites which massacre women: Indian *suttee,* Chinese footbinding, African female genital mutilation, European witchburning, American gynecology. In examining these, I will seek out basic patterns which they have in common, and which comprise the Sado-Ritual Syndrome. . . . There are variations on the theme of oppression, but the phenomenon is planetary.[5]

To Name the connections between gynocidal atrocities and phallic myth is to Touch women spiritually, tearing off mindbindings/spiritbindings, releasing Eye-biting powers. To Name the connections among these apparently unrelated phenomena is to enable women to Realize *our* connections with each Other, and to experience the Terrible Totality of female bonding. It was, in fact, a breaking of the Total Taboo.* Hence the Exorcism accomplished through The Second Passage of *Gyn/Ecology* opens up the possibility of Ecstasy, which is manifested in the Spooking, Sparking, and Spinning of The Third Passage.

Since both Exorcism and Ecstasy are forbidden to women under phallic rule, the Taboo-breaking of all three Passages of *Gyn/Ecology* was altogether eccentric, electric, erratic, and extreme.

In *Pure Lust* I Realized still more fully the resolution of the first counterpoint of my Outercourse. By catching up the ontological/philosophical threads of my earlier work and Weaving these together with Gyn/Ecological Metapatterning, that work moves into a more complex, more sophisticated, and Wilder synthesis of abstract and poetic/Metaphoric modes of Naming.

---

*For the definition of *Total Taboo*, see Chapter Two.

The word *Be-Witching*, which is characteristic of *Pure Lust*, illustrates this phenomenon of Wild synthesis.

Since *Pure Lust* moves farther on the Spiraling paths of Metapatterning its proliferation of Metapatriarchal Metaphors is richer than that of *Gyn/ Ecology*. At the same Time, it Realizes the Elemental specificity of be-ing.[6] It also actualizes more fully than any previous work the Promise of my early intuitions of be-ing, which came from Elemental realities.[7] In *Pure Lust*, then, I Leaped in unprecedented ways toward reconciliation of falsely dichotomized ways of knowing and naming.

THE SECOND COUNTERPOINT

By Spinning *Pure Lust* I reached a further creative resolution of the second contrapuntal movement/dance, which was between my Quest/Lust to become a philosopher and the Call to become a theologian. In writing *Pure Lust* I Realized my deepest choice: to *be* a philosopher. Whereas the subtitle of *Beyond God the Father* is *Toward a Philosophy of Women's Liberation, Pure Lust* IS *Elemental Feminist Philosophy*.

Of course, I had chosen to be a philosopher much earlier. In adolescence and throughout the Moments of Outercourse I was always following this Call. Before the Time of *Pure Lust*, however, I had not fully Realized the implications of this choice. I had to Voyage far on the Subliminal Sea before I could understand the deepest meaning of my Quest, which was to be *my own kind of philosopher*, that is, to be a Dis-coverer of *Elemental Feminist Philosophy*. The Labyrinthine Pathway of this Quest involved seeming digressions, such as being diverted to obtaining the M.A. in English—rather than not going to graduate school at all[8]—and going on for two doctorates in theology—another seemingly strange (really Strange) set of detours.[9] But all of this complex Voyaging was providing necessary material for creating my *own* philosophy.

This creation involved breaking the Total Taboo in more ways than one. It required not only my overcoming of the dualism between abstract and mystical/poetic/mythic thought—which was achieved through Metapatterning—but also transcending the dualism between theology and philosophy. I did not merely choose the latter over the former; I engulfed both in my Elemental Feminist Philosophy. Rejecting the idea of a supernatural order and authority which purportedly transcends nature, I chose to follow my Quest for autonomous knowing.[10] That is, I chose to Spin a philosophy that is in Touch with the Realms of the *Super Natural*○, meaning

> Unfolding Nature or concerned with what Unfolds Nature (an Elemental order which directs History from inside and keeps women and all Biophilic creatures in Touch with the real world through the senses . . .): SUPREMELY NATURAL, PERFECTLY NATURAL (*Wickedary*).

Hence *Pure Lust* represents a Transcendent Third Option, which for me overcomes the foolish/snoolish dichotomy between theology and philosophy. As Pirate I claimed the right to snatch back "the Treasure Trove of symbols and myths that have been stolen and reversed by the theological thieves."[11] Reversing these reversals, reclaiming the results of this process as Metatheological Metaphors, is part of the work of my Craft as Super Natural philosopher.

My experiences of struggling, in the course of The First Spiral Galaxy, to obtain the freedom and the economic support to study (patriarchal) philosophy gave clues that there was some strange and irrational barrier to my obtaining a doctorate in that "field." I did not then understand that I was already bumping up against a taboo against women becoming philosophers. I certainly could not know then that these blockages were functioning as barriers to something vast and deep, that is, to my eventual creation of my own Green Philosophy.

In other words, there was "something" functioning to stop me before I could even get started on the Quest to become a woman-identified philosopher. By the Grace of the Fates I followed the available sidetracks (Pixiepaths) and kept listening for the Call of the Wild. I was spared from the trap of premature absorption into a successful suffocating career as a token female patriarchal philosopher locked into a deadly/deadening department in the "field."

I believe that the "something" that was attempting to block me, even then, was the Total Taboo against the Spiritual Touching Powers of women. For even then, of course, I had the unmitigated gall to reach for the stars. As I have indicated in Chapter Thirteen, by the early 1980s I began to get clues about this Taboo, as it functions to stop even the glimmer of an idea that there might be a woman-identified/nature-identified philosophy and philosopher. The woman who drove me to the airport in California on my way to Australia in the summer of 1981 spoke of her hostile dream and of her fear of me as a philosopher—a fear which she believed to be shared by other women.[12] I thought of this as astonishing and even as absurd, since I had never imagined that I was threatening to women. Upon further reflection, however, I knew that I should take her message seriously.

Not only is it the case that poetry is not prohibited to females, as that acquaintance had suggested, but also even theology, especially in the past two decades, has been open to women.* It became clear to me that the Taboo against women becoming Self-identified philosophers is deeper and more insidious than prohibitions against female theologians.† I think that this is

---

*This has been due in part to fiscal considerations, of course. Divinity Schools in recent years have heavily relied upon large female student populations.

†Of course, women are admitted to graduate schools of philosophy and can even teach the subject if they are not too threatening as autonomous thinkers. The presence of female

related to the fact that the theological tradition implies submission to authority, i.e., of the bible or of a religious institution. A philosopher is an autonomous seeker of wisdom who freely explores and Names reality.

Pure Lust is a Taboo-breaker on many levels. By assuming theology into my own Elemental Feminist Philosophy, decoding its symbols, reversing its reversals, I have challenged directly the authority of the male god in all of his guises. By combining the abstract and even seemingly elitist vocabulary of ontology with Wild, Elemental words I have broken taboos against proper linguistic behavior. Worst of all, by be-ing the originator of my own Green Philosophy, which is the tabooed woman-identified/nature-identified philosophy, I have uttered a Great Refusal of the patriarchal prescription of Self-lobotomy for and by women. I have been better/worse than eccentric and extreme. I have committed the Mortal Sin of following my Quest to be a philosopher.

THE THIRD COUNTERPOINT

The third contrapuntal movement, in the earlier Galaxies, had focused on the odious choice between the ghettoized pseudo-Women's Space of colleges for women (where women were/are "together" but not really together) and the apparently nonghettoized, non-Women's Space of coeducational universities (where women have become even more accessible for harassment and humiliation than they were under the system of segregation). Having experienced the dreariness of the former, I ignorantly chose the latter. By the end of The Second Spiral Galaxy I had begun a risky resolution of this counterpoint by creating Women's Space "on the Boundary" of a patriarchal coeducational institution. My students were brilliant. The classes were sparkling. *Real* teaching and learning were taking place.

In *Pure Lust* I developed my Third Galactic philosophical analysis which serves as theoretical underpinning and legitimation for the Creative Resolution which is Women's Space on the Boundary of patriarchal institutions. A basic premise of this analysis is the fact that patriarchy is a State of Separation. As I explained this in *Pure Lust* there is a disorder at the core of patriarchal consciousness which is engendered by phallocentric myths, ideologies, and institutions. This disorder implies a state of disconnection from Biophilic purposefulness, exemplified in such atrocities as the worldwide rape and massacre of women and of the Third World and the destruction of the planet itself.[13]

Aristotelians, Platonists, Heideggerians, Kantians, Whiteheadians, et cetera may show that some (a few) females can adequately transmit male thought. However, this has always been the role of female teachers in patriarchal institutions. In fact, female conduits can serve to reinforce the message of male intellectual superiority.

This disorder, which I have Named *phallic separatism,* separates women from ourSelves, from our own powers of Knowing and Naming, and from each other. In order to communicate with ourSelves and with each other many of us have found that it is necessary to separate ourSelves in Radical ways from the phallic State of Separation. To put it another way, given the prevailing conditions, some forms of separation are necessary for regaining our integrity and our autonomous powers of communication. As I wrote in *Pure Lust*:

> Women confined in the phallic State of Separation . . . are characterized/crippled by inability to identify the agents of Self-blocking separation. They are victimized by the strategy of reversal. Just as the label "man-hater" in a Woman-Hating Society functions to stop thought, so also the negatively charged use of the label "separatist" within the State of Separation hinders women from Be-Friending.[14]

I chose to use the word *separatism* as a *Labrys*:

> On the one hand, it Names phallic separatism, which blocks and bars Life-Lust—the desire for ontological communication. On the other hand, it Names the choice of women to break from the artificial context of phallic separatism in order to affirm and live our radical connectedness in Biophilic be-ing.[15]

By the use of this Labrys, then, I was enabled to provide the needed philosophical rationale for Women's Studies as a locus for Women's Space in patriarchal universities. I wrote in *Pure Lust:*

> The history of women's struggles to provide and maintain diverse forms of "Women's Space" has been a vivid testimony to the fact that men recognize this to be a crucial issue in the war to control women's minds. . . . Particularly instructive has been the virulent and often vicious undermining by university administrators of the efforts of Feminists to reserve some Women's Studies classes for women only. Such classes can provide the occasion for true encounters with Metamemory, for perceiving and reasoning beyond the schemata of "adult," i.e., male-authored, memories. They can provide contexts for Remembering beyond civilization, for Metapatterning. Therefore, they must be undermined. The radical potential of freely thinking women is a threat to the very meaning of a patriarchal university.[16]

This analysis was inspired, in large measure, by my own experience of teaching Women's Studies courses in a *very* patriarchal university. It was also inspired, and reinforced, by conversations with professors of Women's Studies in many colleges and universities in the 1970s and 1980s. My experience has been that the presence of male students together with women in such classes slows down and in fact blunts the learning process for the women. This is of course in part an effect of learned responses to the presence of males—even of one male—in the class. Eventually I discussed this with the students and began holding separate sessions for women and men.

Everyone has the same reading list and course requirements. Since there have been far fewer men than women in these classes, the former have received more attention. The result, of course, has been extra work for me. However, I enjoy teaching young men as well as women students, and course evaluations have indicated general appreciation of this intellectually challenging experience.[17]

My Third Galactic resolution of the third counterpoint has had a double-edged effect. First, I succeeded in creating a Space on the Boundary of a phallocentric institution where women, and not only men, could express their ideas boldly and creatively, without interference and without blockage from mechanisms of Self-censorship. In addition, by Spinning ideas whose Sources are my own books, I overcame the old academented dichotomy between theory and practice in a special way. Following Crone-logically upon my resolution of the second counterpoint, this New Leap of the third contrapuntal movement involved Acting upon the premises and conclusions of my own philosophy, exercising my philosophical *habitus,* freely exploring and Naming Reality.* I have Dis-covered Elemental Feminist Philosophy in the Presence of my students, Spinning further with them. By the use of this pedagogic method I have totally broken the Total Taboo against exercising the Spiritual Touching Powers of women—overcoming *apraxia* (together with *aphasia* and *amnesia*) on the Boundary of androcratic academia. This has been Dreadful Daring Action.

THE FOURTH COUNTERPOINT

My Third Galactic Resolution of the tension between seeking legitimations and becoming ever more illegitimate became so drastic, especially as I approached The Fourth Spiral Galaxy, that both the dilemma and the Transcendent Third Option required a New vocabulary. Instead of lauding Illimitable Illegitimacy I strove to be Absolutely Wicked and to Name this Metapatriarchal Wickedness for what it *is.* As we have seen, this implies Spinning/Sinning beyond patriarchal "good" and "evil," actively participating in the Unfolding of Be-ing as Good.[18]

As I Journeyed through The Third Spiral Galaxy I became more Active, Breaking into the Background Present. There it was (and is) possible for women to experience *Presence of Presence*○, which is

> Self-Realizing Presence of Prudes and Viragos who communicate Gynergetic Ecstasy (*Wickedary*).

Moreover, I found that to be Present in this way implied actualizing our potential to *Presentiate*○, that is

---

*At this point the reader will have noticed that in The Third Spiral Galaxy the resolution of each counterpoint breaks ground for the resolution of the next.

to Realize as Present the past and future; to Conjure the Presence of Fore-Crones, Fore-Familiars and Other Background beings (*Wickedary*).

Presentiating women are not fixated on dick-tated dichotomies between patriarchal legitimacy and illegitimacy. What is more to the point, we are not stuck in the split between phallocratically defined good and evil. This is precisely because Presentiating implies Dis-closing an integrity that transcends foreground dichotomies.

The Dis-closing of that Original Integrity *is* actively participating in the Unfolding of Be-ing as Good. It is following one's Final Cause. The Final Cause, then, is the beginning, not merely the end of the becoming. It is the First Cause and Cause of causes, which gives an agent the motivation to Act.*[19]

When women are free to be Present to ourSelves and to each Other, we find ourSelves in Touch with our purpose. We are no longer distracted, but rather we are attracted—powerfully—by our Final Cause. We have advanced to the beginning of our Time-traveling Voyage, Realizing as Present the past and future.

Defiantly Wicked women thus are focused on our active participation in the Unfolding of Be-ing. Knowing that to be legitimated is to be assimilated, we reject the role required of us by sadosociety/snooldom, which is the role of *lackey*:

> a servile groveler: one characterized by the lack of everything—integrity, intelligence, passion, humor, courage, vitality, beauty, grace—in short, Potency (*Wickedary*).

Realizing our Elemental Potency, we experience Pure Lust. We choose to Live Now, which means Voyaging *Out*—Outercoursing. Having arrived at the Moment of participation in the Background Present, we Unfold our wings and soar into an expanded Present which is off the calendars, off the clocks of clockocracy.

We skim the surface and dive to the depths of the Subliminal Sea. We toss on the waves of Tidal Time. Having found the Third Hemisphere,[20] we soar Beyond that Beyond.[21] Approaching the Fourth Hemisphere, we find ourSelves at home in The Fourth Spiral Galaxy.

For this Time-traveling feat of arrival at The Fourth Spiral Galaxy we receive no honors, no degrees, no legitimations. We are, however, flooded with Congratulations. Looking around, we See massive crowds of Intergalactic Seals of Approval waving their flippers and barking in contagious Ecstasy. Since Ecstasy is its own reward, we can ask for nothing more. It is Time to enter the Galaxy which bears the Metamysterious number—Four.

---

*As the scholastic philosophers have put it: The final cause is first in the order of intention and last in the order of execution.

BE-DAZZLING NOW:
Moments of Momentous Re-membering
(Off the Calendar, Off the Clock)

Moments of Momentous Re-membering

AHEAD TO THE BEGINNING

The three preceding Galaxies are, in fact, the Prelude to the Fourth, which is also their Beginning.

They are the Prelude because they are the Spiraling Paths of Moments that brought me to this Time of Re-membering. The Fourth comes forth from the chore that has gone before.

They are also the consequence because if I were not in this Galaxy of Momentous Re-membering I could not have traced their pathways. If I were not here in the Be-Dazzling Now, there would be no Recollections from my *Logbook*. If I were not in the Be-Dazzling Now, there would be no *Outercourse*, and there would be no Outercourse to write home about. If I were not home already, I could not have arrived.

But there was such an urgency to arrive! I had to get here even to begin. And it is absolutely necessary that I begin, and that I begin again. Because I know more Now. Not enough, but more.

My Cronies and I—Who are we? A ragged remnant, maybe. But also the Conjurers of a different Course. Staggering on the edge of a doomed world, we soar in our souls . . . sometimes, even often. Basking in Be-Dazzling Light, we ponder the holes out there as they grow, leaking in the sun's kiss of death, the kiss of our Elemental Sister Sun who, like our sisters here, has been turned against us.

Shed tears no more . . . or tears galore. But summon the guts to keep going. My mantra for *Outercourse*: "Keep going, Mary. Go!" Because they want me to stop. They want us to stop. The undead vampire men, the bio-robots gone berserk, the leaders. They want us to stop, because they are winding down.

Keep going. Not really because they want me to stop, want us to stop. But because I am surging with Life. Because, you see, I have arrived here, Now, and I can begin. Because I was born for this Time, and I am strong.

Because my mother said "Go do your own work, dear." Oh, that woman! Because she chose me and because she said that: "Go, do your own work," she sent off a Time bomb, that woman. Because she gave me the taste for Ecstasy, the Lust for It. Because I have It still, and more, and more.

Reach for the Four, the Fourth, the Dimension that was before. From pinoramic to Panoramic—Open the door. And run out, Mary, run. Hug the Green, the Green Grass. Fly with the winds, rush with the waters. Light Her Fire.

And Oh, the desire, the desire for all of It. For the Moment that is Now, Expanding Now. The Now that holds and releases the past, that touches the future. The Now that they can't know about—the undead vampire men, the bio-robots gone berserk, the leaders.

Run right into the Now. There is so much room (no room for gloom). It is so open here, there, everywhere. So full of the sweet, fresh smells of earth and air. Just dare!

CHAPTER SIXTEEN

ON HOW I JUMPED OVER THE MOON

The Moments of The Fourth Spiral Galaxy began when I began working on *Outercourse*. This was during the spring of 1987, after I had handed in the manuscript of the *Wickedary* to the publisher. I do not Re-member the Moments precisely in sequence. I do Re-Call that I was puzzled about the nature of the book that was evolving. I knew that I wanted to write a philosophical work. I also gradually came to know that I wanted to write Recollections from my *Logbook of a Radical Feminist Philosopher.*

A friend from Ireland—Ann Louise Gilligan—suggested something like the latter. We were having lunch in an outdoor café in Newton Centre one day in the summer of 1987. After expressing her appreciation of *Pure Lust* Ann Louise tactfully, in her inimitable fashion, remarked that women would like to know where *Pure Lust* and my other books came from. Essentially, the questions she posed were: "How did it happen? How did you do it?" She posed these queries not so much with the expectation of an immediate response but—as I understood her—as a suggestion for a book that was wanted and needed.

This was not the first or only Time the suggestion had been planted. Various women had asked such questions, and with greater and greater frequency. But in the conversation with Ann Louise the questions of all these women came together for me. They assumed a shape, which was like a summons—or an invitation—to write the story, the autobiography, which would speak to those questions.

While I Sensed more and more that I would like to try this, there was the seemingly conflicting Call, also coming from within my psyche, to move ahead with my own philosophy. It seemed that there were two books crying to be written at the same Time.

Reflecting upon this Now, I see that I was faced with a familiar situation, that is, a dilemma. It was not easy to find the Transcendent Third Option.

In conversations with my friends and in debates with mySelf I wondered which book I should write first. The more I thought about this problem, the more deeply troubled I felt, since there was a double imperative. Then it occurred to me that there would not only have to be two books, but that these would somehow have to be one. But the question was: How to Realize this unity? There was in my mind a growing awareness of an organic unity between the two proposed works, because I did see that the *Logbook of a Radical Feminist Philosopher* should be the primary Source for my expanded philosophizing.

The theme of Living on the Boundary is hardly unfamiliar to the Voyager of *Outercourse*. The important question is: Is my Ground, in the deepest sense, on the Boundaries of patriarchal institutions? The answer is no, not Now.

Oh, yes, I still Fight/Act there, on those Boundaries. But my true Ground, the Ground of that Ground, so to speak, is farther Out, farther Back. Back in the Background. Because I have arrived at the Four, the Fourth, the Dimension that was before, the Source, the Beginning.

Here at the Beginning I have raw, constant knowledge of my Final Cause, the Good who is Self-communicating, who is the Verb from whom, in whom, and with whom all true movements move.

Sure, they can distract me, drag me into their diddling dis-course, but the pull, oh the pull of the Verb—the intransitive One, you know—is so overwhelming that I fly sometimes, fly into the Unfolding, Enfolding arms. The arms of the Spiraling Galaxies, the wings of Spiraling angels. Call them whatever you like.

And just because I said I fly don't think I'm not Grounded. I've hung around academentia long enough to avoid being caught by old word games, old sophistries. *Of course* I mix Metaphors—that's what they're for, to be mixed and rearranged, to shoot the breeze, so to speak. How could I fly if I were not Grounded? How could I be Grounded if I couldn't fly? Everything is connected with everything else.

FED UP

I want to blast out of bore-dom, every way, every day. "That's so extreme," they say. "It is High Time to be Extreme," I say. While we wade knee deep in the blood of women shall I chat about Freud, Derrida, and Foucault? No, I don't think so.

Better to catch a comet by the tail and soar with it. Better to jump bail. The whole foreground is a jail.

'gender studies' . . . blender studies. The men's and women's center at o.u. (Oh, you!)

"No male-bashing!" they say. "That's very bad," they say. "Bad girl."

"Patriarchy is planetary!" I howl.

"That's none of your business," they say. Their eyes are glazed, dazed. "We're not feminists anyway. That's passé."

"Can't you Sense the pain of the footmaimed Chinese women hobbling on mutilated, gangrenous stumps over hundreds and hundreds of years?" I ask.

"It was a different culture," they say.

"Can't you feel the pain of thirty million genitally mutilated African women, today?" I ask.

"It's none of your business," they say. "It's another culture. Bad girl!"

"It's the *same* culture," I say. "Can't you *feel anything*?"

They shrink away, their faces grey. "As white privileged middle-class women we can't possibly imagine . . . "

"Shut up," I say, politely. "You bore me, you gore me. You are killing me with your academented stupidity."

"We feel invalidated by your remarks," they say.

"Well, that's good," I say. Finally.

Oh, here's Sojourner Truth. "Hi Sojourner! They never hooked *you* into postfeminism, fragmentation, or therapeutic, thought-stopping babble, did they? What's that you say?"

"Ain't I a woman?"

"Oh, thank you, Sojourner! I was just about to lose it, but Now you've made my day. My Craft has arrived at The Fourth Spiral Galaxy. But of course I still fight on the Boundaries of patriarchal institutions. Will you help me rock the boat? What? You've been doing that right along? Of course, I knew it, but my knowledge was subliminal. Sometimes I'm kind of dumb, numb, and then I gradually wake up. Anyway, I've been feeling pissed and raw, fed up with the dis-course in the deadzone, so I'm glad you're here. I'm getting things into perspective Now. Your O-Zone—your Aura—is Be-Dazzling. I can see better! And your Cronies are here—lots of them. I mean, I can see them Now. Hi Sappho! Hi Harriet! Hi Matilda! Hi Andrée!"

Sorry if I seem a little out-of-sorts. But things are *so* bad in the fore-ground now. The dimwit in the white house cried on television on the fiftieth anniversary of Pearl Harbor. His voice cracked and everything. He didn't mention Nagasaki and Hiroshima. No one cried about gynocide and geno-cide. I know it's the same old crap. But it's worse.

Yes, of course they're losing. They're all goose-stepping into oblivion. I didn't want to go with them, so I decided to Leap out of the foreground into the Background, into the Expanding Now. And to bring along as many Oth-ers as I could. I'll Now explain how.

BLASTING OUT OF THE FOREGROUND

It's been very Windy lately, in every sense of the word. So I've been thinking about Blasting. When I thought about Blasting out of the foreground I saw mySelf riding a Blast of Wind, in my Craft, of course, which can also be a broom. But what I also wanted to do was to Blast a hole in the wall between the foreground and the Background—a hole so big that everyone who is really Alive can get through. I decided that the way to do that was to just be my Natural Self, who is Extreme.

One day recently a woman, a professional type who is not a Feminist, of course, suddenly began to talk about all the murders reported in the media. Her tone was one of shock. I said, "Yes, and have you noticed how many of the victims are women?" She behaved as if I had just belched and she was politely trying not to notice. After a ten-second pause she said: "I really feel terrible about the children who have been killed."

Now I am not saying that any dynamite I carry is powerful enough to Blast that woman through the hole in the wall. On the other hand, maybe she'll be picked up by the Surge of Wind and just happen to find herSelf there, on the Other side. The point is that there is no Time to hang around and argue. It is Time to Act.

Go, Mary, Go. Hop, Leap, Fly. Our only Chance is Now. Everything is here in the Expanding Now. Get Out from under the undead vampire men, the bio-robots, the leaders/feeders. It's all so simple. Light the Witches' Fires. Go up in smoke. Go for broke. All you really have to do is Care . . . and Dare.

THE COW THAT JUMPED OVER THE MOON

It's all very fine to say "Hop, Leap, Fly." It isn't as if I know where I'm going, exactly. It's like when my mother said not to bother with the dishes—just "Go, do your own work, dear." I didn't have a clear idea of what my work was, but I had to go do it anyway. Eventually I did find out what it was, what it is.

So I have to Hop, Leap, Fly . . . Now. It doesn't matter that I don't have a clear idea *where*. I'll find out. I am finding out. Actually I have a lot in common with the cow that Jumped over the moon. Did *she* know where she was going? I'm sure she didn't, exactly, but she knew she had to do it. It must have been a Strange experience for her. But she refused to be stopped just because her behavior seemed odd. So what if the little dog laughed. What did *he* know?

As I think more about it, I become more and more convinced that the cow knew quite a lot—enough to drive her to Extreme Acts. It is significant, I think, that she Jumped *over* the moon—not just *to* it. She had more imagination than a mere astronaut. Indeed, I conjecture that the cow had a glimpse of the Other side of the moon in her head. She had some clues, some subliminal knowledge, and this was so powerful that it propelled her far into the sky and over the moon. That cow had Wonderlust/Wanderlust, and a person in that condition just can't stop herSelf. It doesn't matter if all the dogs in the world are laughing at her. I can empathize with her situation.

The important thing about real subliminal knowledge, such as that cow had, is that it always sends you to the Other side. If you are hiking and you have the other side of the hill in your head, you know that you can't stop until you get to the other side. If you are a sailor with such a Lust, you have to get all the way across the ocean. Now, the case of the cow was not so different, except that her desire was more powerful, more Extreme.

I have sisterly feelings for that cow. I am sure that she was fed up with domestication. She was stuck in a pasture and seen by some foolish farmer as basically no more than an udder and a breeder, perhaps as a large package of potential hamburger.* Sure, she could have jumped over the fence, but that would have achieved nothing. Her essence and her future were all laid out. The foreground farmers were everywhere, and they would have caught her and dragged her back. So she had to face a dilemma, and she chose a Transcendent Third Option. A cow after my own heart! She chose to Jump over the moon. Far, far up into the sky. Far over the moon to the Other side.

And I think her Sister the moon was Calling and Calling her, saying "Come to me! I'll hide you. Come and be free!" Now I know from experience that the moon can tap you on the shoulder if she wants to, because it has happened to me.[3] So I think that the moon Touched that cow and that the magnetic pull was so strong that the cow was beside herSelf with ecstatic desire. Her heart thumped "Yes, yes." And the moon pulled her so hard that she fairly flew up, up and away. This is perfectly plausible to me.

Also, I am sure that the cow saw many sights on the way. Every Moment was an adventure. Each Moment led to another. Each Moment brought her messages about the Other side. She was following her Final Cause and she felt that she was the Luckiest cow in the world.

Of course, "nobody" has seen that cow since. This proves that she did reach the Other side of the moon. There she was greeted by Sisters of all kinds. I want to meet her and her friends. I want to meet them Now.

And I will, because I can feel the pull of my Sister the moon and I feel mySelf rising, rising. I thought it was a dream until I heard mySelf scream: "Power to the Witch and to the woman in me."[4]

One of the important things about the Other side of the moon is that we know it is there. There would not be a this side if the Other were not there. And because we can see this side, we have big clues about the Other. That's one of the crucial points about subliminal knowledge. You can see what you don't yet see because of what you do see Now. You get there by see-ing/be-ing more and more Now, Here and Now.

HE HAS MADE OF THE WORLD A SHITPILE

The cow who Jumped over the moon deeply understood/understands the words of Valerie Solanas, prophetic Shrew, who published *SCUM Manifesto* in 1967. She wrote:

---

*The cow who Jumped over the moon was actually fairly Lucky, right from the start. She had been brought up on a small, old-fashioned farm and had escaped the hideous destiny of her sisters who die out their lives in misery in "animal factories"—the helpless victims of modern agribusiness. See Jim Mason and Peter Singer, *Animal Factories* (New York: Crown Publishers, Inc., 1980).

The male, because of his obsession to compensate for not being female combined with his inability to relate and to feel compassion, has made of the world
a shitpile.[5]

When Solanas savagely described the patriarchal society and its product
—the shitpile—she could not have explicitly known the extent and contents
of that pile as it is in the foreground now of the 1990s. Waist-deep in hazardous waste, we watch the bad news mount. More than anyone can count.

On CBS knightly news Rather announces with solemn mien that doctors
simply cannot explain the alarming increase in cancer ("the killer") among
children. Are all of the doctors sick in the brain? "Yes!" I proclaim. The shit-
pilers coo: "Drink up your toxic waste, children. It's good for you. See, the
doctor drinks it too."

The world . . . a shitpile! Is it true? Or is there still something I can do?
Is there a Time, a Space . . . of Grace?

This is the Time, the Space. Race, Mary, Race. Into the Expanding Now.
Follow that cow! Jump over the moon, sooner than soon. Now.

You have arrived here already, here on the Other side, at the Beginning.
You just have to let go and Know it. Throw it . . . your Life! Keep on
Throwing it as far as it will go. Re-member what you already Know.

FLYING IN THE DARK OF THE MOON

As I pack up to go to the Now that I Know I remember to bring my typewriter because I have to catch up on Recollections from my *Logbook*. The
Now keeps expanding and I have to account for it. As I have said, I have to
trace the Moments of The Fourth Spiral Galaxy from a Fourth Galactic perspective. I have to Realize my subliminal knowledge of Now.*

Thank heaven for that cow! I can hear her hooves in the distance, far
ahead of me. What a consoling trailblazer! So earthy and solid. So determined, too. She's already on the Other side, of course, but she keeps capering around, kicking up a storm to encourage me on.

The night is very dark. In fact it's the Time of the new moon—the dark
of the moon. They say this is a wonderful Time of New Beginnings. It's a
scary Time, though, for me and my Cronies. Sometimes we all feel abandoned in the dark of the moon—isolated, even. We all know that we are all
out here, somewhere, racing to Jump over the moon. But still it takes a lot
of Fey Faith and Hopping Hope to keep going. Guts, too. We have to trust
what we have already known. Realize it more, that is.

---

*That's why I had to move to the moon—to reflect upon my subliminal knowledge of
Now. This requires *some* distance! The "house move" took place in November 1991, when
I began writing The Fourth Spiral Galaxy.

I still have my Craft, of course—sturdier than ever. And my Cronies all have theirs. It's smooth Sailing in the night sky—with Wild Cat on my shoulder—because of the tremendous pull of the moon. Actually, it would be impossible to fly against it.

And the stars! Oh, the stars are so magnificent, so twinkling. They too reach out and Touch my Craft, Be-Stir my Soul. And even though the moon is dark at this Time, I know that on the Other side it is Be-Dazzling.

GREEN *LOGBOOK* ENTRIES
FROM THE MOON

When Wild Cat and I arrived here on the Other side of the moon the cow was our reception committee. It was love at first sight. We all ran around in Spirals together, sometimes with me hanging on to the cow's tail and sometimes with her butting me from behind. What a mind! That animal never wastes Time on academented dis-course—just goes right to the heart of the matter.

LIFE AT HOME ON THE MOON

When the cow offered to help me with Recollections from my *Logbook* I was deeply Touched. Often she looks over my shoulder as I'm typing. This is not mere curiosity or solicitude. She is actually shooting Elemental Energy through my brain and fingers, through the keys and onto the page. What an electromagnetic connection!

My workshop is on the side of a beautiful mountain with a gorgeous view of the sky. Both Wild Cat and the cow helped me to build it, which wasn't hard, since it's largely a natural formation. The bovine wonder herSelf prefers to sleep outside, but she is always available. Her name, by the way, is Catherine. I guessed it immediately because as a child I had read a great book entitled *Catherine the Comical Cow,* and this cow resembles the heroine of that book. She also resembles the comical cow I met on an Alp in Kleine Scheidegg in the Canton of Bern, Switzerland, in 1976.[1] And she has much in common with Catherine, the Canny/Uncanny cow whom I came to know quite well in Leverett, Massachusetts, in the fall of 1980.[2]

By Now the perceptive reader may well be asking: How does Wild Cat feel about all this cow-identified attraction? To be honest, I must admit that there have been tensions. At first, whenever Catherine came in to look over my shoulder, Wild Cat stalked off to the farthest end of my workshop and sat with her back to us, swishing her tail. I finally sat down with both of them and explained that Wild Cat is always and forever my chosen Domestic Familiar who inspires me ineffably, and that Catherine is our wonderful New friend. Then we all kissed each Other and danced around counterclockwise, meowing, mooing, and howling to the magnificent moon, our home. We have lived together happily ever after.

I'm sure some of my Cronies have arrived by Now, but there's a lot of room here on the moon, and everyone has been eager to settle down and work. I'm sure some have set up their shops on other mountain ranges, in valleys, and in comfortable craters. Really, there's been no Time for a conference. But everyone is aware of everyone else.

COMMUTING TO BOSTON AND ELSEWHERE

I have no trouble commuting to Boston or elsewhere on earth for the purpose of teaching or lecturing or visiting with friends. After you've made the trip once or twice the Jumping is easy. Of course they don't have a clue down there, where I fight on the Boundaries of patriarchal institutions, about where I am commuting *from*. They think I live somewhere in Newton.

More than once I've had to suppress a smile when I've overheard "them" referring to me as "the lunatic." If they only knew! But that's just it. They are incapable of knowing. So I'm safe and invisible here. Wild Cat and Catherine keep each Other company, and they love hearing about my trips each Time I return from these escapades.

None of us loves the bad news that I bring back from the increasingly malignant foreground now. An unspeakable example is the 1990 Halloween night gang attack in Dorchester, Massachusetts, on twenty-six-year-old Kimberly Rae Harbour. According to testimony by a medical examiner the gang-raped woman's death was caused by 132 stab wounds and at least 18 bludgeon wounds. As of December 21, 1991, only one of the eight young men believed to have perpetrated the atrocity had been tried. He was convicted on charges of murder, rape, and robbery. However, he is getting off easy—committed to the Department of Youth Services until his eighteenth birthday, since he was only fifteen years old at the time of the crime.[3]

bad news indeed. a new generation of gynocidal ghouls growing up. armed with guns, too. and women dying out their lives in terror, knowing that no one will believe them that their lives are threatened. not until they're dead. not even then.

So I must know all this and still go, Mary, go. See the Green Light? Green means Time to Go. Go on and on. I will go on with my *Logbook* Now.

GREEN *LOGBOOK* ENTRIES: IRELAND

Sitting here with my friends in my workshop on the Other side of the moon I feel that I am in an ideal situation for Momentous Re-membering of my Real Space Trips to the Emerald Isle which took place in Tidal Time. I have already Momentously Re-membered trips to Ireland which took place in earlier Galaxies.[4] My Third Galactic visit in 1984, especially, was an anticipation of Fourth Galactic travels to that Treasure Island.[5]

The first of these trips occurred in July 1987. Musing over that visit from my Present Lunar/Lunatic perspective I recognize it as a response to a compelling Call of the Wild. Right from the beginning there was an aura of Syn-Crone-icity about the whole adventure.

First of all, I heard "by chance" in the fall of 1986 that an international congress on women was being planned in Dublin. I "heard," that is, misheard, that the title was to be "Women's Words." This struck me as fantastically Timely, since the *Wickedary* would be out in the fall. I was eager to present this New stuff to an international audience, most especially because the location was to be in Ireland.

So I dashed off a "To whom it may concern" letter in October 1986 to the organizers, without having a clue about their identities. I enclosed a proposal for a lecture or workshop and waited. I believe a few phone calls ensued. At any rate, I came to understand that the actual title of the Third International Interdisciplinary Congress on Women was *Women's Worlds.* I received a letter in December 1986 from Katherine Zappone on behalf of the Organizing Committee inviting me to address a plenary session as a Keynote speaker. The letter suggested that I place my present work within the context of my past, narrating the key elements of my past journey and explaining why I see "the linguistic issue" as very significant for the future.

A few weeks later I received a warm letter from Geraldine Moane, also on behalf of the organizing committee, thanking me for my willingness to be one of the Keynote speakers. After a couple more phone calls I found myself in the intriguing situation of having agreed to give a total of three (3) talks, including my Keynote, and I happily wrote up three proposals.

Reading over these proposals Now in my workshop on the Other side of the moon, I am fascinated to see how many of the components of *Outercourse* are already there, for example, "Spiral-like movement through Moments, or clusters of Moments." At that Time, I believed that there were only three such Spirals. The Realization that there are *four* had not yet occurred. Even though I was already in The Fourth Spiral Galaxy and beginning to Realize/actualize it, I did not consciously know that there is a "Fourth" and that I had arrived. I did know, however, that "each of the Moments is revisited and seen from different angles." From my Present perspective it is clear that more nudges of some sort were needed before my Craft would Leap into *conscious* Knowing of The Fourth Spiral Galaxy and of the Expanding Now.

In order to Realize my subliminal knowledge of the existence of The Fourth Spiral Galaxy I would have to go on Living it. In order to Know the Expanding Now I would have to keep on Expanding. The writing of *Outercourse* would be a voyage into such Realization. It would make possible Moments of Momentous Re-membering of Now, Expanding Now. So also would many other activities, including traveling.

So when the Green Light said "Go! . . . to Ireland" I took off for Dublin (on July 1, 1987). I flew directly (by plane) from Boston, really on Fire with excitement about going back there. Ever since my 1984 visit friends have said that I literally light up at the mention of Ireland. Ireland Be-Spells Ecstasy to me.

The five-day Congress was scheduled to begin on July 6, and some Irish women had made exciting travel plans for the free days preceding it. There were also some big ideas brewing for the three days following it.

So it happened that on Friday, July 3, this Irish Background adventure began gently and merrily with explorations in beautiful County Wicklow, as I rambled in a van together with five women and two dogs.* It was a soft and lovely awakening to the Otherworld of Ireland.

The following two days were more intense. With Other new friends I headed West.† We traveled to Pre-Celtic sites with Weird names such as Newgrange, Dowth, and Knowth—which made a Strange threesome. At Dowth, Margaret (Maggie, that is) and I climbed down into a beehive dwelling which both resembled and was different from the ones in Leverett.[6] Mary and Marina waited at the entrance while we continued on down the long dark passage. When we came to the center at the end of the passage we sat down and began chanting "Ba" (as I had frequently done with my friends in Leverett). In contrast to the Leverett experiences, which I had described to Maggie in detail, we heard no bees Buzzing, and were greatly disappointed. However, when we crawled back up the passageway and met Marina and Mary, they announced that they had heard bees Buzzing from inside the structure while we were there. This astonished me, since they did not know the story of Leverett and had not heard Maggie and me chanting.

Puffed up with our success at Dowth, we attempted the same maneuver at Knowth. The site was officially closed, so we climbed over the fence and were greeted by stinging nettles. Luckily my Irish companions knew that the cure for the insufferable stinging is the application of dock leaves, which always grow near the nettles. Quickly cured, we leaped over and around the grassy mounds, over the black plastic bags placed there by some sort of -ologists who were supposedly "studying" the place. We tried chanting "Ba" around the stone structures but did not hear the anticipated Buzzing. The Bees made it known that they are simply not always available on call. Perhaps the stinging of the nettles was their response this Time.

Undaunted, we sped on to *Sliabh na Cailligh*—the Witch's Hill, which is well known to Radical Feminists in Ireland. Running up that hill in the evening light we were welcomed by swallows swooping and stoats scampering, tumbling, playing around the "Hag's Chair."[7]

---

*The women were Marie Davis, Ioma Ax (usually called Io), Joni Crone, Aileen Ryan, and my friend Marisa Zavalloni, who had come from Montreal for the Congress. The dogs were Nellie and Buffie, Familiar friends of Io and Marie.

†These New Companions were Mary Duffy, Margaret Doherty, and Marina Forrestal. Marisa Zavalloni came on this trip as well.

And on we went . . . on to County Sligo. At some point we crossed the River Shannon . . . I don't know where. I was told that when you cross the Shannon, heading West, you come to the place where you can see and hear the fairies. We were all more than ready for this.

Our trip into Sligo was magical—up and over hills on the winding narrow Irish roads in a little car that was filled with sparkling Irish music—from a tape deck. I knew that I was in Fairy Space and Fairy Time as we flew along in the night, carried by the lilting music, coming into the place called Strandhill. The moon was shining on the sea and the mountains were looming on the other side of the bay. In an elated state we found rooms for the night.

The next day we jumped into our magical car and went to Carrowmore. We sat in a circle when we reached the top of the mound which is thought to be Maebh's grave and talked of many things. Then on we went to a stone circle beside the road north of Sligo—at a place called Creevykeel. Each one of us had a strong desire to lie down on the ground there, at various spots. And so we did, and we all had a strong sensation that the earth was magnetizing us, pulling us to her, into her, welcoming us.

Refreshed, we hopped into the car and went on, arriving next at Deerpark Forest, speeding past the rhododendrons we had been told to look for, down the spiraling road to the heart of the forest. Maggie and I jumped out of the car and went striding over the fields there, sensing that the ground was hollow . . . that there was a powerful Presence there. And as I stood on what I knew must be an ancient mound I heard, of all things, the Buzzing of a bee. I looked everywhere, and saw no bees. I called Maggie to come over. When she arrived, the Buzzing stopped, and I was alone with my experience. Such tricksters they are, those bees!

On the way back to Dublin we took the road to Carrowkeel. We drove on a little dirt road into the Green, the Green grass and the bogs . . . and got lost! But there ahead were a little old woman and a little old man who had left their car, apparently collecting peat. The little old woman and the little old man had ruddy, beautiful, ecstatic faces. When we called out, the little old man came walking toward us, smiling. We asked if we were driving on the right road to find the stone mounds (burial places). He replied in the merriest, most musical voice imaginable: "The very one!"

So we continued on the road. It was the wrong one, or rather it was the right one but we were headed in the wrong direction, a fact which he had not pointed out. So we turned around and found the mounds. And the Green, everywhere around there, was the richest Green! Surely only fairy people with merry fairy voices could appear there and confirm us in the wrong direction. And it didn't matter, as my parents would say, because it was all bound to turn out right in the end anyway. And so it did.

And after that we made our way back to Dublin in the East.[8]

In Dublin I was put up in style, in Blooms Hotel, by the organizers of the Congress. My soul was still back in the West, back in the bogs, in

Fairyland. But it was also there in Dublin, which was tingling with excitement. The city had been taken over by Feminists from all over the world. There were about a thousand of us from other countries, and hundreds from all over Ireland itself. Dublin was *our* city, and it felt as if we had taken over the world. Everywhere you looked there were women wearing "Women's Worlds" T-shirts, carrying "Women's Worlds" programs and "Women's Worlds" Congress bags.

Lectures and workshops were being held mainly at Trinity College. I gave my first talk on Tuesday, July 7, in a lecture hall at Trinity. Much of it was from the *Wickedary*. This particular one of my three talks was publicized discreetly—by bulletin board notices rather than in the program—for two reasons. First, no one was supposed to give more than two talks. Second, this one was targeted for a special audience—women who were already familiar with my work.

As it happened, some women who did not meet this qualification sneaked in. One of these was upset by what she perceived as my "hostility" toward men. I was impatient with her and snapped back. I was forgiven for this by most of the women present. However, I was not absolved by the American journalist—Katherine Holmquist—who was assigned by *The Irish Times* to "cover" my talk, since most of the regular staff of Irish reporters were on strike. And indeed she did "cover" it—and me—beyond recognition. Consequently, all hell was raised by women who were Present for the talk. The letters of protest subsequently sent to *The Irish Times* were numerous and thunderous, and they kept on coming for weeks after the Congress.

My Memory of that very exciting meeting at Trinity is primarily of women laughing their heads off. They were more than Wicked enough to appreciate the *Wickedary*. My favorite comment was one I overheard, when a smiling Irish woman exclaimed to another: "I almost wet meself!" "Great!" I thought. This was better than, or at least as good as, the "Arf-Arfing" of Websters' Intergalactic Seal of Approval. So that was a *very* happy afternoon.

On Thursday, July 9, I gave my Keynote Address.* It was an ineffably exciting event for me. When I told Wild Cat and Catherine the story they were moved to meow and moo in harmony, dancing and prancing all over the pages of this chapter, which were soon strewn around my workshop. I had to shoo them out in order to finish writing these Recollections. But first I patiently explained to them that this workshop serves as my Pirate's Cove on the moon and that therefore it is a place for sorting out precious gems of Memories and Insights—a task which requires intense concentration and focus. Hence no distractions are permitted. They try to understand, but they

---

*There were different Keynote speakers each day: Monday: Birgit Brock-Utne (Norway); Tuesday: Kamla Bhasin (India); Wednesday: Monica Barnes, Mary Robinson, Margaret MacCurtain, Ursula Barry (Ireland); Friday: Helen Caldicott (Australia).

are so Charged with Animal Magnetism that they find it virtually impossible to remain calm and collected, or to tear themselves away. At any rate, I am left in peace Now, and so I shall continue.

My speech was scheduled for 4:00 p.m. at the National Concert Hall. Ger Moane and I went early, so the Hall was virtually empty. I have a vivid Memory of our mounting the beautifully carpeted stairway of that magnificent place together. As we walked up, we could hear exquisite Otherworldly/OtherTimely music being played somewhere in the Hall. Neither of us could recognize that piece of music or the composer. It was purely joyous. It was Absolutely Glorious. To me that Momentous Moment of walking up the staircase, my heart dancing with the music, signified something like the Re-membering of our own Splendor across Time—the Grandeur of women. Specifically, I Sensed that we were participating in the Dis-covering and Re-turning of Female Magnificence to Ireland. We were experiencing our Prechristian and Pre-Celtic Gynocentric Reality. We walked up, up, carried by the lilting music. Up to our rightful place, the place of women's Race. I felt tremendous Pride at that Moment. I felt Ecstasy.

Later from backstage I heard the roaring, chattering, laughing of the women as they surged in and took their seats. Soon the huge, elegant hall was filled with women. Women from every continent on earth. Feminists from every continent on earth. "We've all come to the right place!" I thought. "And at this Moment we will be Unerased!"

The "official" audience consisted of about eight hundred academics from around the world, who were supported by their universities. The unofficial audience, to my delight, consisted of about four hundred Irish women from all over Ireland—many of them working-class women who slid in on a sliding scale, so to speak. The vibes were warm and Wild.

The title of my speech was "Be-Thinking, Be-Speaking, Be-Spelling: Re-Calling the Archimagical Powers of Women." There was something from every one of my books, including *Outercourse*,* woven into it. The audience was more than enthusiastic. I felt a strong rapport with them, and so I went all the way.

Afterward, at the Congress Buffet Dinner, which was exquisite, I met women from faraway places. Many told me that they assigned my books in their classes. I was especially moved by the stories of women from India and Japan who told me of their experiences reading and teaching from *Gyn/Ecology.*

Re-membering that dinner Now, I understand that it was really a Pirates' banquet. We had come by means of our Crafts from all over the world in order to feast, strategize, and make merry together. We had docked our

---

*The excerpt from *Outercourse* was from a very early draft of the first chapter of this book.

Crafts at this Emerald Island, where some of us shared and traded our treasures with each Other. We felt at home here. Ireland's great Archaic Gynocentric history is well known among us, for even in dreadful patriarchal times our Truths have not been entirely lost. And after all, the Spirit of the great sixteenth-century Female Irish Pirate, Granuaile, still Lives and Breathes and Sails around these waters and Roams this island. Even little schoolchildren are taught to sing songs about her in Irish.[9]

At one point when I was in the middle of a conversation with Sister Pirates, a man came running through the room exclaiming: "The Lord Mayor is here! The Lord Mayor has arrived!" "So what?" I thought. "Who cares about him?" Then Ger reminded me that the "Lord Mayor" of Dublin at that Time was a woman.[10] And then in she strode, the Lord Mayor in her full regalia. I had the impression that she did not stay very long, but I could be mistaken. There was so much going on! Dinner was followed by a lively concert by Irish women musicians—and then there was a chorus of conversation far into the night.

My final talk, held on Friday, July 10, at the "Mansion House," was entitled "Jumping Off the Doomsday Clock." Ger Moane was the Chaircrone. This session was open to everyone, and a large number of working-class Irish women came and participated. I was excited about the makeup of the audience and decided at some point to hand over the microphone to women who had come to the Mansion House for this special session. I loved the spontaneous comments of the Irish women. One young woman, for example, grabbed the mike and began her comments with the remark: "Well, I heard about this and so I just left me job and came running over!" She then carried on with an impressive analysis of the condition of women in Ireland. Some of the women who were not accustomed to speaking before a large group displayed great courage. For example, after some minutes of discussion back and forth about whether women who had not attended a university could understand philosophical books, one woman who had driven in from her home in the country impatiently took the microphone. She explained that she had never been very verbal and at first had felt that she could never read *Gyn/Ecology.* Then, after her close friend kept prodding her and encouraging her to try to read it, she found that she could indeed understand the book and loved it. So by her courage and articulateness she inspired Self-confidence in others.

Shortly after that session there was a "Reclaim the Night March" through the streets of Dublin.* It was a deeply moving and inspiring experience, marching on those streets to the solemn and relentless beat of a bodhrán

---

*Actually the march was not held at night but in the late afternoon, shortly after my talk at Mansion House. It was a sunny day, as were all the days of the Congress and of my whole visit to Ireland. This good weather added to the atmosphere of optimism that pervaded that Time.

expect some special experience. Yet of course my sense of surprise was total, because I had had no way of knowing which "ordinary" place—if any—would bring me into such a state of Re-membering bliss.

When my friends came out of the take-away place we sped on to the Burren, arriving there for a good part of the sunset. The coloring of the rounded rocks of the area reminded me of the Grand Canyon. They appeared to be a kind of dull rose, and to me at the time there was an aura of sadness about them. I didn't yet know that this was just a first taste of the Burren, which would reveal some of its spectacular Wonders to me several days later.

We drove on to the town of Ballyvaughan in County Clare, where we had a very late and exquisite dinner at Claire's Restaurant. There a Stunning event occurred. It was close to eleven o'clock when the four of us were finally seated at a table with five chairs. At about 11:30 I felt a Presence in the "empty" chair. I explained to my friends that Gladys Custance had promised to visit me in Ireland during this trip.

Well before making that promise she had told me to think of her every evening at about 11:30. So 11:30 had been established as "Gladys's Time." Only a few close friends were aware of this. When Nancy Kelly would be visiting me in the evening and we noticed that it was "Gladys's Time," we would "casually" say: "Hi, Gladys!" So here in Ballyvaughan Gladys subtly made me aware of her Presence. Everyone took it in stride, so to speak. I know that I was very much aware of the "empty" chair.

We stayed at a B and B and took off the next day by the coast road for the Cliffs of Moher, the high astounding cliffs with breathtaking views. By the Time we arrived there we were well into our second Year of Fairy Time on this trip—maybe the second Century—and we were just beginning. As we sat high on the edge of the cliffs a remarkable thing happened. There were several gulls flying around at a distance, but one in particular came over to visit, or rather to "perform." I don't know what else this could be called. The gull swooped and soared, Spiraling around and heading straight for the cliff, then Spiraling away for a bit. She would return again, coasting on the wind, then shoot up and dive down again, while we gasped in Awe of the Bird. This Soaring Performance lasted perhaps half an hour (reckoned by "normal" time).

Most impressive were the Daring of the gull and, I believe, her joy in showing off. I took it personally. What matters is the wonder and joy of it—the bliss and freedom communicated by that gull—who, I Now Realize, Soared her way into the writing of *Outercourse*.[17]

At any rate, it started to rain. Defying the rain and driven by curiosity we headed for a strange-looking stone wall in the middle of a field. Rain-soaked and wet-footed we then drove to a B and B near the town of Doolin. After changing clothes we went for dinner and to a pub in Doolin, which is famous for its authentic live Irish music. After that we went walking in the country, gazing at the fabulous night sky—the starriest sky that I have ever seen. It was not only that there were so *many* stars—far more than were visible even in Leverett, but that they seemed so close, so big and bright and tangible. I saw a shooting star. The night was rather cold and very windy, but we kept on walking.

When we returned to the B and B it was cold and there weren't enough blankets, but it was too late to ask for more. The next Day, Year, Century, I felt the ominous beginnings of a sore throat. But there was so much to see and do!

We headed in the car for a high rock formation near the Cliffs of Moher, known as Hag's Head, whose name alone was enough to make a visit there imperative. Backing away from there in the mud we took off for Kilfenora, Ger's paternal grandmother's birthplace. We then continued on to Corofin, also in County Clare, in order to visit the Corofin Heritage Centre. On the way we saw a road sign pointing the way to "Boston," which it proclaimed to be ten kilometers away. So we jumped out of the car and took each other's pictures under the sign. I was moved to go into a nearby phone box and check for Dalys and Mortimers (Mortimer was my paternal grandmother's name). I didn't call anyone up.*

In the Corofin Heritage Centre I began to pick up some of the Threads that would soon lead to an astonishing adventure. We came upon information (on display in a glass case) about one Donagh Mor O'Dalaigh, Chief of the Bardic School of Ireland (1250) at Finavarra, near Ballyvaughan on the northern edge of the Burren. Since O'Dalaigh is an old form of O'Daly (later shortened to Daly) I felt a special interest in this personage. I Re-membered that my father had had an Uncanny/Canny "way with words."

I was deeply struck by the fact that Donagh Mor O'Dalaigh had lived in the thirteenth century—which for decades has been the century in which I have felt at home. Thomas Aquinas had belonged to that Time, and my studies in Fribourg had focused on the theology and philosophy of that period. Indeed my life there had been suffused with the aura of the thirteenth century. I had not concentrated upon thirteenth-century Ireland, however, until that Moment when it began to come alive for me as I stood in the Heritage Centre in Corofin, gazing into the glass case containing documents concerning the Bard, Donagh Mor O'Dalaigh.

The document in the case informed us that the Bardic School founded by O'Dalaigh continued from 1250 until 1650. There was a poem describing that Bard as a "generous host" and representing his students as "bringing back the old tradition." "How old?" I wondered. "How ancient was the

---

*During my 1984 trip I had tried to track down information on my maternal ancestry, looking for clues about the names Buckley and Falvey, but I didn't get very far. Ireland is, unfortunately, now (in the foreground) part of the patriarchy. I had also looked up Daly and had read in a book of family crests that this is "the greatest name in Irish literature." I could hardly help being proud of this.

tradition they brought back? Was there any Deep Memory of Gynocentric Ireland?"

We noted other things of interest in the museum, such as pictures of famine boats. I read that many starving people were sent to upper New York State. I was beginning to understand more about my people, viscerally and psychically. We all shared a sense of deep sorrow and horror at the suffering of our ancestors.

We left Corofin carrying many treasures—images and ideas. We went, on that same day, to Ennis, also in County Clare. There we met Anne O'Neil, and together with her we went to see the ruins of the cottage of the nineteenth-century Irish Witch, Biddy Early. The site of Biddy's thatched cottage overlooks Kilbarron Lake near Feakle in County Clare. The five of us entered the ruins. After walking around and getting a Sense of the place we found a candle, obviously left by some other visitors. The incident which I am about to relate can be better understood if the reader knows something about the life of Biddy Early.

Born in 1798 in Faha (not far from Feakle), Biddy was a woman of exceptional powers, including clairvoyance and healing powers. She was and is famous throughout Ireland, especially in Clare. Stories of her deeds would fill volumes. Of course she was hated and feared by some priests, who tried in vain to control her. There is a story that when Biddy was near death a priest came and attempted to say the prayers for the dying. However, when he arrived, the paraffin-oil lamp on the wall quenched. When he entered the room where Biddy lay dying the candle in the room quenched. Then he struck a match and lit the candle again but again it quenched. So he could not read the prayers for the dying.[18]

All five of us were aware of this story, since we had been reading from and discussing the biographies of Biddy Early that were sold in the bookshop in Ennis. So we were eager to light the candle we had found there and to have a short celebration/ritual in honor of Biddy. We stood in a circle and one of us lit the candle. Then, lo and behold! It quenched. We stood in silence for what seemed like an eternal second . . . and then the candle flared up again! We accepted this as a very positive omen and carried on with our small celebration. Each of us said a few words and then we blew out the candle and left . . . happily.

We had an intense discussion of patriarchy, racism, and economics during dinner at Brogan's Restaurant in Ennis. After that, Joni, Ger, Aileen, and I parted from Anne and went hunting for a good B and B—a warm one. My sore throat was getting sorer, but I continued to try to ignore it. I went for a walk and was in Ecstasy looking at the night sky. The stars were Stunning!

Thursday, August 27—the fourth Fairy Day of our trip to the West—was even more amazing than the preceding Days. In the morning we went back to the bookshop in Ennis and then drove on to beautiful Lough Gur in County Limerick. Not far from the lake was an incredible Archaic stone

circle—a very large one, with huge stones. It was a gloriously sunny day*
and we excitedly walked and pranced into the grassy center of the circle
examining each enormous stone in turn. One of the largest stones had a zig-
zag (the Rune *Sowelu*) carved into it. This Rune symbolizes wholeness, life
forces, the sun's energy. It did not escape our notice that the stone on which
Sowelu was carved caught the rays of the sun in a special way. It glistened
and glittered, reflecting/refracting the rays, emanating comfort and warmth.

We eventually sat in a circle and began chanting "Ba." The effect of the
exertion, the warm sun, and the chanting was to make us drowsy, so we all
decided to lie down and partially dozed off. I remember that I Saw a rainbow
with my eyes closed. After resting for a little while we gradually "came to."
I don't recall who noticed the Strange phenomenon first, but whoever it was
gasped: "Look!" There, inside the circle with us were eight beautiful calves
standing shoulder to shoulder. Each was a mixture of dark brown and white.
When they moved, they all moved forward together synchronously, as a pha-
lanx, but they kept a safe distance from us. Eventually they grazed a little,
and then they trooped out together in a gap between two of the stones.[19]
Apparently the stone circle was one of their accustomed haunts. We were
intruders, but not too bothersome to them. I will always Re-Call those calves
with Wonder.†

After leaving the stone circle we all went on to Lough Gur itself. There
were strange birds (strange to me, at any rate) unlike any I had seen before,
and they made sounds such as I had never heard before. But Strangeness was
beginning to be expected.

We took off from there in the direction of County Kerry, stopping for dinner in a town called Abbeyfeale, which dumped us back into the foreground.
As we sat waiting endlessly for our dinners in a dingy restaurant I thought
that time had never passed so slowly. When the waiter finally brought us our
wretched repasts, something of the glow of our fantastic experiences preceding this point was temporarily lost. We found ourselves engaged in a futile
foreground discussion of how the media had handled the Congress in
Dublin.

When we emerged from this stuporous state we sped on into County
Kerry and stayed at a B and B someplace outside Killarney. New Miracles
were awaiting us, just around the bend, so to speak. Our goal was to take
a boat the following morning (Friday, August 28) from Port Magee on the
Kerry coast to Great Skellig Island, about eight miles out on the open
Atlantic.

---

*Most of the days of this second 1987 visit were bright and sunny, as had been the case
during my earlier visit that summer.

†And so I am sure will Catherine, who stood tall as I typed the story of the calves, her
pride in her Cowhood ineffably enhanced.

Joni, Aileen, Ger, and I dashed in the little car to Port Magee that Friday morning in a desperate attempt to catch the ferry which was scheduled to depart for Great Skellig at eleven. We lost our way for a few minutes . . . and missed it.

My friends accepted this defeat gracefully. I could not. I ranted and raved that I could not give up. There must be a way! I suggested that we could rent a boat (with boatmen) just for ourSelves. Surely someone would be glad to make a few extra pounds! I was willing to blow all my savings! My stubbornness won out. We did find a boat with two boatmen and by early afternoon we were zooming over the Atlantic headed for the Skelligs.

The sea was rough. The ride was Wild. After a short while it became evident that we were indeed headed for High Adventure. The Skelligs loomed before us in the distance—huge masses of precipitous slate rock. Our specific destination, Great Skellig (or Skellig Michael) is about half a mile long by a quarter of a mile wide. It rises 610 feet in the northeast and 705 feet in the southwest. It was our intention to climb all the way to the top.

Just as we arrived at Great Skellig—Wonder of Wonders!—we saw the rather large group of tourists who had come there on the boat we had missed. They were climbing back into their boat. We waved at them, thrilled that they were leaving. Perfect Timing! We would have the island to our-Selves. What Luck that we had missed that boat! And Now, Re-membering that Lucky Moment, I again hear the words of my parents echoing through my mind: "It's all bound to turn out all right anyway."

There was a guide at the foot of the towering rock who offered his services. We politely declined and began scampering up and up the ancient steps carved out of the solid rock. When we paused in this strenuous endeavor we looked out over the glorious ocean at the vast expanse of the blue sky. Countless gulls were soaring around Small Skellig, which was plainly visible to us. We knew there were many seals, but they seemed to be hiding at times.

When we arrived at the top we found ourSelves in a beautiful Green grassy place. We were interested in an ancient wall with a window overlooking Small Skellig and imagined what might have been the purpose of that. We were fascinated also by a sort of miniature stone circle, so we climbed into it and chanted "Ba." At some point—since we had brought along a bottle of "Ballygowan" spring water, Joni began chanting "Ba-llygowan." We all joined in. I pulled the bottle out of my knapsack and we placed it in the center of the circle. Well, we were being Silly, of course.

In that state of mind we were especially "turned off" by the idea that the idyllic island had been inhabited many hundreds of years ago by monks doing ascetic practices.* What a waste of such a beautiful place! It *must* have

---

*Patriarchal history books and guidebooks insist that this was the case.

had a more appropriate history, even if a few monks did come creeping in at some point.

We saw the remains of what certainly seemed to be beehive structures, which inspired me to think (Bee-think?) about women and bees. I imagined a story about the Skelligs that was quite different from the accounts in the "guide" books. I suggested that many hundreds of years ago Pagan women —adherents of the Old Religion in Ireland—had sought ways to escape the invading christians and their woman-hating religion and laws. Some— perhaps disguised as monks—may have fled in boats to the Skelligs and Realized Great Skellig as an excellent hiding place and home.

Indeed, the place is an excellent fortress. Living on top of Great Skellig, they would have had an expansive view of the ocean all around. They would have been able to spot approaching attackers well in advance of their arrival. Moreover, the long, arduous climb up to the top, which we had just experienced, would have made it difficult for any pursuers to get near them. The women could have hurled rocks or other weapons.

Also, I argued, they could have had a good food supply. There was an abundance of fish, and there could have been room on the grassy top to grow vegetables. Maybe they even kept bees. I also suggested that the presence of the mysterious beehive dwellings in many places, but especially here, made me think of the possibility that such women intended to convey a message to Other women, such as ourSelves, that they had been there. What creatures could be more Female-identified than bees? If a group of women wanted to leave a message or clue of their Presence and identity to women across Time, perhaps to women who would come along a thousand or two thousand years later, and who would speak an altogether different language, what would be a more clue-laden symbol than a beehive structure? This would, at the very least, say: "We, your Sisters, were here before you."

My Cronies thought that my theory, or myth, was interesting and perhaps even plausible. I thought that it came from a genuine intuition and that it was convincing.

While we discussed this we saw our boatmen signaling from down below. We had ignored them as long as possible. It was time to go. So we meandered down the stone steps, relishing the view and the warm sun. The dreary image of the monks had, at any rate, been exorcised, and there was a lot for us to think about during the rough boat ride back. Re-membering that trip Now, I think of it—of course—as an important Piratic expedition. My Craft was loaded with gems of images and inspirational ideas for *Outercourse*.

That evening we stayed at a house on Valentia Island, which belonged to friends of friends, where we made a turf fire and engaged in very intense conversation. I was increasingly aware of my sore throat, especially after the boat ride, but still chose to ignore it. Aileen read aloud an Electrifying passage from Meda Ryan's biography of Biddy Early, which made possible an Intertwining of Threads of our adventure. The passage Aileen read was this:

It is believed that Biddy talked with them [fairies] all her life and did not contradict this impression; she is reputed to have said: "This place between Finevara and Aughanish is the most haunted place in all Ireland."[*20]

When Aileen read these words aloud we all Sensed Electrical Connections. We thought of Donagh Mor O'Dalaigh—"my ancestor"—who hailed from Finavarra; Crossing the River Shannon; Seeing and Hearing fairies; the Wise Woman/Witch, Biddy Early (with whom we all felt some kind of bond). All pointed in the direction of Finavarra. Just one Day later Ger and I would be following these Signals with Fierce Focus, lured on by the Call of . . . Finavarra.

The following morning (Saturday, August 29), we took off for Killarney, where Joni and Aileen would take the train back to Dublin. They were Lucky and got their tickets for half-price. The four of us had elegant sandwiches and tea at Great Southern Hotel, which is near the train station. We were all quite Spacy by this Time. In fact, when I wandered off to find the "Ladies' Room," and was passing by the hotel gift shop, I bumped into a very lifelike dummy that was displaying a new outfit. That would have been all right, but I apologized to the dummy with deep sincerity and continued on. I realized what had happened as I sauntered back from the "Ladies' Room" and saw the thing standing stiffly in front of the gift shop. I found mySelf smiling and suppressing giggles whenever I remembered what had happened.

Fortified by the tea and sandwiches we exchanged good-bye hugs. Then Ger and I started off in the car for our next, and spookiest, adventure. Inspired by Donagh Mor O'Dalaigh and Biddy Early, we began to follow the Intertwining Threads that led, inevitably it seemed, back to County Clare, back to the Burren, and specifically to Finavarra, in Search of "the most haunted place in all Ireland."

VERY BRIEF LUNAR INTERMISSION

I simply must relax a bit here with my companions on the Other side of the moon. I must become grounded here, so to speak, before continuing with the story of Finavarra. The Animals are so comforting and down to earth, I mean, down to moon. "Why don't you get on with the story?" they ask impatiently in sign language, swishing tails and pawing the ground. "Soon," I say, "soon."

Wild Cat and Catherine are excited to hear more, and more. They are amused and befuddled. They would never think of apologizing to a store

---

*There are variant spellings of *Finavarra*, as exemplified in this quotation from Meda Ryan. This is true of many other names, including *Aughinish*, which is also called *Aughanish*.

dummy—or to anyone, for that matter. They just go, go, go. So they constantly remind me to "go, Mary, go." However, they don't understand that I have to catch up with mySelf. After all, I have to get used to the Expanding Now. I must Realize more and more my subliminal knowledge of Now.

It is different for a cat or a cow, especially these two. They have always been there, that is, here. So I can't explain. I just play with them. We run around in circles, counterclockwise, as usual, until I regain my Sense of Direction. When I can howl in harmony with their meowing and mooing I know that I'm ready to begin again.

There! I'm ready to return . . . to County Clare.

GREEN *LOGBOOK* ENTRIES:
IRELAND (FURTHER CONTINUED)

As soon as we had seen off Joni and Aileen, Ger and I drove directly, that is, indirectly, to Finavarra. We took a roundabout route across the Burren, which is filled with winding little roads and crossroads. I was desperate to reach Finavarra before sunset. In the early evening we came to a pub on Aughinish Bay. We entered and asked for directions to Finavarra. The woman bartender replied: "Finavarra—Right down the road!"

We took the road she had indicated, and on this road we met a little man. I opened the car window and asked if he knew any Dalys. He replied by asking which Daly I had in mind. The words that came out of my mouth startled me. I said I was looking for Frank Daly.* His response startled me even more. He said: "Frank Daly in America. Down the road. Turn left and then right, at the crossroads." He then told us that the house where Frank Daly lived was "across from the monument." I thanked him. Then Ger and I turned and stared at each other in wide-eyed wonder. We both felt chills. I was definitely feeling Spooked.

"Frank Daly *in* America . . . Down the road!?" *What* could that mean? We did not know what monument he was talking about, but proceeded. When we arrived at the crossroads, the sign for the "Monument" pointed left. Against our better judgment we followed the sign rather than the directions given us, and soon realized that we were going the wrong way. So we went back to the sign, which had been turned around, and went right, as we had been told. Very soon we met an Other little man on the right-hand side of the road, sweeping with a broom.† We asked for Frank Daly and he said

---

*As the reader of *Outercourse* knows, my father, Frank X. Daly, had died many years before, in Schenectady, New York, when I was in college. See Chapter Two.

†I refer to him, as well as the fellow who had first given directions, as "little," not because they were extraordinarily short, or because I saw them as "wee folk," or "little people," or fairies, exactly. But the way that they appeared and the Timing was so Strange that they did seem to be from some Other dimension.

that Annie Coughlin, who lived in the house down the road, would know everything. We thanked him as he resumed sweeping, and drove on.

Within a minute or two we saw a high Green grassy mound on the left-hand side of the road with a monument on top. I leaped out of the car and ran up to the monument. On it were carved the words:

DONAGH MOR O'DALAIGH

VENERABLE POET

C. 1300 A.D.

Absolutely Stunned, I gazed around. There was a stream nearby with stones in it, shining in the early evening sunlight. The rounded rocks of the Burren to the east looked about the same to me as they had several Days before. It was a lovely place. We drove on, perhaps a hundred yards, and suddenly saw a sign on the right that stated boldly: "Bardic School, 15th century."

The land that was the site of the Bardic School founded by O'Dalaigh was surrounded by an old stone wall. Ger and I got out of the car and climbed over the wall that was adjacent to the road. We climbed up the hilly land, heading toward what appeared to be ruins inside the walls.

At some point we stopped and noticed the sky to the west. It was utterly Rose-colored . . . Rose, Rose. When we turned to the east, we saw that the rounded rocks of the Burren had also turned color to a rich, vivid Rose. It was an utterly Awe-inspiring sunset.* This was a place suitable for a Venerable Poet, and for a Bardic School.

While reveling in the sunset I was distracted by the sudden realization that we were standing in a pasture. In fact, there were several bulls—or bullocks—not far away from us. There were even a couple of them grazing inside the ruin we were approaching. They were looking toward us. I suggested to Ger that we run for it before they became interested in us. We did.

Run, Mary, run. Now! Run, Ger, run. Now! Down the hill, down, down. Keep on going. Over the stone wall. Climb up and over. Get over the wall. Close call!

Actually the animals looked bored, but they could have changed their minds in a second.

And the Roseate Rocks were glowing. The grass was rich, rich Green. The sky was Roseate over All. All over there was Rose, and there was Green.

We asked another little man if there was a restaurant nearby. He said there was. It was called Rose Cottage. We asked if there was a B and B nearby. He said there was. We both heard him say it was called "Sowelu," but we soon found out that it had a Gaelic name that sounded very much like

---

*After other visits to that place at sunset and after talking with some of the inhabitants, I received the impression that the sunset that particular evening was extraordinary. That is, such sunsets do sometimes occur there, but they are not everyday events.

the name of that Rune but which meant "Seat of Mary." We did not stay there, but at another B and B, whose Gaelic name meant "Height of Delight."

We found Rose Cottage and we found Bridget Rose. We approached the door of Rose Cottage—after pausing for a herd of cattle on the road who patiently let us wait while they rubbed up against the car affectionately. Before we reached the door it suddenly opened. A beautiful grey-haired woman with rosy cheeks and sparkly eyes welcomed us to her elegant little establishment. She seemed to have been waiting for us.

Bridget Rose served us a magnificent trout dinner, which we enjoyed while looking out the window of Rose Cottage at the Roseate sky. When we inquired about pubs in the area she said there were two: Linnane's, which was on the Quay, and Mrs. Daly's in Bell Harbour, which was close by. She described Mrs. Daly as "a lovely woman," and her pub as "a lovely place." Tuning into my interest in seeking out Frank Daly in Finavarra, Bridget Rose also suggested a number of people whom I might want to contact during my visit.

After dinner we first went to Linnane's. There we heard local musicians, and after a very short while we left for Mrs. Daly's pub. Mrs. Daly was indeed a lovely woman. She had very white hair and reminded me of my grandmother (my father's mother), whom I had seen only once, when I was about four and she was dying. That Mrs. Daly also had very white hair the one time I saw her. I had been told that she, widowed for many years and with a family of seven children, had been a very shrewd business woman. This Mrs. Daly of Bell Harbour, also a widow, was a shrewd business woman as well. I liked her immediately.

The stars over Finavarra that night were magically bright. Gazing at them I reflected upon the events of that Day. It had been Awesome, that Saturday in Finavarra, providing gems of images that could last . . . forever. No Pirate could possibly have a Treasure Chest huge enough to contain them. They seemed to be spilling over, infinitely. As I Re-member them Now I see those sparkling gems as similar to the stars of that starry night. They seem limitless, lighting pathways into Other worlds, signaling multitudes of possibilities beyond imagining, beyond my Wildest dreams.

That night of Saturday, August 29, my sore throat moved on to becoming a full-fledged cold or flu. I felt sick and feverish most of the night. On Sunday, however, I had sufficient energy for more exploration. First we sought out Annie Coughlin who, strangely enough, told us she knew nothing about O'Dalaigh but suggested we talk to an O'Daly family nearby.* We didn't

---

*As a result of talking with locals I was able to decipher the words which had spooked me on the previous Day: "Frank Daly in America . . . across from the monument." There was a Frank Daly, about seventy years old, who had recently visited his relatives in that area and who had then returned to his home . . . in America. This explanation, however, did not negate the impact or the Power of the Original experience.

CHAPTER EIGHTEEN

DOORS TO FOUR:
LUCKY DIS-COVERINGS
AND HAPPY HOMECOMINGS

As the Voyager of *Outercourse* knows, I flew around the United States throughout the fall of 1987, *Wickedary* in hand, spreading Wicked Words as fast and far as I could. I was already Living in The Fourth Spiral Galaxy, although I didn't know it all the way, that is, overtly. I still had to learn more about Four, more and more about Four . . . The Fourth. The urgency of my need to Know hurled my Craft over the Sea, the Subliminal Sea.

I reached 1988 in a flash . . . a flash of lightning. The sky was brightening as I approached that year. After all, Virginia Woolf had shocked me in December.[1] That Witch! Turning the lights off and on again. Making Electrical Jokes. "Look at her, folks!" she had (in effect) said, making my face turn red. "Trying to imitate *me!*" she had patently said.

O.K., she had her way that day. And she just about pushed me over the brink. I think she was ushering me through the Door, the Door to Four . . . The Fourth Spiral Galaxy, and the Fourth Dimension.

Of course there are many Doors to Four. I had to go through Door after Door to arrive at Four. The move from subliminal to overt is not just one simple hop. I couldn't just pop in one day and say "I'm all the way here!" No. I needed a few more nudges and kicks and lightning bolts and shocking jolts.

Some of these came in 1988. The coast was clear that year. My Crafty Cronies pushed and pulled me through, to the truly Newly New.

LOGBOOK ENTRIES: THE RING FROM GLADYS

On March 27, 1988, my friend Gladys Custance died in Cassadaga, Florida, her winter residence.[2] She was eighty-seven years old.

This was a deep loss. I had no doubt that this spiritually gifted woman could be in Touch with me, and with anyone, whenever and wherever she wanted. But obviously it was not the same. She was no longer on what she would call the "earth plane." I couldn't just call her up in the ordinary way and talk with her. I couldn't go to visit her in Onset (Massachusetts) or in Cassadaga or go out to a restaurant with her, as we frequently had done in recent years.

When I was in Onset later that spring I asked her husband, Kenneth, if I could have something belonging to Gladys as a remembrance. A short while later he gave me an astonishing ring which I had never seen before. I have cherished it ever since, and keep it on the bookshelf in front of the desk on which I am typing this manuscript.

The ring fascinated and surprised me. The band does not form a circle but rather an incipient spiral. That is, the band has two ends which do not join. Rather, they pass each other—parallel each other—with a space between them. Four small identical stones appear, at first glance, to be set in a row on and between these ends.* The sight of these stones, which were opals, startled me, since I did not recall ever having told Gladys (or Kenneth) that my birthday is in October or that the opal is my birthstone.

The fact that this spiral ring was chosen for me was shocking also, because I had never, to my recollection, told Gladys that I was deeply immersed in thinking and writing about spirals or that my forthcoming book would be composed of Spiral Galaxies.

The configuration of this ring and these stones functioned as a kind of koan, nudging me toward further meditation and Musing about spirals and the number four.† Eventually, of course, I came to Realize consciously the existence of The Fourth Spiral Galaxy of *Outercourse,* in which I was already participating.

Inquiring into the history of the ring, I learned that it had been found/purchased in Jamaica. Since Jamaica is a place about which I have happy Memories, and especially since it is an island, this bit of information was also charged for me. As a Pirate I am especially fond of islands, especially Islands where Treasures such as this ingenious spiral ring can be found.

At any rate, the questions about Gladys's ring remain intriguing. Did that ring awaken and/or reinforce images that were already Present in my psyche so that they would find their rightful place in *Outercourse?* I think so. The themes of Spirals, Gems, Treasure Islands, and Piracy were already explicitly there, though not fully developed. But the theme of Four was still hiding under the Subliminal Sea. Gladys's ring helped me to Dis-cover it. As I hold that ring in my hands Now, gazing at it, I wonder what Other secrets it may Dis-close. I Sense that there is still more about Four.

---

*Examining the ring closely I saw that neither end of the band holds all four stones. Rather, each end provides settings for only three. If one thinks of the stones as numbered 1, 2, 3, 4, then, since three of the stones (1, 2, and 3) are set on one end of the band and three (2, 3, and 4) on the other, the effect is that no matter at what angle the ring is held and regarded, the stones, which upon first inspection seem to be just "four in a row," are really in an arrangement of three plus one.

†Given the "three plus one" arrangement of the stones, the "message" to me is that "the fourth" is somehow set apart from the others.

LUNAR REVERIES

During the spring of 1988 I worked as steadily as possible on the first draft of the first two Spiral Galaxies of *Outercourse.* As I Re-member that Time I Realize the intricacy of the Intertwining Threads. As one Moment led to an Other the Momentum increased to a fantastic extent. I could not Realize what I was getting mySelf into until I was into it, and by then I was further out of it, if you know what I mean. And *Now!* As each Moment of Momentous Re-membering tosses my Craft further into the Expanding Now, I feel that I am flying with the speed of Light—Be-Dazzling Light.

This is, in part, the explanation of how I arrived here on the Other side of the moon and am able to commute to and around earth without too much effort. I am just Moving at my own pace out here in space. Moreover, each Moment has a stillness at its center. That's why I am at home here with Wild Cat and Catherine. They don't even mind any more when I take off on lecture tours and such, because they know I'll be back in a jiffy. "No problem!"—as they say in the good old U.S.A.

Right Now I am here in my workshop with my moonmates, Re-membering my travels in the spring of 1988. Of course I hopped around the United States quite a bit that spring, Be-Speaking from the *Wickedary* and Other books.[3] Since the *Wickedary* had just come out in Britain[4] and in Ireland,[5] speaking engagements were arranged for April in England and Scotland by The Women's Press and in Ireland by Attic Press.

As I type my Recollections of that tour, Catherine is standing here (as she often does) looking over my shoulder, electromagnetically shooting Memories of the trip through my brain and onto the pages of this manuscript. I am so Lucky to have such an Archimagical assistant! And Wild Cat's telepathic communications must not be overlooked. Sometimes she sends them through the cow and sometimes directly to me. The complexity of our communications system is mind-boggling. It certainly puts "sophisticated" electronic systems into proper perspective, exposing them for what they are—crude gadgets that are absurd imitations of Bovine, Feline, and, in general, Female abilities.

LOGBOOK ENTRIES: ENGLAND AND SCOTLAND

On Monday, April 18, I boarded a conventional aircraft at Boston's Logan Airport. My destination was London. As usual, of course, I Smuggled my own Craft with me, which presented no problem, since it is invisible to "the authorities." I landed early Tuesday morning at London's Heathrow Airport and was driven to Reeves Private Hotel for Women at Shepherd's Bush Green. This was a delightful and relaxing place, where I stayed for three nights.

Thursday evening was the most exciting time for me on that trip to London. I spoke at Wesley House on Great Queen Street. The talk was organized by Lesbian Line and the Lesbian Archive, and it was a women-only event. I was impressed and moved by the Archive and the women there who told me quite a bit about the oppressive conditions in England under Margaret Thatcher—especially as they affected Lesbians. The Hall was packed with Radical Lesbian Feminists, and the audience was Appreciative, Alive, and Wild. I was Touched by conversations with a number of women and by their gifts, which I cherish—especially the set of tapes given to me by OVA, a talented and Sparky group of Radical Lesbian Feminist musicians. I was very happy that evening, when it was again demonstrated that—even through the hardest times—Wicked Women Live.

The next morning (Friday, April 22) I was "collected" at my hotel and taken to Kings Cross Station, where I caught the midday train for Edinburgh, Scotland. The almost-five-hour ride took me through interesting countryside—interesting to me, at any rate, since I had never taken a train from London to Scotland before. The train trip gave me time to collect my thoughts and prepare for what promised to be an exciting adventure. I also was looking forward to meeting and talking with June Campbell, who was the organizer of "the Edinburgh connection."

June had written to me three years before about *Pure Lust*. She had told me something of her astonishing history, indicating that she had "spent twenty years within the confines of buddhist patriarchy and oppression," and had really only broken free in the early 1980s from the tibetan "buddhist sadospiritualists," as she Named them.[6]

After her escape from this horror, June taught in a college and joined a group of Feminists who opened a bookshop and café for women in Edinburgh called "WomanZone." Beginning in 1986 she and her partner, Benedetta Gaetani, organized "Adventure Trekking," guiding women on long walks through the Himalayas.

When I arrived in the late afternoon in Edinburgh June met me and brought me to the apartment which she shares with Benedetta. We all went out for dinner at a remarkable Chinese restaurant, which served the best Chinese food I have ever tasted. Later that evening and during the next day, with books strewn around us, we talked incessantly.[7]

On Saturday evening I spoke at the Southside Community Centre, which had previously been a church. Although some of the men in the audience were hostile, there were many women present—some of whom had come long distances—who were earnest and eager to know more about Radical Feminism.

On Sunday, April 24, June and I packed in a lot of driving and discussion. It was a rather dull, grey day, but that was no deterrent. We went to Schiehallion, the "she-mountain" of Caledonia (Scotland). As we drove around the mountain, which seemed to represent the Goddess in her grimmer aspects, our conversation also became a bit grim, focusing on the phenomenon of women, including lesbians, attacking women. We were on this foreground subject when we saw a sign announcing that we were entering a town called "Dull." Exactly at this point in time and space a terrible stench—something like the smell of sulfur dioxide—entered the car. After driving on a bit we were roaring with laughter at this peculiar and pungent convergence. I will never forget the place called Dull.

As a parting gift, June gave me a tea leaf reading which proved to be astonishingly accurate over Time. So I had much to think about when I boarded the train heading back to England on Monday, April 25.

On the return trip through England, I first spoke in Sheffield and then went on to Bristol where I gave a talk at The Watershed Arts Centre. Before my talk, when I was dining alone in the cafeteria of the Centre, I noticed several women at a table nearby who were also noticing me. They soon joined me, and I was not surprised to learn that they had come from the Women's Peace Camp at Greenham Common. I liked them immediately and we plunged into conversation. They looked tired and embattled, and our discussion revealed that they had reason to be. To the best of my recollection they all agreed that there was something like "zapping" going on at Greenham. One said that she had virtually lost her short-term memory. I told them about the woman I had met in Dublin in 1987 during the "Reclaim the Night March" who had described conditions at the Camp.

As I write about this connection Now, the Connection clicks in my mind: Pirates exchanging messages again, and again. We had only a brief Time for this, however, before I had to give my speech.

On the following day I was back on the train, headed for London, having come full circle. After I arrived in Paddington Station I went to The Women's Press, where everyone was most gracious, and I was given a ride to Heathrow Airport. Sitting in the airport waiting for my Aer Lingus flight to Dublin I reviewed the events of the trip thus far. I thought of the women at The Women's Press and of their courageous struggle to Survive—Ros de Lanerolle, Katy Nicholson, who had painstakingly arranged for my trip, and Mary Hemming, who drove me through the horrible London traffic to the airport.

I was tingling with excitement at the thought of returning to Ireland. I believe some of the tingling that I feel as I write this Now may be coming from Catherine, who is on the verge of drooling over my shoulder. It is Time for an intermission.

BRIEF LUNAR INTERMISSION

The reason for Catherine's excitement when I mentioned Ireland is obvious. She has fallen in love with the cows there and hopes to hear a few words about them. I told her that this was only a short trip—only five days. But she reminded me telepathically that even one Fairy Day in Ireland can be very, very rich. I have to agree.

Right though she may be, the fact is that I need to have my workshop to mySelf for a Moment, because Something—or rather, Somethings—happened as I was writing the last few pages, and I want to Stop and ponder these events Now. So I must shoo away my wondrous cat and cow. There they go, out the door. Soon enough they'll be back for more.

The Somethings were two of those "coincidences" that can occur in the Expanding Now. They happened precisely when I was typing the lines about Schiehallion, the "she-mountain" of Caledonia. I wanted to know more about this peculiar place name, so I Searched through Barbara Walker's *Woman's Dictionary.* I didn't find what I was looking for (*Schiehallion*), but I did find Something else. Something More was in store.

I kept on browsing in that book, you see, and was nudged through yet an Other Door to Four. One word led to an Other, and before I knew it I had lit upon an entry on "Mary." The word that Jumped off the page from that entry was *lucky.* As the reader of *Outercourse* knows, I have always considered mySelf Lucky. So I read the following with interest:

> One of the symbols of the Virgin Mary reveals the reason that four-leaf clovers were considered "lucky." The four-leaf clover design in Mary's sign . . . points to the four directions. As a pagan design, which it used to be, this probably referred to the four solar turning-points of the year and the nocturnal "eves" when their celebrations were held.
>
> Pagan symbols often became "lucky" in a nonpagan society that refused to recognize their original sense . . . [8]

Much of the material in the entry was already known to me. But the emphasis upon "lucky" rang cosmic bells. My Pagan Luckiness took on a New Look. As defined in *Webster's, luck* means "a purposeless, unpredictable, and uncontrollable force that shapes events favorably or unfavorably for an individual, group, or cause: FATE, FORTUNE." The reversal is astounding. Clearly, my Luckiness has not been purposeless. Quite the opposite is true. It is Stunningly Purposeful—a fact which I have Realized through the living and writing of *Outercourse.* Its Source is my Final Cause. It is connected with the incipient Presence of The Fourth Spiral Galaxy. My Luck is Female, Elemental, Positively Pagan. It has led me through many a Door to Four.

And that isn't all. As I continued browsing in that tome I Lucked upon the entry on "Ba"—a Familiar Word to the readers of this book.[9] According to Walker:

> The *ba* . . . is linked to the ancient, worldwide concept of ancestors and ancestral divinities in bird shapes.[10]

The entry continues:

> Divination by consulting birds (that is, the souls of the dead) was common throughout Greece, Rome, and northern Europe. . . . Folklore in all these areas

emphasized the importance of learning to comprehend the magical language of birds.[11]

Being reminded of "Ba" just before coming to the writing of my 1988 *Logbook* entries on Ireland seems Auspicious. It brings to my mind Memories of encounters with birds in Ireland in 1987, especially the performing gull near the Cliffs of Moher, the Strange birds at Lough Gur, and the multitude of swans near Finavarra.[12] It calls up associations with beehive dwellings and bees. Walker's allusion to ancestors and ancestral divinities Conjures Memories of the Corofin Heritage Centre and explorations at Finavarra the previous summer, and her mention of the magical language of birds brings several Threads together.

So Now that I've contemplated the Somethings that happened when I was writing the last few pages I am prepared to go on with my Recollections of travels in the spring of 1988. I think I hear thumping and scratching outside. My friends are keen to come in for the ride . . . the ride to Ireland.

LOGBOOK ENTRIES: IRELAND AND BACK AGAIN

I was met at the Dublin airport on the evening of Wednesday, April 27, by Joni Crone and Hilary Tierney, who brought me to Buswell's Hotel, where I rested and prepared for the following day, which I knew would be intense.

On Thursday afternoon my book was "launched" by Anne Good in Books Upstairs, an excellent bookshop in Dublin.[13] My role was to meet people, talk about my book and other matters, and sign books. After that I had dinner with a group of women, including Feminist theologians Ann Louise Gilligan, Katherine Zappone, Mary Condren, the well-known writer Nuala Ni Dhomhnaill, as well as Aileen and Joni, at Nico's Restaurant, which has a reputation in Dublin for its fine Italian food. I could not exactly relax during that dinner, since I was scheduled to speak at Trinity College that evening.

My talk at Trinity was arranged by Attic Press, the Feminist press in Dublin which brought out the Irish edition of the *Wickedary*. It was sponsored also by the Trinity Women's Group. I spoke in Edmund Burke Hall, which was packed with an excited and exciting audience.

One vivid Memory of that lecture at Trinity was the sight (and sound) of Ann Louise, who sat near the front and who was really into the spirit of the event. Ann Louise was "acting up," especially when I read some of the "snool" definitions from *Word-Web Three*. For example, when I read the definition of *deadfellows* she shouted out: "Dead right!" After that talk there was a reception which involved very intense conversations with many women. The room was so crowded and the buzzing so loud that it became necessary frequently to go out into the hall in order to hear each other. My Memories of that evening are Positively Revolting.

On Friday I took off with Joni and Aileen for the West. We took the train to Galway, where we "hired a car" to get us to the cottage reserved for the weekend in Bell Harbour, near Finavarra. This was the same cottage we had inhabited the previous summer, and it was beginning to feel like home. Io and Marie came in their van and stayed there also. (Ger was in the U.S. at that Time.)

The experience this Time in Finavarra was one of familiarity, friendship, and fun. We again saw the cows near Rose Cottage and a few of the swans on the lake. We visited the Cliffs of Moher—looking for the special gull, perhaps. She did not show up, but the beauty was invigorating and inspiring.

On Monday, May 2, my friends saw me off at Shannon Airport, where I boarded in a happy mood. I Sensed that more would happen in this Magical place . . . later. I resolved to come back to Ireland as soon as possible . . . specifically to the West.[14]

When I returned to Newton I dived back into work on *Outercourse,* with occasional breaks at the beach. A major event in June was the Third International Feminist Bookfair, which was held at the University of Montreal. I was scheduled to speak at this event and stayed with my friends Marisa Zavalloni and Nicole Brossard. Nicole was the Honorary President of the Fair, which began with a bang: a Great Fiesta with music, balloons, and other colorful attractions held on the top of Mount Royal. Many women from around the world spoke. I was particularly glad to be able to hear my Canadian friends, including Nicole and Marisa, of course, as well as Mary Meigs and Louky Bersianik.

Shortly after that it was Time to start packing for another Great Adventure—my Journey to Switzerland, where I would give a week-long seminar on Elemental Feminist Philosophy in Basel, followed by a lecture in Bern. I was going Home! To an Other Home, for an Other Homecoming!

LOGBOOK ENTRIES: ERIKA'S ISLAND
AND HOMECOMING . . . TO SWITZERLAND

On Wednesday, June 29, I flew by SwissAir from Boston to Zurich. I was in the State of Bliss—a world which I enter sometimes—especially when I think of—or return to—Switzerland. Of course I had been there a few times since my student days in Fribourg, but this Time was especially Momentous. I was going back to teach my own Elemental Feminist Philosophy, not in Fribourg, but in Basel. But I made absolutely sure that I would visit Fribourg and my Other favorite haunts, since I would be so close.

Flying into the sunrise and over the Alps to Zurich is a breathtaking experience, truly a flight into an Other world. My heart leaped up when I saw the Alps, up, up into Ecstasy. It was a particular kind of Ecstasy I have never felt in America—not when flying over the Rockies, not anywhere.

A unique feature of this trip was that I flew out of Zurich the day after I arrived, on my way to spend a week with Erika Wisselinck at her house on a small island near the Portuguese island of Madeira. Erika and Doris Gunn, a Radical Feminist from Switzerland, had plotted this complicated trip.* Erika and I hadn't seen each other for two years, so we had much to discuss as we walked the lovely beaches of the island or sat on the porch of her wonderful stone house. I will begin with the story of this house.

Erika is not rich, to say the least, so she would not be likely to own a house in such an exotic spot. The event that made that possible was that she sued the lutheran church of Bavaria in 1975. She had been teaching for thirteen years in a school owned by the church, and they had tried to "terminate" her by altering her contract, which would have left her almost destitute. She won the case and thus had money to buy the house. So Erika was Lucky![15]

At any rate, there we were, basking in the sun and relaxing in the shade of that island. Erika told me more about the story of *Anna*—her book which was still brewing, but close to completion. I read to her from an early draft of *Outercourse*. We took turns reading from a rather lyrical section in The First Passage of *Gyn/Ecology*. Erika was justifiably proud of her translation of that difficult part, and we read it alternately in English and in German, somewhat puffed up with mutual Self-congratulation.

We swam every day and hiked east and west. Toward the end of my visit we went to a particularly beautiful valley. I remember stopping to talk with some, uh, cows . . . I am Now feeling heavy, hot breathing over my shoulder. . . . There, I've lured her out the door. It's Time to move on with the story of my visit to Switzerland.

On Friday, July 8, Erika saw me off at the little airport, and I was on my way. The restful adventure on the "secret island" had been a great preparation for the arduous week ahead. This began with landing in Zurich and heading immediately for the train station, where I stowed most of my gear in a locker, putting the minimum into my knapsack. I hopped on a train for Bern, with the intention of continuing on to Interlaken, and then up to Wengen and Kleine Scheidegg. I arrived in Wengen in the evening, found a hotel with an awesome view, and looked forward to a glorious day in the Alps.

Saturday began with breakfast on my private balcony, where I gazed at the mountains, thinking that if this were heaven I would be glad to check in, indefinitely. I spent some time walking around Wengen, savoring my Memories, Wonderlusting in the Present as I gazed at the Jungfrau. After awhile I boarded the little mountain train for Kleine Scheidegg and hiked up to where the cows were grazing.

---

*It was Doris who made all the arrangements for the events in Switzerland—but I'll come to that part soon.

The sky and sun and air were glorious, but I knew I had to get going, so I caught the mountain train headed back to Interlaken. I fell asleep and had to be shouted at when it was time to change trains. I continued on to Bern, where I succumbed to the irresistible temptation to walk around and through the arcades. I then boarded the train again for the twenty-five minute trip to Fribourg, where I spent Saturday night.

Fribourg—my medieval wonderland and "hometown"! I wandered around there on Sunday, visiting the university, the *basse ville,* and Bourguillon. Tearing mySelf away I took the train back to Zurich, called Doris Gunn, and picked up my stuff from the locker.

I am sure that I was Spacier than usual from my intense Swiss tour by the time Doris arrived with a friend, Elisabeth Sen-Wenk. They drove me to Hotel Basel, which was not far from the elegant Villa where the seminar would be held. My immediate concern was Survival, as I unpacked my books, notes, and clothes for the week.

Villa Wenkenhof in Riehen bei Basel, literally called a "Lusthaus" (meaning "country seat, or country mansion"), served as the setting for discussions of *Reine Lust (Pure Lust).* This sixteenth-century Villa, now available for a reasonable fee for cultural events, was obtained by Doris through the organization she created, called *Avalun.* Its regal interior and spacious grounds provided a pleasant—though not exactly Wild—environment for Realizing Elemental Feminist Philosophy.

There were over thirty women registered for the seminar. Most were from Switzerland, but some were from Germany, Austria, and the Netherlands. In addition to their sessions with me in the afternoons and often in the evenings, the participants attended working groups in the mornings.[16] Teaching and discussing with this international group of scholarly women was stimulating. These were women who experienced rigorous analysis as well as flights of imagination as fun. I enjoyed hearing their ideas and their responses to *Pure Lust.* Some said that I "think like a European"—which should not be surprising, after my seven years in Fribourg.

Nonchapter Thirteen: "Cat/egorical Appendix" of *Pure Lust* was greatly appreciated, since many of the women were cat lovers. One day, when I was standing in our "classroom" (an exotic parlor in the Villa Wenkenhof) holding forth on ideas from *Pure Lust,* a Strangely Synchronous and Cat/alytic event occurred. Behind me was a table loaded with books and behind that were the huge glass doors that opened out to a porch overlooking the palatial grounds that surrounded the Villa. The doors were ajar. Without my noticing it, a cat, slightly resembling Wild Cat, entered these portals. She came and sat directly in front of me, facing the rows of women. Everyone was smiling and staring at her, so I could not remain oblivious. After receiving the attention that she felt was her due from me, the Feline Familiar made the rounds, visiting various women whom she deemed worthy of being noticed by her. This event was a memorable Cat/atonic for all of us. The cat had come at an appropriate Moment, of course, issuing a Cat/egorical Imperative, a Call of the Wild to Elemental Feminist Philosophers.

I made a number of important connections with women who were taking the seminar. One woman who stands out in my Memory, Adelheid Baumgartner, had a lot of questions. Some of these were interesting, but I was a bit irritated by what I perceived then as her perpetual needling on the question of trinities. "That old christian stuff!" I thought, wishing she would stop. I did not yet know that Adelheid would be coming to Boston that fall, and that she would be sitting in on one of my classes, pursuing her questions. Indeed, Adelheid would have much more to say . . . about Four.*

There were many "extracurricular activities" during the five-day seminar. Among these was a visit with the Swiss Feminist sculptor Bettina Eichen in her studio. Her works include powerful statues of the Muses and of Sophia. I also did a radio interview with Dr. Ursa Krattiger, a well-known Swiss Feminist.

On the evening of Saturday, July 16, I headed to Bern where I was scheduled to give a public lecture. I remember sitting on the speeding train with several of the women who had been at the seminar at Villa Wenkenhof. It was an Electrifying trip, for I was returning to one of my favorite hangouts—the place I had so often visited when studying in Fribourg. I could never have imagined that I would be coming back like this, Charged up to deliver a Fiery Feminist speech in, of all places, Bern.

Excitedly we tumbled off the train and rushed to the place where I would be speaking. The location, as Doris recently reminded me, Be-Laughingly, was a power station.[17] We thought of this as a unique Syn-Crone-icity, especially since the title of my talk was "Re-Calling the Elemental Powers of Women."

When we rushed in, the place was already very crowded and noisy. Since some of my companions were part of the "performance," we decided to go up and sit on the floor of the stage. At the conclusion of my talk, which Lilly Friedberg translated, Doris and two other women "acted out" Nonchapter Thirteen: "Cat/egorical Appendix" to *Pure Lust*. That is, they assumed the roles of Professor Yessir (the Inquisitor) and the two beautiful felines who were handling my interview with him, since I did not want to

---

*One evening in the fall of 1988 I invited Adelheid to go out to dinner with me in Newton, to see if we could achieve a meeting of minds. Although the discussion covered a wide range of topics, it focused in part on the numbers "three" and "four." Adelheid pursued her thoughts in a letter sent to me after her return to Switzerland in January 1989. She wrote: "I didn't like it, to imagine that you could be trapped by the three. I saw you spiraling, in motion, and wanted you to go on as long as possible. . . . There can't be any three without the four. The three grows out of the fourth dimension. . . . If there is no root for trinities, then it's only a play. All threes need a four as ground, e.g., the Pyramids. The four could also be the forgotten things, the unconscious" (Personal communication, January 16, 1989).

be bothered speaking with the snool. This "play" was performed in German, from Erika's translation of *Pure Lust*. The "cats" scampered around the stage delightfully, without missing a line. I think that Bern had never before witnessed such a sight or, rather, sights and sounds.

As we sped back on the train to Basel my companions and I were in a victorious and hilarious mood. There was also some Sense of cosmic connectedness among us. It was the last evening we would all be together on this trip, and the sounds of the *Schnellzug* (fast train) speeding through the night, as well as the sights of the brightly lighted towns and villages as we zipped through them, corresponded to something of what we felt.

Sunday was a mellow and poignant day. Doris and Elisabeth, both of whom had been most gracious throughout my stay, took me out for an elegant dinner. Later, we went for a walk in the country. We walked into Germany. As we hiked in the forest of Riehen, which in Germany becomes the Black Forest, I saw the devastation of many of the trees by acid rain. This brought to mind very forcefully the confrontation between foreground and Background, between elementary man-made horrors and Elemental power, beauty, and strength.

Doris and Elisabeth told me about the hideous fire that had occurred at Sandoz, one of the many chemical companies in Basel, on November 1, 1986. It had blazed all through the night. The air had become utterly contaminated, and a significant number of people who lived and/or worked anywhere near Sandoz died within a short span of time. Others, including Doris, had prolonged illnesses. The fumes were so vile and enduring that many people feared for months that their lives would be endangered if they went outside.

Doris told me that she had had a prophetic dream that the fire would occur. In her dream she had heard or seen the name—in Latin!—of one of the chemicals that would be burning in that hellish conflagration. She also informed me that at least three women, who did not know each other at the time, later reported having had dreams foretelling the fire.

On Monday I flew out of Basel to Zurich in order to catch my international flight for Boston. Doris, who had no ticket, accompanied me. No one questioned her. She shopped with me for souvenirs at the Zurich airport, and after that we each took off—she for Basel and I for Boston. Only later did I find out that Doris had no return ticket for Basel and no money either. But she made it!*

---

*In a recent phone conversation, Doris told me that when she approached the *contrôle* (checkpoint), two men asked to see her ticket. Since she didn't have one, they asked her how she got there. She replied, "Oh, I flew!" The men looked at her as if she were crazy and one of them said to the other in a sarcastic tone: "Oh, she *flew!*" Probably thinking she was a lunatic, they let her go. Such is the Luck of a Lusty Lunatic/Witch (Transatlantic telephone conversation, January 30, 1992).

On the plane I had Time to contemplate the foreground/Background contrasts that had pervaded the "atmosphere" of that trip. During the beautiful sunny days on Erika's island[18] and later in Switzerland we had been exposed to hazardous ultraviolet rays. The "fresh air" of the Villa Wenkenhof still contained residues of chemical contamination. The lives of the women I had met and re-met—brave, creative, joyous, Elemental women—were fraught with complex struggles to Survive against and in spite of the increasingly vile conditions of patriarchal oppression.[19] Our "Time out" at the luxurious Villa was also "Time in" our own Women's Space—to strategize, recoup, Spiral, and Spin. I came back more determined than ever . . . to Win.

CHAPTER NINETEEN

PATRIARCHY ON TRIAL: WHISTLE-BLOWING IN THE FOURTH SPIRAL GALAXY

It is so relaxing here on the Other side of the moon with my Feline and Bovine Familiars! With them around I can reflect with equanimity upon the events of the academented year 1988–89. They can see things in such clear perspective! So I shall gather my thoughts in their company, Now.

When I try to explain *academentia* to the cat and the cow they are dumbstruck. "What," they ask telepathically, "does *that* have to do with . . . Now?"

"Nothing," I reply. "That's why I have to expose it . . . in a Fourth Galactic Light. So I'll begin my *Logbook* Entries on that subject Now, tonight. You see, it is linked with the taming and killing of women and animals and all life—that is, with gynocide and biocide."

Wild Cat and Catherine, shocked and surprised, shut their eyes.

"That's why we came here, to where the coast is clear. We came to See and Name the connections. I shall begin by Momentous Re-membering of specific events. Catherine, assume your Familiar position, looking over my shoulder! Wild Cat, spring up to your favorite place, above the bookcase! All right, Cronies, I shall begin the grim and gory story, which, for us, can only end in glory."

WITCH TRIAL, JESUIT STYLE: *LOGBOOK* ENTRIES ON ACADEMENTIA, 1988–89

When I arrived back in Newton, after my Homecoming to Switzerland, I resumed my writing of *Outercourse*. Since I would be returning to teaching at Boston College in September, I worked as steadily as possible on this book throughout late July and August . . . And then I returned.

By that time Boston College had acquired an increasingly conservative student population. While much of this conservatism manifested itself simply in apathy, there were also aggressive archconservatives, ready to attack, as viciously as their capacities allowed, all those perceived as "radical" or "liberal."

I see that Catherine and Wild Cat are yawning. Yes, well to get on with it . . .

by courageous custodians the following morning. But that was just the beginning.

That morning demonstrators led by Mary Stockton, who was a key figure in all of the protests, marched into Gasson Hall, chanting and beating drums. They knocked on the office door of Dean Barth, knowing that he was inside, "protected" by campus police. When the door was not opened to them they decorated it with a sign containing one word: "Coward." They then paraded outside, where again an impressive demonstration was held on the steps of Gasson facing the library. There were excellent Radical Feminist musicians from Northampton, Massachusetts, who sang songs which they had written for the occasion. Rousing speeches were given by Joyce Contrucci and Bonnie Mann. A nameless figure, officially given a general title such as "the patriarchal enemy," but intended by some to represent certain key administrators, was burned in effigy. From all reports, a good time was had by all.

This was by no means the end of the protests. The students' energy and creativity were hardly exhausted. They felt "high" and empowered. So there was a fourth event, this time in the Dustbowl. They transformed a garbage can into an enormous cauldron and created the "fire" by pouring water over dry ice in the cauldron, which emitted vapors. Joyce Contrucci read a poem written specifically for the demonstration by Robin Morgan, who had mailed it from New Zealand. Joyce also read excerpts from the published *Crone-ology* of my treatment by Boston College.[8] And, of course, there was powerful chanting.*

Then women were invited to throw into the cauldron anything that they wanted to destroy—items representing patriarchal oppression. Each woman made a brief statement of explanation as she hurled her "thing" into the cauldron. Nicki Leone threw in a copy of her thesis, which she had written for her B.A. at Boston College. Others threw in such things as samples of pornography, copies of *The Observer* (BC's right-wing student paper), coat hangers, the bible, styrofoam containers, diet coke cans. Some BC men came over and spat on the women, attempting in various ways—unsuccessfully—to invade and interrupt the event.

Yet a fifth demonstration was held that April, when a group of students decided to hold a "read-in" of my books in the office of the theology department. They entered the office, arms loaded with books, and were promptly herded out. The door was shut in their faces while a campus police officer stayed in the office to guard its inhabitants. Undaunted, the students sat in the hall outside the door and read their favorite selections.

---

*The demonstrators appeared to have an almost inexhaustible supply of chants. Other specimens included: "Freedom to learn, freedom to be, denied to women at BC." Another was "Monan run, but you can't hide, while you're committing gynocide." And there was: "Yessir Professors are given clout, while Mary Daly is being starved out."

Within a week or two the academic year was coming to an end. On the foreground level I had lost, and patriarchal "justice" had prevailed. But had I really lost? The whistle had been blown on BC—nationally and internationally. There had been excellent media coverage.[9] Not only theologians, but also academics in other fields in the U.S. and abroad indicated their wholehearted support.[10] A published letter signed by members of the BC faculty indicated that some had risen to the occasion and could risk taking a stand against an administration which manifestly had no respect for intellectual merit or academic freedom.[11] A published letter signed by about thirty BC graduates (female and male) who had studied with me over the years Re-Called a history of support.[12] A moving letter signed by about forty Irish women scholars, writers, artists, and activists, expressing their disgust at Boston College's actions, exposed the fathers' hypocrisy and pseudo-Irish identity.[13] Innumerable letters from individuals, some of whom had studied with me, were sent to Boston College, with copies to me.[14]

Concomitant with this exposure was the hysteria of the catholic hierarchy about Radical Feminism. It is an interesting "coincidence" that as reported in March 1989 "the term 'radical feminism' surfaced more than once at a recent meeting of 35 U.S. prelates and Pope John Paul II and his Roman curia."[15]

Beyond foreground questions of "winning" and "losing," however, there is a deeper Question: Did all this brilliantly creative activity of resistance prepare the way for Something Else? Did it move women into Moments of Momentous Re-membering? I think the answer is . . . Yes.

For women who were Touched by the insurrection of women at Boston College there was a New Surge of Hope. We were encouraged to see that, in spite of the foreground Age of Dis-memberment of women and the environment, women could and would still Fight Back. And there is More . . . So much Gynergy was generated by these empowering actions that it spilled over into the creation of an Absolutely A-mazing Event—a Pyrotechnic display of Exorcism and Ecstasy which opened Windows and Doors to the Be-Dazzling Now.

The story of this Transcendent Event must Now be told.

LOGBOOK ENTRIES ON "THE WITCHES RETURN: PATRIARCHY ON TRIAL— A DRAMATIC INDICTMENT OF GYNOCIDE, 1989"

Throughout that academic year (1988–1989) countless gynocidal/biocidal atrocities had been reported locally and around the United States. I had continually stressed with my students that since patriarchal scholarship and professions commonly present interrelated events as if they were not connected with each other, they should constantly attempt to See and to Name the connections. That year presented us with an abundance of material to analyze. It was evident that many crimes against women were happening, that the war against women and nature was escalating.*

During that year I had, as usual, spoken at a number of universities.[16] Of particular significance was my visit to Virginia Tech in Blacksburg, Virginia, where I gave the Keynote address for Women's Week on April 6. There I met Evelyn Wight, a Feminist activist whose sister, Rebecca, had been murdered almost one year before (on May 13, 1988) on the Appalachian Trail in Pennsylvania while hiking with her lover, Claudia Brenner. When Evelyn introduced me at Virginia Tech that evening she spoke of the murder of her sister by a man "whose only motive was to destroy the image before him: Two strong women . . . together." Evelyn explained:

> Claudia Brenner's incredible physical strength and mental determination enabled her to hike four miles to the nearest road after being shot five times and still carrying three bullets in her body, and then hitchhike to the nearest police station. She refused attention to her wounds until she was certain the search for Rebecca had begun. They found Rebecca's body where Claudia had left her, covered with a sleeping bag to keep her warm.
>
> Rebecca was dead and the man who killed her was gone. He has since been found and sentenced. Claudia is alive and well today. But this is an unforgettable tragedy. I urge you never to forget it.

I went on and gave my Keynote address, but I could not forget Evelyn's words. Afterward without fully understanding why I was doing it, or how I could make my invitation become Realized, I asked Evelyn if she would come to Boston to speak if we could make it possible. I took her address and phone number, as if I could really make such an event happen. I Now Realize, of course, that the idea of "The Witches Return" was already brewing . . . subliminally.

Soon after that it became clear that it was Time to put patriarchy on trial. I envisioned an Event that would expose the gynocidal/biocidal atrocities and the connections among them, that would publicly bring the criminals to trial, and that would Conjure Nemesis. Women would have an opportunity

---

*Indeed many of my friends were making files of newspaper clippings about atrocities. Many of these occurred in March and/or April 1989: A twenty-eight-year-old woman who was a Wall Street investment banker was gang raped by eight youths, aged fourteen to seventeen, in April. Her skull was fractured by the youths, who used a pipe and a brick. They showed no remorse, sang a rap song, bragged about what they had done, and called their actions "fun." The body of the eighth woman victim of serial killings in the area of New Bedford, Massachusetts, was found that April. Within that time period, two women (Lesbians) from the Boston area who went on vacation together to a small Caribbean island were murdered on the beach there. The Exxon *Valdez* oil spill that spoiled Prince William Sound in Alaska occurred in late March. The two nuclear reactors close to Boston—the Seabrook, New Hampshire, reactor and "Pilgrim" in Plymouth, Massachusetts—were getting back into operation. The list can go on, and on.

to Hex the killers of women and nature and to experience and celebrate Ecstasy.

Together with Cronies and students I Brewed the Event which would be called "The Witches Return." We decided that it would be a women-only multimedia production and that it would be held in Sanders Theatre at Harvard University. The best date that we could arrange for the use of Sanders was Sunday, May 14, 1989, which happened to be Mother's Day.

"The Witches Return" was brought into be-ing through the creative work of strong Witches.[17] We planned the Event rapidly. In this Witch Trial the Witches would be the Judges and the Jury. The accused would be:

Larry Flynt, figurehead for the pornographers

Jack the Ripper, figurehead for serial killers

Exxon, figurehead for Earth-rapers of every kind

The Moronizing Media, figurehead for the Wit Dimmers of the world

Sigmund Freud, figurehead for all professional Mind-fuckers

Boss-town College, figurehead for the Brain-drainers of academia

His Nothingness of Rome and His Arrogance, Cardinal Flaw, figureheads for the Soul-killers of women.

We plotted the construction . . . and destruction of eight wooden dummies representing the accused, each of which would wear appropriate attire and have a suitable balloon head. For example, Larry Flynt would have a suit of $10,000 bills, and Boss-town College would be dressed as a football wearing a roman collar.[18] Gifted women were assigned to make the costumes and props for the cast. We also planned to have music and electrifying sound effects. Together with Joyce Contrucci I wrote the script. We had time for only two rehearsals.

On May 14 hundreds of women poured into Sanders Theatre. The opening address was given by Evelyn Wight, who Stunned the audience as she spoke calmly and movingly of the murder of her sister. At the conclusion of her speech I Pronounced a Nemesis Hex.* After Conjuring the Elemental Powers—Earth, Air, fire, Water—I Conjured also the Presence of Foresisters—Joan of Arc, Harriet Tubman, Matilda Joslyn Gage, Sojourner

---

* NEMESIS HEX:
  On the Earth, in the Air,
  Through the Fire, by the Water
  We are VENGEANCE, Hecate's daughters!

  For peace and love we ever yearned
  But some do wrong and never learn
  This Time it won't be us that burn
  The wrath of Nemesis is here!

> Hold their limbs and stop their mouths
> Seal their eyes and choke their breath
> Wrap them round with ropes of Death.

The entire Witches' Chorus rushed the accused, wrapping them with yarn to signify the muting of the mutilators. After this, as High Chaircrone, I sentenced these figureheads to *de*-heading.

"Off with their heads!" shouted the women, as the jailors, flourishing sharp-edged Labryses, descended upon the accused and popped their balloon heads. As one woman wrote: "The action, intense and furious, was like an enormous exhalation, breathing out pent-up Rage and frustration."[20]

There was an enormous relief of tension as the lights went out and the jailors dumped the de-headed figureheads behind their stand. Then we all left the stage. When the lights went on again Diana Beguine sang her inspiring song, "Celestial Time Tables." I spoke briefly about the Moments of Exorcism and Ecstasy that constitute the Spiral Galaxies of the Voyaging of Wild Women.

The entire cast returned on stage chanting: "POWER TO THE WITCH AND TO THE WOMAN IN ME." Then the whole audience joined in the chanting. As they left Sanders Theatre, with the sounds of "The Witching Hour" in their ears, women's eyes were shining.

As one woman said: "Patriarchy doesn't exist Here, Now."

This statement could have applied to the 1975 Forum on Women and Higher Education.[21] It could also have applied to the 1979 Rally, "We Have Done with Your Education."[22] Both the 1975 and the 1979 events were Sparkling triumphs over patriarchal oppression. They seemed to represent the utmost in transcendence at their respective Times. They were both Third Galactic phenomena.

In fact, however, this Stunning statement was made in 1989, because at this Time Something Other did happen. Our dramatic indictment was created with utterly Fiercely Focused Rage and Elemental, Creative Power. What conditions came together to allow us to bring this about?

On the foreground level the oppression of women and of nature was more atrocious and more obvious. We knew much more about the pornography industry and its vile effects, about serial killers, about the Earth-rapers. We knew more about connections, for example, between the mind-mutilating media and rape. Moreover academic and churchly malevolence did not escape being judged in this context of interconnectedness.

So in 1989, in the foreground Age of Dis-memberment, we Leaped into participation in Nemesis. We—the Witches—returned to judge and mete out the death punishment to the gynocidal killers of women's minds, bodies, and spirits. We Hexed them with Force and Fury. When we de-headed the dummies this was a Metaphor with Terrifying Power. The Witches of Boston had pronounced them GUILTY—without qualification.

Evelyn Wight had spoken to us of the very real, malignant killing of her sister.[23] The Daring Dramatic Production was regal, riotous, and Ragefull. We broke Terrible Taboos.

And after *this* event more than one woman actually did say: "Patriarchy doesn't exist Here, Now." Because this was a Moment, or rather, a cluster of Moments, of Be-Dazzling, many women entered a Door to Four. So it *is* Be-Dazzling Now, in the Expanding Now.

CHAPTER TWENTY

SAILING ON: PORTS OF RE-CALL
ON THE SUBLIMINAL SEA—
PORTS OF ENTRY
INTO THE EXPANDING NOW

Patriarchy does not exist in the Moments of the Expanding Now. It is there, however, in the foreground now. And it is there now, as much as or more than before.

In '89 we knew the score. In December it came, as they say, to the fore. The Montreal massacre ushered in an age of escalating gynocide.

THE GYNOCIDAL MASSACRE IN MONTREAL

On December 6, 1989, a smiling man wearing hunting clothes gunned down and killed fourteen women in the engineering school (École Polytechnique) at the University of Montreal with a semi-automatic rifle. He wounded nine more women in his rampage.* His objective was clear. When twenty-five-year-old Marc Lépine stalked into a classroom at the university he ordered the male students to one side of the room, lined up the women, and said to the latter, "You're all fucking feminists." He then ordered the men to leave and systematically gunned down six women. Lépine had begun by killing a female office worker. He fatally shot three women in the cafeteria and four others in another classroom. Witnesses stated that at one point, while stopping to reload his rifle, he stated, "I want the women." Lépine ended the slaughter by killing himself.

This was the worst mass murder in Canadian history. It was erased (not totally, of course) in the U.S. media. This partial—and therefore very effective—erasure was well noted by columnist David Nyhan in the *Boston*

---

*The press commonly reported that he wounded thirteen "people," while erasing the fact that nine of these were women. See, for example, the article "Massacre in Montreal" in *Newsweek*, December 18, 1989, p. 39.

Sunday Globe. In an article entitled "Shhh . . . 14 Women Were Slaugh-tered," Nyhan wrote:

> They were only women.
>   So it was not such a big deal.
>   Had it been one West German banker . . . or a US diplomat, or a politician from anywhere . . . or a baker's dozen of Blacks, Jews, gays, Palestinians, IRA bombers, Beirut street peddlers, fast-food patrons, airline passengers or vegetarians—I suspect much more would have been made of it. . . .
>   How this story was handled by the media says as much about the relative lack of worth of women as newsworthy victims as does the slaughter itself. . . . The big news is that terrorism against women is not real big news. Why? Because it's so common, ingrained, so garden-variety everyday.
>
>   What does it say about the status of women in 1989, not just that this could happen, but that it could be so quickly shunted off into the "nut" bin, as in: "Oh we don't want that for Page 1, for the top of the newscast, because it was just some nut with a gun, happens all the time"?*[1]

Of course, response to the Montreal massacre cannot be measured by reading/seeing/hearing the male-ordered media. Radical Feminists have our own Network, our own Reality. In Boston, for example, a New Women's Space was opened in December 1989 by Mary Stockton. It was/is known as Crones' Harvest.[2] Mary asked me to give the opening lecture there, on December 21. I spoke about gynocide, as manifested in the Montreal mas-sacre, calling out the names of the victims. We lit candles commemorating these women, and we summoned Courage in ourSelves to keep on fighting and to continue the Journey.[3]

OUTERCOURSING IN THE EARLY NINETIES

Throughout 1990 and 1991 I was on leave from teaching and continued working on *Outercourse*. As I traveled and spoke throughout the U.S., I met many, many women, and I was encouraged and inspired by their ideas and responses to the parts of *Outercourse* that I read or discussed.[4]

   There were visits to Europe that were of special importance for under-standing the Expanding Now. So I will write my *Logbook* entries on these trips as I sit in my workshop on the moon, Now, with the help, of course, of my cat and cow.

The Wall Street Journal, America's biggest newspaper, gave the story forty-seven words. *The New York Times* carried sketchy AP stories, on page 5 one day and on page 14 the next. ABC aired the story ten minutes into the newscast. The picture accompanying the *Newsweek* story is of two men attempting to help a wounded student. It is not immedi-ately clear that the student is a woman. At first glance, at any rate, this appears to be a picture of three men. See *Newsweek*, December 18, 1989, p. 39.

Green Logbook *Entries: Ireland Yet Again*

I departed from Boston's Logan Airport for Shannon, Ireland, on Thursday, September 27, 1990. I checked in at a B and B on Friday, where I was met by Ger Moane. On Saturday we drove to the familiar cottage at Bell Harbour near Finavarra. There we met Io, Marie, Joni, and Aileen. We made the rounds, visiting Mrs. Daly at her pub and Bridget Rose at Rose Cottage. Mrs. Daly gave us a round of free drinks and Bridget welcomed us warmly.

This Time Bridget had special information about the Daly family. She told me about "Castledaly," located between the towns of Gort and Loughrea in County Galway. Since Loughrea was the town in which I had had a power-ful experience of déjà vu in 1987,[5] I was excited to hear about this castle and its location. It was imperative that I go there.

Before going on to Castledaly, however, there was something else we all wanted to investigate—that is, the location of recent "hauntings." Bridget had been quite communicative this Time, so the directions were clear. She told us that within the last couple of years some "sensible lads" had met the ghost of a man wearing a top hat who tipped his hat. The location had been near the old ruined mill where Ger had had her unpleasant encounter with the huge spider in the summer of 1987.[6] It was also in the vicinity of Linnane's pub. So of course we went there. It was a rainy, chilly night and we met no one. But the spot was between Finavarra and Aughinish, which Biddy Early had said was "the most haunted place in all Ireland."

We were ready for a New adventure. So on Tuesday, October 2, we went on to Castledaly. After some searching we found it. The castle was in ruins. I spoke with some neighbors and was told that a Daly family in Dublin lived on that property in the summers in a mobile home. I wanted to see the place very badly, so with my friends I climbed over a fence or two and found mySelf in a Strangely familiar field.

The day was rainy—it was a light, misty rain—but I had to wander and run around on that land, around the trees and clumps of tall grass that had special colors and shapes that reminded me of . . . some distant home. The experience was Ecstatic. It was a Realization of a déjà vu experienced years ago in upper New York State. I was Now Seeing the "already seen" of that Time. I had arrived at a place I had Re-membered long ago—a meadow-like place of bliss. So it seems that I came full Spiral.[7]

Of course I tried to locate the particular Dalys in Dublin who lived there in the summer. I did not succeed. I am not sure whether that matters or even whether it matters if I ever go to Castledaly again. These are foreground details. The Real message is about Expanding Now. It is about Jumping off the calendar, off the clock—entering the Be-Dazzling Now.

We drove on in the rain, stopping for fast food and pushing on to the east. In Blessington I rented a room at the Downshire Hotel, and after dinner my friends went their separate ways for the night. When I was settling into my room I heard loud powerful bird noises. Opening the window I was greeted by absolutely Elemental sights and sounds. A flock of huge awesome dark birds was swooping by in the light of the full moon. They were cawing, Calling, Re-Calling their Ancestral Archaic sounds. They were reassuring, and they were Wild.

That weekend I stayed with Ann Louise Gilligan and Katherine Zappone at "The Shanty," which is their home as well as a center of Feminist activism in Brittas, County Dublin. My traveling companions—Joni, Aileen, Ger, Io, and Marie—and I were invited for dinner at "The Shanty Muse," a separate building believed to be on the site of a former "hedge school."[8] We made merry and became engaged in animated conversation. Ann Louise took me for a memorable drive and a walk through the extraordinarily beautiful nearby countryside. My visit at The Shanty was a Stunning conclusion to a trip that was yet an Other beginning on the Spiral of Expanding Now.

Logbook *Entries:*
Bologna, Italy . . . and Fribourg Again

In the fall of 1990 *Beyond God the Father* came out in Italian.[9] It is an excellent translation by Donatella Maisano and Maureen Lister. Its title sounds delightful in Italian: *Al di là di Dio Padre.* That fall I also published an article in *Leggere Donna,* an Italian Radical Feminist periodical.[10]

It was High Time that *Beyond God the Father* become accessible to women in Italy. In the article in *Leggere Donna* I explained my history of having been a student of catholic theology and philosophy in Fribourg and described my experience of "hanging around" in Rome during the Second Vatican Council, spying on the "godfathers" (roman catholic hierarchy), confronting some of them with questions. I also explained in that article why I thought it was crucial that *Beyond God the Father* be available in Italy in the 1990s: There has been a resurgence of the godfathers' power in Italy, as elsewhere. Moreover, this book does not belong to a forgotten past, but "contains ideas and images that I revisit over and over again as I Spiral farther out from the mindbindings and spiritbindings of patriarchy."[11] I stated that "we cannot Realize [our Elemental Spiritual powers] actively in the world without exorcising the Godfather [god the father] from our psyches."[12]

That fall plans were brewing to bring me to Bologna to give a public lecture a few months after the publication of *Beyond God the Father* in Italian. The First Italian Lesbian Week: "Un Posto per Noi" ("A Place for Us") was scheduled for May 1–5, 1991. I was asked to give a talk—open to all women —within the context of this Lesbian Week, in the Sala dei Notai, famed hall in the heart of the city. It felt absolutely right to me that I would be going to speak in Bologna.

A problem arose, which threatened to block the event, namely, the Gulf War. However, after a period of media-created hysteria over the danger of bombs in airports, the organizers and I decided the coast was clear. I went to Bologna armed with my talk, the title of which was "A Pirate in the Nineties—The Voyage of a Radical Feminist Philosopher."

I was met by Maureen Lister, one of the creators of Lesbian Week, who warmly welcomed me. There were soldiers with machine guns strutting around the airport, but I was not intimidated. I knew I was going to be part of a Momentous occasion. After a nap in my hotel I joined Maureen and the woman who had bravely agreed to translate my speech—Maria Louisa Moretti—who were waiting for me at a table in the hotel coffee shop. It was a comically memorable experience, sitting at that table, cutting up paragraphs and stringing the most translatable parts together with scotch tape. Maria Louisa, who had come to Bologna from Rome for the week's events, was nervous about her role as translator, but on the whole, I would say that our preparations were a hysterically funny episode.

On the evening of Friday, May 5, as I approached the Sala dei Notai to give my talk I was Stunned by the sounds of superb, Otherworldly drumming. Lilly Friedberg, who had driven down from northern Germany for the events of this week, accompanied by Io Ax, who came from Ireland, was standing on the steps of the building, beating out magical rhythmic sounds, welcoming women to this occasion.

As I walked up the steps with Maureen I Re-membered walking up the steps of the National Concert Hall with Ger Moane in Dublin in 1987 and hearing the magical music there. Yes, there it was, though in a different style—the Memory of women coming into our own again—Regally. Pirates coming into our own—in the Expanding Now.

I spoke about the meaning of Radical Feminism, about the Voyage of Crafty Pirates Sailing the Subliminal Sea, about the need for New Virtues, about bringing together Lesbianism and Radical Feminism—which is equivalent to the Dis-covering of Fire. I spoke about Moments of my Own Outercoursing Voyage through Galaxy after Galaxy, farther and farther into Realms of the Wild.

The women were Warm, Wild, and Wise. Their questions and comments were astute. They were Surviving in Italy, in the shadow of the Vatican. They *knew* about oppression of women. The Gynergy there was reminiscent of the energy in Ireland. It also seemed connected with the High Energy of the women in Germany that I had experienced in 1986. And it was definitely connected with the Gynergy in the U.S. in the seventies. The experience was yet an Other reminder of a phenomenon noted earlier in this book, namely, that when Radical Feminism seems to be "down" in one area, it may be Rising Furiously somewhere else.[13] And so, once again, as Voyager/Pirate I am using my Craft Now to carry Tidings/Messages of such varying conditions to Cronies, "reporting my observations of shiftings of the Tides in the Subliminal Sea."[14]

In the course of "Un Posto per Noi," connections were made among women from all over Italy and from many countries. Artists, musicians, writers—Witches of all kinds—shared ideas and images. A Be-Witching closing party was held on the final night at the "home base" of the event—Villa Guastavillani—where Lilly's drumming once again resounded through the halls. The First Italian Lesbian Week was a fantastic success! It was, I think, a harbinger of further Fourth Galactic phenomena.

This event, combined with the New appearance of *Al di là di Dio Padre* speaks volumes about The Fourth Spiral Galaxy. It demonstrates how the Expanding Now encompasses the Moving Past and the Emerging Future in the Be-Dazzling Present. It shows how Doors to Four keep opening and opening, enlarging the Spacious Now.

At the end of the week I went by train with Io to Fribourg. Io had crossed over by boat from Ireland to Germany, where she had arranged to meet Lilly and catch a ride with her to Bologna. It was not only pleasant but also Fourth Galactically important that Io and I made the Journey to Fribourg together.

After what was for me an Ecstatic return trip to Switzerland we arrived in Fribourg and checked into a hotel. The next day we walked down toward the *basse ville* and stopped at a café. Since the subjects of "11:12" and "the little Green Man in my head" were very much on my mind, I began discussing this complex Metamystery with Io, explaining that in my life the two phenomena have been connected. I told her that the "11:12" experience began shortly after my mother's death and continues to involve a variety of "encounters" with clocks and watches whose hands "happen" to have arrived at that Time. I described "the little Green Man" as an imaginary entity whose function—ever since high school and/or college—had been that of Time-keeper. Of course, in hindsight it seems inappropriate that this was a male figure. Except . . . This is patriarchy. So it is not surprising that as an adolescent I imagined this personage as male.

I had thought that "he" was peculiar to me. Years later I discovered that manifestations and depictions of "Green Man" are widespread phenomena.[15] And Io informed me that "Green Man" is all over England—on door knockers, on walking sticks, and, as many report, in the trees. She also told me some of her experiences of Time—Dreams and Visions—and of Green Man.

We both wanted to Search for *Green Women*. We *knew* that they must be everywhere. Under patriarchy people are trained *not* to see such images. The erasure is so total that Green Women—like all Goddesses, Witches, Crones—have been difficult to perceive. I wanted to bring back Green Woman/Green Women from the depths of the Subliminal Sea—back into the Be-Dazzling Light, where we can See.

the little sir nothings have killed the ozone, manufacturing the nozone.[6] combined with the "global warming" they've cooked up, and with massacred rain forests, dis-membered women and animals and trees, and poisoned seas—it's a hell they've made. far worse than the hells of their holy religions.

the necrophiliac "right-to-lifers"—the same cast of vampires, mainly— are at home in the nozone, the no-life zone where the "babies" they mourn can be born to rot. and the women begin to die in back alleys, again.[7]

the millionaire/billionaire right-wing ghouls, their souls gangrenous and stinking with greed, feed on the nozone, making their grabs and gropes for more. The would-be millionaire/billionaire robots follow the score, so they too can get more. more of what? the nozone. the disarmed armies of the homeless, the impoverished sick and aged, grow. more kids are shot to death . . . in school.

the ultimately unnatural becomes the norm (as in "desert storm"). that's the master plan.[8]

that's the normal macho point of view. what else is new? what's the big news? just that there's more of it. exponentially increasing. torture and slaughter of women. torture and slaughter of people of color. torture and slaughter of earth. gynocide, genocide, biocide. it's a roller coaster ride . . . into oblivion.

and there's more on my floor . . . more—always more—on the fore-ground now.

LOGBOOK ENTRIES ON THE FIRST INTERGALACTIC INTERDISCIPLINARY CONGRESS ON THE OTHER SIDE OF THE MOON

I have torn the clippings to shreds. I shall turn my attention to Now. I shall Fiercely Focus on Expanding our Auras, our O-Zones Now. As I roar these words to the cat and the cow I hear a thundering of hooves and feet. I hear a blaring of trumpets and a rolling of drums. Oh, I know what's hap-pening—Here they come! My colleagues and Cronies who toil in their workshops on the Other side of the moon have heard my howling. They've been howling too. The Message swirls around among us: It's Time to hold a Congress on the Other side of the moon. Sooner than Soon.

The Message flies around: We will meet in a conveniently located crater—a large and inspiring "walled plain." We Hear the Call and we Re-Call the Call. Now is the Time; Here is the Place—out in Space. Not so very far out, of course. We are Intergalactic Voyagers all, and could think of star trips millions of light years away. But that's not for today. We want to meet close to the earth, our Home, and our view of her is clear from Here.

I am Now being asked by some of the organizers of this event to write *Logbook* Entries on this "First Intergalactic Interdisciplinary Congress on/of Crones, Cronies, and Their Familiars." They are also asking me to give the

Final Keynote Address, "summing up" and reflecting upon the Elemental Philosophical and Metapolitical import of this Archimagical event. I am honored to accept this invitation, and propose as the title of my own address, "The Great Summation." I Be-Laughingly inform them that I've begun *Logbook* Entries already, anyway. I shall be glad to continue writing these, and to share them with Cronies everywhere.

There are thousands of Cronies gathering with our Crafts, and there are thousands of Fantastic Familiars. The latter immediately begin to organize their own Congress, the Moment we arrive. One who looks something like an armadillo is loudly addressing a crowd, telling them how she Survives and how she Acts as Familiar and Friend of an Amazonian Witch. Wild Cat and Catherine are Wild-Eyed, staring in awe at Other Friendly Familiars. One large baboon, incessantly scratching, has caught the attention of Catherine, who is trying to mimic her, lifting one hoof to her chest. Oops! She falls over. Well, she did her best. A huge gorilla is helping her to her feet and—my Word!—beginning to groom her. These Animals are remarkably sweet and attentive to each Other.

Oh! I see Granuaile—that old Pirate! Of course she's speaking in sixteenth-century Irish, but I think I can say a word or two. "Well, *Céad Míle Failte* (a hundred thousand welcomes), dear Foresister, to you, too!"

Because of Granuaile's status as Transtemporal Pirate, we've just unanimously chosen her to be a Keynote speaker at this Intergalactic Congress of Subliminal Sea Sailors on the moon. We speak literally hundreds of languages from all places and times on planet earth,* but our communication is greatly facilitated by our ability to speak to and understand each other telepathically. So Granuaile has no need of a translator.

For the reader of *Outercourse*, however, I shall gladly serve as translator of Granuaile's remarks. I cannot convey every detail, but I shall do my best to give the gist of her address. Since the readers as well as the writer of this book can be presumed to speak English, I shall employ *Webster's Third New International Dictionary of the English Language* as an aid in translation.

Granuaile is standing on the Speaker's Rock, beginning her address. She is speaking of "The Great Summoning." Her discourse is multileveled and encompasses many meanings of the verb *summon*. She points out, first, that *summon* means "to issue a call to convene: CONVOKE." She explains that The Great Summoning is a Call to Pirates/Subliminal Sea Sailors to convene in the Expanding Now. This Call to convene, she says, is not from any single woman only, not from any "authority," but from all of us who Re-Call Now together.

---

*I think it is important to note here that I have observed a number of participants who do not appear to be earthlings and who do not claim this identity. My understanding is that they are Cosmic Radical Feminist Voyagers who have met and joined our group along the Milky Way and even farther away, in Other Galaxies. We have come together because of Mutual Attraction and Intergalactic Interaction.

She continues by explaining that *summon* also means "to call upon for action." She says we are preparing ourSelves here, on the Other side of the moon, for specified action on our home planet, earth. Yes, we need our workshops on the moon to gain peace and Intergalactic perspective. But we must also continue to commute frequently to Act and Fight and Create on our respective Boundaries on the home planet. We have come here so we can Stand our Ground there. Since we all have our Crafts, this commute is not only instantaneous but also Momentous. And, she says with great emphasis, this is all part of continuing our Intergalactic Voyaging, Expanding Now in The Fourth Spiral Galaxy . . . and, well, perhaps beyond that.

Granuaile is Now pausing. She is raising her arms toward the sky. She is holding her arms toward us and then raising them again, as if summoning the Powers within and without. Then she roars with all her might, Re-Calling that *summon* also means "to evoke, especially by an act of the will: stir or bring to activity: call forth; call up; bring together: CONJURE, AROUSE."

She howls: "Let us summon our Rage. Let us summon our Grief. Let us summon our Disgust. Let us summon our Elemental Powers. It is Time to Act. It is Time to Act together. It is Time to call forth Nemesis!"

The thousands of women are Now standing. We solemnly intone:

> For peace and love we ever yearned,
> But some do wrong and never learn;
> This Time it won't be us that burn;
> The Wrath of Nemesis is Here!

Now the Animals are intoning their own Nemesis Hex. I'd like to be able to translate it, but I don't know how. Oh, it is so powerful, so beautiful, so harmonious, so cacophonous! The frogs, the tigers, the seals, the emus, the elephants, the canaries, the raccoons, the wolves, the whales, the bears, the bats, the squirrels . . . and the trillions of insects and birds. All are chanting their own Words. It must be heard to be Heard. But take my Word for it. Their combined Hexing is enough to grind the foolocrats to dust. And that isn't all. They also harmonize with the Music of the Spheres. They Call and Call and Re-Call . . . Hope. Their Hexing is tough enough to Summon Life.

After the Animals grow silent, Granuaile speaks again. "The Animals have said it. Let us bring forth Life again on earth. We are all Pirates. We have all Sailed the Subliminal Sea. We know the secrets of that Sea. We must summon in Others the Courage to See, to Break Through the Mist, to plunder what is Rightfully ours, and Sail on."

The applause for Granuaile is loud and long. After a brief pause we all call for Hypatia, the great philosopher, mathematician, and astronomer of Alexandria in Egypt, requesting her to Be-Speak. With grace and swiftness of movement, her Aura emanating Intellectual and Moral Power, Hypatia strides to the Speaker's Rock. The whole assembly is aglow with excitement, thrilled to be Here to Hear this eloquent, inspiring teacher.

Hypatia begins: "As some of you know, I was a teacher of philosophy in ancient Alexandria. I taught there in the early part of the fifth century. My students came from all over, because, as you know, word spreads rapidly when there is a teacher somewhere who is actually *interested* in ideas and in communicating them to others. I'm sure many of you understand what I mean!"

The Congress participants laugh uproariously.

Hypatia continues: "And because I was excited by ideas and actually communicated them convincingly, some men who were considered great 'authorities,' including a certain bishop in particular—one Cyril of Alexandria—hated and envied me. They wanted me dead. Those ecclesiastical bureaucrats!"

The audience hisses and groans.

Hypatia laughs. "But you must understand that it was because they knew that they themselves were not very bright! I was not merely 'following the leader,' but actually 'taking off' with my own ideas, and that was too much for them.

"I was and am a Self-identified Pagan Philosopher. You could even call me a Nag-Gnostic Philosopher. There were some churchy types in my classes, who were gradually becoming anxious and suspicious—hateful, even. After I became the head of the Neoplatonist school in Alexandria, some churchmen came to hate me even more than before. They sensed that I was out of their control—that I had broken a Terrible Taboo, and had become a truly autonomous thinker. So they sent a mob to murder and dismember me. I have read in tomes of history that parts of my body were strewn all over Egypt."[9]

The entire audience gasps in horror. There is loud wailing and snarling.

"But my dear friends," says Hypatia, standing proud and tall, "I'm all together Here and Now. I have learned to turn the hate around, and in the Background I still Stand my Ground . . . more Fiercely than before."

Hypatia goes on Be-Speaking strongly and encouragingly to the Congress. "As you know, we are Here to eclipse the foreground now, which is in the most advanced stage of the demonic dis-ease of fragmentation. This is the Stage/Age of Dis-memberment.

"It is no accident that I am Here with you Now. (I Jumped Here, too, as did the cow.) As Crone who has been around . . . and around, I have always Stood my Ground, even unto and beyond dis-memberment."

The philosopher roars Fiercely: "Through and beyond this time of escalating dis-memberment, I call for Re-membering Now!"

After the roars of the crowd subside, Hypatia says: "I see that our Sister, Susan B. Anthony, wishes to speak. Come forward, Susan!"

Susan rushes forward, mounting the Speaker's Rock. "Failure is Impossible!" cries that great crusader. After the applause abates, she says: "I did not fully Realize the meaning of those words when I said them in the nineteenth century. You see, my contemporaries and I could not then fully see the multiracial, multiclass, and planetary dimensions of the women's movement. Nor was it possible to know that our Sister Earth is in mortal danger. And so we could not fully enter the Age of Cronehood of Radical Feminism. We did not know that the Age of Dis-memberment was almost upon us."

Susan continues: "I Now understand the profound connection between the destruction of women and the destruction of the earth. Thus I have joined the New Cognitive Minority of women who Live in the Age of Cronehood. Within this Cognitive Minority there is a Memory-Bearing Group, to which I belong. We are Crones who have 'been around.' Consequently we can Re-Call earlier Moments. Moreover, we can *bear* the memories, learn from them, and open the way for Change. As a result of my Crone-logical Time/ Space Voyaging I am Here to Proclaim that Feminism and Ecology are interconnected. Speaking from this context to this Congress, I am able to say, with Re-Newed confidence, that if you have the Other side of the moon in your head and in your heart you can trust that, in truth, failure is Impossible!"

The entire gathering again breaks into cheers, as well as tears. Then Susan Announces: "Our Sister, Harriet Tubman, has important Words for us Now."

The impressive, dark, ancient Crone approaches the Speaker's Rock. Harriet proclaims: "If you have the Other side of the moon in your head and in your heart you can strategize in Strange ways! You can beat them by means of clever games."

The audience listens in awed silence.

"When I was working on the 'Underground Railroad,' together with Other antislavery stalwarts, I sometimes had warning signals in my head, and I listened to them. At least once I took my party of sisters and brothers and boarded a *southbound* train. I figured no one would suspect us if we were traveling in *that* direction!"

The whole Congress chortles with glee.

Harriet smiles and continues. "If you are a Life Lover, if you are a Dreamer, a Schemer, and a Moonlighter, then you can become Brighter. And before long you are . . . an Invincible Fighter."

The audience is visibly and audibly excited.

Now Harriet pauses. We all Sense that she is about to say something A-mazing. She announces: "I Now propose an Underground Railroad to the Other side of the moon."

The audience is keenly interested.

"Many of our Sisters are still bound in chains," she proclaims. "Worst of all, there are chains on their brains. We must help them catch moonbeams. We must rouse them soon, in the dark of the moon. We must show them our Daring, Wayfaring Ways. We must serve as their Guides. We must help them catch rides on our Crafts that Sail High, to the Other side of the moon. Soon!"

"Now!" cries the cow, the cow who Jumped over the moon.

"Catherine!" I shout. "That's impolite!" But Harriet laughs in pure delight. "The cow is right!" she exclaims. "We'll start tonight!"

And everyone agrees.

Harriet Tubman continues: "I propose as my Partner and Co-Guide for the New expeditions to the Other side of the moon our brilliant and intrepid Native American Sister, Sacajawea, a woman with an unerring Sense of Direction."

The crowd roars approval and calls for Sacajawea—whose name in Hidatsa means "Bird Woman," and in Shoshoni, "Boat Woman."

The powerfully built woman proudly steps forward. She says: "As many of you have heard, I was captured as a slave in my girlhood. Hence I know about chains—chains on the brain. I am known in history books as the one who served as interpreter and guide of the Lewis and Clark expedition to the Pacific Northwest. Of course I had no choice. I did not wish to be the servant of white men.[10] I was young, strong, and adventurous, and I had hopes of seeing my people—the Shoshoni—again. Moreover, I knew how to follow the trails through the mountains, and I longed to see what was on the Other side. I had been told that there was a great ocean, and in my heart I longed to see the sea. Now I wish to use my skills to guide women through the Mist and across the Sea, the Subliminal Sea. I long to speak with them and to bring them to the Other side of the moon. Soon. Or, as the cow says, Now."

While Sacajawea has been addressing the Gathering, a subtle change has come about in the individual and combined Auras of the listening women and their Familiars. There is a tangible Benevolent Presence, a Magnificent Intelligence Here, Now. We are all dumbstruck, as we wait for Her to speak.

My work as translator will be difficult Now. Spider Woman is Here and she is Be-Speaking. She communicates in Other ways, through Other Senses. I shall try to convey her message, which I Sense in our changing Auras. (What an assignment!)

Spider Woman, who is also Thinking Woman, says the world is her brainchild. She began creation by Spinning two threads, east-west, and north-south. Hence the world is divided into four quarters. She says that the sun and the moon are her daughters. Spider Woman says that several Times she has remade the world, as spiders do their webs. She says that she saves only those Wise Ones who keep in contact with her by means of the invisible strands spun to the tops of their heads.[11]

Gazing around Now I see that all of the Cronies and all of the Animals at this Congress on the Other side of the moon do have Luminous strands spun to the tops of our heads. These had been invisible to me before, but since Spider Woman "arrived" (became manifest) the vibrations Here have changed, and the strands have become visible—like moonbeams. So I understand that it is Spider Woman, Primordial One, who is drawing us to the Other side of the moon, her daughter. Here we must Realize our Powers of Spinning so that we can work with her as she remakes the world . . . again.

THE GREAT SUMMATION

Now in this Luminous Gathering there is a Sense in each and in all of us that it is Time for The Great Summation. We express the "sum total" of our Grief by Wailing and of our Rage by Railing.[12] When—save for a few sobs and curses—the noise subsides, many Sisters at the Congress call out names of women whom they hold in esteem. I hear the name of Jiu Jin of China, great woman warrior, poet, fighter for women's rights. I also recognize the name of Hatshepsut, Imposing Queen of ancient Egypt. Multitudes of women are honoring the Amazons of Dahomey in Africa. I hear loud praise for the Australian writer and suffragist Miles Franklin, and for such women of accomplishment as Joan of Arc, Simone de Beauvoir, and Rachel Carson. Hundreds of names are called, and cheers arise from all quarters of the crater.

I stride to the Speaker's Rock and commence my own oration. The following is a summation of my "Great Summation."

> We must not think of our powers to change the world merely by "summing up" our numbers, even though our First Intergalactic Interdisciplinary Congress is impressive in size. Rather, we should focus on our enormous Diversity within our Unity. We are not merely four thousand, or forty thousand, or even forty million. We cannot think that way, because of the enormous variations among us. We are not merely, say, one hundred thousand members within the same "species." We are more like a hundred thousand species. And the more we recognize and develop our unique Elemental powers, the more powerfully we can communicate with each other and Act in the world.
>
> Certain definitions in Webster's may serve to convey my meaning. One definition of summation is "cumulative action or effect; specifically: the process by which a sequence of stimuli that are individually inadequate to produce a response are cumulatively able to induce a nerve impulse." Well, the "nerve impulse" required is the excitement/incitement of women's spirits to Biophilic Actions that defy and overcome the frozen inertia induced by the foreground now. Simply put, it is the Impulse to be Nervy, that is, Bold and Intrepid, showing calm Courage in actions that can transform a necrophilic world.
>
> Because of our Diverse and Varied talents, our Biophilic Energy can increase exponentially. Each variable "factor" depends upon other variable "factors." Hence, I Dare say, each Variable Actor (Unique Biophilic Woman) "depends upon" and is connected with Other Variable Factors/Actors.
>
> In Other words, together, Moonstruck, Metamorphosing Intergalactic Voyagers can change our world. The Great Summation requires cumulative negation of the nothingness of the state of necrophilia (patriarchy). The Great

Summation is following our Final Cause, Realizing our participation in Be-ing. It is cumulative affirmation and celebration of Life.

My very Naming of this phenomenon seems to transmit a Nerve Impulse that darts like Lightning from one Nervy Nagster to an Other. Our Auras are glowing.

The exponential increase of our Energy, which is needed for continuing to Re-member Now, requires more and more Daring and Drastic Action. We must keep on Spiraling farther Out, that is, Outcoursing. We must move on in our Inter-galactic Voyaging. Only in this way can we accurately ascertain our Cosmic Context, continuing to chart the way for Others.

We must have our workshops on the Other side of the moon, and we will have Congresses Here again when the Times are right for these. But we must com-mute continually to earth, working to free our Sisters, carrying on the Fight for Life on earth. Bringing together our many centuries of study and action—as philosophers, astronomers, poets, warriors, healers, musicians, activists, teachers, Survivors of the sadosociety, and Agents of Nemesis—we must convey the Momentous Message. Susan has said it well: "Failure is Impossible!"

"Failure is Impossible!" we all shout out together.

In the blink of an Eye we set off through the sky. We will do or die . . . or do *and* die. But we won't be defeated, ever.

NOTES

INTRODUCTION:
THE SPIRALING MOMENTS OF *OUTERCOURSE*

1. Nancy Kelly first thought of the title *Outercourse* during a conversation we had on a return trip from Rockport, Massachusetts, to Boston one starry night in the fall of 1987. Earlier that day we had been discussing Andrea Dworkin's new book, *Intercourse*, since I had recently received the manuscript. We had moved on to other subjects, and I was then telling Nancy my ideas for a New work, which I was ready to begin pondering, since the *Wickedary* had just been completed. I was describing my ideas of the Intergalactic Voyage of the New book, which would be about the course my life and ideas have taken and are taking. We started to discuss possible titles which would contain the word *course*. I remember that Nancy began intoning, as if in a trancelike state, "Intercourse, Intracourse, Innercourse, Outercourse . . ." "*Outercourse*! That's it, of course!" I yelled. The title was perfect. In a later discussion, Nancy Re-Called her visual experience. She had been looking out the car window at the stars and had seen in her mind's Eye a moving elliptic form in the sky (Telephone conversation, March 11, 1991). The absolute rightness of her intuition was Stunning. The subliminal joke theme—the play on the utterly different foreground term, *intercourse*—was also highly amusing.

2. See *Websters' First New Intergalactic Wickedary of the English Language*, Conjured by Mary Daly in Cahoots with Jane Caputi (Boston: Beacon Press, 1987; London: The Women's Press Ltd, 1988), especially pp. 279–84.

3. Conversation, Newton Centre, Massachusetts, June 1987.

4. Virginia Woolf, *Moments of Being: Unpublished Autobiographical Writings*, ed. and with an introduction and notes by Jeanne Schulkind (New York: Harcourt Brace Jovanovich, 1976), p. 71.

5. Conversation with Jane Caputi, Newton Centre, Massachusetts, June 1988.

6. William J. Kaufmann III, *Galaxies and Quasars* (San Francisco: W. H. Freeman and Company, 1979), p. 76.

7. See Mary Daly, *Gyn/Ecology: The Metaethics of Radical Feminism* (1978; reissued with a "New Intergalactic Introduction by the Author," Boston: Beacon Press, 1990; London: The Women's Press Ltd, 1979, 1991), pp. 1–34.

8. Correspondence on "Women and the Church," *Commonweal* (February 14, 1964), p. 603. See Chapter Four.

9. George Orwell, *1984* (New York: New American Library, 1949), p. 32.

CHAPTER ONE:
EARLY MOMENTS: MY TABOO-BREAKING QUEST—
TO BE A PHILOSOPHER

1. This was Sister Athanasia Gurry, C.S.J., who taught me English throughout my four years of high school at St. Joseph's Academy in Schenectady.

14. One of the battles fought by this organization was its struggle for many years against genital mutilation of women in Africa. These women fought tirelessly —long before the "Second Wave" of Feminism—on behalf of their sisters in Africa. They made information available through their newsletter, *The Catholic Citizen*, and petitioned and lobbied agencies of the United Nations.

15. Although this was an excruciating experience of loss, I Now think it was ultimately a Life-saver. Had I been able to settle down in South Bend and study at Notre Dame, I could have been too comfortable. I would not have been driven to cross the ocean to study in Fribourg. My Be-Dazzling Voyage might indeed have been cut short and tamed into a sort of boat tour or cruise for successful academics.

16. Years later, when I read that prolonged thirst was one of the most effective forms of torture inflicted upon women accused of Witchcraft during the witchcraze in Western Europe, I was able to empathize, even though I have never been forced to endure excruciating physical thirst. During a conversation with Emily Culpepper (Long Beach, California, May 1988) which occurred as I was reading a draft of this part of the manuscript of *Outercourse* to her, she described her own experience of years of stress as feeling heavy stones laid on her chest. Her anxiety had been over finding an appropriate teaching job. When the job materialized, the stones miraculously dematerialized. Emily also had connected her experience of psychic torture (in this case from Feminist-hating academics) with the physical torture of our Foresisters, the Witches. So we had a shared experience of Metamemory.

17. After passing my letter around from one bureaucrat to another—each one "responding" to me that I should write to some other official—they finally did send a curt rejection.

CHAPTER THREE:
STUDENT DAYS IN EUROPE: METAPHYSICAL ADVENTURES
AND ECSTATIC TRAVELS

1. See Thomas Aquinas, *Summa theologiae* I, Q. 30, a. 2. The precise title of the "article" is: "Utrum in Deo sint plures personae quam tres?"—"Whether There Are More Than Three Persons in God?" The actual "problem" for Aquinas and countless other theologians, however, really did boil down to the fact that since they believed that there are four "relations" in God there should, according to a certain logic, be four persons, because a "person" (in God) is a relation. The arguments were long and agonizing. Rereading the article Now convinces me that I must have been in a Stoned/Stunned State to have followed the, uh, logic. Suffice it to say here that behind it all was a complex and elaborate tension between the importance of "three" and "four." Aquinas had to rationalize the "Divine Trinity," or threeness, because that was a dogma of the church. The idea of "Four Divine Persons" was heretical and therefore unthinkable.

2. Unfortunately, the doctoral diploma from St. Mary's was overly modest and feminine. Unlike the large and pompous diplomas from Catholic University and from Fribourg, which were in Latin, the St. Mary's document was small and entirely in English. Worst of all, it was adorned with a little gold seal attached to blue and white ribbons. The ribbons, in particular, had elicited the laugh/sneer of the esteemed professor.

3. Mary Daly, *The Church and the Second Sex* (1968; reissued with an "Auto-biographical Preface to the 1975 Edition" and a "Feminist Postchristian Introduc-

tion," 1975; reissued with a "New Archaic Afterwords," Boston: Beacon Press, 1985), p. 8.

4. Having only recently rediscovered my *Tabella Scholarum*, or record of courses taken, I realize that I had already begun taking philosophy courses at the University of Fribourg in the fall of 1961, while just beginning the theological dissertation, in anticipation of obtaining the doctorate in *philosophy*—years before I actually knew that goal was realistically and financially possible to attain.

5. This means that I was already Moving in the Craft of the Fourth Dimension. That is, I was experiencing an incipient Presence of The Fourth Spiral Galaxy. Through these vivid experiences I was even then retracing earlier Moments with a Pen of Light. See Chapter Six.

6. The word *modernism* has a number of meanings. *Webster's* succinctly defines the roman catholic usage as "a system of interpretation of Christian doctrine developed at the end of the 19th century and condemned by Pope Pius X in 1907 that denied the objective truth of revelation and the whole supernatural world and maintained that the only vital element in any religion and Catholicism in particular was its power to preserve and communicate to others the best religious experiences of the race."

CHAPTER FOUR:
PHILOSOPHICAL CONCLUSIONS AND BEGINNING BE-SPEAKING:
THE SUMMONS TO WRITE *THE CHURCH AND THE SECOND SEX*

1. Correspondence on "Women and the Church," *Commonweal* (February 14, 1964), p. 603.

2. Mary F. Daly, "Catholic Women and the Modern Era," in *Wir schweigen nicht länger!—We Won't Keep Silence Any Longer!*, ed. by Gertrud Heinzelmann (Zurich: Interfeminas Verlag, 1965), pp. 106–10.

3. Mary Daly, "A Built-In Bias," *Commonweal* LXXXI (January 15, 1965), pp. 508–11.

4. Daly, "Autobiographical Preface to the 1975 Edition," *The Church and the Second Sex*, p. 11.

5. My philosophical dissertation was published the next year as a book: Mary F. Daly, *Natural Knowledge of God in the Philosophy of Jacques Maritain* (Rome: Catholic Book Agency, 1966). Even though I had completed all work for the doctorate in July 1965, I was granted only a "Certificat Provisoire" (Provisional Certificate) at that time. This document stated that "according to the regulations regarding the doctoral examination Mademoiselle Mary F. Daly will not have the right to use the title 'Doctor' until after remittance of the Diploma, which will be delivered to her upon reception of 150 printed copies of the Dissertation. This Provisional Certificate is valid for only two years." What this meant was that I was obliged to self-publish and donate 150 copies of my dissertation to the library in order to have evidence that I had earned the degree, and that if I didn't manage to accomplish this within two years, well, that was my loss! It seems that the library used these dissertations in an exchange system with other libraries in order to build up its collection. As for the "Catholic Book Agency," to which I paid several hundred dollars (a fortune to me at the time), I never recouped any of my investment, even though apparently my book was rather widely distributed/sold to libraries in Europe and America.

6. For further astonishing details, see my "Autobiographical Preface to the 1975 Edition," *The Church and the Second Sex*, pp. 5–14.

7. The right of all Swiss women to vote on the Federal level was not won until February of 1971. This victory was largely due to the untiring work of such Feminists as Gertrud Heinzelmann. As of this writing, the women living in the Canton of Apenzell still cannot vote on the local level.

CHAPTER FIVE:
SPIRALING BACK TO BOSTON AND BEYOND

1. There did *exist* such classic analyses as Virginia Woolf's *A Room of One's Own* (1929) and *Three Guineas* (1938)—works of Pure Genius. The point is that these were not taught or even mentioned in my college or graduate school classes. Nor, of course, were the studies and critiques by such brilliant women as Mary Astell, Mary Wollstonecraft, Frances Wright, Margaret Fuller, Matilda Joslyn Gage, Charlotte Perkins Gilman, or Mary Ritter Beard. Because of this erasure, none of these women's thoughts were *really* accessible to me, or to most other women "privileged" to have a patriarchal education (the only formal education available).

2. Daly, "Autobiographical Preface to the 1975 Edition," *The Church and the Second Sex*, pp. 11–13.

3. My analysis of "spooking" is developed in *Gyn/Ecology*. My own experiences, such as this one, gave me important raw material for Dis-covering this mechanism and the many levels of its operation.

4. During 1968 I spoke mainly to religious groups and at catholic colleges, e.g., The College of Saint Rose in Albany, New York, Assumption College in Worcester, Massachusetts, Marist College in Poughkeepsie, New York, Emmanuel College in Boston, Massachusetts, Mount St. Scholastica College in Atchison, Kansas. I gave a week of lectures on the theology of Paul Tillich to clergy at a Pastoral Institute at Immaculate Conception Seminary in Conception, Missouri, and I spoke to the National Conference of Major Superiors of Religious Women in Chicago. I was also "branching out" to secular schools, such as Rutgers University in Camden, New Jersey, and the University of Michigan in Ann Arbor. 1969 was the year I began delivering sermons, for example, at Boston University's Marsh Chapel and at the Community Church of Boston. I was still running around the country speaking at catholic colleges, e.g., St. John's in Cleveland, Rivier in Nashua, New Hampshire, St. Bernard's in Alabama, Marylhurst in Oregon, La Salle in Philadelphia, and Merrimack in North Andover, Massachusetts. That year also I lectured at a few noncatholic institutions, e.g., New York University, Radcliffe College, Brandeis University, and Harvard Divinity School. It is thought-provoking to realize that a number of the catholic colleges at which I spoke are now defunct.

5. As *Outercourse* goes to press it is twenty-three years since that seminar with the "futurist" took place. I still feel compelled to tell the story. One could say that my Hearing of that talk was something like being given a mandate from the Background through this foregrounding fellow to expose the plot and to Name it.

6. See Hannah Tillich, *From Time to Time* (New York: Stein and Day, 1973), especially p. 14.

7. Mary Daly, "Mary Daly on the Church," *Commonweal* XCI (November 14, 1969), p. 215.

8. Mary Daly, "The Problem of Hope," *Commonweal* XCII (June 26, 1970), p. 316.

9. For a detailed report of this event, see "Appendix K: Report of the National Conference on the Role of Women in Theological Education," in *Women's Liberation and the Church,* edited with Introduction by Sarah Bentley Doely (New York: Association Press, 1970), pp. 135–45.

10. Our "research design" for the proposed "Institute on Women" (which later came to be known as "The Women's Institute" and as "The Women's Theological Coalition," and finally as "The Women's Caucus") targeted the fields of theology, ethics, sociology of religion, and church history as major areas for analysis and research concerning the problems and oppression of women. We outlined a curriculum for Women's Studies within the BTI. Our report from this national conference also included careful guidelines for hiring of a woman who would be a trained, competent, and fully committed director of the proposed Institute.

11. There was considerable diversity in my public lectures in 1970. I continued to give sermons, e.g., at the Wellesley College Chapel and at the Charles Street (Boston) Meeting House, and spoke at a variety of churches including the First Parish Church in Cambridge, the North Presbyterian Church in Geneva, New York, and St. Gregory's Parish in Plantation, Florida. Catholic colleges were still on my speaking agenda, including Stonehill College in North Easton, Massachusetts, and Cardinal Cushing College in Brookline, Massachusetts. I spoke at Brandeis University (with Pauli Murray, who was then on the faculty there), at Episcopal Theological Seminary in Cambridge, Massachusetts, and at Wellesley College.

CHAPTER SIX:
REFLECTIONS ON PHILOSOPHICAL THEMES
OF THE FIRST SPIRAL GALAXY

1. See Daly, *Gyn/Ecology*, pp. 57–64.
2. Peter L. Berger, *The Sacred Canopy: Elements of a Sociological Theory of Religion* (Garden City, New York: Doubleday & Company, 1967), p. 17.
3. Daly, *The Church and the Second Sex*, p. 215.
4. Ibid.
5. See "Patriarchal Poetry" (1927), from "BEE TIME VINE" in *The Yale Gertrude Stein*, Selections with an Introduction by Richard Kostelanetz (New Haven and London: Yale University Press, 1980), pp. 106–46.

PRELUDE TO THE SECOND SPIRAL GALAXY:
PIRATING IN THE MIST

1. The resurrection of Marx and Freud (Tweedledum and Tweedledee) as twin theoretical heroes in Women's Studies/"Gender Studies" was a depressing phenomenon of the late 1980s. So also was the fetishizing of such figures as Jacques and Jacques (Lacan and Derrida), the Mock Turtle and Gryphon who began slowly (very slowly) dancing around Alice until she forgot her Wonderlust and dozed off to the refrain: "Men Again, Men Again, Soup, Beautiful Soup." In my view, it is no coincidence that this dull tone has been creeping into and around academic journals and seminars that supposedly have something to do with women's lives, while rape, incest, battering, and murder of women in the real world have been escalating at an indescribably alarming rate.

2. Even patriarchal pirates are absolute outlaws. As an ordinary old encyclopedia states: "In modern times piracy is universally considered a crime against

society, and a pirate may be tried and punished in any country where he [*sic*] may be caught." See "Piracy," *Grolier Encyclopedia* (New York: The Grolier Society, 1957), Vol. XVI, p. 63. So there is a *universally* outlaw character even about patriarchal piracy. As the same article goes on to say: "Piracy is distinguished from privateering through the fact that a pirate bears a commission from no government and attacks the ships of all nations while a privateer bears a commission from a government which authorizes him to attack enemy ships." There are interesting clues also in common depictions of pirates. As every schoolgirl knows, they frequently have an eye patch or a wooden leg. So it is commonly assumed that they are in some way defective—an assumption comparable to ideas about deviant/defiant women. Moreover, pirates are often portrayed as drunk. As Suzanne Melendy commented, the subliminal message is that they are "out of control"—a common idea/fear in patriarchal society concerning deviant women (Conversation, Newton Centre, Massachusetts, September 1989).

CHAPTER SEVEN:

THE TIME OF THE TIGERS: THE HARVARD MEMORIAL CHURCH EXODUS AND OTHER ADVENTURES

1. Mary Daly, "After the Death of God the Father," *Commonweal* XCIV (March 12, 1971), pp. 7–11.

2. Mary Daly, Correspondence on "Women and the Church," *Commonweal* (February 14, 1964), p. 603.

3. Daly, "After the Death," p. 7.

4. The fact that Berger became ever more conservative in later years is, I think, consistent with and confirmative of this interpretation.

5. See Mary Daly, "The Courage to See," *The Christian Century* LXXXVIII (September 22, 1971), pp. 1108–11.

6. Daly, "After the Death," p. 9.

7. See Paul Tillich, *The Courage to Be* (New Haven: Yale University Press, 1952).

8. Daly, "The Courage to See," p. 1110.

9. Ibid., p. 1108.

10. Sermons and talks to church groups in 1971 included participation in a NOW panel on Women and Religion at the Church of the Holy Trinity in New York, a sermon at the Community Church of Boston, a colloquium on "God and the Modern World" at First Church, Cambridge, a lecture at the Cathedral of St. John the Divine in New York, lectures to the Detroit Association of the (catholic) Laity and to the National Association of the Laity at Fordham University in New York, a sermon at Wellesley College Chapel, a talk at Grace Church, Amherst, Massachusetts, and a talk to the "Singles Club" of the First and Second Church in Boston. I gave academic lectures at Union Theological Seminary in New York, at Molloy College in Rockville Center, New York, at the University of Southern Illinois in Edwardsville, and at Emerson College, Boston. I spoke to the Boston Theological Society and to the faculty and students of the Boston Theological Institute.

11. The text of this sermon, together with introductory remarks by me and several letters from "The Exodus Community," were published in my article entitled "The Women's Movement: An Exodus Community," in *Religious Education* LXVII (September–October 1972), pp. 327–35. The letters were written by Emily Culpepper, Linda Barufaldi, Elizabeth Rice, Mary Rodda, and myself.

12. Daly, "The Women's Movement," pp. 332–33.

13. Ibid., p. 334.

14. The word *fembot* first appears in my work in *Gyn/Ecology*, p. 17.

15. See Mary Daly, "The Spiritual Dimension of Women's Liberation," in *Radical Feminism*, edited by Anne Koedt, Ellen Levine, Anita Rapone (New York: Quadrangle Books, 1973), pp. 259–67. This anthology contains a number of articles from *Notes from the Second Year* and *Notes from the Third Year*. The jacket features a reproduction of the collage of two women's faces which I have described.

16. At that time the AAR did not have any special section in which the oppression and aspirations of women could be explored. Occasionally papers had been given on the subject of women and religion, but these were usually presented by men, and they were encapsulated as peripheral parts of other disciplines. This minimizing and encapsulating of the problem of patriarchal religion was not tolerable. It was an obscenity. So we did something about it. When I became program "chairperson" of the section for the following year, I decided that there would be four themes around which papers on women and religion would be grouped: (1) The Women's Revolution and Theological Development; (2) Myth and Sexual Stereotypes; (3) Transvaluation of Values; (4) New Views of History. Subsequently a "call for papers" was sent out, and there were many eager respondents. The "Women and Religion" section still continues to flourish in the 1990s.

17. Mary Daly, "Abortion and Sexual Caste," *Commonweal* XCV (February 4, 1972), pp. 415–19.

18. Ibid., p. 415.

19. Ibid., pp. 415–16.

20. Ibid., p. 416.

21. There was a veritable onslaught of hysterical responses to this article. It was followed by two critical pieces by Peter Steinfels (in the February 18 and March 3 issues) and by an extensive collection of pro and con letters and a reply by me in the April 7 issue. Most of the "con" letters were from men, and these were in extreme contrast to the unanimously favorable response of the women who telephoned, telegrammed, and wrote to me.

22. Mary Daly, "The Spiritual Revolution: Women's Liberation as Theological Re-education," *Andover Newton Quarterly* XII, no. 4 (March 1972), pp. 163–76.

23. Ibid., pp. 170–74.

24. Ibid., pp. 174–75.

25. See Anne Koedt, "Loving Another Woman—Interview," in *Radical Feminism*, pp. 85–93.

26. Ibid., p. 87.

27. Ibid., p. 88.

CHAPTER EIGHT:
THE WRITING OF *BEYOND GOD THE FATHER*—
AND *SOME* CONSEQUENCES!

1. Betty Farians had written an excellent paper entitled "Phallic Worship: The Ultimate Idolatry." Betty became sick and could not make it to the Congress, but her paper was printed together with all of the others in *Women and Religion: 1972*, Proceedings of the Working Group on Women and Religion of the American Academy of Religion, 1972, ed. by Judith Plaskow Goldenberg (Waterloo, Ontario: Waterloo Lutheran University, 1973). The articles by Daly, Farians, MacRae, and

Raymond were reprinted in a revised edition, ed. by Judith Plaskow and Joan Arnold Romero (Missoula, Montana: The Scholars' Press, 1974).

2. Since I departed from my text, the section on "The Most Unholy Trinity" is not in my article, "Theology After the Demise of God the Father: A Call for the Castration of Sexist Religion," in *Sexist Religion and Women in the Church: No More Silence!*, ed. by Alice L. Hageman, in collaboration with the Women's Caucus of Harvard Divinity School (New York: Association Press, 1974). As published in this collection of Lentz Lectures, my article is virtually identical with the 1972 AAR paper that had the same title. The fact that I extemporized a great deal is not discernible from this published piece.

3. The strike against the functioning of the image of the "Holy Spirit" was so explicit that my editor had become nervous and asked me to take part of it out. Instead, I put that material into a footnote. The careful reader did not have to miss it. This is note 50 to Chapter Four of *Beyond God the Father*.

4. That poem was published in Robin's collection of poems, *Monster* (New York: Random House, 1972). In the course of a conversation in Newton Centre, Massachusetts, in October 1989 Linda Barufaldi reminded me that I had read from "Monster" that day, so I was able to Re-member that aspect of the event in Fourth Galactic Time.

5. See Chapters Twelve and Thirteen. See Daly, *Gyn/Ecology*, pp. 37–39, 75–79, 96–98. Reflecting upon the phenomenon Now, it occurs to me that the trinitarian reversal could also be seen as a *triplicity*, defined as "an extreme form of duplicity or double-dealing" (*Webster's*).

6. Together with the christian trinity, the christian cross, especially the crucifix, known also as the "tree of death," legitimates fatherland's endless attempts to put an end to Biophilic Movement, wholeness, and creativity. This sadosymbol legitimates the fathers' *flatland*○, which is "the zone of dullness, sameness, depression: PATRIARCHY, FOREGROUND: the place where Nothing grows" (*Wickedary*). Just as the living, changing Triple Goddess is profoundly unlike the christian trinity, so also the Gynocentric Metaphors of quaternity, e.g., the four phases of the moon, the four seasons, are utterly Other than anything that could be represented by christian crosses or the endless flat squares and graphs of the foreground, which is patriarchal civilization. See *Gyn/Ecology* and *Pure Lust*.

7. See Virginia Woolf, "A Sketch of the Past," *Moments of Being: Unpublished Autobiographical Writings*, ed. and with an Introduction and Notes by Jeanne Schulkind (New York and London: Harcourt Brace Jovanovich, 1976), p. 71.

8. Transcontinental transtemporal telephone conversation with Linda Barufaldi, August 15, 1989.

9. Ibid.

10. For example, I spoke at Southwest Minnesota State College in Marshall, Minnesota, Tufts University in Boston, the University of Rochester in New York State, and Assumption College in Worcester, Massachusetts. I smuggled my heretical views to Colgate Rochester Divinity School, to Yale Divinity School, and to Episcopal Church Women of the Diocese of New Hampshire.

11. Transcontinental telephone conversation with Linda Barufaldi, August 20, 1989.

12. I think it was concerned with rapism and the sexual caste system. I am quite sure that I did not go into a highly intellectual explanation of the language of transcendence. At any rate, the faces in the audience appeared attentive.

13. See Daly, *Beyond God the Father*, p. 180.

14. Ibid., p. 24.

15. Ibid., p. 198.

16. My capitalization and noncapitalization of these words in this list is according to their Original form in *Beyond God the Father*—which does not in all cases coincide with the way I spell them Now. As Gertrude Stein wrote: "Sometimes one feels that Italians should be spelled with a capital and sometimes with a small letter, one can feel like that about almost anything." See Gertrude Stein, "Poetry and Grammar," in *Gertrude Stein: Writings and Lectures 1909–1945,* ed. by Patricia Meyerowitz, with an introduction by Elizabeth Sprigge (Baltimore, Maryland: Penguin Books, 1974), p. 133.

17. I criticized these in later works, which belong to The Third Spiral Galaxy. My purpose here is to understand what was going on then, to place these items in context, and to draw some connections.

18. See Daly, *Pure Lust,* p. 341n.

19. See Mary Daly, "The Qualitative Leap Beyond Patriarchal Religion," in *Quest: A Feminist Quarterly* (Spring 1975), especially pp. 29–32.

20. Daly, *Beyond God the Father,* p. 19.

21. See Daly, "The Qualitative Leap," especially pp. 32–37.

22. Virginia Woolf, *Three Guineas* (New York: Harcourt, Brace & World, Inc., 1938; Harbinger Books, 1966), p. 52.

23. Daly, *Beyond God the Father,* pp. 5–6.

24. So during that semester (Spring 1973) I lectured at United Theological Seminary in Dayton, Ohio, Union Theological Seminary in Richmond, Virginia, Perkins School of Theology at Southern Methodist University in Dallas, McCormick Theological Seminary in Chicago, and St. Paul's Seminary in Kansas City, Missouri. In addition, I spoke in other religious settings, such as the Catholic Centers at East Tennessee State University in Johnson City and at the University of Tennessee in Knoxville. I offered my ideas at Sacred Heart Parish in Watertown, Massachusetts, St. Francis Parish in Metuchen, New Jersey, Holy Family Church in Duxbury, Massachusetts, and First Church in Cambridge, Massachusetts.

25. These included a public address and panel discussions at the "Nobel Conference" held at Gustavus Adolphus College in St. Peter, Minnesota, in January 1973 and lectures at Morningside College in Sioux City, Iowa, McKendree College in Lebanon, Illinois, St. Olaf College in Northfield, Minnesota, and Tufts University in Medford, Massachusetts.

26. In addition, it was reviewed in academic journals, including *Cross Currents, The Journal of Religion, The Drew Gateway, Religious Studies Review, The Washington Book Review, Friends Journal, Ideas of Today, Genesis 2, Growth and Change, Contemporary Psychology. Horizons* devoted a Symposium to it, containing reviews by five theological critics and a response by the author. Positive reviews were published in newspapers and magazines as varying as *The Village Voice, The National Catholic Reporter, Publishers Weekly,* and *The Christian Century.* Many reviews were not published until 1975, 1976, and even later, as the book gained in popularity and respect. The appearance of the earliest newspaper reviews was encouraged greatly by the arduous and devoted work of Mary Lou Shields.

27. In fairness to mySelf I note that the strongest of the overtly Lesbian letters was dated May 14, 1975. This was two and one half years after the actual *writing* of *Beyond God the Father.* Had I been writing it then, it is probable that I would not have included the obscure section on "Heterosexuality—Homosexuality: The Destructive Dichotomy" (pp. 124–27), for 1975 was a very different kind of year from 1972. The Times they were a'changing.

28. Fortunately, there were other celebrations and publication parties for *Beyond God the Father* that were of a happier nature. For example, there was an exciting celebration at Beacon Press and a fascinating party at the home of Feminist author Barbara Seaman in New York.

29. The widespread respect for *Beyond God the Father* among scholars was indicated not only by course adoptions, reviews, panel discussions, and footnote references to it, but by an avalanche of speaking invitations. During that academic year (1973–74), following my "Outer Space" tour to six colleges in Virginia in October, I was an invited lecturer at Southwestern University in Texas, Wellesley College, the Kennedy School of Government at Harvard, Harvard Divinity School, Chatham College in Pennsylvania, University of Connecticut Law School, Rosary College in Chicago, Stanford University, Radcliffe College, the University of Pennsylvania, La Salle College in Philadelphia, Portland State University in Oregon (where I gave a joint lecture with Professor John Cobb of The School of Theology at Claremont, California), Vassar College, and Case Western Reserve in Cleveland, Ohio. I delivered a paper in the Women and Religion section at the Annual Meeting of the American Academy of Religion (November 1973) on "Post-Christian Theology." (I would soon change the spelling to "Postchristian," thereby de-emphasizing *christian*.) In addition, I spoke at less academic events: a workshop at the national conference of the National Association for the Repeal of Abortion Laws at the Park Sheraton in New York, a Planned Parenthood Conference at Yale Divinity School, *The Boston Globe* Book Festival, a Beacon Press panel at Follen Community Church, the annual conference of the Religious Newswriters Association held in conjunction with the United Presbyterian Assembly in Louisville, Kentucky. I wound up the year by giving the Sophia Fahs Lecture at the national convention of the Unitarian Universalist Association in New York on June 23, 1974.

CHAPTER NINE:
MY "FEMINIST POSTCHRISTIAN INTRODUCTION"
TO *THE CHURCH AND THE SECOND SEX*: APPROACHING
THE WATERSHED YEAR

1. In the first of this series of correspondence I was "informed" that the book would be brought out in paperback. Then I informed the editor who had written to me that the rights to the book were now mine. This fact, of course, put me in the position of being able to choose the conditions for this Timely/Untimely reincarnation.

2. Daly, "Autobiographical Preface to the 1975 Edition," *The Church and the Second Sex*, p. 7.

3. Ibid., p. 6.

4. Ibid., p. 6.

5. Ibid., p. 16.

6. Mary Daly, "Post-Christian Theology: Some Connections Between Idolatry and Methodolatry, Between Deicide and Methodicide," *Women and Religion: 1973*, Proceedings of the Working Group on Women and Religion of the American Academy of Religion, 1972, compiled by Joan Arnold Romero (Waterloo, Ontario: Waterloo Lutheran University, 1973), pp. 33–34.

7. Ibid., p. 34.

8. Ibid., p. 35.

9. See Daly, *Pure Lust*, Chapter Eight: "Tidy Demons, Tidal Muses."

10. Daly, "Feminist Postchristian Introduction," *The Church and the Second Sex*, p. 36.

11. Mary Lowry was especially helpful and ingenius, pointing out the merits of "Hobo" and helping me find it and do the paste-up. Mary was a cofounder of New Words Bookstore, a women's bookstore which opened in Cambridge, Massachusetts, in 1974.

12. Daly, *Beyond God the Father*, p. 178.

13. Ibid., p. 198.

14. The sites of my lecturing expeditions that fall included the University of Georgia in Athens, Georgia, Grinnell College in Iowa, Birmingham Temple in Detroit, the University of Delaware, State University of New York/College in Oswego, and a unitarian church in Miami, Florida. The trip to Florida provided an opportunity to try to track down information about Elizabeth Gould Davis, whose A-mazing book, *The First Sex*, published in 1971 by Putnam and in 1972 by Penguin (currently out of print), had rocketed the Feminist movement into New dimensions of imagination and daring. Elizabeth's sudden death in July 1974 had shocked and saddened many. By conversing with one of her friends I gained some insights about the life and thoughts of that heroic woman.

15. See Janice Raymond, Ph.D., "Mary Daly: A Decade of Academic Harassment and Feminist Survival," *Handbook for Women Scholars: Strategies for Success*, ed. by Mary L. Spencer, Monika Kehoe, and Karen Speece (San Francisco: Americas Behavioral Research Corporation, 1982), p. 83.

16. According to the "objective" rules, only course critiques since 1969 counted, since that was when I had acquired the rank of associate professor. What is left out of the picture is the fact that from 1966 to 1969, when my students were virtually all males, the majority of critiques of my courses had been extremely positive. What is also left out is the fact that despite this overwhelmingly positive assessment by male students, I had been denied promotion and tenure in 1969. Only after four months of demonstrations—predominantly by males—was the administration persuaded to reverse its decision. See Chapter Five.

17. Jan Dis-closed the facts concerning this deception and betrayal of confidence by the jesuits in the course of her talk at the "Forum on Women and Higher Education" held at Boston College on February 27, 1975. See Chapter Eleven.

18. Malcolm Boyd, "Who's Afraid of Women Priests?" *Ms.* (December 1974), p. 49.

19. Anne actually did return to the United States in June 1975, after I had gone on leave of absence to write *Gyn/Ecology*. She met Jan Raymond, however, who was then beginning her full-time teaching in Amherst, Massachusetts. Anne studied *Beyond God the Father* in Jan's class at Hampshire College in the fall of 1975. We did meet in the late seventies, and Anne became an important Crony in The Third Spiral Galaxy.

CHAPTER TEN:

REFLECTIONS ON PHILOSOPHICAL THEMES
OF THE SECOND SPIRAL GALAXY

1. Thus my honest attempt, in my article "After the Death of God the Father," to develop and apply Peter Berger's theory brought down that sociologist's wrath, for I had broken the rules and Named the game. In another article of that same year (1971), "The Courage to See," I began—with all due respect—shooting from the hip

at Paul Tillich's inadequacies. Unfortunately he was, like most Great Men, already dead, but his disciples and opponents got the drift. See Chapter Eight.

2. See Daly, *Beyond God the Father*, Chapter Six.

3. This synthesis would become more fully developed in The Third Spiral Galaxy, in *Gyn/Ecology, Pure Lust*, and the *Wickedary*.

4. As explained in *Beyond God the Father*: "Even the term 'method' must be reinterpreted and in fact wrenched out of its usual semantic field, for the emerging creativity of women is by no means a merely cerebral process. . . . Women are now realizing that the universal imposing of names by men has been false because partial. . . . To exist humanly is to name the self, the world, and God. The 'method' of the evolving spiritual consciousness of women is nothing less than this beginning to speak humanly—a reclaiming of the right to name. The liberation of language is rooted in the liberation of ourselves" (p. 8).

5. Ibid., p. 12.

6. Ibid., p. 11.

PRELUDE TO THE THIRD SPIRAL GALAXY:
SPINNING AND WEAVING THROUGH THE MIST

1. I came to the conclusion that the word *anger* is inadequate to Name Woman-identified Rage. *Anger* is a muted term that generally signifies "feelings" that have been displaced and replaced by phallocentric religion, media, and therapy.

2. Daly, *Pure Lust*, pp. 375–76.

3. Pivotal to this pattern-detecting is the *Sado-Ritual Syndrome*, which I Disclosed in the late 1970s. See Daly, *Gyn/Ecology*, pp. 131–33. All five chapters of The Second Passage of *Gyn/Ecology* are expansions/developments of this theme. Also central to my analysis of the *State of Atrocity* is the *Sadospiritual Syndrome*. See Daly, *Pure Lust*, pp. 72–77. All four chapters of The First Realm of *Pure Lust* are explications of the *Sadospiritual Syndrome*. Both of these Syndromes are briefly defined in the *Wickedary*.

4. Virginia Woolf, *Moments of Being: Unpublished Autobiographical Writings*, ed. and with an Introduction and Notes by Jeanne Schulkind (New York: Harcourt Brace Jovanovich, 1976), p. 72.

5. For analysis and definitions of these Virtues see *Pure Lust* and the *Wickedary*.

CHAPTER ELEVEN:
THE QUALITATIVE LEAP BEYOND PATRIARCHAL RELIGION

1. See Chapter Nine.

2. After the reception, Emily, Robin, and I went out to a Viennese Weingarten, and the next day we took off by train for Venice, where we happily drank delicious wine ("Lacryma christi del vesuvio"—"Tears of Christ of Vesuvius") in the Piazza San Marco. A couple of days later I made a complicated series of plane connections in stormy weather and arrived back in Boston just in time to teach my 4:30 class in Feminist Ethics.

3. Mary Daly, "Femminismo radicale: al di là della religione patriarcale," *Vecchi e Nuovi Dei*, a cura di Rocco Caporale (Torino: Editoriale Valentino, 1976), p. 357.

4. Ibid., p. 358.

5. See Chapter Ten.

6. See Mary Daly, "The Qualitative Leap Beyond Patriarchal Religion," *Quest: A Feminist Quarterly*, vol. 1, no. 4, pp. 29–32. Henceforth, all citations are directly from the shortened version published in *Quest*. For the sake of brevity, in the text of this chapter I am referring to the source of these citations simply as "'The Qualitative Leap' article."

7. Ibid., p. 30. In this article I used John Wayne and Brigitte Bardot to illustrate the "scotch-taped" coupledom of androgyny. Later I replaced these with John Travolta and Farrah Fawcett-Majors. See Daly, *Gyn/Ecology*, p. xlv. In speeches throughout the eighties I transmuted them again to Ronald Reagan and Nancy Reagan. The ideal new/old replacement for the nineties has not yet emerged.

8. Daly, "The Qualitative Leap," p. 30.

9. Ibid., p. 30.

10. This idea was common among men who considered themselves to be Feminists in the 1970s. Although it may have been positive for some men that they learned to cry and express their feelings, this did not liberate women. Such 1990s phenomena as Bill Moyers' PBS special on Robert Bly, "A Gathering of Men," aired in the winter of 1990, also failed to address the atrocities perpetrated by males against women and nature, and by rich and powerful white men against Third World people.

11. Daly, "The Qualitative Leap," pp. 31–32.

12. Ibid., p. 29.

13. Ibid.

14. Ibid., p. 24.

15. See Virginia Woolf, *Three Guineas* (New York: Harcourt, Brace & World, Inc., 1938; Harbinger Books, 1966).

16. My whirlwind speaking tours of the winter and spring of 1975 brought me to the Aquinas Institute at Princeton University in Princeton, New Jersey; Denison University in Granville, Ohio; Rutgers University in New Brunswick, New Jersey; Carleton College in Northfield, Minnesota; Barat College in Lake Forest, Illinois; Florida State University in Tallahassee; University of Maine in Orono; Harvard Medical School in Cambridge, Massachusetts; Williams College in Williamstown, Massachusetts; Harvard University in Cambridge, Massachusetts; Keene State College in Keene, New Hampshire. I also spoke at the Cambridge Forum in Cambridge, Massachusetts and at the Woodstock Women's Center in Woodstock, New York.

17. See Chapter Nine.

18. *The Heights*, February 10, 1975.

19. Ibid. See Chapter Nine.

20. See Janice G. Raymond, who cites the proceedings of that meeting in "Mary Daly: A Decade of Academic Harassment and Feminist Survival," in *Handbook for Women Scholars: Strategies for Success*, ed. by Mary L. Spencer, Monika Kehoe, and Karen Speece (San Francisco: Americas Behavioral Research Corporation, 1982), p. 84. This was also reported in an article by Joan Quinlan in *The Heights*, March 3, 1975, p. 3.

21. See Raymond, "Mary Daly," p. 84, which cites the legal memorandum of that meeting. Quinlan's article in *The Heights* (March 3, 1975, p. 3) cites McBrien's pathetic claim that there were "not enough footnotes" in *Beyond God the Father* "in the areas of Christology, Ecclesiology, and the Old Testament." Although it is difficult to have the patience to respond to such charges, I did patiently explain

that the book has more than adequate footnotes. It is noteworthy that the outside experts, whose favorable views of my work were dismissed, were: (1) John Bennett, former President of Union Theological Seminary; (2) John Cobb, renowned theologian on the faculty of The School of Theology at Claremont, California; (3) James Luther Adams, Professor Emeritus associated with Harvard Divinity School. The only persons whose judgments "counted" were members of the Boston College department of theology.

22. We used the term *Foremothers* at that time. Shortly thereafter, many of us began using *Foresisters* instead. This word has seemed more accurate. Not all women are mothers, whereas all can be sisters. *Foresisters* implies an egalitarian relationship, rather than a "maternal" role.

23. The article was published in *The Heights*, February 10, 1975.

24. The women educators who spoke, who were in various "fields" in divers universities, related experiences of discrimination, denial of tenure, and firings at these institutions. In my speech I elaborated upon the nature of Feminist Studies and the ways in which it was thwarted in universities. I proclaimed that 1975 was the Year of the Backlash against women. Jan Raymond made an important point in her speech concerning her own case. "My final and greatest sin was female identification and bonding. I performed the unforgivable act of studying seriously—of identifying professionally—with a woman. In an educational sense, I was not the 'daughter of an educated man,' to use Virginia Woolf's phrase, but the daughter of an educated woman. Had I chosen to study under and seriously associate myself and my work with a renowned and internationally recognized male scholar, my status at BC would undoubtedly be most different today."

25. The Forum was not reported in major newspapers, although reporters had been called. This silence illustrated the fact that 1975 was indeed the year of the beginning of backlash. It was, however, excellently recorded in *The Heights*, March 3, 1975, especially in an article by Maureen Dezell (pp. 1, 15). It was reported also in Feminist media. Most importantly, it was recorded deeply in the Memories of the hundreds of women who were Present.

CHAPTER TWELVE:
THE SPINNING OF *GYN/ECOLOGY*: MY THUNDERBOLT OF RAGE

1. Daly, *Gyn/Ecology*, p. 391.

2. Ibid., pp. 30–31. For further information on the patriarchal soul drama or otherworld journey see Morton W. Bloomfield, *The Seven Deadly Sins: An Introduction to the History of a Religious Concept, with Special Reference to Medieval English Literature* (Michigan State University Press, 1967), especially pp. 7–27. Bloomfield discusses the tradition of the (patriarchal) otherworld journey in connection with the deadly sins. He writes: "The Sins are a by-product of an eschatological belief which has been called the Soul Drama or Soul Journey. . . . The seven cardinal sins are the remnant of some Gnostic Soul Journey which existed probably in Egypt or Syria in the early Christian centuries. But the Soul Journey is itself part of a much vaster eschatological conception, the Otherworld Journey . . ." (p. 12).

3. These did become the core sins of *Pure Lust*, which was published five and one half years after *Gyn/Ecology*.

4. These are to some extent challenged in the *Wickedary*. They are further taken on in this book.

5. A simple example was Dis-covering the etymological connection between the words cosmetic and cosmos, both of which are from the Greek *kosmos*, meaning "order, universe."

6. Daly, *Gyn/Ecology*, pp. 24–25.

7. A couple of New York editors who had seen short sections of the manuscript did, in fact, write very negative and noncomprehending comments to me, which, however, did not succeed in discouraging me. The positive flow of my Muse was much stronger than their negativity.

8. I could not then guess that *Gyn/Ecology* would be received so warmly and so widely upon publication. Nor could I have guessed that this positive response would endure.

9. Sponsoring institutions of my lectures during the long period of work-in-process on *Gyn/Ecology* (fall 1975 through fall 1978) included Colby-Sawyer College in New London, New Hampshire; Beloit College in Beloit, Wisconsin; Williams College in Williamstown, Massachusetts; University of South Dakota in Vermillion; McGill University in Montreal, Canada; Hampshire College in Amherst, Massachusetts; Stephens College in Columbia, Missouri; University of Southern Maine in Portland; Suffolk County Community College on Long Island, New York; Dartmouth College in Hanover, New Hampshire; Rutgers University/Douglass College in New Brunswick, New Jersey; College of Marin in San Rafael, California; Harvard University in Cambridge, Massachusetts; University of Wisconsin in Madison; University of Illinois in Urbana-Champaign; Union Theological Seminary in New York; Trenton State College in Trenton, New Jersey; Trinity College in Hartford, Connecticut; Michigan State University in East Lansing; Indiana University and Purdue University at Fort Wayne; University of Delaware in Newark; Salem State College in Salem, Massachusetts; North Hennepin Community College in North Hennepin, Minnesota; University of Maryland in College Park; University of Massachusetts in Boston; University of Indiana in Bloomington; University of Pittsburgh in Pittsburgh, Pennsylvania; University of New Hampshire in Durham; University of Iowa in Iowa City. I also spoke at the Modern Language Association National Conferences in Chicago and in New York. I gave talks at the Conference on Women and Spirituality held at the University of Massachusetts in Boston; Bread & Roses Restaurant in Cambridge, Massachusetts; The Women's Building in Los Angeles, California; the NOW New Jersey State Conference; The Women's Coffeehouse in Minneapolis, Minnesota; Women's Conference on the Environment in Albany, New York.

10. The insight that *Lesbianism* in the deepest sense implies *Feminism* and that *Radical Feminism* implies *Lesbianism* has been shared by many women. In the seventies, many said this quite succinctly by wearing buttons which carried the witty and bold message: "Fesbian Leminist."

11. Hence I became a Webster and eventually was impelled to write *Pure Lust* and, later, the *Wickedary*. But first, in this Galaxy, there had to be *Gyn/Ecology*.

12. See Chapter Eight.

13. Telephone conversation, August 1990.

14. Indeed, Peggy and I were frequently overtaken by fits of Be-Laughing. This condition escalated during the process of repeated proofreading of the manuscript and galleys of *Gyn/Ecology*. Since Peggy was my "Work-Study student," we put in long, fatiguing hours together, and our condition sometimes resembled a sort of delirium. We drudged together at proofreading, with materials spread out on a dark green card table, which she occasionally described as "the green torture table."

There were certain sentences in the book, however, which invariably threw Peggy into fits of giggling, no matter how many times they had to be read out loud. One outstanding example comes to mind. This was/is in the very last section of the book, entitled "The Celebration of Ecstasy." The sentence (on p. 423) is: "Foxy ladies chase clucking biddies around in circles."

15. Telephone conversation, August 1990.

16. A *Positively Revolting Hag* ◑ is "a stunning, beauteous Crone; one who inspires positive revulsion from phallic institutions and morality, inciting Others to Acts of Pure Lust" (*Wickedary*).

17. Transcontinental telephone conversation, August 1990.

18. We were thinking also of the symbolism of "666" as associated with the "Antichrist."

19. We continued to carry on during eventful evenings. Some uproarious parties were held at Emily's apartment on Sacramento Street in Cambridge. This abode housed a treasured old piano on which she pounded out ludicrous, lugubrious old protestant hymns, while those gathered joined in sing-along sessions. Among our "favorite" monstrous hymns was "Have Thine Own Way, Lord." (See *Gyn/Ecology*, p. 92n.) A rollicking time, including consumption of good food and wine, was had by all.

20. See Chapter Eleven.

21. See Margaret A. Murray, *The Witch-Cult in Western Europe* (Oxford: Oxford University Press, 1921), p. 222.

22. Daly, *Gyn/Ecology*, p. 395.

23. Ibid., p. 396.

24. Of course, I had read and studied about Labryses since the early seventies, for example, in Elizabeth Gould Davis, *The First Sex* (New York: G. P. Putnam's Sons, 1971). When I saw the huge double-axes in Crete, however, these became living Metaphors, taking on Other dimensions.

25. For example, the title *Pure Lust* functions as a Labrys. It is double-sided. Written in lowercase, the expression Names the deadly dis-passion that prevails in patriarchy, the life-hating lechery that rapes and kills the objects of its obsession/aggression. Capitalized, it Names Pure Passion: unadulterated, absolute, simple, sheer striving for abundance of be-ing; unlimited, unlimiting desire/fire. See Daly, *Pure Lust*, pp. 2–3. See also Daly in Cahoots with Caputi, *Wickedary*.

26. Years later, in their maturity, they demonstrated their ability to work together by inspiring "Nonchapter Thirteen: Cat/egorical Appendix," which was published as the conclusion of *Pure Lust*.

27. See Chapter Eight.

28. In contrast to the rather slow though powerful accumulation of reviews that followed the publication of *Beyond God the Father*, the media response to *Gyn/Ecology* was swift as well as massive and predominantly positive. Having pulled out the thick file of reviews I am struck not only by the number but also by the diversity of publications in which these appeared.

These publications included *Publishers Weekly* and *The New York Times Book Review;* scholarly journals such as *Union Seminary Quarterly Review* and *Cross Currents;* christian periodicals such as *The Christian Century* and *Christianity and Crisis;* Feminist periodicals such as *Sojourner, New Directions for Women, Ms., Chrysalis,* and *Feminist Studies* (England). *Gyn/Ecology* was reviewed in newspapers across the United States, including *Harrisburg Weekly, Minnesota Daily, Sun City Arizona News-Sun, San Francisco Bay Guardian.* Many British publications—

including *The London Observer, The Literary Review, New Statesman*, and *Books and Bookmen*—also reviewed this book.

The most pathetic and ludicrous "review" was published by fr. Andrew Greeley, prolific priest-author of junk novels, who, in a syndicated article, "nominated" *Gyn/Ecology* "the worst Catholic book of the year." Obviously Greeley had failed to crack the book as preparation for unashamedly bellowing his priestly pronouncements. He had also failed to grasp the fact that this was no "Catholic book" and that its author had not been a catholic for almost a decade.

29. Electrical connections were manifested among thousands of women when I spoke around the United States and Canada after *Gyn/Ecology* appeared. During the period from January through August 1979 I spoke at the Annual Meeting of the American Association for the Advancement of Science in Houston, Texas; University of Southern California in Los Angeles; Occidental College in Los Angeles, California; Reed College in Portland, Oregon; Stephens College in Columbia, Missouri; California State University in Chico; Smith College in Northampton, Massachusetts; University of Wisconsin in Oshkosh; McGill University in Montreal, Canada; Norfolk State University in Norfolk, Virginia; Concordia University in Montreal, Canada; Pittsburgh Theological Seminary in Pittsburgh, Pennsylvania; Boston University in Boston, Massachusetts; New Jersey State College in Stockton; Mankato State University in Mankato, Minnesota; Southwest State University in Marshall, Minnesota; Saginaw Valley State College in University Center, Michigan. I gave talks at Old Wives' Tales Bookstore in San Francisco, California; The Women's Building in Los Angeles, California; Amazon Sweet Shop in San Diego, California; Giovanni's Room (bookstore) in Philadelphia, Pennsylvania; Womanfyre Books in Northampton, Massachusetts; Mountain Moving Coffee House in Chicago, Illinois; Jane Adams Bookstore in Chicago, Illinois; Amaranth Restaurant in Cambridge, Massachusetts; Women's Bookstore in Worcester, Massachusetts.

30. See Janice G. Raymond, "Mary Daly: A Decade of Academic Harassment and Feminist Survival," in *Handbook for Women Scholars: Strategies for Success*, ed. by Mary L. Spencer, Monika Kehoe, and Karen Speece (San Francisco: Americas Behavioral Research Corporation, 1982), p. 85. See also Judy Appel, "A Brief History," *Affirmations: Newsletter of the Women's Theological Coalition of the Boston Theological Institute*, vol. 6, no. 7 (March 1979), pp. 2–5.

31. Reported in *The Heights* (Boston College Student Weekly), February 26, 1979, p. 8. This was reported also in the Feminist newspaper *Equal Times*, March 18, 1979, p. 10, and in *Valley Women's Voice*, vol. 1, no. 4 (May 1979), p. 8.

32. See *The Heights*, February 26, 1979, p. 8. See also Raymond, "Mary Daly," p. 85. See also *Equal Times*, March 18, 1979, p. 10.

33. By this time Paris's other female accomplice, Sharon Webb, had stopped participating. Her letter of explanation and apology, dated January 25, was published in *The Heights*, March 5, 1979, p. 14.

34. *The Heights*, February 26, 1979, p. 8. See also *Equal Times*, April 15, 1979, p. 11.

35. Ibid., p. 8.

36. Ibid., p. 8. See also Judy Appel, "A Brief History," p. 4.

37. On the morning of February 12 a letter from the Boston College administration informing me that all of my classes would subsequently be monitored was delivered by taxi to my home. This "policy" was implemented that very day. See *The Heights*, February 26, 1979, p. 8. See also *Equal Times*, March 18, 1979, p. 10.

38. See Raymond, "Mary Daly," p. 86. Cited from *The Heights*, March 5, 1979, p. 14. I explained further that whereas Boston College administrators had proclaimed that they were engaged in a "thorough investigation" of the "problem" (which they themselves had created), a "thorough investigation" would have meant a discussion with me, and with the students, right from the start. None of the normal courteous procedures had been followed. The bogus scholastic status of fr. Paris was well known: He was not eligible even to sign up for a course. In sum, I Named the whole affair what it really was: a Witch hunt. The theme of the Witch hunt was developed by Karen A. Hagberg in "Boston Witch Hunt: Feminist Author Persecuted!," *New Women's Times*, vol. 5, no. 8 (April 13–April 27, 1979), pp. 1–2.

39. Published in *The Heights*, March 12, 1979, p. 18.

40. *The Heights*, April 23, 1979, p. 9. See Raymond, "Mary Daly," p. 87. See also *Sojourner: The Women's Forum*, May 1979, pp. 6, 30.

41. This letter was published in *The Heights*, April 23, 1979, p. 9.

42. This title, of course, is from Virginia Woolf, *Three Guineas* (New York: Harcourt, Brace & World, Inc., 1938; Harbinger Books, 1966), p. 36. The exact line in Woolf is: "For we have done with this 'education'!"

43. This event was reported in *New Women's Times*, vol. 5, no. 9 (April 27–May 10, 1979), p. 1. The paper devoted a substantial section of that issue to printing the speeches from the Rally. Excellent coverage was also given in an article by Lisa Sergi in *The Heights*, April 23, 1979, pp. 1, 8–9. At the end of that article I was cited as calling the event "a spiritual triumph," and stating: "We were able to turn the hostility, the oppressiveness, the pettiness of this patriarchal institution into an analytic and energizing event for the hundreds of women present." I stated that the speakers were able to give the evening "a symbolic and mythic significance" by linking the events at BC to a wider world view. "This was a direct contrast to the pettiness and fixation upon detail of the university administrators." One graduate student in particular—Judy Appel, who was cross-registered from Harvard Divinity School into my classes—contributed enormous amounts of time and energy into gathering information about my history at Boston College and spreading the word among Feminists across the United States. Of course, many, indeed most, of my students contributed to this work of publicizing the facts of the case and to making the Rally a great success. See also Pat Harrison, "Daly Support Rally Exhorts, Exhilarates," *Sojourner*, May 1979, pp. 6, 30.

44. At the conclusion of her speech Jan stated:

It is important to remember that tolerance for critics of the system stretches only in certain directions, and these directions are still male-defined. To call the system patriarchy is far different from naming it capitalism. If Mary Daly were a radical humanist, a Marxist, or an anarchist, she would have the support of many of her academic brothers. She could then be defined within the limits of radical tolerance.

But Mary Daly is instead a Spinster, a Fury, a Revolting Hag, a Crone.

This excerpt was published in *New Women's Times*, vol. 5, no. 9 (April 27–May 10, 1979), p. 7. It is substantially the same as the concluding paragraph of Raymond's article, "Mary Daly," pp. 87–88.

45. Woolf, *Three Guineas*, p. 36.

46. Some of the lines from "The Witching Hour" are cited in *Gyn/Ecology*, p. 179. Particularly potent are the words of the chorus:

> In the Witching Hour you come to your power
> You feel it deep inside you, it's rising, rising

And you think it's a dream until you hear yourself scream
Power to the Witch and to the woman in me.
 —*Willie Tyson*   ᵛ
      Debutante (Urana Records)

47. Indeed, Stunning Events that participate in this Other dimension continue to happen. See Chapter Nineteen.

48. Daly, *Gyn/Ecology*, p. 22.

49. Conversation with Emily Culpepper, Newton Centre, Massachusetts, May 1990.

CHAPTER THIRTEEN:
SPINNING BIG: THE EXPLOSION/EXPANSION OF *PURE LUST*

1. For definitions and descriptions of these characters see Daly, *Pure Lust*. See also Daly in Cahoots with Caputi, *Wickedary*. As I wrote in *Pure Lust*: "The noun *snool* means (Scottish) 'a cringing person.' It means also 'a tame, abject, or mean-spirited person' (O.E.D.). In sadosociety, snools rule, and snools are the rule. The dual personalities of these personae—the cast of characters governing and legitimizing bore-ocracy—are unmasked by definitions of the verb *snool*. This means, on the one hand, 'to reduce to submission: cow, bully,' and on the other hand, 'cringe, cower.' Snools are sadism and masochism combined, the stereotypic saints and heroes of the sadostate" (pp. 20–21).

2. *Sadosociety*○ means "society spawned by phallic lust; the sum of places/times where the beliefs and practices of sadomasochism are The Rule; Torture Cross Society: PATRIARCHY, SNOOLDOM" (*Wickedary*).

3. Daly, *Pure Lust*, p. x.

4. Ibid., p. 2.

5. Ibid., p. 3.

6. During that academic year (1979–1980) I spoke at Dartmouth College in Hanover, New Hampshire; Harvard Divinity School in Cambridge, Massachusetts; Rutgers/Douglass College in New Brunswick, New Jersey; Florida State University in Tallahassee; University of Wisconsin in Whitewater; College of Wooster in Wooster, Ohio; Arizona State University in Tempe; San Diego State University in San Diego, California; Oberlin College in Oberlin, Ohio; University of Connecticut in Hartford; University of Rhode Island in Kingston; University of Washington in Seattle; Sacramento State University in Sacramento, California; Stanford University in Stanford, California; University of California in Berkeley. I also gave talks at *The Boston Globe* Book Fair in Boston, Massachusetts; A Room of One's Own Women's Bookstore in Madison, Wisconsin; First Unitarian Church in Houston, Texas; Old Wives' Tales Bookstore in San Francisco, California; A Woman's Place Bookstore in Oakland, California.

7. For more on Divining Familiars, see Chapter Twelve.

8. Indeed that was my last lecture in the United States specifically focused on *Gyn/Ecology*. However, in my lectures abroad during the next several years I did pick up threads from *Gyn/Ecology* while moving on with presenting work-in-process from *Pure Lust*. This was the case when I spoke in Sydney, Australia in 1981 and in the 1982 lectures in Graz, Austria; Munich and Cologne, Germany; Nijmegen, Holland. I continued to catch up these earlier threads, Weaving them with new material, when speaking in Europe into the mid-eighties. This was necessary

because of the "time warp" caused by the fact that my books were published in Europe later than in the United States.

9. Daly, "Autobiographical Preface to the 1975 Edition," *The Church and the Second Sex*, p. 14.

10. This book was eventually published posthumously. See Andrée Collard with Joyce Contrucci, *Rape of the Wild: Man's Violence against Animals and the Earth* (London: The Women's Press, 1988; Bloomington and Indianapolis: Indiana University Press, 1989).

11. Daly, *Pure Lust*, p. 3.

12. At that time there was much talk in the air about "the coming bad years." There were predictions that money would become almost worthless and that owning real estate would be essential for survival.

13. I was teaching in Boston the day The Tornado actually occurred, but I saw its effects shortly afterward. Every detail entered my psyche and made a permanent impression there.

14. Daly, *Pure Lust*, p. 7.

15. Ibid.

16. See also *Pure Lust*, p. 10. The Greek word *stoicheia*, which appears frequently in the epistles of saint Paul, is translated sometimes as "elemental spirits" and sometimes simply as "the elements." Although the pauline epistles may seem to be an improbable springboard for Dis-covering Elemental Feminist Philosophy, the fact is that as Pirate I can and must use improbable re-sources, Righteously Plundering information which belongs to women, placing this in Crone-logical/Be-Dazzling context. I do this here, as elsewhere, with scrupulous scholarship, crediting my re-sources meticulously.

17. See Chapter Two.

18. See Chapters Two and Three.

19. See Chapter Four.

20. See Chapter Four.

21. See Daly, *Pure Lust*, pp. 17–18, pp. 138–39.

22. The intuition and its shocking abruptness are discussed in many of the works of Jacques Maritain. See, for example, Jacques Maritain, *Approaches to God*, trans. from the French by Peter O'Reilly, *World Perspectives*, vol. 1 (New York: Harper and Brothers, 1954). For a thorough analysis of this "shocking" intuition and its implications, see Mary F. Daly, *Natural Knowledge of God in the Philosophy of Jacques Maritain: A Critical Study* (Rome: Officium Libri Catholici—Catholic Book Agency, 1966).

23. This is an allusion to the words of Muriel Rukeyser:

> What would happen if one woman told the truth about her life?
> The world would split open.

See Muriel Rukeyser, "Käthe Kollwitz," III, St. 4, *The Speed of Darkness* (New York: Random House, 1968), p. 103. Rukeyser gives voice to the Power of Truth-telling of one woman about her own life. I am describing the Power of a Truth-telling Time in which not only women are Be-Speaking, but also the Elements.

24. Daly in Cahoots with Caputi, *Wickedary*, p. 276.

25. Ibid., p. 277.

26. See Chapter One.

27. See Virginia Woolf, *Moments of Being: Unpublished Autobiographical Writings*, ed. and with an Introduction and Notes by Jeanne Schulkind (New York: Harcourt Brace Jovanovich, 1976), p. 72.

28. See Chapter Twenty.

29. According to my guide, one theory of the origin of these structures—which can be found throughout New England—was that they were built in approximately the ninth century by Irish monks who were fleeing from Vikings. The latter may have been chasing them in order to steal their treasures—presumably valuable objects that belonged to the church. The "Irish connection" with these "beehives" revealed itself to me several years later during my 1987 visits to Ireland. See Chapter Seventeen.

30. J. C. Cooper, *An Illustrated Encyclopedia of Traditional Symbols* (London: Thames and Hudson, 1978), p. 21.

31. This *bhā* connection was called to my attention by Lilly Friedberg, a Radical Feminist from the U.S. living in Germany (Personal communication, June 1987).

32. Cooper, *An Illustrated Encyclopedia*, p. 20.

33. According to *Webster's, stamina* is from the Latin word *stamina*, plural of *stamen*, meaning "warp, thread of life spun by the Fates."

34. See Daly, *Pure Lust*, pp. 311-14. See also Robert Graves, *The Greek Myths* (Baltimore, Maryland: Penguin Books, 1955, 1960), I.52.2.

35. The chapter which Erika wrote in my house (and on my typewriter) was written originally in English. It was published under the title "Anna—One Day in the Life of an Old Woman," in *Trivia: A Journal of Ideas*, no. 4 (spring 1984), pp. 31–42. In German, the book is entitled *Anna im Goldenen Tor: Gegenlegende über die Mutter der Maria* (Stuttgart: Kreuz Verlag, 1990). In this book the author untwists the patriarchal tales/tails, creating a New—and more probable—legend.

36. See Chapter Twelve. This was implied in the statement the administration had attempted to force me to sign in March 1979 (which I did *not* sign), which contained the stipulation that "during registration periods, University personnel will attend her classes as observers."

37. *The Interpreter's Bible*, 12 vols. (New York: Abingdon-Cokesbury Press, 1952–57).

38. *The Interpreter's Dictionary of the Bible*, 4 vols. (New York: Abingdon Press, 1962).

39. See Daly, *Pure Lust*, especially Introduction and Chapter Four.

40. See Chapter Two and Chapter Five. It is not common for a store owner or employee deliberately to set stopped clocks at twelve minutes after eleven. Although I do not keep journals, when going through materials relevant to this chapter I did find a note that I had written in 1981 describing this incident and confirming the date (Friday, November 13, 1981) and the number of clocks stopped at 11:12, that is, nine clocks.

41. Among the letters in this category were excellent, supportive letters from Nelle Morton and from Howard Clinebell at The School of Theology at Claremont, California.

42. During the winter and spring of 1982, in addition to the University of Wisconsin at La Crosse, I spoke at Fitchburg State College in Fitchburg, Massachusetts; Southern Illinois University in Edwardsville; the University of Montreal in Montreal, Canada; and Linfield College in McMinnville, Oregon. I had refused a number of invitations and deferred others, since I was "in my hermit stage," writing intensively. My talk at the University of Montreal was part of a conference organized by Marisa Zavalloni. The many excellent papers delivered there were later published in a volume entitled *L'Émergence d'une culture au féminin*, ed. by Marisa Zavalloni (Montreal: Les Éditions Saint-Martin, 1987).

43. See Emily Erwin Culpepper, "Philosophia in a Feminist Key: Revolt of the Symbols" (unpublished Th.D. dissertation, Harvard University, 1983). Published on demand by University Microfilms International, Ann Arbor, Michigan, U.S.A. and London, England.

44. In the winter and spring of 1982–83 I gave lectures at Williams College in Williamstown, Massachusetts; Bates College in Lewiston, Maine; Denison University in Granville, Ohio; and the University of British Columbia in Vancouver, British Columbia, Canada. I also gave a talk at Bloodroot Restaurant and Bookstore in Bridgeport, Connecticut.

45. See Ernest G. Schachtel, *Metamorphosis* (New York: Basic Books, 1959).

46. Conversation, Maine, July 1982.

47. Conversation, Leverett, Massachusetts, January 1983.

48. See Chapter Eight.

49. Telephone conversation, September 1991.

50. See Chapter Two.

51. See Chapter One.

52. See Chapter Two.

53. *Pure Lust* is a Realizing of what the twelfth-century Genius Hildegard of Bingen called "viriditas," or Greening Power. See Hildegard of Bingen, *Illuminations of Hildegard of Bingen*, with commentary by Matthew Fox, O.P. (Sante Fe, New Mexico: Bear & Company, 1985). *Outercourse* is an Other Manifestation of Greening Power—and there is more Elemental Power yet to be Realized. But that will be a later story and perhaps also an Other book.

54. Transcontinental telephone conversation, August 1990.

55. The Index was more fully developed by Nilah MacDonald in 1985 for the paperback edition of *Pure Lust*.

56. During the academic year 1983–84 I gave the Samuel F. Salkin Memorial Lecture at the Unitarian Church, sponsored by the First Unitarian Society of Minneapolis, Minnesota. On the following evening I gave another public lecture at the Plymouth Congregational Church, sponsored by the Sojourner Truth School of Women and Religion in Minneapolis. I spoke at Bryn Mawr College in Bryn Mawr, Pennsylvania; University of New Hampshire in Durham; University of Rochester in Rochester, New York; University of Colorado in Boulder; Gettysburg College in Gettysburg, Pennsylvania; University of Kentucky (Women Writers' Conference) in Lexington; Hamilton College in Clinton, New York; Pennsylvania State University in University Park; Emory University in Atlanta, Georgia. I gave talks at the Women's Bookstore in Buffalo, New York; Womanbooks in New York, New York; Giovanni's Room Bookstore in Philadelphia, Pennsylvania.

57. Hester Eisenstein, *Contemporary Feminist Thought* (London: George Allen & Unwin, 1984).

58. See Chapter Ten.

59. See Cecil Woodham-Smith, *The Great Hunger: Ireland 1845–1849* (London: Hamish Hamilton Ltd., 1962), p. 145.

CHAPTER FOURTEEN:
SINNING BIG: THE MERRY MERRY *WICKEDARY*

1. Bloodroot has an excellent selection of books and art objects as well as a superb and ever-changing menu. It is an inspiring Women's Space, and it is frequently visited by travelers en route to and from New York City. Especially popular

are Wednesday evening women's events, including lectures and musical performances. The Bloodroot Collective has published Feminist vegetarian cookbooks containing great recipes and many Feminist quotations which serve as brain food for the reader. As of this writing, the most recent edition is *The Second Seasonal Political Palate* (Bridgeport, Connecticut: Sanguinaria Publishing, 1984). The third will soon be published. Bloodroot is located at 85 Ferris Street, Bridgeport, Connecticut 06605.

2. See Chapters Two, Five, Thirteen, and Twenty.

3. See Daly in Cahoots with Caputi, *Wickedary*, esp. pp. 279–84.

4. Ibid.

5. See *The American Heritage Dictionary*, p. xxi.

6. During the fall of 1984 I spoke at the University of New Brunswick, Canada, in Fredericton; Dalhousie University in Halifax, Nova Scotia, Canada; Bucknell University in Lewisburg, Pennsylvania; the University of Montreal in Montreal, Canada; the National Meeting of the American Academy of Religion in Chicago, Illinois.

7. During the winter and spring of 1985 I lectured at McGill University in Montreal, Canada; the University of Wisconsin in Waukesha; Smith College in Northampton, Massachusetts; the University of Massachusetts in Boston; New England Regional Meeting of the American Academy of Religion at Andover Newton Theological School in Newton Centre, Massachusetts; Memorial University of Newfoundland, Canada; Carleton University in Ottawa, Canada; University of Vermont in Burlington; University of Nebraska in Lincoln; Trinity College in Hartford, Connecticut; Ohio State University in Columbus. I also spoke at A Room of One's Own Bookstore in Madison, Wisconsin, and at the State Historical Society (benefit for the New Feminist Connection Foundation in that city); Readers' Feast Bookstore in Hartford, Connecticut; Womanfyre Books in Northampton, Massachusetts; Women's Music Festival and Writers' Conference in Bloomington, Indiana; NOW Rally in Brighton, Massachusetts, protesting the catholic hierarchy's campaign against birth control and abortion.

8. Suzanne Melendy was Chairhag/Introducer of the WITCH lectures from 1985 to 1987, and she was succeeded by Krystyna Colburn, who has carried on during the succeeding years.

9. Barbara G. Walker, *The Woman's Encyclopedia of Myths and Secrets* (San Francisco: HarperSanFrancisco, 1983), p. 325.

10. Ibid., pp. 324–25.

11. See Chapters Twelve and Thirteen.

12. Daly in Cahoots with Caputi, *Wickedary*, p. xvi.

13. Ibid., p. xvi.

14. Ibid., p. xvii.

15. During the winter and spring of 1985–1986 I spoke in the WITCH Lecture Series in Boston, Massachusetts; at Wesleyan University in Middletown, Connecticut; at Bloodroot Restaurant and Bookstore in Bridgeport, Connecticut; in the Spectrum Lecture Series at West Side Community School in Pittsfield, Massachusetts.

16. The title of my lecture was "From Touchable Caste to Raging Race: New Vices and Virtues—Plastic and Potted Passions."

17. During 1985–1986 Emily was Visiting Assistant Professor of Religion at the University of Massachusetts in Boston. 1986–1987 was an interim year of odd jobs (including teaching in a prison and teaching preschoolers) by which she sustained herSelf while searching for a suitable teaching job. These were indeed times of full-blown backlash—of which we had seen a preview ten years earlier. See Chapter Eleven.

18. This was not my only speaking engagement of the semester. I spoke at Emory University in Atlanta, Georgia; Amherst College in Amherst, Massachusetts; Pennsylvania State University in University Park. I gave other talks at the Radical Feminist Conference on Pornography at New York University; Boston University (sponsored by the WITCH Lecture Series); the Women's Music Festival and Writers' Conference in Bloomington, Indiana.

19. The expression *Third Hemisphere* was suggested to me by the title of a book by the Irish writer Edward (Lord) Dunsany. However, I develop the idea in my own way. See his book, *Tales of Three Hemispheres* (Boston: J. W. Lucas and Company [circa 1919]).

20. Transatlantic telephone conversation with Geraldine Moane in Ireland, November 1991.

21. Ibid.

22. Ibid.

23. Telephone conversation, November 1991.

24. In early July 1987 I gave a Keynote Address and two other talks at the Third International Interdisciplinary Congress on Women which was held in Dublin.

25. In the fall of 1987 I spoke at Northwestern University in Evanston, Illinois; Iowa State University in Ames; Tufts University in Medford, Massachusetts; Radcliffe College in Cambridge, Massachusetts (Gilman Lecture); University of Wisconsin in Waukesha; Duke University in Durham, North Carolina; The School of Theology at Claremont, California; University of California in Los Angeles; Smith College in Northampton, Massachusetts; National Meeting of the American Academy of Religion, Boston, Massachusetts. I also spoke at the Unitarian Church in Davenport, Iowa; the Illinois/Iowa NOW Congress in Moline, Illinois; Mountain Moving Coffee House in Chicago, Illinois; Different Light Bookstore in New York, New York; Somerville Theatre, Somerville, Massachusetts; New Words Bookstore in Cambridge, Massachusetts; A Room of One's Own Bookstore in Madison, Wisconsin; Websters' Bookstore in Milwaukee, Wisconsin; Lammas Bookstore in Washington, D.C.; Page One Bookstore in Sherman Oaks, California; Mama Bear's Bookstore in Oakland, California; Sisterhood Bookstore in Los Angeles, California; Old Wives' Tales Bookstore in San Francisco, California.

26. See Chapters Two, Five, and Thirteen as well as this Chapter on the 11:12 phenomenon.

27. I had thought up and proposed the "Women and Religion Section" at the Annual Meeting of the American Academy of Religion held in Atlanta in 1971, and this time/space for women's Be-Speaking has been sustained since 1972. Therefore, I definitely had the Sense of standing on my own turf then, in 1987. See Chapter Seven.

CHAPTER FIFTEEN:
REFLECTIONS ON PHILOSOPHICAL THEMES
OF THE THIRD SPIRAL GALAXY

1. See Chapter Ten.

2. See Chapter Twelve.

3. I Dis-covered New Words earlier, of course, especially in *Beyond God the Father,* but these were fewer and, on the whole, less Wild.

4. See Chapter Twelve.

5. Daly, *Gyn/Ecology*, p. 111.

6. See Chapter Thirteen.

7. See Chapters One and Two.

8. See Chapter Two.

9. See Chapters Two and Three.

10. This Search for autonomous knowing was evident in my dissertations written in Fribourg. See Chapters Three and Four. It is Outrageously manifested in *Pure Lust*. See Chapter Thirteen.

11. See Chapter Ten.

12. See Chapter Thirteen.

13. Daly, *Pure Lust*, pp. 362–73.

14. Ibid., p. 363.

15. Ibid., p. 364. In the paragraph immediately following the passage just cited I explained my reservations about the term *separatism*: "As a name for the movement of Metamorphosing women . . . *separatism* is what I would call a 'second order' word. For it does not emphasize the direction, or final cause, of our movement, which is ontological Metamorphosis itself, but rather an essential prerequisite of this movement under the conditions of patriarchy. Since, under these conditions, separation from those forces that cut us off from be-ing is necessary, it is not inaccurate for a Radical Feminist to call herSelf a separatist. This name, however, unless used in a context of Lusty words, is inadequate. Since the whole point of Feminist separation is Biophilic communication/participation in Be-ing, it is Bio-logical to conclude that these context-providing words will be Other words—words that signify such transcendent communication, for example, *Spinster, Webster, Brewster, Fate, Muse*."

16. Ibid., p. 372. Sarah Hoagland has written eloquently about this.

17. As I have already explained, I have never refused to teach a registered, *bona fide*, qualified male student who expressed a desire to study with me.

18. See Chapter Fourteen.

19. See Chapter Seven of *Beyond God the Father*.

20. See Chapter Fourteen of *Outercourse*.

21. Ibid.

CHAPTER SIXTEEN:
ON HOW I JUMPED OVER THE MOON

1. See Nicholas D. Kristof, "Stark Data on Women: 100 Million Women are Missing," *The New York Times*, November 5, 1991, pp. C1, C12. Kristof states: "A traditional preference for boys translates quickly—in China, India, and many other developing countries—into neglect and death for girls." Stating that the problem appears to be getting worse in Asia, he cites Harvard economist Amartya Sen: "Professor Sen estimates that considerably more than 100 million females are missing around the world, and he asserts that the reason the shortfall is getting worse in some areas is that girls are not allowed to benefit as much as boys from the improvements in health care and nutrition that are lowering death rates in developing countries." Numerous demographers seem to agree that millions of women die because they're women. As Kristof states: "It is only in the overall statistics that the shortfall becomes clear." In addition to infanticide and neglect of female children, there is another problem, arising from modern technology. Kristof comments: "These days,

technology has presented parents with a tidier option than infanticide: ultrasound tests that determine the sex of a fetus." Kristof writes of a United Nations report which "cited 8,000 abortions in Bombay after the parents learned of the sex of the fetus, *only one of which involved a male* [emphasis mine]." And *Science and Technology* quoted a Chinese peasant as saying: "Ultrasound is really worthwhile, even though my wife had to go through four abortions to get a son."

2. See Chapter Thirteen.

3. See Chapter Thirteen.

4. These words are from a song by Willie Tyson entitled "The Witching Hour," which is on her album *Debutante* (Urana Records). This song is quoted in Daly, *Gyn/Ecology*, p. 179.

5. This work has been republished several times. The most recent edition is Valerie Solanas, *SCUM Manifesto* (London: Phoenix Press, 1991). The words quoted here are on page 5.

CHAPTER SEVENTEEN:

GREEN *LOGBOOK* ENTRIES FROM THE MOON

1. See Chapter Twelve.

2. See Chapter Thirteen.

3. See Doris Sue Wong, "Juvenile Guilty of Murder, Rape in Killing of Harbour," *The Boston Globe*, December 21, 1991, pp. 1, 7.

4. See Chapters Three and Four.

5. See Chapter Thirteen.

6. See Chapter Thirteen.

7. This is the name of a rock formation on Witch's Hill.

8. I owe a debt of gratitude to Mary Duffy for aiding me in Re-membering the many complicated place names with descriptions on this two-day trip to the West—and in the right order! Personal communication, August 11, 1987.

9. This language is the Irish form of Gaelic.

10. The name of the Lord Mayor at that Time was Carmencita Hederman. She was the first woman mayor of Dublin and the only one to date.

11. This sort of shifting around and exchanging messages happened throughout the Congress, of course, in restaurants, on the streets, in hotels, in pubs, in lecture halls. It was nowhere more dramatic, however, than at the "Reclaim the Night March."

12. The Women's Peace Camp at Greenham Common in England was set up in 1981 outside the huge United States Air Force base where they were installing the first Cruise missiles. Over the years thousands of women from all over the world have passed through there. It has been a scene of courageous resistance and struggle, and countless hours of intense discussions. Some women who have been there believe that they were "zapped" by microwaves and that this has had a disorienting effect upon them.

13. A fascinating book about this Female Pirate is Anne Chambers, *Granuaile: The Life and Times of Grace O'Malley, c. 1530–1603* (Dublin: Wolfhound Press, 1979). Perusing the genealogy chart of descendents of Granuaile (Grace O'Malley) recently I was startled to find the name Mary Daly in an outstanding place on the middle of the page. I found that she belongs there because she married someone named Peter, who was the son of Maud Bourke, great-great-granddaughter of Grace

O'Malley. There is no reason to believe—or not to believe—that this Mary Daly is somehow related to me. The point is not about whether I am a descendent of Granuaile in a strict foreground sense. Dis-covering my name on this chart was a jolt, reinforcing my awareness that the Ireland of Granuaile is part of my heritage. I have roots there.

14. Andrée Collard with Joyce Contrucci, *Rape of the Wild: Man's Violence against Animals and the Earth* (London: The Women's Press, 1988; Bloomington and Indianapolis: Indiana University Press, 1989).

15. See Chapter Fourteen.

16. See Barbara G. Walker, *The Woman's Dictionary of Symbols and Sacred Objects* (San Francisco: HarperSanFrancisco, 1988), pp. 343–44.

17. See, for example, Chapter Ten, in which I describe the experience of feeling like a gull sailing the Great Wind.

18. See Edmund Lenihan, *In Search of Biddy Early* (Cork and Dublin: The Mercier Press, 1987), p. 103.

19. It is delightful to me that I have photographs of the eight calves with us in the stone circle. Not that anyone could possibly relegate this magical event to the sphere of hallucination . . . but, all the same . . .

20. See Meda Ryan, *Biddy Early: The Wise Woman of Clare* (Cork and Dublin: The Mercier Press, 1978), p. 99.

21. See Cecil Woodham-Smith, *The Great Hunger: Ireland 1845–1849* (London: Hamish Hamilton Ltd., 1962, 1987). This extraordinary work by Mrs. Woodham-Smith is a rich source of information which is extremely well written and documented.

CHAPTER EIGHTEEN:
DOORS TO FOUR: LUCKY DIS-COVERINGS AND HAPPY HOMECOMINGS

1. See Chapter Fourteen.

2. For other references to Gladys Custance, see Chapters Five, Eight, and Seventeen.

3. In the spring of 1988 I spoke at Miami University in Oxford, Ohio; San Jose State University in San Jose, California; University of Southern California in Los Angeles; Michigan State University in East Lansing; Bowdoin College in Brunswick, Maine; Portland State University in Portland, Oregon; Mount St. Vincent's University in Halifax, Nova Scotia, Canada. I gave a talk at Crazy Ladies Bookstore in Cincinnati, Ohio.

4. The British edition of the *Wickedary* was published in London by The Women's Press in 1988.

5. The Irish edition of the *Wickedary* was published in Dublin by Attic Press in 1988.

6. Personal communication, December 1, 1985. This was confirmed in a transatlantic telephone conversation, January 22, 1992.

7. June compared christianity and buddhism, arguing the case that buddhism is more subtle in its oppression of women and possibly even more thoroughly penetrates women's psyches. To illustrate her point concerning tibetan buddhism she described one meditation which involved "seeing a lama sitting on top of your head, dripping a 'pure' essence (semen) from his body through yours." Conversation,

of Philosophy, edited by Paul Edwards (New York and London: Macmillan Publishing Co., Inc. & The Free Press, 1967).

10. For further insight about the history of Sacajawea, see Paula Gunn Allen's poem, "The One Who Skins Cats," in *Skins and Bones: Poems 1979–1987* (Albuquerque, New Mexico: West End Press, 1988), pp. 14–19.

11. See Barbara G. Walker, *The Woman's Dictionary of Symbols and Sacred Objects* (San Francisco: HarperSanFrancisco, 1988), pp. 419–20.

12. Since we are intensely aware of the foreground now, we have much to Wail and Rail about. The early 1990s continued the escalation of gynocide which Radical Feminists had predicted in the late 1980s. Take 1991, for example. In October of that year mass murderer George Hennard, calling women "treacherous female vipers," opened fire in a restaurant in Killeen, Texas, killing fourteen women and eight men. That same month a New Hampshire man confessed that he had strangled his wife and suffocated his three baby girls. And that October a police officer in Braintree, Massachusetts, was charged with assaulting his blind, diabetic wife who was on kidney dialysis, giving her a separated shoulder and multiple fractures of the knee and elbow. Earlier that year—in late summer—a sixteen-year-old male in Beverly, Massachusetts, was arrested for murdering his fourteen-year-old girlfriend. His parting verbal shot was "It sucks to be you, Amy." As *Boston Herald* columnist Margery Eagan pointed out, more money was spent on the Franklin Park Zoo in Boston than the entire State of Massachusetts spent on sheltering women and children. And, as the same columnist states: "More American women seek emergency treatment for battering than for muggings, rapes, and car accidents combined. Battering is the number one cause of injury to women, who are nine times more likely to be attacked at home than on the street." See Margery Eagan, "Battered Women Deserve Unconditional Protection," *The Boston Herald*, October 24, 1991.

A PARTIAL LIST
OF PUBLICATIONS BY MARY DALY

1963

The Problem of Speculative Theology: A Study in Saint Thomas (unpublished dissertation in theology, University of Fribourg, Switzerland, 1963).

1964

"Women and the Church," *Commonweal* 79 (1964), p. 603. Also published in Gertrud Heinzelmann (editor), *Wir schweigen nicht länger! Frauen äussern sich zum II. Vatikanischen Konzil* (*We Won't Keep Silence Any Longer! Women Speak Out to Vatican Council II*) (Zürich: Interfeminas Verlag, 1965), pp. 106-7.

1965

The Problem of Speculative Theology (Washington, D.C.: Thomist Press, 1965). Also published as "The Problem of Speculative Theology," *The Thomist* 29 (1965), pp. 177–216.

"Catholic Women and the Modern Era," in Gertrud Heinzelmann (editor), *Wir schweigen nicht länger! Frauen äussern sich zum II. Vatikanischen Konzil* (*We Won't Keep Silence Any Longer! Women Speak Out to Vatican Council II*) (Zürich: Interfeminas Verlag, 1965), pp. 108–10.

"A Built-in Bias," *Commonweal* 81 (January 15, 1965), pp. 508–11.

1966

Natural Knowledge of God in the Philosophy of Jacques Maritain (Rome: Officium Libri Catholici, 1966).

1967

"Zeroing in on Freedom," *Commonweal* 86 (June 2, 1967), pp. 316–17.

1968

The Church and the Second Sex (London/Dublin/Melbourne: Geoffrey Chapman, 1968; New York: Harper & Row, 1968).

"Antifeminism in the Church," *Information Documentation on the Conciliar Church*, no. 68–44 (Rome/Geneva: IDO-C, 1968).

"Hans Küng," in William Jerry Boney and Lawrence E. Molumby (editors), *The New Day: Catholic Theologians of the Renewal* (Richmond, Virginia: John Knox Press, 1968), pp. 129–42.

"Christian Mission After the Death of God," in William J. Wilson (editor), *Demands for Christian Renewal* (New York: Maryknoll, 1968), pp. 1–18.

"Dispensing with Trivia," *Commonweal* 88 (May 31, 1968), pp. 322–25.

"Underground Theology" (response to Aquinas M. Ferrara's critique of "Dispensing with Trivia"), *Commonweal* 88 (August 9, 1968), pp. 532–34.

1969

"Return of the Protestant Principle," *Commonweal* 90 (June 6, 1969), pp. 338–41.

"Mary Daly on the Church," *Commonweal* 91 (November 14, 1969), p. 215.

1970

"The Problem of Hope," *Commonweal* 92 (June 26, 1970), pp. 314–17.

"Églises ou tombes de Dieu?" in Philippe Delhaye and Claude Troisfontaines (editors), *L'Église souterraine* (Rome/Genève: IDO-C, 1970), pp. 19–33.

"Women and the Catholic Church," in Robin Morgan (editor), *Sisterhood Is Powerful: An Anthology of Writings from the Women's Liberation Movement* (New York: Vintage Books, 1970), pp. 137–53.

"Toward Partnership in the Church," in Mary Lou Thompson (editor), *Voices of the New Feminism* (Boston: Beacon Press, 1970), pp. 136–51.

1971

"The Courage to See," *The Christian Century* 88 (September 22, 1971), pp. 1108–11.

"After the Death of God the Father: Women's Liberation and the Transformation of Christian Consciousness," *Commonweal* (March 12, 1971), pp. 7–11. Also published in Carol P. Christ and Judith Plaskow (editors), *Womanspirit Rising: A Feminist Reader in Religion* (San Francisco: Harper & Row, 1979), pp. 53–62.

"The Spiritual Dimension of Women's Liberation," in Ann Koedt and Shulamith Firestone (editors), *Notes from the Third Year: Major Writings of the Radical Feminists* (New York, 1971), pp. 75–79. Also published in A. Koedt, E. Levine, A. Rapone (editors), *Radical Feminism* (New York: Quadrangle, 1973), pp. 259–67.

1972

"Abortion and Sexual Caste," *Commonweal* 95 (February 4, 1972), pp. 415–19.

"The Spiritual Revolution: Women's Liberation as Theological Re-education," *Andover Newton Quarterly* 12 (March 1972), pp. 163–76. Also published in *Notre Dame Journal of Education* 2, no. 4 (1972), pp. 300–312.

"The Women's Movement: An Exodus Community," *Religious Education* 67 (September–October 1972), pp. 327–35.

"A Call for the Castration of Sexist Religion," *The Unitarian Universalist Christian* 27 (Autumn/Winter 1972), pp. 23–37. Also published as "Theology After the Demise of God the Father: A Call for the Castration of Sexist Religion," in Alice L. Hageman (editor), in collaboration with The Women's Caucus of Harvard Divinity School, *Sexist Religion and Women in the Church: No More Silence!* (New York: Association Press, 1974), pp. 125–42. Also published under the same title in Judith Plaskow (editor), *Women and Religion 1972* (American Academy of Religion and The Scholars' Press–University of Montana at Missoula, 1972), pp. 7–33.

1973

Beyond God the Father: Toward a Philosophy of Women's Liberation (Boston: Beacon Press, 1973).

"Post-Christian Theology," in Joan Arnold Romero (editor), *Women and Religion 1973* (American Academy of Religion and The Scholars' Press–Florida State University at Tallahassee, 1973), pp. 33–38.

1974

"God Is a Verb," *Ms.* (December 1974), pp. 58–62, 96–98.

1975

"Autobiographical Preface to the Colophon Edition" and "Feminist Postchristian Introduction," in *The Church and the Second Sex: With a New Feminist Postchristian Introduction by the Author* (New York: Harper & Row, 1975), pp. 5–51.

"The Qualitative Leap Beyond Patriarchal Religion," *Quest* 1, no. 4 (Spring 1975), pp. 20–40. Also published in Lee A. Jacobus (editor), *A World of Ideas: Essential Readings for College Writers*, 3d edition (Boston: Bedford Books of St. Martin's Press, 1990), pp. 605–29.

"A Short Essay on Hearing and the Qualitative Leap of Radical Feminism," *Horizons* 2 (1975), pp. 120–24.

1976

"Feminismo radicale: al di là della religione patriarcale," in Rocco Caporale (editor), *Vecchi e nuovi dei: Studi e riflessioni sul senso religioso dei nostri tempi. Dagli atti del Secondo Simposio Internazionale sulla Credenza organizzato dalla "Fondazione Giovanni Agnelli" (Vienna, 7–11 gennaio 1975)* (Torino: Editoriale Valentino, 1976), pp. 357–88.

1977

"The Courage to Leave: A Response to John Cobb's Theology," in D. R. Griffin and T. J. J. Altizer (editors), *John Cobb's Theology in Process* (Philadelphia: Westminster Press, 1977).

"Radical Feminism, Radical Religion," in Elizabeth Clark and Herbert Richardson (editors), *Women and Religion* (New York: Harper & Row, 1977), pp. 259–71.

1978

Gyn/Ecology: The Metaethics of Radical Feminism (Boston: Beacon Press, 1978).

1980

"Vorwort zur deutschen Ausgabe von Beyond God the Father," in Mary Daly, *Jenseits von Gottvater, Sohn & Co.: Aufbruch zu einer Philosophie der Frauenbefreiung* (München: Frauenoffensive, 1980), pp. 5–10.

1982

Notes pour une ontologie du féminisme radical, traduit par Michèle Causse (Québec: L'Intégrale, 1982).

"Gyn/Ecology: Spinning New Time/Space," in Charlene Spretnak (editor), *The Politics of Women's Spirituality: Essays on the Rise of Spiritual Power Within the Feminist Movement* (New York: Anchor Press/Doubleday, 1982), pp. 207–12.

1984

Pure Lust: Elemental Feminist Philosophy (Boston: Beacon Press, 1984; San Francisco: Harper San Francisco, 1992).

1985

"New Archaic Afterwords," in *The Church and the Second Sex: With the Feminist Postchristian Introduction and New Archaic Afterwords by the Author* (Boston: Beacon Press, 1985), pp. xi–xxx.

"Original Reintroduction," in *Beyond God the Father: Toward a Philosophy of Women's Liberation. With an Original Reintroduction by the Author* (Boston: Beacon Press, 1985), pp. xi–xxix.

1987

"Pouvoirs élémentaux des femmes: re-mémoration/re-membrement," in Marisa Zavalloni (editor), *L'émergence d'une culture au féminin* (Montréal: Les Éditions Saint-Martin, 1987), pp. 133–46.

Websters' First New Intergalactic Wickedary of the English Language (Conjured by Mary Daly in Cahoots with Jane Caputi) (Boston: Beacon Press, 1987).

1988

"Reine Lust: Laster, Tugenden, neue Verhaltensweisen—Plastik und Bonsai Leidenschaften," in Marlies Fröse (editor), *Utopos—Kein Ort: Mary Daly's Patriarchatskritik und feministische Politik; Ein Lesebuch* (Bielefeld: AJZ, 1988), pp. 114–30.

"Be-Laughing," *Woman of Power*, no. 8 (Winter 1988), pp. 76–80.

1989

"Be-Friending: Weaving Contexts, Creating Atmospheres," in Judith Plaskow and Carol P. Christ (editors), *Weaving the Visions: New Patterns in Feminist Spirituality* (San Francisco: Harper & Row, 1989), pp. 199–207.

1990

"Spiraling into the Nineties," *Woman of Power*, no. 17 (1990), pp. 6–12.

"New Intergalactic Introduction," in *Gyn/Ecology: The Metaethics of Radical Feminism. With a New Intergalactic Introduction by the Author* (Boston: Beacon Press, 1990), pp. xiii–xxxv.

1993

Outercourse: The Be-Dazzling Voyage. Containing Recollections from My Logbook of a Radical Feminist Philosopher (Be-ing an Account of My Time/Space Travels and Ideas—Then, Again, Now, and How) (San Francisco: Harper San Francisco, 1993).

INDEX

Aalfs, Joann, 263, 268
Abbeyfeale (Ireland), 363
Abod, Susan, 230, 231
abortion, 408, 453; and sexual caste system, 142ff; speaking out for repeal of anti-abortion laws, 108, 136–37, 142–43
academia/academentia, 95ff, 385ff; lack of Feminist analysis of, in sixties, 89ff
academic freedom, struggle for, 95ff, and *passim*
Act, Original Capacities to, 195n
Acts of Seeing, 222
Adams, Carol, 207
Ad Hoc Hagographers, 229
African Americans, 35, 100. *See also* women of color
Age of Cronehood, 412
Age of Dis-memberment, 9, 10, 12, 210, 339, 393, 398, 412
Aggression (anger/malevolent male violence), 212, 240, 273
Agnelli Foundation, 183, 200
Alchemy, Spiritual/Intellectual, 157–58
A-mazing: and *Gyn/Ecology*, 224–25; defined, 225
Amazons, 211; and Plundering, 205
Amazons of Dahomey (Africa), 414
American Academy of Religion, 141, 174, 319ff, 388; lecture about *Pure Lust*, 297; Women and Religion section, 141–42
amnesia, 6n, 7, 27, 106, 130, 190, 231, 328
Anamnesia/Unforgetting, 106, 133, 140, 150
Andover Newton Theological School, 167, 170, 189, 299
androgyny, 203; as male-functioning malapropism, 160ff; 1975 critique of, 203ff
anger. *See* Rage
Animal Guides, in *Wickedary*, 295n, 301–5
animals: in Australia, 260–62; in Ireland, 349, 350, 360, 363, 365, 368, 369, 403; as guides in *Wickedary*, 301–5;

in Leverett, MA, 246, 253–55, 270; destruction of, by patriarchy, 21, 147n, 222n, 230, 243, 343n, 385, 407–8, *and throughout book*; in Onset, MA, 217–18; on Other side of the moon, 409ff; in Switzerland, 218, 380, 381; in woman-centered society, 219. *See also* Familiar; Wild Cat
Anthony, Leigh, 390, 391, 450
Anthony, Susan B., 411–12
anti-abortion laws: and misogynism of church, 142–43; speaking out for repeal of, 108; testimony for repeal of, 136–37
Antichrist, Second Coming of women as, 159
"Anti-Modernist Oath," 69–70, 99n
"anxiety of nonbeing," 159
aphasia, 116, 117, 122, 130, 190, 328; defined, 6
Appel, Judy, 438
apraxia, 6n, 8, 184, 195, 197, 210, 234, 235, 237, 238, 267, 274, 290, 309, 321, 322, 328, 391; defined, 6
Aquinas, Thomas, 51, 52, 59, 90, 141, 157, 245, 361
Aran Islands (Ireland), 354; and Piracy and Pirate's Craft, 355; and Subliminal Sea, 354
Archaic Background of words, 294
Archaic Gynocentric tradition, 51
Archaic knowledge, 269
Archaic meanings, 221
Archaic Memory, 19
Archaic Origins, 221
Archaic, Prechristian, Pagan Source, 406
Archaic Reality, Deep Memories of in Europe, 65n
Archaic time, glimpses of in Egypt, 83
Archespheres, 268–69; defined, 268n
Archimage, in *Pure Lust*, 275
Aristotle, 157
Ashe, Sister Kaye, 59
assimilation, 7, 95, 132, 186, 203, 212; defined, 116
Assimilators, 116, 131
Athena, 205

Athleticism, Spiritual/Intellectual, 157–58, 219
atrocities of patriarchy, 150n, 195, 197, 212, 213, 221, 227, 229, 230, 308, 323, 326, 339, 343–44, 393, 399, 400–401, 407–8, 433, 451, 453, 454
Attic Press (Dublin, Ireland), 378
Aughinish (Ireland), 370
Augustine, saint, 141
Aura, 58, 63, 64, 92, 104, 149, 154, 211, 217, 240, 241, 242, 244, 250, 252, 257, 263, 280, 284, 341, 348, 355, 360, 361, 408, 410
Australia, 259ff, 325
Averroes, 245
Avicenna, 245
Ax, Ioma (Io), 349, 358, 370, 379, 402–5

"Ba," 255n, 349, 363, 364, 378; etymology of, 256; meaning of, 377
Bachofen, J. J., 157
Background, 1, 132, 149, 158, 163, 182, 195, 208, 312, 322, 339, 340, 341, *and throughout book*
backlash, 170–71, 262, 434, and *passim*
Ballyvaughan (County Clare, Ireland), 360
Bardic School of O'Dalaigh, 361, 368
Barracuda, 92, 166
Barrett, Eileen, 182
Barufaldi, Linda, 3, 11n, 137, 139, 146, 152, 153, 155, 156, 207, 428. *See also* Tigers
basse ville (Fribourg, Switzerland), 58, 66, 406
Battle of Principalities and Powers, 266, 277, 280; and writing of *Pure Lust*, 241
Baumgartner, Adelheid, 382
Beauvoir, Simone de, 55, 112, 158, 174, 414
Beaven, Betsey, 279n, 293
Be-Dazzling, 6, 8, 12, 13, 21, 108, 150, 155, 175, 225, 251, 294, 312, 341, 345, *and throughout book*; defined, 5
Be-Dazzling Light, 9, 196, 205, 222, 234, 238, 312n, 320, 321, 335, 374, 405; of Female Fire, 231; of The Third Spiral Galaxy, 250
Be-Dazzling Now, 8ff, 210, 335ff, 393, *and throughout* The Fourth Spiral Galaxy
Be-Dazzling Voyage, 5, 10, 12, 20, 46, 88, 244, *and throughout book*
beehive, symbolism of, 255–56
beehive structures: and "Ba," 378; in Ireland, 349, 365; in Leverett, MA, 254ff

bees: in Ireland, 349–50, 365; in Leverett, MA, 254ff
Bees, Spelling, as Animal Guides to *Wickedary*, 304
Be-Falling, 7, 130, 133, 139, 164; defined, 7
Be-Friending, 197, 327
Beguine, Diana, 297, 305, 398
Be-ing, 3, 6, 21, 133, 158, 187, 196, *and throughout book*; and *Beyond God the Father*, 158; defined, 158n; participation in, 152, 275, 415; and *Pure Lust*, 275; as Verb, 158, 161
be-ing: Background, 175, 251; defined, 158n; Ecstatic, in Third Passage of *Gyn/Ecology*, 221; intuition of, 113, 158, 160, 161, 323; intuition of, and The Tornado, 252; intuition of, and clover blossom, 23, 113, 117–18, 251; Re-Claiming Elemental, 254; and Sinning, 292; as verb, 418
Be-Laughing, 21, 90, 100, 175, 199, 216, 252, 274
Be/Leaving, 94, 121
Belfast (Ireland), 281
Bell Harbour (Ireland), 370, 379, 402
Bellamy, Suzanne, 260–62
Beltane, 165
Be-Musing, 152–54, 214–20, 310
Berger, Peter, 112, 135, 157
Bern (Switzerland), 66, 67, 381, 382
Bersianik, Louky, 6n, 244n, 379
Be-Speaking, 10, 46, 112, 119, 139, 144, 148, 174, 213, 229, 238, 319, *and throughout book*; and *amnesia*, 130; and *aphasia*, 130; as Be-Falling, 130; and *The Church and the Second Sex*, 77, 91; of clover blossom, 23, 51, 113, 117–18, 160, 251, 276; defined, 7; in early Moments, 6; of hedge, 51, 114, 251, 277; Original Moment of (letter to *Commonweal*), 77; and *Wickedary*, 313
Be-Witching, 205, 224; defined, 196; Power, 149, 196, 324, *and throughout book*
Be-words, in *Pure Lust*, 275, 276
Beyond God the Father, 7, 59, 132, 146ff, 174, 187, 190, 195, 203, 206, 222, 260; as beginning of Elemental Radical Feminist Philosophy, 158; and *The Courage to Be* (Tillich), 159; and "Father-Mother God" of Mary Baker Eddy, 135; and "Feminist Postchristian Introduction" to *The Church and the Second Sex*, 133; from Fourth Galactic perspective, 155; index of, 165; inspired by Rage and rationality, 163; Italian publication of, 403;

letters about, 167ff; malapropisms in, 160ff; Prophesying *Gyn/Ecology* and *Pure Lust*, 163; publication of, 167, 170; reviews of, 167ff; and Smuggling, 157; subtitle of, 132, 164, 188; unifying theme of, 159–60; and words used in *Wickedary*, 296

Bhā², 256

Bielefeld, University of, 307

biocide, 11, 385, 393–94, 408

Biophilia, 238, 293, 310, 326, 327, *and throughout book*; defined, 294

Biophilic Actions, 414

Biophilic Bonding, 199, 232, 233, 238, 269

Biophilic Bounding, 4

Biophilic Energy, 414

Biophilic Powers, 242

Biophilic women, 131, 198

Black Forest (Germany), 383

Blake, William, "Tyger! Tyger! burning bright," 147, 150

Blasting, out of the foreground, 341

Blavatsky, Madame, 257

Blessington (Ireland), 402

Bloodroot Restaurant and Bookstore (Bridgeport, CT), 279n, 293

Blooms Hotel (Dublin, Ireland), 350

Blue Mountains (Australia), 260

Bologna (Italy), 403–6

Bonding, Female, 20, 45, 85, 114, 133, 138, 166, 185, 225, 232, 233ff, 238, 239, 269, 323

books: in childhood, 30, 35; and Magical encounters, 257; Radiant Realm of Books, 26; World of Glowing Books, 26

Boon Companion, defined, 68n

bore-dom, 339, 340

bore-ocracy, 200

bore-words, 275

Boston (in Ireland), 361

Boston Theological Institute (BTI), 53, 137, 153, 279n, 299; Women's Institute, 141; Women's Studies at, 103, 298

Boundary, 120, 147, 152, 159, 175, 188, 189, 199, 347; and Radical Feminist Thought, 148; between dreams and "reality," 155; and Women's Space, 326–28

Boundary Living, 40, 46, 121, 189, 218, 240, 283, 340, 341; defined, 46

Bourguillon (Switzerland), 60, 381, 406

Brainstorms, 163, 215, 225

Breakthrough and Re-Calling, Moments of, 129, 137, 140, 143, 143n, 144, 146, 147, 150, 175, 182, 184, 185, 190, *and throughout* The Second Spiral Galaxy

breast implants, 407

Brenner, Claudia, 394

Briffault, Robert, 157

Briggs, Katharine (*Encyclopedia of Fairies*), 354n

Brighton (MA), 54, 104, 152, 164

Broom, 95n, 110, 165, 189, 197, 211, 221, 341

Brossard, Nicole, 244n, 280, 379

bulls/bullocks (in Ireland), 368

bull-jumping, fresco in Herakleion Museum (Crete), 219

Burke, Adrienne, 390

Burren (Ireland), 359–61, 366–70

Buswell's Hotel (Dublin, Ireland), 281, 378

Cahill, Jane Furlong, 94

Call of the Wild, 23, 27, 46, 80, 114, 133, 152, 246, 249, 325, 348; defined, 221; and *Gyn/Ecology*, 221ff

Call of the Wild, The, 25, 30

calves (in Ireland), 363

Campbell, June, 375–76, 447

Canterbury (England), 65

Caputi, Jane, 8, 182, 216, 276, 293ff, 315, 317, 417, 453

Cardinal Cushing College (Brookline, MA), 54

Cardinal Flaw, on trial in "The Witches Return," 395

Carrowmore (Ireland), 350

Carson, Rachel, 257, 414

Castledaly (County Galway, Ireland), 402ff

Cat/atonic, defined, 220n

Cat/egorical Appendix (*Pure Lust*), 274; "acted out" at Bern seminar, 382

Cat/egorical Imperative, 220n, 301

Catherine (in Leverett, MA), 246, 346

Catherine (The Cow That Jumped over the Moon), 342ff, 346–47, 351–52, 357, 358, 363n, 366–67, 371, 374, 376, 385, 388, 396, 401, 407, 408ff

catholic church, 76, 90, 282ff, 393

Catholic University of America (Washington, D.C.), 48, 55, 114, 118

Cat-words, 275

Causse, Michelle, 280

Chapman, Geoffrey (London, England), publisher, 78

Chautauqua Institution (Chautauqua, NY), 106

Chelland, Fran, 182, 259, 263, 270

Chernobyl: discussions in Germany about, 307; media reporting of, 306; and Sado-Ritual Syndrome, 308, 309

"Children of All Lands" stories (Madeline Frank Brandeis), 25

"Christian Feminism": my dismissal of position, 176; and Postchristian Feminism, 181; promoted by catholic hierarchy, 450; and Radical Feminism, 164, 393, 450

christianity, 173; Departure from, 153; myths and symbols of, 111, 135, 148, 181, 187, 188, 189, 322

Christolatry, analyzed in *Beyond God the Father*, 159

christmas tree, 31

Church and the Second Sex, The, 6, 71ff, 79, 84, 102ff, 111, 118, 122, 157, 206, 242, 249; as an Act of Be-Speaking, 91; my mother's Presence during writing of, 92; "Autobiographical Preface to the 1975 Edition," 62, 77, 102n, 172, 180, 186; and *Beyond God the Father*, 133; cover of 1975 edition, 176; "Feminist Postchristian Introduction" to the 1975 edition, 7, 8, 102n, 132, 133, 172ff, 180, 184, 186, 190, 195; First Coming of, 77; frontispiece of 1975 edition, 176; initial writing of, in Fribourg (Switzerland), 80; letters about, 100–101; as Originally Radical, 91n; paperback edition of, 172ff, 185; publication of, 93–94; publicity for, 93–94

Civil Rights movement, 90

Clare, County (Ireland), 359; Daly family roots, 359

class differences, in college, 45

Cleveland Circle (Boston, MA), 87

Cliffs of Moher (Ireland), 360, 378, 379

clover blossom, 41, 113, 117, 276; and becoming a Radical Feminist Philosopher, 23; Be-Speaking of, 251; Call of the, 24, 78; and hedge, 51, 276; and intuition of be-ing, 23, 113, 117–18, 251

Cobb, Ann, 259

Cobb, Irwin, 95n

Cobb, John B., Jr., 389

coeducation, 119ff, 189, 326–28

cognitive minority, 315; of one, 53, 111ff, 238

Colburn, Krystyna, 279n, 396, 443

Collard, Andrée, 103, 216, 230, 303, 341, 356, 360, 396; and conversations about animals and nature, 269; death of, 310; dedication of *Wickedary* to, 310; paean to Moon-Cow Goddess, 358; *Rape of the Wild*, 243, 356

Cologne (Germany), 271

Commonweal, 50, 101–11, 142–43; letter to (1964), 6, 77, 134, 187

communication, interspecies, 216ff. *See also* animals; Elemental Encounters; moon

Condren, Mary, 378

connectedness: Dis-covering lost threads of, 210, 219; in The First Spiral Galaxy, 113; longing for, in eighties, 285; Re-Weaving threads of, 221; Spinning threads of, 300

Connemara (Ireland), 354

Connors, Denise, 182, 207, 211, 217, 218, 220, 242, 246, 270, 272, 274; and conversations about *Pure Lust*, 269; and title *Metamorphospheres*, 272; and Wild Eyes, 220

"Continued existence." *See* hedge

contrapuntal movements, in Spiral Galaxies, 115ff, 187ff, 321ff

Contrucci, Joyce, 310, 392, 395, 396, 397

Conway Hall (London, England), 285

Cork (Ireland), 282

Corofin Heritage Centre (County Clare, Ireland), 361–62, 378

cosmic covenant, 160, 185, 188

counterpoint, 60, 323. *See also* contrapuntal movements

Courage, 130, 159, 160, 197, 414; Ontological, 198, 275

Courage to Be, The (Tillich), 136, 159

Courage to Leave, 139, 198

Courage to Live Wildly, 198

Courage to Sail, 130, 187–90, and *passim*

Courage to See, 136ff, 198

Courage to Sin, 130, 198

Courage to Spin, 198, 219

Courage to Write, 168, 239

Course, 2, 80, 113, 129, 132, 197

Course, True, 1, 3

cow/cows: in Ireland, 369, 370, 371, 376, 379; in Kleine Scheidegg (Switzerland), 346; in Leverett, MA, 246; magical encounter in Switzerland, 218ff; and moon, in Archaic myths, 357; that jumped over the moon, 342ff, *and throughout* The Fourth Spiral Galaxy. *See also* Catherine

Craft, 3ff, 6, 13, 109ff, 129, 129n, 147, 149, 151, 154, 157, 163, 168, 184, 185, 187, 189, 190, 196, 200, 205, 221, 225, 250, 257, 267, 293, 309, 312, 314, 320, 321, 322, 325, 341, 345, 348, 352, 355, 374, *and throughout book;* defined, 109. *See also* Pirate

Creevykeel (Ireland), 350

Crete, 72ff; influence on *Gyn/Ecology*, 72n, 218; Treasures of, 151n

Crone, 2, 10, 11, 12, 90, 199, 212, 223, 229, 256, 300, 309, 311, 314, 329, 338, 396ff, 405, 408, 411, 412

Crone, Joni, 281, 282, 284, 349, 354, 358, 359, 366, 370, 378, 402, 403

Crone-logical context, 239, 294, 295n, 314, 316, and *passim*

Crones' Harvest (Boston, MA), 401, 451

Crone-words, 224

Cronies, 182, 190, 199, 214, 244n, 335, 339, 341, 344, 345, 347, 365, 370, 372, 385, 395, 405–13, *and throughout* The Fourth Spiral Galaxy

Crystal Lake (Newton, MA), 278, 293, 294, 301, 304, 305

Culpepper, Emily, 43, 108n, 113n, 137, 138, 146, 148, 153, 155, 156, 176, 183, 201, 207, 215, 230, 259, 264, 269, 272, 278, 298n, 300, 303, 310, 311n, 319, 356, 396, 397, 436, 439. *See also* Tigers

Cushing, Cardinal, of Boston (MA), 56

Custance, Gladys, 106, 107, 156, 355, 360; "Gladys's Time," 360; death of, 372; gift of spiral ring, 373

"Daily, Daily, Sing to Mary," 24, 94

Daly, Anna, 19, 27ff, 34–36, 44–45, 47, 51, 54, 56–57, 67–68, 71–74, 80, 84–86, 87, 91ff, 104, 335, 342, 350, 364

Daly family: female Presence, 29; Irish roots of, 29, 359, 361, 402; Search for, in Finavarra (Ireland), 367

Daly, Frank, 26–29, 34, 36, 40, 44–45, 67, 92, 350, 364, 367ff, 418

Daly, Mary: books: *See Church and the Second Sex; Beyond God the Father; Gyn/Ecology; Pure Lust; Wickedary; Outercourse*; other publications of: "Abortion and Sexual Caste," 142–43, 427; "After the Death of God the Father," 134–35, 426; "Autobiographical Preface to the 1975 Edition" of *The Church and the Second Sex*, 62, 77, 102n, 172, 180, 186; "Built-in Bias, A," 77, 423; "Courage to See, The," 136, 426; "Feminist Postchristian Introduction" to *The Church and the Second Sex*, 7, 8, 102n, 132, 133, 172ff, 180, 184, 186, 190, 195; Foreword to Andrée Collard's *Rape of the Wild*, 356; *Natural Knowledge of God in the Philosophy of Jacques Maritain* (doctoral dissertation in philosophy), 74, 75; "Post-Christian Theology," 174–75, 430; "Problem of Hope, The," 102, 424; *Problem of Speculative Theology, The* (doctoral dissertation in theology), 63, 66, 69; "Radical Feminism: The Qualitative Leap Beyond Patriarchal Religion," 183–84, 200–205, 432–33; "Spiritual Dimension of Women's Liberation, The," 140–41, 427; "Spiritual Revolution: Women's Liberation as Theological Re-education, The," 143, 427; "Theology After the Demise of God the Father: A Call for the Castration of Sexist Religion," 147, 428; "Women and the Catholic Church," 141, 426; "The Women's Movement: An Exodus Community," 426

Daly, Mrs., pub (Finavarra, Ireland), 369, 370, 402, 419

Daring, 224, 244, 277, 360

Daring Deeds, 208

Daring Ecstasy, 277

Davis, Charles, 101–2

Davis, Elizabeth Gould, 158, 247n

Davis, Marie, 349, 358, 370, 379, 402, 403

Deadly Sins of the Fathers, 8, 131, 195n, 210, 211, 212, 223, 240; defined, 116n; in *Pure Lust*, 275; in "Qualitative Leap" article, 205

deception, 60n, 212, 223, 240,

Deerpark Forest (Ireland), 350

Defiance, Act of, 203

Dellenbaugh, Anne, 19n, 182, 244, 253, 268, 276n, 431

demons, 5, 7, 9, 90, 118, 123, 205, 210, 240, 280

Depression, the Great, 28, 33–34, 36

Dhomhnaill, Nuala Ni, 378

Dines, Gail, 397n

Dis-covering, 56, 78, 157, *and throughout book*

Dis-memberment, Age of, 9, 10, 12, 210, 339, 393, 398, 412

dis-memberment, 9, 10, 21, 75, 223, *and throughout book*

Disgust, 199, 240, 293, 410

Diversity in Unity, 414

Dixon, Marlene, 103

Doctor Doolittle, 30

"Doctor," vs. "Miss" as title, 53

Doherty, Margaret, 349, 354, 370

dolphins, on walls of Knossos (Crete), 218–19

Doolin (Ireland), 360

"doomsday clock," 294, 308, 353; stopped by Elemental forces, 294

Downshire Hotel (Ireland), 402

Dowth (Ireland), 349

Dracula, 32–33

Dream of Green, 48, 50, 114, 276; and 11:12 phenomenon, 105n

dualisms, 276

Dublin (Ireland), 86, 280, 348, 350, 358

Duffy, Mary, 349, 354

Dull (Scotland), 376
Dunaengus (Ireland), 355
Dworkin, Andrea, 417

Early, Biddy, 362ff, 402; biography by
    Meda Ryan, 365
Earth: dangers to, 244; Elemental
    Biophilic Powers of, 242
Earth-rapers, 398
Ecology, connection with Radical Femi-
    nism, 108, 160, 163, 177ff, 243, 412,
    and throughout book
Ecstasy, 5, 63ff, 156, 195, 197, 323, 335,
    339, 349, 352, 362, 379, *and through-
    out book*; Breaking Taboo of, 277;
    Daring Ecstasy, 277; Gynocentric,
    212; Lust for, 274; Metapatriarchal
    Journey of, 9, 222ff; Moments of, in
    Pure Lust, 277; from Nature and the
    Realm of Books, 61; and Otherworld
    Journey, 205
Eddy, Mary Baker, and "Father-Mother
    God," 135
Edelmann-Klittich, Helga, 307
Edinburgh (Scotland), 375
Egypt, 82ff
Eichen, Bettina, 382
Electrical connections, 259, 289, 290,
    320, 346, 366
Electrical powers, 224, 235, 320
Elemental connectedness, for creation of
    Pure Lust, 262
Elemental connections, and *Wickedary*,
    293, 301
Elemental Encounters, 22–23, 26–27, 41,
    51, 114, 251, 252, 267, *and throughout
    book*
Elemental Feminist Philosophy, 9, 114,
    158, 198, 251, 276, 324, *and through-
    out book*; and *Beyond God the Father*,
    158; Dis-covering, 248ff; and The
    Tornado, 250
Elemental Integrity, 144, 321
Elemental, meanings of, 248
Elemental Memory, 131; defined, 256
Elemental Ontology, Realizing, 274–77
Elemental Passion, 240ff
Elemental Powers, 280, 320, 395, 398,
    410, 414
Elemental Reality, 106, 324; Dis-covering
    and communicating in *Pure Lust*,
    250; distinguished from elementary
    world, 250
Elemental Rhythms, defined, 272
Elemental Sounding, defined, 257
Elemental Sounds, 257, 314
Elemental Spirits, 277; defined,
    256–57

Elemental Spirits/Animals/Angelic
    beings, 245
Elemental Time, 4
Elemental world and Inhabitants, 267
elementaries, defined, 250
Elements, 151 and *passim*; defined, 249;
    Other Dimensions of, 254; Powers of,
    261
11:12 phenomenon, 104ff, 157n, 264,
    294, 405, 441; and *Appendicular Web
    Four* of the *Wickedary*, 105n; as cata-
    lyst for Leaps of Re-membering, 105;
    and Dream of Green, 105n; and little
    Green Man/Woman, 105n; marking
    Moments in the Be-Dazzling Voyage,
    105; and Syn-Crone-icities, 105
El Greco, 64
elimination (envy), 8, 189, 203, 212;
    defined, 131
Eliminators, 131, 190
E-motion, 197, 208, 234–35, 294; vs.
    plastic passion, 250
E-motional, 89, 118, 169, 175, 190, 357,
    371, *and throughout book*
energy, women's, 152. *See also* Gynergy
England, visits to, 65, 279–80, 284–85,
    374–76
Ennis (County Clare, Ireland), 362
environment: destruction of, linked to
    oppression of women, 108, 222n;
    "1974–1984, Decade of Choice"
    (Richland, WA), 177; "Women and
    the Environment" symposium
    (Spokane, WA), 177
envy, 131, 212
e-racer, defined, 190n
erasers of women, 129
Erasure, State of, 130
erasure, 190, 207; of Green Women, 405;
    of Self, 186, 188; of women, 46, 131;
    of women's Past, 152
Erigena, Johannes Scotus, 245
"eternal feminine" and "eternal mascu-
    line," 203
Exorcism, 5, 9, 156, 195, 197, 323, 339,
    398; of *amnesia*, 7; of *aphasia*, 6;
    of *apraxia*, 8, 321; of demons. *See*
    demons; Metapatriarchal Journey of,
    in *Gyn/Ecology*, 222ff; and Otherworld
    Journey, 205; in *Wickedary*, 304
exorcism, of christian symbolism, 148
Expanding Now, 336, 338, 339, 341, 348,
    374, 399, 400, 401, 405, *and through-
    out* The Fourth Spiral Galaxy
extra-environmentals, women as, 159
Exxon, on trial in "The Witches Return,"
    395
Eye-Opening, 100–101, 197
Fairyland (in Ireland), 350ff

Fairy Space: defined, 313; in Ireland, 350. *See also* Third Hemisphere

Fairy Time, 66, 354, 360; in Ireland, 350, 355, 362, 376; defined, 314. *See also* Fourth Hemisphere

"Fall, the": Radical Feminist analysis of, 146; and women's victimization, 151

Familiar: Divining, 217–19, 242, 303ff, 349–50, 356, 360, 378; Domestic, 216–17, 220, 245, 346

Famine, Irish, 362

Farians, Betty, 53, 81, 103, 141, 143, 158, 427

Fates, 296, 325; and *Pure Lust*, 256

Fearful Symmetry, 147, 150

female friendship, 39, 45–46, 100, 107, 163, 223, 259

fembotism, 140

Feminism: Age of Cronehood, 10; "First Wave" of, 10; "Second Wave" of, 9, 11, 77, 88

Feminist Studies, 166, 180. *See also* Women's Studies

Feminist University, dream of, 44, 209

Festival of Irish Women's Arts and Culture (Dublin, Ireland), 354

Fey Faith, 199, 269, 344

Fiercely Focusing, 137, 184, 244, 260, 398

Final Cause, 2, 3, 151, 155, 158n, 159, 160, 188, 195n, 273, 275, 329, 340, 343, 377, 415; defined, 114

Fina, Mary Jane, 44

Finavarra (Ireland), 361, 369, 378, 379, 402; Electrical Connections, 366, 367ff; Search for roots, 367; swans, 370, 378–79

Fire, 196, 212, 262, 268, 276, 335, 342, 348; Dis-covering, 404; of *Pure Lust*, 244; reclaiming, 229; of women-identified energy, 231

Fire of Rage, 184, 197

First Cause, 329. *See also* Final Cause

First Intergalactic Interdisciplinary Congress on the Other Side of the Moon, 408ff

First International Feminist Bookfair (London, England), 279ff

First Italian Lesbian Week ("Un Posto per Noi"), 403

Fitzpatrick, Kay, 44

Fletcher, Melissa, 396, 397n

Flynt, Larry, on trial in "The Witches Return," 395

foreground, 1, *and throughout book*; Blasting out of, 341–42; conditions in late eighties, 357; exposed by *Wickedary*, 312; illusions and fears blocking Background Future, 116; inhabitants of, illuminated by *Wickedary*, 312; Naming connections among phenomena of, 221; now, 339ff, 407ff; in the nineties, 407; time, 4

Foresisters, 11, 131, 155, 395, 434

Forrestal, Marina, 349

Forum on Women and Higher Education, 207–8, 311, 398

Fosdick Chair (Union Theological Seminary), 164

Four, 329, 335, 340, 348, 372–73, 377, 382, 422; Doors to, 372, 373, 377, 382n, 399, 405

Fourth Dimension, 64, 109, 110, 150, 151, 340, 372, 423

Fourth Hemisphere, 314, 329. *See also* Fairy Time

fragmentation, 8, 9, 75, 186, 195, 198, 210, 212, 221, 321

François, 153

Frankfurt (Germany), 306, 308

Franklin, Linda, 182, 207

Franklin, Miles, 414

Frauenoffensive (German publisher), 271

Freire, Paulo, 157

Freud, Sigmund, on trial in "The Witches Return," 395

Freya, Goddess, Mistress of Cats, 302

Fribourg (Switzerland), 55–56, 58–70, 71–86, 90, 99, 117, 187, 249, 250, 269, 270, 310, 361, 379, 381, 405–6, 418, 421, 422, 423, 445; teaching in junior year abroad programs, 56, 61, 62, 63

Fribourg, University of, 58, 99n, 118, 387

Friday the 13th, 302

Friedberg, Lilly, 307, 382, 404, 441

Friendship, Fire of Female, 223

Frye, Marilyn, 290

Furie, Noel, 279n, 293

Furies, 197

Furry, defined, 301

Fury, 199, 213, 233, 322. *See also* Rage

Future, Background, 4, 7, 9, 26, 41, 83, 116, 117, 121, 152, 219, 405

future, foreground, 6–7, 100, 123, and *passim*

Gage, Matilda Joslyn, 10, 43, 158, 341, 395

galaxy, etymology of, 5, 357

Gallup, Gerda, 309

Galway (Ireland), 354, 379

Gawain and the Green Knight, 49, 105n

geese, Wild, 304

Gelles, Elizabeth, 298, 391

"gender studies," 340

King's Canyon (Australia), 261
Kleine Scheidegg (Switzerland), 68, 346, 380
Knossos, Palace of (Crete), 72, 218
Knowledge, 115, 225; Archaic, 269; Background, Realizations of, 111, 150; E-motional, 89, 169; New, 175, 190; Original, 21, 150; subliminal, 112, 166, 169, 338, 342
Knowth (Ireland), 349
König, Cardinal, 8, 200ff
KPFA (San Francisco, CA), tape of Berkeley lecture, 243
Krattiger, Dr. Ursa, 382

Labrys, 151, 156, 211, 241, 269, 275, 277, 327, 391, 396–97; double-edged pairs of words, 223, 322; *Gyn/Ecology* as, 239; in Herakleion (Crete), 219; as inspiration for New Words, 219; *Pure Lust* as, 241, 436; and Smuggling, 219; Thomistic training as, 75
Labyrinthine Sense, defined, 314
lackey, defined, 329
La Drière, James Craig, 49
Lake, Jan, 356
Lammas, 261
Lanerolle, Ros de, 285, 376
language differences between Irish and American English, 359
language of transcendence, New, 161
Larson, Anna, 450
Lauer, Rosemary, "Women and the Church" (*Commonweal*), 6, 76, 144
Laughing Out Loud, 199, 218; and *Wickedary*, 293, 313
Leap, 78; into The Second Spiral Galaxy, 107; Spiraling, and move to Leverett (MA), 249; to Fribourg (Switzerland), 187
Leaping. *See* Qualitative Leaping
Leggere Donna, 403
Leone, Nicki, 392, 450
Lesbian Archive (London, England), 375
Lesbian Identity, 143ff, 170, 211–12, 214, 234n, 281, 375, 429
Lesbianism, and Radical Feminism, 375, 404, 435, *and throughout book. See also* Crone; Fury; Hag; Harpy; Integrity, Woman-identified; Spinster; Terrible Taboo; Total Taboo; Touching Powers; Woman-identification; Women-Touching Women
Lesbian Line (London, England), 375
letters: about *Beyond God the Father*, 167ff; about *The Church and the Second Sex*, 100ff, 167; about

Gyn/Ecology, 233ff; about *Pure Lust*, 285ff; about *Wickedary*, 314ff
Leverett (MA), 258, 277; and beehive structures, 254ff; collapse of barn, 268; description of cabin and land, 246ff; the loft, 263; poisoning of house, 272; Re-Weaving connections with early experiences, 254; and Spinning of *Pure Lust*, 246ff, 263ff; and Spiraling Leap, 249; The Tornado, 247
Liberty Hall (Dublin, Ireland), 66n, 281
Lieberman, Marcia, 207
Light. *See* Be-Dazzling Light
Lily Dale (New York), 107
Linnane's pub (Finavarra, Ireland), 369, 402
Lister, Maureen, 404, 406; and Donatella Maisano, Italian translation of *Beyond God the Father*, 403
Living Dead, State of the, 198
Logbook of a Radical Feminist Philosopher, Recollections from, 1, 11–13, 19, 109, 113, 337–38, 344, 346ff, 374, 378, *and throughout book*
London Bridge, 64
"Looking Glass Society," 177
Lord Mayor of Dublin, 353
Lorde, Audre, 232–33
Lost Senses, Search for, 106–7. *See also* Senses
Lough Gur (County Limerick, Ireland), 362; birds at, 378
Loughrea (Ireland), 359, 402
Lowry, Mary, 176, 431
Luck, 85, 87, 364; definition, 377
Lucky, 29, 32, 34, 55, 63, 65, 70, 72, 76, 83n, 92, 93, 173, 187, 258, 343, 349, 356, 364, 366, 374, 377, 380, 386, 419
"Lunatic Fringe," 199, 314
Lust, 196, 203, 208, 335, 342; to be a philosopher, 117, *and throughout book*; for Intellectual/E-motional/Spiritual Integrity, 117; for Metamorphosis, 391. *See also* Pure Lust
Lust-words, 275
Luxembourg, Strange occurrence with Pontiac, 67

McCafferty, Nell, 281
McCarthy, Mary Ellen, 279n
McDargh, John, 391
MacDonald, Nilah, 450
MacEoin, Gary, 79
McGillicuddy, Frances, 80
McMahon, Pat, 182, 207
McNamara, Melody, 354
MacRae, Jean, 137, 146. *See also* Tigers

Madeleva, Sister, 50, 53
Maebh, grave of (Ireland), 350
magical ceremonies, 217, 242; and writing of *Wickedary*, 303
Maisano, Donatella, 406; and Maureen Lister, Italian translation of *Beyond God the Father*, 403
malapropisms, male-functioning, in *Beyond God the Father*, 160ff
"Malleus Maleficarum," 317
Malone, Sara, 390
-*mancy* words, 254
Mann, Bonnie, 392, 397n
Mansion House (Ireland), 353
Mantra: for writing of *Beyond God the Father*, 214; for writing of *Gyn/Ecology*, 214, 216, 239; for writing of *Outercourse*, 335
maple tree, crooked, 248, 257, 274; and *Pure Lust*, 274
Marcuse, Herbert, 157
Maritain, Jacques, 23, 74, 440
Martin, Corinne, 354
Mary: image of, 188; shrines to, in Europe, 60, 406; as symbol, analyzed in *Beyond God the Father* and *Pure Lust*, 275; symbols of, 377
Matter, E. Ann, 290
maze, defined, 225
mazes of the masters, 212
Media, Moronizing, 309; on trial in "Witches Return," 395
Medora A. Feehan Fund, 56, 62, 78n
Meigs, Mary, 379
Melendy, Suzanne, 278, 279, 426, 443, 450
Memories, as Galvanizing Intergalactic Gallops, 110; in the Expanding Now, 338; as precious gems, 351
Memory: Archaic, 7; Deep, 13, 110, 131–33, 231, 254; Ecstatic, of Fribourg, 90; Elemental, 131, 256; of the Future, 7, 9, 26, 41, 209, 219; and *Logbook*, 11; Re-Called and Remembered through *Wickedary*, 313, *and throughout book*
Memory and Writing conference (New Brunswick, Canada), 244n
Memory-Bearing Group, 10, 11, 412
Messenheimer, Susan, 450
Meta-etymologies, in *Wickedary*, 297
Meta-words, 275
Metadictionary, 294; defined, 293
Metaknowledge, in doctoral dissertation in theology, 69
Metalanguage, 213
Metamemory, 327; defined, 52
Metamorphosis, 137, 163, 186, 197, 251; Lust for, 391; Sense of, in letters, 238

Metamorphospheres, 270, 272; defined, 270
Metamystery, defined, 295n
Metapatriarchal, defined, 157n
Metapatriarchal Metaphors, 60n, 275, 322, 324; defined, 223; in *Pure Lust*, 251, 275; list of, 223
Metapatterning, 249; defined, 222; in *Gyn/Ecology*, 222–24, 322–24; in *Pure Lust*, 249, 274, 275, 324, 327
metaphor, etymology of, 139–40
Metaphoric event, 139–40
Metaphoric expression, 188, 195
Metaphor, Metatheological, 188
methodicide, 159
methodolatry, 159, 188, 190
Middle East, 81ff; and Glowing World of Books, 82; Strange "coincidences" in, 82
Milhaven, Annie Lally, 450
Milky Way, 357; and Be-Dazzling connections, 257; Track of the White Cow in Celtic lands, 358
mindbindings, 44, 60, 75, 322, 323; defined, 313; exorcised in *Gyn/Ecology*, 322
mind-pollutants, 150
Miriam, Kathy, 269
Miriam, Selma, 279n, 293
misogynism, 76, 90, 117, 141–42
Mist, 129–31, 133, 149, 151, 152, 155, 164, 188, 190, 195, 196, 205, 222, 354; of Subliminal Sea, 149, 150, 157, 250; Pirating in the, 129, 131, 185
Moane, Geraldine, 111n, 311, 348, 352–55, 358, 359, 366–70, 379, 402, 403, 404, 419, 420
Moate (Ireland), 359
Molloy, Siobhan, 281
Moltmann, Jürgen, 157
Moments, 1–13, 276, 319, 320, 321, 324, 336, 337, 338, 348, *and throughout book*
Montreal (Canada) massacre, 400–401
moon, 13, 197, 247, 249, 254, 256, 257, 272, 314, 337, 343, 344, 345, 347, 350, 371, and *passim*; in Australia, 261, 262; childhood experiences of, 31, 117; commuting from, 347; and cow, in Archaic myths, 357–58; at Crystal Lake, 293, 294; in Leverett (MA), 246–47; life at home on, 346ff. *See also* Other side of the moon
Moon-Cow Goddess (Io), 357, 358
Moore, Leslie, 172
Moretti, Maria Louisa, 404
Morgan, Robin, 141, 149, 158, 207, 260, 300n, 392

Promise (and Prophecy), 6–7, 77, 121, *and throughout* The First Spiral Galaxy; broken, 45, 46, 48, 119, 189; broken, in women's colleges, 44, 84, 119; broken, transcended by Gynergy, 95; Moment of, 95, 276; Original, 119; Realizing deep, 121
prostitution, conference on, 141–42
Prudish Prudence, 199, 269, 283
pseudogeneric, 102 and *passim*
psychic powers, 169. *See also* Senses
Pure Lust, 8, 59, 66n, 197, 198, 204, 209, 240–91; and *Beyond God the Father* and *Gyn/Ecology*, 240, 274–75; Cat/egorical Appendix, 274; continuity with *Beyond God the Father*, 275; Dis-covering Elemental Feminist Philosophy, 248–51; double-rootedness, 274; Index of, 279; Index of New Words, used in *Wickedary*, 296; inspired by Wanderlust/Wonderlust in Fribourg (Switzerland), 56; as Labrys, 241; letters about, 285ff; Metamorphosphere, Spinning of, 272; as philosophical successor to *Beyond God the Father*, 252; Prophesied in *Beyond God the Father*, 163; Pyrospheres, Spiraling into, 267–69; reconnecting with early experiences, 254; reviews of, 290ff; unifying theme of, 274–77; Weaving threads from earlier books, 323ff
Pure Lust, 329; Background meaning, defined, 241; as Virtue, 269
pure lust: defined, 273; patriarchal, ontologically evil, 241
Purple sky, 114, 117, 254
Pyrogenesis, defined, 276
Pyrogenetic Focus, 151
Pyrogenetic Passion, 46
Pyrogenetic Powers, 163
Pyrogenetic Virtues, 196ff
Pyro-ontology, 276
Pyrosophical Temperance, 199, 269
Pyrosophy, 276
Pyrospheres, 270; defined, 268n
Pyro-words, 268, 275

Qualitative Leaping, 4, 5, 8, 13, 47, 94, 161, 184, 189, 196, 203ff
quaternity. *See* Goddess
Quest, 109, 158, 198; to be a philosopher, 22ff, 26, 55, 113, 118, 251, 324, 326, *and throughout book*

Race, life regarded as a, 2
Race of Wild Women, 20, 277, 308
racism, 21, 35, 100, 233, 235, 311, 362

Radiant Realm of Books, 26
Radical Feminism, 10, 104, 140, 147, 155, 188, 190, 195, 201ff, 204, 233, *and throughout book*; backlash against, 207–9, 260, 262; and Boundary, 148; bringing together with Lesbianism, 404, 435; condition of, in eighties, 280, 297; connection with Ecology, 243; in Germany, 309; in "Qualitative Leap" article, 205
Radical Feminist Conference on Prostitution (1971), 141–42
Radical Feminist Identity, 1, 2, 3, 21, 249 *and throughout book*
Radical Feminist Philosophy, 2, 21, 78, 119, 157, 284, *and throughout book*
Radical Feminists, 140, 243, 281, 283, 298, *and throughout book*; Cosmic, 409n; in Ireland, 281ff; Surviving in mid-eighties, 300, 310
Rage, 112n, 208, 216, 221, 231, 410; Deep Volcanic, 240; Fiercely Focused, 398; and *Gyn/Ecology*, 233; Gynergizing Focus of, 233; Illuminating, 197; against racism, 233; about religion courses in college, 46; Virtue, 196ff; Volcanic, in letters, 239
"Raggedy Ann" stories, 25
Rakusin, Sudie, 293, 313n, 315
Ramsay, Janet, 260–61
rape: of environment, 13, 177, 398; Refusal of rapism, 177; of women, 120n, 144n, 148, 150n, 230, 323, 326, 339, 347, 354
Rattlesnake Gutter Road (Leverett, MA), 256–57
Raymond, Charlotte Cecil, 215
Raymond, Jan, 103, 137, 141n, 142, 143, 146, 155, 156, 166, 180, 206, 207, 230, 431, 434, 438. *See also* Tigers
Real Eyes, 295; defined, 274
Reality: Background, vs. foreground, 283; Elemental, 106; Gynocentric, Prechristian and Pre-Celtic, 352; reclaiming, 152; vs. unreality, 241
Realize, defined, 274
Realizing, 274, 283
Realms of *Pure Lust*. *See* Archespheres; Pyrospheres; Metamorphospheres
Realms of the Wild, 199
Re-Calling, 7, 190, 313; defined, 130n; of the Wild, 164; of Prepatriarchal/ Metapatriarchal Reality, 130
Re-Call, Ports of, 406
"Reclaim the Night March" (Dublin, Ireland), 353
Recollections, from My *Logbook of a Radical Feminist Philosopher*, meaning of, 11–13, *and throughout book*

Re-membering, 3, 9, 11, 12, 174, 313; of
    Future and Past, 9; Lost Senses, 78;
    Momentous, 9–11, 110, 210, 335, 347,
    and throughout The Fourth Spiral
    Galaxy; of Voyage, 11; of women's
    splendor, 352
reproductive technologies, 222n
reversals, patriarchal, 20, 117, 188; of
    Aristotelian-Thomistic analysis, 269;
    of Background Reality, 150; of chris-
    tianity, 322; christian trinity as, 150;
    as patriarchal strategy, analyzed in
    Beyond God the Father, 159; as patri-
    archal strategy, analyzed in *Pure Lust*,
    275; of phallic morality, 196n; revers-
    ing, 60n, 75, 109, 150, 151, 325;
    unraveling, 221
reviews: of *Beyond God the Father*, 167,
    429; of *Gyn/Ecology*, 436–37; of *Pure
    Lust*, 290–91; of *Wickedary*, 317
revolution, false meaning of, 151
Rice, Liz, 138
Rich, Adrienne, 165, 207, 230
Richland (WA), 177–78
Riesterer, Beate, 259
Righteously ripping off, 129
Ring of Kerry (Ireland), 66
Roberson, Marge, 305
Roberts, Jane, 257
Rockefeller Foundation Humanities
    Grant, 212, 225
rocks, 248, 256
Rome (Italy), 64, 78ff
Room of Our Own, 231
Rose, Bridget, 369, 370, 402
Rose Cottage (Ireland), 368–69, 379,
    402
Rosemary (classmate), death of, in first
    grade, 24
Rossaveel (Ireland), 354
Ross Castle, 66
Ryan, Aileen, 281, 349, 354, 355, 358,
    359, 366, 378, 402, 403

Sacajawea, 413
Sacred Canopy, The (Berger), 135
Sado-Ritual Syndrome, 221n, 223, 233n,
    273, 308, 323
sadosociety, 10, 221n, 240, 245, 263, 293,
    329; defined, 439
Sadospiritual Syndrome, 263, 267, 274
sado-words, 275
Sagaris (VT), 209, 217
sailing, 21, 71, 112ff, 119, 120, 129, 130,
    133, 166, 187ff, 190, 195, 198, 225,
    239, 345, 354, 387, 400, 404, 406
Saint Joan's International Alliance, 53,
    80, 424

Saint John the Evangelist School
    (Schenectady, NY), 24ff
Saint Joseph's Academy (Schenectady,
    NY), 26, 38
Saint Mary's College (Notre Dame, IN),
    50ff, 114, 118, 249
Saint Rose, College of (Albany, NY), 22,
    42–45
Sanders Theatre (Harvard University,
    Cambridge, MA), 395
Sandoz (Basel, Switzerland), chemical
    fire, 383
Sappho, 20, 43, 341
Sara (spider), 303–4, 356
SARAH (Women's Center, Stuttgart,
    Germany), 309
Scales, Ann, 391
scapegoat syndrome, 277; analyzed in
    Beyond God the Father, 159
Schachtel, Ernest G. (*Metamorphosis*),
    and *Pure Lust*, 272
Schenectady (NY), 22ff, 39, 251, 254
Schiehallion (Scotland), 375
Schlafly, Phyllis, 20
Scotland, visit to, 375–76
Schultz, Mary, 269, 244n
SCUM Manifesto, 343
Sea of subliminal knowledge. *See*
    Subliminal Sea
Search, for the Lost Senses, 106
"Second Coming," of women, 130,
    159
Second Vatican Council, 78
Seeing, Acts of, 222
Seeing/Sensing, Origin of European art
    and architecture, 64
Self, 197
Self-censor, 197, 260
Self-elimination, 132, 189, 203
Self-erasure, 203
Self-hatred, female, 277
Sen-Wenk, Elisabeth, 381
Sense of Direction, 27ff, 40, 110, 113–16,
    150, 174, 187, 314
Sense of Intention, 110
Sense of Outrage, 53
Sense of Purpose, 260
Sense of Timing, 47
Senses, 197; Lost, 65, 78, 105–7, 253–54;
    Other, 252, 267, 413; Psychic, 82–83,
    197
separatism, 326–28, 445, and *passim*
separatism, phallic, 326–28. *See also*
    State of Separation
Seti I, tomb of, 83
"sexist," use of term, 162–63
sexual caste system, 136; and abortion,
    142ff; and Realizing Touching Powers,
    275; and universalization, 162

Shannon, River (Ireland), 350; Crossing over, 370; crossing to Other dimensions, 359

Shanty, The (Brittas, County Dublin, Ireland), 403

Shape-shifting, 9, 133, 268, 312, 391; defined, 212; of *Gyn/Ecology*, 224

Sheffield (England), 376

Shields, Mary Lou, 139, 165

Shrewish Shrewdness, 199, 269

Silly, 316; defined, 215

Simone de Beauvoir Conference (NY), 232

Simpson's Gap (Australia), 261

sin, etymology of, 292

Sinning, 198, 292, 326

Sisterhood, 9, 20, 133, 158, 159, 185, 187, 188; as antichurch, 160; as cosmic covenant, 143n, 160; as revolution, 159

Sisterhood Is Powerful (Robin Morgan), 108, 141, 300n

"sisterhood of man," 143

Sisters: religious, 26, 27–28, 42, 49, 418, 421; elementary school teachers: Sister Mary Arthur, 25; Sister Mary Clare of the Passion, 24–25; Sister Mary Edmund, 24; high school teachers: Sister Athanasia Gurry, C.S.J., 22, 41, 417; Sister Genevieve Greisler, C.S.J., 37, 41, 419, 420

skein: defined, 304; words in *Wickedary*, 304

Sliabh na Cailligh (Witch's Hill, Ireland), 349

Sligo, County (Ireland), 350

sloth, 195n, 212

Smuggling, 78, 110, 129–31, 132, 154, 157, 188, 197, 202n, 221, 267, 374; of Background information, 132; and Labrys, 219; Source of, 132; Treasures of Crete, 219. *See also* Piracy; Plundering

Smyth, Ailbhe, 281

Snake-Goddesses, Minoan (Crete), 219

snow (Elemental), 23, 114, 116, 267–68

Solanas, Valerie, 343–44

south wind (of Aquinas), vs. Great Wind, 52n

Sparking, 221, 223, 323

Spider Woman (Thinking Woman), 413–14

spiders: in Ireland, 370; and *Wickedary*, 303. *See also* Sara

Spin, defined, 210

Spinning, 8–9, 60, 147, 163, 195, 196, 199, 200, 205, 210, 211, 218, 219, 221, 223, 231, 240, 241, 249, 293, 299,

300, 307; and be-ing, 292; connections, in letters, 239; conversations, vs. academented babble, 250; defined, 195; and Exorcism, 9; Moments of, 184, 205, 222; and Sinning, 292; and Weaving, in The Third Spiral Galaxy, 321, 322, 323, 324; Webs, and Voyaging through Time, 314

Spinsters, 28, 195, 210, 211, 213, 217, 223, 224, 300, 315, 322, 338

Spiral Galaxies, 4, 5; Background and, 5; The First Spiral Galaxy, 6, 19ff; The Fourth Spiral Galaxy, 9, 319, 320, 335ff, 348; interconnectedness, 10; Intertwining Threads of, 374; and Moments of Exorcism and Ecstasy, 398; The Second Spiral Galaxy, 7, 129ff; The Third Spiral Galaxy, 8, 195ff, 312, 338

Spiraling, 1, 4, 150, 162, 185, 203, 235, 299, *and throughout book*; Courage, 197; with Craft, 109; into Elemental Feminist Philosophy, 277; of Outercourse, 244, 254, 338; Quest, 158; of women's movement, 208

Spiritual Frontiers Society, 106

Spiritualism, 106–7, 156, 373, and *passim*

spiritualization, 159, 188

Spokane (WA), 177

Spooking, 221, 223, 307, 318, 319, 323

Stag-nation, 88, 109, 198, 219

Stamina, 249, 256; defined, 441

Standing My Ground, 262, 283, 339–40, 410

Standley Chasm (Australia), 261

Stanley, Sandra, 279

Starchase, 257

Star-Lust, 257

stars, 247, 250, 254, 257, 270, 314, 325, 345, 360–61, 362

State of Atrocity, 197, 229

State of Bliss, 379

State of Bondage, 3

State of Boredom, 23

State of Possession, 147n, 149, 322

State of Reversal, 225

State of Separation, 221, 327, 357

State of Severance, 197, 221

Stathopoulou, Georgia, 450

Stendahl, Brita and Krister, 167

Stockton, Mary, 392, 401, 450

stone circle at Lough Gur (County Limerick, Ireland), 362–63; calves at, 363

stone mounds (Ireland), 350

Strandhill (County Sligo, Ireland), 350

Stuttgart (Germany), 309

Styrian Academy, 271

subliminal knowledge, 7, 12, 13, 46, 111–12, 131, 157, 342, 343; of The Fourth Spiral Galaxy, 348; of holidays, in childhood, 31; of Now, 338, 344; Realization of, 238

subliminal meanings, in patriarchal texts, 130

Subliminal Sea, 13, 40, 129, 149, 150, 151, 152, 154, 157, 168, 188, 195, 196, 200, 205, 219, 222, 231, 233, 234, 236, 238, 250, 285ff, 293, 309, 313, 320, 321, 329, 338, 404; contamination of, 13; not to be confused with Jung's "collective unconscious," 112n; and Prepatriarchal Heritage, 283; Ports of Re-Call on, 400ff; Sailing, 112, 387, *and throughout book*

Subliminal Sensing, 182

subliminal undermining, 98–100

summon, etymology of, 409

Sun, 335, 363

Super Natural, defined, 324

Surviving, 300, 357, 376, 384, 404

Swidler, Arlene, 103

Switzerland, Ecstatic living, 66. *See also* Basel; Bern; Fribourg; Kleine Scheidegg; Wengen; Zurich

Sydney (Australia), 262

symbols, of patriarchy, 60n, 134ff, 195, *and throughout book*

Symposium on Belief, Second International, 183ff, 200

Syn-Crone-icities, 12, 236, 252, 278, 286, 316, 348, 382; and 11:12 phenomenon, 105; Sense of, in letters, 238; during Spinning of *Wickedary*, 293, 301

Szasz, Thomas, 157

taboos: breaking, 130, 326; against women as philosophers, 260, 325, 418; against women as theologians, 260

Tae Kwon Do, 95

tense, problems of, 6

Terrible Taboo, defined, 45n

Terrible Taboo/Total Taboo, 45, 111, 144–45, 198, 325, 418; breaking, 144, 313, 321, 323, 324, 328, 399

Thatcher, Margaret, 20, 375

"theology of hope," 102

Theoret, France, 244n

Third Eye/I, 78

Third International Interdisciplinary Congress on Women (Dublin, Ireland), 348–54

Third Hemisphere (Fairy Space), 311, 329; defined, 311

Thirteen, 294, 302, 305, 314

thirteenth century, importance of, 361

Thirteenth Hour, defined, 302

Threshold/Limen: of Background knowledge, 115; Spiraling toward, 116

Tidal Time, 2, 4, 175, 211, 214, 219, 231, 272, 314, 329, 347; defined, 269; vs. tidy time, 269

Tides, shifting, 309

tidy time, defined, 269

Tierney, Hilary, 378

Tigers, the, 137, 146, 148, 152, 155, 156, 158, 164, 165, 176, 182, 189, 200ff, 220

Tillich, Hannah, 101

Tillich, Paul, 54, 136, 148, 157

Tillis, Carole, 450

Time, 12; Green, 157; Momentous, 132; of New Beginnings, 344; vs. time, 314; Volcanic, 200; Voyaging through, and Spinning Webs, 314

Time Bombs, 132, 167, 205, 335; "Autobiographical Preface" and "Feminist Postchristian Introduction" to *The Church and the Second Sex* (1975 ed.), 177–80

Time, Elemental, 4

Time, Fairy. *See* Fairy Time

time, foreground, 4, 11, 294, 314

Time, Real, 175

Time/Space, 115, 207

Time-Space, New, 110, 183

Time, Tidal. *See* Tidal Time

time, tidy. *See* tidy time

Time Travel, 1, 2, 9, 11, 109, 172, 251, 314

time warp, 182

Timing, Sense of, 157

Toadal Time, defined, 305

tokenism, 20, 88ff, 121, 131, 137, 163, 166, 186, 189, 203, 231, 277, 307, 325, and *passim*

Tokenism, Age of, 84

toms, dicks, and harrys, 199

Tornado, The, 247–48, 249–50; and Discovery of Elemental Feminist Philosphy, 250; and Elemental Encounters, 252; etymology of *tornado*, 252; and Great Wind, 249; and intuition of being, 252; and Metamorphosis, 251; and Naming foreground conditions, 252; as a Word, 252

Total Taboo, 144–45, 260, 323, 324, 325, 328; defined, 45n

touchable caste: defined, 144n; women as, 267, 275

Touching Powers, 144, 214, 275, 325, 328; defined, 144n

transcendence, 151

Transcendent Third Option, 321, 322, 343; in The Fourth Spiral Galaxy, 337, 338; in *Pure Lust*, 325; in The Second Spiral Galaxy, 186, 189; in The Third Spiral Galaxy, 203, 204

transcendental, use of word, 418

Treasures, 188, 325; of Crete, 219; of Ireland, 232, 369, 371; on Islands, 373

Treasure Islands, 151n, 232, 347, 373

Tree of Life, 322

trees, 116–17, 247n, 248, 256, 257, 274

Tribe of Wild Women, 165, 168, and *passim*

Tribes of Words, 224, 297; *Crone*-Tribe, 224; *Gyn*-Words, 224; *Hag*-Tribe, 224; in *Pure Lust*, 275

trinity, christian, 51, 59, 148, 150, 205, 322; as reversal of Triple Goddess, 150ff

Trinity College (Dublin, Ireland), 66, 351, 378

Triple Goddess, 51, 150, 150n, 223, 322, and *passim*

triplicity, defined, 428

trivialization, 159, 188

True Course, 1, 3, 116, 164, 166, 185, 189

Trujillo, Jen, 391

Truth, Sojourner, 10, 341ff, 396

Tubman, Harriet, 341, 395, 412–13

Turtle Café, 214

Tyson, Willie, 230, 231

Unfolding, 109, 209; of Be-ing, 198, 328; of *Gyn/Ecology*, 212; of New Be-ing, 187

Union Theological Seminary (New York, NY), 164

universalization, 159, 188; and sexual caste system, 162

Valentia Island (Ireland), 365

Valley of the Winds (Australia), 261

vampirism, 33n

Vatican Council, Second, 78ff

Velosolex motor bicycle, 62

Venice (Italy), 64

Vertigo, 214

Vices, Naming in *Pure Lust*, 269

Victoria, Queen, 20

Vienna (Austria), 183ff, 200ff

Villa des Fougères, 58, 63

Villa Wenkenhof, 381

Virtues: Biophilic Bonding, 269; Courage, 197–98; Disgust, 199, 240, 293; Fey Faith, 269; Hopping Hope, 269; Laughing Out Loud, 199, 218; Nagging, 253; Naming in Pure Lust, 269;

Nemesis, 269; New, need for, 404; Prudish Prudence, 269; Pure Lust, 269; Pyrogenetic, 197; Pyrosophical Temperance, 269; Shrewish Shrewdness, 269; Wicked, 197

Volcanoes, 111, 132, 242ff, and *passim*

Votteler, Ginster, 271

Voyage, 46, 88, 188, 196, 207, 221; into the Background, through Europe, 65; contrapuntal movement of, 115ff, 187ff, 321ff; early Moments of, 109; Lust to, 274; Metapatriarchal, 214; Moments marked by 11:12 phenomenon, 105; Original phase of, 19ff; of Outercourse, 4, 244, 329; of Pirate, 162 and *passim*; of Radical Feminist Philosopher, 2ff, 3, 12, 78; Remembering, 11; Spiraling, 86, 109; of Spiraling Paths, 3, 4

Voyaging: Be-Dazzling, in letters, 239; foreground tracks/traps blocking, 225; Intergalactic, 408, 414; of Wild Women, 398

Walker, Alice, 257

Walsh, Ann, 48

Wasteland: escape from, in Australia, 262; Passage through, in early eighties, 259

Watershed Year, 8, 182, 200ff

Way, Peggy, 103

weavers, significance of, at Canterbury, England, 65

Weaving, 198, 249, 321, 338

Webs: of connections, 110; Re-Weaving, 9; in *Wickedary*, 296, 303, 311, 314. *See also* Word-Webs

Webster, defined, 292n

Webster, Noah, 317–19

Websters' First New Intergalactic Wickedary of the English Language. See Wickedary

"Websters' Intergalactic Seal of Approval," 274, 293, 329, 351

"We Have Done with Your Education," 229, 398

Wehr, Demaris, 290

Welch, Sharon, 279n

Wengen (Switzerland), 68, 380

Wesley House (London, England), 374

Whistle-Blowing, 385ff

Whitehead (Alfred North), 157

Wicked, defined, 292

Wickedary, 8, 59, 198, 204, 209, 292ff, 372, 409; blurbs for jacket, 318; breaking Terrible Taboo/Total Taboo, 313; brewing of, 292; British and Irish publication of, 374; "Canny

Comments" in, 297n; "Cockaludicrous Comments" in, 297n; Core, 296ff; defined, 292n; Elemental inspiration for, 294; essays in, 294ff; and Jane Caputi, 293ff; and Laughing Out Loud, 313; and Naming and Hearing, 313; purpose of, 294; Spooking incidents surrounding publication of, 317ff; unifying theme of, 311–14; Word-Webs in Core, 297

Wicklow, County (Ireland), 349

Wight, Evelyn, 394–95, 399, 451

Wight, Rebecca, 394

Wild Cat, 220ff, 245, 257, 258, 268, 270, 302, 345, 346–47, 351–52, 357, 358, 366–67, 371, 374, 377, 385, 396, 401, 407, 408; and Angels, 245; as Animal Guide in *Wickedary*, 301; and Background Glimpses, 245; communication with, 258; defined, 302; as Furry, Glamour Puss, Magnifi-cat, and Grimalkin, 301; as Pyrognostic/Pyrosophical Cat, 268

Wild Eyes, 220ff, 245, 270; and Angels, 245; and Background Glimpses, 245

Wilson, Bill, 91, 310

Wilt, Judith, 391

Wind, Great. *See* Great Wind

Wisselinck, Erika, 270–71, 280, 306ff, 380, 441, 448; *Anna: Several Days in the Life of an Old Woman*, 259, 380; German translation of *Gyn/Ecology*, 258, 380; translator of lectures, 307

WITCH, as acronym for Radical Feminist groups, 300n

WITCH (Feminist lecture series), 300

witchburnings, 230, 323

Witchcraft, 198

witchcraze: in Germany, 308; of early nineties, 317

Witches, 205, 224, 342; of Boston, 398; feast of Lammas, 261; Primal Powers of, 314, 343; Spell, 214

"The Witches Return: Patriarchy on Trial," 393ff

Witch, Great Original, 308, 316. *See also* Archimage

Wittig, Monique (*Les Guérillères*), 397

Wollstonecraft, Mary, 158

woman as vessel, 109–10

Womanchurch, 143n

woman-identification, 95, 132, 145, 166, 182

woman-identified, 20, 43, 75, 157, 160, 190n, 196, 204, 229, 231, 260, 325, 326

women of color, 222n, 232, 233, 323, 340, 408

Women's Army Corps (W.A.C.), 39

Women's Institute. *See* Boston Theological Institute

women's movement, 143; early Moments in sixties and seventies, 23n; erasure by media of, 208; as exodus community, charismatic community, communicating community, 160; as Final Cause, 160; in Germany, 308; as Metapatriarchal Journey of Exorcism and Ecstasy, 275; as ontological movement, 159ff, 222, 275

Women's Peace Camp (Greenham Common, England), "zapping" of women at, 354, 376, 446

Women's Press, The (London), 285, 374, 376

Women's Space, 95, 119, 120, 141, 189, 231; on the Boundary, 326–28; in coeducational colleges, 326–27; defined, 95n; in women's colleges, 326

Women's Studies, 43, 103, 132, 137, 141, 189, 208, 298, 327

Women's Time, 231

Women-Touching Women, 143ff, 162, 170, 211, 214, *and throughout book*

Wonderlust/Wanderlust, 109, 114, 342, and *passim*

Woolf, Virginia, 3, 53, 150, 162, 197, 205, 231, 320, 372, 396

Words, Wicked, 204, 292ff, *and throughout book*

Words, double-edged. *See* Metapatriarchal Metaphors

Words, invention of, transitional, 204

Word-Webs: hidden, Dis-covering in ordinary dictionaries, 294; Spinning of, 305; of *Wickedary*, 297, 300ff

Wright, John (Cardinal), 56, 62, 67

Writing, Act of, 175, 213

"X-factor," 100, 179

Yahweh & Son, 160

Yancey, Josephine, 310

Yugoslavia, 73

Zappone, Katherine, 348, 358, 378, 403

Zavalloni, Marisa, 280, 349, 379

Zurich (Switzerland), 379